Cracking the GRE:
Chemistry Exam

THE PRINCETON REVIEW

Cracking the GRE:
Chemistry Exam

By Monique Laberge, PhD

RANDOM HOUSE, INC.
NEW YORK

www.randomhouse.com/princetonreview

Princeton Review Publishing, L.L.C.
2315 Broadway
New York, NY 10024
E-mail: comments@review.com

ISBN: 0-375-75346-X
ISSN: 1521-9453

Editor: Rachel Warren
Production Coordinator: Robert McCormack
Illustrations: Carmine Raspaolo

Manufactured in the United States of America on partially recycled paper.

9 8 7 6 5 4 3 2 1

ACKNOWLEDGMENTS

The author would like to thank Dr. J. Fidy, for generously giving her time to work on the book. She would also like to thank her editor, Rachel Warren; production coordinator, Robert McCormack, for the beautiful layout; and Carmine Raspaolo, for rendering the art quickly and accurately.

CONTENTS

I. ANALYTICAL CHEMISTRY

II. INORGANIC CHEMISTRY

IV. PHYSICAL CHEMISTRY

I. ANALYTICAL CHEMISTRY

DATA ACQUISITION AND USE OF STATISTICS

WHY ARE STATISTICS USED IN CHEMISTRY?

Statistics are used to check the accuracy of collected experimental data, to compare two experimental methods, to compress data, and to express the precision of a result.

SIGNIFICANT FIGURES

Significant figures are the *number of digits required to express a given quantity with precision*. When we say that a number is expressed to a given number of significant figures, this means that the last digit in the number always has an uncertainty of one. So, a number expressed to 4 significant figures has an uncertainty of one in its last digit.

The following numbers are all expressed to five significant figures (the uncertainty expressed in the last number is in boldtype):

$$0.1308\mathbf{3}$$
$$1308.\mathbf{3}$$
$$0.0130\mathbf{8}$$

Example of an addition:

$$
\begin{array}{r}
310.3 \\
8.418 \\
0.1609 \\
\hline
318.8789
\end{array}
$$

Is this result correct, or is 318.**8** correct?

Neither. The correct answer is 318.9, because the first term of the addition, 310.3, which is expressed to 4 significant figures, has an uncertainty of one in its last digit; because of this, it invalidates the number of digits after the decimal in the other two terms. 318.8 is also incorrect, because the 8 must be raised to 9, since the digit that follows the 8 (7) is > 5.

ROUNDING OFF NUMBERS

210.04 = 210.0
210.06 = 210.1
210.05 = 210.0
210.15 = 210.2

The numbers above have been rounded off correctly: 210.04 is rounded off to 210.0 because the 4 is smaller than 5; similarly, 210.06 is rounded off to 210.1 because the 6 is greater than 5; 210.05 is rounded off to 210.0 because the 0 before the 5 is an even number; and 210.15 is rounded off to 210.2 because the 1 before the 5 is an odd number.

PERCENT ERROR

$$\% \text{ error} = \frac{\text{actual} - \text{measured}}{\text{actual} \times 100\%}$$

Consider the following expression: $\dfrac{(22.64 \times 0.3402 \times 0.06400)}{3.1433} \times 100\%$

The % error for each term is:

Term	% Error
22.64 ± 0.01	0.0442
0.3402 ± 0.0001	0.0294
0.06400 ± 0.00001	0.0156
3.1433 ± 0.0001	0.0032

Adding up the % errors: 0.0442 + 0.0294 + 0.0156 + 0.0032 = 0.0924%, and

$$\frac{(22.64 \times 0.3402 \times 0.06400)}{3.1433} \times 100\% = 15.6821236 \text{ with } 0.0924\% \text{ error, or}$$

$$\frac{15.6821236 \times 0.0924}{100} = 0.0145, \text{ reported as } 15.68 \pm 0.01.$$

We use the largest possible error (22.64 ± 0.01 or 1 in 2264) seen in the lot above with respect to significant figures.

Two types of errors can affect the accuracy of a measured quantity. They are

i) *determinate errors*: These are errors that are instrumental, operative and in methodology; these errors can be avoided or corrected;

ii) *indeterminate errors*: accidental and random, these errors cannot be estimated or predicted except by mathematical probability theory, which states that indeterminate errors follow a Gaussian distribution. Statistics deals with this type of error.

Basic Statistics in Chemistry: Definitions

Some basic statistical definitions are illustrated below using the following series of numbers:

$$2, 4, 5, 6, 7, 8, 8, 9, 9, 9, 11, 11, 12$$

- **Median:** 9 is the median, ie, the number seen the most frequently in the group.

- **Arithmetic mean** (x) — The sum of the numbers (x_i), divided by their quantity N:

$$x = \frac{\sum x_i}{N} = \frac{101}{13} = 7.77$$

- **Geometric mean** (m_g) — The product of the numbers, raised to the power $\frac{1}{N}$ or

$$m_g = (x_1 x_2 ... x_i)^{\frac{1}{N}}$$

$$(2 \cdot 4 \cdot 5 \cdot 6 \cdot 7 \cdot 8 \cdot 8 \cdot 9 \cdot 9 \cdot 9 \cdot 11 \cdot 11 \cdot 12)^{1/13} = 7.08$$

- **Mean deviation** — The value of a measurement in a series minus the arithmetic mean of the series: $x - x$

- **Absolute deviation** — The absolute value of the mean deviation: $|x - x|$

- **Standard deviation** (S) — $S = \sqrt{\sum (x_i - x)^2} / N - 1$

Example:

Given a series of data points (8, 11, 12, 13, 16), find the standard deviation:

First tabulate the data; start by calculating the statistical quantities you need to use the standard deviation equation $S = \sqrt{\sum (x_i - x)^2} / N - 1$:

x	$x - x$	$|x - x|$	$(x - x)^2$
8	−4	4	16
11	−1	1	1
12	0	0	0
13	+1	1	1
16	+4	4	16
Total:	0	$\sum/N = 10/5 = 2$	$(x - x)^2 = 34$

The arithmetic mean is: $x = \dfrac{\sum x_i}{N} = \dfrac{1}{5}(60) = 12$

And the standard deviation is $S = \dfrac{\sqrt{\sum (x_i - x)^2}}{N - 1} = \sum = \dfrac{\sqrt{34}}{5 - 1} = 2.915$

- Standard deviation (S) $S = \dfrac{\sqrt{N\sum x_i^2 - \left(\sum x_i\right)^2}}{N(N-1)}$

This is an alternate standard deviation formula that does not require calculating of the mean. Using the values of the previous example with this formula, we see that

$S = 2.915$ since $N = 5$, $\sum x_i = 60$; $(\sum x_i) = 64 + 121 + 144 + 169 + 256 = 754$

- Variance: The square of the standard deviation: S^2

- Standard error of the mean: $\dfrac{S}{\sum N}$

- The confidence level: $1 - \alpha$, where $\alpha = 0.05$ if a 95% level of confidence is desired, 0.01 for a 99% level, and 0.001 for a 99.9% level.

Chemists report their results at any one of these three confidence levels. At a confidence level of 95%, the measurement is referred to as "significant"; at 99%, it is "highly significant" and at 99.9%, it is "very significant."

- The confidence limit: $x \pm \dfrac{tS}{\sqrt{N}}$, where t is a statistical factor that is dependent on the desired confidence level and on the number of degrees of freedom.

Example:

A chemist makes 118 distinct measurements of the dielectric constant of ethanol. The mean value obtained is $x = 32.70$ debye and $S = 0.07$. At a 99% level of confidence, what is the true dielectric constant of ethanol?

t values for confidence testing

Degrees of Freedom	Confidence level 95% ($\alpha = 0.05$)	Confidence level 99% ($\alpha = 0.01$)
1	12.706	63.657
2	4.303	9.925
3	3.182	5.841
4	2.776	4.604
5	2.571	4.032
6	2.447	3.707
7	2.365	3.500
8	2.306	3.355
9	2.262	3.250
10	2.228	3.169
25	2.060	2.787
∞	1.960	2.576

Because the desired confidence level is 99%, $\alpha = 0.01$, and $N = 118$, so the number of degrees of freedom equals $N - 1 = 117$. Because $N - 1$ exceeds 25, the infinity value is used from the table of t values: for $N = \infty$, the t value is 2.576 at a confidence level of 99%. And the true dielectric constant of ethanol is equal to

$$x \pm \frac{tS}{\sqrt{N}} = 32.70 \pm \left[\frac{2.576 \times 0.07}{\sqrt{95}}\right] \text{debye} = 32.70 \pm 0.0185 \text{ debye}$$
$$= 32.70 \pm 0.02 \text{ debye}$$

DATA COLLECTION: THE METHOD OF LEAST SQUARES

When plotting data, we get a group of data points made up of x and y values. The x values are *independent* variables and the y values are *dependent* variables. The data do not usually plot in a straight line, more often *scatter* is present due to experimental error.

Since many chemical processes can be described by a straight line of the type $y = mx + b$, a method has been developed to obtain the best possible straight line from a series of experimental data points (which contain a degree of scatter).

This is called the **method of least squares**, which involves two equations. The first is used to calculate the slope m.

$$m = \frac{\dfrac{\sum x_i y_i - (\sum x_i \sum y_i)}{n}}{\dfrac{\sum x_i^2 - (\sum x_i)^2}{n}} \qquad\qquad b = y - mx$$

where: n = number of data points

x = mean of x values = $\dfrac{\sum x_i}{n}$

y = mean of y values = $\dfrac{\sum y_i}{n}$

$\sum x_i$ = sum of x values

$\sum y_i$ = sum of y values

Example:

NADH has a strong absorbance at 340 nm; a calibration curve is prepared by recording the absorbance at that wavelength with samples of different concentrations. Get the best straight line from the experimental measurements using the method of least squares, and determine the concentration of a solution of NADH with absorbance at 340 nm, equal to 0.501, based on $y = mx + b$.

The values obtained for the different concentrations are as follows:

Concentration (mg/mL)	A_{340}
0.00	0.002
10.00	0.121
20.00	0.242
30.00	0.268
40.00	0.402
50.00	0.483
60.00	0.612
70.00	0.711
80.00	0.821
90.00	0.921
100.00	1.011

Rearranging	x_i	y_i	$x_i{}^2$	$x_i y_i$
	0.00	0.002	0.00	0.00
	10.00	0.121	100.00	1.21
	20.00	0.242	400.00	4.84
	30.00	0.268	900.00	8.04
	40.00	0.402	1600.00	16.08
	50.00	0.483	2500.00	24.15
	60.00	0.612	3600.00	36.72
	70.00	0.711	4900.00	49.77
	80.00	0.821	6400.00	65.68
	90.00	0.921	8100.00	82.89
	100.00	1.011	10000.00	101.10

and

$$\Sigma x_i = 550.00$$

$$\frac{\Sigma x_i}{n} = \frac{550.00}{11} = 50 = x$$

$$\Sigma y_i = 5.594$$

$$\frac{\Sigma y_i}{n} = \frac{5.594}{11} = 0.508 = y$$

$$(\Sigma x_i)^2 = 302500.00$$

$$\Sigma x_i^2 = 38500.00$$

$$\Sigma x_i y_i = 390.48$$

Then,

$$m = \frac{\dfrac{\Sigma x_i y_i - \left(\Sigma x_i \Sigma y_i\right)}{n}}{\dfrac{\Sigma x_i{}^2 - (x_i{}^2)^2}{n}}$$

$$= \frac{\dfrac{390.48 - (550.00 \cdot 5.594)}{11}}{\dfrac{38500.00 - 302500.00}{11}}$$

$$= 0.01$$

and $b = y - mx$

$$= 0.508 - (0.01 \times 50)$$

$$= 0.008$$

Then the straight line is $y = mx + b$

$$y = 0.01x + 0.008$$

And the graph looks like this:

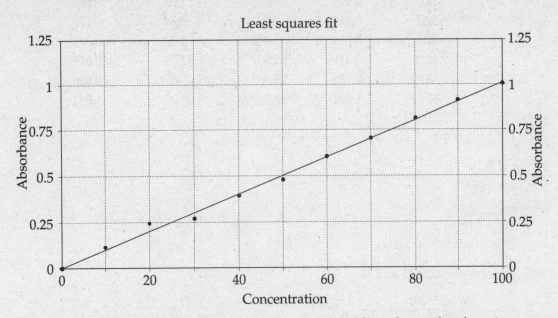

The concentration of the NADH sample can be extrapolated from the graph or by using $y = mx + b$, $0.501 = 0.01x + 0.008$, and $x = $ concentration $= 49.30$ mg/mL.

THE CORRELATION COEFFICIENT

The correlation coefficient defines the correlation between two variables. It expresses a relationship between *observed* values and *probable* values. The higher the correlation between observed and probable values, the better the data.

The correlation coefficient r is calculated from two sets of data points as follows:

$$r = \frac{\sum x_i y_i - nxy}{\sqrt{(\sum x_i^2 - nx^2)(\sum y_i^2 - ny^2)}}$$

When r is between 0.90 and 0.95, the correlation is fair; when r is between 0.95 and 0.99, the correlation is good; and it's excellent when $r > 0.99$

Example:

A calibration curve was prepared by plotting the concentration of benzhydroxamic acid vs. its absorbance at 280 nm. Calculate the correlation coefficient.

[BHA] µM	A_{280}
10.0	0.203
20.0	0.412
30.0	0.614
40.0	0.819
50.0	0.953
60.0	1.201

Rearranging:

x_i	y_i	x_i^2	$x_i y_i$	y_i^2
10.0	0.203	100.0	2.03	0.041
20.0	0.412	400.0	8.24	0.170
30.0	0.614	900.0	18.42	0.377
40.0	0.819	1600.0	32.76	0.671
50.0	0.953	2500.0	47.85	0.908
60.0	1.001	3600.0	60.06	1.002

and

$n = 6$

$x = 35.0$

$y = 0.667$

$\sum y_i^2 = 3.169$

$\sum x_i^2 = 9100.0$

$\sum x_i y_i = 169.36$

and the correlation coefficient is

$$r = \frac{\sum x_i y_i - nxy}{\sqrt{(\sum x_i^2 - nx^2)(\sum y_i^2 - ny^2)}}$$

$$r = \frac{169.36 - (6)(35.0)(0.667)}{\sqrt{[9100.00 - (6)(35.0)^2][3.169 - (6)(0.667)^2]}}$$

$r = 0.99$

So the correlation is excellent.

SOLUTIONS AND STANDARDIZATION

GENERAL TERMS

The following terms are found in expressions for concentration:

- molecular formula: indicates the number and type of atoms present in a given molecule

- molecular weight: the sum of the atomic weights of all of the atoms in a molecule

- mole: a mole of a substance is the amount in grams of that substance that's numerically equal to its molecular weight.

- equivalent weight: that weight required to react completely with one mole of another substance

One mole of any substance contains the same number of molecules or atoms: 6.02252×10^{23}. This is Avogadro's number.

The concentration of solutions is expressed as follows:

- molar concentration (M): number of moles of substance in one liter of solution

- normal concentration (N): number of equivalent weights of a substance in one liter of solution

- molality (m): number of moles of substance per 1 kg of solvent

- % by weight: weight of solute/weight of solution $\times$ 100%

Dilutions are calculated using this formula:

$$Concentration_{final} \cdot Volume_{final} = Concentration_{initial} \cdot Volume_{initial}$$

Example:
Calculate the volume of 0.1 M HCl needed to prepare 50 ml of 0.05 M HCl.

$C_i V_i = C_f V_f$

$V_i = C_f \times V_f / C_i$

$V_i = 0.05 \text{ M} \times 50 \text{ mL} / 0.1 \text{ M}$

$V_i = 25 \text{ ml}$

So 25 mL of 0.1 M HCl should be diluted to 50 mL, i.e., 25 mL of 0.1 M HCl + 25 mL H_2O.

VOLUMETRIC ANALYSIS

Volumetric analysis is an analytical method that involves a known *reaction* between a solution of *unknown* concentration (the **analyte**) and a solution of *known* concentration (the **titrant**). The process of adding the titrant to the analyte is called a **titration**.

When the volume of titrant that's been added is the amount required to completely react with the analyte, an **equivalent point** has been reached. At this point, the total weight of analyte can be calculated from the volume and concentration of titrant used in the titration. The **end point** of the titration is determined by an **indicator**, which is a reagent that's added; indicators change color to signal the end of a reaction.

Volumetric methods can be classified as follows:

- Acid–base titrations

- Oxidation–reduction titrations

- Complexometric titrations

STANDARD SOLUTIONS

Standard solutions are prepared by dissolving an accurately massed amount of a primary standard in a known volume of solution, using volumetric glassware. A **primary standard** is a chemical of very high purity (> 99.99%). Potassium acid phthalate is a primary acid standard which is commonly used to standardize base solutions. Na_2CO_3 is a standard base used to standardize acid solutions.

If the chemical substance is not pure enough, it can be reacted with a primary standard. For example, NaOH is not a primary standard because it absorbs water easily, i.e., it is hygroscopic. But its reaction with potassium acid phthalate—itself a primary standard—turns it into a standard solution that can be used as a titrant:

$$NaOH + \text{(benzene ring with COOH and COOK)} \longrightarrow \text{(benzene ring with COO}^-\text{+Na and COO}^-\text{+K)} + H_2$$

Standardized solution
used to titrate

Now the concentration of the NaOH solution can be determined with a high degree of accuracy. Similarly, Na_2CO_3 (primary standard) is used to standardize sulfuric acid.

MEASUREMENT OF VOLUME

Volume is measured using volumetric glassware (pipets, beakers, graduated cylinders).

The most accurate glassware are

Volumetric flasks: calibrated to contain a known volume of solution at a given temperature (20 or 25° C)

Burets: calibrated to deliver a known volume of solution (50 mL to 0.1 mL)

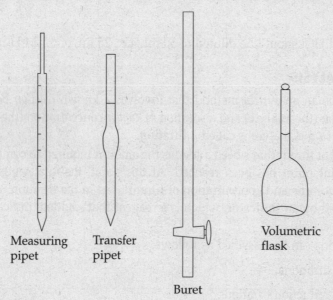

Measuring
pipet

Transfer
pipet

Buret

Volumetric
flask

CHEMICAL EQUATIONS

$$Na_2SO_4 + BaCl_2 \rightarrow BaSO_4 + 2NaCl$$

This equation shows the quantities of reagents that react in this chemical reaction. For example, by the law of conservation of mass, 142 g (1 mole) of Na_2SO_4 will react with 208 g (1 mole) of $BaCl_2$ to yield 233 g of $BaSO_4$ (1 mole) and 117 g of NaCl (2 moles). Notice that 142 g + 208 g = 233g + 117 g.

MOLAR CALCULATION

For any substance, number of moles $= \dfrac{weight\ (in\ grams)}{molecular\ weight}$

Example:

How can the mass of SO_3 be determined in solution?

1. SO_3 exists in solution as a part of the following equilibrium:

$$SO_3(g) + H_2O(l) \leftrightarrow H_2SO_4 \, (aq)$$

2. Adding NaOH will cause all of the $SO_3(g)$ to be converted first to $H_2SO_4 \, (aq)$ and then, via this neutralization, into the soluble sodium sulfate salt.

$$NaOH + H_2SO_4 \rightarrow Na_2SO_4 \text{ (soluble)} + H_2O$$

3. $Na_2SO_4 + BaCl_2 \rightarrow BaSO_4 + 2NaCl$ The amount of SO_3 is determined by calculating the mass of SO_4^{2-}, since there is a 1:1 molar ratio of SO_3 to SO_4^{2-} in solution:

So the mass of $SO_3 = = \dfrac{\text{mass of precipitate} \times \text{molecular weight } SO_3}{\text{molecular weight } BaSO_4}$

HOMOGENOUS EQUILIBRIA

Homogeneous equilibria describe systems that are present in only one phase. Three topics are covered under this heading: acids and bases, oxidation–reduction, and complexometry. These are three types of reactions that are used in volumetric titrations.

ACIDS AND BASES

- The **Brönsted-Lowry** definitions of acids and bases are as follows

Acids are proton donors (e.g., they donate protons to H_2O or NH_3)
Bases are proton acceptors (e.g., they accept protons from H_2O or NH_3)

which means	Acid $\leftrightarrow$ Base + H^+
Some common acids:	HCl, H_3PO_4, H_2O, NH_4^+, H_3O^+, $H_2PO_4^-$
Some common bases:	H_2O, NH_3, OH^-, $SO_4^{\,2-}$, $Fe(H_2O)OH^{2+}$

Both H_2O and SH^- can either accept or donate a proton: they are *amphoteric electrolytes* or *ampholites.*

LEWIS ACIDS AND BASES

This is the definition of a **Lewis acid**: An acid is any molecular or ionic species that can accept a pair of electrons in the formation of a covalent bond.

By definition, a **Lewis base** is any molecular or ionic species that can donate a pair of electrons in the formation of a coordinate covalent bond.

CONJUGATE ACID-BASE PAIRS

$$HCl + NH_3 \Leftrightarrow NH_4^+ + Cl^-$$
$$\text{acid} \quad \text{base} \qquad \text{base} \quad \text{acid}$$

Conjugate acid-base pairs are related to each other by the loss or gain of one proton; the conjugate pairs are: HCl/Cl^- and NH_3/NH_4^+.

Example:

Which of the four H_3PO_4 and $H_2PO_4^-$, or H_3PO_4 and HPO_4^{2-} constitute a conjugate pair?

Only $H_3PO_4/H_2PO_4^-$, because the other pair involves the gain/loss of more than one proton.

$$\underset{\text{acid}}{H_3PO_4} \Leftrightarrow \underset{\text{base}}{H_2PO_4^-} + H^+$$

STRENGTH OF ACIDS AND BASES

Acids are classified as strong or weak. A strong acid or base completely dissociates in water:

$$HCl + H_2O \rightarrow Cl^- + H_3O^+$$

HCl is a strong acid, this dissociation proceeds fully to the right. One example of a strong base is NaOH, which also fully dissociates to its constituent ions in water:

$$NaOH + H_2O \rightarrow Na^+ + OH^-$$

A weak acid only partially dissociates in water; notice the double arrows:

$$CH_3COOH + H_2O \Leftrightarrow H_3O^+ + CH_3OO^-$$

and a weak base does not completely dissociate in water either:

$$C_6H_6NH_2 + H_2O \Leftrightarrow C_6H_6NH_3^+ + OH^-$$

THE ACID AND BASE DISSOCIATION CONSTANTS

K_a and K_b express the relative ability of an acid to donate a proton and the ability of a base to accept one. The dissociation for an acid HA (general term) in water can be expressed as follows:

$$HA + H_2O \Leftrightarrow A^- + H_3O^+$$

The hydronium ion H_3O^+ is the form in which the transferred proton H^+ is loosely bonded to water. A simplified equation is

$$HA + H_2O \Leftrightarrow A^- + H^+$$

The dissociation constant for this expression can be expressed as a ratio of equilibrium concentrations of products to reactants. Note that the concentration of H_2O is not in the expression because the concentration of H_2O in $H_2O = 1$.

$$K_a = \frac{[A^-][H^+]}{[HA]}$$

This is the equilibrium expression for a base dissociating in water, $A^- + H_2O \rightarrow HA + OH^-$, and the base dissociation constant is

$$K_b = \frac{[HA][OH^-]}{[A^-]}$$

Strong acids and bases have high K_a's and K_b's because the equilibrium concentrations of the products is so much greater than the equilibrium concentrations of the reactants.

THE SELF-IONIZATION OF H_2O

The following equilibrium exists in all aqueous solutions:

$$2H_2O \Leftrightarrow H_3O^+ + OH^-$$

$$\text{or} \qquad H_2O \Leftrightarrow H^+ + OH^-$$

and the dissociation constant or ionic product of water is expressed as

$$K_w = [H^+][OH^-]$$

This product increases with temperature and is equal to 1.008×10^{-14} M at 25°C, to 1.139×10^{-15} at 0°C and to 5.474×10^{-14} at 50°C.

So, at room temperature (this is true of pure water), the product of the concentrations of H^+ and OH^- is roughly equal to 1.0×10^{-14} M.

And then because of the 1:1 mole ratio in the equilibrium reaction,

$$[H^+] \times [OH^-] = 1.0 \times 10^{-14} \ M$$
$$[H^+] = [OH^-] = 1.0 \times 10^{-7} \ M$$

And: $\qquad\qquad [H^+] = 1.0 \times 10^{-7} \ M$

Similarly, $[OH^-] = 1.0 \times 10^{-7} \ M$

THE CONCEPT OF pH

The pH or pOH of a solution expresses the concentration of H^+ or OH^- ions present and is defined as

$$pH = - \log [H^+]$$
$$pOH = - \log [OH^-]$$

The pH of a solution that contains $[H^+] = 1.0 \times 10^{-7}$ M is 7.0.

We can combine the dissociation constants for water as follows:

$$K_a K_b = K_w = [H^+][OH^-] = 10^{-14}$$

Taking logarithms of both sides,

$\quad -\log K_w = -\log ([H^+] [OH^-]) = -\log [H^+] -\log[OH^-] = 14$

$pK_w = pH + pOH = 14$

and $pK_a + pK_b = 14$ at 25°C

Example:

What is the pH of a 0.010 M solution of formic acid (HCO_2H) in water at 25°C if the $pK_a = 3.74$?

$\qquad pK_a = -\log K_a$

And $\qquad K_a = 1.80 \times 10^{-4} \ M$

For the dissociation reaction, we can write

$$HCO_2H \Leftrightarrow H^+ + HCO_2^-$$

And the concentrations can be expressed as follows:

initial $[HCO_2H]$:   0.010 M

initial $[H^+]$ 0

initial $[HCO_2^-]$ 0

equilibrium $[HCO_2H]$ 0.010 $- x$

equilibrium $[H^+]$ x

equilibrium $[HCO_2^-]$ x

and $K_a = \dfrac{[H^+][HCO_2^-]}{[HCO_2H]}$

$$1.80 \times 10^{-4} = \frac{(x)(x)}{0.010 - x} = \frac{x^2}{0.010 - x}$$

$$x^2 + 1.80 \times 10^{-4}x - 1.80 \times 10^{-6} = 0$$

and x is 2.50×10^{-3} and is equal to the $[H^+]$.

Since: pH $= -\log[H^+]$, then the pH of a 0.010 M formic acid solution is 2.6.

BUFFERS

A buffer solution is a solution that acts to resist a pH change upon addition of a small quantity of acid or base.

It is made up of either: a weak acid and its salt (or conjugate base) or

a weak base and its salt (or conjugate acid).

The Henderson-Hasselbach equation describes the pH of a buffer solution of a weak acid and its conjugate base.

$$pH = pK_a - \log \frac{[HA]}{[A^-]} \quad \text{or}$$

$$pH = pK_a - \log \frac{[salt]}{[acid]}$$

And for a buffer solution of a weak base and its conjugate acid,

$$pOH = pK_b - \log \frac{[salt]}{[base]}$$

i)   if you know the pK_a and the concentrations of the salt and the acid, the Henderson-Hasselbach equation can be used to find the pH of a solution;

ii) if [salt] = [acid], then the pH of the buffer is equal to the pK_a of the acid;

iii) all buffers have maximum buffering capacity at pH $= pK_a$, and this holds true over a pH range of roughly $pK_a \pm 1$

Example:

What are the pH and pOH of a solution that is 0.100 M in NH_4Cl and 0.080 M in NH_3 given that the pK_b of NH_3 is 4.76?

$$NH_3 + H_2O \Leftrightarrow NH_4^+ + OH^-$$

$$pOH = pK_b - \log \frac{[salt]}{[base]}$$

$$pOH = 4.76 - \log \frac{0.100}{0.080}$$

$$pOH = 4.66$$

And: pH = 14 – 4.66 = 9.34

POLYPROTIC ACIDS

$$H_2A \Leftrightarrow H^+ + H_2A^- \qquad K_{a1}$$
$$H_2A^- \Leftrightarrow H^+ + HA^{2-} \qquad K_{a2}$$
$$HA^{2-} \Leftrightarrow H^+ + A^{3-} \qquad K_a$$

When acids can donate more than one proton, they are called polyprotic acids. Adding bases to polyprotic acids results into two or more proton dissociation steps. For example, an acid with three ionizable protons has three different equilibria (and three different K_a's).

H_3A is the fully acidic form, A^{3-} is the fully basic form, and H_2A^- and HA^{2-} are intermediate forms.

Example:

Calculate the pH of a 0.050 M solution of H_3PO_4. Phosphoric acid has a $K_{a1} = 1.1 \times 10^{-2}$, a $K_{a2} = 7.5 \times 10^{-8}$ and a $K_{a3} = 4.8 \times 10^{-13}$.

We can write the equilibrium equation for the dissociation of the first proton:

$$H_3PO_4 \Leftrightarrow H^+ + H_2PO_4^-$$
$$0.050 - x \qquad x \qquad x$$

So $K_{a1} = 1.1 \times 10^{-2} = \dfrac{[H^+][H_2PO_4^-]}{[H_3PO_4]}$

and then $x^2 = (1.1 \times 10^{-2})(0.050 - x)$ and

$$x^2 + 0.011x - 5.5 \times 10^{-4} = 0$$

Using the quadratic formula to solve for x, $x = 0.019\ M = [H^+]$, and the acid is 38% ionized. Because the other two dissociation constants are sufficiently different, i.e., they differ from the first and each other by more than 10^3, they can be neglected, and the pH of the solution is

$$pH = -\log[1.9 \times 10^{-2}] = 1.73$$

ACID-BASE TITRATIONS

STRONG ACID/STRONG BASE TITRATION (NEUTRALIZATION TITRATION)

In an acid-base titration, an acid is reacted with an equivalent amount of base. This is called a neutralization reaction. Here's an example of this type of reaction:

$$HNO_3(aq) + NaOH(aq) \rightarrow NaNO_3 (aq) + H_2O(l) \text{ or}$$

acid   base

$$H^+ + NO_3^- + Na^+ + OH^- \rightarrow Na^+ + NO_3^- + H_2O$$

By monitoring pH as a function of titrant added, a titration curve can be generated. The titration curve below was obtained by titrating 100 mL of 0.1 M HNO_3 with 0.1 M NaOH:

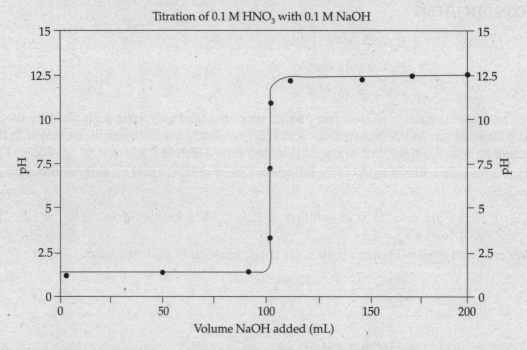

Titration of 0.1 M HNO_3 with 0.1 M NaOH

The **equivalence point** of an acid-base titration is the point at which exact stoichiometric amounts of reacting acid and base are present. In the example above, the equivalence point is achieved when the number of moles of base is equal to the number of moles of the acid present, because there is a 1:1 molar ratio in the balanced neutralization reaction.

- pH values before neutralization (i.e., before the equivalence point) are determined by the amount of acid present (not yet neutralized by base).

- At the equivalence point, the only source of H^+ and OH^- is from the dissociation of H_2O, and so the pH is 7.0.

- The pH after the equivalence point is determined by the amount of NaOH that continues to be added.

The end point, which is ideally the equivalence point—when stoichiometrically equivalent amounts of acid and base have combined—is determined using (i) a pH meter or (ii) an acid-base indicator.

ACID-BASE INDICATORS

Acid-base indicators are weak acids or bases that change color over a specific pH region,

$$H^+ + In^- \Leftrightarrow InH$$
$$\text{red} \qquad\qquad \text{orange}$$

For example, phenolphthalein is used for the 8–10 pH range; it is colorless at pH 8 (InH) and purple at pH 10 (In^-).

WEAK ACID/STRONG BASE TITRATION

The titration of acetic acid by sodium hydroxide is an example of a weak acid-strong base titration:

$$CH_3COOH(aq) + NaOH(aq) \rightarrow CH_3COO^- (aq) + Na^+ + H_2O(l)$$
$$\text{acid} \qquad\qquad \text{base} \qquad\qquad \text{base}$$

In this case, the salt of the weak acid (conjugate acid) is produced at the end of the titration.

$$CH_3COO^- + H_2O \Leftrightarrow CH_3COOH + OH^-$$

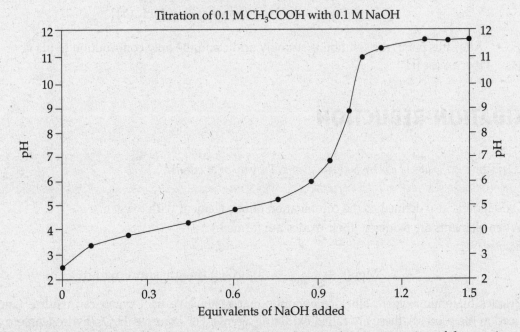

Titration of 0.1 M CH$_3$COOH with 0.1 M NaOH

So before the titration begins, the pH is > 7.0 (depending on the concentration of the starting acid) and, as the base is added, the titration curve will look like this:

- At the beginning of the titration, the pH depends on the K_a of the acid. The addition of NaOH results in a mixture of CH_3COOH (not neutralized) and its salt, CH_3COO^- (from the neutralized reaction).

- Upon addition of half the equivalence of base, pH = pK_a, and the acid is half-hydrolyzed. This is the midpoint of the titration ($x = 0.5$ equiv.).

- At the equivalence point, all the CH_3COOH has reacted and now the solution contains the salt CH_3COO^- and Na^+. The pH is weakly basic because the anion of the conjugate base CH_3COO^- is weakly basic.

- After this point, the solution is strongly basic and the only contribution to pH is the excess [OH^-] from $CH_3COO^- + H_2O \leftrightarrow OH^- + CH_3COOH$

WEAK BASE/STRONG ACID TITRATION

$$NH_3\,(aq) + HCl(aq) \Leftrightarrow NH_4Cl(aq)$$

$$NH_3 + H^+ + Cl^- \rightarrow NH_4^+ + Cl^-$$

The titration of a weak base with a strong acid is the same process as the previous case except that the titration curve is the reverse of that obtained for the titration of a weak acid with a strong base.

- At the beginning of the titration, the pH is basic and depends on the K_b of the base. The addition of acid results in a mixture of the base $[NH_3]$ and of $[NH_4^+]$ the conjugate acid, and the solution becomes less basic.

- Upon addition of half the equivalence of acid, pH = $14 - pK_b$ and $[NH_3] = [NH_4^+]$. This is the midpoint of the titration.

- At the equivalence point, all of the NH_3 has reacted, and the pH is acidic because it is determined by the concentration of $[NH_4^+]$

$$NH_4^+\,(aq) + H_2O(l) \leftrightarrow H_3O^+ + NH_3\,(aq)$$

- After this point, the solution is strongly acidic and the only contribution to pH is the excess $[H^+]$

OXIDATION-REDUCTION

Oxidation is the loss of electrons. Reduction is the gain of electrons.

Oxidation is also defined as the combination of one element with oxygen.
When elements are oxidized, their oxides are formed.
Example:

$$2Mg(s) + O_{2(g)} \rightarrow 2MgO(s) \text{ (magnesium oxide)}$$

Besides diatomic oxygen, other compounds that easily give up oxygen can oxidize (and are reduced in the process); these are called **oxidizing agents**. For example, H_2O_2 (hydrogen peroxide), CuO (Cu(II) oxide), $KMnO_4$ (potassium permanganate), and all of the halogens (all of which need only a few electrons to complete their outer valence electron shell) readily give up oxygen and are also excellent oxidizing agents because they readily gain electrons.

When oxygen is removed from an oxide, the reaction is called a **reduction**, and the element that lost the oxygen is said to have been reduced. The compound that gains the oxygen is called a **reducing agent** and is oxidized in the process. Examples of reducing agents include carbon, CO (carbon monoxide), hydrogen, sodium, magnesium, aluminum, and the alkaline-earth elements (Group I), which have few electrons in their outer electron valence shell and readily give up these outer electrons.

Oxidation and reduction contribute to a single combined process called a **redox reaction:**

$$CuO_{(s)} + H_{2(g)} \rightarrow Cu_{(s)} + H_2O_{(g)}$$

Here CuO is the oxidizing agent; it's reduced to Cu, and H_2 is the reducing agent; it's oxidized.

REDOX REACTIONS

In the oxidation of magnesium, magnesium gives two electrons to oxygen:

$$Mg \rightarrow Mg^{2+} + 2e^- \quad \text{(electron loss = oxidation)}$$
$$2e^- + O \rightarrow O^{2-} \quad \text{(electron gain = reduction)}$$

During this reaction, magnesium is oxidized, and oxygen is reduced. Mg is the reducing agent, and oxygen is the oxidizing agent.

You should also know that elements other than oxygen can gain electrons:

$$Fe_2O_3(s) + 2Al(s) \rightarrow Al_2O_3(s) + 2Fe(s)$$

$$2Al \rightarrow 2Al^{3+} + 6e^- \quad \text{(oxidation)}$$

$$2Fe^{3+} + 6e^- \rightarrow 2Fe \quad \text{(reduction)}$$

In this reaction, iron oxide containing Fe(III) is reduced to iron metal, Fe (0). The reducing agent is aluminium oxide, which is oxidized in the process.

> *Oxidizing agents are substances that gain electrons and are reduced in the process. Reducing agents are substances that lose electrons and are oxidized in the process.*

Whether a substance behaves as a reducing or oxidizing agent depends on the substance it is reacting with. For example, bromine (Br_2) and iodide ion (I^-) are both halogens and are commonly known as oxidizing agents. But when they react together, Br_2 acts as the oxidizing agent (because it is more electronegative than (I^-) and therefore attracts electrons more:

$$2I^- \rightarrow I_2 + 2e^- \quad \text{(oxidation)}$$
$$\underline{Br_2 + 2e^- \rightarrow 2Br^- \quad \text{(reduction)}}$$
$$Br_2 + 2I^- \rightarrow 2Br^- + I_2$$

And when Br^- is reacted with chlorine Cl, Br becomes the reducing agent and chlorine (which is more electronegative) is the oxidizing agent:

$$2Br^- \rightarrow Br_2 + 2e^- \quad \text{(oxidation)}$$
$$\underline{Cl_2 + 2e^- \rightarrow 2Cl^- \quad \text{(reduction)}}$$
$$Cl_2 + 2Br^- \rightarrow 2Cl^- + Br_2$$

> *Oxidizing agents are electron acceptors. Reducing agents are electron donors.*

In a redox reaction, every oxidizing agent has a corresponding reducing agent, which has at least one more electron than the oxidizing agent. An oxidizing agent and its reducing agent are called a **redox pair**.

REDOX POTENTIALS

$$Fe^{2+} + Ce^{4+} \Leftrightarrow Fe^{3+} + Ce^{3+}$$

The energy from this spontaneous reaction could be harnessed in an **electrochemical cell**. An electrochemical cell can be created by connecting the Fe^{2+} and Ce^{4+} solutions with a platinum wire, both ends of which function as electrodes. This would separate the above reaction into two oxidation-reduction reactions, called the **half-cell reactions**:

$$Fe^{2+} \to Fe^{3+} + e^- \qquad \text{(oxidation)}$$

$$Ce^{4+} + e^- \to Ce^{3+} \qquad \text{(reduction)}$$

The platinum wire-electrode side at which oxidation occurs is called the **anode**, and the electrode at which reduction occurs is called the **cathode**. The electrical potential, defined by the capacity of ions to accept or lose electrons, is referred to as the **electrode potential**.

The electrode potential of hydrogen has been assigned a value of 0 volts at a pressure of 1 atmosphere:

$$2H^+ + 2e^- \Leftrightarrow H_2 \qquad E°(V) = 0$$

This is called the **standard hydrogen electrode (SHE)**. Potential differences between this half-cell reaction value and that of others ions are called **standard electrode potentials**.

Some standard electrode potentials

Half-reaction	$E°$ (V)
$Mg^{2+}(aq) + 2e^- \leftrightarrow Mg(s)$	–2.37
$Fe^{2+}(aq) + 2e^- \leftrightarrow Fe(s)$	–0.44
$Cr^{3+}(aq) + e^- \leftrightarrow Cr^{2+}(aq)$	–0.41
$Sn^{4+}(aq) + 2e^- \leftrightarrow Sn^{2+}(aq)$	+0.15
$MnO^{4-}(aq) + e^- \leftrightarrow MnO_4{}^{2-}(aq)$	+0.56
$Fe^{3+}(aq) + e^- \leftrightarrow Fe^{2+}(aq)$	+0.77
$Br_2(aq) + 2e^- \leftrightarrow 2Br^-(aq)$	+1.07

> *The higher (or more positive) the standard electrode potential of a redox pair, the weaker a reducing agent the reduced form, and the stronger an oxidizing agent the oxidized form.*

In the above table, the strongest reducing agent is Mg (it is most readily oxidized), and the strongest oxidizing agent is Br_2 (it is most readily reduced).

Example:

Consider the following half-reactions:

$$Cu^{2+}(aq) + 2\ e^- = Cu(s) \qquad E° = +0.34 \text{ V}$$

$$Fe^{3+}(aq) + e^- = Fe^{2+}(aq) \qquad E° = +0.77 \text{ V}$$

Fe(III) ions can oxidize copper ions while being reduced themselves:

$$Cu^{2+}(aq) + 2\,e^- = Cu(s) \qquad\qquad E^o = +0.34\ V$$
$$Ox_1 \qquad\qquad\qquad Red_1$$

$$2Fe^{2+}(aq) = 2Fe^{3+} + 2e^- \qquad\qquad E^o = -0.77\ V$$
$$Red_2 \qquad\quad Ox_2$$

$$Cu^{2+}(aq) + 2Fe^{2+}(aq) = Cu(s) + 2Fe^{3+}(aq) \qquad E^o = -0.43\ V$$

Notice that reversing the Fe^{2+} half-reaction also reverses the sign of the potential, which changes from +0.77V to –0.77V. Also notice that two electrons are required to oxidize copper, so the Fe^{2+} half-reaction must also be doubled to provide them.

Thus, in a given redox system, one half-reaction *always* reacts in the direction of oxidation, and the other reacts in the direction of reduction:

Oxidizing agent 1 + electron → reducing agent 1   (oxidation)

Reducing agent 2 → oxidizing agent 2 + electron   (reduction)

Oxidizing agent 1 + reducing agent 2 → reducing agent 1 + oxidizing agent 2

or

$$Ox_1 + e^- \to Red_1 \qquad \text{(oxidation, half-reaction 1)}$$
$$Red_2 \to Ox_2 + e^- \qquad \text{(reduction, half-reaction 2)}$$

$$Ox_1 + Red_2 \to Red_1 + Ox_2$$

The sum of the standard electrode potentials of the half-reactions is called the **redox potential**, so in our example above, the redox potential is –0.43 V.

Example:

In the following redox pair, $Sn^{2+} \leftrightarrow Sn^{4+} + 2e^-$, Sn^{2+} is the reduced form, and the reducing agent and Sn^{4+} is the oxidized form and the oxidizing agent.

COMPLEXOMETRY

COMPLEX METAL-ION PAIRS

In complexometric titrations, the titrant is typically a **chelating agent**, which is an organic complexing agent that's used to bind the analyte, usually a metal ion. This analytical method is used to determine metal ions. The most widely used chelating agent is ethylenediaminetetraacetic acid (EDTA) which has the structure:

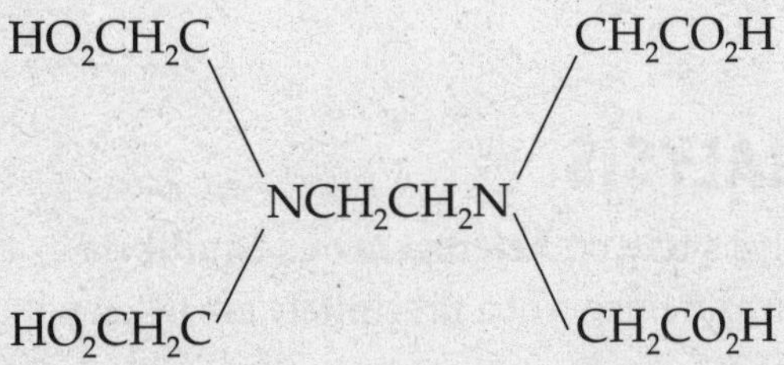

$$HO_2CH_2C \qquad\qquad\qquad CH_2CO_2H$$

$$NCH_2CH_2N$$

$$HO_2CH_2C \qquad\qquad\qquad CH_2CO_2H$$

EDTA has four complexing groups (CH_2CO_2H) that allow it to wrap around a metal ion. This complex (EDTA wrapped around a metal ion) is an example of a **chelate,** which can take part in the following equilibrium:

$$\text{Complexation (chelate)} \quad \underset{\text{complex dissociation}}{\overset{\text{complex formation}}{\longleftarrow\!\!\!\!\longrightarrow}} \quad \text{metal ion + ligands}$$

In the preceding sections, we discussed acid-base pairs and redox pairs: these are similar to **complex-metal ion pairs**.

Here's an example:

$$[Ag(CN)\,2]^-(aq) \Leftrightarrow Ag^+(aq) + 2CN^-(aq)$$

This **anionic** complex has an overall charge of –1.

Uncharged complexes also exist:

$$[Ag(CN)](aq) \Leftrightarrow Ag^+(aq) + CN^-(aq)$$

Cationic complexes have overall positive charges:

$$Ag^+(aq) + 2NH_3(aq) \Leftrightarrow [Ag(NH_3)_2]^+(aq)$$

FORMATION CONSTANTS

Complexation reactions are often reversible and occur stepwise, and each step has a unique formation constant K_f.

For example, the formation of cationic $[Ag(NH_3)_2]^+$ occurs in two steps:

$$Ag^+ + NH_3 \leftrightarrow [Ag(NH_3)]^+ \qquad\qquad K_{f1} = \frac{[Ag(NH_3)]^+}{[Ag^+][NH_3]}$$

$$[Ag(NH_3)]^+ + NH_3 \leftrightarrow [Ag(NH_3)_2]^+ \qquad\qquad K_{f2} = \frac{[Ag(NH_3)_2]^+}{[Ag(NH_3)^+][NH_3]}$$

And the overall formation constant is the product of the formation constants of the two steps:

$$K_f = (K_{f1})(K_{f2})$$

HETEROGENEOUS EQUILIBRIA

Equilibrium systems that contain only one phase are called homogeneous equilibria. When more than one phase is encountered, the systems are called heterogeneous equilibria. Four topics are covered under this heading: gravimetric analysis, solubility, precipitation titrations, and chemical separations.

GRAVIMETRIC ANALYSIS

Gravimetric methods of analysis rely on **heterogeneous equilibria**.

In these methods, mass measurements of a **precipitate** are taken with a precise analytical balance.

Gravimetry involves the following steps:

1. preparation of the analyte solution
2. precipitation
3. digestion of the precipitate
4. filtration and washing of the precipitate
5. drying and weighing of the precipitate
6. determination of amount of analyte present

Here's an example of gravimetric analysis, the precipitation method used for determining the mass of calcium in water:

(i) An excess of oxalic acid ($H_2C_2O_4$) is added to a precisely known volume of natural water, and the subsequent addition of ammonia forms the oxalate ion:

$$H_2C_2O_4 + 2NH_3 \rightarrow C_2O_4^{2-} + 2NH_4^+$$

(ii) The oxalate ion then causes the precipitation of calcium oxalate:

$$Ca^{2+}(s) + C_2O_4^{\ 2-}\ (aq) \rightarrow CaC_2O_4\ (s) \downarrow$$

(iii) The precipitate is collected in a crucible, weighed, dried, and then heated to 500°C to yield calcium oxide:

$$CaC_2O_4(s) + \Delta \rightarrow CaO(s) + CO(g) + CO_2(g)$$

(iv) The crucible and the calcium oxide are then cooled and the mass of CaO is determined by subtracting the known mass of the crucible. (The number of moles of CaO is equivalent to the number of moles of calcium.)

Here's an example of a sample calculation:

Example:

A sample of 5.00 mL of water containing calcium is treated with an excess of oxalic acid in the presence of ammonia. The precipitate is filtered, dried, and then heated to 500°C. Its mass is determined to be 3.50 mg. Calculate the concentration of calcium in the sample in g/L.

Answer: The solid obtained after heating is CaO (molar mass = 56.1 g/mol). The stoichiometry of the reaction is such that the number of moles of CaO obtained is equal to the number of moles of calcium initially present in the water sample. So,

$$\text{Mass of Ca} = \left(\frac{\text{mass of CaO}}{\text{molar mass of CaO}}\right)\text{molar mass of Ca}$$

$$= \left(\frac{0.00350g}{56.1g/mol}\right)40.1g/mol$$

$$= 2.5\ mg$$

$$\text{and } [Ca^{2+}] = \frac{2.5\ mg}{5.00\ mL} = \frac{0.5\ mg}{mL} = 0.5\ g/L$$

Gravimetric analysis can also involve **volatilization methods**. A volatile product can be collected and massed, or the mass of a volatile product can be determined by the mass loss of a certain sample.

For example, the gravimetric determination of the hydrogen carbonate content of antacid tablets is as follows:

$$NaHCO_3(aq) + H_2SO_4(aq) \rightarrow CO_2(g) + H_2O(l) + NaHSO_4(aq)$$

Carbon dioxide is collected in a tube containing an absorbent substance that retains it. The mass of CO_2 is then obtained by difference, and because the stoichiometry of reaction is one mole of $NaHCO_3$ per mole of CO_2, the amount of hydrogen carbonate can be determined.

PROPERTIES OF PRECIPITATES AND PRECIPITANTS

- **Specificity and selectivity**. A good precipitant for gravimetric analysis should be *specific*: it should react with only one chemical species.

Dimethylglyoxime is highly specific; it precipitates only the Ni^{2+} ion. If not specific, a precipitating agent should at least be highly *selective* and react with a very limited number of species.

For example, silver nitrate is a selective reagent because the only common ions it precipitates out of acidic solutions are Cl^-, Br^-, I^-, SCN^-.

SOME IMPORTANT POINTS ABOUT GRAVIMETRIC ANALYSIS

- **Ease of recovery of analyte**. A good reagent should also react with the analyte to form a precipitate that is easy to filter and wash, sparingly soluble so that there is no significant loss during the filtration and washing steps, unreactive with constituents of the atmosphere, and of known composition.

- **Particle size**. Precipitates made of large particles are easy to filter and are usually purer than those made up of small particles.

- **Colloidal and crystalline suspensions**. Colloidal suspensions are made of small particles (10^{-7} to 10^{-4} cm in diameter), that are invisible to the naked eye. These particles do not tend to settle to the bottom of the solution and can be difficult to filter. Crystalline suspensions are made of particles 0.1 mm or more in diameter. These particles tend to settle spontaneously and are easily filtered. It is preferential to choose reactions that produce a crystalline suspension.

- **Factors determining particle size**. These factors are experimental variables, such as precipitate solubility (S), reactant concentration, solute concentration (Q), and the rate at which the reactant is added. Particle size is related to a property of the system called relative supersaturation, which depends on the variables just mentioned.

$$\text{Relative supersaturation} = \frac{Q - S}{S}$$

Particle size varies inversely with supersaturation over the time period in which the reagent is added.

When $\frac{Q-S}{S}$ is large, the precipitate tends to be colloidal; when $\frac{Q-S}{S}$ is small, the precipitate tends to be crystalline.

- **Experimental conditions** should be chosen to minimize Q (by using dilute solutions and slowly adding the reagent) and to maximize S (run the reaction at elevated temperature). Note that colloidal solids can be precipitated from hot, well-stirred solutions that contain an electrolyte that ensures coagulation. In this context, an electrolyte is a solid upon whose surface colloidal particles are adsorbed.

- **Mechanism of precipitate formation.** Precipitates form in two ways: by nucleation or by particle growth. During *nucleation*, a small number of particles join together to produce a small solid. This nucleus may grow by the further accumulation of particles: this is particle growth.

  In precipitation, existing nuclei grow, and additional nucleation takes place. If nucleation predominates in the precipitation process, the precipitate is made of a large number of small nuclei and tends to be colloidal. If particle growth predominates, a fast settling and easy-to-filter precipitate is obtained.

TREATMENT OF GRAVIMETRIC DATA

The results obtained from gravimetric analysis are usually obtained from two experimental measurements: the mass of the sample and the mass of a product of known composition.

SOLUBILITY

- The **solubility of a substance** is the number of grams of solute necessary to form a saturated solution in one kilogram of water.

The fundamental rule of solubility:

Like dissolves like.

A polar solvent can be used to dissolve a polar solute, and a nonpolar solvent can be used to dissolve a nonpolar solute.

- **Here are the steps of the dissolution process:**

1. The solute disperses in individual particles when its intramolecular forces rupture. This process requires the input of energy $(\Delta H_1 > 0)$;

2. The intramolecular forces in the solvent also rupture; this causes its expansion and allows greater accessibility to the solute particles. This process is also endothermic $(\Delta H_2 > 0)$;

3. Interaction of solute with solvent molecules, which forms a solution. This step is usually exothermic $(\Delta H_3 < 0)$.

The change in enthalpy that accompanies the formation of a solution is called the **heat of dissociation**. It can be either positive or negative.

$$\Delta H_{diss} = \Delta H_1 + \Delta H_2 + \Delta H_3$$

Processes that require a lot of energy (ie, they have a high ΔH_{diss}) do not tend to occur spontaneously.

Take a look at the solubility of NaCl in water. The first step in the dissociation of NaCl requires a lot of energy, because of the great strength of the ionic bond between Na and Cl:

$$NaCl(s) \rightarrow Na^+(g) + Cl^-(g) \qquad \Delta H_1 = 790 \text{ kJ/mol.}$$

The second step of the dissolution process (ΔH_2) is solvent expansion; it also requires a lot of energy because the hydrogen bonds of water must be broken. The third step (ΔH_3) describes solute-solvent interaction:

$$H_2O(l) + Na^+(g) + Cl^-(g) \leftrightarrow Na^+(aq) + Cl^-(aq)$$

It is high and negative because the interaction between the ions and water is very strong. The combined second and third steps is referred to as the heat of hydration:

$$\Delta H_{hydr} = \Delta H_2 + \Delta H_3 = -785 \text{ kJ/mol}$$

Overall,

$$H_{diss} = \Delta H_1 + \Delta H_{hydr} = 790 \text{ kJ/mole} - 785 \text{ kJ/mol}$$
$$\Delta H_{diss} = 5 \text{ kJ/mol}$$

The dissociation enthalpy is small, but positive.

So why does salt dissolve so readily in water? It is because of favorable energetic conditions and the increase of disorder as a result of the process.

FACTORS INFLUENCING DISSOLUTION

- **Structure**: Solubility increases if both the solute and the solvent have similar polarities (like dissolves like!).

  Because molecular structure determines the polarity of a compound, there is a clear relationship between structure and solubility.

  Example:

  Vitamin A is liposoluble (fat-soluble). It is mostly composed of carbon and hydrogen and is nonpolar.

  For this reason, it is soluble in nonpolar body fat and not in water, which is a polar molecule.

  On the other hand, vitamin C contains several C–O and O–H bonds, which makes it polar and enables it to dissolve easily in water, but not in body fat.

- **Pressure**: Pressure exerts very little influence on the solubility of solids and liquids, but it has a remarkable effect on the solubility of gases. The influence of pressure on the solubility of gases is best expressed by **Henry's Law**: *In the absence of chemical reaction between the solute and the solvent, the quantity of gas dissolved in a solution is directly proportional to the pressure of the gas above the solution.*

- **Temperature**: The dissolution of solids occurs more rapidly at higher temperatures, but the quantity of solid that can be dissolved can either increase or decrease. Generally, the solubility of solids increases with temperature, but two notable exceptions to this rule are cerium and sodium sulfate. The solubility of gases in water always decreases with increasing temperature.

SOLUBILITY PRODUCT CONSTANT

In a saturated solution of a slightly soluble ionic compound, an equilibrium exists between the solute and its ions:

$$PbI_2(s) \leftrightarrow Pb^{2+}(aq) + 2I^-(aq)$$

You would think that the equilibrium constant for this reaction would be: $K_{eq} = [Pb^{2+}][2I^-]/[PbI_2]$ but, because the concentration of the solute remains constant in a saturated solution at a given temperature, the $[PbI_2]$ constant can be combined with the regular equilibrium constant to form a new constant K_{sp}, called the **solubility product constant**. For the above reaction,

$$K_{sp} = [Pb^{2+}][I^-]^2$$

It is defined as the product of the concentrations of the ions of a chemical in a saturated solution of that chemical. The solubility product constant is related to the **solubility (s)**, which is defined as the number of moles of a substance that dissolves in 1 liter of water. Keep in mind that this equation shows that the equilibrium is independent of the amount of solute present.

Some Solubility Product Constants at $T = 25\ ^{\circ}C$

Substance	K_{sp}
Aluminum hydroxide, $Al(OH)_3$	2.0×10^{-32}
Barium carbonate, $BaCO_3$	8.1×10^{-9}
Calcium carbonate, $CaCO_3$	8.7×10^{-9}
Ferrous hydroxide, $Fe(OH)_2$	8.0×10^{-16}
Ferric hydroxide, $Fe(OH)_3$	4.1×10^{-38}
Lead sulfide, PbS	8.0×10^{-28}
Magnesium hydroxide, $Mg(OH)_2$	1.2×10^{-11}
Mercurous bromide, Hg_2Br_2	5.8×10^{-23}
Silver bromide, AgBr	4.0×10^{-13}
Zinc sulfide, ZnS	1.0×10^{-21}

Example:

Calculate the solubility of PbI_2 at 25°C. The K_{sp} of PbI_2 is 7.1×10^{-9}.

Answer: When PbI_2 ionizes, one mole of Pb^{2+} and two moles of I^- are formed:

$$PbI_2 \rightarrow Pb^{2+} + 2I^- \text{ and } K_{sp} = [Pb^{2+}][I^-]^2$$

Let s represent the molar solubility of PbI_2. Since each mole of PbI_2 that dissolves yields one mole of Pb^{2+} and two moles of I^-, then $[Pb^{2+}] = s$ and $[I^-] = 2s$,

and $\quad [Pb^{2+}][I^-]^2 = 7.1 \times 10^{-9}$

or $\quad (s)(2s)^2 = 7.1 \times 10^{-9}$ and

$$s = \left(\frac{K_{sp}}{4}\right)^{\frac{1}{3}} = \left(\frac{7.1 \times 10^{-9}}{4}\right)^{\frac{1}{3}} = 1.2 \times 10^{-3} M$$

So the solubility in g/L is 1.2×10^{-3} moles/liter × 461.0 g/mole = 0.55 g/L

PRECIPITATION TITRATIONS

The formation of a fairly insoluble compound occurs in precipitation reactions:

$$A(aq) + B(aq) \leftrightarrow AB(s)$$

$$K_{sp} = [A] \times [B]$$

Silver nitrate is one titrimetric agent that's widely used in precipitation reactions to determine halides, certain divalent anions, and mercaptans, which precipitate as silver salts. Silver nitrate is one of the few reagents that reacts rapidly enough to be useful.

There are three stages in the titration curve for a precipitation reaction: preequivalence points, the equivalence point, and postequivalence points.

Example:

Consider the titration of an analyte A^-, which has the concentration C_A, with $AgNO_3$, which has the concentration C_{AgNO3}.

The reaction is $A^-(aq) + Ag^+(aq) \rightarrow AgA(s)$, and $K_{ps} = [Ag^+] \cdot [A^-]$, so this K_{sp} looks pretty much the same as the K_{sp} for a slightly soluble ionic compound.

- **Preequivalence points:** Up to the equivalence point, A^- will be present in excess, as a result of both precipitate formation and dilution. Two steps are required to calculate the preequivalence point concentration of $[A^-]$.

    1. The concentration of analyte, C_A, after addition of a volume V_{AgNO_3}, is given by

    $$[A^-] = \frac{(V_{A^-} \cdot C_{A^-}) - (V_{Ag^+} \cdot C_{Ag^+})}{V_{A^-} + V_{Ag^+}}$$

The precipitate formed, AgA, will dissolve in accordance with its K_{sp}, and the amount of A^- released back in solution will be equal to the amount of Ag^+ that's simultaneously formed:

$$[Ag^+] = K_{sp}/[A^-]$$

    2. A correction factor is then added to the preceding equation (because not all of the Ag^+ added will form a precipitate with the A^- in solution; AgA is only slightly soluble).

    $$[A^-] = \frac{\left(V_{A^-} \cdot C_{A^-}\right) - \left(V_{Ag^+} \cdot C_{Ag^+}\right)}{V_{A^-} + V_{Ag^+}} + \frac{K_{sp}}{[A^-]}$$

The correction factor takes into account only the concentration of A^- ions that result from the dissociation of AgA.

$$\text{Correction factor} = [A^-]_{diss} = [Ag^+]_{diss} = \frac{\dfrac{K_{sp}}{[AgA]}}{[A^-]}$$

However, this correction term is necessary only when K_{sp} is relatively large, if the solutions are very dilute, or if the point considered is very near the equivalent point.

Having calculated $[A^-]$, we can then calculate the silver ion concentration using: $[Ag^+] = K_{sp}/[A^-]$ and then pAg, which is defined as:

$$pAg = \log[Ag^+]$$

- **Equivalence point.** At the equivalence point, neither A^- nor $AgNO^3$ is in excess: they exist in stoichiometric proportions: $[Ag^+] = [A^-] = \sqrt{K_{sp}}$.

- **Postequivalence points.** Now the titrant is in excess.

The concentration of silver ions is $\left[Ag^+\right] = \dfrac{\left(V_{Ag^+} \cdot C_{Ag^+}\right) - \left(V_{A^-} \cdot C_{A^-}\right)}{V_{A^-} + V_{Ag^+}} + \dfrac{K_{sp}}{\left[Ag^+\right]}$.

taking into account that $[A^-][Ag^+] = K_{sp}$ (AgA).

The correction term also applies here, although it is usually negligible. The value of pAg can be obtained easily from the result of the calculation above.

FACTORS THAT AFFECT THE EQUIVALENCE POINT ON A GRAPH

- Equivalent points, or end points, are sharp and easy to locate; small additions of titrants at these points cause large changes in the titration curve.

- End-point determination and precision also improve when the analytical reaction is nearer to completion. Therefore, the largest changes are observed for the reaction products that are the least soluble (small value of K_{sp}; these products form precipitates well and do not redissolve into solution).

CHEMICAL SEPARATIONS

Few analytical methods are so specific as to be completely free of interference.

In a chemical analysis, an **interference** is a species that behaves similarly to the analyte; this causes an error in the final analysis. Several procedures are available that overcome interferences, such as use of a **masking agent,** which reacts with an interference and prevents it from causing error in analysis or separating the analyte and the interference through separate phases with **solvent extraction, ion exchange,** or **electrolysis.**

Here's an example of this: The Fe^{3+} ion is an interference in the iodimetric determination of Cd^{2+}. The F^- ion is used as a masking agent because it complexes with Fe^{3+} and not Cd^{2+}.

Example:

The selective precipitation of metal sulfides can involve hydrogen sulfide as the precipitant. A saturated solution of H_2S is approximately 0.10 mol/liter. Hydrogen sulfide is a diprotic acid and it dissociates as follows:

$$H_2S(aq) + 2H_2O \rightarrow S^{2-}(aq) + 2H_3O^+(aq)$$

with

$$(K_1)(K_2) = \frac{[H_3O^+]^2[S^{2-}]}{[H_2S]} = 6.8 \times 10^{-23}$$

The desired concentration of S^{2-} ion is achieved by controlling the pH of the solution. If the pH = 1.00, then $[H_3O^+] = 1.00 \times 10^{-1}\,M$ and $[S^{2-}] = 6.8 \times 10^{-22}\,M$.

The sulfide ion content of a saturated H_2S solution is inversely proportional to the square of the hydronium concentration.

Take a look at this example:

How can a saturated solution of H_2S be used to separate Cd^{2+} from Tl^+ in a solution that's 0.1 M in each cation? CdS has a $K_{sp} = 2 \times 10^{-28}$ and Tl_2S has a $K_{sp} = 1 \times 10^{-22}$.

CdS precipitates at lower Cd^{2+} concentration than Tl_2S. If we arbitrarily decide that

1. CdS is less soluble than Tl_2S and therefore at the same concentration of S^{2-}, CdS will precipitate first. The criterion for removal of Cd^{2+} is 10^{-4} M, then the required concentration of S^{2-} to carry out this removal is

$$[S^{2-}] = \frac{2 \times 10^{-28}}{[Cd^{2+}]} = 2 \times 10^{-24}$$

If we maintain $[S^{2-}]$ at this level or higher, quantitative removal of Cd^{2+} (which we desire) is achieved. Then the precipitate can be filtered from the solution. The $[H_3O^+]$ concentration at which this value of $[S^{2-}]$ is achieved is

$$[H_3O^+] = \frac{\sqrt{6.8 \times 10^{-23} \times [H_2S]}}{2 \times 10^{-24}} = 1.8\,M$$

To initiate precipitation of Tl_2S from the filtration liquid, the required concentration of S^{2-} is

$$[S^{2-}] = \frac{1 \times 10^{-22}}{[Tl^+]} = 1.0 \times 10^{-20}$$

Precipitation of Tl_2S will be induced when the solubility constant is exceeded, that is, when $[S^{-2}] \geq 1 \times 10^{-20}$.

The concentration of $[H_3O^+]$ at which this condition is achieved is

$$[H_3O^+] = \frac{\sqrt{6.8 \times 10^{-23} \times [H_2S]}}{1 \times 10^{-20}} = 0.03\,M$$

This means that, by maintaining $[H_3O^+]$ between 0.03 M and 1.8 M, CdS can be quantitatively separated from Tl_2S.

INSTRUMENTAL METHODS

Five topics are covered under this heading: electrochemical methods, spectroscopic methods, chromatographic methods, thermal methods, and the calibration of instruments.

ELECTROCHEMICAL METHODS

The two most important electrochemical methods are potentiometry and voltammetry.

Potentiometry

Potentiometry refers to a group of techniques that involves the measurement of emf (electromotive force) compared to a standard zero current. The measurement of potential provides quantitative information about the compounds in a sample. There are two forms of potentiometry: **indicator electrode potentiometry** and **potentiometric titration.**

- **Indicator electrode potentiometry** uses an indicator electrode, the *ion-selective electrode*, that measures ion activity directly when it is immersed in an analyte solution, and is selectively sensitive to the element being determined. An ideal indicator electrode responds rapidly and accurately to changes in the concentration of the analyte ion. It is used in conjunction with a *reference electrode*, which is insensitive to the composition of the analyte and has a known and constant potential.

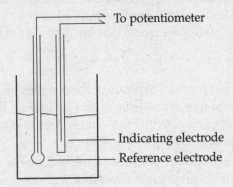

Setup for potentiometric measurement

There are two types of indicator electrodes: *metal* and *membrane*.

Metal electrodes function by sensing the transfer of electrons at the interface between electrode and solution.

Membrane electrodes function by sensing the transfer of ions from one side of a selectively permeable membrane to the other. These electrodes contain both a test solution and a reference electrode. The *glass electrode* used for pH measurements is an example of a membrane electrode, but glass electrodes that detect ions other than protons have been developed. Now Na^+, K^+, Rb^+, Cs^+, Li^+, Ag^+, and NH_4^+ can be potentiometrically measured by glass electrodes. Membrane electrodes can be either liquid or gas sensing. Like glass, crystals can also be used as membrane materials. An example of this is the solid-state fluoride electrode, in which the membrane consists of a single crystal of $LaCl_3$ doped with Eu(II) to increase its electrical conductivity. This electrode is 1000 x more selective toward fluoride than toward chloride, iodide, and bromide.

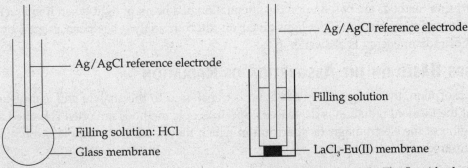

The glass pH electrode

An ion-selective electrode: The fluoride electrode

- **Potentiometric titration** uses electrodes, which can be either highly selective or universal, as indicators for determining the end points of titrations. These electrodes measure the potential as a function of the amount of titrant added, and a rapid change of potential usually indicates the end point of the titration.

Voltammetry

Voltammetry is the name given to a family of techniques in which electrolysis is carried out so that the analyte is completely oxidized (or reduced) to a product of known composition. The two main voltammetric methods are *electrogravimetry* and *coulometry*. These two techniques differ from potentiometry in that they require application of a current throughout the entire process.

- In **electrogravimetry**, a potential ensures that continual electrolysis is applied across carefully weighed electrodes. The current is administered and maintained at a high value, until the species is quantitatively deposited at one of the electrodes (the **working electrode**). Metals are reduced at the cathode to yield a metal deposit:

$$M^+(aq) + e^- \rightarrow M(s)$$

The elements Ag, Pb, and Mn produce deposits of their oxides on the anode; this method is not useful in solutions of these metal ions. The deposits may be impure if several reducible species are present in solution and if the applied potential is too high. This method is used for the quantitative determination of a small range of elements.

For example, the electrolysis of Cu^{2+} produces a deposit of Cu on a Pt cathode in an acidic solution, and the electrolysis of Br^- produces a deposit of AgBr on a silver anode.

In this case, the anode reaction is $Ag(s) + Br^- \rightarrow AgBr(s) + 1 e^-$ and reduction occurs at the cathode.

- **Coulometric procedures**

Coulometry measures the quantity of electricity required for the quantitative electrolysis of an analyte. Coulometric procedures do not require that the product of the electrochemical reaction be a weighable solid, because the quantity of electricity consumed during the process is proportional to the amount of analyte present, if only one species is involved.

During a coulometric analysis, the electrolytic current is recorded as a function of time. The analysis of the curve thus obtained gives the number of coulombs and subsequently the number of equivalents of the analyte.

SPECTROSCOPIC METHODS

Spectroscopic methods of analysis are based upon the measurement of electromagnetic radiation that's absorbed or emitted by an analyte.

Absorption methods are based upon the attenuation of a beam of light when it interacts with an analyte. In **emission** methods, the light given off after an analyte has been excited by thermal, electrical or radiant energy is analyzed.

METHODS BASED ON THE ABSORPTION OF RADIATION

During absorption, the energy of the radiation is transferred to the analyte and, consequently, the energy of the incident radiation is decreased. Spectroscopic methods are often classified according to the region of the electromagnetic spectrum in which they work, for example, X-ray, ultraviolet, visible, infrared, etc., spectroscopy.

- **Visible and Ultraviolet Spectrometry**

In VIS or UV spectroscopy, the absorption (or emission) process results in an electronic rearrangement within atoms or molecules. The UV region of the spectrum ranges from the far UV (10–200 nm) to the near UV (200–400 nm). The VIS region extends from 400 to 750 nm. During the absorption process, the molecules are first in their ground electronic state. Upon absorbing incident radiation, they reach an excited state.

The emission process is the reverse of absorption; a molecule already in an excited state returns to a ground electronic state by the emission of radiant energy.

Terms used in absorption spectroscopy:

- Transmittance (T)   the fraction of incident radiation transmitted by the solution. $T = P/P_0$, where P_0 and P represent the power of the beam before (P_0) and after passage (P) through the solution. It is a measure of the attenuation of a beam of radiation by an absorbing solution.

- Absorbance (A)   quantity defined by $A = -\log T = \varepsilon b c$, where ε is the molar absorptivity (which depends on the identity of the solution), b is the length of the measuring cell, and c is the molar concentration of the solution.

This equation is referred to as the Beer-Lambert law:

$$A = -\log T = \varepsilon b c.$$

The absorbance is directly proportional to the amount of analyte present. The concentration of an analyte can be derived by comparing its absorbance to that of a standard of known concentration.

Infrared (IR) Spectrometry

Infrared spectrometry is the study of the absorption of radiation that has wavelengths of 1 to 1000 mm (usually reported in cm^{-1}). Absorption spectra in the infrared region occur because of transitions between vibrational and rotational energy levels of molecules in their ground electronic state.

IR is used in qualitative analysis and allows the identification of characteristic groups and the subsequent confirmation of molecular structure by comparison with standard spectra.

Quantitative study in the infrared region is based on the Beer-Lambert Law. For a particular absorption band, a calibration curve is constructed by plotting A against c for solutions of known concentration.

Raman Spectrometry

Raman spectroscopy is another form of vibrational spectroscopy in the IR region of the EM spectrum; it complements IR. When monochromatic light is directed at a cell that contains a particular compound, the scattered, emergent light contains frequencies that differ from the original one. These differences correspond to changes in the vibrational and rotational states of the molecular species.

With small molecules, less symmetric vibrations tend to yield intense infrared bands, whereas more symmetric vibrations often lead to strong Raman bands. Raman spectrometry may be used for identification purposes, as well as for quantitative studies. As with IR, the intensities of the lines of interest are compared with the intensities of standard lines to determine quantities.

Microwave Spectrometry

The microwave region of the electromagnetic spectrum encompasses radiation that has wavelengths ranging from 1 mm to several centimeters. Absorption of this type of radiation causes changes in the rotational frequency levels of gaseous polar molecules. Microwave spectrometry is used to determine structural information.

Nuclear Magnetic Resonance (NMR)

In NMR spectroscopy, radio-frequency radiation is absorbed by the nuclei of certain isotopes when they are placed in a magnetic field. The frequency of radiation required for NMR absorption depends on the isotope and its chemical environment.

The isotopes suitable for NMR spectroscopy include ^1H, ^{13}C, ^{19}F, and ^{31}P.

The number of absorption peaks that appear on the spectra for the magnetic nuclei in a molecule depends on the spatial position of neighboring magnetic nuclei in that molecule. Also, the intensity of an absorption peak is proportional to the number of existing nuclei. NMR is a very valuable technique for structural elucidation, especially of organic compounds.

Mass Spectrometry

Mass spectrometry concerns the determination of mass in the identification of compounds, specifically the mass to charge ratio (m/e) of gaseous ions.

The sample to be analyzed is first ionized, then bombarded with a beam of electrons. In this process, charged particles are formed, and these particles may be elemental, molecular, or fragmental in nature. The mass spectrometer then separates the ions according to their m/e ratio and determines the relative abundance of these ions. Structural information can be deduced from the observed ratios, and quantitative information can be derived from the relative abundance of each species.

Mass spectrometry is widely used in the structural determination of hydrocarbons. The ionization of the **parent molecules** (RS) in the vapor state by a beam of high-energy electrons can be described as follows:

$$R{:}S + e^- \rightarrow 2e^- + R{\cdot}\ S^+ \rightarrow R{\cdot} + S^+$$

In a first step, the parent molecules ionize, yielding parent cation-radicals ($R{\cdot}\ S^+$), which then dissociate to yield other cations or neutral species. The resulting **mass spectrogram** will show peaks at the (m/e) values of the cations generated by ionization. The relative peak heights are proportional to the relative abundance of the cations. The largest observed m/e value is that of the parent RS molecule, and the masses of the fragment cations then provide clues as to the possible structure of RS.

METHODS BASED ON THE EMISSION OF RADIATION

Atomic Spectrometry

Atomic spectrometric techniques, for the most part, are based on the emission of radiation after absorption of energy by a solute. Because the electronic transitions are associated with large dipole changes, the techniques are very sensitive and are used primarily in the field of *elemental trace analysis*. The first step of an atomic spectrometric procedure is **atomization**. During this process, the sample is volatilized and decomposed to produce particles, which can either be atoms or ions. An example of the use of atomic spectrometry is in the determination of lead, tin, and zinc in brasses (copper alloys). The sample is first dissolved in acid and, after dilution of the solution, a known volume is injected into the spectrometer. Then volatilization separates the component ions or atoms for subsequent analysis.

Some of the techniques based on atomic spectrometry are: Ark/spark emission spectrometry, in which electronic excitation is produced by electrical discharge and detection is accomplished by a photomultiplier; glow discharge atomic emission spectrometry; plasma emission spectrometry; flame emission spectrometry, atomic fluorescence spectrometry; and X-ray emission spectrometry.

Fluorimetry

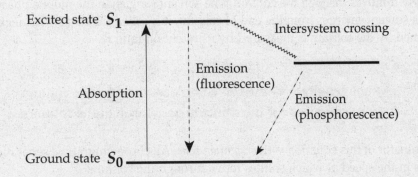

Fluorescence is caused by the absorption of radiant energy and reemission of some of this energy in the form of light. The light emitted is almost always of higher wavelength (i.e., lower energy) than the radiant energy initially absorbed. In true fluorescence, emission takes place in a short time ($10^{-12} - 10^{-9}$ sec), because the radiation is emitted from the same excited state energy level in which absorption took place and the molecule has the same singlet spin multiplicity in both the ground state and in the excited state. But if intersystem crossing occurs to a state of different multiplicity (triplet), the light is emitted with a time delay ($> 10^{-8}$ sec), and the phenomenon is known as *phosphorescence*. Both of these phenomena are designated by the term *photoluminescence*.

Fluorescence has many practical uses in analytical chemistry. The electronic transitions involved are of the type $n \to \pi^*$ (an electron in a nonbonding orbital is promoted to a π-antibonding orbital, which leads to very weak fluorescence), and $\pi \to \pi^*$ (π-bonding to π-antibonding, which leads to very strong fluorescence).

The total fluorescence intensity F is given by

$$F = I_0 \times 2.3\varepsilon cl\phi_f$$

where I_0 is the intensity of the incident light,

          ε is the molar absorptivity,

          c is the concentration,

          l is the cell length, and

          ϕ_f is the quantum yield of fluorescence.

In absorbance (or UV-VIS) photometry, the sensitivity is limited by ε, and the minimum detectable concentration is 10^{-8} M. In fluorescence spectrometry, the sensitivity is limited only by the maximum intensity of the exciting light source; the limit of detection of this method is around 10^{-12} M.

CHROMATOGRAPHY

Chromatography is a method for physically separating mixtures based on the varying solubility and structural properties of the components. This technique separates mixtures of substances by using a *stationary* phase and a *mobile* phase. The stationary phase is the immobile material with which the column is packed. The more time a component (the mobile phase) spends adsorbed onto that phase, the more slowly it moves through the column. The solvent (or gas) in the mobile phase is called the *eluent*. When a solvent emerges from the end of column, it is called the *eluate*. The degree to which a solute is retained by the column is measured by its retention ratio R:

$$R = \frac{\text{time required for the solvent to pass through the column}}{\text{time required for the solute to pass through the column}}$$

The denominator of this equation is the *retention time*. All chromatographic separations are based on differences in the speed at which solutes move through the column.

The equilibrium involved in the column can be described quantitatively by the partition coefficient K:

$$K = \frac{C_S}{C_M}$$

where C_s is the molar concentration of the solute in stationary phase and C_m is its concentration in the mobile phase.

In chromatography, it can be imagined that the column that contains the stationary phase is divided into N segments, in each of which one equilibrium occurs. Each of these imaginary segments is called a *theoretical plate*. If the total length of the column is L, the height equivalent of a theoretical plate (HETP) is

$$\text{HETP} = \frac{L}{N} = A + \frac{B}{v} + C \cdot v$$

where A, B, and C are coefficients and v is the mobile phase velocity. This is called the *van Deemter* equation. A is related to eddy diffusion, B to longitudinal diffusion, and C to mass transfer. These coefficients can be evaluated using other equations. The smaller the HETP is, the better the separation.

Chromatographic results are presented in a **chromatogram**, which plots the elution profile of the separation achieved. The x axis is the time and the y axis is the detector response. In a typical chromatogram, the number of peaks indicates the number of components separated by the chromatographic procedure. The intensity of the peaks is proportional to the concentration of the separated substances, and their order of appearance will depend on the selected chromatographic principle. For example, in a size exclusion chromatogram, the heavier components appear first.

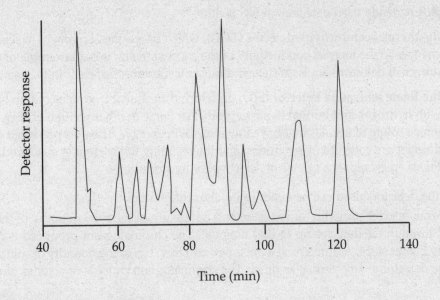

GAS CHROMATOGRAPHY (GC)

In *gas chromatography*, a volatile liquid or gaseous solute is carried by a gaseous mobile phase called the *carrier gas*.

The stationary phase is usually a relatively nonvolatile liquid adsorbed on a solid support, and the moving phase is usually helium or hydrogen gas. This most common form of GC is called *gas-liquid partition* chromatography.

When solid particles on which the solute can be adsorbed serve as the stationary phase, this is called *gas-solid adsorption* chromatography.

During a standard GC procedure, a volatile liquid sample is vaporized and swept into the column by the carrier gas. After passing through the column which contains the stationary phase, the solutes are separated from each other. Finally, the gas stream flows through a detector, which sends a signal to a recorder. Although He and H_2 are the most common carrier gases in GC, N_2, CO_2, and Ar are also used. The lighter gases (H_2 and He) allow for more longitudinal diffusion (diffusion parallel to the direction of flow of the carrier gas) of solutes, which tends to decrease the column efficiency. The best carrier gases for difficult separations are heavier gases such as N_2 or CO_2, because they reduce the flow rate and increase column efficiency.

Detectors

The function of the detector is to sense and measure the small amounts of the separated components that are present in the carrier gas as it leaves the column. Some of the important properties of a detector in GC include

1. **sensitivity** to the concentration of the analyte;

2. **linearity**, which refers to the concentration range over which the signal is directly proportional to the concentration of the analyte and not distorted;

3. **stability**, the extent to which the signal output remains constant with time;

4. **universal or selective response** to the components present in the mixture.

The most frequently used detectors in GC include

1. **the thermal conductivity detector (TCD)**, which uses a metal filament to sense changes in the thermal conductivity of the carrier stream; it is an example of a universal detector because it detects almost all substances present in the sample;

2. **the flame ionization detector (FID)**, in which the effluent from the column is mixed with hydrogen and burned in air to produce a flame that has enough energy to ionize solute molecules that have low ionization energy. The ions produced in the detector are collected at electrodes, and the resulting ion current is measured. The FID is an example of a detector selective for hydrocarbons.

In GC, the detectors used can be either integral or differential.

An integral detector provides (at any moment) a measure of the total quantity of the solute that has passed through the detector up to that moment. The chromatogram produced is composed of successively higher steps. A differential detector gives a measure of the quantity of solute that passes through the detector at any particular time. The chromatogram consists of a series of peaks rather than steps.

ANALYSIS OF GC CHROMATOGRAMS

For *qualitative analysis*, the peaks of a chromatogram can be identified by their retention times. For *quantitative analysis*, the area under each peak of interest is measured and correlated with the quantity of each component in the mixture.

It may happen that two solutes in a given sample have very similar retention times. Then the chromatogram will show overlapping peaks.

The resolution (R) of the peaks is determined by:

$$R = \frac{2\left(t_{R_2} - t_{R_1}\right)}{\left(W_{b_1} - W_{b_2}\right)}$$

where t_{R_2} is the retention time for substance 2,

t_{R_1} is the retention time for substance 1, and

W_{B_1} and W_{B_2} are the respective bandwidths of each peak.

R indicates how effectively a given column separates two solutes. The separation factor S is equal to the ratio of the retention times and the ratio of the partition coefficients of the two solutes:

$$S = \frac{t_{R_2}}{t_{R_1}} = \frac{K_2}{K_1}$$

LIQUID CHROMATOGRAPHY

Classical liquid chromatography uses gravity-fed columns (in **size exclusion** chromatography) and ionic resins (in **ion-exchange** chromatography). The first method separates the components of a mixture according to their molecular weights, whereas the second method separates them on the basis of their charge. **Molecular sieve gels** are used to pack size exclusion columns, and the elution of the components proceeds with the heavier components eluting first, followed by the lighter ones. In ion-exchange separations, the column is packed with an **anionic** or a **cationic resin**, depending on the charge of the sample's components.

High-performance liquid chromatography (HPLC) uses a high pressure that forces the liquid through the column, which is packed with particles of very small diameter. HPLC is much more efficient than conventional liquid chromatography but cannot perform large-scale separations. The most common stationary phase contains nonpolar groups covalently bonded to 5- to 10-mm silicon particles. *Single-solvent elution* or *gradient elution* (in which solvents with decreasing polarity are used) is employed in liquid chromatography.

Detectors

The most frequently used detector in LC is the ultraviolet detector. UV-VIS absorption is monitored as the effluent from the column passes through the detector, which is held in a radiation beam. Changes in the light transmittance indicates that a solute is being eluted. The detector is highly sensitive, with detection limits of concentrations as low as 1×10^{-9} M for highly absorbing material. Other detectors include the fluorescence detector (for fluorescent solutes), the electrochemical detector, which measures the current associated with the oxidation or reduction of solutes, and the refractive index detector. This last detector can be used only for pure mobile phases (therefore it is not suitable for gradient elution) and has poor sensitivity.

THERMAL METHODS

In thermal methods of analysis, the effect of heat on a sample is studied and provides qualitative and quantitative information about the sample.

Certain thermal events act as indicators for substances; these include phase transitions and glass transitions. Recording the change in the phase property as the temperature is varied results in a thermal analysis curve called a *thermogram*.

THERMOGRAVIMETRY (TG)

Thermogravimetry is the study of the change in mass of a sample as its temperature is varied.

Many substances undergo weight changes that result in characteristic curves when they are heated over a certain temperature range. If the change can be linked to a particular event, the thermogram can be used for quantitative analysis, but this technique requires a **thermobalance**, which has a sample support inside a furnace so that its temperature can be easily controlled. This method is useful for inorganic substances and polymers but is limited to substances that undergo weight changes. Precision is usually around 1%.

Here's an example:

When heated to 1000°C, calcium oxalate monohydride undergoes three changes, all of which are accompanied by weight loss. Its thermogram plots sample weight vs. temperature, and it displays four plateaus, each lower than the previous one. The temperatures at which curve drops are observed are the transition temperatures. In the case of $CaC_2O_4 \cdot H_2O$, the thermogram reflects the following reactions:

1. Between 22 and 200 °C, loss of water:

$$CaC_2O_4 \cdot H_2O \rightarrow CaC_2O_4 + H_2O$$

2. Between 400 and 500 °C, loss of carbon monoxide and formation of calcium carbonate:

$$CaC_2O_4 \rightarrow CaCO_3 + CO$$

3. Between 700 and 800 °C, loss of carbon dioxide and formation of carbon oxide:

$$CaCO_3 \rightarrow CaO + CO_2$$

DIFFERENTIAL THERMAL ANALYSIS (DTA)

This method is based upon the measurement of the temperature difference between the sample and an inert reference material such as Al_2O_3, when they are both heated uniformly. The temperature of the reference sample rises steadily and linearly, and the same thing happens to the sample, except that a peak is observed when an exothermic process takes place and a depression is recorded when an endothermic process takes place. The deviation in temperature can be qualitatively and quantitatively analyzed, as displayed in the **differential themogram**, which is a diagram of ΔT vs. furnace temperature. The curve remains flat, as long as no endothermic or exothermic process occurs. When such processes take place, they are reflected in the thermogram as positive peaks (exotherms) or negative peaks (endotherms).

The instrumentation involves a single furnace containing both the sample and the reference. The temperature of the sample and the reference are measured separately by sensitive thermocouples. Precision is usually about 1%.

CALIBRATION OF INSTRUMENTS

In quantitative analysis, an analytical measurement must be accurately related to the composition of the sample. Only when the relationship between measurement and analyte obeys a strict and measurable proportionality can the amount of analyte be derived from the measurement. This proportionality must be established in *calibration procedures*.

For a simple calibration, a range of standards that contains varying amounts of the analyte is prepared. Then a calibration curve of signal against amount of analyte is plotted, and the results for samples of unknown concentration are interpolated from this calibration curve. An ideal calibration curve would be smooth over a wide range of analyte concentrations, but deviations must be expected at higher and lower ranges, and this means loss of precision.

ENVIRONMENTAL APPLICATIONS

ANALYSIS OF ATMOSPHERIC SAMPLES

The atmosphere is primarily a mixture of O_2, N_2, and Ar; together, these make up more than 99.9% of dry air. The atmosphere also contains variable amounts of water vapor and a number of minor and trace gaseous components, such as ozone, carbon monoxide, methane, nitric oxide, nitrogen dioxide, sulfur dioxide, and Freons, which are either naturally present or result from industrial activity. Chemical reactions occur and affect the composition of the atmosphere by changing the concentration of one or more of these components and generating new ones. Most analytical methods used to study atmospheric samples fall into one of three categories:

- monitoring of components of ambient air;

- monitoring industrial emissions; and

- measuring the specific toxicity of airborne substances.

Many analytical methods are available for the analysis of atmospheric samples. The following are the most common:

GAS CHROMATOGRAPHY

Gas chromatography involves the separation of gaseous mixtures using the selective adsorption of the components of interest on solids such as alumina, silica gel, or a molecular sieve, etc. Conventional detectors are used, including flame ionization detectors (FID) and electron capture detectors (ECD), but detectors that measure very low concentrations of specific contaminants may also be used.

SPECTROMETRIC METHODS

These methods are widely used in gas analysis. All gases that contain covalent bonds, except non-polar diatomic molecules (O_2, N_2, Cl_2) possess characteristic absorption spectra in the infrared UV region. Their absorption depends on the concentration of the molecules and follows the Beer-Lambert law. Certain gas molecules fluoresce after they are stimulated to an excited state in a process called *chemiluminescence*. Analysis of atmospheric samples often involves measurements at very low concentrations, so that highly sensitive and selective analyzers such as the dual-beam non-dispersive infrared (NDIR) or ultraviolet (NDUV) analyzer are necessary. Typically, for sample cells with path lengths of 100–200 mm, detection limits are at the ppm level.

FOURIER TRANSFORM SPECTROMETRY

Fourier transform spectrometry is a technique used for nondispersive measurement of spectra. It is usually applied in the infrared region (FTIR). In FTIR spectrometry, the entire frequency range is monitored simultaneously, so that several atmospheric components can be measured together. FTIR spectrometers are often used as GC detectors.

LIDAR (LIGHT DETECTION AND RANGING)

LIDAR operates similarly to radar. A pulse of light is emitted directly into the atmosphere by a high-power laser and is scattered by aerosols. A proportion of the scattered light is absorbed and reemitted by the target analyte in the air and back-scattered along the transmission line. Then a detector receives the pulse, and information on the nature and position of the absorbing and scattering species can then be derived by measuring the time it takes for the pulse to return to the detector. Information on the chemical composition of the atmosphere is obtained by a LIDAR system, which operates in a differential mode (DIAL). Because the intensity of the scattered light is weak, LIDAR and DIAL are usually operated at UV or VIS lengths. These methods are currently used for monitoring NO, NO_2, O_3, and CO_2 and some organic molecules in air.

PHOTOACOUSTIC SPECTROMETRY (PAS)

In photoacoustic spectrometry, the sample is contained in a sealed chamber and irradiated with pulses of IR or UV light. Some of the energy is absorbed by the target molecule and released as heat, causing the temperature and pressure inside the chamber to rise, and microphones detect the pressure pulses thus produced. Specificity is achieved by selecting a radiation corresponding to a specific absorption band of the gas. The amplitude recorded by the microphone can be used in quantitative measurements of the target gases. PAS is applicable to a wide variety of gases and organic molecules (i.e. toluene) and is highly sensitive; the response is linear over a wide range of concentrations. Detection limits are very low; for instance, 150 ppb for carbon monoxide, 3 ppm for carbon dioxide, and 70 ppb for formaldehyde.

OTHER SPECTROMETRIC METHODS

Correlation spectrometry is an analytical method in which the molecules to be analyzed are used to specify the analytical wavelength. *Tunable diode laser spectrometry* is similar to conventional IR absorption spectrometry, but the source is a diode laser with a very narrow line width, which enables the vibration lines of the target molecule to be resolved. This increases both the sensitivity and the selectivity of the technique.

ELECTROCHEMICAL SENSORS

When a gas is introduced in an electrochemical device that consists of a cell and two electrodes in contact with an electrolyte, a reaction may happen at one of the electrode-electrolyte interfaces. A current will be generated and correlated with the concentration of the gas. The sensing electrode may be made selective to a particular gas by enveloping the sensing electrodes in a suitable membrane through which the gas diffuses. Electrochemical sensors are available for the following gases: H_2, O_2, NO_2, NO, Cl_2, CO, SO_2, and HCN.

An example of electrochemical sensor is the CO_2 sensor. Its design incorporates an indicating/reference electrode pair placed inside a tube that contains a solution of sodium hydrogen carbonate as internal electrolyte. The tube is sealed with a gas-permeable membrane. When the sensor is immersed in the sample solution which contains the CO_2 to be determined, diffusion of the carbon dioxide occurs through the membrane until equilibrium is reached, the point at which the concentration of CO_2 in the sample solution is equal to that of the internal electrolyte. Any change in the electrolyte's CO_2 concentration will also change its pH, and this pH change is detected by the electrode pair and converted to carbon dioxide concentration.

CHEMICAL METHODS

Most pollutant gases in the atmosphere are reactive and can be monitored by selective absorption from an air sample of known volume, followed by chemical analysis. For instance, SO_2 can be monitored by following its absorption into an H_2O_2 solution, and then its titration. Chemical methods often involve *gas detector tubes*, which are tubes packed with a reagent system suitable for analysis. After a gaseous sample is introduced into a gas detector tube, a reaction takes place (which can be redox, acid-base, etc.), and a color change occurs in the column packing. The concentration of the sample can be deduced from the length of the stain and comparison with calibration data. Gas detector tubes provide quick information, but they are not very specific.

ANALYSIS OF WATER SAMPLES

Because water has excellent solvent properties, it is recognized as the ultimate *sink* for pollutants. The common analytical tests performed on water samples include pH measurements and qualitative determinations, such as measurements for dissolved oxygen, total organic carbon, metals, salts, and trace organic substances.

pH, Acidity, and Alkalinity

pH is a measure of the acidity or basicity of water; it runs on a scale of 0 – 14, and pH = 7 is neutral.

Three methods of pH measurement are commonly used: stick paper coated with a sensitive dye, dye solutions, and the H^+ glass electrode. Acidity refers to the capacity of water to neutralize OH^- ions. It can be determined by titration with sodium hydroxide and a suitable color indicator. Alkalinity is the capacity of water to neutralize H^+ ions, and it is usually determined by titration with a strong acid such as HCl in the presence of an indicator.

Determination of Dissolved Oxygen and Oxygen Demand

The amount of dissolved oxygen in water depends on the ambient temperature and pressure. Dissolved oxygen can be decreased or depleted by the biochemical breakdown of organic material in the water. These organic materials can be from animal, industrial, or agricultural sources. **The biochemical oxygen demand (BOD)** of certain organic processes can be determined by measuring the amount of O_2 present in water before and after the incubation of a sample for five days at 20°C. Dissolved oxygen is determined by using a dissolved oxygen electrode.

A titrimetric method called the Winkler method is also used, in which dissolved oxygen is used to oxidize Mn^{2+} to Mn^{4+}. The Mn^{4+} formed by this oxidation is then reduced in acidic solution in the presence of I^-, to form I_2, which is then titrated with sodium thiosulfate. The concentration of dissolved oxygen is obtained from the result of this titration. The sequence of reactions is

$$MnO \cdot H_2O + 1/2\ O_2 \rightarrow MnO_2 \cdot H_2O$$
$$MnO_2 \cdot H_2O + 2I^- + 4H^+ \rightarrow Mn^{2+} + I_2 + 3H_2O$$
$$I_2 + 2S_2O_3^{2-} \rightarrow S_4O_6^{2-} + 2I^-$$

One mole of $S_2O_3^{2-}$ is equivalent to 0.25 mole of O_2.

Total Organic Carbon

The BOD test described above gives us information on the oxidizability of the dissolved oxygen, but not on the total organic contents of the sample. To determine the total organic contain of a sample, a total organic carbon (TOC) test is performed. Several methods exist for this, but routine analysis is done by quantitative oxidation of the carbon to CO_2 with an ionization detector, such as those used in GC. The CO_2 can be formed from organic matter as follows:

1. by quantitative oxidation of the organic carbon after acidification to remove interferences from carbonates and bicarbonates;

2. by oxidation of the organic carbon in a gas stream passed through a heated tube; and

3. by oxidation of the organic carbon with potassium peroxydisulfate.

Determination of Metals

Quantitative determination of metals is easily achieved by atomic spectroscopic methods such as flame emission spectrometry (FES), atomic absorption spectrometry (AAS), inductively coupled plasma-atomic emission spectrometry (ICP-ES), and inductively coupled plasma-mass spectrometry (ICP-MS).

Dissolved Salts

Water is an excellent solvent for ionic substances. The concentrations of dissolved substances in water can be determined with good sensitivity by electrical conductivity measurements. However, the determination of the concentrations of certain species may require individual reactions or chemical separation prior to these measurements. *Water hardness* refers to the properties of certain dissolved substances that lead to the formation of metal carbonate deposits in water, e.g., Ca^{+2}, Mg^{+2}, Pb^{+2}. Although all ionic species can be determined separately, total hardness is the quantity most regularly measured. This determination is performed by complexometric titration with EDTA at pH 10. Anionic species in water are measured and identified by chromatographic separation, followed by nonselective measurements such as conductivity. Ion-exchange chromatography is the method usually used for this.

RADIOCHEMICAL METHODS

There are three main reasons for which **radiotracers** are so useful in chemical analysis.

1. A chemical species can be labeled with a radioisotope, so that it becomes distinguishable from the unlabeled species. The radioisotope does not usually affect the chemical behavior of the labeled species. Tritium labels are an exception because of the significant mass difference between $_1^1H$ and $_1^3H$.

2. Chemical environment does not influence the radioactive characteristics of an atom, so that a label can be detected wherever it appears.

3. During radioactive decay, particles and radiation are emitted with high energy and can be easily detected. Radiochemical analysis can be made from only 10^{-12} of an analyte.

The relative stability of a nucleus depends on both the total and relative number of neutrons and protons it contains. Unstable nuclei may decay in several possible ways; a nucleus with a mass number $A > 207$ will adjust to a more stable state by emitting a relatively large particle known as an α-particle $\left(_2^4He\right)$. For heavy nuclei with $A > 238$, nuclear fission becomes an important mode of decay. In nuclear fission, two smaller nuclei of roughly equal mass are emitted. For every mass number a stable neutron to proton ratio exists, which varies from 1 to 1.5 as A increases. Any nuclei with a ratio outside this range are unstable and decay to achieve a more stable ratio.

The most important modes of radioactive decay are α-decay, β^--decay, κ-electron capture, β^+-decay, and γ-decay. All of these modes of decay are covered in a later chapter.

Instrumentation

In all radioactive methods, emissions are measured by a detector, which in turn emits a series of electrical pulses. Electrical pulses generated by the detector are amplified and sent to a recording device. When the detector is calibrated with standard sources, the proportionality between the activity of the source and the number of pulses generated by the detector within a given time (i.e., the count) can be determined; this gives a measure of the radioactivity of the source.

The three main types of detectors used in radiochemical methods are gas ionization detectors, semiconductors, and sodium iodide and liquid scintillation detectors.

GAS IONIZATION DETECTOR

In this mode of detection, the ionizing radiation interacts with an ionizable gas, usually argon. The gas is maintained within a closed tube through which a thin wire anode courses. The anode is connected to a high voltage supply (300–3000V), and when the ionizing radiation penetrates the tube, argon ions (Ar^+) and electrons are produced. The electrons are accelerated toward the anode, producing secondary ionization and an increase in the number of collisions between accelerated electrons and atoms. Electrical pulses are generated when electrons hit the anode.

Two types of gas ionization detectors exist.

1. The Geiger-Müller counter operates on high voltages, which leads to complete ionization of the filling gas; this saturates the detector. Under these conditions, the number of electrons produced is independent of the applied potential. Furthermore, the sizes of the pulses produced are all similar, irrespective of the nature and energy of the radiation.

2. The proportionality counter operates at lower voltages; here the size of the pulse is proportional to the energy of the radiation.

SEMICONDUCTOR DETECTORS

With these detectors, the ionizing radiation hits the semiconductor atoms and lifts electrons into their conduction bands. The electrons can then travel very quickly toward the positive electrode. The positive species produced during the ionization cannot move freely, but the electrons (under the influence of high voltages (3–5 kV), can move freely and are discharged at the anode to produce well-defined electrical pulses. There is a direct relationship between the energy of the radiation and the pulse size, which makes this detector an excellent choice for nuclear spectrometry.

SODIUM IODIDE DETECTOR

In this type of detector, sodium iodide absorbs the radiation from the source and reemits it as UV light. Electrical pulses are then produced by a photocathode and a photomultiplier. The UV radiation exists at a strain center within the NaI crystal. To increase the efficiency of the detector, approximately 1% of the Na^+ ions is often replaced by the much larger Tl^+ ion; this creates more strain centers within the crystal.

LIQUID SCINTILLATION COUNTER

Some organic compounds can also absorb ionizing radiation and reemit it as UV light. The most common organic scintillators are conjugated aromatic compounds. They are frequently studied in solution, in these cases they are called *liquid scintillators*. The counting technique is used primarily with sources that are β-emitters with low particle energy. Some β⁻-emitters include $_1^3H$, ^{14}C and ^{35}S.

Liquid scintillation counting also requires the use of counting cocktails, which are made up of four components:

1. a solvent, which is usually toluene. Water is used with samples that are ionic.

2. an emulsifying agent that ensures good contact between the sample and the scintillator.

3. a primary scintillator that receives the energy (emitted by the source) and transfers it via its molecular orbitals to a secondary scintillator.

4. a secondary scintillator, that reemits the absorbed energy at a longer wavelength in a region in which the photomultipliers are most efficient.

Interferences are often associated with liquid scintillation counting. Chemoluminescence arises when a chemical or biochemical reaction within the counting cocktail stimulates the emission of radiation. The sample can be refrigerated to slow down the process, heated to bring it to completion, or the interfering chemical can be removed—all of these procedures can attenuate the phenomenon. Chemical quenching arises when a chemical within the sample interacts with the scintillating radiation. Removal of the interfering chemical is the only solution for this. Color quenching occurs when a colored compound absorbs the scintillating radiation. Bleaching of the sample solution can solve this problem.

APPLICATIONS

STUDY OF CHEMICAL PATHWAYS

Chemical analyses frequently require separating an analyte from an interfering material, and specific quantitative procedures are used to achieve these separations. These procedures include solvent extraction, chromatography, and selective precipitation. The progress of these procedures is followed with radiotracers, which are very sensitive. So very small amounts of reactants are required to follow a chemical pathway. During the individual separation steps, the distribution of the species can be determined by simple measurements; the tracer indicates the efficiency or degree of completion of the procedure.

RADIOIMMUNOASSAY (RIA)

Immunogens are substances that have molecular masses of 6,000 or more and provoke an immunological response in animals. In RIA, a specific immunochemical reagent is used in sub-stochiometric amounts to determine the presence of a wide range of immunogens. This method relies on the specificity of immunochemical responses and the high sensitivities of radiotracer detectors. To design an RIA protocol, the appropriate antibody, or binding agent, must be obtained. This is achieved by forcing the immunogen to enter the bloodstream of an animal; this triggers the animal's natural defense system. Antibodies (binding agents) that are highly specific to the immunogen are produced by the animal, and these binding agents are sufficient for use in RIA. After an incubation period of of 10 to 12 weeks (or until a sufficient amount of antibodies has been produced), blood is taken from the animal, and the serum containing the antibodies is separated. This serum is often called antiserum. The production of the antiserum is always the longest and most difficult step in the RIA procedure.

The rest of the procedure involves four main steps.

1. The binding agent must be mixed with measured amounts of the labeled analyte and the antiserum to analyze the sample.

2. This solution must be incubated at 2–4°C for one to two hours to allow a state of equilibrium to be established.

3. The bound and the free analyte must be separated; this is done by adsorption of the free analyte on activated charcoal or precipitation of the bound analyte with ammonium sulfate.

4. The activity ratio (A) between the bound and free analyte must be measured. The activity ratio is given by $A = \dfrac{Z}{X + Y - Z}$ where X is the amount of analyte in the sample (the quantity to be determined), Y is the amount of labeled analyte added, and Z is the amount of antiserum added. RIA is extremely useful in determining small amounts of organic compounds in complex matrices. RIA methods are not as complex as conventional procedures, because they use extremely specific binding agents and because analysis can be performed at the picogram level. RIA methods are extensively used in medicinal and forensic investigations, as well as in the determination of drugs (amphetamines, barbiturates, morphine, nicotine, penicillin, etc.), steroids (androgens, estrogens, progesterones, etc.), and hormones (growth hormone, insulin, etc.). RIA methods are sensitive, specific, and simple to apply, but specific binding agents may be difficult to obtain, cross-reaction (interference) with molecules similar to the analyte can sometimes occur, and precision is generally about 1-3%.

ANALYTICAL CHEMISTRY: WORKED-OUT PROBLEM SET

1. Which of the following acids is the weakest?

    (a) CH_3COOH $K_a = 1.75 \times 10^{-5}$
    (b) C_6H_5COOH $K_a = 6.30 \times 10^{-5}$
    (c) HCOOH $K_a = 1.76 \times 10^{-4}$
    (d) HNO_2 $K_a = 5.10 \times 10^{-4}$
    (e) HF $K_a = 6.70 \times 10^{-4}$

    (A) Acetic acid (CH_3COOH) is the weakest acid because it has the smallest K_a. This is indicative of less dissociation in solution.

2. What is the volume of 0.5 N NaOH required to prepare 100 mL of 0.1 N NaOH?

    (a) 5 mL
    (b) 10 mL
    (c) 15 mL
    (d) 20 mL
    (e) 25 mL

    (D) The correct answer is (d): $V_i = \dfrac{V_f \times V_c}{C_i} = 100 \text{ mL} \times \dfrac{0.1N \text{ NaOH}}{0.5N} = 20 \text{ mL}$

3. What is the pH of a 1.0×10^{-7} M solution of HCl?

    (a) 2
    (b) 4
    (c) 7
    (d) 9
    (e) 11

    (C) Since HCl is a strong acid, we can assume that 100% of the HCl is dissociated and therefore the $[H^+] = 1.0 \times 10^{-7}$, pH = $-\log[H^+]$

    $$= -\log [1.0 \times 10^{-7}]$$
    $$= 7$$

4. Write a net ionic equation for the equilibrium established between the following ionic compounds and their ions. For each case, write the solubility product expression in terms of concentration and solubility.

(a) CuI

$$CuI(s) \leftrightarrow Cu^+(aq) + I^-(aq)$$
$$K_{sp} = [Cu^+][I^-] = s \times s = s^2$$

(b) $Ba(IO_3)_2$

$$Ba(IO_3)_2(s) \leftrightarrow Ba^{2+}(aq) + 2IO_3^-$$
$$K_{sp} = [Ba^{2+}][IO_3^-]^2 = s(2s)^2 = 4s^3$$

(c) $Pb_3(PO_4)_2$

$$Pb_3(PO_4)_2(s) \leftrightarrow 3Pb^{2+}(aq) + 2PO_4^{3-}(aq)$$
$$K_{sp} = [Pb^{2+}]^3[PO_4^{3-}]^2 = (3s)^3(2s)^2 = 108s^2$$

(d) $La(IO_3)_3$

$$La(IO_3)_3(s) \leftrightarrow La^{3+}(aq) + 3IO_3^-(aq)$$
$$K_{sp} = [La^{3+}][IO_3^-]^3 = s(3s)^3 = 27s^4$$

(e) $La_2(C_2O_4)_3$

$$La_2(C_2O_4)_3(s) \leftrightarrow 2La^{3+}(aq) + 3C_2O_4^{2-}(aq)$$
$$K_{sp} = [La^{3+}]^2[C_2O_4^{2-}]^3 = (2s)^2(3s)^3 = 108s^5$$

5. The following titration curve is representative of which of the following titrations?

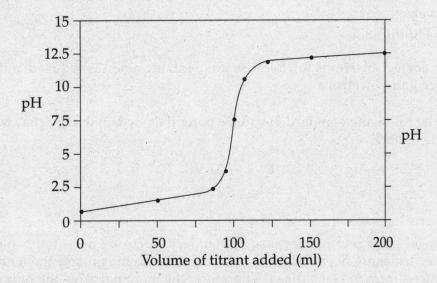

(a) HCl with NaOH
(b) CH_3COOH with NaOH
(c) HCl with NH_3

(**A**) The correct answer is (A) because it is the titration of a strong acid with a strong base. The end point is reached quickly, and the curve is steep as the titration reaches it.

6. Which of the following acids are polyprotic?

   (a) CH_3COOH

   (b) H_2SO_4

   (c) $HOCl$

   (d) HNO_3

   (e) All of them

(**B**) Carbonic acid is a polyprotic acid because it has more than one ionizable proton. Polyprotic acids dissociate according to the following equilibria:

$$H_xA \leftrightarrow XH^+ + A^{x-} \qquad\qquad K_a = K_{a1} + K_{a2} + ...+ K_{ax}$$

where x is the number of ionizable protons. When $x = 2$, a polyprotic acid can be called diprotic.

H_2CO_3 has $x = 2$ and dissociates as follow:

   1. $H_2CO_3 \leftrightarrow H^+ + HCO_3^-$ $\qquad K_{a1} = 4.3 \times 10^{-7}$
   2. $HCO_3^- \leftrightarrow H^+ + CO_3^{2-}$ $\qquad K_{a2} = 4.8 \times 10^{-11}$

7. During a redox reaction, the oxidizing agent will

   (a) lose electrons

   (b) be oxidized

   (c) gain electrons

   (d) none of the above

(**C**) The correct answer is (c), because an oxidizing agent is reduced and therefore gains electrons.

8. Given the following standard electrode potentials, which will be the strongest reducing agent?

$Mg^{2+} + 2e^- \leftrightarrow Mg$	$E^\circ = -2.37$ V
$Fe^{2+} + 2e^- \leftrightarrow Fe$	$E^\circ = -0.44$ V
$Cr^{3+} + e^- \leftrightarrow Cr^{2+}$	$E^\circ = -0.41$ V

The answer is magnesium because its standard electrode potential is the most negative. The more negative the standard potential, the greater the tendency of the reduced form to be oxidized. Therefore, the more negative the reduction potential, the weaker an oxidizing agent the oxidized form is, and the stronger a reducing agent the reduced form is.

9. Given the solubility product constant of barium iodate, $Ba(IO_3)_2$, calculate the solubility in g/L and the molar concentration of the ions at equilibrium.

$K_{sp} = 1.6 \times 10^{-9}$; molar mass = 487 g/mol

$Ba(IO_3)_2(s) \leftrightarrow Ba^{2+}(aq) + 2IO_3^-$

Answer:

$K_{sp} = [Ba^{2+}][IO_3^-]^2 = s(2s)^2 = 4s^3$

$$s = \left(\frac{K_{sp}}{4}\right)^{\frac{1}{3}} = \left(\frac{31.6 \times 10^{-9}}{4}\right)^{\frac{1}{3}} = 7.4 \times 10^{-4} \text{ mol/L}$$

$s = (7.4 \times 10^{-4} \text{ mol/L})(487 \text{ g/mol}) = 2.36 \text{ g/L}$

$[Pb^{2+}] = s = 7.4 \times 10^{-4} \text{ mol/L}$

$[IO_3^-] = 2s = 1.5 \times 10^{-3} \text{ mol/L}$

10. Calculate the solubility product constant of bismuth (III) sulfide. The solubility is $s = 5.1 \times 10^{-13}$ g/L and the molar mass is 514 g/mol.

$Bi_2S_3(s) \leftrightarrow 2Bi^{3+}(aq) + 3S^{2-}(aq)$

Answer:

$K_{sp} = [Bi^{3+}]^2[S^{2-}]^3 = (2s)^2(3s)^3 = 108s^5$

$$s = \frac{5.1 \times 10^{-13} \text{g/L}}{514 \text{ g/mol}} = 9.9 \times 10^{-16} \text{ mol/L}$$

$K_{sp} = 108s^5 = 108(9.9 \times 10^{-16})^5 = 1.0 \times 10^{-73}$

11. When $In_4[Fe(CN)_6]_3$ is dissolved until a saturated solution is attained, the molar concentration of In^{3+} ions is 6.4×10^{-7} mol/L. Calculate the K_{sp} of the salt and its solubility in mg/L. (Molar mass = 1109 mol/L.)

$In_4[Fe(CN)_6]_3(s) \leftrightarrow 4In^{3+}(aq) + 3Fe(CN)_6^{4+}(aq)$

Answer:

$K_{sp} = [In^{3+}]^4[Fe(CN)_6^{4+}]^3 = (4s)^4(3s)^3 = 6912s^7$

$$s = \frac{1}{4}[In^{3+}] = \frac{1}{4}(6.4 \times 10^{-7} \text{ mol/L}) = 1.6 \times 10^{-7} \text{ mol/L}$$

$s = (1.6 \times 10^{-7} \text{ mol/L})(1109 \text{ g/mol}) = 1.8 \times 10^{-4} \text{g/L} = 0.18 \text{ mg/L}$

$$K_{sp} = 6912(1.6 \times 10^{-7})^7 = 1.9 \times 10^{-44}$$

12. A chemist mixes 700 mL of a solution of $Ce(NO_3)_3$, 3.5×10^{-3} mol/L with 250 mL of a solution of KIO_3, 2.5×10^{-2} mol/L. Will a precipitate form upon mixing both solutions together? K_{sp} $Ce(IO_3)_3 = 1.9 \times 10^{-10}$.

Answer:

$$Ce^{3+}(aq) + 3IO_3^-(aq) \leftrightarrow Ce(IO_3)_3(s)$$

$$[Ce^{3+}] = \frac{700 \text{ mL}(3.5 \times 10^{-3} \text{ mol/L})}{700 \text{ mL} + 250 \text{ mL}} = 2.6 \times 10^{-3} \text{ mol/L}$$

$$[IO_3^-] = \frac{250 \text{ mL}(2.5 \times 10^{-2} \text{ mol/L})}{700 \text{ mL} + 250 \text{ mL}} = 6.6 \times 10^{-3} \text{ mol/L}$$

$$\text{Ionic product} = [Ce^{3+}][IO_3^-]^3 = (2.6 \times 10^{-3})(6.6 \times 10^{-3})^3 = 7.5 \times 10^{-10}$$

Because this value is greater than the solubility product constant of the cerium(III) iodate salt, a precipitate will form when the two solutions are mixed.

13. A solution contains 1.0×10^{-1} mol/L of Cu^+ and 2.0×10^{-3} mol/L of Pb^{2+}. If I^- ions are added to the solution, which salt will precipitate first, PbI_2 or CuI? Can quantitative separation of these two cations be achieved by adding I^- to this solution? $K_{sp}(PbI_2) = 1.4 \times 10^{-8}$ and $K_{sp}(CuI) = 5.3 \times 10^{-12}$

Answer:

First calculate the minimum concentration of I^- that will initiate precipitation of PbI_2 :

$$K_{sp} = [Pb^{2+}][I^-]^2 = 1.4 \times 10^{-8}$$

$$[I^-] = \sqrt{\frac{K_{sp}}{[Pb^{2+}]}} = \sqrt{\frac{5.3 \times 10^{-8}}{1.0 \times 10^{-4}}} = 2.6 \times 10^{-3} \text{ mol/L}$$

PbI_2 will precipitate when $[I^-] \geq 2.6 \times 10^{-3}$ mol/L. Then calculate the minimum concentration of I^- that will initiate precipitation of CuI:

$$K_{sp} = [Cu^+][I^-] = 5.3 \times 10^{-12}$$

$$[I^-] = \frac{K_{sp}}{[Cu^+]} = \frac{5.3 \times 10^{-12}}{1.0 \times 10^{-4}} = 5.3 \times 10^{-8} \text{ mol/L}$$

Therefore CuI will precipitate, and Pb^{2+} will stay in solution if 5.3×10^{-8} mol/L $\leq$ $[I^-] < 2.6 \times 10^{-3}$ mol/L. I^- can therefore be used to achieve separation of the two cations.

14. A solution is 0.010 mol/L in each of the following ions: Cu^{2+}, Ni^{2+}, Mn^{2+}, and Hg^{2+}. If a 0.10 mol/L solution of H_2S is slowly added at pH 0.50, determine which of the cations will precipitate. $K_a = 6.8 \times 10^{-23}$.

Answer:

First, calculate $[S^{2-}]$ at pH 0.50:

$$H_2S(aq) \leftrightarrow 2H^+(aq) + S^{2-}(aq)$$

$$K_a = \frac{[H^+]^2[S^{2-}]}{[H_2S]} = 6.8 \times 10^{-23}$$

and

$$[S^2] = \frac{K_a \cdot [H_2S]}{[H^+]^2} = \frac{(6.8 \times 10^{-23}) \cdot (0.10)}{(10^{-0.5})^2} = 6.8 \times 10^{-23} \, mol/L$$

For each cation, at 0.010 M, calculate the minimum concentration of S^{2-} that will initiate precipitation, and compare it to the calculated concentration of S^{2-}.

(a) Cu^{2+} ion

For CuS, $K_{sp} = 8.5 \times 10^{-45}$.

$$[S^{2-}] = \frac{K_{sp}}{[Cu^{2+}]} = \frac{8.5 \times 10^{-45}}{0.01} = 8.5 \times 10^{-43} \, mol/L$$

Under the current conditions, CuS will precipitate.

(b) Ni^{2+} ion

For NiS, $K_{sp} = 3.0 \times 10^{-21}$.

$$[S^{2-}] = \frac{K_{sp}}{[Ni^{2+}]} = \frac{3.0 \times 10^{-21}}{0.01} = 3.0 \times 10^{-19} \, mol/L$$

The concentration of S^{2-} is too low to initiate the precipitation of NiS.

(c) Mn^{2+} ion

For MnS, $K_{sp} = 2.3 \times 10^{-13}$.

$$[S^{2-}] = \frac{K_{sp}}{[Mn^{2+}]} = \frac{2.3 \times 10^{-13}}{0.01} = 2.3 \times 10^{-11} \, mol/L$$

The concentration of S^{2-} is too low to initiate the precipitation of NiS.

(d) Hg^{2+} ion

For HgS, $K_{sp} = 1.6 \times 10^{-54}$.

$$[S^{2-}] = \frac{K_{sp}}{[Hg^{2+}]} = \frac{1.6 \times 10^{-54}}{0.01} = 1.6 \times 10^{-52} \, mol/L$$

Under the current conditions, HgS will precipitate.

15. Determine if it is possible to separate the ions in a solution that is 0.0020 mol/L in Cd^{2+} ion and 0.0065 mol/L in ions using OH^- ions as a precipitant. Assume that 1.0×10^{-6} or less constitutes a quantitative removal. Calculate the range between which the concentration of OH^- ions should be maintained. K_{sp} $Al(OH)_3$ $= 2.0 \times 10^{-32}$, and K_{sp} $Cd(OH)_2 = 5.9 \times 10^{-15}$.

Answer:

$$Al(OH)_3(s) \leftrightarrow Al^{3+}(aq) + 3OH^-(aq) \qquad K_{sp} = [Al^{3+}][OH^-]^3 = 2.0 \times 10^{-32}$$
$$Cd(OH)_2(s) \leftrightarrow Cd^{2+}(aq) + 2OH^- \qquad K_{sp} = [Cd^{2+}][OH^-]^2 = 5.9 \times 10^{-15}$$

It is clear that $Al(OH)_3$ should precipitate first in the presence of hydroxide ions because it has a lower solubility product. Thus Al^{3+} can be separated from Cd^{2+} by precipitation. Since lowering the concentration of Al^{3+} ions to 1.0×10^{-6} or less constitutes a quantitative separation, calculate the required $[OH^-]$ necessary to lower $[Al^{3+}]$ to this level:

$$[OH^-] = \sqrt[3]{\frac{K_{sp}}{[Al^{3+}]}} = \sqrt[3]{\frac{2.0 \times 10^{-32}}{1.0 \times 10^{-6}}} = 2.7 \times 10^{-9} \, mol/L$$

The required concentration of hydroxide ions to effect a quantitative removal of ions is 2.7×10^{-9} mol/L. Then calculate the concentration of hydroxide ions that will initiate the precipitation of Cd^{2+} ions at the given concentration of 2.3×10^{-3} M:

$$[OH^-] = \sqrt{\frac{K_{sp}}{[Cd^{2+}]}} = \sqrt{\frac{5.9 \times 10^{-15}}{2.0 \times 10^{-3}}} = 1.7 \times 10^{-6} \, mol/L$$

Separation is feasible if 2.7×10^{-9} mol/L $\leq [OH^-] < 1.7 \times 10^{-6}$ mol/L.

16. Generate a titration curve (pAg or pI vs. V_{Ag+}) for the titration of 50.0 mL of KI (0.0750 mol/L) with $AgNO_3$ (0.150 mol/L, K_{sp} AgI $= 8.3 \times 10$. Here the p means $-\log[x]$.

Answer:

(a) At 0.00 mL of $AgNO_3$ added, pAg is indeterminate.

$$pI = -\log[I^-] = -\log(0.075) = 1.12$$

(b) At 5.00 mL of $AgNO_3$ added. After adding $AgNO_3$, $[I^-]$ decreases because of precipitation and dilution.

$$[I^-] = \frac{(V_{I^-} \cdot C_{I^-}) - (V_{Ag^+} \cdot C_{Ag^+})}{(V_{I^-} + V_{Ag^+})} + \frac{K_{sp}[AgI]}{[I^-]}$$

The second term of this equation is very small and can be neglected. FIX UNITS

$$[I^-] = \frac{(50.0 \, mL \cdot 0.075 \, mol/L) - (5.00 \, mL \cdot 0.150 \, mol/L)}{(50.0 \, mL + 5.0 \, mL)} = 5.45 \times 10^{-2} \, mol/L$$

$$pI = -\log[I^-] = -\log(5.45 \times 10^{-2}) = 1.26$$

pAg can be calculated in either of the two following ways.

1. $K_{sp} = [Ag^+][I^-]$

$$\left[Ag^+\right] = \frac{K_{sp}}{\left[I^-\right]} = \frac{8.3 \times 10^{-17}}{5.45 \times 10^{-2}} = 1.52 \times 10^{-15}\, mol\,/\,L$$

$$pAg = -\log[Ag^+] = -\log(1.52 \times 10^{-15}) = 14.82$$

2. $pAg + pI = pK_{sp}$

$$pAg = pK_{sp} - pI = -\log(8.3 \times 10^{-17}) - 1.26 = 16.08 - 1.26 = 14.82$$

Note that the titration curve can be generated by plotting either pAg or pI against V_{Ag^+}. The first case will produce a descending curve, and the second an ascending curve.

(c) At 10.0 mL of $AgNO_3$ added.

$$\left[I^-\right] = \frac{(50.0\ mL \cdot 0.0750\ mol\,/\,L) - (10.0\ mL \cdot 0.150\ mol\,/\,L)}{(50.0\ mL + 10.0\ mL)} = 3.75 \times 10^{-2}\, mol\,/\,L$$

$$pI = -\log[I^-] = -\log$$

$$pAg = pK_{sp} - pI = 16.08 - 1.43 = 14.65$$

(d) At 20.0 mL of $AgNO_3$ added.

$$\left[I^-\right] = \frac{(50.0\ mL \cdot 0.0750\ mol\,/\,L) - (20.0\ mL \cdot 0.150\ mol\,/\,L)}{(50.0\ mL + 20.0\ mL)} = 1.07 \times 10^{-2}\, mol\,/\,L$$

$$pI = -\log[I] = -\log(1.07 \times 10^{-2}) = 1.97$$

$$pAg = pK_{sp} - pI = 16.08 - 1.97 = 14.11$$

Now we will pick two points directly preceding and two points directly following the equivalence point because this will be the steep part of the curve.

(e) At 24.0 mL of $AgNO_3$ added.

$$\left[I^-\right] = \frac{(50.0\ mL \cdot 0.0750\ mol\,/\,L) - (24.0\ mL \cdot 0.150\ mol\,/\,L)}{(50.0\ mL + 24.0\ mL)} = 2.02 \times 10^{-3}\, mol\,/\,L$$

$$pI = -\log[I^-] = -\log(2.02 \times 10^{-3}) = 2.69$$

$$pAg = pK_{sp} - pI = 16.08 - 2.69 + 13.39$$

(f) At 24.9 mL of $AgNO_3$ added.

$$[I^-] = \frac{(50.0\ mL \cdot 0.0750\ mol/L) \cdot (24.9\ mL \cdot 0.150\ mol/L)}{(50.0\ mL + 24.9\ mL)} = 2.00 \times 10^{-4}\ mol/L$$

pI = $-\log[I^-]$ = $-\log(2.00 \times 10^{-4})$ = 3.70

pAg = pK_{sp} − pI = 16.08 − 3.70 = 12.38

(g) At 25.0 mL of AgNO$_3$ added. At the equivalence point, neither KI nor AgNO$_3$ is in excess, and the only source of ions is the solid AgI itself. Therefore,

$$[I^-] = [Ag^+] = \sqrt{K_{sp}} = \sqrt{8.3 \times 10^{-17}} = 9.11 \times 10^{-9}\ mol/L$$

pI = pAg = $-\log(9.11 \times 10^{-9})$ = 8.04

pAg = pK_{sp} − pI = 16.08 − 8.04 = 8.04

Note the sharp decline in pAg at the equivalence point.

(h) At 25.1 mL of AgNO$_3$ added.

$$[Ag^+] = \frac{(V_{Ag^+} \cdot C_{Ag^+}) - (V_{I^-} \cdot C_{I^-})}{(V_{Ag^+} + V_{I^-})}$$

$$[Ag^+] = \frac{(25.1\ ml \cdot 0.150\ mol/L) - (50.0\ ml \cdot 0.0750\ mol/L)}{(25.1\ ml + 50.0\ ml)} = 2.00 \times 10^{-4}\ mol/L$$

pAg = $-\log[Ag^+]$ = $-\log(2.00 \times 10^{-4})$ = 3.70

pI = pK_{sp} − pAg = 16.08 − 3.70 = 12.38

(i) At 35.0 mL of AgNO$_3$ added.

$$[Ag^+] = \frac{(35.0\ mL \cdot 0.150\ mol/L) - (50.0\ mL \cdot 0.0750\ mol/L)}{(35.0\ mL + 50.0\ mL)} = 1.76 \times 10^{-2}\ mol/L$$

pAg = $-\log[Ag^+]$ = $-\log(1.76 \times 10^{-2})$ = 1.75

pI = pK_{sp} − pAg = 16.08 − 1.75 = 14.33

(j) At 50.0 mL of AgNO$_3$ added.

$$[Ag^+] = \frac{(50.0\ mL \cdot 0.150\ mol/L) - (50.0\ mL \cdot 0.0750\ mol/L)}{(50.0\ mL + 50.0\ mL)} = 3.75 \times 10^{-2}\ mol/L$$

pAg = $-\log[Ag^+]$ = $-\log(3.75 \times 10^{-2})$ = 1.43

pI = pK_{sp} − pAg = 16.08 − 1.43 = 14.65

The titration curve looks like this:

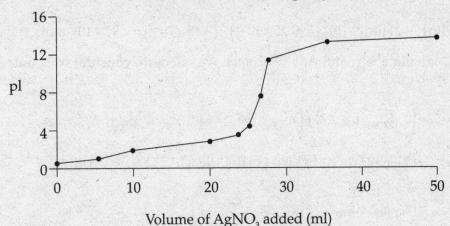

Titration of Kl with AgNO₃

17. The acid-base dissociation for the indicator HIn is

$HIn(aq) + H_2O \leftrightarrow H_3O^+(aq) + In^-(aq)$, for which

$$K_a = \frac{[H_3O^+][In^-]}{[HIn]}$$

The absorption spectrum for the equilibrium system shows two bands with maxima at wavelengths 440 nm and 620 nm.

For HIn, $\varepsilon_{440} = 2206$, and $\varepsilon_{620} = 780$.

For In^-, $\varepsilon_{440} = 410$, and $\varepsilon_{620} = 3375$.

Calculate the absorbance at 440 nm and 620 nm for a solution that contains 3.25×10^{-4} mol/L of HIn and is maintained at pH 4.26. Assume a 1.00-cm cell path length.

First, calculate [HIn] and [In⁻] at pH = 4.26

$[H_3O^+] = 10^{-4.26} = 5.50 \times 10^{-5}$ mol/L

At equilibrium, $[HIn]_{eq}$ and $[HIn]_0 - [In^-]_{eq}$ where $[HIn]_0 = 3.25 \times 10^{-4}$ mol/L

$$K_a = \frac{[H_3O^+] \cdot [In^-]}{[HIn]} = \frac{[H_3O^+] \cdot [In^-]}{[HIn]_0 - [In^-]}$$

$$K_a \cdot [HIn]_0 - K_a[In^-] = [H_3O^+] \cdot [In^-]$$

$$K_a \cdot [HIn]_0 = [In^-] \cdot \{K_a + [H_3O^+]\}$$

$$[In^-] = \frac{K_a[HIn]_0}{K_a + [H_3O^+]} = \frac{(6.6 \times 10^{-6}) \cdot (3.25 \times 10^{-4})}{(6.6 \times 10^{-6}) + (5.50 \times 10^{-5})} = 3.48 \times 10^{-5} \, mol/L$$

$$[HIn]_{eq} = [HIn]_0 - [In^-] = (3.25 \times 10^{-4}) - (3.48 \times 10^{-5}) = 2.90 \times 10^{-4} \, mol/L$$

Then, calculate A_{440} and A_{620}. For each wavelength, consider the contribution of each species:

$$A_{440} = \left(\varepsilon_{440(HIn)} \cdot C_{HIn} \cdot \ell\right) + \left(\varepsilon_{440(In^-)} \cdot C_{In^-} \cdot \ell\right)$$

$$A_{440} = (2206)(2.90 \times 10^{-4})(1.00) + (410)(3.48 \times 10^{-5})(1.00) = 0.656$$

$$A_{620} = \left(\varepsilon_{620(HIn)} \cdot C_{HIn} \cdot \ell\right) + \left(\varepsilon_{44620(In^-)} \cdot C_{In^-} \cdot \ell\right)$$

$$A_{440} = (780)(2.90 \times 10^{-4})(1.00) + (3375)(3.48 \times 10^{-5})(1.00) = 0.344$$

18. Calculate the mass of $Ag_2Cr_2O_7(s)$ (molar mass = 432 g/mol) produced from 2.65 g of $AgNO_3$ (molar mass = 170 g/mol) in solution with an excess of $Cr_2O_7^{2-}$.

The reaction is $2Ag^+(aq) + Cr_2O_7^{2-} \leftrightarrow Ag_2Cr_2O_7(s)$.

$$\text{Mass of } Ag_2Cr_2O_7 = \frac{\text{mol of } AgNO_3}{2} \cdot \text{molar mass of } Ag_2Cr_2O_7$$

$$\text{Mass of } Ag_2Cr_2O_7 = \frac{\text{mass of } AgNO_3}{2 \cdot \text{molar mass of } AgNO_3} \cdot \text{molar mass of } Ag_2Cr_2O_7$$

$$\text{Mass of } Ag_2Cr_2O_7 = \frac{2.65 \, g}{2 \cdot 170 \, g/mol} \cdot 432 \, g/mol = 337 \, g$$

19. What mass of KIO_3 (molar mass = 214 g/mol) will precipitate 4.50 g of $Ba(IO_3)_2$ (molar mass = 487 g/mol)?

The reaction is $Ba^{2+}(aq) + 2IO_3^-(aq) \leftrightarrow Ba(IO_3)_2(s)$.

$$\text{Mass of } KIO_3 = 2 \cdot \text{mol of } Ba(IO_3)_2 \cdot \text{molar mass of } KIO_3$$

$$\text{Mass of } KIO_3 = 2 \cdot \frac{\text{mass of } Ba(IO_3)_2}{\text{molar mass of } Ba(IO_3)_2} \cdot \text{molar mass of } KIO_3$$

$$\text{Mass of } KIO_3 = 2 \cdot \frac{4.50 \, g}{487 \, g/mol} \cdot 214 \, g/mol = 3.96 \, g$$

20. Treatment of a 0.8189 g sample containing Na_2SO_4 (molar mass = 142 g/mol) in an excess of $BaCl_2$ yielded 0.4847 g of $BaSO_4$. Evaluate the % content of Na_2SO_4 in the sample.

The reaction is $Na_2SO_4(aq) + BaCl_2(aq) \rightarrow BaSO_4(s) + 2NaCl(aq)$

$$\% \text{ composition} = \frac{\dfrac{1 \text{ mol of } Na_2SO_4}{1 \text{ mol of } BaSO_4} \cdot \text{mol of } BaSO_4 \cdot \text{molar mass of } Na_2SO_4}{\text{mass of the sample}} \cdot 100$$

$$\% \text{ composition} = \frac{\dfrac{1 \text{ mol of } Na_2SO_4}{1 \text{ mol of } BaSO_4} \cdot \dfrac{\text{mass of } BaSO_4}{\text{molar mass of } BaSO_4} \cdot \text{molar mass of } Na_2SO_4}{\text{mass of the sample}} \cdot 100$$

$$\% \text{ composition} = \frac{1 \cdot \dfrac{0.4867 \text{ g}}{233 \text{ g/mol}} \cdot 142 \text{ g/mol}}{0.8189 \text{ g}} \cdot 100 = 36.22\%$$

II. INORGANIC CHEMISTRY

GENERAL CHEMISTRY

There are 105 elements and all matter consists of these elements or compounds composed of them. Chemistry is the study of how these elements form compounds and, in turn, how they react with each other. Four topics are covered under this heading: atomic and electronic structure of the elements, periodic trends of the elements, oxidation states, and nuclear chemistry.

ATOMIC AND ELECTRONIC STRUCTURE OF THE ELEMENTS

PROTONS, NEUTRONS, AND ELECTRONS

Atoms consist of nuclei and electrons, and atomic nuclei are composed of two different types of particles of almost equal mass: protons, which have a positive charge and a mass equal to 1.6726×10^{-24} g and neutrons, which are neutral, have no charge, and have a mass of 1.6750×10^{-24} g. The nucleus of the lightest element, hydrogen, consists of a single proton.

The mass of an electron is 9.1094×10^{-28} g. The electron has the same charge magnitude as a proton: 1.6022×10^{-19} coulombs, but is negatively charged.

Atoms are neutral; the number of protons in their nuclei equals the number of electrons.

This number is called the atomic number (Z).

An element is a substance in which all atoms have the same atomic number Z; this means that they are all identical.

Electrons can be removed from some elements to yield positively charged ions, called cations.

ELECTRONIC ENERGY LEVELS

Electrons can be thought of as being arranged in successive shells of increasing energy around the nucleus. This view is called the **Bohr model** of the atom; below you can see a Bohr representation of sodium (Na):

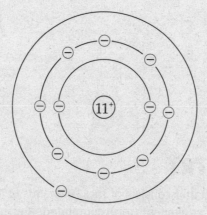

The atomic number of Na is 11; this means that sodium has 11 electrons occupying concentric energy levels around its nucleus, which consists of 11 protons.

When the first electron shell is filled with its maximum number of *s* electrons (2), the second shell is then filled with its maximum number of *s* electrons (2) and *p* electrons (6). The last electron occupies the third shell.

In the **orbital model** of the atom, each energy level (*n*) has one *s* orbital, which contains a maximum of 2 electrons. In every energy level, the **s-orbitals** (they are spherical) are always filled first and named as follows by order of increasing energy:

- The *s* orbital of the first energy level (*n* = 1) is called **1s**
- The *s* orbital of the second energy level (*n* = 2) is called **2s**
- The *s* orbital of the third energy level (*n* = 3) is called **3s**, and so on.

Starting with the second energy level ($n = 2$), **p orbitals** start being occupied:

Hydrogen has 1 electron:	$1s^1$
Helium (He) has 2 electrons:	$1s^2$
Lithium (Li) has 3 electrons:	$1s^2\,2s^1$
Beryllium (Be) has 4 electrons:	$1s^2\,2s^2$
Boron (B) has 5 electrons:	$1s^2\,2s^2\,2p^1$
Carbon (C) has 6 electrons:	$1s^2\,2s^2\,2p^2$

Another representation is

H ⬚

He ⬚

Li ⬚ ⬚

Be ⬚ ⬚

B ⬚ ⬚ ⬚

      $1s$ $2s$ $2p$

The half-arrows represent electrons and their spin states. The orbital electronic occupancy of atoms is expressed in the following way:

$$1s^2$$

In this example, 1 refers to the energy level ($n = 1$), s to the type of orbital occupied (an s orbital), and the superscript 2 to the number of electrons in the orbital.

Orbitals can be represented as follows:

s

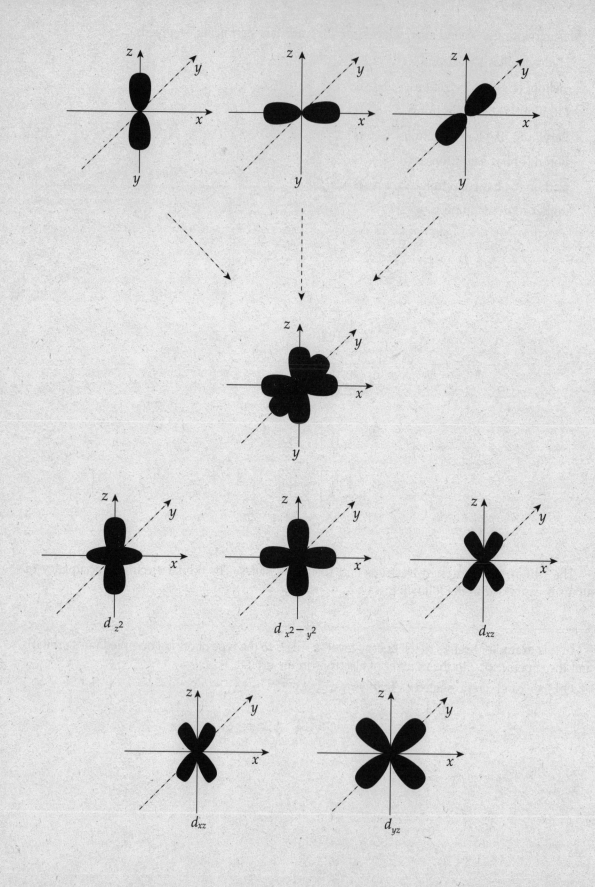

There are three kinds of p orbitals (p_x, p_y and p_z) and they can each accommodate two electrons for a total of six for the p orbitals of a given energy level. The axes (and subscripts) x, y, z refer to the magnetic properties of the electron.

There are five d orbitals, and they start becoming filled at the third energy level ($n = 3$). Two are illustrated above; they can accommodate a total of 10 electrons. There are seven f orbitals and they start becoming occupied at the fourth ($n = 4$) energy level.

Electrons are added according to the following filling order, according to the **aufbau principle**:

Main Energy Level, n	Energy Sublevel, l	Type of orbital	Name of orbital	Number of orbitals	Number of electrons
1	0	s	$1s$	1	2
2	0	s	$2s$	1	2
	1	p	$2p$	3	6 = 8
3	0	s	$3s$	1	2
	1	p	$3p$	3	6
	2	d	$3d$	5	10 = 18
4	0	s	$4s$	1	2
	1	p	$4p$	3	6
	2	d	$4d$	5	10
	3	f	$4f$	7	14 = 32

This can be represented using the following energy level diagram:

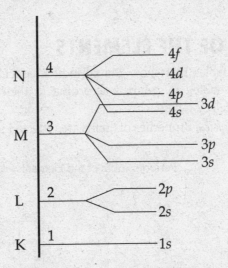

New electrons always occupy the next unoccupied, lowest energy level (1, 2, 3, 4...) or sublevel ($1s$, $2s$, $2p$...). Since the $3d$ sublevel is of higher energy than the $4s$, the order of filling electrons is

$1s$ $2s$ $2p$ $3s$ $3p$ $4s$ $3d$ $4p$

When the lowest energy levels are occupied by the electrons of an atom, it is said to be in the **ground state**. The addition of energy, for example, heat, can promote electrons to higher energy levels. The atom is then said to be in an **excited state**.

The following **Bohr table** illustrates the periodicity of the elements as their respective electronic levels are being filled:

Z	Element	1s	2s	2p	3s	3p	3d	4s	4p	4d	4f
1	H	1									
2	He	2									
3	Li	2	1								
4	Be	2	2								
5	B	2	2	1							
6	C	2	2	2							
7	N	2	2	3							
8	O	2	2	4							
9	F	2	2	5							
10	Ne	2	2	6							
11	Na	2	2	6	1						
12	Mg	2	2	6	2						
13	Al	2	2	6	2	1					
...											
19	K	2	2	6	2	6		1			
20	Ca	2	2	6	2	6		2			
21	Sc	2	2	6	2	6	1	2			
22	Ti	2	2	6	2	6	2	2			
23	V	2	2	6	2	6	3	2			
24	Cr	2	2	6	2	6	5	1			
25	Mn	2	2	6	2	6	5	2			

PERIODIC TRENDS OF THE ELEMENTS

Elements can be grouped in tables that show the periodic characteristics that result from their electronic structure (the Bohr table) or grouped according to their relative atomic masses and chemical properties (the Mendeleev table).

This means that trends in *physical* properties of atoms are reflected in their chemical behavior and reactivity.

Periodic Table of the Elements

1 H 1.0																	2 He 4.0
3 Li 6.9	4 Be 9.0											5 B 10.8	6 C 12.0	7 N 14.0	8 O 16.0	9 F 19.0	10 Ne 20.2
11 Na 23.0	12 Mg 24.3											13 Al 27.0	14 Si 28.1	15 P 31.0	16 S 32.1	17 Cl 35.5	18 Ar 39.9
19 K 39.1	20 Ca 40.1	21 Sc 45.0	22 Ti 47.9	23 V 50.9	24 Cr 52.0	25 Mn 54.9	26 Fe 55.8	27 Co 58.9	28 Ni 58.7	29 Cu 63.5	30 Zn 65.4	31 Ga 69.7	32 Ge 72.6	33 As 74.9	34 Se 79.0	35 Br 79.9	36 Kr 83.8
37 Rb 85.5	38 Sr 87.6	39 Y 88.9	40 Zr 91.2	41 Nb 92.9	42 Mo 95.9	43 Te (98)	44 Ru 101.1	45 Rh 102.9	46 Pd 106.4	47 Ag 107.9	48 Cd 112.4	49 In 114.8	50 Sn 118.7	51 Sb 121.8	52 Te 127.6	53 I 126.9	54 Xe 131.3
55 Cs 132.9	56 Ba 137.3	57 *La 138.9	72 Hf 178.5	73 Ta 180.9	74 W 183.9	75 Re 186.2	76 Os 190.2	77 Ir 192.2	78 Pt 195.1	79 Au 197.0	80 Hg 200.6	81 Tl 204.4	82 Pb 207.2	83 Bi 209.0	84 Po (209)	85 At (210)	86 Rn (222)
87 Fr (223)	88 Ra 226.0	89 †Ac 227.0	104 Unq (261)	105 Unp (262)	106 Unh (263)	107 Uns (262)	108 Uno (265)	109 Une (267)									

*Lanthanide Series:	58 Ce 140.1	59 Pr 140.9	60 Nd 144.2	61 Pm (145)	62 Sm 150.4	63 Eu 152.0	64 Gd 157.3	65 Tb 158.9	66 Dy 162.5	67 Ho 164.9	68 Er 167.3	69 Tm 168.9	70 Yb 173.0	71 Lu 175.0
†Actinide Series:	90 Th 232.0	91 Pa (231)	92 U 238.0	93 Np (237)	94 Pu (244)	95 Am (243)	96 Cm (247)	97 Bk (247)	98 Cf (251)	99 Es (252)	100 Fm (257)	101 Md (258)	102 No (259)	103 Lr (260)

In the periodic table, each element is designated as follows:

17	Cl
chlorine	
35.457	

The above notations are for chlorine (symbol = Cl), which has the atomic number 17 and an atomic mass of 35.457.

The elements are arranged in **groups**, **subgroups** (columns) and **periods** (rows) in the periodic table. For example, in the 4th period, you can see that 10 subgroups are inserted between groups II and III. Some of the groups that have names are

Group IA   *alkali metals*

Group IIA   *alkaline earth metals*

Group VII   *halogens*

Group VIII   *noble gases*

In the 4th period, elements with atomic numbers 22 to 30 are known as the **transition metals**.

In the 6th period, elements with atomic numbers 57 to 70 are known as the **lanthanides**.

In the 7th period, elements with atomic numbers 89 to 102 are known as the **actinides**.

Some of the most important atomic properties are listed below.

IONIZATION ENERGY (IE)

The ionization energy is the minimum energy required to remove one electron from an atom in its ground state.

The **valence**—or outermost—electrons are primarily responsible for chemical behavior. In the periodic table, the group number corresponds to the number of valence electrons an atom has; it ranges from one, for the alkali metals (Group I), to the stable, nonreactive, full complement of eight in the noble gases (Group VIII).

It is relatively easy to remove an electron from an alkali metal such as sodium (Na), but it becomes increasingly difficult as you move across a period.

The ionization energy increases across the periodic table, from left to right.

Let us consider some elements of the periodic table; their ionization energy is graphed below, as a function of their atomic number. With the second row elements, a low point occurs when there is a lone electron in the outer s orbital; this is the case with Li ($1s^2 2s^1$), and you can see that the third point on the graph is Z = 3. As the outer orbital fills, with two electrons, Be($2s^2$), Z = 4, its stability is increased by the presence of this $2s$ orbital. The next element, B ($2s^2 2p^1$), Z = 5, has a lone electron in a $2p$ orbital which can be removed with less energy. Therefore, the ionization energy dips from Be to

B. With the $2p$ orbitals filling according to Hund's rule (only one electron in each orbital before pairing occurs), ionization energy increases from $B\left(2s^2 2p_x^1\right)$ to $C\left(2s^2 2p_x^1 2p_y^1\right)$, $Z = 6$, and to $N\left(2p_x^1 2p_y^1 2p_z^1\right)$, $Z = 7$. There is a dip from N to O $\left(2s^2 2p_x^2 2p_y^1 2p_z^1\right)$, $Z = 8$, due to a less stable electronic configuration. Then the ionization energy increases for F $\left(2s^2 2p_x^2 2p_y^2 2p_z^1\right)$, $Z = 9$, until the $2p$ orbitals are completely filled with paired electrons for Ne $\left(2s^2 2p_x^2 2p_y^2 2p_z^2\right)$, $Z = 10$. The same pattern is observed for the representative elements of periods 3, 4, 5, and 6.

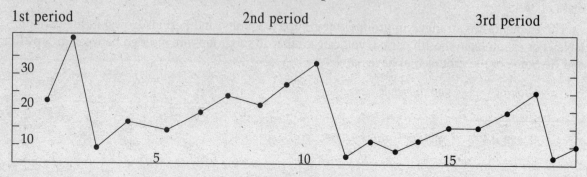

1st period   2nd period   3rd period

Z (increasing atomic number)

The graph shows that it's easier to remove a single electron from Ar ($Z = 18$, IE = 25.21×10^{-19} joules) than it is to remove one from Ne ($Z = 10$, IE = 34.52×10^{-19} joules). This is because in Ar ($1s^2 2s^2 2p^6 3s^2 3p^6$), the outermost electrons are in a shell that's further away from the attraction of the positive nucleus, compared to Ne ($1s^2 2s^2 2p^6$). With each successive noble gas, a more distant p orbital is involved; this makes it easier to remove an electron from the attractive force of the nucleus. Furthermore, as more energy levels and electrons are added to the electronic structure, a screening effect takes place, which further decreases the attraction of the nucleus. This trend in ionization energy is generally valid within a group.

ELECTRON AFFINITY

As we have said, if energy is required to remove an electron from an atom, and it is also true that energy is released when an electron is added to an atom.

Electron affinity refers to the energy change that occurs when an electron is added to a neutral atom:

$$M(g) + e^- \rightarrow M^-(g)$$

Halogens are reactive nonmetals; they have very strong electron affinities because of their strong tendency to accept an eighth valence electron and thus form a stable octet like the noble gases, which are highly stable:

Fluorine (F)	$1s^2\, 2s^2\, 2p^5$
Chlorine (Cl)	$1s^2\, 2s^2\, 2p^6\, 3s^2\, 3p^5$
Bromine (Br)	$1s^2\, 2s^2\, 2p^6\, 3s^2\, 3p^6\, 3d^{10}\, 4s^2\, 4p^5$

Oxygen has about half the electron affinity of fluorine, and elements to the left have even less affinity. It is easier to add electrons in elements to the rightmost section of the periodic table, because electrons are attracted more strongly to their greater nuclear charge.

The trend in electron affinity across a period is similar to that of ionization energy; the presence of eight electrons in a shell (ns^2np^6) represents the most stable atomic arrangement, but two (ns^2) or five (ns^2np^3) are also relatively stable. Elements with these electron configurations have lower electron affinities than do those with the stable octet. In a given group of elements, electron affinity generally decreases with increasing atomic number. However, this trend is more slight than the one observed across periods, and the exceptions are numerous.

IONIC AND ATOMIC RADII

The dimensions of elements and ions can be determined by x-ray crystallography. The following terms are used to refer to the sizes of atoms and ions:

- atomic radius: radius of an element including its nucleus and electron cloud

- Ionic radius: distance between the nuclei of two ions bound by ionic forces in a stable crystal

- van der Waals radius: distance of closest approach between the nuclei of two atoms or molecules that are not bound to one another

- covalent radius: half of the distance between nuclei of two atoms of the same element bonded by a covalent bond

The ionic radius of a cation is smaller than that of the corresponding atom

For instance,

sodium: $r_{Na} = 157$ ppm $r_{Na+} = 97$ ppm

magnesium: $r_{Mg} = 136$ ppm $r_{Mg+} = 75$ ppm

The ionic radius of an anion is larger than that of the corresponding atom

For instance,

chlorine: $r_{Cl} = 99$ ppm $r_{Cl-} = 181$ ppm

sulfur: $r_S = 104$ ppm $r_{S2-} = 184$ ppm

Cations are formed when metals lose electrons. Because of this loss of negative charge, the nuclear charge pulls the remaining electrons in closer. So the cationic radii of metals are smaller than their atomic radii. Nonmetals usually gain electrons to form anions. This added negative charge increases electron repulsion, making anionic radii larger than atomic radii.

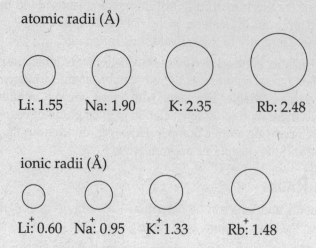

atomic radii (Å)

Li: 1.55   Na: 1.90   K: 2.35   Rb: 2.48

ionic radii (Å)

Li$^+$: 0.60   Na$^+$: 0.95   K$^+$: 1.33   Rb$^+$: 1.48

Now let's consider a series of *isoelectronic* ions (ions of different species that have the same number of electrons): N^{3-}, O^{2-}, F^-, Ne^0, Na^+, Mg^{2+}. The greater the positive nuclear charge, the greater the attraction exerted on the electrons. Therefore, these ions exhibit a steady decrease in size from first to last in our list. Furthermore, ionic radii increase from top to bottom in a group because of the addition of electron shells. The radii of neutral atoms show a less marked decrease to the right across anyone period. Although the number of electrons increases across a period, nuclear charge also increases. This charge pulls in electronic shells more strongly and causes a small decrease in size. This attraction balances the repulsion between the added electron and the other electrons. To sum up, atomic radii decrease from left to right across a period and from top to bottom in a group.

ELECTRONEGATIVITY

Electronegativity is the measure of the *relative* tendency of an atom to gain electrons in a chemical bond.

- **Electronegative** elements have many electrons in their outermost shell and tend to easily accept electrons and become negatively charged. Electronegative elements hold strongly to their valence electrons; they have a high electron affinity;

- **Electropositive** elements have few electrons in their outermost shell and tend to easily lose them and become positively charged. Electropositive elements do not hold strongly on to their valence electrons; they have a low electron affinity.

The lower the electronegativity, the less the atom holds on to its valence electrons

- The most electronegative group of elements of the periodic table are the Group VII elements, the halogens.

- The least electronegative group of elements of the periodic table are the Group I elements, the alkalis.

- Bonds between atoms that have a large electronegativity difference, such as sodium (0.9) and chlorine (3.0), have a predominantly ionic character.

- Bonds between atoms that have similar electronegativity, such as carbon (2.5) and hydrogen (2.1), are predominantly covalent, ie, methane (CH_4)

Most chemical bonds have partial covalent and partial ionic character; the relative contributions of covalent and ionic bonding depend on the electronegativity difference between atoms.

> *The electronegativity of elements in the periodic table decreases down groups and increases from left to right across periods.*

OXIDATION STATE

OXIDATION NUMBER AND VALENCE

The periodic properties of the elements, such as ionization energy and electron affinity, indicate that atoms attempt to have their valence shell completed by giving away, capturing, or sharing one or several electrons (their *valence* electrons).

- When an atom *gains* electrons to fill its valence shell, its **oxidation number** is equal to the number of electrons gained, and a negative sign is assigned to it.

Example:

Fluorine (F) has seven valence electrons ($1s^22s^22p^5$). It needs to gain only one in order to fill its outer shell and form the F⁻ ion ($1s^22s^22p^6$), which has the oxidation number –1.

- When an atom loses valence electrons, its oxidation number is equal to the number of electrons lost, and a positive sign is assigned to it.

Example:

Mg has two valence electrons ($1s^22s^22p^63s^2$). It must lose these two electrons to form an Mg^{2+} ion with a filled outer shell ($1s^22s^22p^6$). In this state, its oxidation number is +2.

- Metals often have positive oxidation numbers that are equal to their group numbers in the periodic table.

- Nonmetals often show negative oxidation numbers equal to eight *minus* their group number.

Periodic trends are observed in oxidation numbers:

Group I: alkali metals usually have an oxidation number of +1

Group II: alkaline-earth metals usually have an oxidation number of +2

Group VII: halogens usually have an oxidation number of –1

O and S have oxidation numbers of –2, N and P, of –3. Many elements' oxidation numbers depend on the compound in which they are found. For instance, in HCl, H is +1 and Cl is –1, but in ClO_3^-, if O is –2, the oxidation number of Cl must be +5 in order for the ion's net charge to be –1.

However, this does not imply that chlorine loses five electrons to oxygen. Oxidation numbers cannot be taken as indicators of actual ion transfers. The numbers are merely used as a way of keeping track of chemical reactions and balancing equations (particularly redox equations).

RULES ABOUT OXIDATION NUMBERS

An element in any compound can be assigned an oxidation number according to the following rules:

1. The oxidation number of any free element or atom in its elemental state is zero. Fe, Na, H_2, O_2, N_2, H, O and N all of the atoms have zero oxidation numbers.

2. The oxidation number of any one-atom ion is equal to its charge: Na^+ has an oxidation number of +1, Mg^{2+} of +2, Cl^- of –1.

3. Hydrogen has an oxidation number of +1 in all compounds except metallic hydrides (MH), where its oxidation number is –1.

4. Oxygen has an oxidation number of –2 in all compounds except peroxides, where its oxidation number is –5, and in OF_2 where it's +2 (and F is –1).

5. In combinations of nonmetals that don't involve H or O, the nonmetal that is either to the right of or above the other in the periodic table (so the least metallic, or most electronegative element) is assigned an oxidation number that has the same value as the charge of its most commonly encountered negative ion. For instance, in CCl_4, Cl would be –1 and C is +4. However, in CH_4, H is +1 and C is –4. In SF_6, F is –1 and S is +6, but in CS_2, S is –2 and C is +4. CS_2 is a borderline case. C is above S in the periodic table, but S is to the right of C. The oxidation numbers above are assigned because S is farther to the right of C, than C is *above* S.

6. The algebraic sum of the oxidation numbers of all atoms in the formula of a neutral compound must be zero. For example, in NH_4Cl, the oxidation number of H is +1 and that of Cl is –1, so N's must be –3 in order for the sum of all oxidation numbers to be 0.

7. The algebraic sum of oxidation numbers of all atoms in the formula of an ion must equal the charge of the ion. So in SO_4^{2-}, O is –2 and S must be +6 in order for the sum of all oxidation numbers to be equal to –2.

8. In chemical reactions, the *total oxidation number is conserved*.

> *If the oxidation number of an element **increases** during a chemical reaction, the element is **oxidized**; if it **decreases**, the element is **reduced**.*

In a balanced chemical equation, *oxidation and reduction must balance each other exactly.*

TRENDS IN OXIDATION NUMBERS

Many elements have characteristic oxidation numbers because of their positions in the periodic table. The *maximum* oxidation number generally increases across a period from +1 to +7.

- **Representative metals**: The metals in Groups I–III form ions with positive charges that are numerically equal to the numbers of their respective groups.

- **Nonmetals**: Nonmetals often have more than one oxidation number. Their *most common* oxidation number is usually –(8–gn) where *gn* represents the group number.

Examples:

Sulfur (S), –(8–gn, which is 6) = –2, and S can combine with two hydrogens (+1) to form H_2S, but in SO_3 and H_2SO_4, S is +6.

Most nonmetals also have intermediate oxidation numbers. If you examine the oxidation numbers of the elements from Na to Cl, you can see clearly the periodic trend in maximum oxidation numbers:

Na (+1), Mg (+2), Al (+3), Si (+4), P (+3, +5), S(+4, +6), Cl (+1, +3, +5, +7).

- **Transition Metals**: The general electronic structure of transition elements is $(n-1)d^x ns^2$ where $n \geq 4$ and $x = 1$–10. Transition elements are characterized by deeply buried d orbitals.

Examples:

All first-row transition elements, starting with $_{21}$Sc, have the same core electronic configuration; $1s^2 2s^2 2p^6 3s^2 3p^6$. For example $_{21}$Sc($3d^1 4s^2$), $_{22}$Ti($3d^2 4s^2$), etc., with irregularities observed at $_{24}$Cr($3d^5 4s^1$) and $_{29}$Cu($3d^{10} 4s^1$) consistent with the greater stability of half-filled sublevels.

The electrons in the $3d$ and $4s$ sublevels are very close in energy. This leads to the possibility that some or all of the $3d$ electrons will be involved in chemical bonding, which in turn means that transition elements can exhibit *variable* oxidation numbers. Early members of the series of transition elements exhibit *maximum* oxidation numbers of increasing magnitude, from +3 (for Sc) up to +7 (for Mn in MnO_4^{2-}), which correspond to the group numbers. The maximum oxidation number usually falls by *one* unit for each step to the right across the second half of the transition elements: Sc (+3), Ti (+2, +3, +4), V (+2, +3, +4, +5), Cr (0, +2, +3, +5, +6), Mn (0, +1, +2, +3, +4, +5, +6, +7), Fe (0, +2, +3, +6), Co (0, +2, +3, +4), Ni (0, +1, +2, +3, +4), Cu (0, +1, +2, +3), Zn (+2).

- **Inner transition elements**. The general electronic structure of inner transition elements is $(n-2)f^x ns^2$ where $n \geq 6$ and $x = 1$ to 14. Inner transition elements are characterized by very deeply buried $4f$ orbitals, for lanthanides ($_{57}$La to $_{70}$Yb), and $5f$ or actinides ($_{89}$Ac to $_{102}$No). Their chemical properties are less variable than those of the transition elements because the orbitals being filled are less exposed to other atoms. These elements have virtually identical outer electronic structures and therefore nearly identical chemical properties. All lanthanides form compounds that have an oxidation number of +3, whereas actinides show increasing oxidation numbers Ac^{3+} to U^{6+}. All elements beyond $_{94}$Pu exhibit +3 oxidation numbers, as do the lanthanides.

NUCLEAR CHEMISTRY

NUCLIDES AND ISOTOPES

- Nuclei consist of protons and neutrons. The number of protons an atom contains is called the *atomic number*, Z.

- An element consists of a nucleus and electrons. Identical elements have the same atomic number, Z.

- The total number of protons and neutrons in a nucleus is its *mass number, A.* The mass of the nucleus is measured in *atomic mass unit (amu).* One amu is one-twelfth of the mass of one $_6^{12}C$ isotope (1 amu = 1.660244 $\times10^{-24}$ g).

Example:

Hydrogen (H) has atomic number of 1. It has one proton and one electron. It occurs as three different isotopes, in which the nucleus has 0, 1, or 2 neutrons. In the notation used below, the superscript refers to the mass number and the subscript, to the atomic number. Tritium has A = 3 and Z = 1, so, it has 3 – 1 = 2 neutrons.

$$_1^1H \qquad\qquad _1^2H \qquad\qquad _1^3H$$
hydrogen $\qquad$ deuterium $\qquad$ tritium

More common for isotopes is the notation that omits the atomic number, Z: ^{14}C, ^{12}C, etc.

Listed below are some elements and the number of protons and neutrons that make up their most common isotopes:

Hydrogen	1 proton			=	1 nucleon
Helium	2 protons	+	2 neutrons	=	4 nucleons
Lithium	3 protons	+	4 neutrons	=	7 nucleons
Beryllium	4 protons	+	5 neutrons	=	9 nucleons
Carbon	6 protons	+	6 neutrons	=	12 nucleons
Nitrogen	7 protons	+	7 neutrons	=	14 nucleons
Oxygen	8 protons	+	8 neutrons	=	16 nucleons

- Size and shape of the nucleus

Neutron scattering experiments have shown that the radius of a nucleus is proportional to the cubic root of its mass number:

$$r = \left(1.33\times10^{-13}\right)\cdot\sqrt[3]{A}\ \text{cm}$$

The entire atomic radii, including the electron clouds, are about twenty thousand times these figures. Many nuclei are spherical, and many are elongated like footballs.

- Binding energy

An atom of a stable isotope weighs *less* than the sum of the masses of its constituents. For instance, the total mass of the particles in an $_{80}^{200}Hg$ atom is 201.66588 amu, but the observed atomic mass of $_{80}^{200}Hg$ is only 199.9683 amu! The missing 1.6975 amu of matter has been converted to the energy that's required to overcome proton–proton repulsion and hold the nucleus together. In the case of $^{200}_{80}Hg$, the *binding energy* is $E_{bind} = 931$ MeV or 7.90 MeV/nucl. The binding energy of elements 1–8 (including $^{16}_{8}O$) is low and proportional to the number of protons and neutrons (nucleons). For the elements from $^{16}_{8}O$ to $^{238}_{92}U$, the binding energy of the stable isotopes is almost constant at about 8 MeV per nucleon. The energies involved in nuclear reactions far exceed those involved in chemical reactions. For the former, the interconversion of mass and energy is normal. For the latter, it is negligible. In nuclear reactions, the *total mass and energy* of the reacting species does not change during the course of the reaction.

NUCLEAR DECAY

- Many nuclei do not decay, and they are referred to as **stable isotopes**.

- **Radioactive isotopes** represent nuclei that break down spontaneously into new elements.

During nuclear decay, particles and radiation are emitted, which means that the values of Z and A of the product might differ from those of the reactants. The most common types of radioactive radiation are

1. **Alpha particles**: An α-particle is a helium nucleus (2 protons and 2 neutrons). Its symbol is $^{4}_{2}He$.

2. **Beta particles (β)**: Beta particles are electrons travelling at very high velocities, close to the speed of light (3×10^8 ms^{-1}); they result from the breakdown of a neutron into a proton and an electron.

3. **Gamma radiation (γ)**: Electromagnetic radiation (consisting of high-energy photons) of very short wavelength.

There are five types of nuclear decay, all associated with loss of mass and the liberation of energy.

1. **Electron emission**. Electron emission is also called β^- decay. In spontaneous β^- decay, one of the neutrons of the nucleus decomposes into a proton and a fast electron, for example; $^{228}_{88}Ra \rightarrow ^{228}_{89}Ac + ^{0}_{-1}e$. One neutron is lost, but one proton is gained, and A remains the same.

In β^+ decay, Z always increases by one.

2. **Electron capture**. One electron from the cloud that surrounds the nucleus is captured by the nucleus and combines with a proton to form a neutron $\left(^{1}_{+1}p + ^{0}_{-1}e \rightarrow ^{1}_{0}n \right)$.

For example:, $^{207}_{84}Po + ^{0}_{-1}e \rightarrow ^{207}_{83}Bi$.

In electron capture, Z always decreases by one.

3. **Positron emission.** A positron is a particle that has the mass of an electron, but a unit positive charge. Its symbolized by $^{0}_{+1}e$ or β^+. During β^+ emission, a proton decomposes to form one neutron and one positron $\left(^{1}_{+1}p \rightarrow ^{1}_{0}n + ^{0}_{+1}e\right)$. For example, $^{207}_{84}Po \rightarrow ^{207}_{83}Bi + ^{0}_{+1}e$.

In positron emission, Z always decreases by one.

4. **Alpha-particle emission.** α-particle emission occurs for heavier elements ($A > 200$). For example, $^{232}_{90}Th \rightarrow ^{207}_{88}Ra + ^{4}_{2}He$.

In α-particle emission, the atomic nucleus decreases by two, and A by four.

5. **Gamma emission during alpha decay.** γ-rays are high-energy photons that are emitted in a stream during nuclear decay. In this reaction: $^{238}_{92}U \rightarrow ^{234}_{90}Th + ^{4}_{2}He$, α-particles of two different energies—4.18 MeV and 4.13 MeV are liberated. The alpha emission is accompanied by electromagnetic radiation in the form of γ-rays, whose energy is equal to 0.05 MeV. The 4.13 MeV α-particle is emitted when $^{238}_{92}U$ is converted to $^{234}_{90}Th$ that's in an *excited* nuclear state. When $^{234}_{90}Th$ falls to its *ground* state, 0.05 MeV of γ radiation is liberated. The 4.18 MeV α-particle is emitted when $^{238}_{92}U$ is converted to $^{234}_{90}Th$ in its *ground* nuclear state.

STABILITY AND HALF-LIFE

The total number of nuclei that decay in a given time is proportional to the total number of nuclei present.

- The probability that a nucleus will decay in a given time is constant and independent of the surrounding of the nucleus. This is called a **first-order** decay. The expression that relates the number of nuclei n that remain at time t to the number originally present, n_0, at time $t = 0$ is $n = n_0 e^{-kt}$, where k is a first-order rate constant. In a **first-order decay**, the time required for any amount of material to decay by half is constant and independent of the amount originally present. From the previous equation, we can derive: $t_{1/2} = \ln 2 / k = 0.693 / k$. If the half-life of a radioactive substance is one day, then this means that one day is required for 1mg, 1g, 1kg or 1 ton of that substance to decay to half of its original mass.

Artificial Transmutation

Artificial transmutation is the process by which one element is transformed into another. The first artificial transmutation was carried out in 1919 by Sir E. Rutherford, and it looked like this: $^{14}_{7}N + ^{4}_{2}He \rightarrow ^{17}_{8}O + ^{1}_{1}H$. To bring positively charged nuclei together close enough for a fusion to take place, high energies are needed. One method of fusing 2 nuclei is to use a **particle accelerator**.

- When an accelerated particle such as a neutron strikes a target nuclei, the nucleus can split into 2 or more fragments, in a process called **nuclear fission**.

- When an accelerated particle is captured by a target nucleus to produce a larger nucleus, this process is called nuclear fusion.

- When $^{235}_{92}U$ is bombarded by slow neutrons, fission occurs, resulting in several fission products: $^{235}_{927}U + ^1_0n \rightarrow ^{139}_{56}Ba + ^{94}_{36}Kr + 3^1_0n$. The ^{235}U fission is a potential **chain reaction** because it produces three fast neutrons for every one that's used to initiate the fission of one nucleus. Each fission of a nucleus liberates neutrons that will cause the fission of more than one nucleus.

IONIC SUBSTANCES

Ionic substances are charaterized by ionic bonding. Five topics are covered under this heading: ionic bonding; lattice geometries, ionic radii, radius ratio effects, and lattice energies.

IONIC BONDING

IONS AND ELECTRONS

Ionic bonding occurs as a result of the transfer of electrons from an atom of one element to an atom of another.

Ionic bonds only occur between electropositive and electronegative elements (atoms).

- Electropositive elements have few electrons in their outer shells and can easily lose them, becoming positive ions in the process (Na^+, Ca^{2+}, Al^{3+}).

- Electronegative elements have many electrons in their outer shells; they tend to draw electrons in, to become negative ions (Cl^-, S^{2-}, F^-).

- In ionic bonding, the number of electrons lost by the atoms of one element always equals the number of electrons gained by the atoms of the other element.

Atoms become charged ions through the loss or gain of electrons.

Stable electronic valence shell occupancy is achieved when an electropositive metal gives off its valence electron to an electronegative nonmetal. The most stable ionic bonds exist when the respective s and p orbitals of valence shells are completely filled.

In the orbital model of the atom, this can be represented by the following electronic configurations:

Na:	$1s^2$	$2s^2$	$2p^6$	$3s^1$	
Cl:	$1s^2$	$2s^2$	$2p^6$	$3s^2$	$3p^5$
Na$^+$:	$1s^2$	$2s^2$	$2p^6$		
Cl$^-$:	$1s^2$	$2s^2$	$2p^6$	$3s^2$	$3p^6$

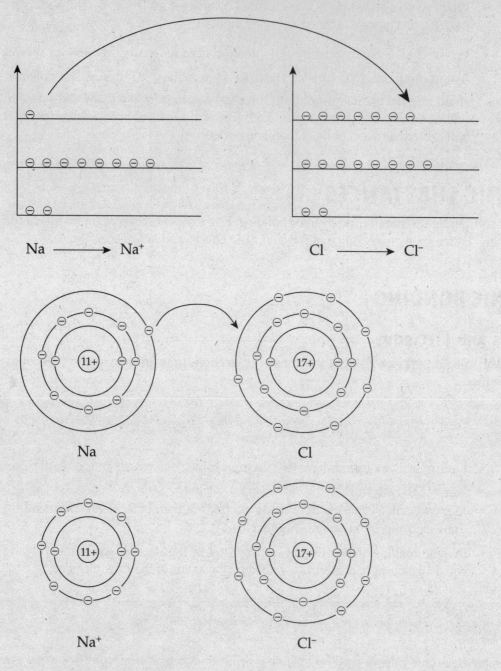

Another representation would be:

$$Na\cdot \quad + \quad \cdot\ddot{\underset{..}{Cl}}: \quad \longrightarrow \quad [Na]^+ \quad + \quad [:\ddot{\underset{..}{Cl}}:]^-$$

In order for the atoms of two elements to undergo ionic bonding, the difference in their electronegativities must be at least 1.7.

RULES FOR IONIC BONDING

Example: Al and O:

1. Write down the electronic configuration of the highest, occupied energy level of the elements involved:

   Al: $3s^2$ $3p^1$

   O: $2s^2$ $2p^4$

2. Determine how many electrons the electropositive element can lose and how many the electronegative element can accept:

   Al must give off three electrons to gain the electronic configuration of the closest noble gas in the periodic table, Ne ($2s^2 2p^6$) and O must gain two electrons to fill its highest energy level. This gives us Al^{3+} and O^{2-}.

3. Determine how many atoms of each element are required to yield the same amount of electrons gained and lost. This is the product of the respective number of electrons gained or lost by each element:

   3 electrons (to be lost by Al) $\times$ 2 electrons (to be gained by O) = 6

4. How many atoms of Al are required to give off a total of six electrons and how many of O can gain a total of six?

   For Al: $\dfrac{6}{3}$ electrons = 2 atoms

   For O: $\dfrac{6}{2}$ electrons = 3 atoms

5. Use the resulting numbers to balance the formula:

   $2Al^{3+} +$ $3O^{2-}$ $\rightarrow$ Al_2O_3

6. Verify that the charge is the same on both sides of the equation:

   The charge of $2Al^{3+}$ is $2 \times (+3) = +6$ and that of $3O^{2-}$ is $3 \times (-2) = -6$, so the total charge for the left side of the equation is $6 - 6 = 0$. The total charge of Al_2O_3 is 0.

Example:

The unit cell of NaCl contains Na^+ and Cl^- ions in a 1:1 ratio, and the unit cell of Al_2O_3 contains Al^{3+} and O^{2-} ions in a 2:3 ratio.

PROPERTIES OF IONIC SUBSTANCES

- The reaction between an electropositive metal and an electronegative nonmetal yields a salt:

Examples:

$$2Na + Cl_2 \rightarrow 2NaCl \text{ (sodium chloride)}$$

$$Fe + S \rightarrow FeS \text{ (iron (II) sulfide)}$$

Ionic bonding is typical for salts.

Other inorganic compounds also display ionic bonding, for exampl,e the metal oxides (Al_2O_3) and hydroxides (NaOH). Ionic bonding is characterized by a coulombic attraction force that acts equally in all directions. The consequence of this type of bonding is that the ions will distribute according to charge in the ionic lattice, which will be stabilized by the action of the coulombic force.

- Ionic substances are solid at room temperature. The application of heat will loosen the ionic lattice until a point is reached when it falls apart; this is the melting point.
- Ionic substances have relatively high melting (mp) and boiling points (bp).

Examples:

NaCl: mp = 800 °C   bp = 1440 °C

KBr: mp = 728 °C   bp = 1376 °C

- Molten salt solutions are very good electricity conductors, as are salts dissolved in aqueous solution; compounds that conduct electricity are called **electrolytes**.

Example:

$$NaCl \rightarrow Na^+ + Cl^-$$

Electrolytic dissociation takes place in an aqueous solution of NaCl. If electrodes are introduced and a current is applied, the Na^+ cations will migrate to the negative electrode (cathode) and the Cl^- anions will migrate to the positively charged electrode (anode).

Cations are positive and migrate to the cathode; anions are negative and migrate to the anode.

Cations commonly used in electrolytic cells include:

- all metals (eg. Na^+, Al^{3+}, Fe^{2+}...)
- the hydrogen ion, H^+, and the hydronium ion, H_3O^+
- the ammonium ion, NH_4^+

Anions commonly used in electrolytic cells include:

- all acidic ions (eg. Cl^-, SO_4^{2-}, NO_3^-...)
- the hydroxide ion, OH^-

LATTICE GEOMETRIES

CRYSTAL LATTICES

- If a metal that has low electronegativity (meaning that it is electropositive) combines with a nonmetal, with high electronegativity (it's electronegative), the product is a solid that consists of positive metallic ions and negative nonmetallic ions held together by strong electrostatic forces in a regular pattern called a **crystal lattice**.

- The energy of these electrostatic interactions is called **lattice energy** (U).

- The term **crystal** refers to this type of solid. The array that constitutes the crystal lattice is regular—it repeats itself periodically.

- The smallest unit that repeats itself indefinitely in three dimensions is called the **unit cell**.

- Crystallography is the branch of chemistry that studies the structure of **unit cells**.

TYPES OF CRYSTAL LATTICES: THE CRYSTAL SYSTEMS

There are seven types of crystalline structures, each of which possesses a characteristic unit cell that repeats itself to give a solid structure without voids.

The size and geometry of a unit cell is denoted by the lengths (a, b and c) of the three axis and the three angles (α, β, and γ) that occur between pairs of intersecting axis (b and c, a and c, a and b, respectively).

The seven crystal systems are:

1. **Cubic.** Cell edges: $a = b = c$; cell angles: $\alpha = \beta = \gamma = 90°$; example: NaCl.

2. **Tetragonal.** Cell edges: $a = b \neq c$; cell angles: $\alpha = \beta = \gamma = 90°$; example: $Hg(CN)_2$.

3. **Hexagonal.** Cell edges: $a = b = c \neq d$; cell angles: $\alpha = \beta = \gamma = 120°$, the edge d is perpendicular to the plane described by edges a, b and c; example: PbI_2.

4. **Rhombohedral.** Cell edges: $a = b = c$; cell angles: $\alpha = \beta = \gamma \neq 90°$; example: $NaNO_3$.

5. **Orthorhombic.** Cell edges: $a \neq b \neq c$; cell angles: $\alpha = \beta = \gamma = 90°$; example: K_2CrO_4.

6. **Monoclinic.** Cell edges: $a \neq b \neq c$; cell angles: $\alpha = \gamma = 90°$, $\beta \neq 90°$; example: $K_3Fe(CN)_6$.

7. **Triclinic.** Cell edges: $a \neq b \neq c$; cell angles: $\alpha \neq \beta \neq \gamma$; example: $CuSO_4 \cdot 5H_2O$.

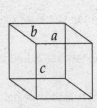

cubic: $a = b = c$

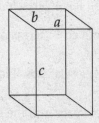

tetragonal: $a = b \neq c$

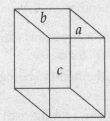

orthorhombic: $a \neq b \neq c$

Most of these basic systems may be divided further. For instance, a simple cubic primitive unit cell (P) exists that contains atoms only at the corners, a body-centered unit cell (bcc or I) that contains atoms at the corners as well as at the center of the unit cell, and a face-centered unit cell (fcc or F) that contains atoms at its corners and in the center of each of the six faces.

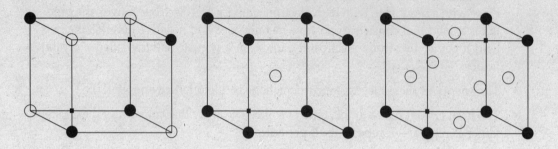

CLOSE PACKING OF SPHERES

There are three types of crystalline solids:

- **ionic solids**, which are made of positive and negative ions arranged in regular arrays; each ion is surrounded by ions of the opposite charge (eg, NaCl, CaF_2). The unit cells are held together by coulombic forces that act between the cations and anions. These solids are hard, brittle, and have high melting and boiling points. They are poor conductors of electricity and heat.

- **covalent solids** are made of atoms that are held together by very strong covalent bonds (eg, quartz, SiO_2). They are very hard, and have high melting points. They are poor conductors of heat and electricity. Sometimes different forms of covalent crystals occur, but are made up of the same element (eg, graphite and diamond are two covalent solids that are made of carbon).

- **molecular solids** are made of neutral molecules (like H_2O, SO_2, sucrose, I_2, P_4); they are held together by weak van der Waals forces or hydrogen bonds. They are soft, and are poor conductors of electricity and heat.

- **metallic solids** are made of one closely-packed metal element. Each lattice point of the unit cell in metallic solids is occupied by a metal cation. (The atom without its outershell electrons). The free valence electrons circulate around the metallic cations; this makes them very good electricity and heat conductors. They can be soft or hard, depending on the element, and have variable melting points.

The structures of many solids can be described in terms of the regular stacking of spheres that represent the ions or atoms

In some metals, the atoms pack together as close as possible; these metals are called **close-packed structures**.

This geometry allows for the least waste of space and the maximum number of neighbors.

TYPES OF CLOSE PACKING

Spheres in a close-packed structure have several layers. In the first layer, a single sphere is surrounded by six neighbors:

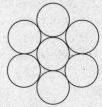

In the second layer, the spheres are not placed directly above those of the first layer, but o-rather occupy the voids between adjacent spheres:

Four spheres (three in the first layer, in triangular formation, and one above) create a regular tetrahedron about a void, which is called *tetrahedral hole (or T-hole)*. A second kind of hole, bound by six spheres (three in the first layer, in triangular formation, and three in the second layer, above, also in triangular formation but offset by 60° with respect to the three spheres in the first row) is also generated. These are called *octahedral holes (or O-holes)* and they are illustrated below. The atoms of the first layer are labeled 1 and those of the second layer, 2:

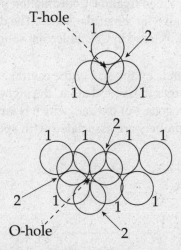

A third kind of hole is also defined, which is between three adjacent spheres in the same layer, and this is called a *triangular hole*. For spheres of equal diameter, the size of the holes varies in the following order: triangular < tetrahedral < octahedral. The third layer can be arranged in either of two ways and can therefore lead to two possible structures. In one of the possible structures, the spheres of the third layer lie directly above the spheres of the first layer. This packing of layers gives a lattice with a **hexagonal unit cell** and is known as **hexagonal close packing (hcp)**. In the second of the two possible structures, the spheres of the third layer are placed directly above the holes of the second layer. In this arrangement, the third layer lies over neither of the previous two. The fourth layer would go directly above the first one, in an abcabc... type of arrangement. This arrangement corresponds to a lattice with a *face-centred cubic unit cell*. The crystal structure is therefore a *cubic close packing (ccp)* or, more accurately, *face-centred cubic (fcc)*.

If there are N atoms in a crystal, there are N O-holes and $2N$ T-holes. The O-holes are the larger of the two and can each accommodate a sphere of radius up to 0.41 times that of the largest sphere without causing distortion of the structure. The T-holes are much smaller and can only accommodate spheres of radius up to 0.23 times those of the close-packed spheres.

CALCULATING UNIT CELL VOLUMES

For a simple cubic close packing cell, with its spheres in each of the eight corners touching their immediate neighbors, the length of one edge of the cubic cell is equal to twice the radius of the sphere: $L_{ccp} = 2r$ and $V_{ccp} = L^3 = 8r^3$.

The **body-centred cubic cell (bcc)** has one sphere in each corner and one in the middle of the cell. The cell in the middle prevents those in the corners from touching each other. Instead, the spheres touch each other along the **body diagonal**. The length of this diagonal is equal to $4r$. The lengths of the edges of the cell are: $L_{bcc} = \dfrac{4}{\sqrt{3}} r$ and $V_{bcc} = \left(\dfrac{4}{\sqrt{3}} r\right)^3 = \dfrac{64}{3\sqrt{3}} r^3$

For the face-centred (fcc) cell, the atoms touch along the **face diagonal**. The length of this diagonal is $4r$ and the lengths of the edges of the cell are: $L_{fcc} = \dfrac{4}{\sqrt{2}} r$ and $V_{fcc} = \left(\dfrac{4}{\sqrt{2}} r\right)^3 = \dfrac{32}{\sqrt{2}} r^3$

COORDINATION NUMBER

The coordination number (CN) of an atom (or an ion) is its number of closest neighbors within the lattice. These closest neighbors are called **ligands**. Coordination numbers range between 8 and 12 for metals, 4 and 8 for ionic solids, 1 and 6 for molecular solids. The densities of the three types of solids are reflected to a certain extent by this trend in CN; molecular solids are the lightest solids and metals the most dense.

The coordination number depends on the size of the central atom, as well as that of the ligands. The smaller the ligands and the larger the central atom, the higher is the possible CN. For example, nitrogen can coordinate four hydrogens, but oxygen, which is larger, can coordinate a maximum of three hydrogens. **Coordination numbers are associated with specific geometries:**

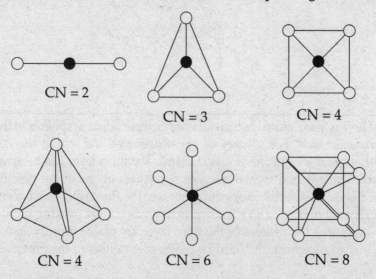

CN = 2

CN = 3

CN = 4

CN = 4

CN = 6

CN = 8

So, CN = 2 defines a linear geometry,

CN = 3 defines a trigonal pyramidal geometry,

CN = 4 defines a tetrahedral or planar (rare) geometry,

CN = 6 defines an octahedral geometry, and

CN = 8 defines a bipyramidal geometry.

IONIC SOLIDS AND CLOSE PACKING OF SPHERES

The crystal structure of many ionic solids is usually described in terms of the systematic filling of O- and/or T-holes in a close-packed structure of ions (usually anions) by smaller ions (usually cations). Ionic substances tend to adopt a few basic structures. Most can be seen as lattices in which the anions (usually the largest ions) stack together in cubic patterns, with cations (usually the smallest ions) occupying the T- or O-holes.

The basic structures of ionic solids are

1. **The rock-salt, or halite structure: NaCl**, AgCl, AgBr, KBr, LiCl, RbI, TiO, MgO, CaO, etc. In NaCl, the structure is based on a cubic array of bulky chloride ions, with the cations (Na^+) occupying all of the **O- holes**.

2. **The zinc-blende, or sphalerite structure: ZnS**, CdS, HgS, CuCl, etc. In ZnS, the structure is based on a cubic array of Zn^{2+} ions, with S^{2-} ions occupying **half of the T-holes**.

3. **The fluorite structure: CaF_2**, $BaCl_2$, PbO_2, HgF_2, etc. The structure of CaF_2 is based on a cubic array of F^- ions, with Ca^{2+} ions occupying all of the T-holes.

4. **The anti-fluorite structure: K_2O**, K_2S, Li_2O, Na^2O, etc. This structure is the inverse of the fluorite structure; the positions of the cations and anions are reversed. The structure of K_2O is based on a cubic array of O^{2-} ions, with K^+ ions occupying **all of the T-holes**.

5. **The wurzite structure: ZnS**, ZnO, MnS, BeO, etc. The structure of ZnS, another polymorph of zinc sulfide, is based on a hexagonal array of Zn^{2+} ions, with the S^{2-} ions occupying **half of the T-holes**.

6. **The nickel-arsenide structure: NiAs**, NiS, CoS, FeS, etc. The structure of NiAs is based on a hexagonal array of As^{3-} ions, with the Ni^{3+} ions occupying **all of the O-holes**.

7. **The rutile structure: TiO_2**, MnO_2, MgF_2, SnO_2, NiF_2, etc. The structure of TiO_2 is based on a hexagonal array of O^{2-} ions, with Ti^{4+} ions occupying **half of the O-holes**.

IONIC RADII AND IONIC RADIUS RATIO EFFECTS

In an ionic solid, ideal packing is that which allows the creation of maximum electrostatic attraction between ions of opposite charges, and minimum repulsion between ions of identical charge.

To understand the structure of ionic solids, it is important to remember the general trends in atomic radii:

- Ionic radii increase down groups on the periodic table.

- The radii of ions of the same charge decrease across a period.

- The radius of a given ion increases with increasing coordination number. For example, the ionic radius of a Ca^{2+} ion depends on its environment; it can be 1,00 Å (CN = 6), 1.12 Å (CN = 8), 1.28 Å (CN = 10), or 1.35 Å (CN = 12).

- The ionic radius of a given element decreases with increasing oxidation number. For example, $Fe^{2+} > Fe^{3+}$.

- A positive charge means a dominant nuclear attraction, which means that cations are usually smaller than ions.

For cations and anions to participate in a stable structure, the cation must be sufficiently large to hold the anions in their respective positions, while still allowing them to come into close contact with one another.

Example:

Given a cation with CN = 6 (six anionic neighbors, four in the same plane as the cation, one above and one below), if the cation is too small, the anion–anion repulsion will be strong and the cation-anion attraction weak. This system will therefore seek to reduce its coordination number. If the cation is too large, the anions are not in contact, which means that more anions could be accommodated around it. In this case, the coordination number wants to increase. In the limiting case, when all seven ions are just in contact, the attractive and repulsive forces are balanced. It can be shown by simple geometry that in this limiting case, the ratio $r_+/r_- = 0.414$. A similar type of reasoning and calculation can be applied to the other possible types of coordination numbers:

CN of cation	Shape	r_+/r_- limits	Structure type
3	planar trigonal	0.155–0.225	SO_3
4	tetrahedral	0.225–0.414	ZnS
6	octahedral	0.414–0.732	NaCl
8	cubic	> 0.732	CsCl

If the radius ratio falls below a minimum, the ions of opposite charge will not be in contact, and ions of identical charge will touch. A lower coordination number, which would allow the contact of oppositely charged ions, is restored and then becomes favorable. It is therefore possible to predict the structure type that some binary ionic compounds will adopt, frm cation/anion ratios. But at times, radius ratios only provide a rough guide to what is *possible* rather than what actually happens. Here are some examples in which the radius ratio values work quite well:

Examples:

1. MgO: $r_{mg^{2+}} = 0.072$ nm, $r_{O^{2-}}, = 0.140$ nm and $r_+/r_- = 0.51$; predicted structure: identical to NaCl, observed structure: identical to NaCl.

2. MgI: $r_{mg^{2+}} = 0.072$ nm, $r_{Te^{2-}} = 0.221$ nm and $r_+/r_- = 0.33$; predicted structure: identical to ZnS, observed structure: identical to ZnS.

3. MgS: $r_{mg^{2+}} = 0.072$ nm, $r_{s^{2-}} = 0.185$ nm and $r_+/r_- = 0.39$; predicted structure: identical to ZnS, observed structure: identical to NaCl.

The radius ratio structure prediction works well except near the limiting values (which is the case with ZnS).

Lack of reliability of this prediction method is due to the following factors:

- First, ionic radii cannot be measured directly. X-ray diffraction measurements give internuclear spacing $r_+ + r_-$ rather than r_+ or r_-.

- Second, ions are not hard spheres. The amplitude of the wave function that describes their electronic distribution does not suddenly drop to zero at a given value of r.

- Third, the radius of an ion increases whenever the coordination number increases.

LATTICE ENERGIES

THE BORN-HABER CYCLE

When an ionic solid is formed between mutually attractive cations and anions, the overall energy of the solid is lower than that of the free ions. The difference in energy between the two forms is called the **cohesive energy**.

The **lattice energy** is the sum of the energies of interaction of the ions in a crystal. It cannot be measured directly, and is the result of two main contributions: the coulombic interactions between ions and the van der Waals repulsive energy.

The coulombic interaction can be evaluated theoretically using compressibility data, and it is called the **Madelung constant**. To get around the impossibility of measuring the lattice energy directly, experimental thermochemical data can be used in conjunction with a **Born-Haber cycle**. The Born-Haber cycle is a calculation of the total energy of a crystal by considering all of its formation steps, and it includes a lattice energy contribution.

As an example of a Born-Haber cycle, we will discuss the formation of sodium fluoride from its constituting elements:

The reaction is

$$Na_{(s)} + \frac{1}{2}F_{2(g)} \rightarrow NaF_{(s)}$$

The energetic factors associated with each step are obtained by decomposing the reaction into different steps.

Step 1:   Sublimation of solid sodium

$Na(s) \rightarrow Na(g)$ $\Delta H_{sublimation}$ = +109 kJ/mol

Step 2:   Ionization of gaseous sodium atoms

$Na(g) \rightarrow Na^+(g)$ $\Delta H_{ionization}$ = +496 kJ/mol

Step 3:   Dissociation of fluoride molecules

$F_2(g) \rightarrow 2F(g)$ $\Delta H_{dissociation}$ = +154 kJ/mol

For one mole of F atoms, the enthalpy is +77 kJ/mol.

Step 4:   Formation of fluoride ions (electron affinity)

$$F(g) + e^- \rightarrow F^-(g) \qquad\qquad \Delta H_{ionization} = -328 \ \text{kJ/mol}$$

Step 5: Formation of sodium fluoride from gaseous sodium and fluoride ions

$$Na^+(g) + F^-(g) \rightarrow NaF(s) \qquad \Delta H_{lattice} = -923 \ \text{kJ/mol}$$

The sum of the five processes represents the global reaction, and the sum of the five individual enthalpy values is equal to the total energy value.

$$Na(s) + \frac{1}{2}F_2(g) \rightarrow NaF(s) \qquad \Delta H_{total} = -569 \ \text{kJ/mol}$$

COULOMBIC CONTRIBUTIONS TO LATTICE ENERGIES

To calculate the lattice energy of an ionic solid, we need to take into account the attractions and repulsions between ions. The lattice energy, also defined as the energy released when one mole of the free gaseous ions come together from infinite interionic separation to make up the crystal, can be calculated from the Born-Landé equation:

$$U = \frac{N_A \cdot z_+ z_- \cdot e^2}{4\pi\varepsilon_0 (r_+ + r_-)} \cdot \left(1 - \frac{1}{n}\right) \cdot M$$

where N_A is Avogadro's number ($6.022 \times 10^{-23} \ \text{mol}^{-1}$), z_+ and z_- are the charges of the positive and negative ions, e is the charge of the electron (1.602×10^{-19} C), ε_0 is the vacuum permittivity constant ($9.95 \times 10^{-12} \ \text{C}^2\text{J}^{-1}\text{m}^{-1}$), $(r_+ + r_-)$ is the equilibrium distance between the ions, M is the Madelung constant, and n is Born's exponent.

The value of n generally lies between 7 and 10, and is related to the size of the ions. The Madelung constant, M, is the sum of an infinite series, and it represents the effect on the ion of its neighboring ions. It reflects the relative positions of ions within the crystal, and is therefore dependent on the geometry of the crystal. For the structural types described in the previous section, the values of M are cesium chloride (1.763), fluorite (2.519), rock salt (1.748), rutile (2.4008), sphalerite (1.638) and wurtzite (1.641). The Born-Landé equation only takes into account the attractive component of the total potential energy of the solid. The *Born-Mayer* equation, however, takes both the attractive and repulsive components into account.

$$U = \frac{N_A \cdot z_+ z_- \cdot e^2}{4\pi\varepsilon_0 (r_+ + r_-)} \cdot \left(1 - \frac{d^*}{d}\right) \cdot M$$

where d^* is a constant estimated from measurements of compressibility, usually set at 0.345 Å.

CONSEQUENCES OF LATTICE ENERGIES

The two equations shown above tell us that, for a given crystal type (or for a given value of M), the lattice enthalpy increases with increasing ionic charge and decreasing ionic radii.

The effects of lattice energies and ionic charges and radii on three physical properties of ionic solids are listed below.

- **Thermal stability**—In general, large anions are stabilized by large cations, and large cations, by large anions. For example, let us consider the decomposition temperature of thermally unstable carbonate compounds. Magnesium carbonate decomposes at 300 °C, whereas barium carbonate does not decompose until a temperature of 800 °C is reached.

- **High oxidation numbers and small ions**—Cations with high oxidation numbers are stabilized by small anions. For example, the only known halides of Ag(II), Co(II), and Mn(IV) are fluorides. The heavier halides of heavy metals with high oxidation numbers, such as copper (II) iodide and iron(III) iodide decompose at room temperature. To explain this, let's examine the redox reaction:

$$MX + \frac{1}{2}X_2 \rightarrow MX_2,$$ where X is a halogen. The conversion of $\frac{1}{2}X_2$ to X^- is more exothermic for F_2 than for the heavier Cl_2, and the lattice energy plays a major role in this. In the conversion of MX to MX_2, the charge of M goes from +1 to +2, so the lattice enthalpy increases according to the Born-Mayer equation. As the radius of the anion increases, the difference in the two lattice energies diminishes. So to have an *increase* in thermodynamic stability, the radius of the anion must decrease.

- **Solubility**—In general, compounds that contain ions with widely different radii are generally soluble in water. Consider the sulfate of the alkaline earth elements: the sulfate ion is large, and the solubilities of the alkaline-earth metal sulfates decrease, from magnesium to barium sulfate. As a matter of fact, the barium ion is used in the gravimetric determination of sulfate ions. In contrast, the solubilities of alkaline-earth metal hydroxides increase, from magnesium to barium hydroxide.

COVALENT MOLECULAR SUBSTANCES

Covalent molecular substances are held together by covalent bonds, which form when two atoms share electrons in mutually held molecular orbitals. Seven topics are covered under this heading: Lewis diagrams, molecular point groups, valence bond description, molecular orbitals and hybridization, VSEPR concepts, bond strengths, and intermolecular forces.

LEWIS DIAGRAMS

The existence of many compounds could not be explained by ionic bonding, for example, diatomic fluorine. The fluorine molecule, F_2, consists of two F atoms that have the electronic configuration: $1s^2\ 2s^2\ 2p^5$.

It is not possible for these two atoms to achieve the electronic configuration of the nearest noble gas—Ne ($1s^2\ 2s^2\ 2p^6$)—by transferring valence electrons. But it is possible to achieve it by sharing a pair of electrons, in what is called a **bonding pair**:

$$:\!\overset{\displaystyle ..}{\underset{\displaystyle ..}{F}}\!\cdot \quad + \quad :\!\overset{\displaystyle ..}{F}\!\cdot \quad = \quad :\!\overset{\displaystyle ..}{\underset{\displaystyle ..}{F}}\!:\!\overset{\displaystyle ..}{\underset{\displaystyle ..}{F}}\!:$$

The American chemist G.N. Lewis first suggested this bonding scheme in 1916, and representations like the one above, in which valence electrons are represented by dots, are called **Lewis diagrams**. These bonding representations are all equivalent:

$: \overset{\cdot\cdot}{\underset{\cdot\cdot}{F}} : \overset{\cdot\cdot}{\underset{\cdot\cdot}{F}} :$ Each electron is represented by a dot.

$|\overline{F} - \overline{F}|$ Each electron pair is represented by a line.

$F - F$ Only the shared electrons are represented by the line.

Covalent bonds occur when two atoms share electrons in shared molecular orbitals.

Examples:

Methane: Carbon has 4 valence electrons and forms 4 covalent bonds with the lone electrons of 4 hydrogen atoms:

$$\begin{array}{ccc} & H & \\ & | & \\ H\!:\!\overset{\cdot\cdot}{\underset{\cdot\cdot}{C}}\!:\!H & \quad H-C-H \\ & | & \\ & H & \\ H & & H \end{array}$$

Water: Oxygen has 6 valence electrons and forms 2 covalent bonds with the electrons of 2 hydrogen atoms. Four electrons are left, they are not involved in the bonding and are called **nonbonding electrons** or **lone pairs**:

$$H\!:\!\overset{\cdot\cdot}{\underset{\cdot\cdot}{O}}\!:\!H \qquad H-\overline{O}-H$$

Ammonia: Nitrogen has 5 valence electrons and forms 3 covalent bonds with the electrons of 3 hydrogen atoms. Two electrons do not participate in the bonding and make up a lone pair.

$$\begin{array}{ccc} & H & \\ & | & \\ H\!:\!\overset{\cdot\cdot}{N}\!:\! & \quad H-N| \\ & | & \\ H & H \end{array}$$

This leads to a statement of the octet rule:

Molecules in the second or third row of the periodic table are most stable when each atom of the second or third row is surrounded by four bonding or nonbonding electron pairs. Elements in the first row require only one pair of electrons.

MOLECULAR POINT GROUPS

Before going further with the various theories for covalent bonding, we should introduce **symmetry** concepts, which are used to define the geometries of compounds and their orbitals.

SYMMETRY ELEMENTS AND OPERATIONS

A molecule XY_4 can be represented using its symmetry elements in this way:

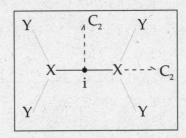

- **Identity (E):**   All molecules have identity, ie, they can rotate about 360° and yield the same, indistinguishable configuration.

- **Center of symmetry (i):**   A line that divides a molecule into two identical parts, such that every atom through i meets equivalent atoms at a distance equidistant from i:

- **Rotation axis (C_n):**   Rotation about $360°/s^- = n$ yields the same configuration; above, there are two axes of rotation about 180° or $360°/180° = C_2$. The molecule above has two C_2 axes. This is expressed as $2C_2$.

- **Mirror plane (σ):**   Reflection through a mirror plane yields the same configuration. The molecule above has two mirror planes; the one shown above and another perpendicular to it along the vertical C_2 rotation axis. This is expressed as $2\sigma\sigma_{v'}$ where the subscript v stands for "vertical." The molecule above also has a third mirror plane, called a $\sigma_{h'}$ where the h stands for horizontal. This plane is perpendicular to the plane of the paper and to the σv shown, and includes the horizontal C_2 reflection axis.

- **Rotation-reflection axis (S):**   Some molecules exist such that rotation about an axis, followed by a reflection through a plane perpendicular to the axis, yields the same configuration.

When these reflections are applied to a molecule and result in a representation that's indistinguishable from the starting configuration, they are called **symmetry operations**.

The group of all possible symmetry operations that can be performed on molecules of a given configuration is called a **molecular point group**. All molecules and ions can be assigned to a specific point group. A few examples are given in the following table. When a molecule has no symmetry at all—besides E—it is assigned to the C_1 point group.

Pt. Group	Elements	Examples
C_1	E	CHFClBr
C_2	E, C_2	H_2O_2
C_{2v}	$E, C_2, 2\sigma$	CH_2Cl_2, NO_2, H_2O
C_3	E, C_3	NH_3
C_{3v}	$E, C_3, 3\sigma$	$CHCl_3, NH_3$
D_{2h}	$E, C_2, 2C_2, 3, i$	C_2H_4
D_{3h}	$E, C_3, 3C_2, 3\sigma, i$	BF_3, cyclopropane
T_d	$E, 3C_2, 4C_3, 6\sigma, 3S_4$	$CH_4, NiCl_4{}^{2-}$
O_h	$E, 3C_4, 4C_3, 8C_2, 9\sigma, 3S_4, 4S_6, i$	$PtCl_6{}^{2-}, SF_6$

COVALENT BOND DESCRIPTION, MOLECULAR ORBITALS, AND HYBRIDIZATION

COVALENT BONDING

- Occurs in elemental gases (eg, H_2, Cl_2, not including the noble gases); a few non-salt inorganic compounds (eg, HCl, NH_3, CO_2), but mostly in organic compounds, ie, the compounds of carbon which is *electroneutral* (neither electronegative nor electropositive).

- Since these molecules carry no charge, covalent substances do not conduct electricity; they are not electrolytes.

- Before covalent molecules can react, their strong covalent bonds must be broken, which is why organic reactions as a rule are slower than inorganic ones;

- Covalent substances generally have low melting and boiling points.

Types of Covalent Bonds and Molecular Orbitals

Italic letters are used to describe molecular orbitals and Greek letters are used to describe the type of covalent bonding.

s-*s*-σ bonding

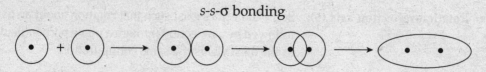

Example: $H + H \rightarrow H_2$

When two H atoms approach one another, their respective $1s^1$ orbitals overlap, and energy is lost. As they overlap still more, they reach the lowest possible energy state, which dictates the bond length of the covalent *s*-*s*-σ bond. This creates a new orbital, which contains both electrons and belongs to both atoms.

Energy is required to break this bond in the hydrogen molecule—the same amount as was required to create the bond, 435 kJmol^{-1}. This is the **binding energy**.

> *When atoms combine to form molecules, they attempt to achieve the lowest energy level.*
>
> *In covalent bonding, two single atomic orbitals combine to become a molecular orbital.*

p-p-σ bonding

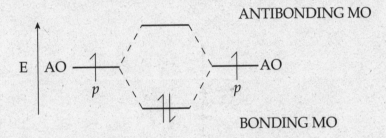

p orbitals can also overlap and form molecular orbitals. The plus and minus signs are not charges, they refer to the sign of the wave function used to mathematically construct the orbitals. An overlap of orbitals is only possible between orbitals that have the same description or sign. When the positive or negative halves of two p orbitals overlap, a rotation-symmetric molecular orbital is formed; the p-p-σ bond. The resulting molecular orbital is at a lower energy than the single p orbitals:

ANTIBONDING MO

E | AO —— p —— AO

BONDING MO

In the above representation, two atomic orbitals (AO), p orbitals, combine to form a p-p-s orbital, the bonding MO, which contains the two p electrons, now shared by the molecule.

Example: $Cl + Cl \rightarrow Cl_2$

$$:\overset{\cdot\cdot}{\underset{\cdot\cdot}{Cl}}\cdot \quad + \quad :\overset{\cdot\cdot}{\underset{\cdot\cdot}{Cl}}\cdot \quad = \quad :\overset{\cdot\cdot}{\underset{\cdot\cdot}{Cl}} : \overset{\cdot\cdot}{\underset{\cdot\cdot}{Cl}}:$$

The electronic configuration of a Cl atom is: $1s^2\ 2s^2\ 2p^6\ 3s^2\ 3p^5$

In each Cl atom, one of the $3p$ orbitals contains only one electron, and they can combine to form a p-p-σ orbital, which covalently binds both atoms into a molecule of chlorine, Cl_2.

s-p-σ bonding

An atomic s-orbital and a p-orbital can also overlap to form a molecular s-p-σ orbital:

The wavefunction of the s-orbital can only be positive, so the overlap is always with the positive half of the p-orbital. The resulting rotation-symmetric molecular orbital is a *s-p-σ* orbital, which yields an *s-p-σ*-bond.

Example: $H + Cl \rightarrow HCl$

$$H\cdot \quad + \quad \cdot \ddot{\underset{..}{Cl}} \cdot \quad = \quad H \cdot \ddot{\underset{..}{Cl}} :$$

The singly-occupied s orbital of hydrogen and the singly occupied p orbital of the three 3p orbitals of Cl form a molecular *s-p-σ* orbital.

p-p-π-bonding

There are three p orbitals, designated p_x, p_y, and p_z. When two atoms approach one another along an axis x, overlap can only occur with their respective p_x orbitals. This yields a *p-p-σ* bond. But when p_y and p_z orbitals approach one another along x, this yields a *p-p-π* orbital which, unlike the *s-p-σ* orbital, is not rotation-symmetric. Rather, *p-p-π* orbitals are symmetric about a plane that contains the x axis. This type of orbital overlap yields *p-p-π* bonding and the corresponding bond is called a π bond:

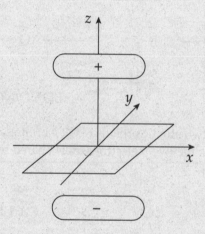

A maximum of three covalent bonds are allowed between two atoms:

- One *p-p-σ* bond (p_x-p_x-σ); and
- two *p-p-π* bonds (p_y-p_y-π; p_z-p_z-π)

One example of covalent bonding is the formation of molecular oxygen, as shown in the following molecular orbital diagram:

Example: $O + O \rightarrow O_2$

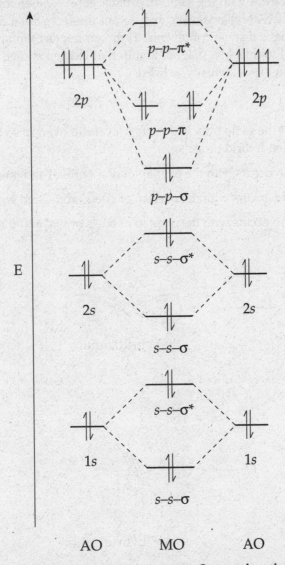

E

AO   MO   AO

Molecular oxygen (O_2) consists of two oxygen atoms. Oxygen has the following x‹ectronic configuration: $1s^2\, 2s^2\, 2p^4$. In the diagram above, the corresponding atomic orbitals (AO) and molecular orbitals (MO) are represented by horizontal bars, and the electrons that they contain, by arrows. The diagram illustrates the bonding between the 8 electrons of one oxygen atom with the 8 electrons of another to form molecular oxygen with 16 electrons. The AO's are shown left and right of the central MO. The lower MO levels are filled first. Each oxygen atom has two electrons in its s orbitals ($1s$ and $2s$, for a total of 4 s electrons). These four electrons go into the bonding (s-s-s) and antibonding (s-s-s^*) molecular orbitals of O_2. Since both bonding and antibonding s MO's are completely filled, $1s$ and $2s$ s-bonding cancel out.

The next MO level (p-p-σ) can accommodate two electrons, and the next (p-p-π), accomodates four. The remaining two electrons go into the p-p-π^* antibonding orbital. There are a total of six electrons in the pi bonding orbitals, but two are in the p-p-π^* antibonding orbital, so two electrons cancel out in the bonding orbitals, and the bond order of molecular oxygen is $4/2 = 2$. Of the 16 electrons of molecular oxygen, 14 are paired, and two are unpaired in the p-p-π^* orbitals because of Hund's rule, which states that two electrons with the same spin must go in separate orbitals. Unlike molecules with paired electrons, which are diamagnetic and do not interact with a magnetic field, molecules with unpaired electrons have magnetic moments. They can interact with a magnetic field, and are said to be paramagnetic. From its MO diagram, molecular oxygen is predicted to have a magnetic moment, and this has been experimentally verified.

HYBRIDIZATION

The *s* and the *p* orbitals of the same principal energy level can overlap so that new types of orbital types result; these are called **hybrid** orbitals:

- *sp*-**hybridization** occurs with the overlap of one *s* orbital and one *p* orbital;
- *sp*^{2}-**hybridization** occurs with the overlap of one *s* orbital and two *p* orbitals;
- *sp*^{3}-**hybridization** occurs with the overlap of one *s* orbital and three *p* orbitals.

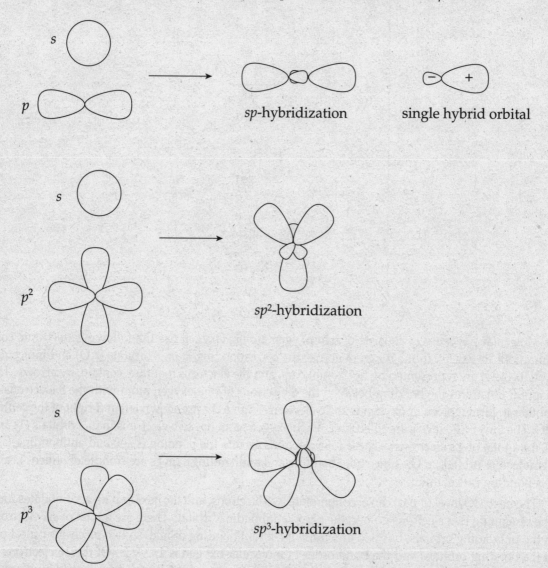

VSEPR CONCEPTS

Valence-shell electron-pair repulsion concepts can be used to refine the hybridization model and accounts for some forms of covalent bonding. It describes the specific geometry adopted by some covalent substances and is based on the following rule:

> *Pairs of electrons in a valence shell are arranged in the geometry most likely to maximize their separation.*

Examples:

H_2O:

$$H:\overset{\displaystyle\cdot\cdot}{\underset{\displaystyle H}{O}}:$$

VSEPR accounts for the 104.5° H–O–H angle experimentally observed in water: all four orbitals are sp^3 hybridized, but the two lone pairs lie closer to the oxygen atom, and there is more repulsion between them than between a lone pair and a bonding pair. It is to minimize this repulsion that the angle adopts this value.

CH_4:

$$\overset{\displaystyle H}{H:\overset{\displaystyle\cdot\cdot}{\underset{\displaystyle\cdot\cdot}{C}}:H}$$

The methane molecule has four equivalent sp^3 hybridized orbitals. They are arranged in a tedrahedral geometry, and all C–H angles are equal to 109.47°.

NH_3:

$$\overset{\displaystyle H}{H:\overset{\displaystyle\cdot\cdot}{\underset{\displaystyle H}{N}}:}$$

In ammonia, the four orbitals are also sp^3 hybridized. Without hybridization, the tetrahedral angles would be 90°. With hybridization and electron repulsion, the actual angle is measured at 107.3°.

BOND STRENGTHS

CARBON BONDS

All of organic chemistry relies on two properties of the carbon atom:

- Each carbon atom can form four covalent bonds, ie, share four valence electrons;
- Carbon atoms like to bind each other and form carbon chains.

The electronic configuration of carbon in the ground state is

$$1s^2\ 2p^6\ 2s^2\ 2p^2$$

In the ground state, the 2s orbital is fully occupied and cannot participate in bonding. But in the first excited state, ie, when one 2s electron is promoted to the 2p energy level, the electronic configuration becomes:

$$1s^2 \, 2p^6 \, 2s^1 \, 2p^3$$

This provides carbon with four singly occupied orbitals that can share their electrons and form four covalent bonds.

So the carbon atom has three ways in which it can arrange four single valence electrons for bonding:

- *sp* hybridization: two electrons in two *sp* hybrid orbitals and two electrons in two *p*-orbitals; this yields linear, triple-bond geometries.

- *sp²* hybridization: three electrons in three *sp²* hybrid orbitals and one electron in a *p* orbital; this yields trigonal, double-bond geometries.

- *sp³* hybridization: four electrons in four *sp³* hybrid orbitals; this yields tetrahedral, single-bond geometries.

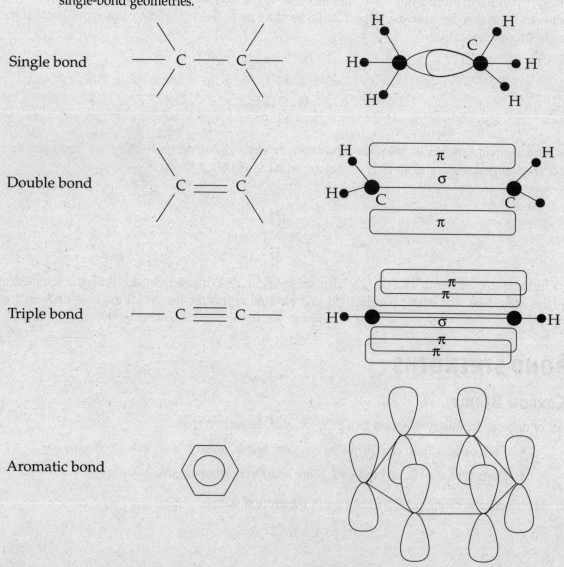

The bond strengths vary, depending on the type of bonding and elements involved:

Type of bond	Bond strength, kJ/mol^{-1}
C–C	348
C=C	682
C–C	962
C–H	413
C–O	351
C=O	732
H–H	435
N–H	392

INTERMOLECULAR FORCES

Intermolecular forces are essentially electrostatic; ie, they're the result of the forces that electrical charges regularly exert on one another All atoms and molecules are subject to them, whether they are in a vacuum or in a medium.

Intermolecular forces include all interactions that occur in the absence of orbital overlap, and become possible when molecules are charged, have a dipole moment, or are placed in electric fields.

A molecule that has two oppositely charged ends is a dipolar molecule.

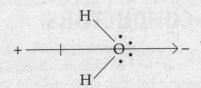

the dipolar water molecule

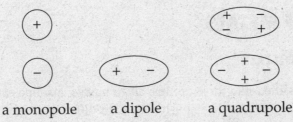

a monopole   a dipole   a quadrupole

1. Charge-charge interactions: occur between groups that have a net charge; the force is nondirectional and depends on the distance between the charges. It is important in proteins which have charged amino acid sidechains.

2. Monopole-dipole interactions: occur between a group that has a charge (a monopole) and a dipolar group.

3. Monopole-quadrupoles: occur between a charged group and a quadrupolar group.

4. Dipole-quadrupoles: occur between dipolar and quadrupolar groups.

5. Quadrupole-quadrupoles: occur between quadrupolar groups.

6. Induced polarization: atoms and molecules are polarizable: when placed in an electric field they become dipolar and can be involved in electrostatic interactions.

7. Van der Waals interactions: This interaction occurs between all molecules, including those that have no net charge or are not polarizable. It is due to the motions of electrons as they approach each other, as well as to their tendency to repel one another. It is the sum of three contributions: the induction force, the orientation force, and the dispersion force.

8. Hydrogen bonding: H-bonding is due to the fact that when hydrogen is covalently bound to O (as in water) or N or another electronegative element, the electron density is shifted to the electronegative element, which confers a partial positive charge to the hydrogen. This allows formation of H-bonds between the now positive hydrogen and the electronegative or negatively charged groups of other molecules.

METALS AND SEMICONDUCTORS

All elements can be classified as metals, nonmetals, metalloids or noble gases. The chemical properties of metals result from the type of bonding that occurs among atoms in the solid state. Three topics will be covered under this heading: properties and structures of metals, band theory, and physical and chemical consequences of band theory.

PROPERTIES OF METALS

CLASSIFICATION OF METALS

- Metals are classified into three groups: alkali metals, alkaline-earth metals, and transition metals, and are distinguished by their different properties.

- Alkali metals are good oxidizing and reducing agents.

- Alkaline-earth metals are also good oxidizing and reducing agents, but do not react as readily as the alkali metals.

- Transition metals can have many different oxidation states.

- All the elements from Group IA to IIB are metals, except hydrogen.

- Group IIIA contains four metals (Al, Ga, In, Tl) and one metalloid (B).

- Group IVA contains two metals (Sn, Pb), two metalloids (Si, Ge), and one non-metal (C).

- Group VA contains one metal (Bi), two metalloids (As, Sb), and two nonmetals (N, P).
- Group VIA contains two metalloids (Te, Po) and three nonmetals (O, S, Se).
- Group VIIA contains one metalloid (At) and four nonmetals (F, Cl, Br, I).

PROPERTIES OF METALS

- All metals are solid at room temperature, except mercury (Hg).
- All metals are good conductors of heat and electricity.
- All metal are malleable (they can easily be hammered into sheets).
- All metal are ductile (they can be drawn into wires).
- Metals generally have high melting points.

PROPERTIES OF METALLOIDS (B, Si, Ge, As, Sb, Tl, Po, At)

- Metalloids have variable properties: they have both metallic and nonmetallic character.
- Some metalloids conduct electricity (Si, Ge, As, Sb).
- Some metalloids have low melting points (As).
- Some metalloids have high melting points (B, Si, Ge).
- Metalloids have various degrees of hardness (hard metals: B, Si, Te; soft metals: As, Sb).

ELECTRICAL CONDUCTIVITY

Solids may also be classified into three types according to their electrical conductivity:

- **Metals** conduct electricity very easily.
- **Insulators** consist of discrete, small molecules with large ionization energies. Most ionic solids, as well as solids with infinite covalent bonding (network solids) such as diamond and quartz, are good insulators.
- **Semiconductors** are metalloids, such as Si and Ge, and compounds formed from two elements that lie between these elements on the periodic table, such as GaAs. Their electrical properties are intermediate between metals and insulators.

PERIODIC PROPERTIES OF METALS

Group	Name	Properties	Elements
IA	Alkali metals	1 valence electron, easily lost; good reducing agents; very reactive with water and O_2; exist as salts in nature, not in metallic form; Na and K have great biological importance	Na, K, Li, Rb, Cs, Fr

IIA	Alkaline-earth metals	2 valence electrons, easily lost; often in +2 oxidation state; not as reactive as alkali metals; slowly form hydroxides with H_2O; exist as salts in nature; Ca and Mg have great biological importance	Be, C, Mg, Sr, Ba, Ra
IIIB to II B	Transition Metals	4th row TMs have electrons in the 4th shell and an incomplete 3rd shell; 5th row TMs have electrons in the 5th shell and an incomplete 4th shell; many oxidation states possible; mostly occur as salts in nature; also occur as pure elements (Cu, Au); biologically important as trace elements (Cu, Zn, Co); can form coordination compounds with anions or neutral molecules	4th row: Sc to Zn 5th row: Y to Cd
IIIA		Al is the most abundant metal on earth; mostly have +3 oxidation state; fairly reactive	Al, Ga, In
IVA		very soft and malleable; low melting point; fairly reactive; amphoteric, can act as acids or bases	Pb, Sb

BAND THEORY

Metals are crystalline solids in which identical atoms occupy all the lattice sites. Obviously, these **atoms** are not bound by electrostatic forces like those encountered between cations and anions in ionic solids. Weak van der Waals forces could not account for the high melting and boiling points of metals. Furthermore, the high coordination numbers of metals do not agree with the presence of localized covalent bonds between each atom and its neighbors.

METALLIC BONDING

The exceptionally high electrical conductivity of metals provides us with insight into the nature of metallic bonding. If we examine the electronic configuration of common metals, we see that they always have more valence orbitals than valence electrons to fill them. For example, Li ($1s^2$ $2s^1$) has only one valence electron for its $2s$ and $2p$ orbitals. Therefore this electron is relatively free to move through the crystal lattice structure. One model of metallic structure is that the lattice of positive metallic ions exists in a **sea of electrons** that holds the ions tightly together. The atoms in the crystal structure can easily be displaced in planes with respect to each other, which explains the malleability and ductility of metals. The displacement in the sea of electrons provides a constant shield between the positive ions and does not allow the development of strong repulsive forces.

BAND THEORY

A more detailed model of metallic bonding is provided by the **band theory**, in which the metal is thought of as a giant molecule in which delocalized molecular orbitals cover the entire structure.

Example:
Sodium (Na): $(1s^2\ 2s^2\ 2p^6\ 3s^1\ 3p^0)$

When the $3s$ orbital of one Na atom overlaps the $3s$ orbital of its immediate neighbor, two molecular orbitals (MO), one bonding (with lower energy) and one antibonding (with higher energy) are formed. When a third atom joins the first two, a third molecular orbital is created: the central MO is nonbonding and is surrounded by a bonding and a nonbonding one, at lower and higher energy levels, respectively. When N atoms come together in a single line, N molecular orbitals are formed, with N distinct energy levels. These N molecular orbitals are very closely spaced in energy and form a virtually **continuous band** covering a range of energies, as shown below:

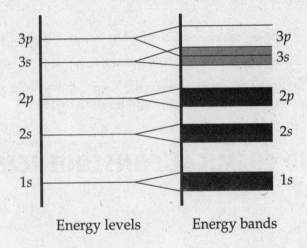

The gray band is the **valence band** ($3s$). It contains the freely moving valence electrons.

The empty band ($3p$) that overlaps the valence band is the **conducting band**; if electrons jump into it, the material will be able to conduct electricity.

This model leads us to the following points:

- when a valence band is not fully occupied, valence electrons can move in many energy states;

- valence electrons can jump into the conducting band;

- the width of the band depends on the degree of overlap of the atomic orbitals between neighboring atoms: the greater the overlap, the wider the band;

- a band is thus a near continuum of a finite number of energy levels;

- the band constructed from the overlap of s orbitals is called an **s band**. Similarly, *p* **bands** and *d* **bands** can be constructed.

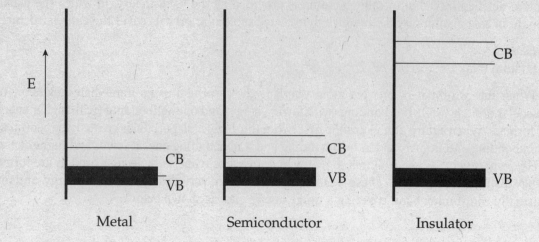

| Metal | Semiconductor | Insulator |

- a metal has overlapping valence and conducting bands (VB and CB);

- insulators have a big gap between their VB and CB;

- a semiconductor has a small gap between the VB and CB; adding energy (heat, light) can then excite electrons that can jump from VB to CB.

PHYSICAL AND CHEMICAL CONSEQUENCES OF BAND THEORY

INSULATORS

- Partially filled bands of delocalized orbitals account for electrical conduction in solids.

- A solid in which electrons saturate a band and a considerable gap exists between the completely filled band and the next available one is called an **insulator.**

- Insulators do not conduct electricity under normal conditions.

- Boron and carbon (diamond) are insulators.

Example: Carbon in diamond.

When the delocalized sp^3 orbitals interact with each other, two bands of delocalized orbitals are formed; one from bonding orbitals and one from antibonding orbitals. There are just precisely enough valence shell electrons to fill these bonding orbitals, and this makes the bonding in diamond incredibly strong. The valence band that contains electrons does not overlap the next band, which has completely unfilled orbitals, and there is a **forbidden energy gap** between the valence band and the conduction band. If a sufficiently large amount of energy is provided to promote electrons from the valence to the conduction band (across the forbidden energy gap), an insulator can be made to construct electricity. In diamond, the gap between the top of the valence band and the bottom of the conduction band takes about 120 kcal/mol of energy to overcome.

SEMICONDUCTORS

- Semiconductors have electrical properties that are intermediate between those of metals and insulators.

- Silicon, germanium, and gray tin all possess the same structure as diamond. However, the forbidden energy gap in these solids is much smaller than in diamond: 25 kcal/mol for Si, 14 kcal/mol for Ge, and 1.8 kcal/mol for Sn. If an appropriate amount of energy is provided to promote electrons from the valence band to the conduction band, the solid can conduct electricity.

- In semiconductors, this relatively small amount of energy can be supplied by thermal means or by a moderate electrical field. The number of excited electrons increases with increasing temperature, which is opposite from the trend seen in metals.

> *Unlike metals, semiconductors are substances with electrical conductivities that increase with increasing temperature.*

- The main difference between a semiconductor and an insulator depends on the size of the band gap in the insulator.

Because insulators can be made to conduct electricity if sufficient energy is provided to send electrons across the forbidden energy gap, the distinction between insulators and semiconductors is considered artificial and is often ignored. Silicon is a good example of this. Because of its energy gap of 25 kcal/mol, it is sometimes considered an insulator in the pure state, and sometimes a semiconductor. But a silicon crystal is considered a semiconductor when it's mixed with certain impurity atoms.

INTRINSIC SEMICONDUCTORS

An intrinsic semiconductor is a solid in which the band gap is so small that some electrons from the valence band will occupy energy levels in the conduction band. This slight electron population in the conduction band will result in the introduction of **negative carriers** (electrons) into the upper level and **positive holes** into the lower. As a result, the solid is conducting: the electrons sent into the conduction band can move freely, and the positive holes left in the valence band move in one direction, as electrons jump to fill them from adjacent bonding pairs in the opposite direction. But at room temperature, a semiconductor has a much lower conductivity than a metal because of the small number of electrons and holes that can act as carriers. The temperature dependence of the **conductance (G)** of a solid follows the following expression:

$$G = G_0 \cdot e^{-E_g/2KT}$$

where E_g is the energy gap between the valence and conduction bands. Silicon and germanium are intrinsic semiconductors because they are semiconducting in the pure state.

EXTRINSIC SEMICONDUCTORS

A substance that is normally an insulator can become semiconducting if small amounts of other atoms are introduced into the lattice, rendering it impure. The result of this is a substance called **an extrinsic semiconductor.**

Example: Silicon (Si)

The structure of a silicion solid is similar to that in which carbon participates, in diamond. But in silicon the energy gap is much smaller: $E_g = 25$ kcal/mol. This gap can be narrowed if impurities such as boron or phosphorus (a few ppm) are substituted for some silicon atoms in the crystal lattice. The process of introducing the impurity is called **doping.** Phosphorus and astatine (Group V) possess five valence electrons, one more electron than silicon. After four of them have covalently bonded with neighboring silicon atoms, one extra electron is left and is available for each substituting dopant atom. If the donor atoms are far apart from each other, the donor band will be very narrow. In a silicon crystal doped with phosphorus atoms, the energy of the extra electron is close to that of the conduction band. The donor band is close to the conduction band, and the thermal excitation of electrons from the donor band to the empty conduction band enables a current to flow. Only 0.25 kcal/mol is required to free the donated electron of phosphorus and make silicon a semiconductor. This process is called **n-type conductivity** because the charge carriers are negative electrons. N-type semiconductors are formed when a doping atom possesses more external electrons than the parent atom. A similar effect can be achieved if boron or gallium (Group III) is introduced in the silicon lattice instead of phosphorus. Boron has one fewer electron than silicon. For each boron atom introduced in the crystal lattice, a vacancy is created in the valence band. The dopant atoms form a very narrow and empty **acceptor band** that lies close and above the filled Si valence band. At a temperature of T = 0K, this acceptor band is empty, but at higher temperatures, thermal excitation promotes Si electrons into it, effectively creating holes in the Si valence band. This process allows other electrons in the band to become mobile; an electron from a neighbor of a boron atom drops into its empty orbital, which creates a vacancy that can be filled by an electron from the next Si atom. This creates a cascade or domino effect, in which an electron from each of a row of atoms moves one place toward the neighboring atom. So electrons become mobile both in the valence and the acceptor bands. The process in the valence band can also be seen as a hole moving across a row of atoms, in the direction opposite to the flow of electrons. This is called **p-type conductivity** because the charge carriers are now positive holes.

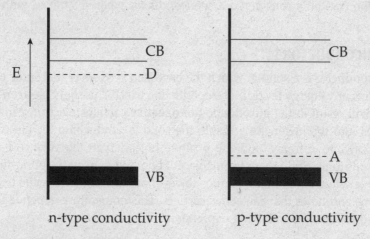

n-type conductivity   p-type conductivity

SEMICONDUCTOR APPLICATIONS

- The most important applications of band theory are based on **p-n junctions**.

- A p-n junction consists of a p-type semiconductor that's in close contact with an n-type semiconductor. In the p-type, the charge carriers are the holes, and in the n-type, the charge carriers are extra electrons.

- At the interface between both semiconductors, a few electrons of the n-zone migrate spontaneously toward the p-type zone. This migration confers a negative charge to the p-zone (because of gained electrons) and a positive charge to the n-zone (because of lost electrons and holes created in the low energy MO).

- This accumulation of charge is called contact, or **junction potential**.

- If the p-zone is connected to the negative pole of a battery and the n-zone to the positive pole, the electrons are attracted to the (+) pole and the holes to the (–) pole, which is opposite the normal direction of the displacement of electrons and holes at the junction. The junction offers a resistance to the current flow and is said to be **inversely polarized**. No current can flow through the system.

- If the p-zone is connected to the positive pole, and the n-zone to the negative pole of the battery, the flow of electrons takes place in the normal direction at the junction. The junction is then **directly polarized**. The current can flow freely.

- A p-n junction makes an excellent **rectifier**. When inserted in a circuit in which the electrical potential alternates continually, a p-n junction allows the current to flow only in the direction of direct polarization, so an alternative current (ac) can be transformed into a direct current (dc). Before p-n junction technology was available, vacuum tubes were used as rectifiers. They were large, fragile, and unreliable. Today, all solid state electronic components in TV sets, calculators, computers, etc., use p-n junction technology.

Transistors are another important application of p-n junctions. A n-p-n transistor is made by inserting a p-type semiconductor between two n-type semiconductors; this creates two interfaces—and attaching the (+) and (–) poles so that one applied potential increases the supply of carriers for another potential. An n-p-n transistor inserted between two circuits can then take the current in one circuit and produce a proportional current in the other one at a higher power level, thus acting as an amplifier.

CHEMISTRY OF THE MAIN GROUP ELEMENTS

The elements of the s and p blocks of the periodic table are collectively referred to as main group elements. All of the elements in this block (Groups I and II) are metals, and seven of the p-block elements are usually considered metals. This section outlines the occurrence and recovery, as well as the physical and chemical properties of main group elements. Five topics are covered under this heading: electronic structure and atomic term symbols, Groups I and II, Groups III and IV, Groups V and VI, and Groups VII and VIII.

GROUP I (ALKALI METALS) AND GROUP II (ALKALINE EARTHS)

OCCURRENCE AND RECOVERY

- **Sodium (Na) and potassium (K)** are the sixth and eighthmost abundant elements, respectively, in the Earth's crust.

- The low abundances of **rubidiumb (Rb) and cesium (Cs)** are associated with the lesser nuclear stability of the heavy elements.

- Because the alkali are all highly reducing, their recovery requires expensive technology, for instance, the electrolysis of molten salts: **Lithium (Li)** is found in the mineral spodumene $LiAl(SiO_3)_2$, and is recovered by electrolysis of molten LiCl and KCl.

- **Sodium** is found in rock salt (NaCl) and seawater, and is recovered by electrolysis of molten NaCl.

- **Calcium (Ca) and magnesium (Mg)** are, respectively, the fifth and seventh most abundant elements found in the Earth's crust. Like alkali, metals are mostly recovered by the electrolysis of molten salts.

- **Beryllium (Be)** is found in beryl, $Be_3AlSi_6O_{18}$, and is recovered by the electrolysis of molten $BeCl_2$.

- **Magnesium** is also found in dolomite $CaMg(CO_3)_2$, and it is recovered by the reaction, at 1200 °C, of $MgCaO_2$ with FeSi.

- **Calcium** is also recovered from limestone, $CaCO_3$, by the electrolysis of molten $CaCl_2$.

PHYSICAL PROPERTIES

- The properties of lithium and its compounds differ markedly from those of the other members of its group.

- The alkali metals are all soft and silvery-white.

- The melting and boiling points of compounds formed from alkali metals decrease down the group, varying from 180 °C and 1340 °C for Li to 40 °C and 680 °C for Cs, respectively.

- They crystallize in the body-centered cubic crystal structure.

- As can be expected from their electronic configuration, the first ionization energy of alkali metals is very low, the product is an ion that has the much more stable rare-gas structure, and the second ionization energy is much higher than the first. Consequently, the chemistry of these elements is dominated by their low electronegativities (1.0 for Li, to 0.7 for Cs), the ease with which they form ions, and the structure of the ions formed.

- The majority of the compounds of these elements are ionic.

- The ionization energies of the alkali elements decrease with increasing atomic radius.

- In spite of their differences in electronic configuration, there is a remarkable uniformity between the behavior of alkaline-earth metals and that of the alkali metals.

- Alkaline-earth elements are all metallic in appearance.

- Their melting and boiling points are higher than those of alkali. These values also decrease down the group, varying from 1280 °C and 2700 °C for compounds of Be to 960 °C and 1140 °C for compounds of Ra, respectively.

- The first four elements crystallize in close-packed structures. Be and Mg crystallize in the hexagonal close-packed structure, Ca is hexagonal and face-centered, and Sr is face-centered. Ba exhibits a body-centered structure.

- The first two ionization energies of the alkaline-earth elements, meaning the removal of the ns^2 electrons, are rather low, and there is a considerable gap between the second and the third. As is the case in the alkali metals, the IEs decrease with increasing atomic radius.

- Their electronegativities vary from 1.5 for Be, to 0.9 for Ba, which indicates that they will form compounds that have strong ionic character.

CHEMICAL PROPERTIES

- The standard potentials of alkali metals are very uniform and only vary from −3.04 V (for Li) to − 2.92 V (for Cs). This tells us that they are all capable of being oxidized by water (−0.83V): $M_{(s)} + H_2O_{(l)} \rightarrow M^+_{(aq)} + OH^-_{(aq)} + \frac{1}{2}H_{2(g)}$. This reaction is very rapid and exothermic for sodium and the heavier alkali, and the hydrogen that's generated is combustible.

- All alkali form binary compounds with halogens. Most of the alkali halides have a (6,6)-coordination rock-salt structure, except CsCl, CsBr, and CsI, which have the more closely packed (8,8)-structure. At high pressures the halides of Na, K, and Rb undergo a transition from a (6,6) to an (8,8)-structure.

- Most simple alkali salts are soluble in water, except the larger cations (K^+ to Cs^+) combined with heavier anions. For instance, the solubility of caesium perchlorate is only 0.10 mol/L, whereas that of lithium perchlorate is 4.5 mol/L.

- The complexes formed with the alkali ions arise from the coulombic attraction created by small donors possessing O or N atoms. For the *s* group elements, the smaller the ion and the greater its charge, the greater the stability of the complex formed.

- The most common stable complexes of Group I cations are formed with polydentate ligands such as 18-crown–6 ether or bicyclic 2.2.1 and 2.2.2 cryptate ligands.

- The standard potentials of alkaline-earth metals vary a little more than those of the alkali metals: from −1.98V for Be to −2.93 for Ba. They are also capable of being oxidized by water: $M_{(s)} + 2H_2O_{(l)} \rightarrow M^{2+}_{(aq)} + 2OH^-_{(aq)} + H_{2(g)}$. This reaction is less rapid for the alkaline earths than for the alkali metals.

Example:

Which forms the most stable carbonate, a magnesium or a barium ion? Is there a trend in solubility?

$MgCO_3$ is more soluble than $BaCO_3$. Compare the relative size of the two cations with that of a carbonate ion. Large anions are generally stabilized by large cations. The radius of the carbonate ion is of the same order of magnitude as that of the barium element. The solubility of carbonates should decrease from the smaller to the larger elements in a group.

GROUP III AND IV ELEMENTS

OCCURRENCE AND RECOVERY

- **Boron (B)** is a rare element (~9 ppm). It is found in hydrated sodium borates, such as borax, $Na_2B_4O_5(OH)_4 \cdot 8H_2O$.

- **Aluminium (Al)** is much more abundant (~80,000 ppm). It is primarily found in bauxite, which consists of various hydrates of aluminum oxide, $Al_2O_3H_2O$.

- **Carbon (C)** and **silicon (Si)** are also very abundant (~180 ppm and 270,000 ppm, respectively). Carbon is recovered as diamond or graphite. Silicon is recovered from the reduction of silica (SiO_2), with carbon, at very high temperatures.

- **Germanium (Ge)** is not very abundant and is recovered in the treatment of zinc ores.

- **Tin (Sn)** is recovered from the reduction of cassiterite (SnO_2) with carbon in a furnace, and **lead (Pb)** is recovered from lead sulfides, which are converted to oxides and reduced with carbon.

- As in Groups I and II, the low abundance of the heavier elements is due to the decrease in the nuclear stability of elements after iron.

PHYSICAL PROPERTIES

- The lightest members of Group III and IV are nonmetals, and the heaviest are metals.

- Boron and silicon have very similar physical properties. In compounds, they are both chemically hard (there is a big difference between their ionization energies and their electron affinities). In their elemental form, they are hard, semiconducting solids.

- Carbon and boron, like most of the elements in the p block, are polymorphous. All of the carbon atoms in diamond are covalently bonded to four neighbors and form a tightly bonded three-dimensional structure. Because of this, diamond is very hard and is a very poor electrical conductor. Graphite, however, consists of layers of planar sheets made up of the overlap of sp^2 hybrids of carbon atoms. The overlap of the remaining p orbitals forms a p conduction band, which makes graphite a good electrical conductor. Because of the weak van der Waals forces between sheets of carbon atoms, graphite is slippery and is often used as a lubricant.

- Thallium and lead, the last elements of Groups III and IV, respectively, crystallize into a close-packed structure and can therefore be considered metals. There is wide structural diversity within the boron group. In solid boron, the icosahedral B_{12} units are the basis of its chemistry.

CHEMICAL PROPERTIES

- The majority of the compounds of most elements of the two groups contain the elements in the +3 oxidation state, for Group III and +4 for Group IV.

- Thallium and lead are exceptions; their oxidation numbers are equal to their group number minus two: +1 for thallium and +2 for lead.

- The chemical properties of boron, carbon, silicon, and germanium are typical of those of nonmetals.

- The first two elements of each group easily form compounds with oxygen and fluorine, as evidenced by the large number of oxanions they form: borates, aluminates, carbonates, and silicates.

- Boron forms simple trihalides BX_3, which are remarkable as Lewis acids. These halides undergo nucleophilic displacement reactions to form BR_3 compounds (R = alkyl groups). In boron nitrogen compounds, BN is isoelectronic with C–C. One form of BN resembles diamond, and the other resembles graphite. Molecular compounds including the BN bond include Lewis acid-base couples, alkenes, and aminoboranes.

- Boranes are a very large group of compounds that fall into three different classes: closoboranes $[B_nH_n]^-$, nidoboranes B_nH_{n+4}, and arachnoboranes, B_nH_{n+6}.

- Carbon plays a central role in organic chemistry and is also a member of a great number of inorganic and organometallic compounds.

- Carbon compounds include hydrocarbons and halogenated hydrocarbons, as well as oxygen and nitrogen compounds.

- Saline carbides are largely ionic solids, and are formed by the elements of Groups I and II and by aluminum. Metallic carbides are formed by d- and f- block elements. They are electric conductors.

- Metalloid carbides are formed by boron and silicon and are covalent solids. Halides of silicon and germanium are mild Lewis acids due to hypervalence of their central atoms.

- Silicates are compounds that contain metals and the tetrahedral SiO_4 structure. In silicates, the SiO_4 building block may share one or two oxygen atoms with an adjacent SiO_4.

- Aluminosilicates are similar to silicates except that aluminum atoms replace some of the silicon atoms.

Example:

Is $B_{10}H_{14}$ a closo-, nido-, or arachnoborane?

It is a nido borane because it conforms to the general nido borane formula (B_nH_{n+4}).

GROUP V AND VI ELEMENTS

OCCURRENCE AND RECOVERY

- **Nitrogen (N)** and **oxygen (O)** are obtained by the distillation of liquid air at very low temperatures.

- Nitrogen is converted into **ammonia** by the Haber process, which occurs at high temperatures and pressures. $N_2 + 3H_2 \rightarrow 2NH_3$

- **Phosphorus (P)** is extracted from fluorapatite, $Ca_5(PO_4)_3F$, and hydroxyapatite, $Ca_5(PO_4)_3OH$. White phosphorus exists as a tetrahedral P_4 molecule. Red phosphorus exists as an amorphous solid. Phosphoric acid is obtained by the reaction of these phosphate rocks with sulfuric acid.

- **Arsenic (As)**, **antimony (Sb)**, and **bismuth (Bi)** are usually found in sulfide ores. These elements exist as several allotropes.

- **Sulfur (S)** is found in its native form in an S_8 ring and in metal sulfides.

- **Selenium (Se)**, **tellurium (Te)**, and **polonium (Po)** are found in metal sulfide ores.

PHYSICAL PROPERTIES

- Nitrogen and oxygen are the only members of their groups that exist in gaseous form and as diatomic molecules under normal conditions.

- All of the other elements of Groups V and VI are solids.

- Metallic character increases down these groups.

- As opposed to other group elements, the coordination numbers of N and O in compounds are generally lower.

- Oxygen has two allotropes: O_2, which possesses a double bond and a triplet ground state, and ozone, O_3, which is a highly unstable and strongly oxidizing agent.

CHEMICAL PROPERTIES

- Nitrogen and oxygen are among the most electronegative elements in the periodic table (3.04 and 3.44 respectively).

- Their chemical properties are markedly different from those of the other group elements. Oxygen never achieves the rest of the group's maximum oxidation state (+6), but nitrogen does (+5), under strong oxidizing conditions.

- Because of their small radii, nitrogen and oxygen rarely have coordination numbers greater than 4, but the heavier members of Groups V and VI can reach +5 and +6. (SeF_6 and PCl_5 for example.)

- Because of its triple bond, N_2 is highly unreactive. Under extreme conditions, certain strong oxidizing agents can transfer electrons to the molecule and break the bond. For example, the slow reaction of lithium with N_2 at room temperature yields Li_3N.

- The halides of nitrogen and oxygen are few due to their resistance to oxidation.

- The halides of the heavier elements are more numerous. For Group V, formulas are generally of the type EX_3 and EX_5, and for Group VI, they're EX_2, EX_4 and EX_6, where X is a halide.

- The two most important oxanions of nitrogen are NO_3^- (oxidation number = +5) and NO_2^- (+3). N(V) is found in nitric acid, HNO_3, N(III) is found in nitrous acid (HNO_2), and N(IV) is found in a gaseous equilibrium mixture: $N_2O_{4\ (g)} \leftrightarrow 2NO_{2\ (g)}$.

- The oxides of phosphorus include P_4O_4 and P_4O_{10}, which are both cage compounds.

- The important oxanions are $H_2PO_2^-$ (oxidation number = +1), HPO_3^{2-} (+3), and PO_4^{3-} (+5).

- There are many known compounds that contain a PN bond (isoelectronic with SiO). For example, phosphazenes are rings or chains that contain R_2PN units.

- The oxanions of sulfur include the unreactive sulfate ion, SO_4^{2-} (S = +6), the reducing sulfite ion, SO_3^{2-} (+4) and the oxidizing peroxosulfate ions, $S_2O_8^{2-}$ ($O_3S-OO-SO_3^{2-}$).

Example:

What is the probable structure of $AsCl_5$?

Trigonal bipyramid. To answer this question, you need to consider that As belongs to Group V, and that one of the electrons of the lone pair must be promoted to a $4d$ orbital. The five unpaired electrons thus produced can form covalent bonds with five chlorine atoms, and the most stable geometry (creating the least repulsion between electron pairs) is trigonal bipyramid.

GROUP VII (HALOGENS) AND VIII ELEMENTS (RARE GASES)

OCCURRENCE AND RECOVERY

- Because of their high reactivity, halogens are found only as halides in nature.

- **Iodine (I)** , the most easily oxidized, is also found as the iodate (IO_3^-).

- The primary sources of **fluorine (F)** are insoluble deposits of calcium fluoride.

- Chlorides, bromides, and iodides are soluble and found primarily in ocean water. The elements are produced by the oxidation of the halides.

- Most of the **helium (He)** on the planet is produced by alpha emission and is found in gas wells.

- **Argon (Ar)** and **neon (Ne)** are the most abundant rare gases in the atmosphere and, like **krypton (Kr)** and **xenon (Xe)** , are obtained by the distillation of liquid air.

Example:

Helium is the second most abundant element in the universe—why is there so little of it on Earth?

Because helium is the lightest of the noble gases and is not easily retained by the earth's gravitational field.

PHYSICAL PROPERTIES

- The structures of the elements of each of these groups display a remarkable uniformity.

- The halogens are all nonmetals and diatomic molecules, and the rare gases are all atomic gases with very low reactivity.

- The halogens show a displacement of the maximum absorption toward the longer wavelengths of the light spectrum from fluorine to iodine: fluorine is colorless, chlorine is green, bromine is red, and iodine is purple.

Example:

Which of the following two species is the most stable: NaI_3 or CsI_3?

CsI_3 is more stable. I^- is a large ion and will be stabilized by an ion of similar size. Remember the rule: Large anions are stabilized by large cations.

CHEMICAL PROPERTIES

- The halogens are among the most reactive of the nonmetallic elements, and the rare gases (their neighbors) are the least reactive.

- Fluorine is the most reactive, the most electronegative, and the strongest oxidant of all of the halogens.

- Fluorine stabilizes metals ions in their highest oxidation state; AgF_4^- (Ag = +3), BiF_5 (Bi = +5), PtF_6 (Pt = +6). Therefore, metal fluorides, as well as fluorocarbon polymers, are usually used to contain and handle fluorine and reactive fluorine compounds.

- The molecular fluorine compounds tend to be very volatile; much more so than their chlorine counterparts and some of their hydrogen counterparts.

- The fluorine atom is very small; its electrons are strongly held by the nucleus. This gives fluorine compounds a very low polarizability and a weak dispersion interaction.

- Because of its high electronegativity (3.98), the fluorine atom tends to attract the electrons of neighboring atoms very strongly in covalent compounds. This effect gives rise to the enhanced acidity of fluorine-containing acids.

- Iodine can form aggregates described by the formula I_n^-. I_3^-, for instance, can be seen as an aggregate of I_2 and I^-.

- There are several known interhalogens (compounds containing a halogen-halogen bond). These compounds are in the forms XY, XY_3, XY_5, and XY_7, where X is generally Cl, Br, or I and Y is F.

- Most halogen oxides are unstable (OF_2, Cl_2O). The halogen oxyanions and oxyacids, however, are numerous and stable.

- The strength of oxacids grows along with the number of oxygen atoms: HClO is less acidic than perchloric acid $HClO_4$.

- The halogen oxyanions form metal complexes, particularly metal perchlorates and periodates. Halogen oxyanions and oxides are mostly very powerful oxidizing agents.

- The most important compounds of noble gases are the xenon fluorides: XeF_2, XeF_4, and XeF_6. Compounds that contain bonds between xenon and oxygen, carbon, and nitrogen are also known. The compounds of the other noble gases are much less common.

Example:

What is the shape of the Cl_2O molecule?

Angular. Each chlorine atom forms a covalent bond with the oxygen atom. This yields four electron pairs (two bonding and two nonbonding).

Example:

What is the geometry of XeF_2?

Linear. One of the Xe electrons must be promoted into a vacant $5d$ orbital. The two unpaired electrons form covalent bonds with the fluorine atoms. The remaining three lone pairs of the xenon atom are positioned in a plane at 120° angles, and the two Xe–F bonds are above and below that plane.

CHEMISTRY OF THE TRANSITION ELEMENTS

The elements found in Groups IIIB to IIB of the periodic table are called transition metals. They are characterized by special properties that arise from their d- and f-electron shell configurations. Three topics are covered under this heading: electronic structure; physical and chemical properties of transition metals, lanthanides, and actinides; and coordination chemistry.

ELECTRONIC STRUCTURE OF TRANSITION METALS

VALENCE ELECTRONS OF TRANSITION METALS

The periods of the periodic table reflect the electron occupancy of orbitals by valence electrons:

1st period	$1s^2$	2 elements
2nd period	$2s^2\,2p^6$	8 elements
3rd period	$3s^2\,3p^6$	8 elements
4th period	$4s^2\,4p^6\,3d^{10}$	18 elements
5th period	$5s^2\,5p^6\,4d^{10}$	18 elements
6th period	$6s^2\,6p^6\,5d^{10}\,4f^{14}$	32 elements
7th period	$7s^2\,7p^6\,6d^{10}\,5f^{14}$	32 elements

Thus, valence electrons distribute as follows:

- Main group elements: s- and p orbital occupancy;

- Transition metals: s- and d orbital occupancy;

- Lanthanides and actinides: s-, d-, and f orbital occupancy.

- Starting with the 4th period, there are five possible d orbitals per energy level and each can accommodate 2 electrons, for a possible total of 10 d-electrons.

- Starting with the 6th period, there are seven possible f orbitals per energy level and each can accommodate 2 electrons, for a possible total of 14 f electrons.

- These orbitals all have the same energy in the gaseous metal ion, the free ion.

- The five d orbitals are divided into two groups, called t_{2g} and e_g respectively; these names are derived from the symmetry of the orbitals in the octahedral or tetrahedral point groups.

- 4th and 5th row transition metals can adopt several oxidation states.

Example: Iron (Fe)

In the 0 oxidation state—or pure, elemental state, the electronic configuration of iron is $3s^2$, $3p^6$, $3d^6$, $4s^2$.

Note that the 4s level is located at a lower energy level than the 3d level, which is why it contains 2 electrons before the d shell is fully occupied (capacity: 10 electrons).

In the +2 oxidation state—or when it loses 2 electrons, its configuration becomes $3s^2$, $3p^6$, $3d^6$, $4s^0$ or simply d^6.

In the +3 oxidation state—or when it loses 3 electrons, its valence configuration is $3s^2$, $3p^6$, $3d^5$, $4s^0$ or simply d^5.

4th row transition metals are designated "d_n" systems where n is equal to the number of electrons present in the 3d shell. This number varies with the oxidation state of the transition metal.

The following table lists some of the 4th row d systems. In the zero oxidation state, their $4s$ level has 2 electrons; when they are oxidized to the +2 oxidation state, they lose the two $4s$ electrons, which is why their d-level occupancy remains unchanged:

Oxidation state:	0	+2	+3
Element			
Sc	d^1	d^1	
Ti	d^2	d^2	d^1
V	d^3	d^3	d^2
Cr	d^4	d^4	d^3
Mn	d^5	d^5	d^4
Fe	d^6	d^6	d^5
Co	d^7	d^7	d^6
Ni	d^8	d^8	d^7
Cu	d^9	d^9	d^8
Zn	d^{10}	d^{10}	d^9

CRYSTAL FIELDS

- d orbitals are degenerate orbitals; they lie at the same energy. Under the influence of an approaching **crystal** or **ligand field**, consisting of charged ligands, the energy of these orbitals will be split by the electric field into two or more groups groups that will have different designations, depending on the symmetry of the resulting orbitals:

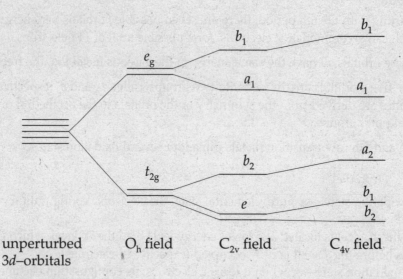

- Some of the common point groups to which transition metal complexes belong are the octahedral (O_h), tetrahedral (T_d), square planar (C_{4v}) and rhombic (C_{2v}).

- In the case of octahedral symmetry, there are two ways to fill the d orbitals; designated **high spin** (HS) and **low spin** (LS), respectively. Whether a complex will be HS or LS depends on the strength of the crystal field interactive energy, ie, whether the approaching ligands are strong or weak. When the ligands are strong, they interact strongly with the d orbitals, and this results in a larger splitting of the e_g and t_{2g}

orbitals. Electrons will then fill only the lower t_{2g} orbitals, because the gap is too large. When the ligands interact weakly with the d orbitals, the splitting will be smaller and the electrons will then occupy the orbitals following the aufbau principle: the five orbitals all take one electron before any of them accepts a second one.

Example: Filling of d-orbitals by the 6 electrons of the Fe^{2+} ion under octahedral symmetry:

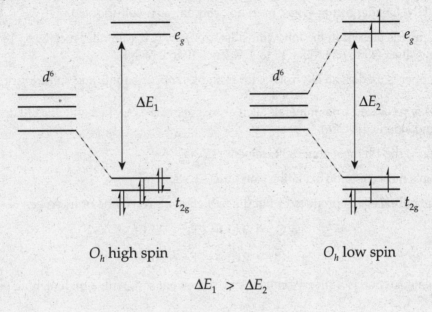

$$\Delta E_1 \; > \; \Delta E_2$$

PROPERTIES OF TRANSITION METALS

- Important elements in this group include **iron (Fe)**, **copper (Cu)**, **nickel (Ni)**, and **zinc (Zn)**.

- They are recovered as ores, and the pure elements are extracted and purified by various metallurgical means (crushing, flotation, smelting, etc); they also occur as salts.

- The metals in the 4th row (Sc to Zn) have electrons in their 4th shell but incomplete 3rd shells (vacancies in the $3d$ orbitals).

- The metals in the 5th row (Y to Cd) have electrons in their 5th shell but incomplete 4th shells (vacancies in the $4d$ orbitals).

- Transition metals have different oxidation states. This allows them to form different compounds with the same element (for example, FeO formed from Fe^{2+} and Fe_2O_3 formed from Fe^{3+}.

- These different oxidation state are made possible by the fact that electrons can be lost from two different valence shells; in the 4th period, these are: $4s$ or p and $3d$.

- The electronegativity increases from left to right across the periodic table; transition metals with higher electronegativity are less reactive than alkali metals.

- Transition metals form both covalent and ionic compounds.

Copper (Cu) is recovered from minerals such as chalcopyrite ($CuFeS_2$), bornite (Cu_5FeS_4), cuprite (Cu_2O), and azurite ($2CuCO_3.Cu(OH)_2$. It is a reddish, soft metal that can be hardened by hammering; it has a high melting point, 1083 °C.

- Next to silver, copper is the best conductor of electricity and heat; its common oxidation states are +2 and +1.

- Copper is more electropositive than hydrogen and is only soluble in oxidizing acids, in HNO_3 under nitrogen gas, or in hot, concentrated sulfuric acid.

- Copper is present in the following alloys: bronze (Cu + another metal, i.e., 10% Sn), new silver (45 to 67% Cu + 12 to 45% Zn + 10 to 26% Ni).

- Copper is used as an electrolyte, for example, copper sulfate and sulfuric acid.

Iron (Fe) is recovered from minerals such as magnetite (Fe_3O_4), hematite (Fe_2O_3), pyrite (Fe_2S), and siderite ($FeCO_3$).

- Iron is the 4th most abundant element (4.7 %)

- Iron's most common oxidation states are +3. +2;

- The pure metal is produced from the reduction of iron oxide or hydrogen:

$$Fe_2O_3 + 2Al \rightarrow 2Fe + Al_2O_3$$

$$Fe_2O_3 + 2Al \rightarrow 2Fe + Al_2O_3$$

- Elemental iron is a silvery-white metal, somewhat soft, with a high melting point, 1535 °C;

- It is used in several alloys, the most famous being **steel**, which has a carbon content that varies between 0.02 to 2.06%.

Manganese (Mn) has oxidation numbers +2 and +7 in acidic media and +4 and +6 in basic media.

- Manganese is recovered from minerals such as manganite (MnO(OH), pyrolusite (MnO_2), and hausmannite (Mn_3O_4);

- It is purified in the following way: $3MnO_4 + 8Al \rightarrow 9Mn + 4Al_2O_3$.

- It is used in the production of alloys and manganese steel, which contain about 10–15% Mn.

- Mn(II) forms sulfates ($MnSO_4$), chlorides ($MnCl_2$), oxides (MnO), and sulfides (MnS).

- Mn(III) forms oxyhydrates ($Mn_2O_3 \cdot xH_2O$) and oxides (Mn_2O_3).

- Mn(IV) also forms oxides (MnO_2), and Mn(V) forms another oxide, Mn_2O_7

Chromium (Cr) is recovered from minerals such as chromite ($FeO.Cr_2O_3$) and krokoite ($PbCrO_4$);

- The pure metal is obtained from

$$Cr_2O_3 + 2Al \rightarrow Al_2O_3 + 2Cr$$

- It has oxidation states of +6, +4, + 3, and +2.

- Cr(II) forms chlorides ($CrCl_2$), and Cr(III) forms oxides (Cr_2O_3) and oxyhydrates ($Cr_2O_3 \cdot xH_2O$), as well as chlorides ($CrCl_3$) and sulfates ($Cr_2(SO_4)_3$);

- Cr(IV) and Cr(VI) both form oxides, CrO_2 and CrO, respectively.

Zinc (Zn) is recovered form minerals such as zincblende (ZnS) and smithsonite ($ZnCO_3$).

- Zinc has one oxidation state, +2.

- The metal is purified by electrolysis of the oxide, obtained from

$$2ZnS + 3O_2 \rightarrow 2\ ZnO + 2SO_2$$

and then reduced with coal:

$$ZnO + C \rightarrow Zn + CO$$

- It is a bluish-white, soft metal. Its compounds are zinc oxides (ZnO), hydroxides ($Zn(OH)_2$), chlorides ($ZnCl_2$), and sulfides (ZnS).

Nickel (Ni) is recovered from minerals such as chloanthite (Ni, Co, Fe)As_3 and $NiAs$;

- Nickel has the oxidation states +2, +3, and +4;

- The metal is obtained by aluminothermal methods:

$$3NiO + 2Al \rightarrow 3Ni + Al_2O_3$$

- Ni(II) forms oxides (NiO), chlorides ($NiCl_2$), sulfates ($NiSO_4$), carbonates ($NiCO_3$), and hydroxides (Ni $(OH)_2$); Ni(III) forms oxyhydrates ($Ni_2O_3 \cdot xH_2O$).

LANTHANIDES AND ACTINIDES

- Together with **scandium (Sc)**, **yttrium (Y)**, and **lutetium (Lu)**, the lanthanides are called **rare metals** and their oxides, **rare earths**.

Z	Symbol	Name
57	La	lanthanum
58	Ce	cerium
59	Pr	praseodymium
60	Nd	neodymium
61	Pm	prometheium
62	Sm	samarium
63	Eu	europium
64	Gd	gadolinium
65	Tb	terbium
66	Dy	dysprosium
67	Ho	holmium
68	Er	erbium
69	Tm	thulium
70	Yb	yttrium

- They are recovered from various minerals such as gadolinite, cerite, and monazite.

- The oxidation state of lanthanides is generally +3. Ce and Tb also occur as +4; and Eu, Sm, and Yb, as +2.

- Their properties are the result of incomplete f-electron shells.

- All **actinides** are radioactive elements.

Z	Symbol	Name
89	Ac	actinium
90	Th	thorium
91	Pa	protactinium
92	U	uranium
93	Np	neptunium
94	Pu	plutonium
95	Am	americium
96	Cm	curium
97	Bk	berkelium
98	Cf	californium
99	Es	einsteinium
100	Fm	fermium
101	Md	mendelevium
102	No	nobelium

- The actinides up to Z = 94 are naturally occurring, others are produced in nuclear reactors;

- **Uranium (U)** is recovered from minerals like uranium pitchblende ($mUO_2 \cdot nUO_3$);

- The U_{235} isotope can undergo nuclear fission;

- U has oxidation states +6 and +4; uranium hexafluorate, UF_6, is used to separate U-isotopes.

- **Thorium (Th)** has an oxidation state of +4 and forms ThO_2 (which has a very high melting point, 3390 °C) as well as complex thorates ($Na_6[Th(CO_3)_5]$).

COORDINATION CHEMISTRY

- Coordination chemistry is the chemistry of transition metals that are bonded to ligands. These are called **complexes** or **coordination compounds**, and are usually brightly colored.

- The transition metals can coordinate a wide variety of ligands due to their incompletely filled d shells; this provides them with several oxidation states and renders them capable of forming paramagnetic compounds when unpaired electrons are present.

- The preferred coordination numbers are 4 and 6, but 3 and 5 also occur very often. This leads to preferred geometries, which are listed in the following table.

System	Oxidation state	Coordination number	Geometry of the complex
Cu, d^{10}	+1	2	Linear
		3	Planar
		4	Tetrahedral
Cu, d^9	+2	4	Square planar
		4	Tetrahedral
		5	Square pyramidal
		5	Trigonal bipyramidal
		6	Octahedral
Ni, d^8	+2	4	Square planar
		4	Tetrahedral
		5	Trigonal bipyramidal
		6	Octahedral
Fe, d^6	+2	4	Tetrahedral
		6	octahedral

- The geometry adopted by a given coordination compound will depend on the strength of the incoming ligands; i.e., to what extent the charge interaction between the central coordinating metal and the ligands will favor the adoption of a specific geometry.

- The formation of a complex can be expressed as follows:

$$M^{n+} + L \rightarrow ML^{n+} \qquad K_{eq} = [ML^{n+}]/[M^{n+}][L]$$

- The stability of the complexes formed with divalent ions follows the **Irving-Williams series**, in which K_{eq} increases from left to right: $Ba^{2+} > Sr^{2+} > Ca^{2+} > Mg^{2+} > Mn^{2+} > Fe^{2+} > Co^{2+} > Ni^{2+} > Cu^{2+} > Zn^{2+}$.

- The **spectrochemical series** provides an estimate of the ability of incoming ligands to cause the splitting of d orbitals: $< Br^- < Cl^- < SCN^- < F^- < OH^- < oxalate < H_2O < NH_3 < pyridine < NO_2^- < CN^- < CO$.

So in octahedral symmetry, complexes formed with Br^- ions will have a smaller splitting of d-orbitals and will be low spin; complexes formed with CO as a ligand will have a large d-orbital splitting and will be high spin.

The main reactions that coordination compounds undergo are:

1. Ligand substitution: a coordinated ligand is replaced by another one; $[ML_nX] + Y \rightarrow [ML_nY] + X$; where L, X, and Y are different ligands.

   Example: $[Co(NH_3)_5Cl]^{2+} + OH^- \rightarrow [Co(NH_3)_5OH]^{2+} + Cl^-$

2. Redox reactions: electron transfer processes in which the oxidation state of the metal changes: $Cr^{2+} + Co^{3+} \rightarrow Cr^{3+} + Co^{2+}$

   Example: $[Co(NH_3)_5Cl]^{2+} + [Cr(H_2O)_6]^{2+} \rightarrow [Co(NH_3)_5H_2O]^{2+} + [Cr(H_2O)_5Cl]^{2+}$

THE *TRANS* EFFECT

Ligand substitution in square, planar Pt complexes can yield either *cis* or *trans* products. This depends on the nature of the ligand *trans* to the incoming ligand. Ligands can be arranged in a series of increasing *trans* effect: $H_2O < OH^- < NH_3 < Cl^- < Br^- < I^- < NO_2^- < CO < CN^-$.

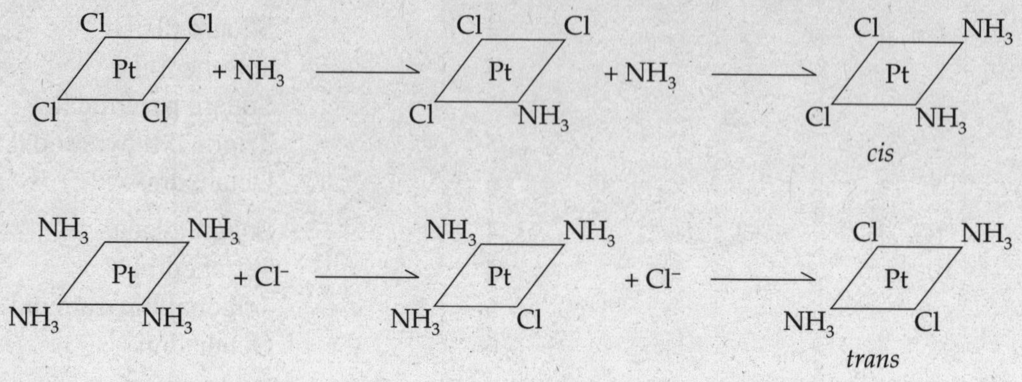

SPECIAL TOPICS

Five special inorganic chemistry topics are covered under this heading: organometallic chemistry, environmental chemistry, catalysis, applied solid-state chemistry, and bioinorganic chemistry.

ORGANOMETALLIC CHEMISTRY

- An **organometallic** compound is a substance that contains at least one metal-carbon bond. The suffix "metallic" includes main group metals, metals of the *d*- and *f*-blocks as well as metalloids such as boron, silicon, and arsenic.

- Any one of four possible M–C forming reactions can be used to obtain most organometallic compounds:

1. Metal + organohalide: $2M + RX \rightarrow MR + MX$, where R is an alkyl group and X is halogen.

Example:

The synthesis of a **Grignard** reagent, which is an organometallic compound:

$$Mg + CH_3Br \rightarrow CH_3MgBr$$

2. Transmetallation: $M + M'R \rightarrow MR + M'$, where M is a metal that is more electropositive than M';

3. Double displacement: $MR + EX \rightarrow MX + ER$, where E is a *p*-block metalloid and M is more electropositive than E.

Example:

The synthesis of tetramethyl silicon:

$$Li_4(CH_3)_4 + SiCl_4 \rightarrow 4LiCl + Si(CH_3)_4$$

4. Hydrometallation: $MH + H_2C = CH_2 \rightarrow MH_2C\text{-}CH_3$. In the case of unsymmetrical alkenes, the M group attaches to the less hindered carbon atom, and the smaller H attaches to the most hindered C.

Example:

Predict the products of the reaction of gallium with dimethylmercury. What kind of reaction is this reaction? Write the balanced equation.

Gallium is a Group III element; it's more electropositive than mercury. It's likely to undergo a transmetallation reaction with dimethylmercury, yielding a trivalent covalent compound:

$$2Ga + 3Hg(CH_3)_2 \rightarrow 2Ga(CH_3)_3 + 3Hg$$

- The s-block elements form organometallic compounds that have highly polar M^+–C^- bonds. The ionic character of these bonds increases for the heavier elements.

- The organometallic compounds of group III (B to Tl), are more polar in nature than are those of the s-block elements.

- BR_3 and GaR_3 compounds are unassociated planar trigonal molecules. The trend in their nucleophilic character is as follows: $AlR_3 > GaR_3 > BR_3$.

- The organometallic compounds of the Group IV metals (Si to Pb) are electron-poor. The bonds in these organometallic compounds are not very polar. These elements form MR_4 compounds with tetrahedral geometry. The low polarity of their bonds and the steric hindrance around the central atom accounts for the resistance of these compounds to hydrolysis.

- The organometallic compounds of Group V (As to Bi) are electron-rich. This Lewis basicity arises due to the presence of a lone pair of electrons on the central atom. AsR_3, $:SbR_3$ and $:BiR_3$ are all trigonal pyramidal. The central atom may exist in oxidation states of +3 and +5, as in AsR_5, although ER_5 compounds are much less common. The AsR_3 compounds and some SbR_3 compounds may form complexes with some d-block metals.

- The term **heptacity** is often used to describe organometallic compounds in the d- and f groups. The heptacity (η) is the number of carbon atoms of an organic ligand that are attached to a metal atom. Heptacity ranges from η^1 to η^8.

- Organometallic compounds of the d-block elements in Groups VI, VII, and VIII generally have 18 valence electrons around their central metal atom. For Groups 9 and 10, valence electrons number 16 or 18. Complexes that obey these rules are generally stable.

THE 18 ELECTRON RULE

The first thing to bear in mind is that this rule is a "rule of thumb" and that it does not necessarily reflect the actual distribution of electrons in the complex. It is used to predict reactivity or stability and it works as follows:

   i) assign to the metal its number of valence electrons (and do not consider its oxidation state);

ii) for the ligands, assign electrons as per the following table:

iii) add up both contributions.

iv) when the organometallic complex has a charge, consider a positive charge as an electron deficiency and subtract it from the total; similarly, consider a negative charge as an excess of electrons and add the corresponding number to the total.

Ligand	Electrons Donated to M
H, CH_3, CH_2CH_3, CN, OH, Cl, NO	1
PR_3, NH_2, NH_3, CO, RCN, ROOR´	2
Cyclopentadienyl, indenyl	5
Benzene	6
cyclooctatetraene	8

Here are more examples of electron-counting (refer to the above table for ligand contributions):

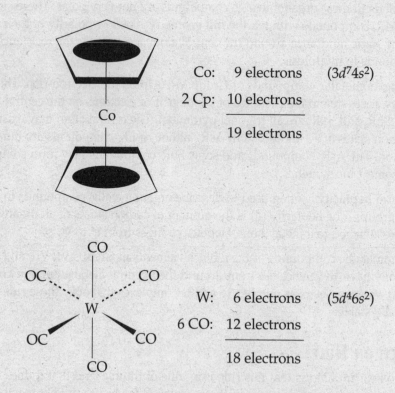

Co: 9 electrons $(3d^74s^2)$

2 Cp: 10 electrons
_____

19 electrons

W: 6 electrons $(5d^46s^2)$

6 CO: 12 electrons
_____

18 electrons

Cr: 6 electrons $(3d^5 4s^1)$

6 NH$_3$: 12 electrons

18 electrons

Rh: 9 electrons $(4f^8 5s^1)$

2 CO: 4 electrons

1 Indenyl: 5 electrons

18 electrons

Example:

Do (a) Ni(CO)$_4$, (b) [Fe(CO)$_4$]$^{2-}$ and (c) [Fe(η^5–C$_5$H$_5$)$_2$]$^+$ obey the rule above?

Answer: (a) yes, (b) yes (c) no. In each case, consider the number of valence electrons around the metal atom, the number of electron donated by the ligand, and the charge of the ion, if applicable. Ex. (c) 8 + 5 + 5 – 1 = 17, and not 18, as expected for a complex of a Group VIII metal.

ENVIRONMENTAL CHEMISTRY

Over the past twenty years, the commercial use of organometallic compounds has increased to the point where their interaction with the natural environment has become inevitable. For example, fuel additives (methyllead), polymers (organosilicons) and pesticides (organomercury and organotin) now all affect our environment.

- The major classes of **toxic organometallic** compounds found in the environment include organomercury, organotin, organolead, organoarsenic, and organosilicon compounds, as well as some organometallic compounds of the metals and metalloids of the *p* block (antimony, germanium, thallium, etc). The presence of toxic compounds of cobalt, manganese, and cadmium has also been reported.

- Organometallic compounds are usually more toxic than their parent inorganic metal compounds. Mercury, lead, and tin are prime examples. (Arsenic is an exception.)

- Many natural, aromatic, coordinating ligands exist in soil water and in sediments, and can bind very strongly to metals and organometallic substances. This binding increases the stability of the coordinated organometallics.

- Radicals are often present in the air, and many airborne particulate species can act as catalysts for the decomposition of the organometallic species.

- Toxic effects are maximum for the monopositive species (obtained from the neutral saturated organometallics that have lost one organic group). Examples of these include R_3Pb^+, R_3Sn^+, and CH_3Hg^+.

- The toxicity of neutral organometallics (ie, R_4Sn) comes from their conversion to monocations by the organism that absorbs them. One of the most striking toxic effects of this in higher animals is the reduction of the myelin coating of nerve fiber, which leads to damage of the central nervous system.

- Some organometallic compounds may be created in the environment starting from inorganic precursors, often through the process of **biomethylation**. Methylation of mercury and arsenic in the environment is well known. Methyltin has been found in ocean water and rivers. Biomethylation usually takes place as a result of the reaction of methyl carbanions CH_3^-, from naturally occurring biological agents such as cobalamin; CH_3CoB_{12}. The methylation of mercury from CH_3CoB_{12} is as follows: $CH_3CoB_{12} + Hg^{2+} \rightarrow CH_3Hg^+ + H_2OCoB_{12}^+$. Bacteria found in sediments can also cause the methylation of mercury, and species such as $Hg(CH_3)_2$ and $[Hg(CH_3)]^+$ can easily penetrate cell walls, thus entering the food chain.

CATALYSIS

A catalyst is a substance that increases the rate of a chemical reaction without being consumed.

Catalysis is a **cyclic process**. A catalyst introduces new reaction mechanisms (pathways), which causes the catalyzed reaction to possess a lower Gibbs free energy of activation than a noncatalyzed reaction. However, the Gibbs free energy of the overall reaction (being a state function) is not affected by a catalyst. A catalyst also does not influence the position of a chemical equilibrium.

Catalysis can be classified as either **homogeneous** or **heterogeneous.**

- In **homogeneous catalysis**, the catalyst and the reagents are present in the same phase.

- In **heterogeneous catalysis**, the catalyst is present in a phase different from that of the reactants. Most heterogeneous catalysts are solids and are easily separated from the products of the reaction. This makes them more attractive than homogeneous catalysts from an economic point of view.

Example:

Determine if the following processes are examples of homogeneous or heterogeneous catalysis: (a) The hydrogenation reaction of vegetable oil by powdered nickel; (b) The oxidation of SO_2 by oxygen, in the presence of nitrous oxide (NO).

Solution: (a) Heterogeneous; (b) Homogeneous.

Homogeneous catalysts have the same phase as that of the reactants, whereas heterogeneous catalysts do not.

- The **turnover frequency**, N, of a catalyst is defined as the ratio of the rate of the reaction (v) over the concentration of the catalyst ($[C]$ in homogeneous catalysis) or the amount of catalyst (in heterogeneous catalysis): $N = v/[C]$. In heterogeneous catalysis, the surface area of the catalyst can replace $[C]$.

In order to be successful, a catalytic process must possess four distinct characteristics.

(1) The reaction to be catalyzed must be thermodynamically favorable; each step of the catalyzed process must have a lower Gibbs energy of activation (ΔG^{++}) than that of the uncatalyzed reaction. Stable catalytic intermediates must not be formed during the process. Impurities may slow down catalysis by coordinating with the active sites of the catalyst; these impurities are called catalyst poisons.

(2) The reaction must be fast enough to be useful when it is catalyzed.

(3) The catalyst must be selective and yield a high proportion of the desired product and a minimum of side products.

(4) The catalyst must have a long lifetime and go through a great number of cycles without being altered or used up by side reactions.

Five reaction types, or steps, account for most of the homogeneous catalytic processes of hydrocarbon transformation.

(1) Coordination and dissociation of reactants (ligands) with the catalyst. Both processes must have low activation energy.

(2) Migration of an alkyl or hydride ligand to an unsaturated ligand: $L + H-MR_2-(CH_2=CH_2) \rightarrow L-MR_2-CH_2CH_3$.

(3) Nucleophilic attack on a coordinated ligand: $L_5M-CO + OH^- \rightarrow (L_5M-(CO)-OH)^- \rightarrow (L_5M-H)^- + CO_2$.

(4) Oxidation and reduction. The metal ion of metal complexes used in the catalytic oxidation of organic substances may alternate between two different oxidation states.

(5) Oxidative addition: $L_4M + AX \rightarrow A-(L_4M)-X$ and reductive elimination, the reverse process. One of the best known catalytic systems is the Wilkinson's catalyst, $RhCl(PPh_3)_3$, which is used for the hydrogenation of alkenes. This process involves some of the steps mentioned above.

APPLIED SOLID-STATE CHEMISTRY

- Solid-state chemistry is sometimes also called materials chemistry. It is concerned with the synthesis, structure, properties, and applications of solid materials.

- The materials involved are usually, but not exclusively, inorganic. Areas of interest include metals, crystal defects, solid solutions, phase transition, and phase diagrams.

- The majority of inorganic solids are nonmolecular. Their structure and properties are based on how the atoms or ions are situated in three dimensions. In contrast, the structure and properties of molecular substances are attributed to the individual molecules. Because minerals are naturally occurring, they are included in the scope of solid-state chemistry. The materials of interest are usually crystalline, but the study of glass is also an important part of this science.

- The **defect structure** of solids constitutes an important field of solid-state chemistry. All solids contain defects of some sort that greatly influence such properties as electrical conductivity, mechanical strength, corrosion and chemical reactivity.

- **Point defects** occur at single sites, whereas **extended defects** occur in one, two, or three dimensions. These defects can be intrinsic or extrinsic.

- **Intrinsic defects** are present for strictly thermodynamic reasons: the presence of defects in a solid introduces disorder in a perfect structure, increasing the entropy of the system. The formation of defects is an endothermic process, which raises the enthalpy, H, of the system. The Gibbs free energy, $G = H - TS$, is usually lowered by the presence of defects, as long as $T > 0$.

- Two types of intrinsic point defects have been recognized: the **Schottky defect** and the **Frenkel defect**. The former corresponds to a vacancy; a point defect in which an atom or ion is missing from its usual site. This does not change the overall stoichiometry of the solid. The latter corresponds to a point defect in which an atom or ion has been displaced to an interstitial site in the lattice. This also does not alter the stoichiometry of the solid. Frankel defects are more common in open structures, in which the coordination numbers are low. The presence of Schottky or Frenkel defects can be determined by density measurements.

Example:

The theoretical density of titanium monoxide, TiO is $d = 5.7$ g/cm^3. Its measured density is $d = 4.9$ g/cm^3. Does the solid contain defects? If so, of which type?

Solution: The solid contains vacancies on the cation and the anion sites in equal numbers. A defect caused by vacancies should lower the measured density of the solid from that predicted, whereas a defect caused by the displacement of an atom should not.

- **Extrinsic defects** are not determined by thermodynamics and can be controlled by synthetic conditions and purification of the solid. An example of this is that electron-rich As atoms are introduced into silica to increase its electrical conductivity.

- Introducing defects in solids has provided chemists with a way to change the **optical properties** of solids. For example, adding Cr(III) to colorless Al_2O_3 yields red ruby, the color is a result of the splitting the d orbitals of Cr(III). Ruby absorbs light in the UV region and emits a strong red radiation that can be used in **laser** technology.

- Nonstoichiometric compounds are substances that have variable composition but constant basic structure. Their formulae deviate from whole-number ratios. They are encountered among the halides of the early d-block metals and among the oxides of metals that can have more than one oxidation number. For instance, the composition of wüstite (FeO) can vary from $Fe_{0.90}O$ to $F_{0.95}O$ at 1000 °C.

- In solid electrolytes, one or several types of ions can diffuse across the lattice, for instance, Ag_2HgI_4, in which the Ag$^+$ ion can diffuse at an appreciable rate. Applications of this phenomenon include electrochemical cells such as batteries, fuel cells, and electrochemical sensors.

- **Superconductors** are another important class of solids; they possess the ability to conduct electricity without resistance. Until recently, substances such as mercury had to be cooled to below 20 K to become superconducting. Since 1986, high-temperature superconductors (HTSC) such as $YBa_2Cu_3O_7$, which become superconducting at a temperature above the boiling point of current refrigerants such as liquid nitrogen, have been used. The superconductors have structures that are related to that of perovskite.

BIOINORGANIC CHEMISTRY

Bioinorganic chemistry studies the function of metals and nonmetals in biological processes. It can also be defined as the biochemistry of the function of the elements traditionally studied by inorganic chemists.

The following table lists some of the metals that are important for biological functions:

Metal	Biological role
Na^+, K^+	Charge carriers in essential body electrolytes required to maintain homeostasis; required for nerve synapses Na^+ is main cation of extracellular fluids; K^+ is main cation of intracellular fluids .
Mg^+, Ca^{2+}	Ca is main component of bone and teeth Critical for blood coagulation and transmission of nerve impulses Mg^{2+} is an enzyme activator; Ca^{2+} acts as a trigger in nerve signal transduction.
$Fe^{3+/2+}$	Present in heme proteins such as myoglobin (O_2 storage in muscle), hemoglobin (O_2 carrier in blood), and the cytochromes (electron transfer in mitochondrial respiratory chain).
Zn^{2+}	pH control, liver function, synthesis of DNA.
Co^{2+}	Essential component of vitamin B_{12}.
Mn, Cr, Ni, Mo	Other essential trace elements.

CELL MEMBRANES

Cells are surrounded by a membrane barrier that separates their interior and exterior. Some substances are produced inside the cell and need to be exported through the cell wall. These can be substances that are required for body biochemistry or unwanted byproducts. Alkali cations function as **carriers** of molecules across the cell membrane.

CALCIUM BINDING PROTEINS

8, 7, and 6-coordinate calcium is found in many so-called calcium binding proteins, such as parvalbumin, troponin, staphylococcal nuclease, thermolysin, and concavallin. They have various functions, including acting as receptors for intracellular calcium and structural intermediates for enzyme catalysis.

METALLOENZYMES

Enzymes are **biological catalysts**. Metalloenzymes are an important class of enzymes characterized by the presence of a metal ion that is an essential participant in catalyzed reactions. Examples are:

Carboxypeptidase A: catalyzes the hydrolysis of the C-terminal residues in peptide chains with participation of Zn^{2+}.

Carbonic anhydrase: zinc metalloenzyme found in plants, animals, and micro-organisms. It catalyzes the reversible hydration of CO_2.

HEME PROTEINS

Heme proteins have several biological functions. They are involved in electron transfer reactions (cytochrome *c* , cytochrome *c* oxidase, cytochrome P450), they act as oxygen carriers (myoglobin, hemoglobin), and many heme proteins catalyze a variety of biochemical reactions (peroxidases). All are characterized by an active group, the **heme**, which is embedded in a protein matrix that consists of folded, linked amino acid chains. The heme is a macrocyclic porphyrin ring that contains iron as its central metal and whose chemistry is influenced by ring substituents that differ from one type of heme protein to another. The iron can be 4, 5 or 6-coordinate and is always coordinated to four nitrogens in the porphyrin ring. There are two additional coordination sites, above and below the plane of the ring. In hemoglobin, the 5th ligand coordination occurs with the nitrogen of the sidechain of a histidine residue, and the 6th ligand can be oxygen or carbon monoxide.

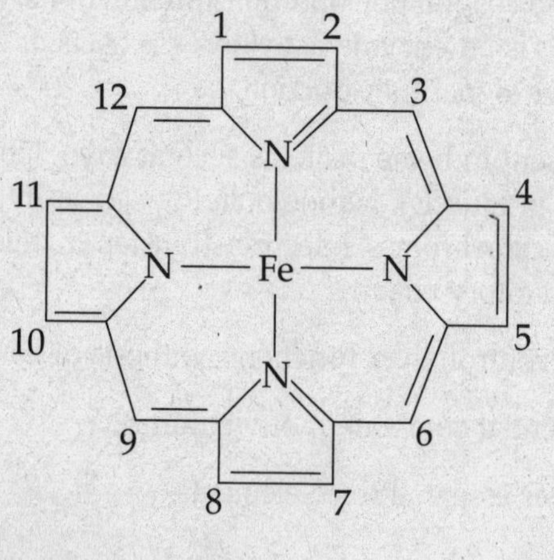

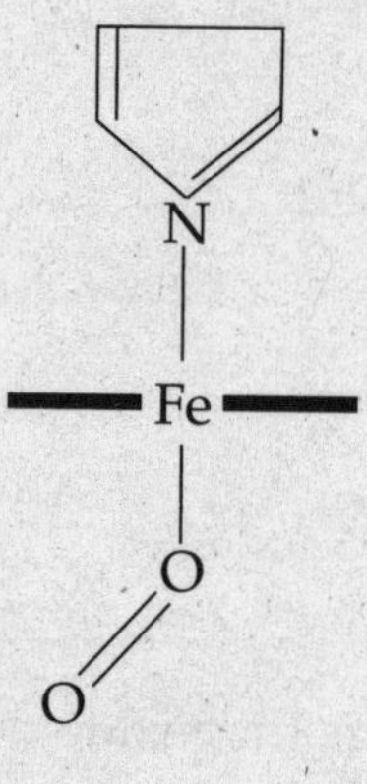

BLUE COPPER PROTEINS

Blue copper proteins (azurin, plastocyanin, stellacyanin, and umecyanin) are involved in electron transport and copper strorage functions. Their active group consists of a copper ion coordinated to amino acid residues in a distorted tetrahedral geometry.

INORGANIC CHEMISTRY: WORKED-OUT PROBLEM SET

1. What is the coordination number of the central in SiF_6^{2-}?

   (A) +2

   (B) +4

   (C) +6

   (D) –6

   (E) –4

   (C) To answer this question you have to remember that the oxidation number of halogens is –1 and that the algebraic sum of *all the oxidation numbers* is equal to zero in a neutral atom or to the charge of the ion, as is the case here. Therefore: oxidation number (Si) = –2 –6(–1) = +4.

2. What is the coordination number of the central atom in $[Co(NO_3)_5]^+$?

   (A) +2

   (B) +3

   (C) +4

   (D) +5

   (E) +6

   (E) The nitrate ion has an oxidation number of –1. According to the rule stated above, oxidation number (Co) = +1 – 5(–1) = +6

3. What is the oxidation state of the underlined elements in the following compounds? Use the following answer choices:

   (A) +1

   (B) –1

   (C) +3;

   (D) –3

   (E) +5

      (a) $\underline{P}H_3$

      (b) $\underline{P}_2O_7^{4-}$

      (c) $K\underline{N}O_2$

      (d) $Mg_3\underline{N}_2$

      (e) $\underline{I}Cl_5$

(f) $[\underline{Mn}(H_2O)_3Br_3]^{2+}$

(g) $\underline{Ag}(NH_3)_2^+$

(h) $Li\underline{H}$

(i) $H_2\underline{O}_2$

The answers are (a) D, (b) E, (c) C, (d) D, (e) E, (f) E, (g) A, (h) B, (i) B. Most of these should be fairly self-evident, but here are explanations for some odd cases:

In question (a), for $P_2O_7^{4-}$, (P) $= \dfrac{1}{2}[-4 - 7(-2)] = +5$; for question (f), when a complex ion contains a neutral ligand, such as in $[Mn(H_2O)_3Br_3]^{2+}$ and $Ag(NH_3)_2^+$, the oxidation number of that ligand is zero; for question (h), the oxidation number of H in a hydride is –1; and the oxidation number of a peroxide is also –1, for question (i).

4. $CsXeF_7$ is one of the ionic substances formed with xenon. Which of the following answers gives the charge of the F ion, the coordination number, and the oxidation number of xenon in this ion?

    (A)   Charge = +1, CN = 6, ON = +7

    (B)   Charge = –1, CN = 7, ON = +6

    (C)   Charge = –1, CN = 6, ON = +4

    (D)   Charge = –1, CN = 8, ON = +6

    (E)   Charge = +1, CN = 8, ON = +6

(B) Recognize that Cs is an alkaline metal and the charge of its ion is +1. Therefore the anion is XeF_7^-. Then determine the oxidation number of Xe: $-1 - 7(-1) = +6$, and count the number of atoms bonded to the Xe (7 fluorine atoms).

5. What change of oxidation number do the underlined elements undergo, in the following reaction?

$$\underline{N}H_3 + \underline{O}_2 \rightarrow \underline{N}\underline{O} + H_2\underline{O}$$

    (A)   N $(-3 \rightarrow -1)$, O $(-2 \rightarrow 0)$

    (B)   N $(+3 \rightarrow -2)$, O $(-2 \rightarrow 0)$

    (C)   N $(0 \rightarrow +2)$, O $(-2 \rightarrow 0)$

    (D)   N $(-3 \rightarrow +2)$, O $(0 \rightarrow -2)$

    (E)   N $(+3 \rightarrow +2)$, O $(0 \rightarrow +2)$

(D) Determine the oxidation number of N and O in both the reactants and the products. Rule 1: the oxidation number of a free element or atom in its elemental state is zero.

6. In the reaction $2MnO_4^- + 6H^+ + 5H_2S \rightarrow 2\,Mn^{2+} + 8H_2O + 5S$, determine the oxidation number of Mn in MnO_4^-, which element is oxidized, the oxidizing element, and whether this element is oxidized or reduced.

    (A)   +7, S, Mn, reduced

    (B)   +4, Mn, S, oxidized

    (C)   +7, S, Mn, oxidized

    (D)   +7, Mn, S, oxidized

    (E)   +4, Mn, S, reduced

(A) Determine the oxidation number of Mn. Then examine this redox equation to see which other element undergoes a change of oxidation state (S: $-2 \rightarrow 0$). When an atom in a molecule or ion is oxidized, its oxidation number increases, and during a reduction, it decreases (Mn: $+7 \rightarrow +2$).

7. Which of the following statements is the most accurate about the first ionization energies of atoms?

    (A) IEs decrease regularly from left to right across a period.

    (B) IEs increase regularly from left to right across a period.

    (C) IEs decrease from left to right across a period except for irregularities in atoms with three and six valence electrons.

    (D) IEs increase from left to right across a period except for irregularities in atoms with three and six valence electrons.

    (E) IEs increase with increasing atomic number (Z) in a group.

(D) In a period, all the valence electrons possess the same principal quantum number (n). As the number of electrons increase, so does the nuclear charge that binds them more strongly to the nucleus. There is also greater stability associated with half-filled orbitals (np^3 and a resulting decrease of IE from np^3 to np^4 configurations) and filled orbitals (ns^2 and np^6 and a resulting decrease from ns^2 and ns^2np^1 configurations).

8. Which of the following statements is the most accurate about the trends in atomic radii?

    (A) Atomic radii decrease with increasing atomic number (Z) from left to right across a period, but increase with increasing Z down a group.

    (B) Atomic radii increase with increasing Z across a period, but do not change in a column.

    (C) Atomic radii decrease with increasing Z across a period, but decrease with increasing Z down a group.

    (D) Atomic radii decrease with increasing Z across a period, but do not change in a group.

    (E) Atomic radii increase with increasing Z across a period and also increase with increasing Z in a group.

(A) Across a period, all of the valence electrons are at the same energy level, which is pulled together more strongly as the atomic number increases. In a group, the addition of successive energy levels causes the valence electrons to be farther from the nucleus as n increases.

9. Which of the following species has the largest ionic radius?

   (A) Ga^{3+}

   (B) Tl^{3+}

   (C) B^{3+}

   (D) Al^{3+}

   (E) In^{3+}

(B) All of these ions are formed from group (III) elements. Down a group, atomic and ionic radii increase.

10. Which of the following elements is more likely to form covalent compounds?

   (A) K

   (B) Be

   (C) Al

   (D) Cs

   (E) C

(E) Covalent compounds are formed between nonmetallic elements (ie, with similar electronegativities) and ionic compounds are formed between metals and nonmetals (elements with a wide difference in electronegativity). Carbon is the only nonmetal among the above elements.

11. Which elements are more likely to form strong bases?

   (A) s-block metals
   (B) p-block metals
   (C) p-block nonmetals
   (D) d-block metals
   (E) f-block metals

(A) An indication of the metallic character of an element is the strength of the base formed from the reaction of its oxide with water. For instance, $Li + \frac{1}{2}O_2 \rightarrow$ Li_2O and $Li_2O + H_2O \rightarrow 2\,Li^+ + 2OH^-$. Oxides of the elements at the upper right of the periodic table react with water to form acids: $SO_3 + 3H_2O \rightarrow H_3O^+ + SO_4{}^{2-}$.

12. What is the most reactive nonmetal in period 2?

    (A) C

    (B) N

    (C) O

    (D) F

    (E) Ne

    (D) Fluorine is the most electronegative element and can react violently with elements having very low electronegativities, such as Cs.

13. Which of the following atoms has the greatest tendency to capture an additional electron?

    (A) F

    (B) Na

    (C) Cl

    (D) S

    (E) Ne

    (A) The elements in the upper right corner of the periodic table possess the highest electron affinities of all elements. By capturing an additional electron, flourinecompletes its valence shell and thus acquires the structure and stability of a noble gas.

14. ^{214}Po and ^{210}Po differ by four

    (A) isotopes

    (B) protons

    (C) valence electrons

    (D) neutrons

    (E) electrons

    (D) These are the isotopes of polonium. They have the same atomic number, 84, (thus 84 protons and electrons) but differ by their *mass number*, which is the number in the upper left corner of the atomic symbol. The mass number A is the sum of the number of protons and neutrons in the nucleus: $A = n + p$.

15. When an element disintegrates by beta emission, the atomic number of the resulting element

    (A) decreases by 1
    (B) increases by 1
    (C) decreases by 2
    (D) increases by 2
    (E) does not change

(B) During beta, or electron emission, one neutron decays into a proton, which stays in the nucleus, and a fast electron is ejected from the nucleus (the beta emission). The mass number A of the new element is the same, but the atomic number has increased by one.

16. Which of the following particles are essential to sustain a nuclear fission chain reaction?

    (A) the neutrons
    (B) the alpha particles
    (C) the electrons
    (D) the protons
    (E) the beta particles

(A) During a nuclear fission reaction, one *slow* neutron is required to initiate the reaction and three fast neutrons are produced; this perpetuates the chain reaction.

17. Which of the following statements is false?

    (A) Of the four common subatomic particles (protons, neutrons, alpha and beta particles), the beta particle has the smallest mass.
    (B) An applied electrical field does not affect gamma rays.
    (C) Nuclear fusion on the sun converts hydrogen to helium, with a release of energy.
    (D) During nuclear decay, mass is converted to energy.
    (E) ^{14}C is an isotope of ^{14}N.

(E) Isotopes are atoms of *the same element*, that have the same Z, but different values of A.

18. Brass is an alloy of copper and zinc. It has a face-centered cubic (fcc) cell with the copper at the faces of each unit cell and the zinc at the corners. How many atoms of each element does each unit cell contain?

  (A) 3 Cu and 1 Zn
  (B) 1 Zn and 3 Cu
  (C) 1 Zn and 1 Cu
  (D) 3 Zn and 3 Cu
  (E) 2 Zn and 2 Cu

(B) In a face-centered cubic cell, the atoms that occupy each of the eight corners belong to eight adjacent cubic cells. Or, each corner of one cubic cell contains half an atom. The atoms at each of the six faces belong to only two unit cells, or each face has half an atom. Summing up, we have $8 \times \dfrac{1}{8} = 1$ atom (Zn), and $6 \times \dfrac{1}{2} = 3$ atoms (Cu).

19. The atomic radii of Cu and Zn are 1.25×10^{-10} m and 1.35×10^{-10} m, respectively. What is the volume of a unit cell of brass?

  (A) 4.22×10^{-23} cm^3
  (B) 5.36×10^{-23} cm^3
  (C) 4.98×10^{-23} cm^3
  (D) 1.08×10^{-22} cm^3
  (E) 7.38×10^{-23} cm^3

(C) The atoms along a face diagonal touch slightly. The diagonal is then equal to the sum of the atomic radii ($d = 2,60 \times 10^{-10}$ m). The length of the cubic cell can then be evaluated by simple geometry, using the Pythagorean theorem: $l = d/2$. The volume of the cell is $V = l^3$.

20. Which of the following factors contributes to increased electrical conductivity in semi-conductors?

   I. An increase of temperature.
   II. Exposition to light.
   III. Addition on an impurity (doping)

  (A) I only
  (B) II only
  (C) III only
  (D) I and III only
  (E) I, II, and III

(E) An increase in temperature makes the electrons more mobile. They can also absorb light and "jump" into a conduction band. The addition of impurities to a semiconductor can either increase the number of negative carriers (like the electron-rich phosphorus atoms introduced into a silicon crystal) or the number of positive holes (like the electron-deficient boron introduced in a silicon crystal).

21. What is the correct expression for the heat of formation (Q) of sodium fluoride if the following thermochemical values are available?

    S = heat of sublimation of sodium

    I = ionisation energy of sodium

    D = energy of dissociation of fluorine

    E = electron affinity of fluorine

    U = lattice energy

    (A) $Q = S + I + \dfrac{1}{2}D - E - U$

    (B) $Q = S + I + D - E - U$

    (C) $Q = S + I + \dfrac{1}{2}D + E - U$

    (D) $Q = S + I - \dfrac{1}{2}D - E - U$

    (E) $Q = S + I - D - E - U$

(A) Q is the sum of the heat produced in every step of the formation of NaF from solid sodium and gaseous fluorine atoms. The processes corresponding to S, I, and D are endothermic and are assigned a positive sign in the sum. Because only one fluorine atom is required, the value of D must be divided by two. Fluorine is the element with the highest electron affinity and taking an electron is an exothermic process. U is the energy released when a gaseous sodium ion binds a gaseous fluorine ion. E and U are exothermic processes and are assigned negative signs.

22. Which of the following statement(s) is/are true?

    I.   Magnesium carbonate decomposes at a higher temperature than barium carbonate.
    II. Iron (III) fluoride decomposes at a higher temperature than iron (III) iodide.
    III. Rubidium iodide is less soluble than sodium iodide.

    (A) I and II only

    (B) I only

    (C) I and III only

    (D) II and III only

    (E) I, II, and III

(D) Large cations are stabilized by large anions. Ba^{2+} and CO_3^{2-} are comparable in size, but Mg^{2+} is much smaller than CO_3^{2-}. Therefore, magnesium carbonate should decompose at a lower temperature than barium carbonate. Cations with high oxidation numbers are stabilized by small anions. Compounds that contain ions with very different ionic radii are generally more soluble.

23. A compound has the formula XF_4. The element X cannot be

   (A) Sn

   (B) Si

   (C) Sc

   (D) C

   (E) Ge

   (C) Sn, Si, C, and Ge all belong to Group IV and have four valence electrons (ns^2np^2), thus allowing tem to form four covalent bonds with fluorine atoms. Sc belongs to Group IIIB and has the electronic configuration $[Ar]3d^14s^2$.

24. An element has the electronic structure $1s^22s^22p^63s^2$. To which group does this element belong?

   (A) Group I

   (B) Group II

   (C) Group III

   (D) Group VI

   (E) Group VIII

   (B) This element only has two electrons in its highest electron shell ($n = 3$). Therefore it is an alkaline-earth.

25. When element 118 is made, it is likely to be

   (A) an alkali

   (B) a transition element

   (C) an inner transition element

   (D) a halogen

   (E) a rare gas

   (E) The element with 118 electrons should have the following electron configuration: $[Rn]5f^{14}6d^{10}7s^27p^6$. The completely filled sublevels $7s$ and $7p$ would make this element a noble gas.

26. An atom in Group IIIA of the periodic table of the elements is most likely to

   (A) form a 3+ ion
   (B) form a 3– ion
   (C) be a poor conductor of heat and electricity
   (D) be a nonmetal
   (E) have an oxide of the general formula RO

   (A) Elements in this group have the electronic configuration ns^2np^1 and are more likely to form cations by losing their valence electrons (metals) than anions. All group IIIA elements are metals, with the exception of boron, and they're all good conductors.

27. Which of the following must happen to form cations from neutral atoms?

   (A) protons must be gained
   (B) protons must be lost
   (C) electrons must be gained
   (D) electrons must be lost
   (E) neutrons must change

   (D) A cation is a species with a number of electrons inferior to the nuclear charge. The formation of cations involves the loss of valence electrons, usually through transfer to atoms with high electron affinities, such as fluorine.

28. Which of the following elements is a metal that does not react with acids?

   (A) uranium
   (B) helium
   (C) sodium
   (D) iron
   (E) gold

   (E) Gold offers a very good resistance to acid and is known as a noble metal.

29. Select one of the following answers to for questions (a) to (e):

   (A) Group I
   (B) Group II
   (C) Group VI
   (D) Group V
   (E) Group VIII

(a) The elements of his group react with water to form hydrogen gas.

(A) This behavior is characteristic of the reactive alkali metals, which readily react with water to form hydroxides and hydrogen. For example,

$$2Na(s) + 2H_2O(l) \rightarrow 2NaOH(aq) + H_2(g)$$

(b) The elements of this group are characterized by atoms that are gaseous at STP.

(E) Rare gases have completely filled outer energy levels and are nonreactive under normal conditions. Under STP conditions, very weak interactive forces exist between individual atoms.

(c) The elements of his group are characterized by half-filled p orbitals.

(D) The elements of Group V are characterized by the electronic configuration ns^2np^3. In accordance with Hund's rule which states that pairing can only occur after all individual orbital of a given sublevel have received one electron, the np^3 configuration corresponds to the half-filling of these orbitals.

(d) The elements of this group are characterized by the start of pairing p electrons.

(C) Pairing of electrons in a p, d, or f orbital can only start after each orbital has received one electron.

(e) The elements of this group are characterized by very reactive metals.

(A) With their ns^1 electronic configuration, alkali metals have the lowest ionization energy and react very rapidly with nonmetals possessing high electron affinities.

Select one of the following answers for questions (f) to (i):

(A) amorphous compound

(B) nonpolar covalent compound

(C) polar covalent compound

(D) metal

(E) ionic substance

(f) Solid lithium is a...

(D)

(g) Methane is a...

(B) Examine the symmetry and structure of the CH_4 molecule. Although each of the four C–H bonds is polar, their respective orientation is such that the resultant dipole moment of the molecule is zero.

(h) Gaseous hydrochloric acid is a...

(C) The difference in electronegativity between the H and Cl atoms is about 0.5. Therefore the diatomic HCl molecule is polar. HCl in aqueous solution is considered a strong acid and dissociates completely.

(i) Lithium chloride is a...

(E) LiCl consists of an active metal and an active nonmetal; the difference in their respective electronegativities is 2.5, characteristic of ionic substances.

30. Which of the following bonds are ionic?

    I. H – Cl
    II. Rb – Cl
    III. S – Cl

    (A) I only

    (B) II only

    (C) III only

    (D) I and II only

    (E) none of the above

(B) Examine the difference of electronegativity between the atoms. Rb and Cl also belong to opposite ends of the periodic table.

31. Which of the following statements is true?

    (A) A catalyst modifies the enthalpy of a system.

    (B) A catalyst modifies the nature of the product of a reaction.

    (C) A catalyst modifies the entropy of a system.

    (D) A catalyst modifies the activation energy of a system

    (E) A catalyst modifies the equilibrium position of system

(D) A catalyst increases the rate of chemical reaction by lowering the activation energy.

32. Which of the following types of reactions is used to synthesize the organometallic Grignard reagent?

    (A) metal and organohalide

    (B) transmetallation

    (C) double displacement

    (D) hydrometallation

    (E) none of the above

(A) A Grignard reagent is obtained by the reaction of a metal with an organohalide according to $2M + RX \rightarrow MR + MX$.

III. ORGANIC CHEMISTRY

STRUCTURE, BONDING, NOMENCLATURE

Organic chemistry is the study of carbon, its compounds, and the reactions they undergo. Four topics are covered under this heading: configuration and stereochemical notation, conformational analysis, systematic IUPAC nomenclature, and spectroscopy (IR and ^{1}H and ^{13}C NMR).

CONFIGURATION AND STEREOCHEMICAL NOTATION

ORGANIC MOLECULAR SYMMETRY

The distinction of molecular chirality and nonchirality is made on the grounds of symmetry.

A chiral molecule is dissymmetric; it has no reflection symmetry.

Previously, we saw that molecular point groups are groups of different symmetry classes characterized by particular combinations of symmetry elements.

There are three main symmetry elements: the reflection plane (s), the rotation axis (C_n) and the rotation-reflection axis (S_n).

Using the σ, C_n and S_n symmetry elements, we can group organic molecular conformations into five distinct categories:

No reflection symmetry	Examples	With reflection symmetry	Examples
1. no σ, no C_n, no S_n	C_1	1. One σ, no C_n, no S_n	C_s
2. One or more C_n	C_n, D_n	2. One S_n, no σ	S_n
		3. One or more C_n, One or more σ	C_{nv}, C_{nh}, D_{nd}, O_h

Organic Conformations That Have No Reflection Symmetry

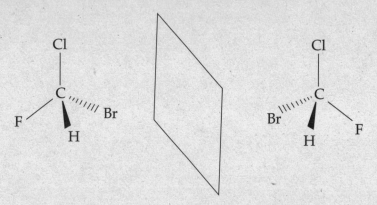

CHFBrCl belongs to the C_1 point group. It has no symmetry elements except E (identity), and reflection through a mirror plane (s) produces mirror images that are distinct and nonsuperimposable. This is the case every time carbon has four different substituents. The carbon in these cases is called **asymmetric** (C^*), and molecules of this type (which have no reflection symmetry) are **chiral**. They are **optically active**, which means that their solutions turn the plane of polarized light.

Example:

The biphenyl series of compounds:

This molecule is asymmetric even though it does not contain an asymmetric carbon: its mirror images are not superimposable. Molecules like this often belong to the C_2 point group.

Organic Conformations With Reflection Symmetry

Molecules that have reflection symmetry are **achiral**. Most achiral molecules have σ planes and C_n axes of symmetry. In achiral molecules, reflection through a σ plane yields conformations that are superimposable and indistinguishable.

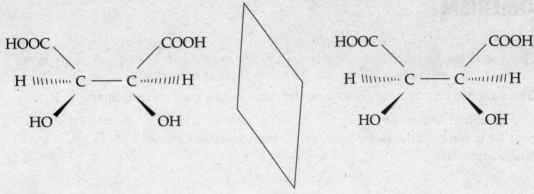

Example:

meso-tartaric acid.

This molecule belongs to the S_2 point group; it has an S_2 reflection-rotation axis. This symmetry operation is double: first the molecule is reflected through a mirror plane.

The mirror image, when rotated 180° about the S_2 axis, is then converted back to the starting configuration of the molecule:

Some Point Groups	Some Point Groups
Representative of chiral molecules without reflection symmetry	**Representative of achiral molecules with reflection symmetry**
C_1 = asymmetry C_n = C_n axis only D_n = C_n + nC_2 only	C_s = σ plane only S_n = S_n + some C_n, no σ C_{nv} = C_n, +$nσ_v$ C_{nh} = C_n, + $σ_v$ D_{nd} = C_n + nC_2 + $nσ_v$ D_{nh} = C_n + C_2 + $nσ_v$ + $σ_h$ T_d, O_h, etc.
Chiral molecules can exist as a pair of enantiomers and show optical activity	**Achiral molecules are not optically active**

ISOMERISM

Isomers are different molecules that have the same constituent atoms, but in different arrangements.

There are two broad classes of isomers: **structural isomers** and **stereoisomers**.

1. Structural isomers

Structural isomers differ in the positions of their constituent atoms:

Chain isomerism:

The carbon chain on the left-hand side is a normal, linear chain. The one on the right hand side is an **iso-C chain**.

Positional isomerism:

The bromine atom substitutes for hydrogen at different carbons in the chain.

Example: Tautomerism:

These two molecules (porphyrins) are **tautomers**. Tautomeric molecules differ in the position of their respective H atoms, as shown above.

2. Stereoisomers

Stereoisomers differ in their spatial, 3-D arrangements. The different types of stereoisomers are:

- **Geometrical isomers**, which arise when rotation about a bond—or bonds—is not possible:

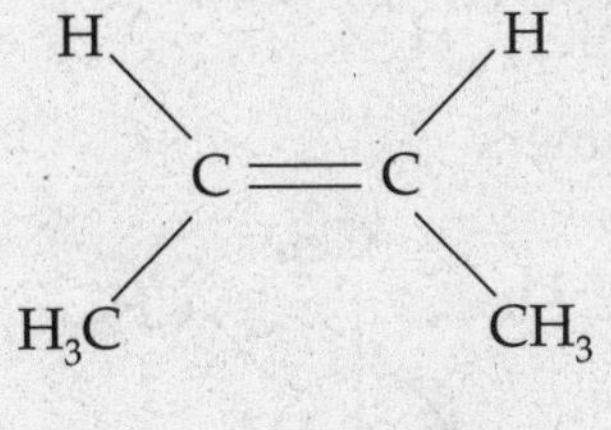

cis-2-butene 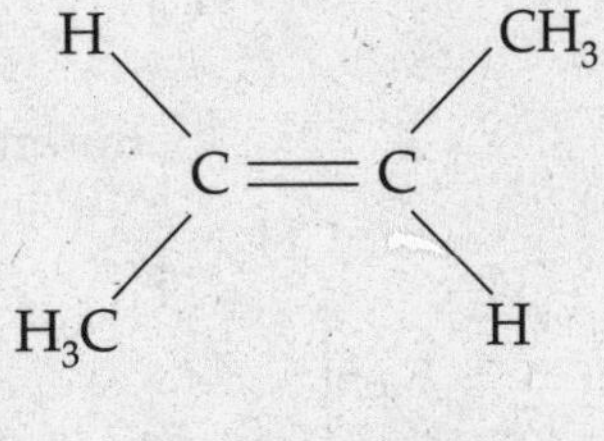   trans-2-butene

- **Enantiomers**, which are nonsuperimposable, chiral mirror images.

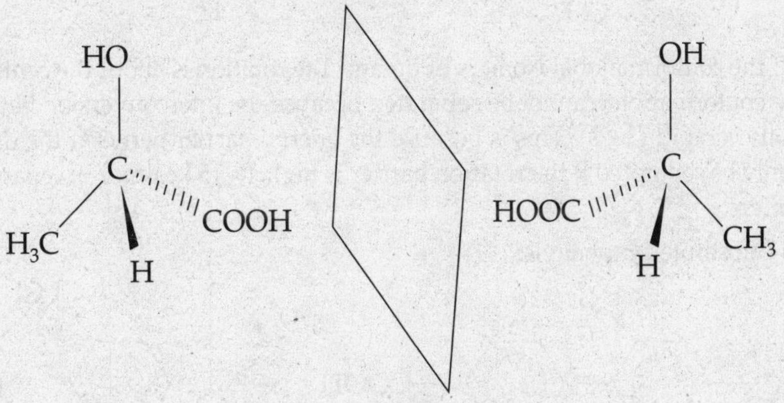

lactic acid

- **Diastereomers**, which are stereoisomers that are not mirror images of each other.

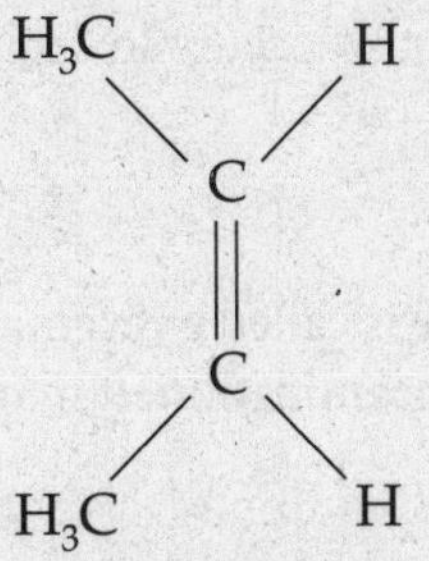

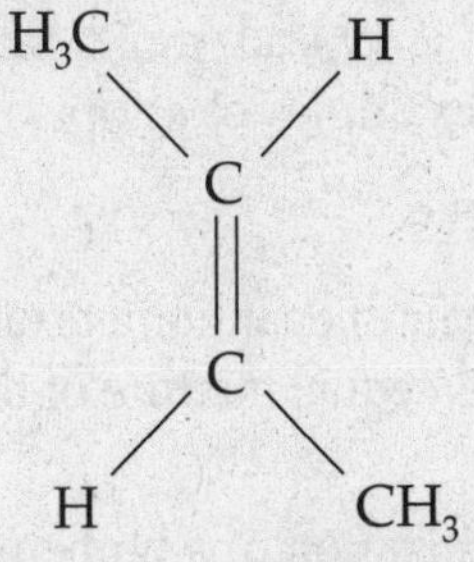

Geometrical isomers are also diastereomers.

Enantiomers have identical physical and chemical properties; they are not easy to separate. Diastereomers have different physical and chemical properties; they are easy to separate by conventional means (distillation, chromatography, and crystallization).

- **Conformers** or **conformational isomers**, which are stereoisomers that differ by a rotation—or rotations—about a single bond:

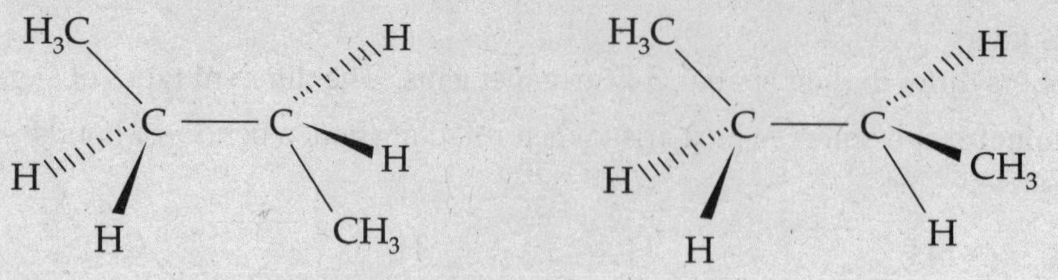

Butane conformers

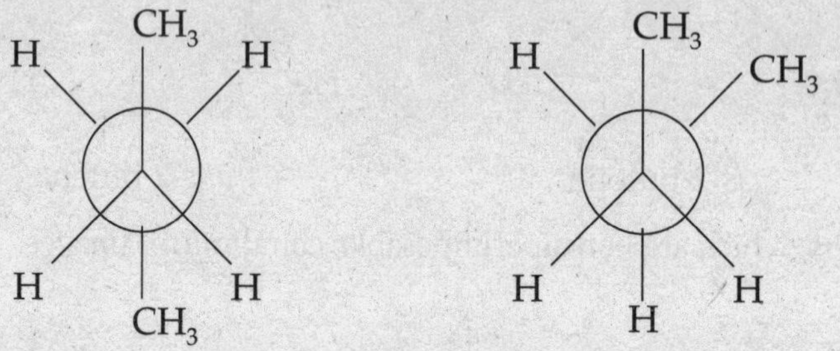

In the case of the conformational isomers of butane, the rotation is about the central C–C bond. A mixture of these conformations cannot be separated because the interconversion between the different conformations is rapid (10^9 s). This is because the energy barrier between the different forms is low. They can only be separated if the rotation barrier is high (> 15 kcalmol^{-1}); separable isomers are called **atropisomers**.

Example: Substituted biphenyls:

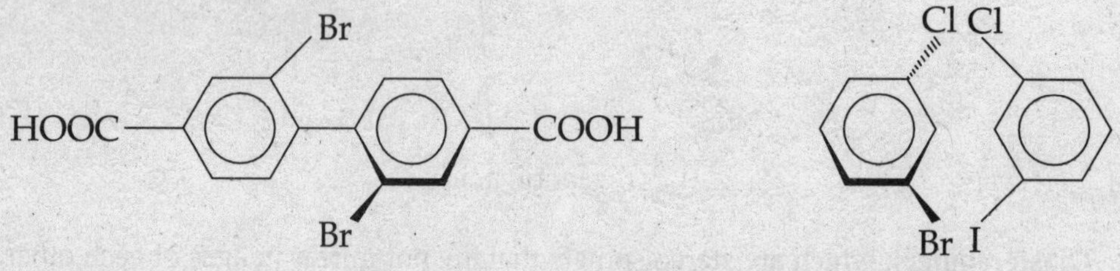

Large ortho substituents, such as Br, hinder rotation about the C–C bond in biphenyls. In this case, the barrier to rotation is 19 kcal/mol^{-1}. Restricted rotation also occurs in amines and polypeptides, which contain many examples of atropisomers.

RACEMIC MIXTURES

A 50-50 mixture of a pair of enantiomers of a chiral molecule is called a racemic mixture. Conversion of one enantiomer to an equal mixture of the two is called **racemization**. It may be catalyzed by heat, light, H$^+$, or OH$^-$.

Example: Racemization of a biphenyl derivative:

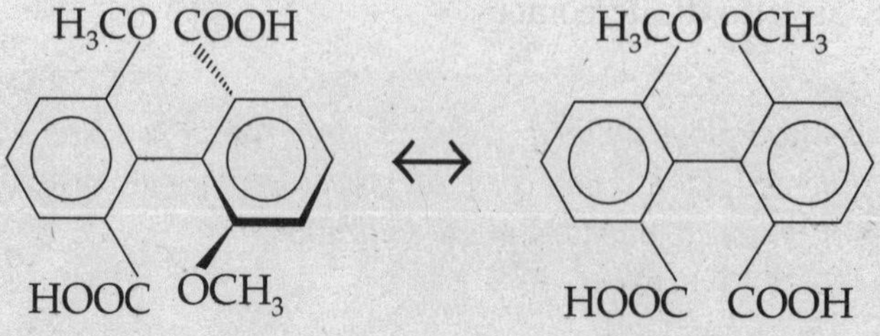

The half-time for this racemization is 78 minutes in boiling acetic acid, which means that in 78 minutes, half of the derivative will be racemized.

- **The *R* and *S* convention to identify enantiomers:**

The actual 3-D arrangement of atoms about an asymmetric center (C*, N*, S*, P*,...) is called the **absolute configuration** of the molecule (as opposed to the **relative configuration**), which describes the ligand arrangment of an asymmetric center, relative to another asymmetric center. This convention involves a set of rules used to describe the absolute configuration of each asymmetric center in a molecule in terms of (*R*) and (*S*) prefixes, which stand for "right" and "left" respectively. The rules are:

(a)   Substituent ligands at an asymmetric center are given a priority based on *increasing* atomic number, thus: $I > Br > Cl > S > P > Si > F > O > N > C > H >$ lone pair;

(b)   If two or more substituents have the same type of atom directly bonded to the asymmetric center, the priority is decided by considering the other atoms of the subsitutent, thus: $CH_2\underline{F}_3 > CH_2\underline{C}H_3 > CH_2\underline{N}H_2 > CH_2\underline{H}$. The same applies to

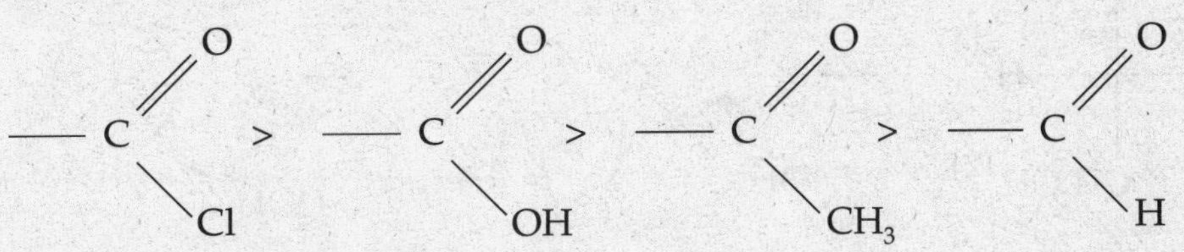

(c)   Multiple bonds are treated like multiple substituents, ie,

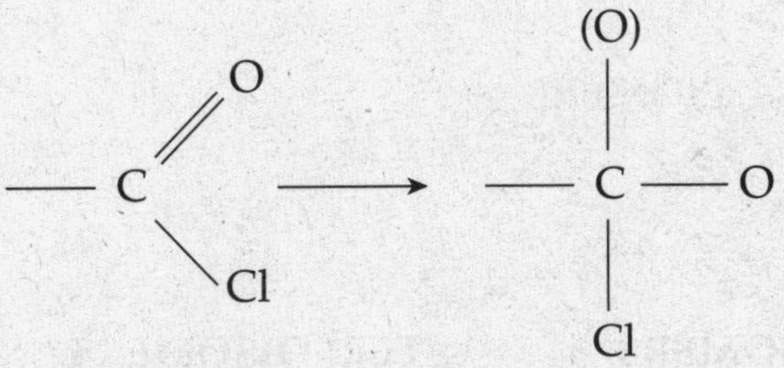

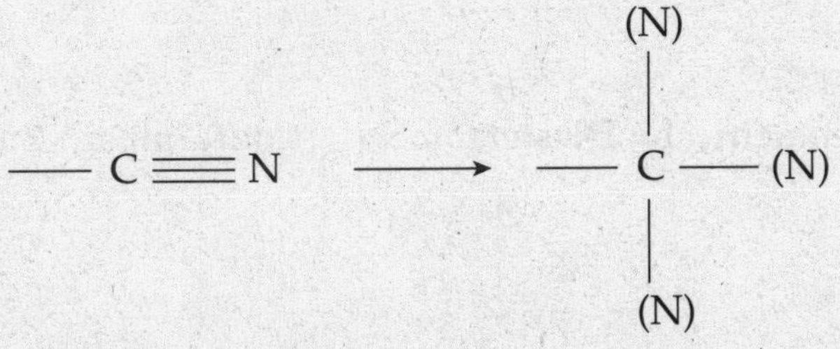

Hence, C=O takes precedence over alcohols and tertiary alcohols, over secondary.

The priorities assigned to the substituents of an asymmetric center are numbered (1) to (4); (1) has the highest priority. The Fisher projection *has the (4) substituent away from the viewer, and the remaining three substituents are viewed. If the sequence (1) to (3) is* counterclockwise, *the configuration is S. If the sequence (1) to (3) is* clockwise, *the configuration is R.*

Example: Glyceraldelhyde

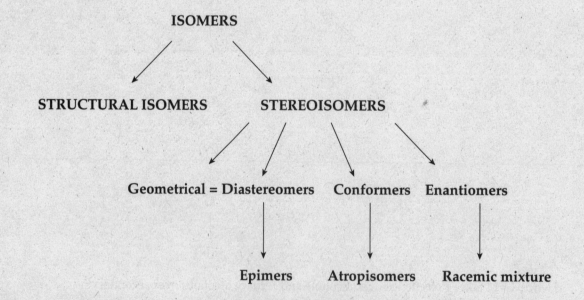

Isomerization can be summarized as follows:

ISOMERS

STRUCTURAL ISOMERS   **STEREOISOMERS**

Geometrical = Diastereomers   **Conformers**   **Enantiomers**

Epimers   **Atropisomers**   **Racemic mixture**

The barriers to rotation vary with the different isomers:
Geometrical isomers > Atropisomers > Conformers
> 35 kcal-mol^{-1} 35-15 kcal-mol^{-1} < 15 kcal-mol^{-1}

CONFORMATIONAL ANALYSIS

Conformational analysis is a methodology used to determine the most probable conformation(s) of a given compound.

- **Ethane**

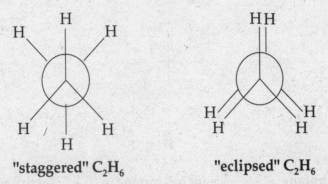

"staggered" C_2H_6 "eclipsed" C_2H_6

The "eclipsed" conformation has a higher rotation barrier (3 kcal-mol⁻¹) than the "staggered" conformation ("E" and "S," respectively, in the diagram below).

Energy profile for the C–C bond rotation in ethane

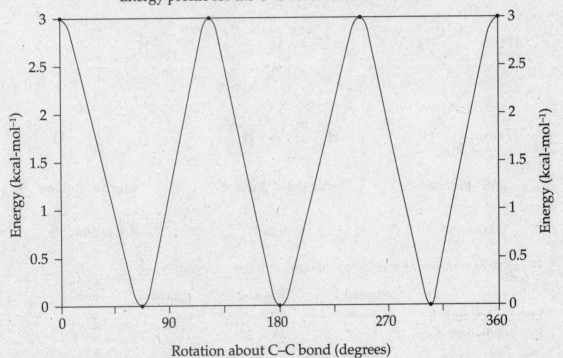

The relative populations of eclipsed (E) and staggered (S) ethane conformers can be estimated by using:

$$K = e^{-\Delta G/RT}$$

where ΔG = 3 kcal-mol⁻¹, T = 300 K, R = 1.987 cal/deg K/mol, K = 1/159 = [E/S], and 99.375% of the ethane molecules are in the staggered form at 25 °C.

- **Butane**

There are more conformational isomers of butane than of ethane, and they are shown below with their respective rotation barriers (the energy required for successful rotation). The barrier for ethane's eclipsed conformation is 3.5 kclmol^{-1}; and that of eclipsed-1 butane is higher (5 kcal/mol^{-1}) due to the bulkier methyl groups.

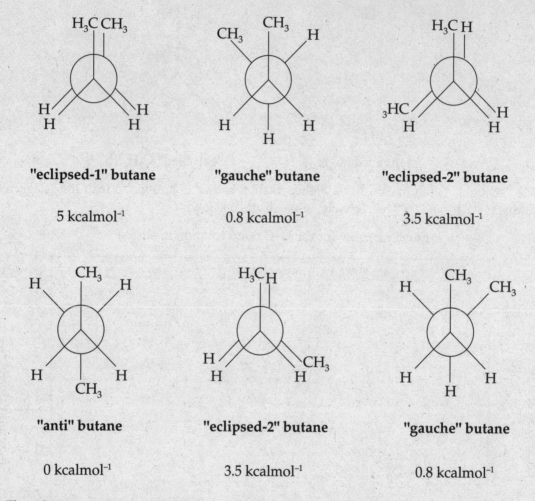

"eclipsed-1" butane	"gauche" butane	"eclipsed-2" butane
5 kcalmol^{-1}	0.8 kcalmol^{-1}	3.5 kcalmol^{-1}

"anti" butane	"eclipsed-2" butane	"gauche" butane
0 kcalmol^{-1}	3.5 kcalmol^{-1}	0.8 kcalmol^{-1}

The relative populations distribute as follows at room temperature:

	eclipsed-1	eclipsed-2	gauche	anti
Energy (kcal-mol^{-1}):	5	3.5	0.8	0
Rel. population:	1	13 × 2	1203 × 2	4644
%:	0.01	0.37	34.00	65.62

The relative populations of conformational isomers are temperature-dependent, as are their physical properties.

- **Cyclohexane**

Planar cyclohexane is not very stable because of the ring strain associated with maintaining planarity. To relieve ring strain, cyclohexane undergoes eclipsing effects, which yield three main nonplanar conformers with almost no ring strain. They are called:

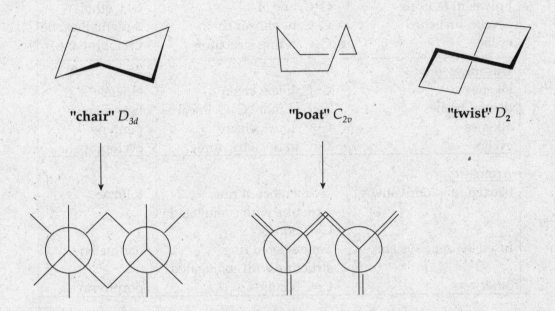

"chair" D_{3d} "boat" C_{2v} "twist" D_2

The lowest energy isomer—and the most stable—is the chair configuration, followed by the twist conformer, at 5.5 kcalmol^{-1} above the chair conformer, and the boat at 6.4 kcalmol^{-1} above the chair conformer. The twist conformation is not detectable at room temperature. The relative populations are as follows:

	twist	chair
At 25 °C:	1	10,000
At 800 °C:	1	3

The boat conformation represents a transition state between two different twist conformations.

IUPAC NOMENCLATURE

The International Union of Pure and Applied Chemistry (IUPAC) regulates the systematic nomenclature of all organic compounds. In this section, we will review the basic principles of hydrocarbon nomenclature. The nomenclature of functional groups will be described in a later section, as specific compounds are introduced. Hydrocarbons are classified as follows:

Hydrocarbon	Characteristic	Examples
Saturated:		
acyclic, unbranched	C–C, linear chain	CH_4 ethane
univalent radicals	C–C, one H lot	CH_3 ethyl
acyclic, branched	C–C, nonlinear chain	3-methylhexane
cyclic	C–C in ring structures	cyclopropane
Unsaturated:		
alkenes	C=C, linear chain	ethene
dienes, trienes	Two or more C=C, linear	hexadiene
alkynes	C=C, linear chain	pentyne
cyclic	C=C in ring structures	cyclopropene
Aromatic:		
benzene and derivatives	six-membered ring structure with conjugated C=C bonds;	toluene
fused benzene system	x-membered ring structure with conjugated	naphtalene
other	C=C bonds	porphyrin

SATURATED HYDROCARBONS

- Acyclic, unbranched alkanes

Acyclic hydrocarbons have their carbons arranged in chains. They have only single C–C bonds, which is why they are designated "saturated"; the carbons bind the maximum number of hydrogens possible. They are also called **alkanes**. Their names consist of a numerical prefix with the ending -*ane*.

n	Name	Formula
1	Methane	CH_4
2	Ethane	C_2H_6
3	Propane	C_3H_8
4	Butane	C_4H_{10}
5	Pentane	C_5H_{12}
6	Hexane	C_6H_{14}
7	Heptane	C_7H_{16}
8	Octane	C_8H_{18}
9	Nonane	C_9H_{20}
10	Decane	$C_{10}H_{22}$

- Univalent radicals

Univalent radicals are obtained by removing one hydrogen from an alkane. They are called **alkyls** and they are named by replacing the -*ane* ending of the alkane by -*yl*. The carbon atom with the free valence is assigned the number 1.

$$\overset{4}{CH_3}\!-\!\!-\!\overset{3}{CH_2}\!-\!\!-\!\overset{2}{CH_2}\!-\!\!-\!\overset{1}{CH_2}\!-\!\!-$$

Butyl

$$\overset{10}{CH_3}\!-\!\!-\![CH_2]_8^{9\text{-}2}\!-\!\!-\!\overset{1}{CH_2}\!-\!\!-$$

Decyl

Examples:

- Branched alkanes

These compounds are named after the longest carbon chain in the molecule. The name is prefixed by a term describing the side chain and the number of the carbon it's attached to.

Examples:

2-Methylpentane

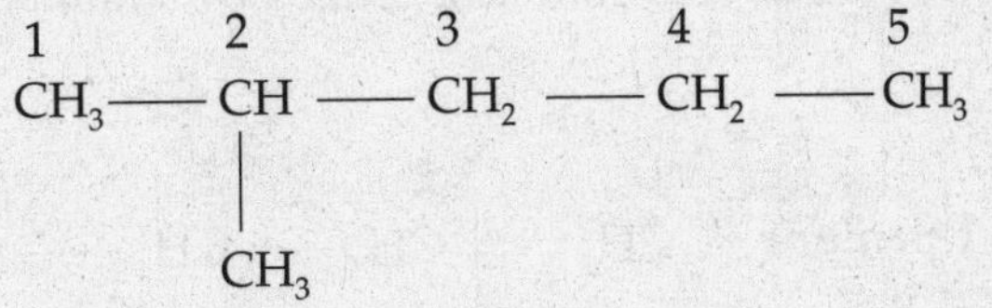

$$\overset{1}{CH_3}\!-\!\!-\!\overset{2}{CH}\!-\!\!-\!\overset{3}{CH_2}\!-\!\!-\!\overset{4}{CH_2}\!-\!\!-\!\overset{5}{CH_3}$$
$$|$$
$$CH_3$$

1, 3, 5-Trimethylhexane

$$\overset{6}{CH_3}\!-\!\!-\!\overset{5}{CH}\!-\!\!-\!\overset{4}{CH_2}\!-\!\!-\!\overset{3}{CH}\!-\!\!-\!\overset{2}{CH}\!-\!\!-\!\overset{1}{CH_3}$$
$$|\qquad\quad|\qquad\ |$$
$$CH_3\qquad CH_3\quad CH_3$$

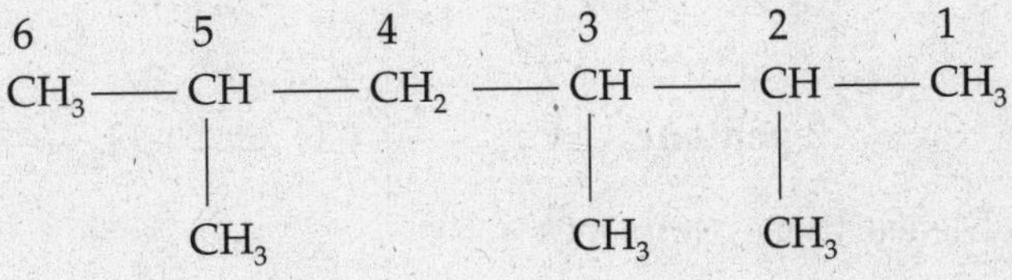

Naming alkanes:

—*use the longest C-chain to name the alkane;*
—*assign numbers to the carbons starting with the end nearest a branch;*
—*the substitutent groups (-yl) prefix the name of the alkane;*
—*and they are prefixed by the number of the carbon to which they are attached;*
—*if they are different, they are listed in alphabetical order;*
—*if they are the same, they are prefixed di-, tri-, tetra-, etc*

- Cycloalkanes

Alkanes closed in a ring structure are called **cycloalkanes**. They are named like the acyclic alkanes and prefixed with *cyclo-*. In cycloalkenes, the carbons are listed alphabetically and numbered in the direction that gives the lowest possible number to the other substituents:

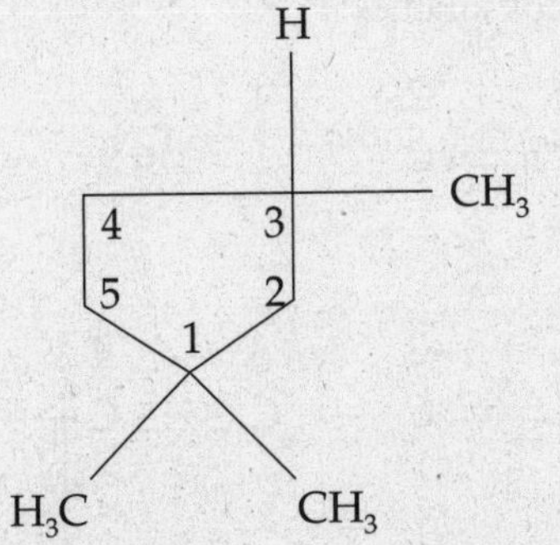

1, 1, 3-trimethylcyclopentane

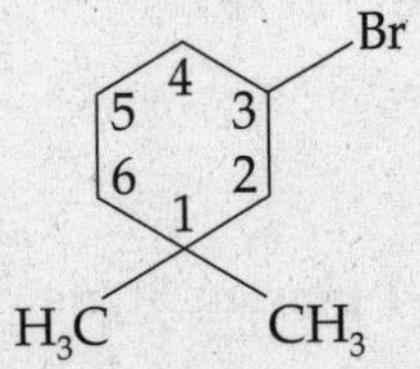

3-bromo-1, 1-dimethylcyclohexane

Unsaturated Hydrocarbons

- Alkenes

Alkenes contain at least one double C=C bond and are unsaturated because, unlike alkanes, they can react easily with hydrogen. The C=C bond is called an **element of saturation** because it decreases the number of hydrogens of the corresponding unsaturated alkane by two.

So ethane, C_2H_6, has no element of saturation, and ethene, C_2H_4, has one element of saturation: the C=C bond (removes 2 H's).

They are named in the same way as alkanes, but the ending *-ene* is used to indicate the presence of the double C=C bond. So, eth*ane* is CH_3–CH_3 and eth*ene* is CH_2=CH_2. With chains that exceed three carbons, the location of the double bond is indicated by a number.

Examples:

1-pentene

$$\underset{1}{CH_2} = \underset{2}{CH} - \underset{3}{CH_2} - \underset{4}{CH_2} - \underset{5}{CH_3}$$

2-pentene

$$\underset{1}{CH_3} - \underset{2}{CH} = \underset{3}{CH_2} - \underset{4}{CH_2} - \underset{5}{CH_3}$$

- Dienes, trienes, tetraenes

Alkenes with two double bonds are called **dienes**, alkenes with three are called **trienes,** and four, **tetraenes**. Numbers are used to locate the double bonds and the substituents:

1,3-pentadiene

$$\underset{1}{CH_2} = \underset{2}{CH} - \underset{3}{CH} = \underset{4}{CH} - \underset{5}{CH_3}$$

2-Methyl-1,4-pentadiene

$$\underset{1}{CH_2} = \underset{2}{C} - \underset{3}{CH_2} - \underset{4}{CH} = \underset{5}{CH_2}$$
$$|$$
$$CH_3$$

- Alkynes

Alkynes contain a triple C≡C bond. They are named after their parent alkane, but have the ending *-yne*. They are named following the same rules as for alkenes:

1-Bromopropyne

$$\underset{3}{CH_3} = \underset{2}{C} \equiv \underset{1}{C} \quad :\overset{..}{\underset{..}{Br}}:$$

2-Methyl-1-penten-3-yne

$$\underset{1}{CH_2} = \underset{2}{C} - \underset{3}{C} \equiv \underset{4}{C} - \underset{5}{CH_3}$$
$$|$$
$$CH_3$$

- Cyclic unsaturated hydrocarbons

Alkenes also form ring structures, called **cycloalkenes**. Likewise, dienes form **cyclodienes**. In the nomenenclature, the position of the double bonds and ring substituents are noted:

1,3-Cyclohexadiene

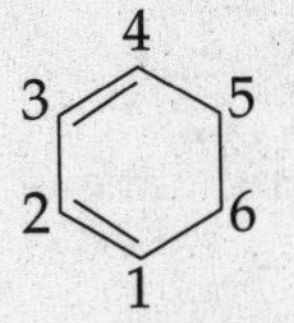

3-Nitrocyclohexene

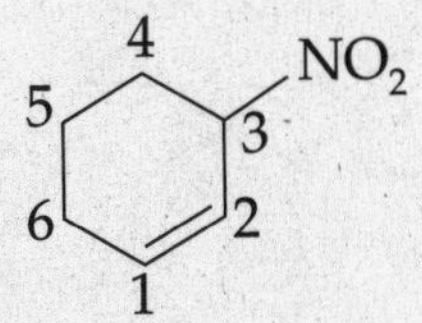

1,3,5,7-Cyclooctatetraene

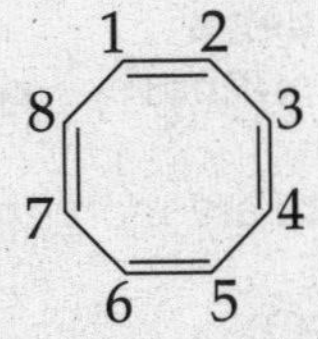

1-Ethylcyclopentene

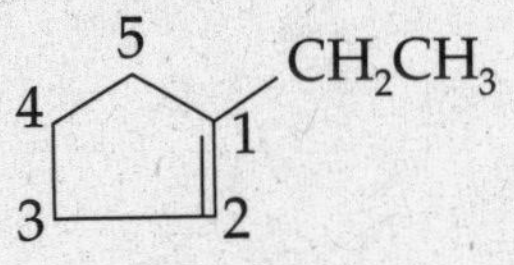

AROMATIC HYDROCARBONS

- Benzene and derivatives

Benzene derivatives are named using the following convention for two substituents:

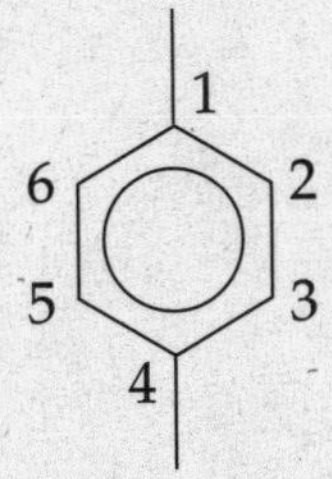

1, 4 or *para* 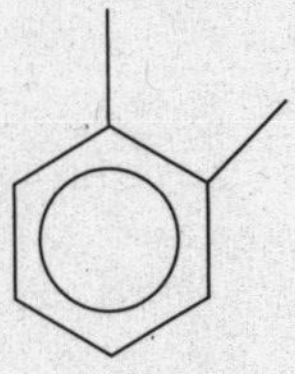   **1, 2 or** *ortho* 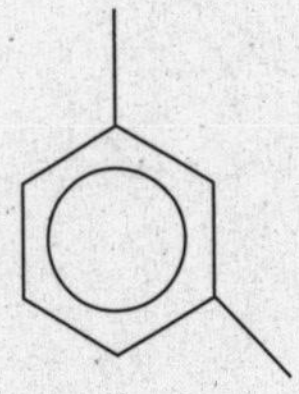   **1, 3 or** *meta*

The benzene derivatives are often referred to by their common names, which are as follows (the second name given is the systematic name; these are rarely used):

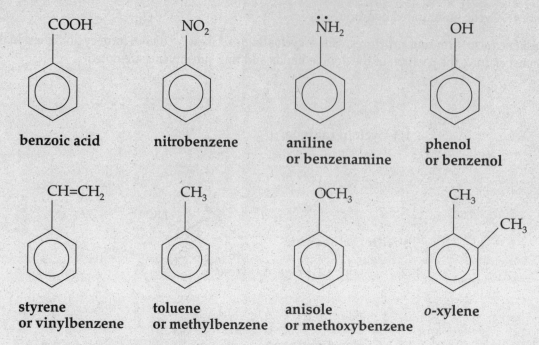

benzoic acid   nitrobenzene   aniline
or benzenamine   phenol
or benzenol

styrene
or vinylbenzene   toluene
or methylbenzene   anisole
or methoxybenzene   o-xylene

Numbers are used when there are more than two substituents:

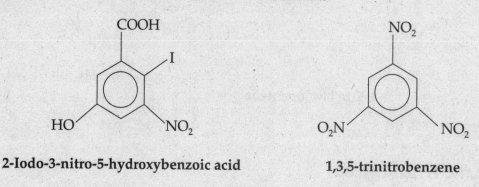

2-Iodo-3-nitro-5-hydroxybenzoic acid   1,3,5-trinitrobenzene

3,4-dinitrophenol   2,4,6-trichloroaniline

- Fused aromatic ring systems

These compounds consist of two or more fused benzene rings that share a common C–C bond. They are also called **polynuclear aromatic hydrocarbons**.

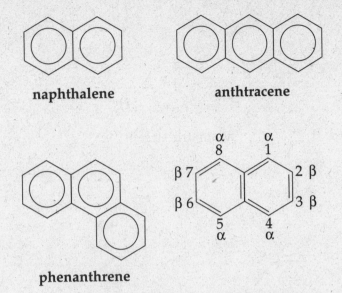

naphthalene

anthtracene

phenanthrene

Their substituent compounds are named using the above convention, either with numbers or greek letters.

- Larger aromatic ring systems

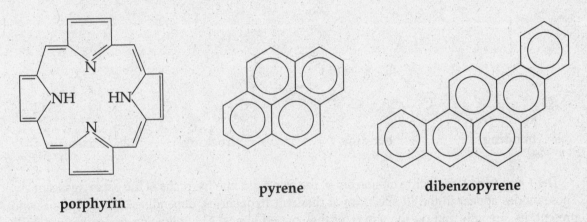

porphyrin

pyrene

dibenzopyrene

SPECTROSCOPY—IR AND ¹H AND ¹³C NMR

Infrared (IR) and nuclear magnetic resonance (NMR) are two spectroscopic techniques routinely used in organic chemistry to characterize the structures (and often identity) of compounds.

INFRARED SPECTROSCOPY (IR)

Molecules absorb light in the IR region of the spectrum, which ranges from 30 to 3000 cm^{-1}.

The bands they produce in their IR spectra are due to vibrations of the molecule, which cause a change in dipole moment during absorption of IR radiation. The band shapes and positions depend on the symmetry of the molecule's vibrations, called **modes of vibration**. Illustrated below are different types of IR-active modes that are observed at different frequencies (ν) in the IR spectra:

symmetric stretch   **symmetric stretch**   **asymmetric stretch**

twist   **wag**

bending   **bending**   **rocking**   **scissoring**

The + and – symbols refer to motion out of the plane and into the plane of the paper, respectively. These modes appear in the IR spectrum at different frequencies, depending on the type of bond present, its strength, and on the nature of the bonded atoms. The following trends are generally observed and are used by chemists to characterize compounds:

- The higher the bond order, or the bond strength, the higher the IR frequency. So $\nu_{C\equiv C} > \nu_{C=C} > \nu_{C-C}$.

- The heavier the atoms involved in the vibrating bond, the higher the frequency.

- Hydrogen bonding shifts the spectrum to lower frequencies.

In addition to specific modes of vibration that occur at specific IR frequencies, **group frequencies** are also observed. Group frequencies are associated with specific groups of atoms producing IR bands that are composite modes of vibration. Several of these groups of atoms consist of organic **functional groups** (see section C).

One useful range of IR absorption is the **fingerprint region** (between 1500 and 700 cm^{-1}) where several characteristic vibrations are observed for different functional groups.

The functional groups are very sensitive to their molecular environments. For example, it is possible to distinguish between a carbonyl or ester C=O group (stretch between 1690 and 1750 cm^{-1}), the C=O group of a carboxylic acid (stretch between 1700 and 1725 cm^{-1}), and that of an acid chloride (stretch between 1770 and 1820 cm^{-1}). Similarly, the C–H stretch is observed between 2800 and 3000 cm^{-1} in alkanes, but at ~ 3300 cm^{-1} if the carbon is in acetylene, at ~ 3050 cm^{-1} if it is in ethylene, and at ~3000 cm^{-1} if it is attached to an aromatic ring.

A few well-known correlations between IR band position and structure are summarized in the following table:

Group	IR v (cm^{-1})
OH, NH, CH	3700–3100
Aryl, olefinic CH	3100–3000
Aliphatic CH	3000–2700
Acidic COOH	3100–2400
C=O	1900–1550
C=C and C=N	1700–1550
N=O	1660–1450
Aromatic N=O	1330–1530
NH_2 and CNH	1660–1500
CH_2 and CH_3	1500–1250
NO_3^- and CO_3^-	1470–1310
SO_2 and SO_3^-	1400–1000
C≡O	1300–1000
SO_2	1150–1360
C–H wag, olefinic	1000–600
C–H wag, aromatic	900–700

¹H NMR

Organic chemists also use NMR (nuclear magnetic resonance) as a common spectroscopic technique for structural determination. In NMR, one of the useful quantities measured is the **chemical shift (d)**, which allows for the identification of the bonding environment of specific hydrogen atoms. This chemical shift arises as follows: Atoms with an odd number of protons have magnetic moments. The hydrogen nucleus (1 proton) has two isoenergetic spin states, denoted +1/2 and –1/2. When placed in an external magnetic field, the nuclear spin states are split and no longer have the same energy. The higher energy state aligns its magnetic moment *against* the applied field and the lower energy state aligns *with* the field. The difference in energy between the two states is in the radio-frequency range, and radiation in that range can excite the nuclei, inducing spin flips between the higher and lower energy states. This is called **resonance**. NMR spectroscopy features a fixed radio frequency (usually 60 MHz) and a magnet that applies a varying magnetic field. When the resonance condition is met, ie, when the spin flip occurs, a peak is recorded in the spectrum. The ability of the external magnetic field to affect the spin state of the hydrogen nuclei will depend on the extent to which the nuclei are shielded by surrounding electron clouds. The signals of more shielded protons will appear **upfield** in the spectrum, and the signals of less shielded protons will appear **downfield**. The chemical shift is usually expressed relative to a standard such as TMS, trimethylsilane, $(CH_3)_4Si$, whose signal is assigned zero ppm on the d-scale.

The δ-scale chemical shift (ppm) is calculated as shift downfield from TMS (Hz)/total NMR spectrometer frequency (MHz)

Common NMR spectrometer frequencies:

- 60 MHz ≡ 14,092 gauss
- 100 MHz ≡ 23,486 gauss
- 200 MHz ≡ 46,972 gauss

Shown below is the ^{1}H-NMR spectrum of ethanol (CH_3CH_2OH):

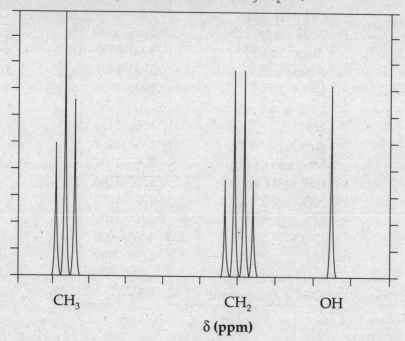

δ (ppm)

The signals from the protons reflect their differing magnetic environments: the signals of the more shielded protons appear first (upfield) to the right in the spectrum, followed by the signals of less shielded protons. This trend is also illustrated in the following table, which lists a few characteristic chemical shift values:

H attached to:	δ (ppm)	Examples	Substituent group
Cyclic C	0.2–0.3	Cyclopentane	
1° carbon	0.9	$-CH_3$	Methyl-
2° carbon	1.3	$R-CH=CH_2$	Ethenyl-
3° carbon	1.5	$-C\equiv CH$	Ethynyl-
C–C	3.0	$-CH_2-C\equiv CH$	Prop-2-inyl
C–I	3.0	$-I-CH_3$	Iodide
C–Br	3.5	$-Br-CH_3$	Bromide
CX–COOH	2.6	CH_2-COOH	Carboxyl
CX–C=O	2.7	$CH_2-C=O$	Carbonyl
C bound to aromatic C	2.9	C_6H_6-C-H	Benzylic
ROCH	4.0	$R-O-CH_3$	Ether

¹H-NMR Chemical Shifts Generally Depend on the Following Factors

1. The proximity of electronegative atoms (N, O, I, Br...) to the H in question decreases its shielding and results in a signal shift downfield; conversely, electropositive atoms increase H shielding;

2. The most shielded H's are found in alkanes.

3. The proximity of electron-withdrawing groups (C=O, aromatic carbons, C=C, C≡C,...) also shift ¹H signals downfield.

4. The signals of hydrogens involved in H bonding are also shifted downfield.

Another feature of proton signals in high-resolution NMR spectra is that they are indicative of **spin-spin splitting**. In the example above, the signal for CH_3 is split into three peaks, and that for CH_2 into 4 peaks. This is due to the coupling between the nuclear spins of the different protons, that is, each proton's magnetic environment is slightly different than that of its neighbor in a given group.

Spin-spin splitting is usually indicative of the magnetic nonequivalence of protons located on *adjacent* **carbon atoms.** $N + 1$ **peaks are observed in the splitting of a given proton signal if** N **magnetically equivalent protons are found on the adjacent carbon.**

In the methyl group, the protons have four possible sets of spins, which will affect the magnetic environment of the two CH_2 protons, splitting their signal into four lines. Likewise, the CH_2 protons have three different sets of spins, so the CH_3 proton signal is split into three peaks.

Applying the splitting rule, CH_2 has two equivalent protons, so if its carbon is bonded to a methyl carbon, the CH_3 proton signal will be split into $N + 1$ peaks, or $2 + 1 = 3$. Similarly, CH_3 has three equivalent protons so the signal for CH_2 will split into $N + 1$ peaks, or $3 + 1 = 4$ peaks. By convention, magnetically unequivalent hydrogens are assigned a and b superscripts.

Example: NMR can be used to distinguish between the diastereomers of 1-dibromo-2-methylethanoic acid:

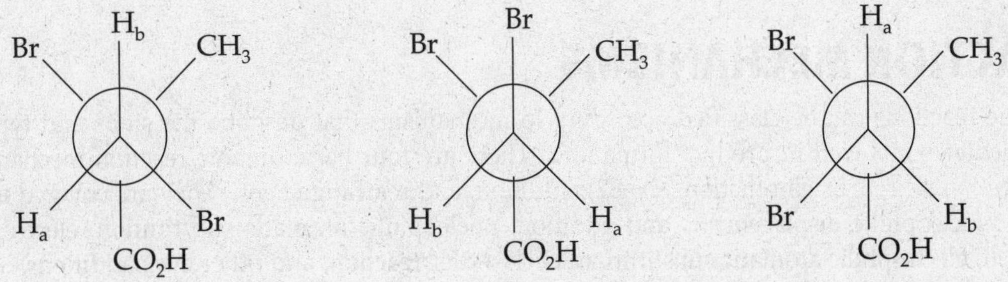

A   B   C

Three staggered conformations are possible; in each of them, however, H_a and H_b are always in different environments. They are magnetically nonequivalent, and each will give rise to a doublet ($N + 1 = 2$). The number of doublets observed is indicative of the number of conformational isomers present, as seen below:

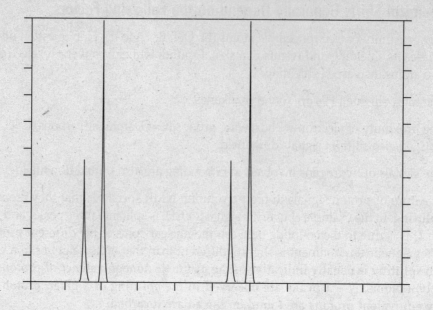

¹³C NMR

The naturally occurring isotope of carbon, ^{12}C, is not NMR-active, since it has an even number of protons, but the ^{13}C isotope is. ^{13}C-NMR is a more intricate technique than ^{1}H-NMR because, in addition to ^{13}C spin-spin coupling, ^{13}C-^{1}H coupling also occurs. But techniques are available to obtain **proton-decoupled** spectra, which are then analyzed in terms of the ^{13}C chemical shifts. In this case, the information will be similar to that obtained from ^{1}H-NMR spectra, ie, characteristic d-values are associated with the different types of ^{13}C present in the molecule. The **proton coupled** spectra will yield more information, because the number of protons bound to each ^{13}C present can also be determined.

REACTION MECHANISMS

Organic reactions can be classified according to mechanisms that describe the steps and types of intermediates involved in product formation. There are four basic organic reaction mechanisms: substitution (S_N1, S_N2), elimination (E1, E2), addition, and rearrangement. They are covered in this order: Nucleophilic displacements and addition, nucleophilic aromatic substitution, electrophilic addition, electrophilic aromatic substitution, Diels-Adler reaction, and other cycloadditions.

SUBSTITUTION (ALSO KNOWN AS NUCLEOPHILIC DISPLACEMENT)

In a substitution reaction, one atom, ion, or group of atoms is substituted for another, and a **nucleophile** (Nu), which is a species that has an unshared pair of electrons, becomes attached to an alkyl group.

$$Nu\!:^- \;\; + \;\; R\ddot{X}\!: \;\; \longrightarrow \;\; NuR \;\; + \;\; :\ddot{X}\!:^-$$

A fragment, called the **leaving group** is displaced from the alkyl group, taking with it the electrons that bonded it to the carbon atom. This type of bond breakage is called **heterolytic cleavage** because the leaving group retains both electrons from the broken bond.

$$HO^- + CH_2 \text{---} Br \longrightarrow HO \text{---} CH_2 + Br^-$$
$$\qquad\quad | \qquad\qquad\qquad\qquad |$$
$$\qquad\quad CH_3 \qquad\qquad\qquad\quad CH_3$$

Nucleophilic displacement could theoretically occur by any of the following three mechanisms:
(1) Formation of a Nu–C bond, followed by C–X bond cleavage:

$$Nu^- + R\text{---}X \longrightarrow \left[Nu\text{---}R\text{---}X \right]^- \longrightarrow Nu\text{---}R + X^-$$

This mechanism, however, is unlikely because the intermediate species would require that there be ten electrons in the valence shell of carbon;
(2) Simultaneous Nu–C bond formation and C–X bond cleavage:

$$Nu^- + R\text{---}X \longrightarrow \left[\overset{\delta^-}{Nu}\text{----}R\text{----}\overset{\delta^-}{X} \right]^- \longrightarrow Nu\text{---}R + X^-$$

In this case, the rate of the reaction would depend on the concentration of both Nu$^-$ and RX, because they are both involved in the transition state. This is the mechanism that does indeed occur, and it is called S_N2, in which S_N stands for nucleophilic substitution and the 2 indicates that the rate-determining step is bimolecular:

$$rate_{SN2} = k[Nu][RX]$$

(3) Heterolytic cleavage of the C–X bond, followed by the formation of a Nu–C bond:

$$RX \longrightarrow X^- + \left[R^+ \right] \xrightarrow{Nu^-} NuR$$

This is a two-step process that involves the formation of a **carbocation,** and it occurs in nature. The rate of the reaction depends only on the rate of ionization of RX, and is independent of the concentration of Nu$^-$. This process is called an S_N1 reaction, and the 1 indicates that the rate-determining step is unimolecular:

$$rate_{SN1} = k[RX]$$

Example:

What is the product of the reaction of ethyl bromide with potassium cyanide? Write a mechanism and clearly identify the nucleophile, the substrate, the product, and the leaving group.

In potassium cyanide, the nucleophile is the negatively charged cyanide ion, CN$^-$. A nucleophilic substitution of bromide by cyanide occurs, and the product is ethyl cyanide.

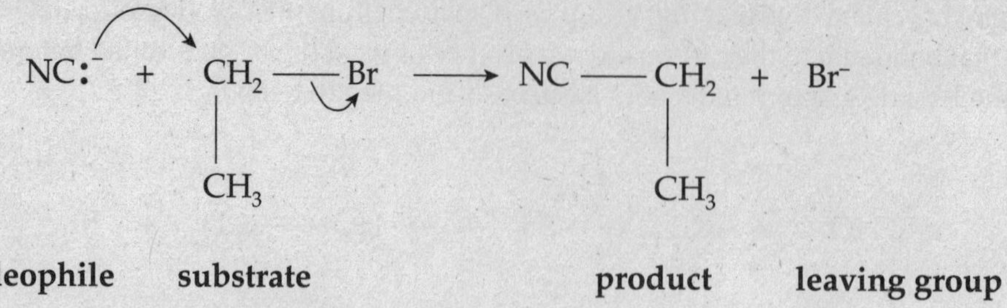

$$NC:^- \ + \ CH_2 \text{---} Br \ \longrightarrow \ NC \text{---} CH_2 \ + \ Br^-$$

$$\underset{CH_3}{|} \qquad\qquad\qquad\qquad \underset{CH_3}{|}$$

nucleophile   **substrate**   **product**   **leaving group**

In an S_N2 reaction, the nucleophile collides with the substrate on the side opposite the bond between the carbon atom and the leaving group. This back-side displacement occurs with inversion of configuration around the carbon atom (called a Walden inversion).

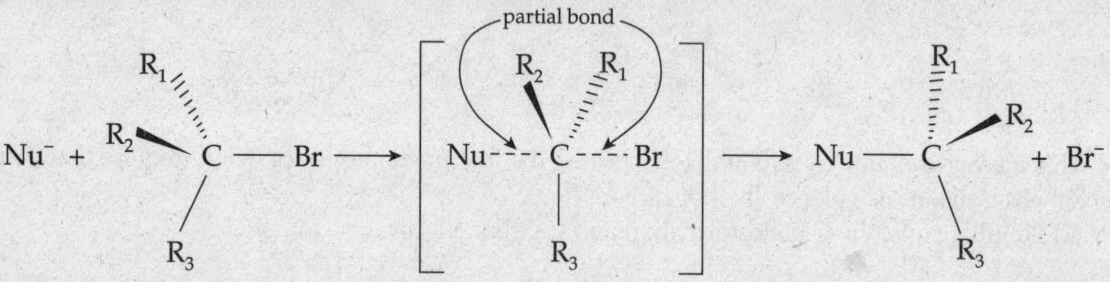

During a rear attack such as this, the nucleophile bonds via the backside lobe of a carbon sp^3 orbital. This mechanism is called "concerted" because the formation of the Nu–C bond and the cleavage of the C–Y bond occur simultaneously. During the reaction, the reactants reach a transition state of high potential energy, which features a sp^2-hybridized carbon with the p-orbital perpendicular to the plane of the central carbon and its three substituents. If the substrate is optically active, the product will have the opposite configuration.

Steric hindrance is the most important factor in determining the rate of an S_N2 reaction.

The potential energy needed to form a crowded transition state is much higher than that for a transition state with less spatial crowding. The relative rates of S_N2 reactions are as follows:

methyl > primary > secondary > tertiary

(these terms refer to zero, one, two, and three alkyl substituents on the carbon atom, respectively). Methyl, primary and secondary halides almost always undergo S_N2 reactions, while bulkier tertiary halides react exclusively according to the S_N1 mechanism.

Example:

Which of the following compounds would undergo the fastest S_N2 reaction? Explain.

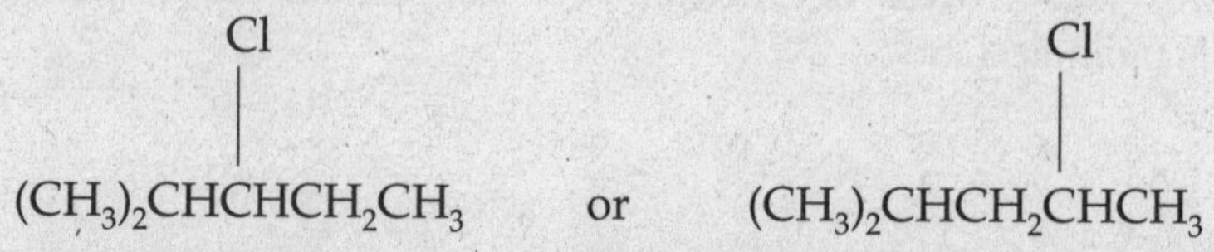

$$\underset{(CH_3)_2CHCHCH_2CH_3}{\overset{Cl}{|}} \qquad or \qquad \underset{(CH_3)_2CHCH_2CHCH_3}{\overset{Cl}{|}}$$

To answer this question, you must examine the space around the carbon atom bearing the leaving group. In the second compound, the substituents of the carbon atom are smaller than those of the first compound. There is less steric hindrance, and this compound will therefore undergo the faster S_N2 reaction.

Because of steric hindrance, tertiary alkyl halides undergo S_N1 reactions. This process first involves a slow ionization step to form a **carbocation**, followed by bonding of the carbocation to a nucleophile with an unshared pair of electrons:

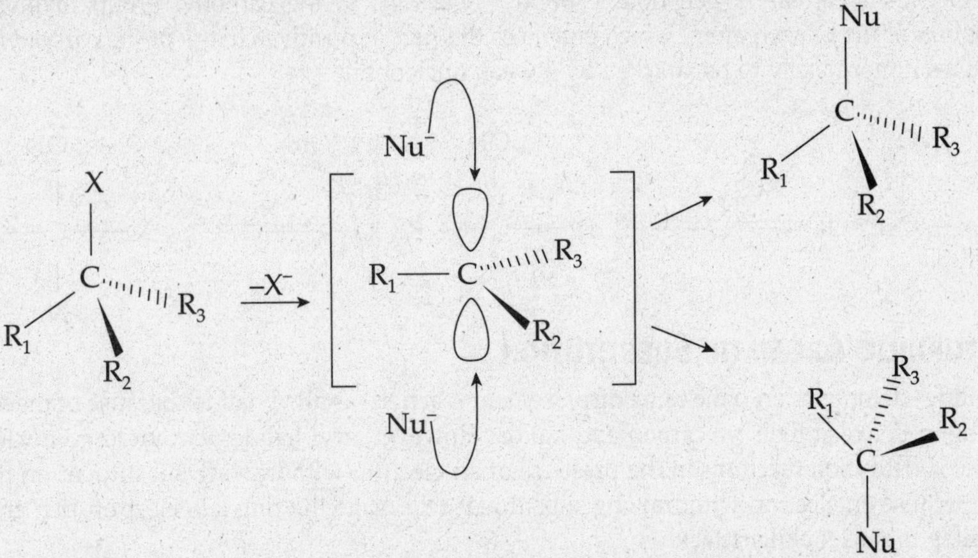

The sp^2-hybridized carbocation has a plane of symmetry, and nucleophilic attack is equally likely to happen on both sides. If the substrate contains a chiral C–X bond, the product of the reaction will be racemic (50% R and 50% S), and without inversion (unlike in S_N2 reactions). The order of reactivity of alkyl halides is:

$$\text{tertiary} > \text{secondary} > \text{primary}$$

Carbocations are a very reactive species, but they do, however, have a certain degree of stability due to factors that contribute to the dispersion of their positive charge, such as inductive effects or steric assistance. For instance, the alkyl groups of tertiary alkyl halides are electron donors and inductively stabilize carbocation intermediates:

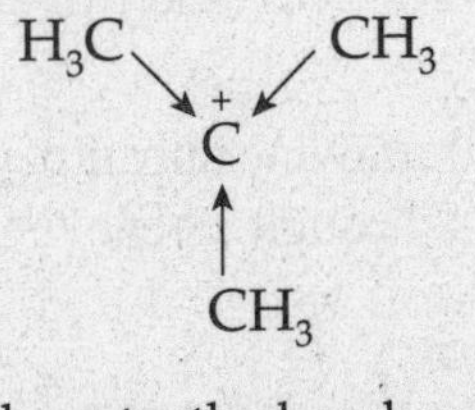

Furthermore, as the leaving group departs, the bond angles of the sp^2-hybridized intermediate expand from ~ 109° to 120°, which relieves strain during the reaction with the substrate. This lowers the activation energy of highly substituted, compared to unsubstituted, halides.

Example:

List the following carbocations in order of increasing stability:

(a) $(CH_3CH_2CH_2)_3C^+$ (b) 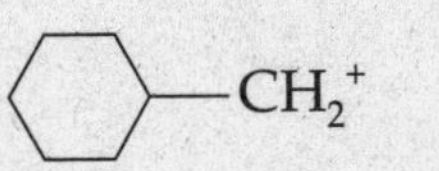 $-CH_2^+$ (c) $(CH_3CH_2CH_2)_2CH^+$

The answer is b < c < a.

The greater the number of alkyl substituents, the greater the inductive effect and steric assistance, and the greater the stability of the carbocation.

NUCLEOPHILIC ADDITION

Nucleophilic addition is a typical reaction mechanism for alhehydes and ketones because of the polarity of their carbon-oxygen double bond. Reactions of the carbonyl group involve initial protonation of the oxygen atom, which enhances the partial positive charge of the carbonyl carbon and makes it more likely to be attacked by a weak nucleophile.

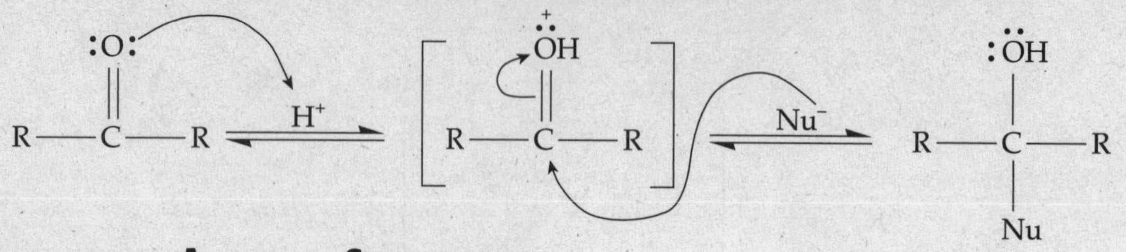

NUCLEOPHILIC AROMATIC SUBSTITUTION

Aryl halides do not undergo the same displacement reactions as alkyl halides because of the strength of the bond between their sp^2 carbon and halide. However, aryl halides can undergo nucleophilic aromatic substitution reactions in the presence of an electron-withdrawing substituent on the ring. This is because an electron-withdrawing substituent will make the ring less electron-rich and more susceptible to nucleophilic attack.

There are two major mechanisms for nucleophilic aromatic substitution:

(1) Addition of a nucleophile and formation of a carbanion intermediate, followed by the loss of the halide ion:

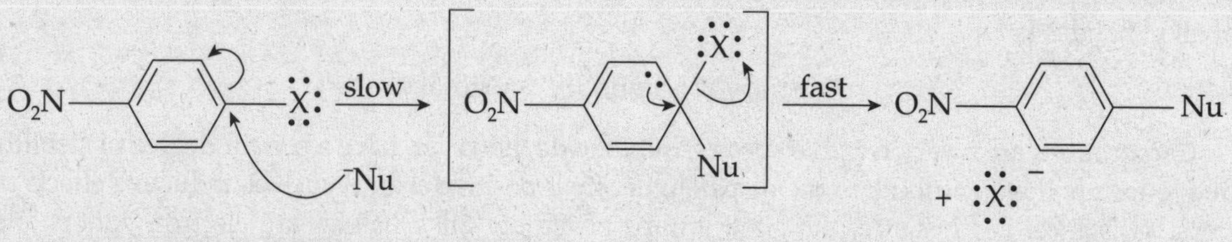

The carbanion is stabilized by resonance and the removal of negative charge by the electron-withdrawing group. Electron-withdrawing *ortho-* and *para-*substituents stabilize the carbanion intermediate more than *meta-*substituents.

(2) In the absence of electron-withdrawing substituents, nucleophilic aromatic substitution is very rare and proceeds through a benzyne intermediate:

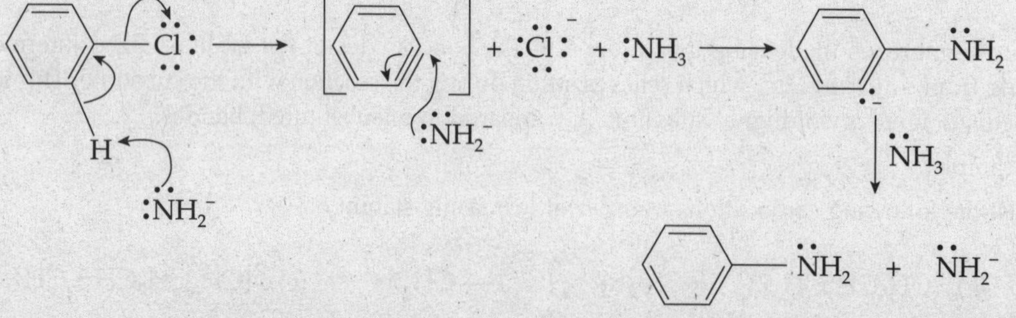

The benzyne triple bond is made of an sp^2-sp^2 sigma bond, a p-p overlap (from the pi cloud) and a side-to-side overlap of the two sp^2 orbitals of the starting C–H and C–X bonds. Because of the rigid geometry of the ring and of the angle between these two sp^2 orbitals, the overlap is not very good and this intermediate is highly reactive.

ELECTROPHILIC ADDITION

Addition reactions are characteristic of unsaturated compounds. The pi-electron cloud represents a far more reactive electron system than a σ bond, so the electrons of multiple bonds behave as Lewis bases toward Lewis acids. During addition reactions, the substrate does not lose any atoms. For instance, the reaction of an alkene with the highly polarized HCl molecule proceeds in two steps: initial attack by the **electrophile** (electron-deficient species such as H^+, CH_3^+, Br^+, NO_2^+ and HSO_3^+) to form a carbocation, followed by reaction with the negative halide ion.

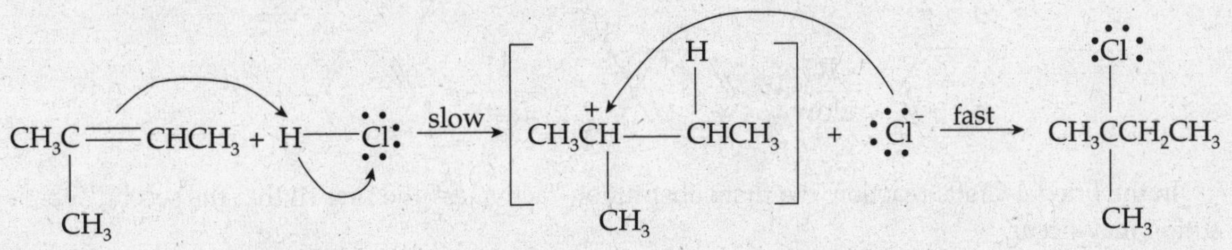

The reaction is called an **electrophilic addition** reaction because the initial attack is by an electrophile. If the alkene is unsymmetrical, the addition follows Markovnikov's rule, ie, in additions of HX to unsymmetrical alkenes, the H^+ of HX goes the sp^2 carbon with the greatest number of hydrogens.

Example:

What is the product of the reaction between 1-methylcyclohexene and HI?

Answer: 1-iodo-1-methylcyclohexane.

The sp^2 carbon that bears the methyl group does not have an attached hydrogen atom. The sp^2 carbon at position 2 has one hydrogen atom. Therefore, the H^+ is added at position 2 and I^- at position 1.

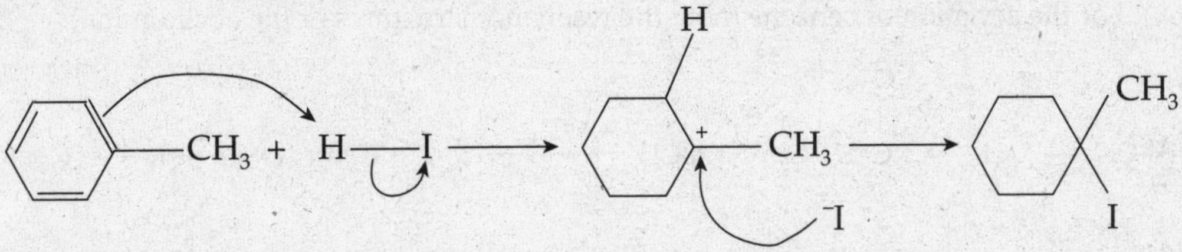

Electrophilic Aromatic Substitution

Aromatic rings, with their electron-rich pi-electron clouds, are easily attacked by electrophiles, but electrophilic additions are not likely because they lead to the rupture of the aromaticity of the ring. Instead, electrophiles generally substitute for a hydrogen atom according to the following general mechanism:

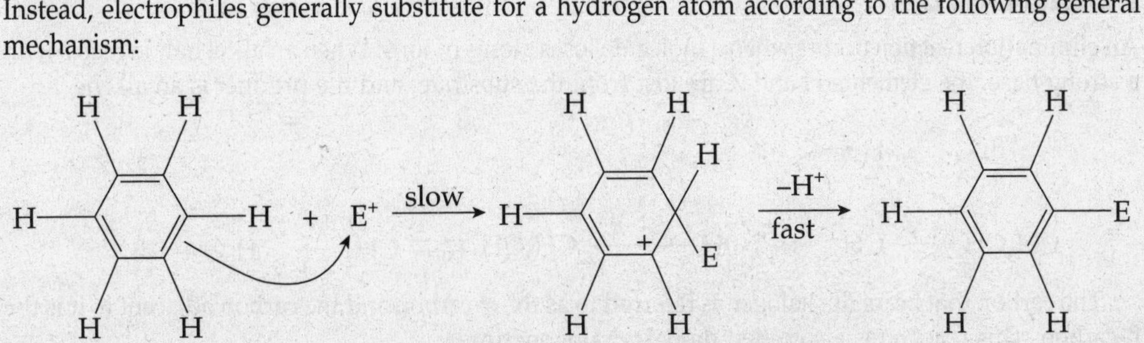

(The required electrophile is generated by a specific reaction, prior to the electrophilic substitution step; it's obtained through the reaction between a Lewis acid and a reagent.)

Example: The alkylation of benzene (a Friedel-Crafts reaction).
The first step is the generation of a carbocation:

$$R\!-\!\ddot{\underset{\cdot\cdot}{Cl}}\!: + AlCl_3 \longrightarrow R^+ + AlCl_4^-$$

The second step is the electrolytic attack on benzene to form an alkylbenzene:

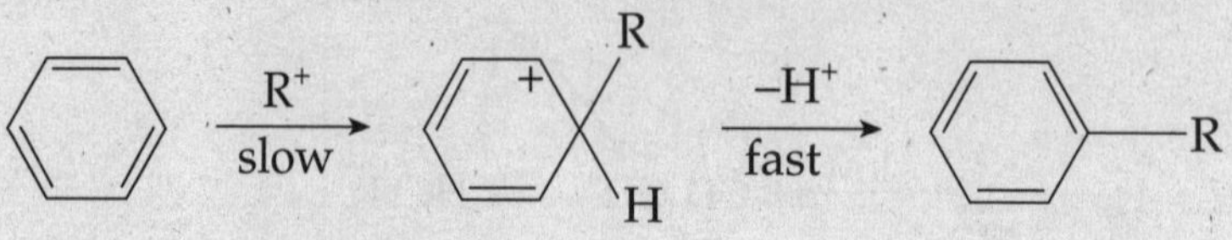

In the Friedel-Crafts reaction, the first substitution "activates" the ring so that the second substitution may occur.

In aromatic electrophilic substitutions, electrophiles can be generated via the following reactions:

1. For the halogenation of benzene:

$$:\ddot{\underset{\cdot\cdot}{Br}}\!-\!\ddot{\underset{\cdot\cdot}{Br}}\!: + FeBr_3 \rightleftharpoons :\ddot{\underset{\cdot\cdot}{Br}}^+ + FeBr_4^-$$

2. For the nitration of benzene:

$$H\ddot{\underset{\cdot\cdot}{O}}\!-\!NO_2 + H_2SO_4 \xrightleftharpoons{-HSO_4^-} H_2\overset{+}{\underset{\cdot\cdot}{O}}\!-\!NO_2 \rightleftharpoons H_2\ddot{O}\!: + NO_2$$

3. For the acylation of benzene (note the resonance structures of the acylium ion):

$$R\overset{O}{\overset{\|}{C}}\!-\!\ddot{\underset{\cdot\cdot}{Cl}}\!: + AlCl_3 \rightarrow R\overset{O}{\overset{\|}{C}}\text{----}Cl\text{----}AlCl_3 \xrightarrow{-AlCl_4^-} \left[R\text{----}C\!=\!\overset{+}{\underset{\cdot\cdot}{\ddot{O}}} \longleftrightarrow R\!-\!C\!\equiv\!\overset{+}{O}\!:\right]$$

4. For the sulfonation of benzene:

$$H_2SO_4 + SO_3 \longrightarrow \overset{+}{HSO_3} + HSO_4^-$$

ELIMINATION

An elimination reaction occurs when a molecule loses atoms or ions. When an alkyl halide reacts with a strong base, the elements H and X are lost from the substrate, and the product is an alkene.

$$\underset{CH_3CH}{\overset{:\ddot{Br}:}{|}}\!-\!\underset{CH_2}{\overset{H}{|}} + :\ddot{\underset{\cdot\cdot}{O}}H^- \longrightarrow CH_3CH\!=\!CH_2 + H_2O + :\ddot{\underset{\cdot\cdot}{Br}}:^-$$

The carbon that bears the halogen is referred to as the α-carbon and the carbon adjacent to it is the β-carbon. This reaction is also called **dehydrohalogenation**.

Two mechanisms are possible for elimination reactions, **E2 elimination** or **E1 elimination.**

E2 Elimination

In this mechanism, a base removes a hydrogen atom; the C–H bond cleaves heterolytically. The adjacent carbons form a carbon-carbon double bond by ejecting the halide as an anion. The reaction does not involve a carbocation intermediate: it is a concerted reaction, just like the S_N2 reaction:

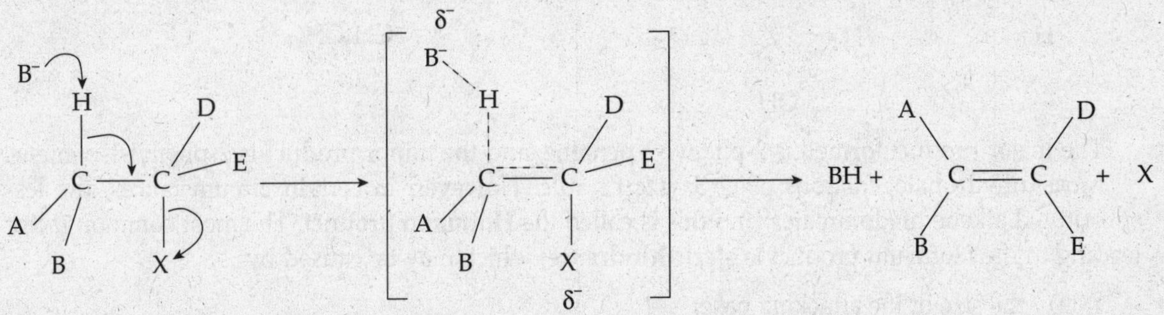

In E2 reactions, the 2 refers to the two reactants involved in the transition state. The rate of reaction is proportional to the concentration of both base and substrate:

$$rate_{E2} = k[base][substrate]$$

E2 reactions generally obey **Saytzeff's rule**, which states that when more than one β-carbon bears hydrogen atoms, it is the most substituted carbon that undergoes elimination. This rule is mostly valid for leaving groups such as X or OH.

Another consideration in E2 reactions is **anti-elimination** or anti-positioning, which determines the stereochemistry of the alkene product. For example, 1-bromo-1,2-diphenylpropane has two chiral carbons (C1 and C2). The possible enantiomers are (1R, 2R), (1S, 2S), (1R, 2S) or (1S, 2R) but in only one of these possible conformations are the H and the Br in an *anti* position. If either the (1R, 2R) or (1S, 2S) react, the *anti* alignment of H and Br places both phenyl groups on the same side of the molecule, and a (Z)-alkene is obtained (also called a *cis*-alkene). If the (1R, 2S) or (1S, 2R) react, (E)-alkenes are produced, ie, with the phenyl groups on opposite sides (or *trans* to each other).

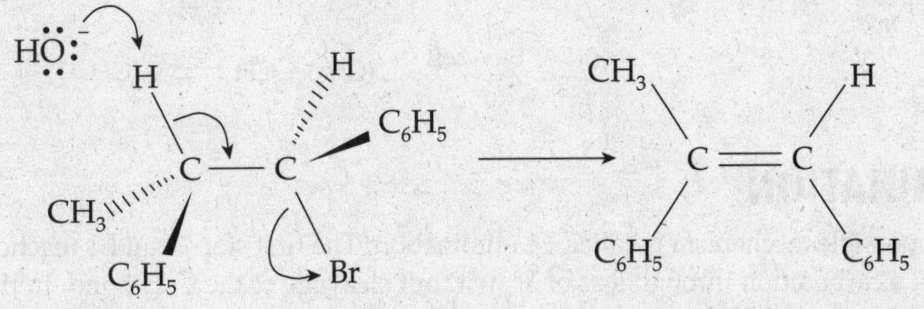

(1S, 2S)-1-bromo-1,2-diphenylpropane   (Z)-1,2-diphenyl-1-propene

This reaction is **stereospecific** because different stereoisomers of the substrate yield stereoisomerically different products.

Example:

What are the products of the reaction of 2-bromo-2-phenylpentane with KOH? Which alkene product should predominate?

Answer: C1 and C3 are the two β-carbon atoms. Of these, C3 is the most substituted and so should lose a hydrogen atom.

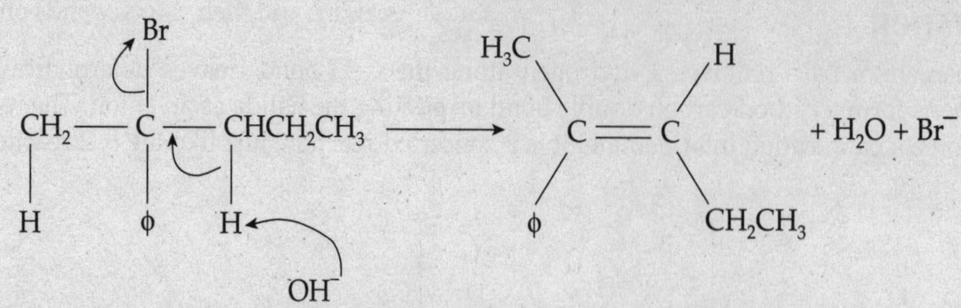

The major product formed is 2-phenyl-2-pentene, and the minor product is 2-phenyl-1-pentene. Most dihydrohalogenations obey Saytzeff's rule. However, in certain circumstances, the less substituted alkene predominates, and this is called the **Hofmann product**. The most common factor leading to the Hofmann product is **steric hindrance**, which may be caused by

(a) the size of the attacking base;

(b) the size of the group surrounding the leaving group;

(c) the size of the leaving group.

Example:

Write the Saytseff and Hofmann product of the E2 reaction of 2-Bromo-2,4,4-trimethylpentane with potassium ethoxide. Which product should predominate?

Answer: According to Saytseff's rule, C3 is the most substituted β-carbon. However, that side of the leaving group is bulkier than the other, and does not facilitate the attack of the base. The Hofmann product should predominate.

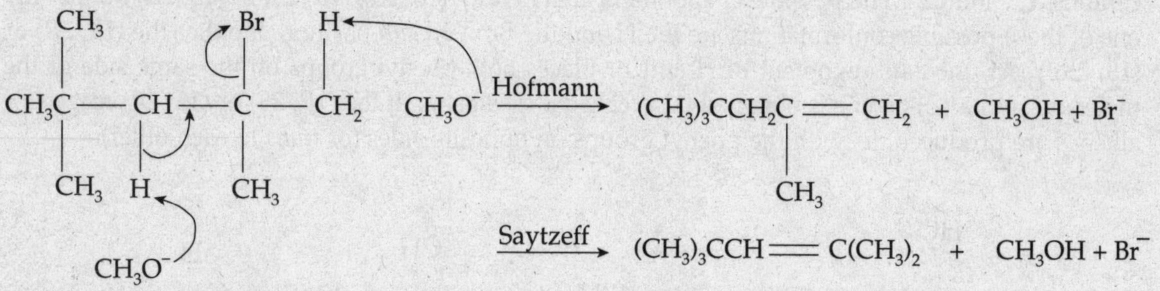

E1 ELIMINATION

The second possible mechanism is called E1 elimination. The first step of an E1 reaction involves the formation of a carbocation through loss of X^-, without cleavage of the C–H bond. In the second step, a weak base removes an H^+ ion from the carbon atom adjacent to the positive carbon:

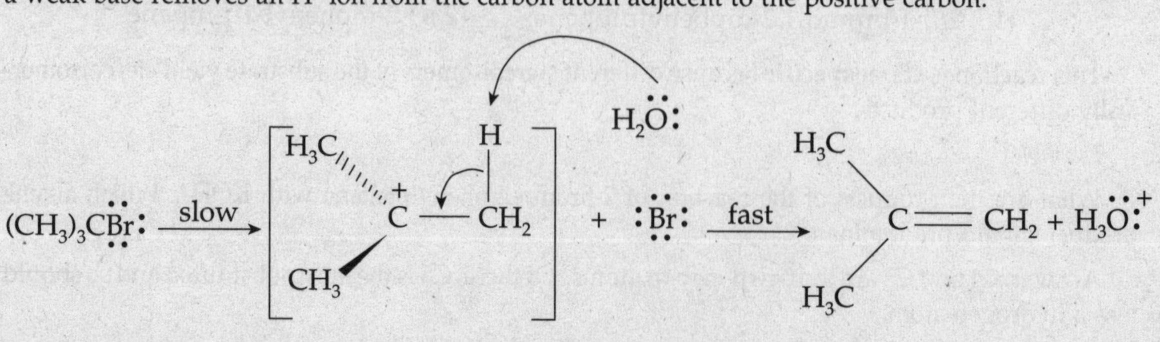

As is the case in S_N1 reactions, E reactions are first order reactions and their rate depends only on the concentration of the substrate:

$$\text{rate}_{E1} = k[\text{substrate}]$$

Tertiary halides undergo E1 elimination faster than the other alkyl halides. Since the reactions conditions are the same for both S_N1 and E1 reactions (eg. a weak base, a polar solvent, etc.), these reactions compete.

In the case of alkyl halides, the S_N1 mechanism usually predominates. In the case of secondary and tertiary alcohols, the E1 reactions predominate; the first step involves protonation and loss of a water molecule, followed by a second step in which a weak base transfers a H^+ ion to a β-carbon. Saytzeff's rule is obeyed and the most stable alkene is produced.

Example:

What is the product of the reaction of 1-methyl-1-cyclohexanol with H_3PO_4? Write one possible mechanism.

Answer: The compound is a tertiary alcohol and will undergo dehydration through an E1 mechanism. According to Saytseff's rule, a hydrogen atom on the C2 carbon of the cyclohexane ring will be eliminated:

THE DIELS-ALDER REACTION AND CYCLOADDITIONS

The Diels-Alder reaction belongs to a class of reaction called **pericyclic reactions**, which are characterised by a cyclic transition state. In the Diels-Alder reaction, a conjugated diene is heated and reacted with an alkene or an alkyne, called **dienophiles** ("lover of dienes") to yield a six-membered ring.

The Diels-Alder reaction is also referred to as a **4 + 2 cycloaddition**, because the ring produced is the result of the interaction of four pi-electrons in the diene with two pi-electrons in the dienophile.

diene   dienophiles

Y is an electron-withdrawing group; usually a group that contains a C=O or a C≡N. The diene is an electron-rich species, and the dienophile is an electron-poor species. The reactivity of the diene is improved when it incorporates electron-donating groups such as alkyl or –OR groups. A good dienophile should have at least one electron-withdrawing group (designated Y, above), and preferably more than one to pull the electron density from the pi bond.

Two examples of substituted dienophiles and their possible reactions are:

The diene must have a *cis* conformation in the transition state, so *cis*-substituted dienophiles are preferred. As shown above, the product of a Diels-Alder addition always contains one more ring than is present in the reactants.

The stereoselectivity of the Diels-Alder reaction is illustrated below. The isomer in which the $-CO_2CH_3$ group is *syn* with respect to the bridge is called the **endo** isomer and is derived from a transition state in which the unsaturated group of the dienophile has a *syn* rather than an *anti* orientation with respect to the diene.

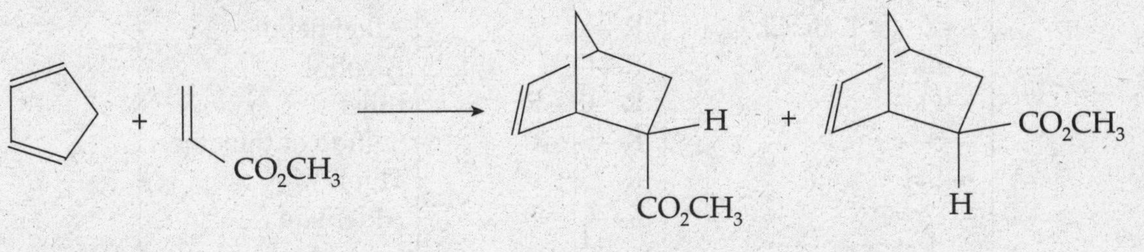

Endo isomer   Exo isomer

Example:

Suggest a Diels-Alder reaction that would lead to the formation of 4-cyanocyclohexene.

Answer: Deduce the structure of the starting diene and dienophile by using the arrows in the reverse order, starting with the double bond of the six-membered ring:

Other pericyclic reactions include electrocyclic reactions, in which a compound with conjugated double bonds undergoes cyclization.

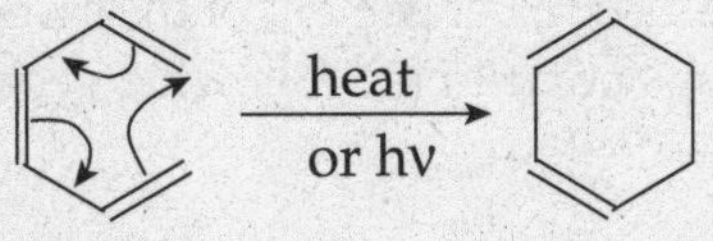

FUNCTIONAL GROUPS

The study of organic chemistry is basically the study of the interactions of functional groups of organic compounds, which is the topic covered under this heading: Alkanes, alkenes, dienes, alkyl halides, alcohols, thiols, ethers, epoxides, sulfides, aromatic compounds, aldehydes, ketones, carboxylic acids, and amines.

A **functional group** is the reactive part of an organic molecule. There are two types of functional groups:

(i) functional groups defined by the types of carbon-carbon bond they contain (C–C, C=C or C≡C);

(ii) functional groups defined as specific atoms or groups of atoms that replace an hydrogen in a hydrocarbon.

Important functional groups in organic chemistry

Functional group	Formula	Name
C—C	C_nH_{2n+2}	Alkane
C=C	C_nH_{2n}	Alkene
C≡C	C_nH_{2n-2}	Alkyne
C=C=C		Diene
—X, X = F, Br, Cl, I	R—X	Alkyl halide
—OH	R—OH	Alcohol
—O—	R—O—R	Ether
—S—	R—S—R	Sulfide or thioether
—SH	R—SH	Thiol
—C=O with H below	R—C=O with H below	Aldehyde
—C=O with R below	R—C=O with R below	Ketone
—C=O with OH below	R—C=O with OH below	Carboxylic acid

ALKANES

Alkanes are acyclic hydrocarbon chains with the general formula C_nH_{2n+2}. They are characterized by **single C–C** bonds and are called **saturated** because their carbons bind as many hydrogens as possible; a maximum of four. **Alkyl groups** are symbolized as **R** in general formulas. Two prefixes are used to specify the geometry of alkyls: $n\text{-}C_nH_{2n+1}$ where n stands for a normal, linear C-atom chain and $i\text{-}C_nH_{2n+1}$ where i stands for an "iso" arrangement of the carbons, ie, where the second carbon in the chain has a branch. Alkyl groups occur in the following geometries:

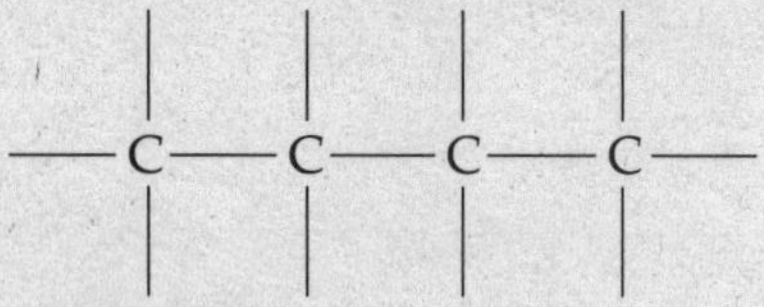

n-butyl

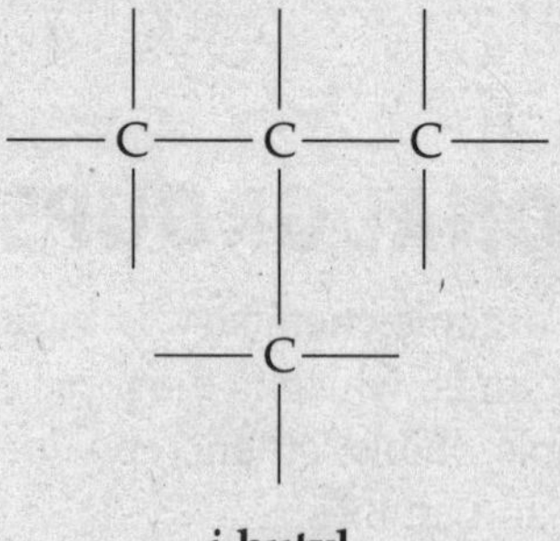

i-butyl

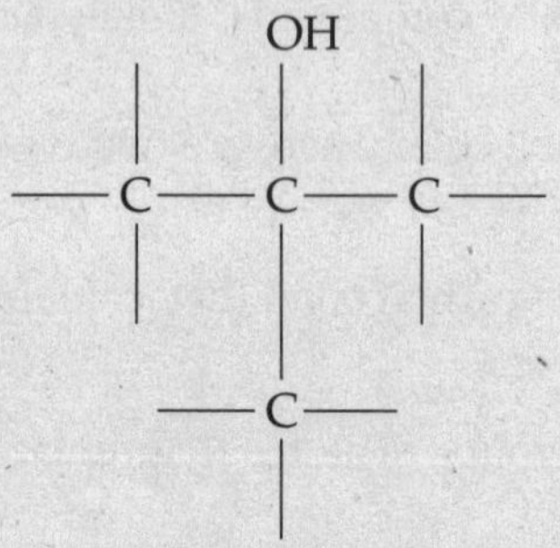

tert-butyl alcohol

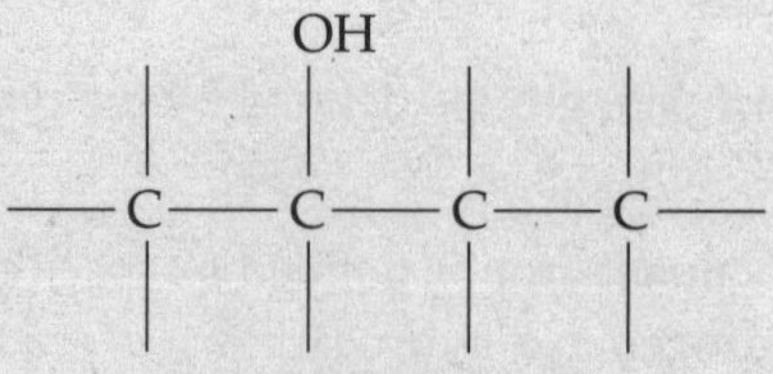

sec-butyl alcohol

SYNTHESIS OF ALKANES

1. Reduction of Alkyl Halides (RX)

1.1 $RX + Zn + H^+ \rightarrow RH + Zn^{+2} + X^-$

Example: $CH_3Cl + Zn + H^+ \rightarrow CH_4 + Zn^{+2} + Cl^-$

1.2 $4RX + LiAlH_4 \rightarrow 4RH + LiX + AlX_3$

Example: $4CH_3Cl + LiAlH_4 \rightarrow 4CH_4 + LiCl + AlCl_3$

1.3 $RX + (n\text{-}C_4H_9)_3SnH \rightarrow RH + (n\text{-}C_4H_9)_3SnX$

Example: $CH_3Cl + (n\text{-}C_4H_9)_3SnH \rightarrow RH + (n\text{-}C_4H_9)_3SnX$

1.4 $RX + 2Li \xrightarrow{\text{under dry ether}} R^-{:}(MgX)^+ + H_2O \rightarrow RH + (MgX)^+(OH)^-$

Example: $CH_3Cl + + 2Li \rightarrow CH_3^-{:}(MgCl)^+ + H_2O \rightarrow CH_4 + (MgCl)^+(OH)^-$

Reaction 1.4 above involves an intermediate step, the formation of a **Grignard reagent**, $R^-{:}(MgX)^+$. These reduction reactions all feature the replacement of a halogen (X) by a hydrogen, and the number of carbon atoms in the products equals that of the reactants.

2. Catalyzed Hydrogenation of Alkenes and Alkynes to Produce Alkanes

$$CH_3\!-\!\overset{\overset{\textstyle CH_3}{|}}{C}\!=\!CHCH_3 + H_2 \xrightarrow{\text{Pt or Ni}} CH_3\!-\!\overset{\overset{\textstyle CH_3}{|}}{C}\!=\!CH_2CH_3$$

2-Methyl-2-butene   **2-Methylbutane**

$$CH_3C\!\equiv\!CCH_2CH_3 + 2H_2 \xrightarrow{\text{Pt or Ni}} CH_3CH_2CH_2CH_2CH_3$$

2-Pentyne   **Pentane**

3. Corey-House Synthesis

(a) $2R\!-\!Li + CuI \xrightarrow{\text{under dry ether}} R_2CuLi + LiI$

(b) $R_2CuLi + R'\!-\!X \rightarrow R'\!-\!R + RCu + LiX$

Example: $CH_3CH_2Cl + CuI \rightarrow (CH_3CH_2)_2CuLi + LiI + C_2H_5Cl \rightarrow$
$$CH_3CH_2CH_2CH_3 + CH_3CH_2Cu + LiCl$$

In the Corey-House synthesis, the product always has more carbons than the reactants: Two alkyls are combined to yield the larger alkane under lithium dialkylcuprate (R_2CuLi above).

THE MAJOR REACTIONS OF ALKANES

Alkanes are not very reactive; significant energy must be consumed in order for the reaction to happen.

1. Thermal Dehydrogenation

$C_nH_{2n+2} + \xrightarrow{\text{heat}} \text{mixture of smaller chain alkanes}$

2. Combustion

$$C_nH_{2n+2} + 2O_2 \rightarrow CO_2 + 2H_2O$$

3. Halogenation

$$RH + X_2 + \xrightarrow{\text{heat}} RX + HX$$

This halogenation reaction proceeds by radical formation and is stepwise, in three major steps:

- The *initiation step*: in which a **reactive intermediate** is generated, in this case a **free radical** of the halogen atom. The radicals are generated by the absorption of light. Radicals lack an octet of electrons and are extremely reactive, as well as **electrophilic,** because they are electron-deficient;

- The *propagation steps*: in the presence of an alkane, the radical formed will break one of the C–H bonds. One electron remains on the alkane, which becomes an alkyl radical since it loses a hydrogen and an electron, and the other electron forms the bond in the newly formed H–X molecule. In a second propagation step, the alkyl radical formed reacts with a halogen molecule to form the halogenated alkane.

- The *termination steps*: the reaction is over when the free radicals are used up and no new ones are formed. So a termination step produces fewer radicals than it uses up.

Example: Bromination of methane: $CH_4 + Br_2 \rightarrow CH_3Br^+ + HBr$

1. Initiation step:

$$:\ddot{Br}:\ddot{Br}: \xrightarrow{\text{uv}} :\ddot{Br}\cdot + \cdot\ddot{Br}:$$

bromine atom   two bromine radicals

2. Propagation steps:

methane   bromine radical   methyl radical   hydrogen bromide

methyl radical   bromine atom   bromomethane   bromine radical

3. Termination steps:

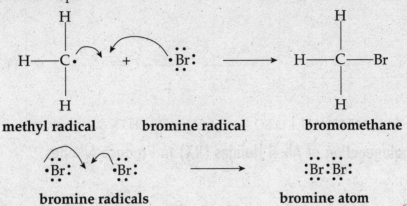

methyl radical   bromine radical   bromomethane

bromine radicals   bromine atom

ALKENES

Alkenes are acyclic hydrocarbon chains with the general formula C_nH_{2n}. They are characterized by double C=C bonds and are said to be unsaturated because they react with hydrogen to produce saturated alkanes. Alkenes contain one element of saturation, the double C=C.

- The number of elements of saturation in a given compound is calculated using

$$\frac{[2X_c + 2 - X_H]}{2}$$

where X_C is the number of carbons and X_H is the number of hydrogens.

For example, C_7H_{14} (heptene) has $\frac{(2 \times 7) + 2 - 14}{2} = 1$ element of saturation.

Similarly, C_7H_{16} (heptane) has $\frac{(2 \times 7) + 2 - 16}{2} = 0$ elements of saturation.

- Alkenes easily undergo **polymerization**, which produces **polymers**, which are large molecules made of chain-linked starting molecules called **monomers** or **mers**.

$$CH_2=CH_2 \longrightarrow$$

styrene monomer

polystyrene

SYNTHESIS OF ALKENES

1. Dehydrogenation of alkanes to produce alkenes

$$\longrightarrow \overset{|}{\underset{|}{C}}-\overset{|}{\underset{|}{C}} \longrightarrow \quad \xrightarrow{\text{heat, Pt or Pd}} \quad \longrightarrow \overset{|}{C}=\overset{|}{C} \longrightarrow \quad + \quad H$$

Example: $CH_3CH_2CH_2CH_3 \rightarrow$ 1-Butene + mix of *cis*- and *trans*-2-Butene + 1,3-Butadiene + H_2

2. Dehydration of alcohols (ROH) to produce alkenes

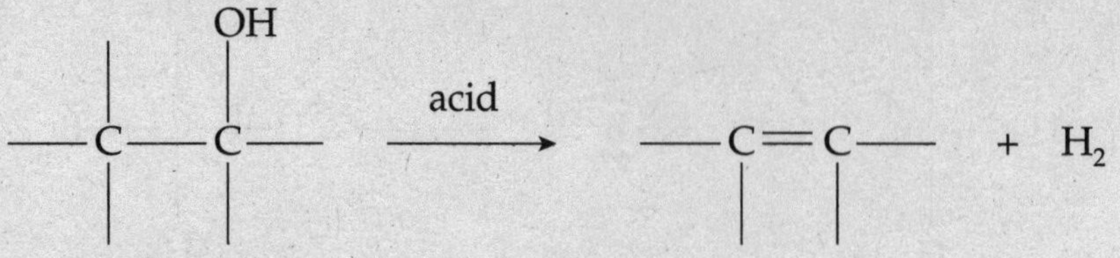

Example: $CH_3CHOHCH + H_2SO_4 \rightarrow CH_3CH{=}CH_2 + H_2O$

3. Dehydrohalogenation of Alkyl Halides (RX) to Produce Alkenes

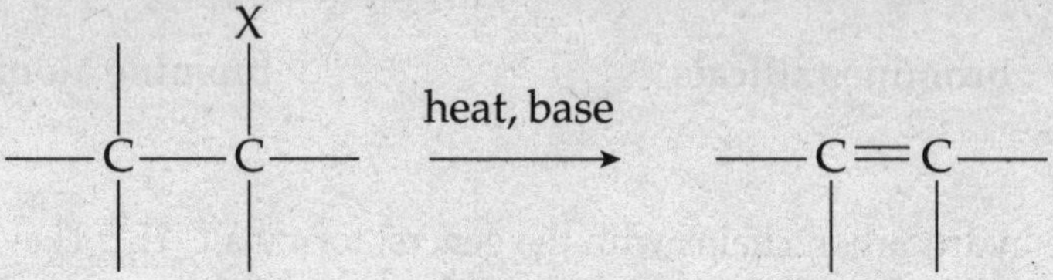

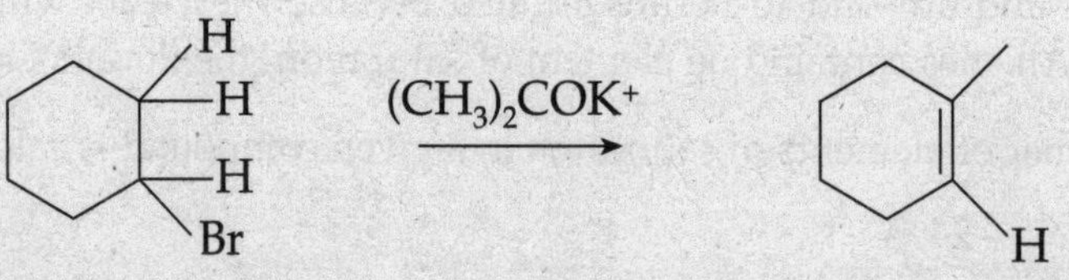

cyclohexyl bromide   cyclohexene

4. Dehalogenation of vicinal dihalides to produce alkenes

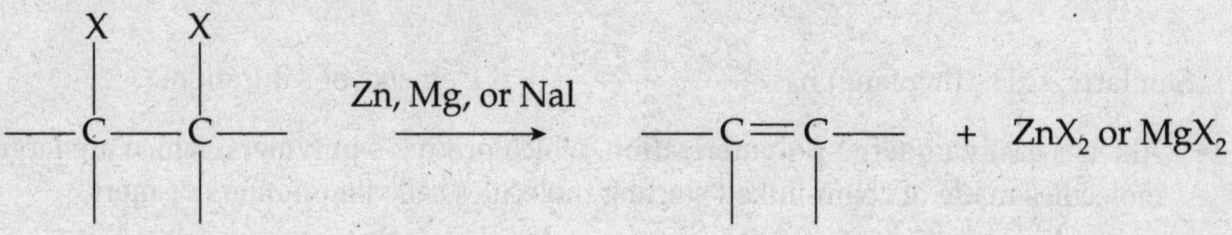

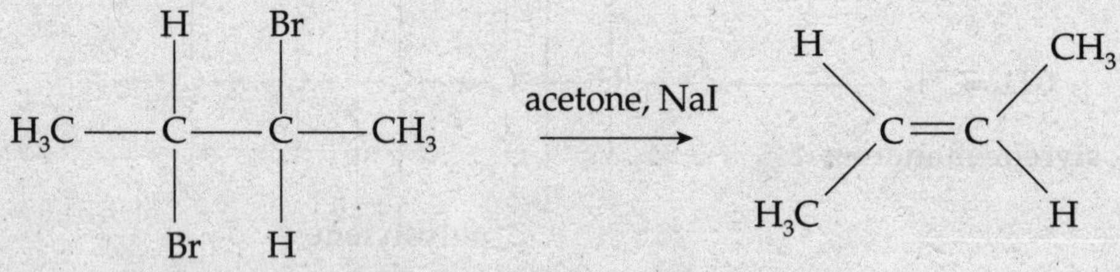

5. Reduction of alkynes (RC–CR) to produce alkenes

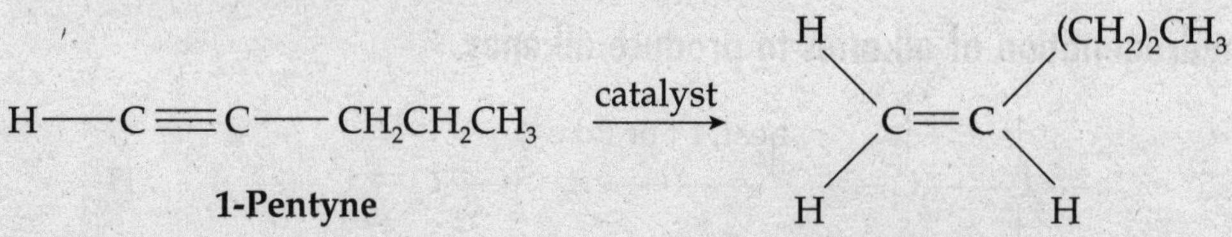

1-Pentyne

1-Pentene

REACTIONS OF ALKENES

1. Addition of hydrogen halides (HX) across double bonds

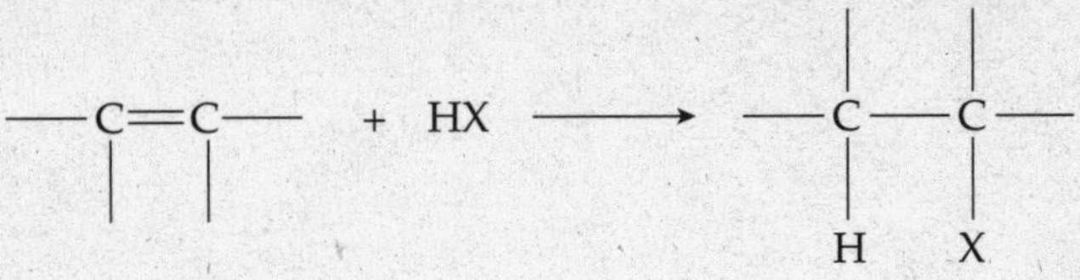

Example:

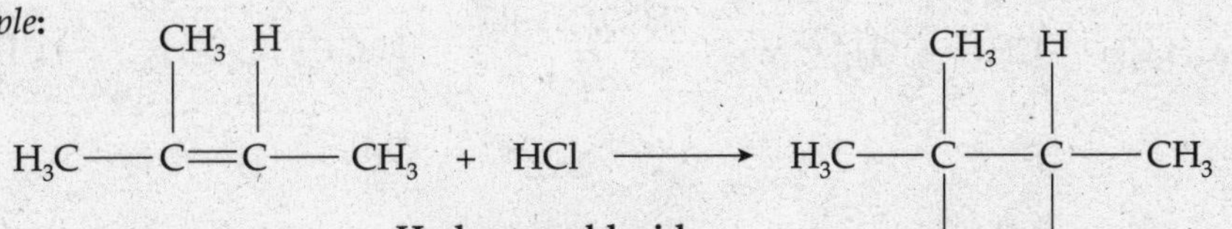

2-Methyl-2-butene   Hydrogen chloride   2-Methyl-2-chlorobutane

> **Markovnikov's rule** *states that addition of a proton to the double bond of an alkene yields a product in which the proton is bonded to the carbon atom that already bears the greater number of hydrogens bonded.*

2. Hydration of alkenes to produce alcohols

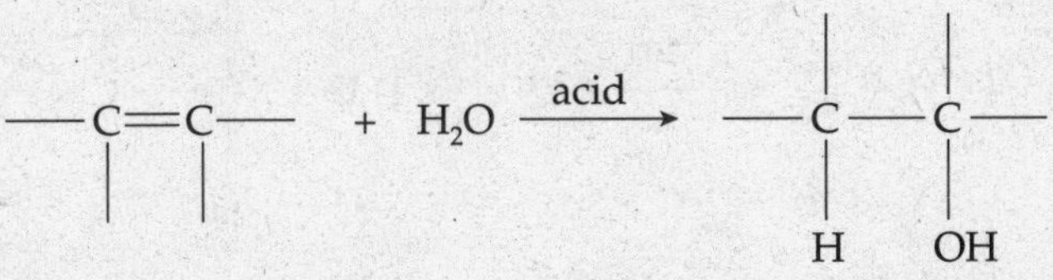

Example:

$$CH_3CH_2CH=CH_2 \ + \ H_2O \ \xrightarrow{H_2SO_4} \ H_3C-C-C-CH_3$$

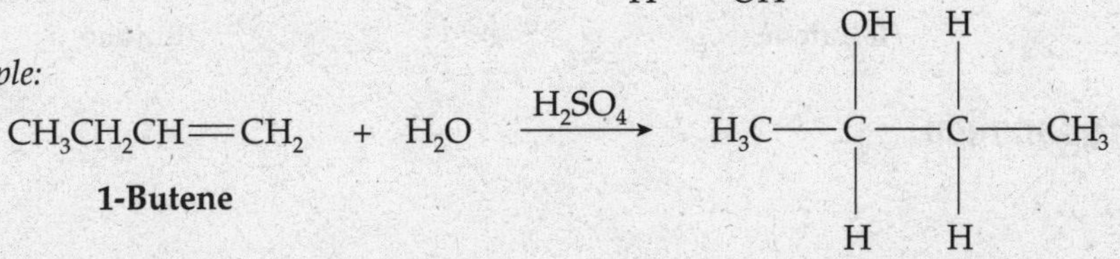

1-Butene

2-Butanol

3. Addition of H_2SO_4 to alkenes to produce alcohols

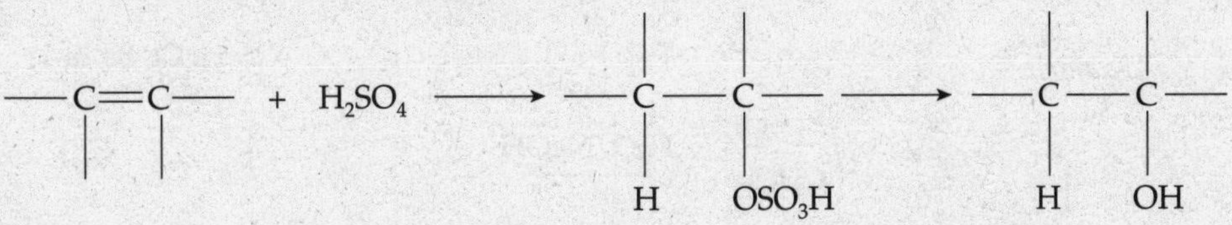

Example:

$$CH_3CH_2CH=CH_2 \ + \ H_2SO_4 \ \longrightarrow \ H_3C-C-C-CH_3$$

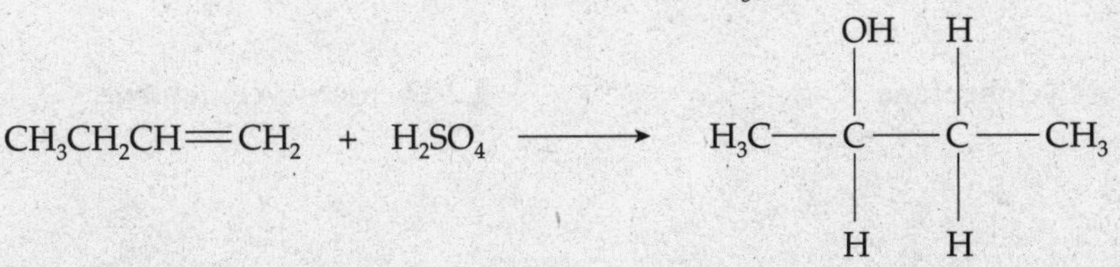

1-Butene

2-Butanol

4. Oxymercuration-demercuration of alkenes to produce alcohols

$$-\overset{|}{C}=\overset{|}{C}- \ + \ Hg(OAc)_2 \ \xrightarrow{H_2O} \ -\overset{|}{\underset{H}{C}}-\overset{|}{\underset{HgOAc}{C}}- \ \xrightarrow{NaBH_4} \ -\overset{|}{\underset{H}{C}}-\overset{|}{\underset{OH}{C}}-$$

Example:

$$CH_3CH_2CH{=}CH_2 \ + \ Hg(OAc)_2 \ \xrightarrow{H_2O/NaBH_4} \ H_3C{-}\overset{OH}{\underset{H}{C}}{-}\overset{H}{\underset{H}{C}}{-}CH_3$$

1-Butene   **2-Butanol**

5. Catalytic hydrogenation of alkenes to produce alkanes

$$-\overset{|}{C}=\overset{|}{C}- \ + \ H_2 \ \xrightarrow{Pt,\ Ni\ or\ Pd} \ -\overset{|}{\underset{H}{C}}-\overset{|}{\underset{H}{C}}-$$

Example:

$$CH_3CH_2CH{=}CH_2 \ + \ H_2 \ \xrightarrow{Pt} \ H_3C{-}\overset{H}{\underset{H}{C}}{-}\overset{H}{\underset{H}{C}}{-}CH_3$$

1-Butene   **Butane**

6. Cyclopropanation

$$-\overset{|}{C}=\overset{|}{C}- \ + \ \overset{X_1 \quad X_2}{\underset{\ddot{C}}{}} \ \longrightarrow \ \triangle\overset{X_1}{\underset{X_2}{}}$$

$X_1, X_2 = H, Cl, Br, or I$

Example:

Cycloheptene + $CHCl_3$ $\xrightarrow{H_2O/NaOH}$ 1,2-Dichlorocycloheptene (with two Cl)

Cycloheptene   **1,2-Dichlorocycloheptene**

7. Allylic substitution

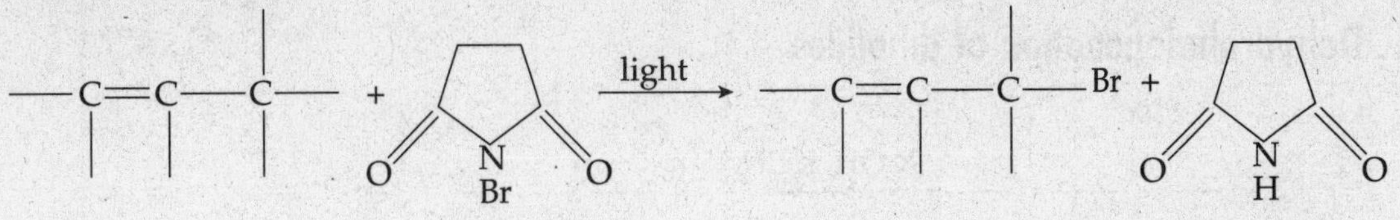

N-bromosuccinimide → Succinimide

Example:

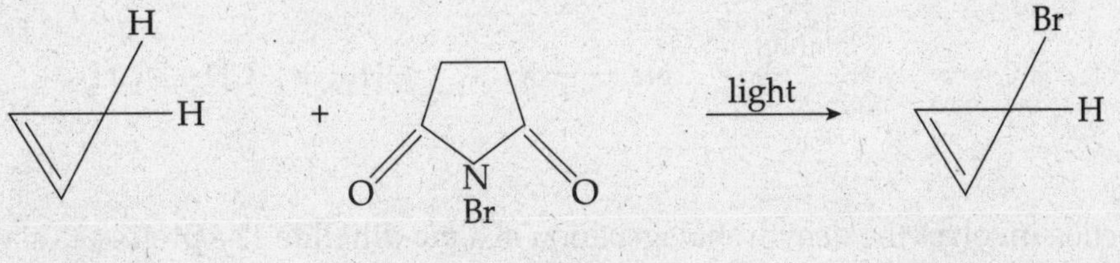

Cyclopropene   N-bromosuccinimide   3-bromocyclopropene

8. Ozonolysis of alkenes to produce carbonyl groups

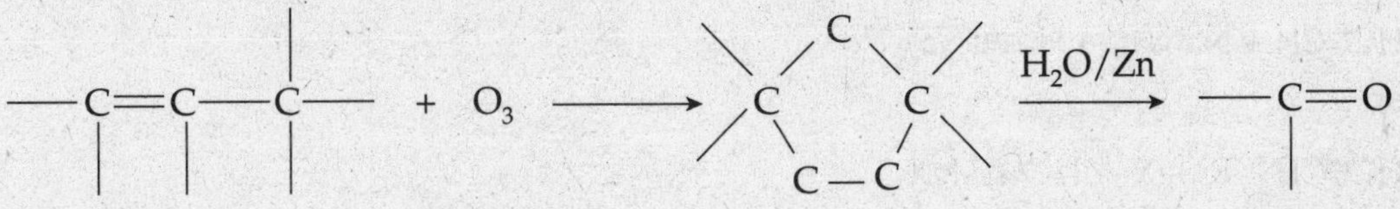

Ozonide

Carbonyls

ALKYNES

Alkynes are acyclic hydrocarbon chains with the general formula: C_nH_{2n-2}. They are characterized by **triple $C\equiv C$** bonds. The reactivity of alkynes is somewhat comparable to that of the alkenes. One of the most important alkynes is ethyne ($CH\equiv CH$), which is usually called acetylene.

As is the case for alkenes, an alkane can yield several alkynes, depending on where the triple bond is formed:

Example: Possible alkynes from hexane:

n-Hexane
$CH_3CH_2CH_2CH_2CH_2CH_3$

3-Hexyne
$CH_3CH_2C\equiv CCH_2CH_3$

4-Methyl-2-pentyne
$CH_3CHC\equiv CCH_3$
$\quad\quad |$
$\quad\quad CH_3$

1-Hexyne
$CH\equiv CCH_2CH_2CH_2CH_3$

i-**Hexane**
$CH_3CHCH_2CH_2CH_3$
$\quad |$
$\quad CH_3$

4-Methyl-1-pentyne
$CH_3CHCH_2C\equiv CH$
$\quad |$
$\quad CH_3$

2-Hexane
$CH_3C\equiv CCH_2CH_2CH_3$

PREPARATION OF ALKYNES

1. Dehydrohalogenation of dihalides

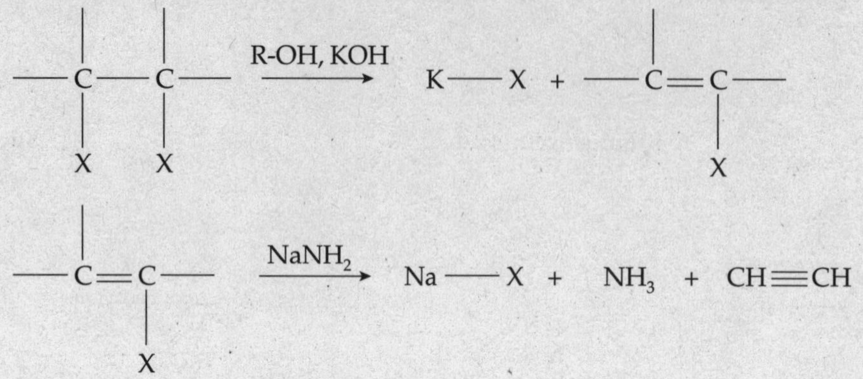

The above reaction involves the dehydrohalogenation of a ***vic*-dihalide**. The prefix *vic-* stands for *vicinal* and it describes in this case halogens on adjacent carbons. If the halogen molecules (X) are bound to the same carbon, the dihalide is then called a *geminal* or ***gem*-dihalide**. Alkynes can also be prepared by the dehydrohalogenation of *gem*-dihalides.

2. Alkyl Substitution

$HC \equiv CH + NaNH_2 \rightarrow HC \equiv CNa$

or

$HC \equiv CH + RMgX \rightarrow HC \equiv CMgX$

REACTIONS OF ALKYNES

1. Addition of hydrogen chloride across the triple bond

$HC \equiv CH + HCl \rightarrow CH_2 = CHCl$ (vinyl chloride)

2. Addition of hydrogen cyanide across the triple bond

$HC \equiv CH + HCN \rightarrow CH_2 = CHCN$ (acrilonitrile)

3. Addition of acetic acid across the triple bond

$HC \equiv CH + CH_3COOH \rightarrow 2CH_3 - CO - O - CH = CH_2$ (vinyl acetate)

4. Addition of alcohols (ROH) across the triple bond

$HC \equiv CH + ROH \rightarrow CH_2CHOR$ (alkylvinyl ether)

5. Hydration of the triple bond

$HC \equiv CH + CO + H_2O \rightarrow CH_2 = CH - COOH$ (propenoic acid)

6. Dimerization

$2\ HC \equiv CH \rightarrow H_2C = CHC \equiv CH$

DIENES

Some alkenes have more than one carbon double bond (C=C) in their formulas, for instance, **dienes**, which have **two C=C** bonds, or trienes with three and tetraenes with four. Some important dienes are:

$$CH_2 = CH — CH = CH_2$$
1,3-Butadiene

$$CH_2 = CCH_3 — CH = CH_2$$
2-Methyl-1,3-butadiene

$$CH_2 = CH — CH = CH — CH_3$$
1,3-Pentadiene

$$CH_2 = CH — CH_2 — CH = CH_2$$
1,4-Pentadiene

When double bonds are separated by only one single bond, they are said to be **conjugated**. If they are separated by more than one C–C bond, they are **isolated**. In the above examples, 1,3-butadiene, 2-methyl-1,3-butadiene and 1,3-pentadiene are all **conjugated dienes**. Compounds containing conjugated double bonds are more stable than ones that contain isolated bonds because the double bonds can interact with each other.

SYNTHESIS OF DIENES

1. Dehydration of diols

$$HOCH_2CH_2CH_2CH_2OH \xrightarrow{-2H_2O} CH_2=CH–CH=CH_2$$

2. Dehydrogenation of alkanes (see p. tktk)

3. Dehydrogenation of alkenes

$$CH_2=CHCH_2CH_3 \xrightarrow{-2H_2} CH_2=CH–CH=CH$$

4. Dehydrohalogenation of dihalides

$$CH_3CHXCH_2CH_2X \xrightarrow{+R-OH/KOH} CH_2=CH–CH=CH_2$$

REACTIONS OF DIENES

1. Addition of hydrogen
$$CH_2=CH–CH=CH_2 + 2H_2 \rightarrow CH_3CH_2CH_2CH$$

2. Diels-Alder reaction

$$CH_2 = CH — CH = CH_2 + CH_2 = CH_2 \xrightarrow{heat}$$

1,3-Butadiene   **Ethylene**   **Cyclohexene**

ALKYL HALIDES

When an alkane loses a hydrogen, the hydrogen can be replaced by a halogen atom (F, Cl, Br, I), so that a compound known as an **alkyl halide** is formed. Alkyl halides are usually abbreviated **RX**, with X = F, Cl, Br, or I.

PREPARATION OF ALKYL HALIDES

1. Alcohol (ROH) + HX

$$R-OH + HX \rightarrow RX + H_2O$$

2. Alcohol + PX₃

$$3R-OH + PX_3 \rightarrow 3RX + H_3PO_3$$

3. Addition of HX to alkenes

$$R_1-CH=CH-R_2 + HX \rightarrow R_1-CH_2-CHX-R_2$$

Example: $CH_3CH=CH_2 + HI \rightarrow CH_3-CHI-CH_3$

4. Halogenation of alkanes with Cl₂ or Br₂

$$RH + X_2 \rightarrow R_x + HX$$

REACTIONS OF ALKYL HALIDES

1. Synthesis of higher alkanes

Step 1. $R-CH_2-X + 2Na \rightarrow R-CH_2-Na + NaX$

Step 2. $R-CH_2-Na + X-CH_2-R \rightarrow R-CH_2-CH_2-R + NaX$

2. Synthesis of R—OH using NaOH

$$R-CH_2-X + NaOH \rightarrow R-CH_2-OH + NaX$$

3. Elimination

$$R-CH_2-X + KOH \xrightarrow{\text{ethanol}} RCH=CH_2$$

4. Synthesis of Grignard Reagents (GR)

$$RX + Mg \xrightarrow{\text{ether}} RMgX$$

Example: $CH_3Br + Mg \rightarrow CH_3MgBr$

USE OF GRIGNARD REAGENTS

- Formaldehyde + GR → primary alcohol

$$H_2C=O + CH_3MgX \rightarrow CH_3-CH_2-(O^-MgX)^+ + H_2O \rightarrow CH_3-CH_2OH + MgX(OH)$$

- Aldehyde + GR → secondary alcohol

$$RCOH + R'MgX \rightarrow RCH(O^-MgX^+)R' + H_2O \rightarrow RCH(OH)R' + MgX(OH)$$

- Ketone + GR → tertiary alcohol

$$RCOR' + R''MgX \rightarrow RR'R''C(O^-MgX^+) + H_2O \rightarrow RR'R''COH + MgX(OH)$$

- Nitrile + GR → ketone

$$RC\equiv N + R'MgX \rightarrow RC=N(MgX)R' + H_2O \rightarrow RCOR' + NH_3 + MgX(OH)$$

- Carbon dioxide + GR → carboxylic acid

$$CO_2 + RMgX \rightarrow RCOOMgX + HCl \rightarrow RCOOH + MgXCl$$

ALCOHOLS

An alcohol is defined as a compound that has an **–OH functional group** bound to a carbon. The alcohols of alkanes are saturated, acyclic compounds with general formula $C_nH_{2n+1}OH$ and are abbreviated **ROH**. If the –OH group is bound to an aromatic carbon, the compound is a **phenol**, abbreviated **ArOH**:

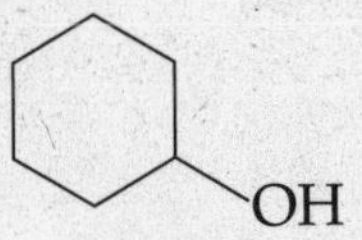

Cyclohexanol 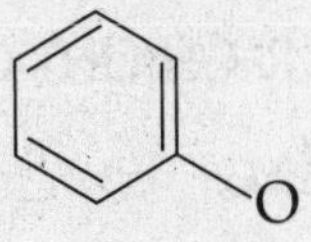   **Phenol**

- Depending on the location of the –OH group, alcohols are called

| Primary | R–CH$_2$(OH) | Ex: CH$_3$CH$_2$OH (ethanol) |

Secondary $R_1 \longrightarrow C(OH) \longrightarrow R_2$ Ex: $CH_3CHOHCH_2CH_3$ (2-butanol)

$$| \atop H$$

Tertiary $R_1 \longrightarrow C(OH) \longrightarrow R_2$ Ex: $(CH_3)_3COH$ (2-methyl-2-propanol)

$$| \atop R_3$$

- A primary alcohol has its –OH group bound to a primary carbon, ie, a carbon that's bound to only one other C atom.

- A secondary alcohol has its –OH group bound to a secondary carbon, ie, a carbon bound to only two other C atoms.

- A tertiary alcohol has its –OH group bound to a tertiary carbon, ie, a carbon bound to three other C atoms.

When alcohols have triple and double carbon bonds, they are named by adding the suffix –ol to the corresponding alkene/alkyne name so that the lowest carbon number is that to which the –OH group is attached:

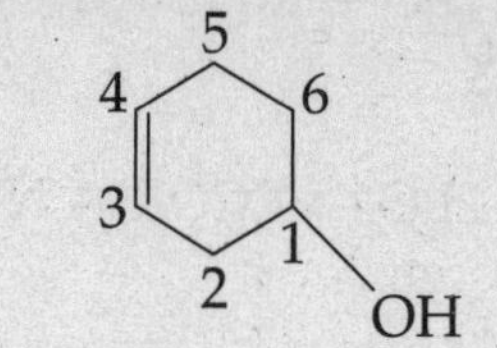

3-Cyclohexene-1-ol 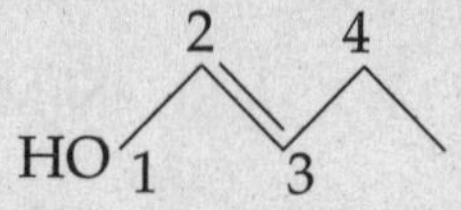   *trans*-**2-Penten-1-ol**

- The proton of the –OH group of alcohols is weakly acidic and can be removed by a strong base to yield an **alkoxide ion**:

$$H-\overset{\cdot\cdot}{\underset{\cdot\cdot}{O}}-H \ + \ B\overset{\cdot\cdot}{:}^- \ \rightleftharpoons \ R-\overset{\cdot\cdot}{\underset{\cdot\cdot}{O}}\overset{\cdot\cdot}{:}^- \ + \ B$$
  alcohol   base   alkoxide ion

SYNTHESIS OF ALCOHOLS

1. Hydration of alkenes

$$R\text{–}CH=CH_2 + H\text{–}OH \rightarrow R\text{–}CH(OH)\text{–}CH_3$$

2. Hydrolysis of alkyl halides

$$RX + OH^- \rightarrow ROH + X^-$$

3. Preparation from Grignard Reagents (GR)

- Formaldehyde + GR → primary alcohol

$$H_2C=O + CH_3MgX \rightarrow CH_3\text{–}CH_2\text{–}(O^-MgX)^+ + H_2O \rightarrow CH_3\text{–}CH_2OH + MgX(OH)$$

- Aldehyde + GR → secondary alcohol

$$RCOH + R'MgX \rightarrow RCH(O^-MgX^+)R' + H_2O \rightarrow RCH(OH)R' + MgX(OH)$$

- Ketone + GR → tertiary alcohol

$$RCOR' + R''MgX \rightarrow RR'R''C(O^-MgX^+) + H_2O \rightarrow RR'R''COH + MgX(OH)$$

4. Oxymercuration-demercuration of alkenes

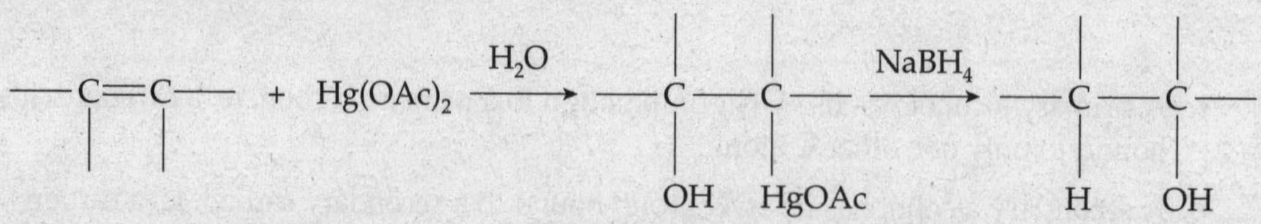

Example:

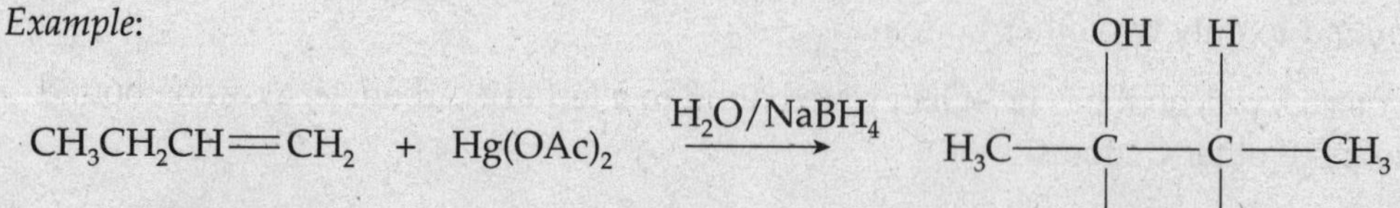

$$CH_3CH_2CH=CH_2 + Hg(OAc)_2 \xrightarrow{H_2O/NaBH_4} $$

1-Butene

2-Butanol

5. Hydroboration-oxidation of alkenes

$$RCH{=}CH_2 + (BH_3)_2 \rightarrow (RCHCH_2)_3{-}B + H_2O_2/OH^- \rightarrow RCHCH_2$$
$$\qquad\qquad\qquad\qquad\quad | \qquad\qquad\qquad\qquad\qquad | \;\; |$$
$$\qquad\qquad\qquad\qquad\; H \qquad\qquad\qquad\qquad\qquad H \;\; OH$$

REACTIONS OF ALCOHOLS

1. Oxidation of primary alcohols to carboxylic acids

$$R{-}CH_2{-}OH + \xrightarrow[\text{H}_2\text{SO}_4]{\text{Na}_2\text{Cr}_2\text{O}_7} R{-}COOH$$

2. Oxidation of primary alcohols to aldehydes

$$R{-}CH_2{-}OH \xrightarrow[\text{pyridine}]{\text{CrO}_3} R{-}COH$$

3. Oxidation of secondary alcohols to ketones

$$R_1{-}C(OH){-}R_2 \xrightarrow[\text{H}_2\text{SO}_4]{\text{Na}_2\text{Cr}_2\text{O}_7} R_1{-}COOR_2$$
$$\qquad\quad |$$
$$\qquad\quad H$$

4. Reduction of alcohols to alkanes

$$R{-}OH \xrightarrow{\text{LiAlH}_4,\ \text{TiCl}_4} R{-}H$$

5. Synthesis of alkyl halides

$$R{-}OH + HX \rightarrow R{-}X$$

6. Dehydration to alkenes

7. Dehydration to ethers

$$2R{-}OH + H^+ \rightarrow R{-}O{-}R + H_2O$$

8. Tosylation

tosyl chloride   alkyl tosylate

9. Acylation

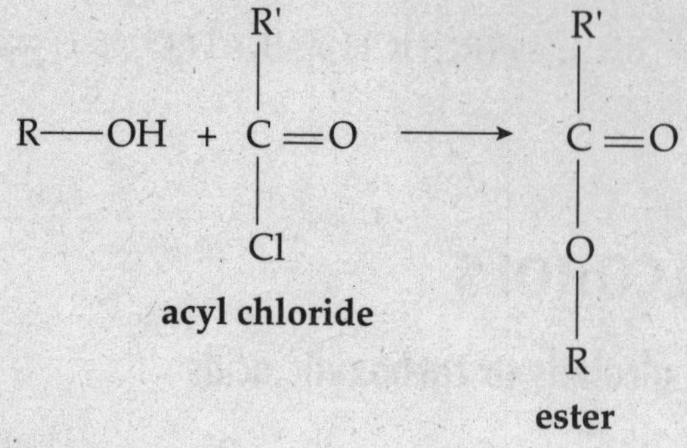

$$R\text{---}OH \; + \; \underset{\substack{| \\ Cl}}{\overset{\substack{R' \\ |}}{C}}=O \; \longrightarrow \; \underset{\substack{| \\ O \\ | \\ R}}{\overset{\substack{R' \\ |}}{C}}=O$$

acyl chloride   **ester**

10. Deprotonation to alkoxide

R–OH + Na → R–O$^-$ $^+$Na

R–OH + K → R–O$^-$ $^+$K

Example: CH_3CH_2–OH + K → K$^+$$^-OCH_2CH_3$ (potassium ethoxide)

THIOLS

Thiols or **mercaptans** have an **–SH (sulfhydryl) functional group** bound to a carbon. Their general formula is $C_nH_{2n+1}SH$, and they are abbreviated **RSH**.

Examples:

$CH_3CH(CH_3)CH_2CH_2SH$ 3-methyl-1-butanethiol

$CH_3CH=CHCH_2CH_2SH$ 3-pentene-1-thiol

SYNTHESIS OF THIOLS

1. From alkyl halides and HS⁻

RX + HS$^-$ → X$^-$ + RSH

2. From disulfides

R–S–S–R (+ Li and liquid NH$_3$) → RSH

3. From alkenes

R′CH=CH$_2$ + H$_2$S (+ RO$^-$) → RSH

REACTIONS OF THIOLS

1. Synthesis of thioesters

RSH + R′–COCl → R′–COSR

2. Synthesis of thioethers

RSH + OH$^-$ + R′X → R–S–R′

3. Synthesis of thioacetals

RSH + R′–CH=O → R′–CH(SR$_2$)

4. Synthesis of sulfonic acids

RSH + KMnO$_4$ → R–SO$_3$H

ETHERS

Ethers can either be **simple** ethers, **R-O-R** or **Ar-O-Ar**, when the R or Ar groups are identical, or **mixed** ethers, **R-O-R'** or **Ar-O-Ar'** or **R-O-Ar**, when the groups bonded to the oxygen are not the same. For the most part, they are named by using the names of the R or Ar group to which is added "ether." The IUPAC nomenclature names ethers as substituted alkanes.

$$CH_3CH_2OCH_2CH_3$$
diethyl ether

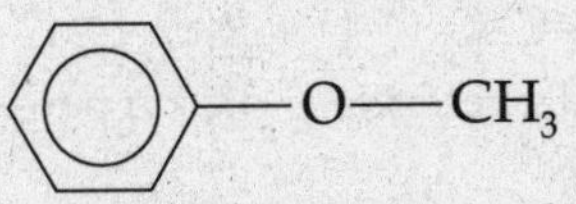

methyl phenyl ether

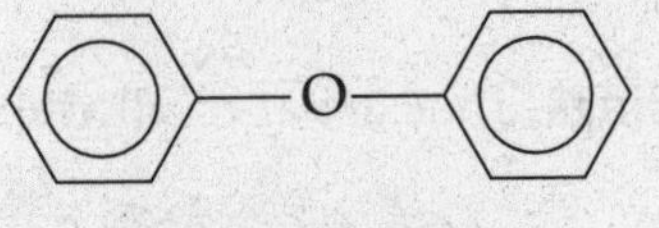

diphenyl ether

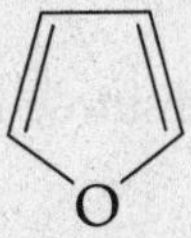

furan

tetrahydrofuran

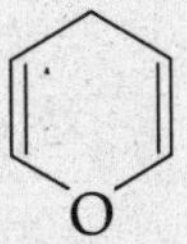

pyran

SYNTHESIS OF ETHERS

1. Williamson synthesis

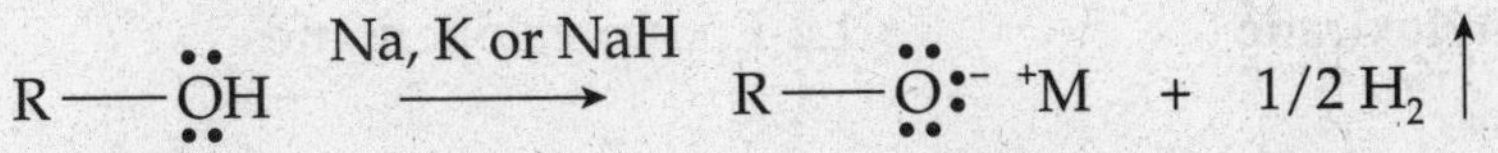

$$R - \overset{..}{\underset{..}{O}}H \xrightarrow{\text{Na, K or NaH}} R - \overset{..}{\underset{..}{O}}:^- {}^+M \ + \ 1/2\,H_2 \uparrow$$

alcohol   **alkoxide**

$$R - \overset{..}{\underset{..}{O}}:^- \qquad R' - \overset{..}{\underset{..}{X}}: \longrightarrow R - \overset{..}{\underset{..}{O}} - R' \ + \ \overset{..}{\underset{..}{X}}:^-$$

alkyl halide or tosylate   **ether**

Example: $(CH_3)_3 - OH \xrightarrow{\text{Na}} (CH_3)_3 - O^- {}^+K \xrightarrow{CH_3CH_2CH_2Br} (CH_3)_3 - OCH_2CH_2CH_3$

2. Intermolecular dehydration

$$2ROH + H_2SO_4 \rightarrow ROR + H_2O \quad \text{(R is primary)}$$

REACTIONS OF ETHERS

1. Cleavage by HBr or HI

$$ROR' + HX \rightarrow RX + R'X \qquad\qquad X = Br \text{ or } I$$

The reaction occurs in two steps:

Step 1:   ROR' + HX → RR'OH → RX + R'OH

Step 2:   ROH + HX → RX + R'X

2. Oxidation to peroxides

RO–C–H + O_2 → RO–C–O–O–H + R–O–O–C–H

                         hydroperoxide   dialkyl peroxide

EPOXIDES

Epoxides are **cyclic ethers** with **three-membered rings.** They are also called **oxiranes.**

Examples:

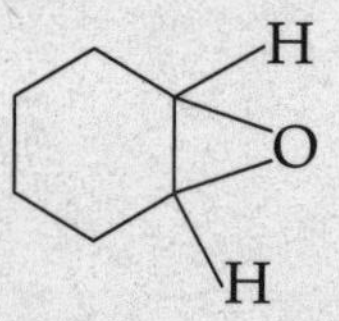

Epoxycyclohexane 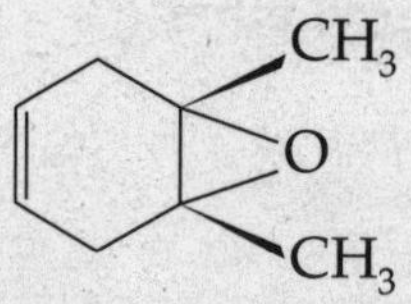   *cis*-**4,5-Epoxy-4,5-dimethylcyclohexene**

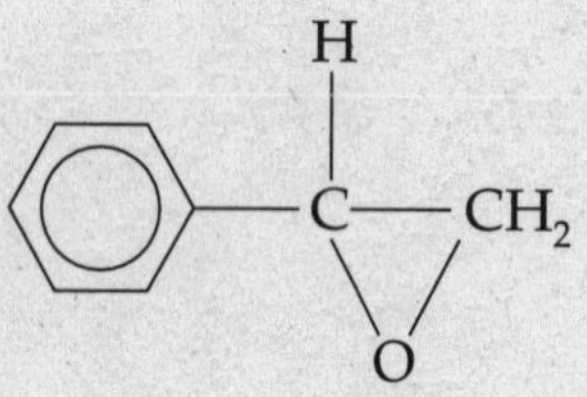

1-Phenyloxirane 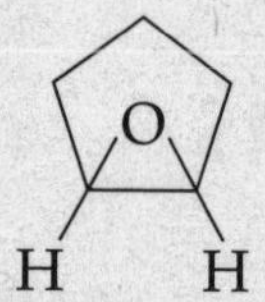   **1,2-Epoxycyclopentane**

SYNTHESIS OF EPOXIDES

1. Peroxyacid epoxidation

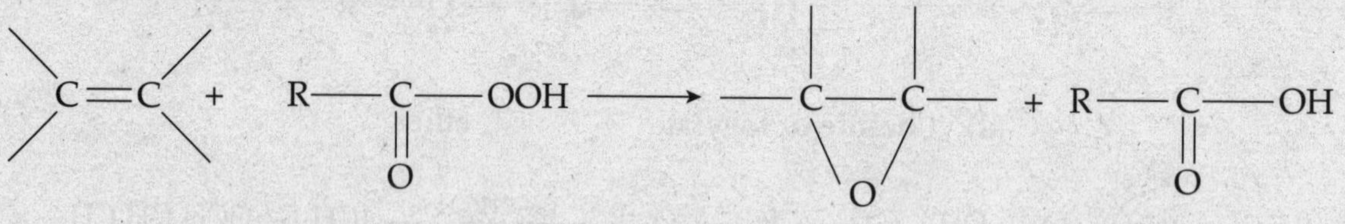

2. From halohydrins

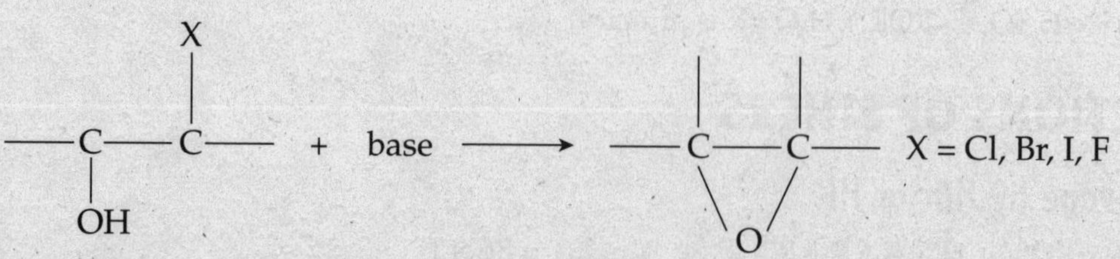

X = Cl, Br, I, F

REACTIONS OF EPOXIDES

1. Acid-catalyzed cleavage

with H_2O:

$$\xrightarrow{H^+/H_2O}$$ *anti*-diol

with ROH:

$$\xrightarrow{H^+/ROH}$$

with hydrohalic acids:

$$\xrightarrow{H-X} \qquad \xrightarrow{H-X}$$

2. Base-catalyzed cleavage

with alkoxides:

$$\xrightarrow{RO-}$$

with organometallic compounds:

$$\xrightarrow{R-M/H_2O}$$

SULFIDES

Sulfides or **thioethers** contain a sulfur atom between R groups. They are abbreviated **R–S–R** and, like ethers, they can be simple or mixed, depending on whether the R groups are identical or not.

Examples:

$CH_3SCH_2CH_3$ ethyl methyl sulfide

CH_3SCH_3 dimethyl sulfide

$CH_3CH_2SCH_2CH_3$ diethyl sulfide

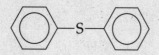 diphenyl sulfide

SYNTHESIS OF SULFIDES

Williamson displacement of RS

Step 1: $RSH + NaOH \rightarrow RS^-$

Step 2: $RS^- + R'X \rightarrow R-S-R' + NaX$

REACTIONS OF SULFIDES

1. Synthesis of sulfonium salts

$R-S-R + R'Br \rightarrow R_2R'S:^+X^-$

Example: $(CH_3)_2S: + CH_3CH_2:Br \rightarrow [(CH_3)_2SCH_2CH_3]^+Br^-$

2. Hydrogenolysis

$R-S-R' + H_2 \xrightarrow{\text{Raney Ni catalyst}} RH + R'H + H_2S$

AROMATIC COMPOUNDS

Aromatic compounds are **cyclic, unsaturated** compounds that have **conjugated** double bonds. The archetypal aromatic compound is benzene (C_6H_6).

As shown above, benzene, as was first proposed by Kekulé consists of a cyclic structure with alternating double bonds. But double bonds are shorter than single bonds, so this picture was modified to account for the fact that the carbon bonds in benzene are all the same length (1.397 Å) by introducing the **resonance** representation, in which the π electrons are assumed to be delocalized over the whole ring. This also explained some of the unexpected properties of benzene and its derivatives, such as its low degree of reactivity and resistance to oxidation.

But the resonance model could not fully account for the unusual stability of the benzene ring. To understand further reasons for its stability requires **molecular orbital theory**, which includes a description of π-electron delocalization.

According to this view, benzene is a planar ring consisting of six sp^2 hybridized carbon atoms, each s-bonded to two carbon neighbors and one hydrogen. Each carbon also has an electron in a p orbital, perpendicular to the plane of the ring. These p orbitals overlap with adjacent p orbitals to form a π-bonding system above and below the plane of the ring:

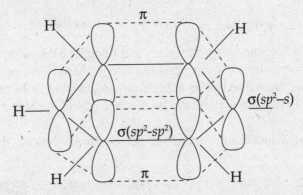

The six p orbitals form six π molecular orbitals. The lowest in energy are the bonding orbitals that contain the six π electrons.

The higher energy antibonding orbitals π^* in the diagram below are empty. The distribution of π electrons over the bonding p orbitals makes them **delocalized** over all six carbon atoms. This configuration of completely filled bonding orbitals is energetically very favorable and is what confers on benzene its stability and resulting chemical properties.

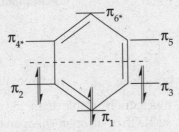

AROMATICITY

Molecular orbital theory accounts for the properties of benzene and also for the properties of any compound designated as having **aromatic character**. That term implies the following:

- A cyclic structure with conjugated π bonds containing unhybridized p orbitals that can overlap with other ring carbons to form the delocalized pi electron system.

- Delocalization of the π-electron system lowers the total electronic energy.

- The structure can be described by **Hückel's rule**:

A compound is aromatic *if the number of its π electrons is equal to 2+4n where n is zero or an integer and represents filled electron shells. For* n = 0, 1, or 2, *aromatic systems have 2, 6, and 10 π electrons.*

Examples:

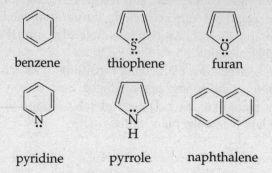

benzene   thiophene   furan

pyridine   pyrrole   naphthalene

In the above examples, pyridine, pyrrole, furan, and thiophene are heterocyclic compounds with an aromatic character. Pyrrole has six π electrons and two unshared electrons on the N atom overlap in the π system. Likewise, furan also has six π electrons, and two electrons on the O atom overlap in the π system of the ring. In the case of pyridine, the electron pair of the N atom does not overlap with the π electron system.

When the π electron delocalization increases the electronic energy, the compound is called **antiaromatic**.

A compound is antiaromatic *if the number of its π electrons is equal to 4n where n is an integer. For* n = 1, 2, or 3, *antiaromatic systems have 4, 8, and 12 π electrons.*

Example:

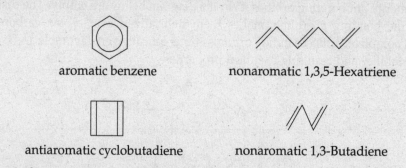

aromatic benzene   nonaromatic 1,3,5-Hexatriene

antiaromatic cyclobutadiene   nonaromatic 1,3-Butadiene

The aromatic benzene ring is much more stable than its open chain analog; however, the antiaromatic cyclobutadiene is less stable than its open chain analog.

Applying Huckel's rule to cyclobutadiene yields the following: it has four sp^2 hybrid carbons and four overlapping unhybridized *p*-orbitals. The structure has two double bonds; therefore it has four π electrons and 4n = 4 with *n* = 1; it is antiaromatic.

Benzene has six sp^2 hybrid carbons and six overlapping unhybridized *p* orbitals. The structure has three double bonds, so six π electrons and 6 = 4*n* + 2; it is aromatic.

Cyclooctatetraene has eight sp^2 hybrid carbons and eight overlapping unhybridized *p* orbitals. It has four double bonds, so eight π electrons and should be a 4*n* system with *n* = 2 and an antiaromatic character. But it does exhibit antiaromatic unstability and is clearly not aromatic. In fact, it is nonaromatic and has a folded ring shape that prevents good overlap of the π-bond system. This has been confirmed by experiments in which it behaves as an alkene.

SOME BENZENE DERIVATIVES

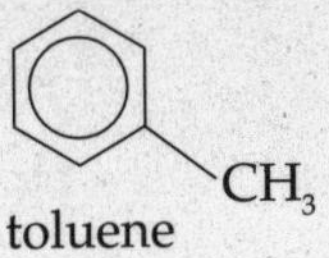

toluene

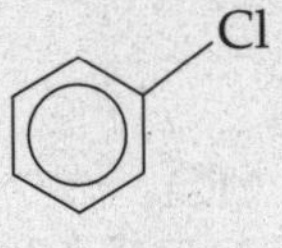

chlorobenzene

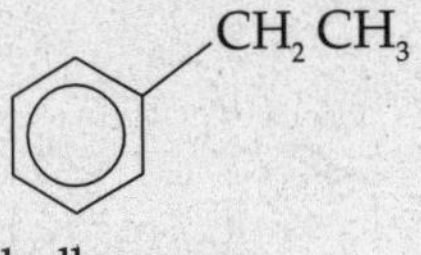

ethylbenzene

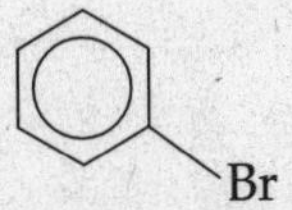

Bromobenzene

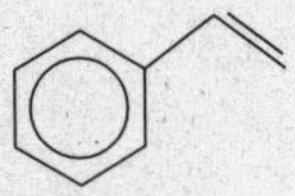

styrene

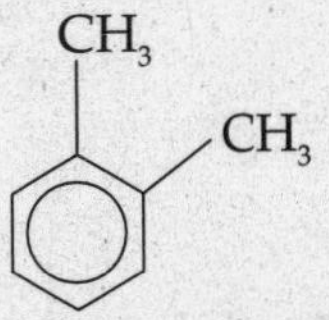

1,2-dimethylbenzene

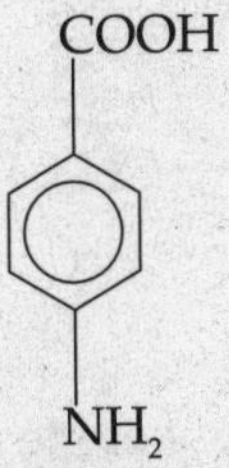

p-aminobenzoic acid

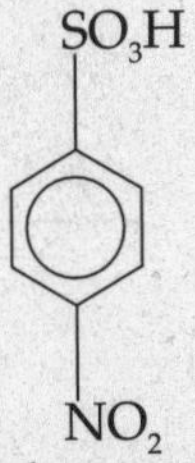

p-nitrobenzenesulfonic acid

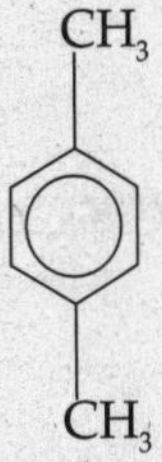

p-xylene

REACTIONS OF BENZENE AND ITS DERIVATIVES

1. Halogenation

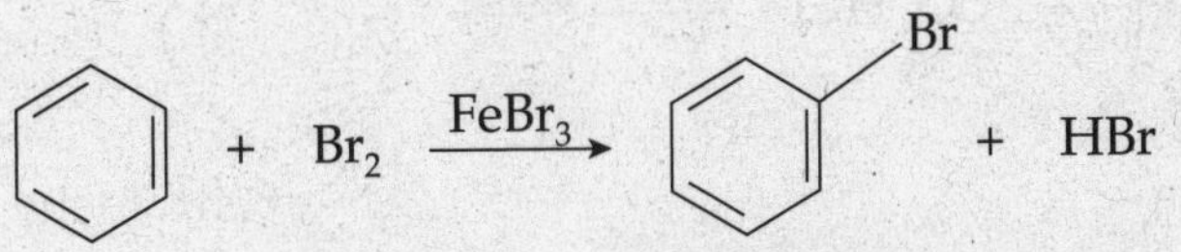

Benzene $+ Br_2 \xrightarrow{FeBr_3}$ Bromobenzene $+ HBr$

2. Nitration

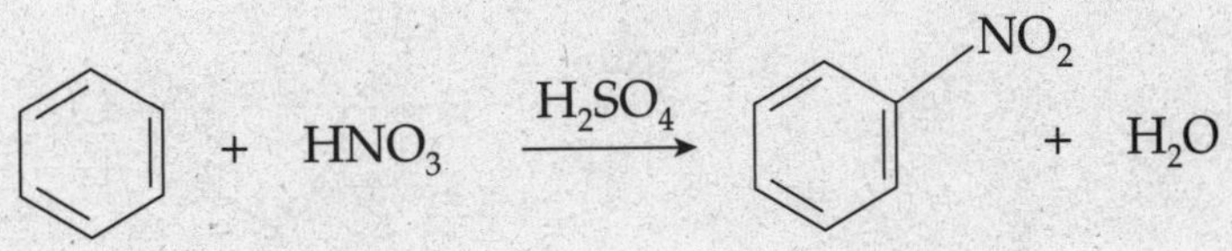

Benzene $+ HNO_3 \xrightarrow{H_2SO_4}$ Nitrobenzene $+ H_2O$

3. Sulfonation

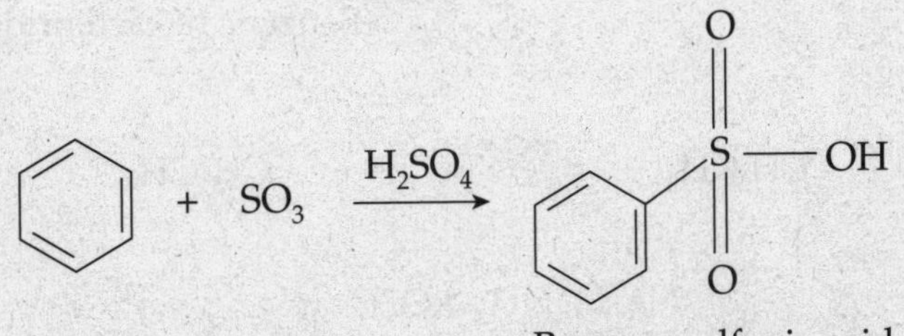

Benzene $+ SO_3 \xrightarrow{H_2SO_4}$ Benzenesulfonic acid

4. Alkylation (Friedel-Crafts)

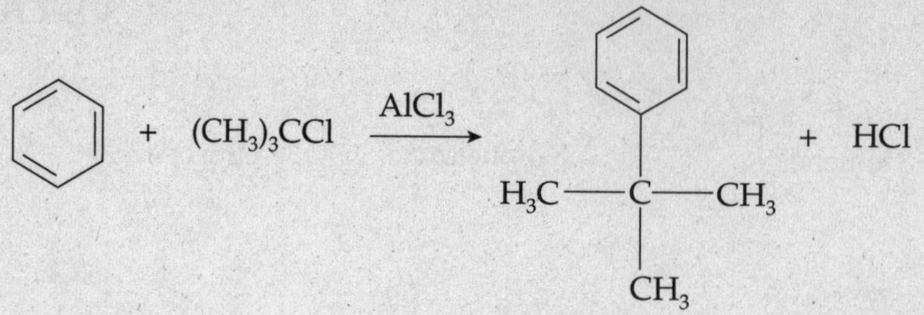

t-Butylbenzene

5. Acylation (Friedel-Crafts)

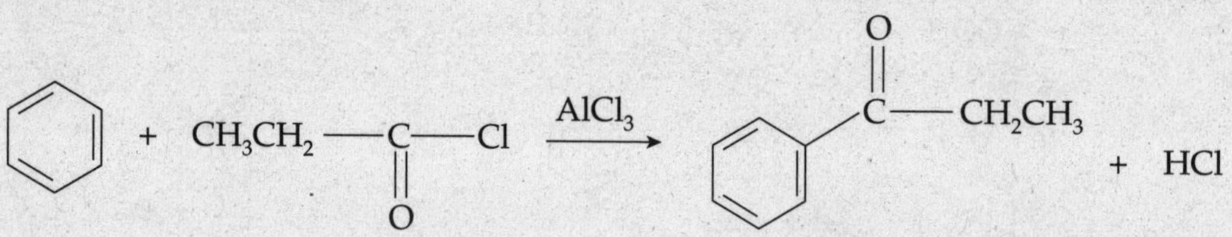

Phenyl ethyl ketone

6. Gatterman-Koch synthesis

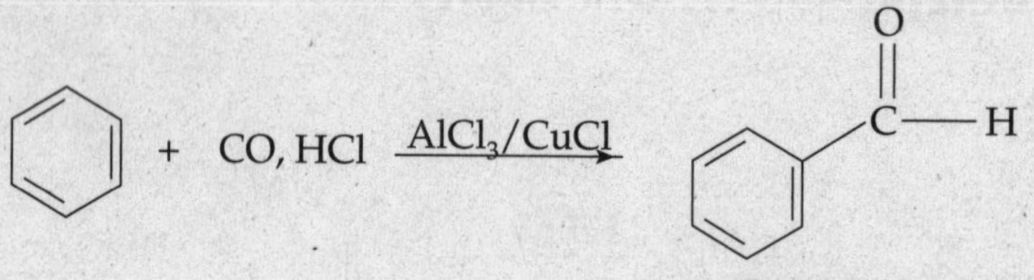

Benzaldehyde

7. Chlorination

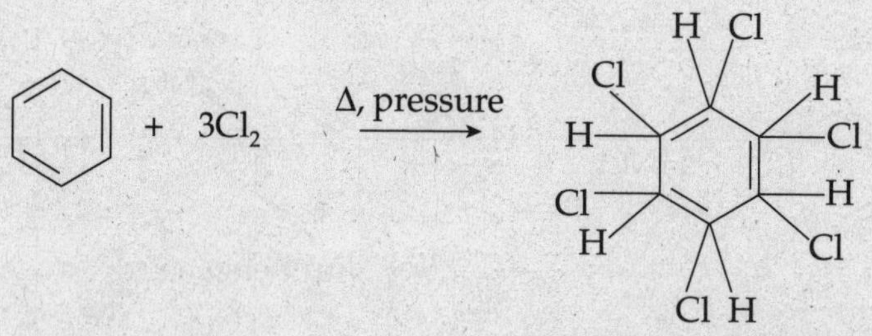

Hexachlorocyclohexane
(Benzene hexachloride)

8. Birch reduction

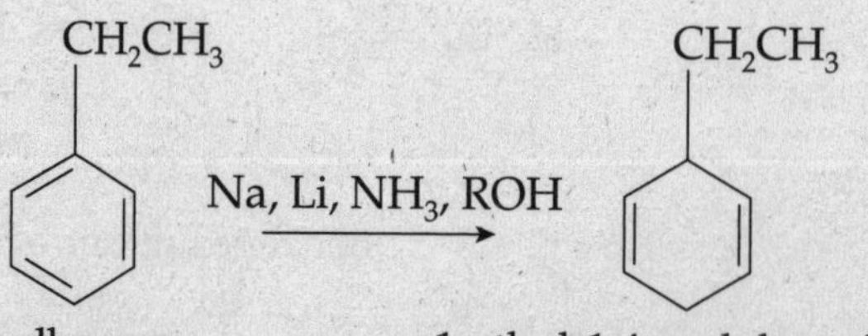

ethylbenzene   1-ethyl-1,4-cyclohexadiene

9. Catalyzed hydrogenation

o-diethylbenzene + 3H$_2$ $\xrightarrow{\text{Ru/Rh, }\Delta\text{ + pressure}}$ 1,2-diethylcyclohexane

10. Clemmensen reaction

acylbenzene $\xrightarrow{\text{Zn, Hg/HCl}}$ alkylbenzene

11. Oxidation by KMnO$_4$

alkylbenzene $\xrightarrow{\text{KMnO}_4/\text{H}_2\text{O}}$ benzoic acid salt

12. Halogenation of side chain

alkylbenzene $\xrightarrow{\text{X}_2\text{, light}}$ halogenated alkylbenzene

13. Hydrogenolysis of alcohols

benzyl alcohol $\xrightarrow{\text{H}_2/\text{Pd}}$ toluene

14. Hydrogenolysis of ethers

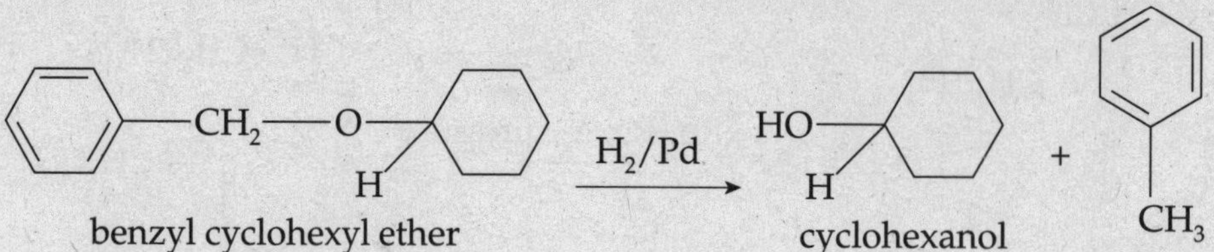

benzyl cyclohexyl ether $\xrightarrow{H_2/Pd}$ cyclohexanol + toluene

ALDEHYDES

Aldehydes, abbreviated **RCOH**, contain a **carbonyl (C=O)** functional group bonded to **one alkyl or aryl group and a hydrogen**. The IUPAC names of aldehydes are obtained by replacing the final "e" in alkanes by the suffix *–al* (for one C=O group) or *–dial* (for two C=O groups). Carbons are numbered starting with the carbonyl C, which is assigned 1. Common names are derived from carboxylic acid IUPAC names, replacing the suffixes *–ic, –oic* or *–oxylic acid* by *–aldehyde*. Greek letters are used to identify the carbons; the first after the C=O group is the α carbon, and the second is the β carbon, etc.

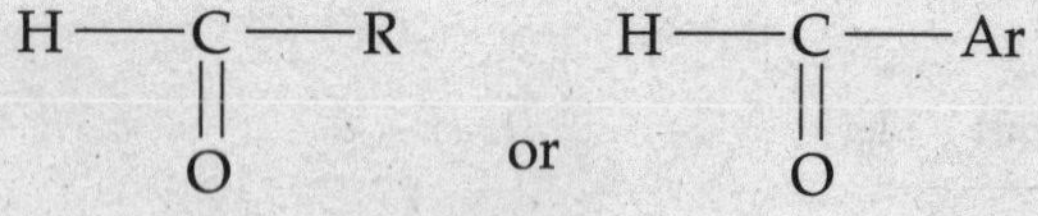

aldehyde

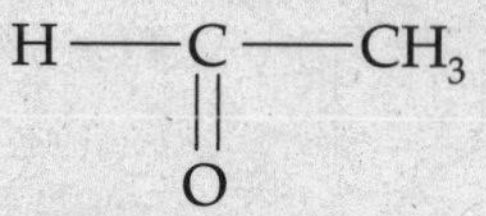

acetaldehyde
(ethanal)

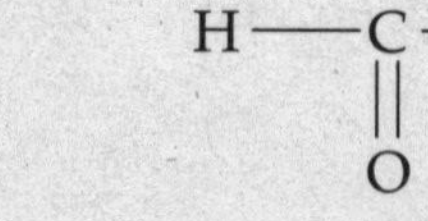

formaldehyde

propionaldehyde
(propanal)

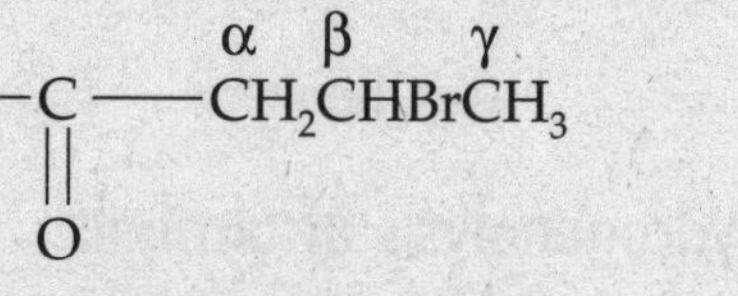

β-methylbutyraldehyde
(3-methylbutanal)

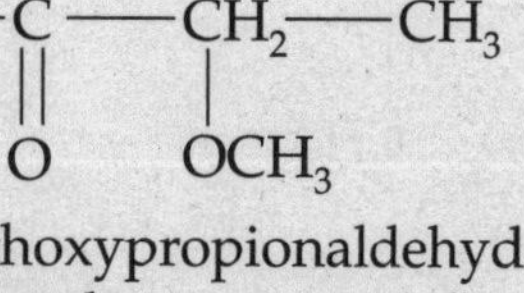

benzaldehyde

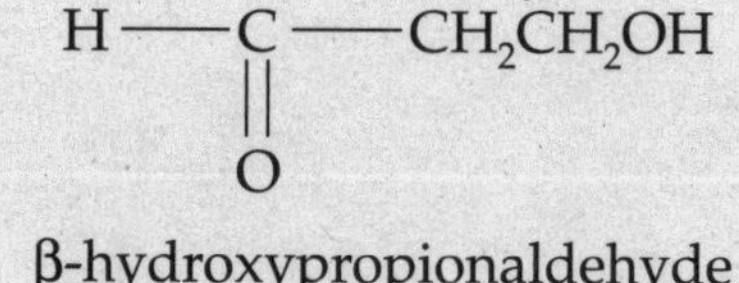

β-bromobutyraldehyde
(3-Bromobutanal)

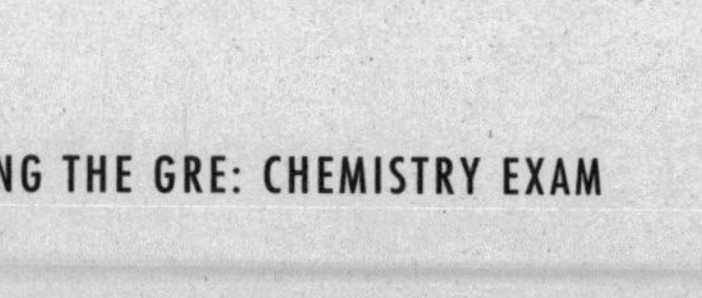

α-methoxypropionaldehyde
(2-methyoxypropanal)

β-hydroxypropionaldehyde
(3-hydroxypropanal)

The chemistry of aldehydes is governed by the carbonyl group, in which the carbon is sp^2–hybridized. It is σ–bonded to oxygen, hydrogen and to an R atom in one plane, and the unhybridized π orbital overlaps with an oxygen p orbital to form a π bond in a plane perpendicular to the σ bond network. Oxygen is more electronegative than carbon; so π electron density is greater on the oxygen. This confers a partial positive charge on the carbon and a large dipole moment (~ 2.7 Debye) on the C=O bond):

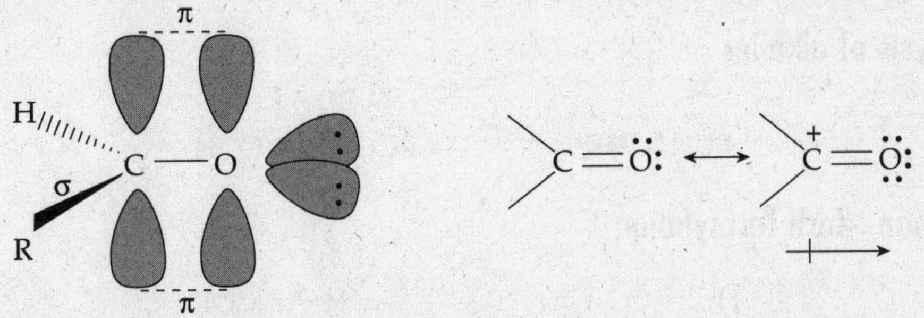

Aldehydes are very reactive: the carbon can act as an electrophile and the oxygen as a nucleophile, because of its two nonbonding pairs of electrons

ACIDITY AND BASICITY OF ALDEHYDES

The electronic properties of the carbonyl group allow it to react either as an acid or a base; it is **amphoteric**. This means that it acts as a base when the oxygen nonbonding electrons bond with a H$^+$ or other positive species, and as an acid when the partial positive charge of the carbon accepts a pair of electrons from a nucleophile.

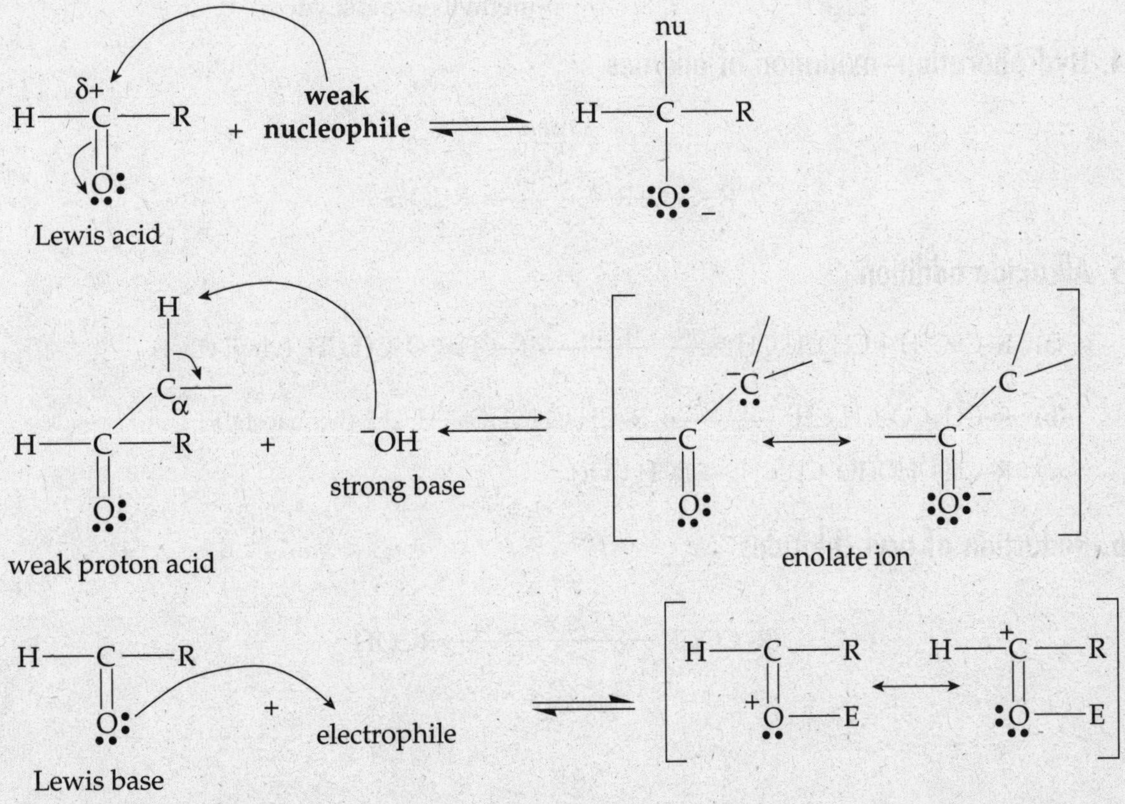

SYNTHESIS OF ALDEHYDES

1. Oxidation of primary alcohols

$$R-CH_2OH \xrightarrow[\text{H}]{\text{K}_2\text{Cr}_2\text{O}_7} RCOH$$

2. Ozonolysis of alkenes

$$RCH=CHR \xrightarrow[\text{(CH}_3)_2\text{S}]{\text{O}_3} RCOH + R'COH$$

3. Gatterman–Koch formylation

$$HCl + CO + Ar-H^+ \xrightarrow{\text{AlCl}_3} H-Ar-COH$$

Example:

toluene   CO, HCl, AlCl₃   *p*-methylbenzaldehyde

4. Hydroboration–oxidation of alkynes

$$R-C\equiv C-R \xrightarrow[\text{NaOH}]{\substack{(1)\ \text{BH}_3 \\ (2)\ \text{THF} \\ \text{H}_2\text{O}_2}} RCOH$$

5. Alkoxide addition

(a) $R-C\equiv C-H + CH_3CH_2OH \xrightarrow{\text{(NaOCH}_2\text{CH}_3)} R-CH\equiv CO-CH_2CH_3$ (vinyl ether)

(b) $R-CH\equiv CO-CH_2CH_3 \xrightarrow{\text{(H}_3\text{O}^+)} R-CH_2CHOHO-CH_2CH_3$ (hemiacetal)

(c) $R-CH_2CHOHO-CH_2CH_3 \rightarrow RCH_2COH$

6. Reduction of acyl chlorides

$$R-COCl \xrightarrow{\text{(H}_2,\ \text{Pd},\ \text{BaSO}_4,\ \text{S})} RCOH$$

REACTIONS OF ALDEHYDES

1. Hydration

$$RCOH + H_2O \rightarrow RCH(OH)_2 \qquad \text{(hydrate)}$$

2. Addition of Grignard reagent

$$RCOH + R'MgX \rightarrow RCHR' \qquad \text{(OMgX)}$$

3. Reduction

a) $RCOH + NaBH_4/LiAlH_4 \rightarrow RCHHO^- \qquad$ (alkoxide)

b) $RCHHO^- + H^+ \rightarrow ROH \qquad$ (alcohol)

4. Synthesis of cyanohydrins

$$RCOH + HCN \rightarrow RCHOHCN \qquad \text{(cyanohydrin)}$$

5. Synthesis of imines

$$RCOH + R'NH_2 \rightarrow RCH=NR + H_2O \quad \text{(imine or Schiff base)}$$

6. Synthesis of oximes

$$RCOH + H_2NOH \rightarrow RCH=NOH \qquad \text{(oxime)}$$

7. Synthesis of acetals

$$RCOH + 2ROH \rightarrow RCHOR'OR' + H_2O \qquad \text{(acetal)}$$

8. Oxidation

$$RCOH \xrightarrow{(KMnO_4,\ Ag^+...)} RCOOH \qquad \text{(acid)}$$

9. Clemmensen reduction

$$RCOH + Zn(Hg) \xrightarrow{(HCl)} RCH_3$$

KETONES

Ketones, abbreviated **RCOR'**, contain a **carbonyl (C=O)** functional group bonded to **two alkyl or aryl groups**. The IUPAC names are obtained by replacing the final "e" in alkanes by the suffix –*one*. In open chain ketones, carbons are numbered starting with the carbon closest to the carbonyl C. Numbering in cyclic ketones starts with the carbonyl carbon. Common names are derived from carboxylic acid names; the suffixes –*ic*, –*oic*, or –*oxylic acid* are replaced by –*ketone*. Some systematic names are never used. For example, dimethyl ketone is called acetone. Ketones containing a phenyl group use the suffix –*phenone*.

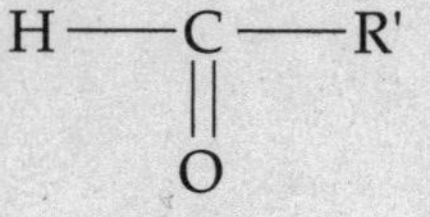

H—C—R' (ketone)

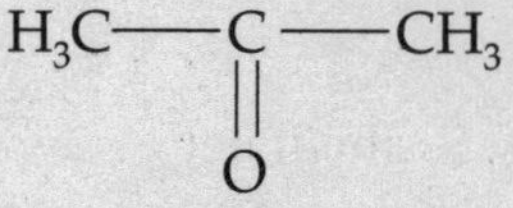

$\underset{\text{O}}{\text{||}}$

ketone

H_3C—C—CH_3

acetone
(dimethylketone)

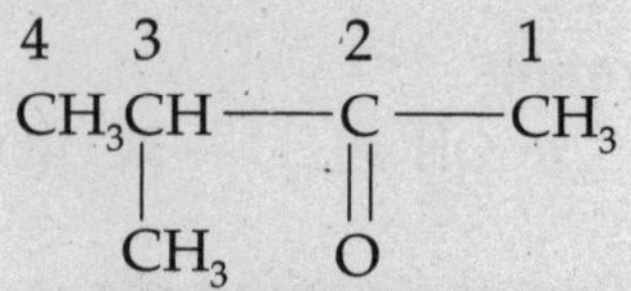

4   3   2   1
CH_3CH—C—CH_3
      | ||
     CH_3 O

methyl isopropyl ketone
(3-methyl-2-butanone)

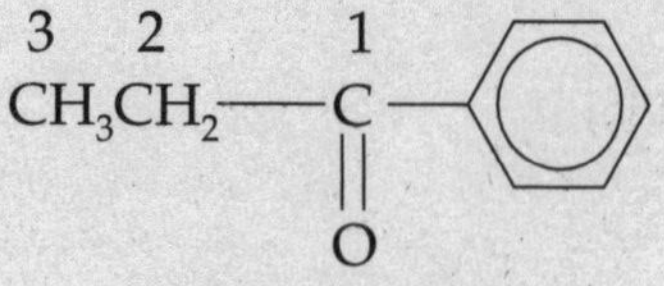

3   2   1
CH_3CH_2—C—⬡
           ||
           O

ethyl phenyl ketone
(1-phenyl-1-propanone)
(propriophenone)

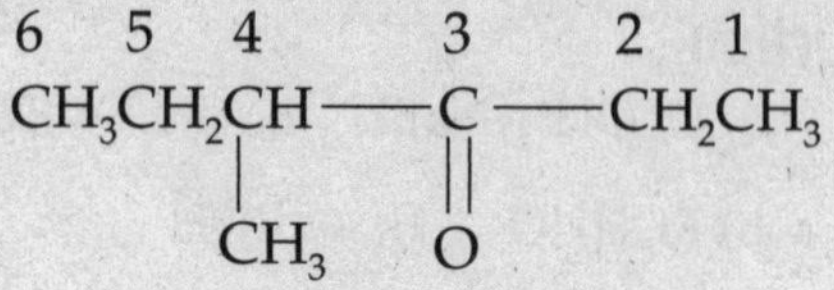

6   5   4   3   2   1
CH_3CH_2CH—C—CH_2CH_3
          | ||
         CH_3 O

ethyl *sec*-butyl ketone
(4-methyl-3-hexanone)

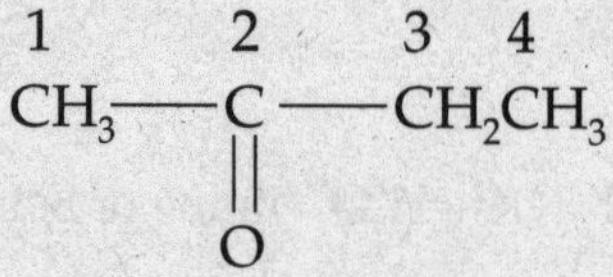

5   4   3   2   1
CH_3C=CH—C—CH_3
   | ||
  CH_3 O

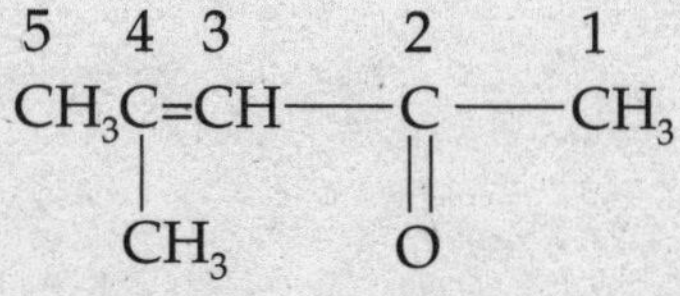

mesityl oxide
(4-methyl-3-penten-2-one)

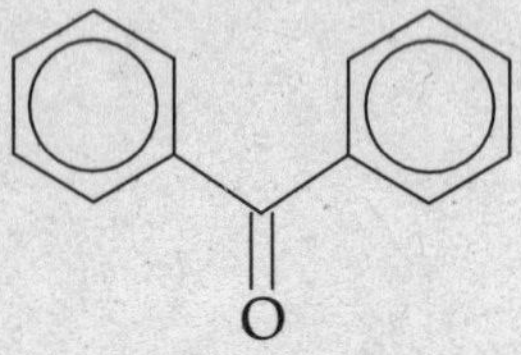

1   2   3   4
CH_3—C—CH_2CH_3
       ||
       O

methyl ethyl ketone
(2-butanone)

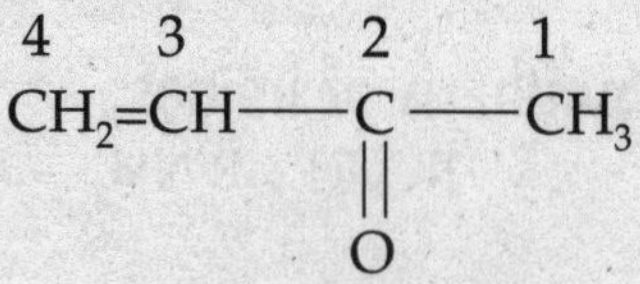

4   3   2   1
CH_2=CH—C—CH_3
           ||
           O

methyl vinyl ketone
(3-buten-2-one)

benzophenone

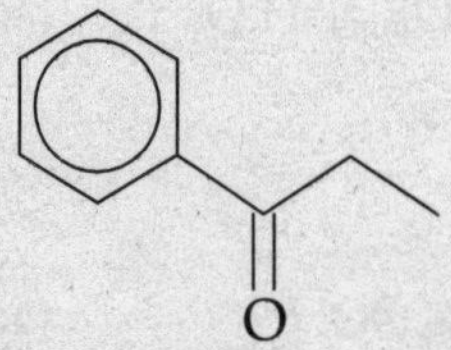

propriophenone

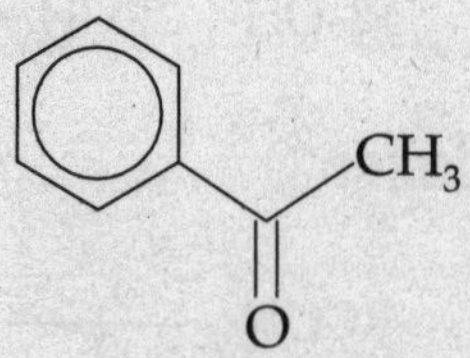

acetophenone

Like aldehydes, the properties of ketones are governed by their **carbonyl group**. Aldehydes and ketones have similar chemistries. For example, they are both **amphoteric**, but the presence of two electron–donating R groups in ketones—instead of one—lowers the electrophilicity of the carbonyl carbon, so ketones are generally less reactive than their corresponding aldehydes because there is less partial positive charge on the C=O carbon.

SYNTHESIS OF KETONES

1. Oxidation of secondary alcohols

$$\text{R–CHOH–R}' \xrightarrow[\text{H}^+]{\text{K}_2\text{Cr}_2\text{O}_7} \text{RCOR}'$$

2. Ozonolysis of alkenes

$$\text{RCH=CR}'\text{R}'' \xrightarrow[\text{(CH}_3)_2\text{S}]{\text{O}_3} \text{RCOR}' + \text{R}'\text{COR}''$$

3. Acylation of arenes

(a) $RCOHCl \xrightarrow{AlCl_3} RC^+=O + AlCl_4^-$ \qquad (acylonium ion)

(b) $RC^+=O + ArH \rightarrow HArC=OR \xrightarrow{H^+} ArC=OR$

4. Alkylation of 1,3-Dithianes

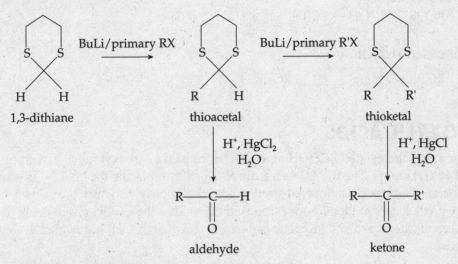

1,3-dithiane \qquad thioacetal \qquad thioketal

aldehyde \qquad ketone

5. Synthesis from organolithium and carboxylic acids

$RCOOH + 2R'Li \rightarrow RCR'(OLi) + H_3O^+ \rightarrow RCOR'$

6. Synthesis from nitriles

$RC\equiv N + R'MgX \rightarrow RC=NMgXR'$ (Mg salt of imine) $+ H_3O^+ \text{ Æ } RCOR'$

REACTIONS OF KETONES

1. Hydration

$RCOR' + H_2O \rightarrow RC(OH)_2R'$ \qquad (hydrate)

2. Addition of Grignard reagent

$RCOR' + R''MgX \rightarrow RCR'(OMgX)R''$ (alkoxide) $+ H_3O^+ \rightarrow RCR'R''OH$ \qquad (alcohol)

3. Reduction

(a) $RCOR' \xrightarrow[LiAlH_4]{NaBH_4} RCHR'O^-$ \qquad (alkoxide)

(b) $RCHR'O^- + H^+ \rightarrow RCHR'OH$ \qquad (alcohol)

4. Synthesis of cyanohydrins

$RCOR' + HCN \rightarrow RCHOR'CN$ \qquad (cyanohydrin)

5. Synthesis of imines

$$RCOR' + R''NH_2 \rightarrow RC=NR''R' + H_2O \qquad \text{(imine or Schiff base)}$$

6. Synthesis of oximes

$$RCOR' + H_2NOH \rightarrow RC=NOHR' \qquad \text{(oxime)}$$

7. Synthesis of ketals

$$RCOR' + 2R''OH \rightarrow RC(OR'')_2R' + H_2O \qquad \text{(ketal)}$$

8. Clemmensen reduction

$$RCOR' + Zn(Hg) \xrightarrow{\ \ HCl\ \ } RCHR'H$$

CARBOXYLIC ACIDS

Carboxylic acids, abbreviated **RCOOH** or **ArCOOH**, contain a **carboxyl** functional group bonded to **one alkyl or aryl group**. The IUPAC names are obtained by replacing the final "e" in alkanes by the suffix *–oic acid*. Carbons are numbered starting with the carboxyl C, which is assigned 1. Common names use greek letters to identify the carbons, the first after the COOH group being the a carbon, and the second, the b carbon. Aromatic carboxylic acids (ArCOOH) are named as derivatives of benzoic acid.

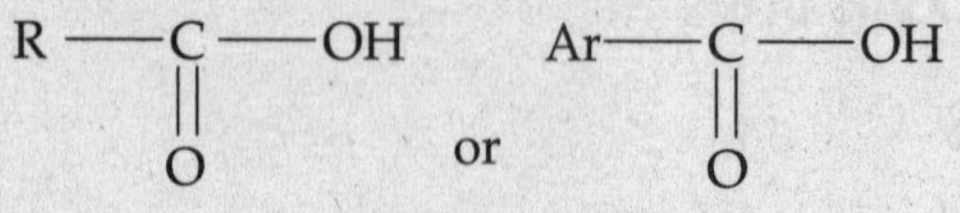

carboxylic acid

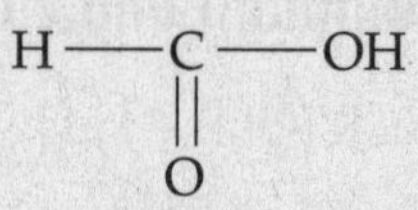

formic acid
(methanonic acid)

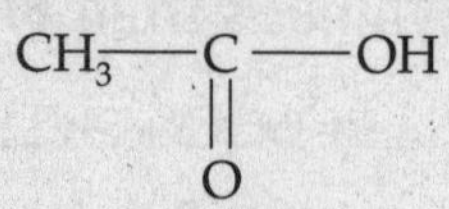

acetic acid
(ethanonic acid)

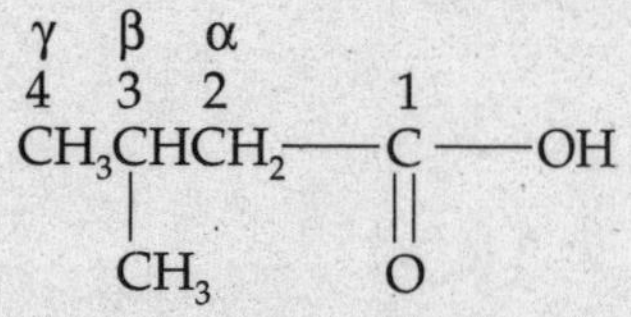

isovaleric acid
β-methylbutyric acid
(3-methylbutanoic acid)

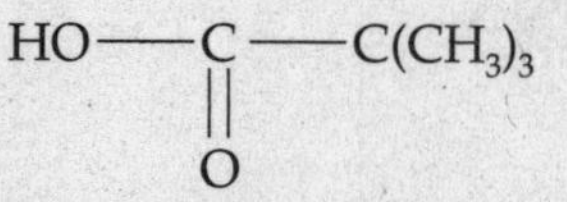

pivalic acid
trimethylacetic acid
(2,2-dimethylpropanoic acid)

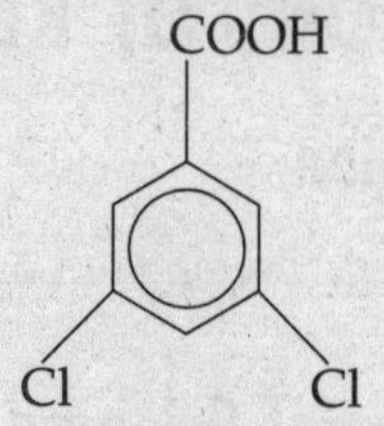

3,5-dichlorobenzoic
acid

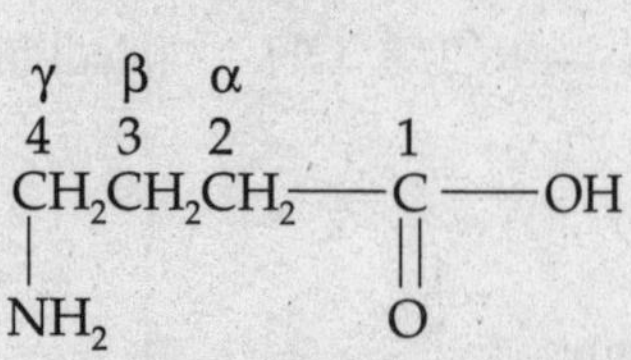

γ-aminobutyric acid
(4-aminobutanoic acid)

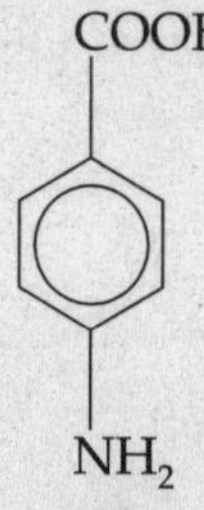

p-aminobenzoic
acid

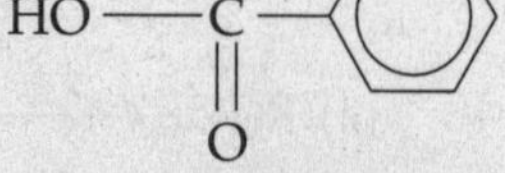

benzoic acid

SYNTHESIS OF CARBOXYLIC ACIDS

1. Oxidation of primary alcohols and aldehydes

$$RCH_2OH \xrightarrow[KMnO_4]{H_2CrO_4} RCOH$$

2. Carboxylation of Grignard reagents

$$RX \xrightarrow[ether]{Mg} RMgX \xrightarrow{O=O=O} RCOO^- {}^+MgX + H^+ \rightarrow RCOOH$$

3. Hydrolysis of nitriles

$$RCH_2X \xrightarrow[acetone]{NaCN} RCH_2C\equiv N \xrightarrow[H_2O]{H^+} RCH_2COOH$$

4. Oxidation of alkylbenzenes

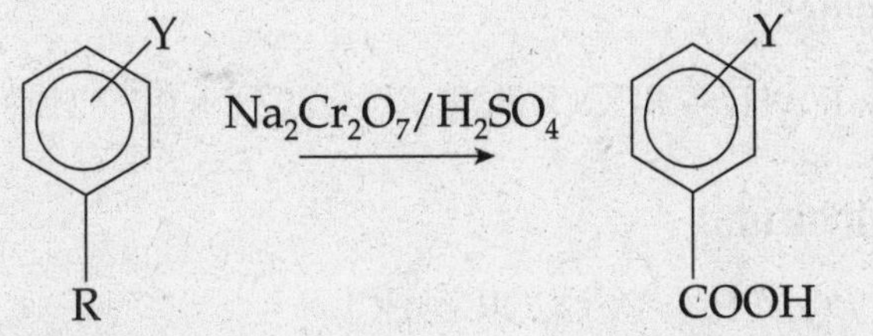

$$\xrightarrow{Na_2Cr_2O_7/H_2SO_4}$$

Alkylbenzene
(Y can resist oxidation)

a Benzoic acid

5. Oxidative cleavage of alkenes and alkynes

$$RCH=R'CR'' \xrightarrow{\cdot KMnO_4} RCOOH + R'COR''$$ (acid + ketone)

REACTIONS OF CARBOXYLIC ACIDS

1. Conversion to salts

$$RCOOH \xrightarrow{strong\ base} RCOO^-{}^+Y + H_2O$$

Example:

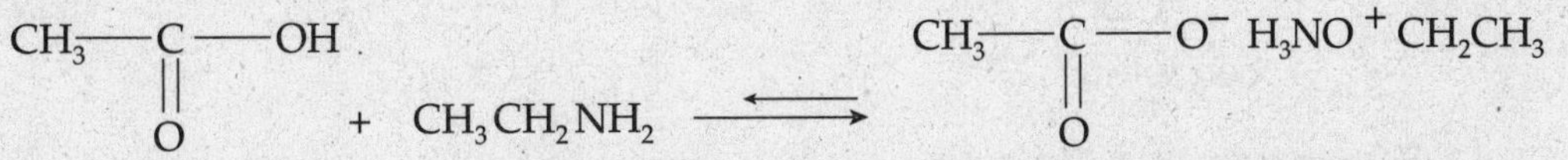

Acetic acid   +   **Ethylamine**   ⇌   **Ethylammonium acetate**

2. Synthesis of acid chlorides

$$RCOOH + SOCl_2 \rightarrow RCOCl + SO_2 + HCl$$

Example:

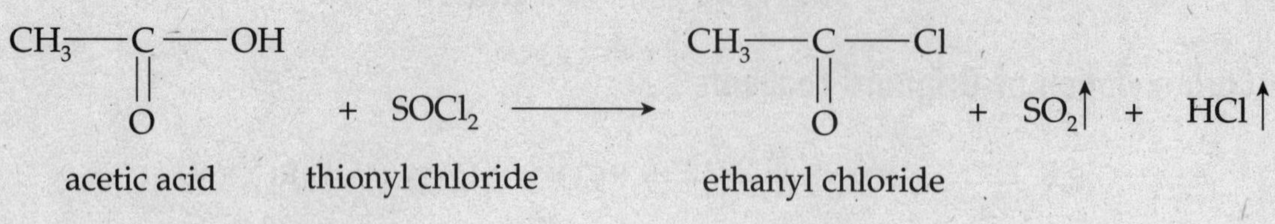

CH$_3$—C(=O)—OH + SOCl$_2$ ⟶ CH$_3$—C(=O)—Cl + SO$_2$↑ + HCl↑

acetic acid   thionyl chloride   ethanyl chloride

3. Esterification

$$RCOOH + R'OH \rightarrow RCOOR' + H_2O \qquad \text{(ester)}$$
$$RCOOH + CH_2N_2 \rightarrow RCOOCH_3 + N_2 \qquad \text{(methyl ester)}$$

4. Synthesis of amines

$$RCOOH + R'NH_2 \rightarrow RCOO^- H_3N^+\text{-}R' \rightarrow RCONHR' + H_2O$$

5. Synthesis of anhydrides

$$RCOCl + R'COOH \rightarrow RCOCOR' + HCl$$

6. Synthesis of primary alcohols

$$RCOOH \xrightarrow[H_2O]{LiAlH_4} RCH_2OH \qquad \text{(primary alcohol)}$$

7. Synthesis of ketones (alkylation)

$$RCOOH \xrightarrow[H_2O]{RLi} RCOR' \qquad \text{(ketone)}$$

Example:

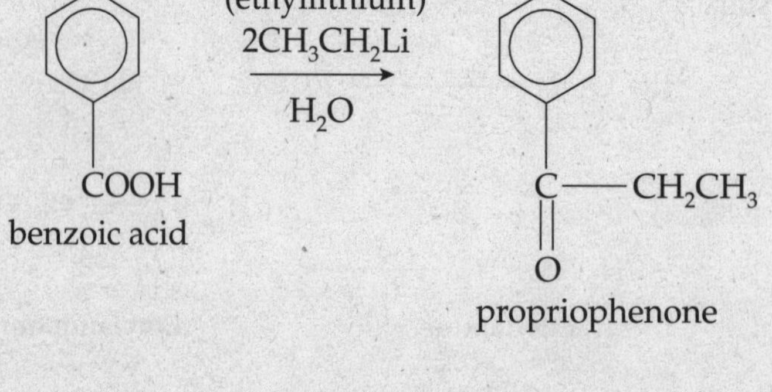

benzoic acid   (ethyllithium) 2CH$_3$CH$_2$Li / H$_2$O ⟶ propriophenone

AMINES

Amines contain the **amine (NH_2)** functional group. Depending on how many alkyl or aryl groups are bonded to the nitrogen atom, they are classified as primary, secondary or tertiary:

Primary amine:

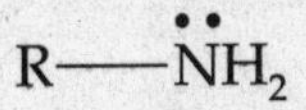

$$R \overset{\cdot\cdot}{-NH_2} \qquad\qquad \text{or} \qquad\qquad Ar \overset{\cdot\cdot}{-NH_2}$$

$$CH_3CH_2 \overset{\cdot\cdot}{-NH_2}$$

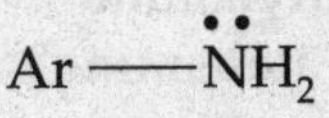

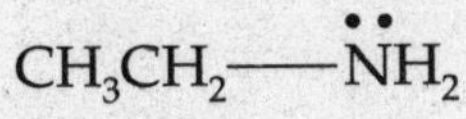

Ethylamine

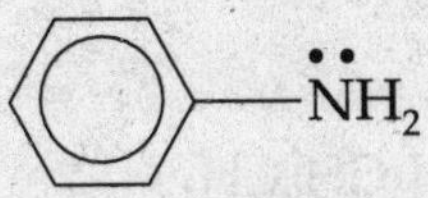

Aniline

Secondary amine:

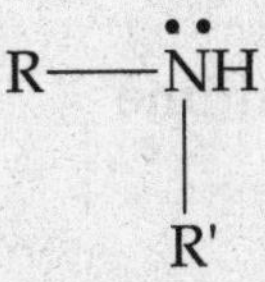

$$R \overset{\cdot\cdot}{-NH} \qquad\qquad \text{or} \qquad\qquad R \overset{\cdot\cdot}{-NH}$$

$$CH_3 \overset{\cdot\cdot}{-NH}$$

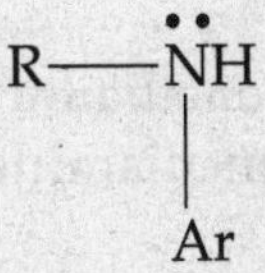

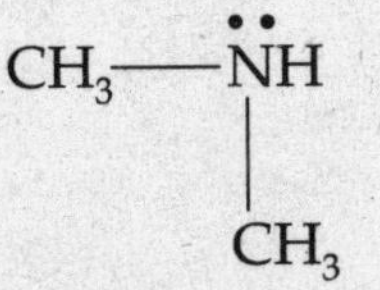

Dimethylamine

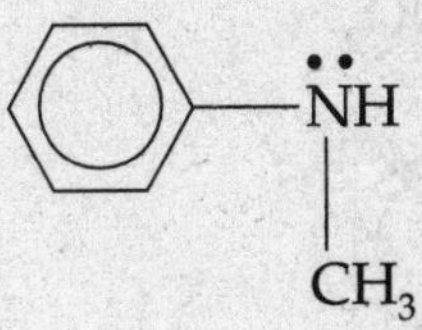

Methylaniline

Tertiary amine:

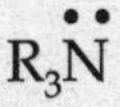

$$R_3\overset{\cdot\cdot}{N} \qquad\qquad \text{or} \qquad\qquad R \overset{\cdot\cdot}{-N-} R'$$

$$CH_3 \overset{\cdot\cdot}{-N-} CH_3$$

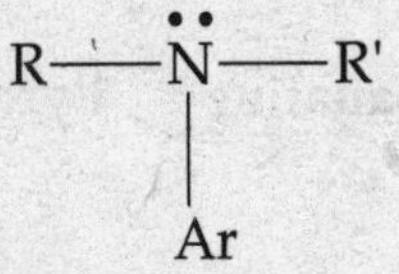

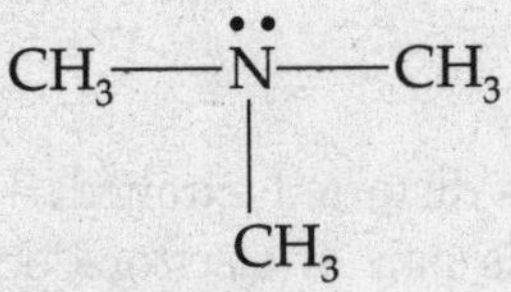

Trimethylamine

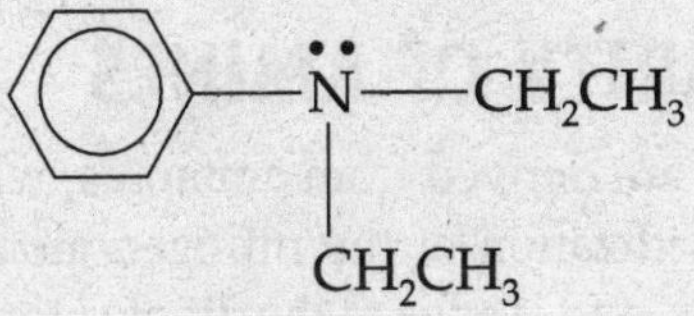

Diethylaniline

The IUPAC names are obtained by replacing the final "e" in alkanes by the suffix *–amine*. The longest carbon chain provides the root name and a number indicates the location of the amine group in the chain. Substituents on the nitrogen atom are identified with the prefix *N–*. Common names use the name of the alkyl group bonded to nitrogen and followed by the suffix *–amine*. The prefixes *di*, *tri*, and *tetra* are used for identical substituents. Aromatic and heterocyclic amines have historical common names.

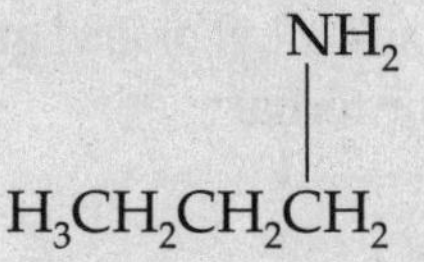

Butylamine
(1-butanamine)

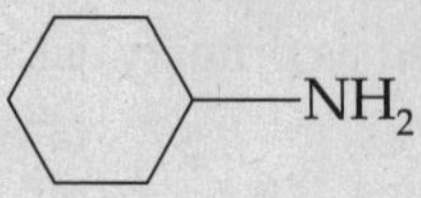

$H_3CH_2CH_2CH_2$ with NH_2

Cyclohexylamine

—NH_2

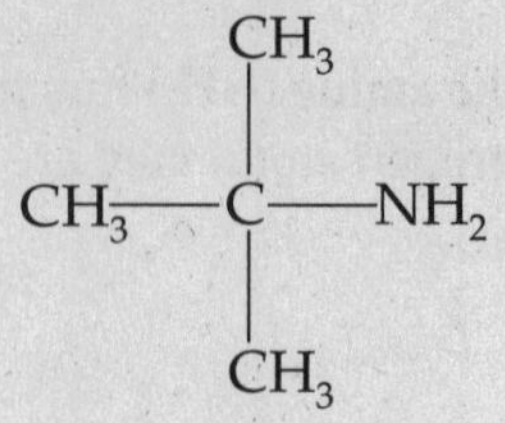

t-Butylamine
(2-methyl-2-proponamine)

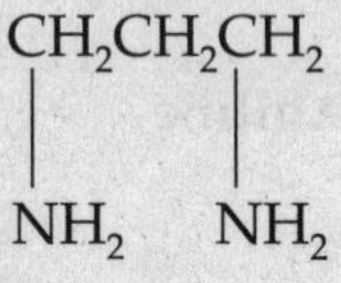

CH_3—C—NH_2 with CH_3, CH_3

Trimethylenediamine
(1,3-propanediamine)

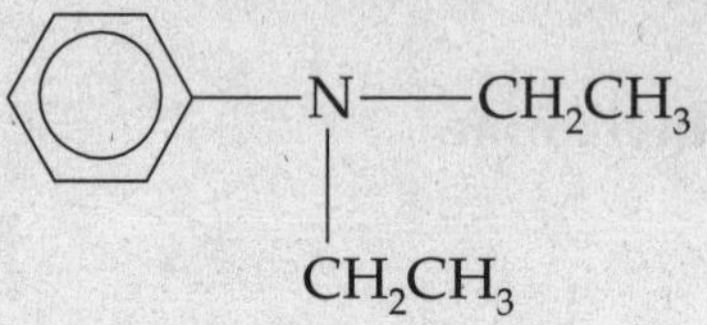

$CH_2CH_2CH_2$, NH_2, NH_2

N,N-Diethylaniline

—N—CH_2CH_3 with CH_2CH_3

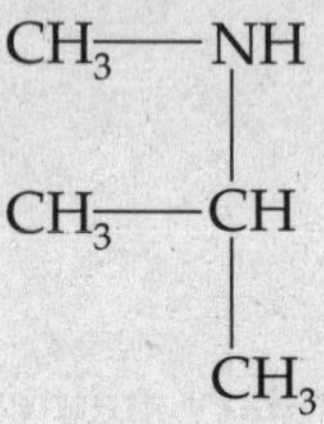

Methylisopropylamine
2-(N-methylamino)propane

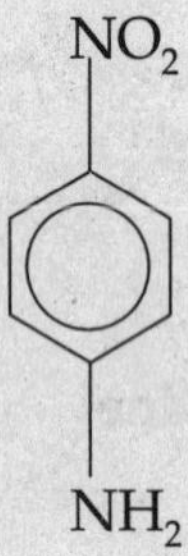

CH_3—NH, CH_3—CH—CH_3

p-Nitroanaline

NO_2 ... NH_2

Pyrrolidine

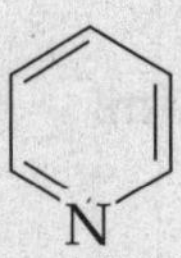

N
H

Pyridine

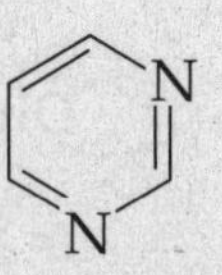

N

Pyrimidine

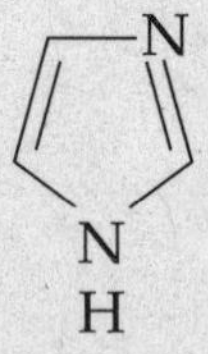

N, N

Imidazole

N
N
H

POLARITY OF AMINES

Amines are derived from ammonia, which has a distorted tetrahedral symmetry, resulting from the sp^3–hybridization of the nitrogen atom. A lone pair of electrons occupies one of the tetrahedral positions, and it adds to the dipole moments of the N–C and N–H bonds. Thus amines are very polar molecules.

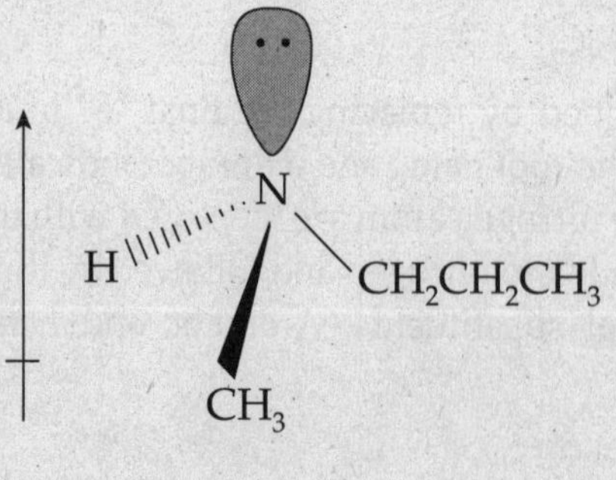

N
H ..... $CH_2CH_2CH_3$
CH_3

Since they have N–H bonds, primary and secondary amines can form H–bonds and act both as acceptors or donors. Because they lack N–H bonds, tertiary amines can act only as acceptors.

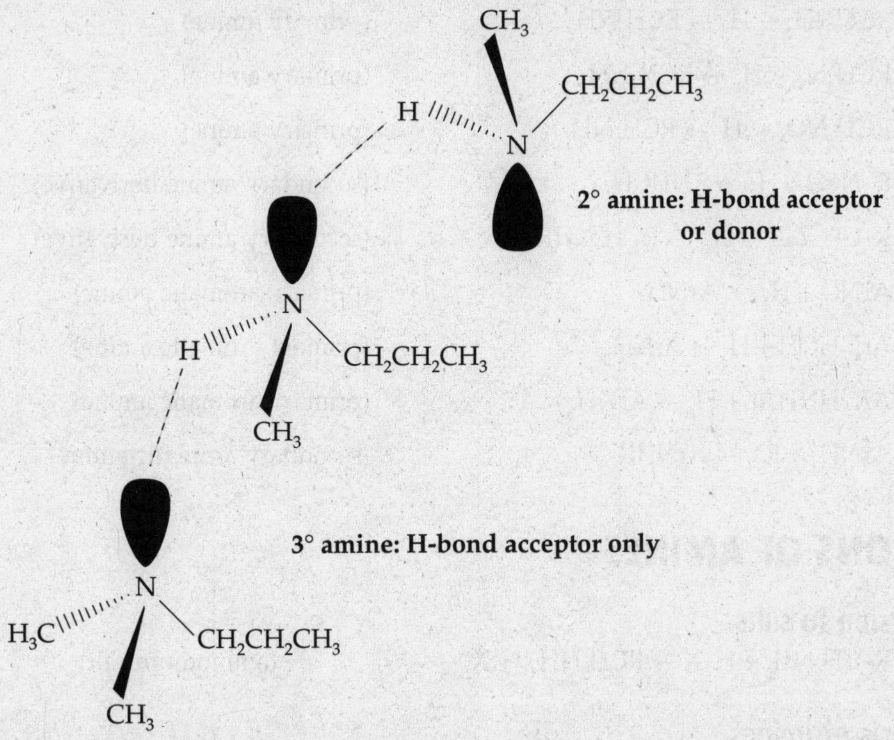

$$CH_3$$

$$CH_2CH_2CH_3$$

H ⫽⫽⫽ N

2° amine: H-bond acceptor or donor

N

H ⫽⫽⫽ CH_2CH_2CH_3

CH_3

3° amine: H-bond acceptor only

H_3C ⫽⫽⫽ N CH_2CH_2CH_3

CH_3

The lone pair of nonbonding electrons on the nitrogen of amines allows them to act as Lewis bases and bind electrophiles. They can also act as proton bases by accepting an H^+ from an acid:

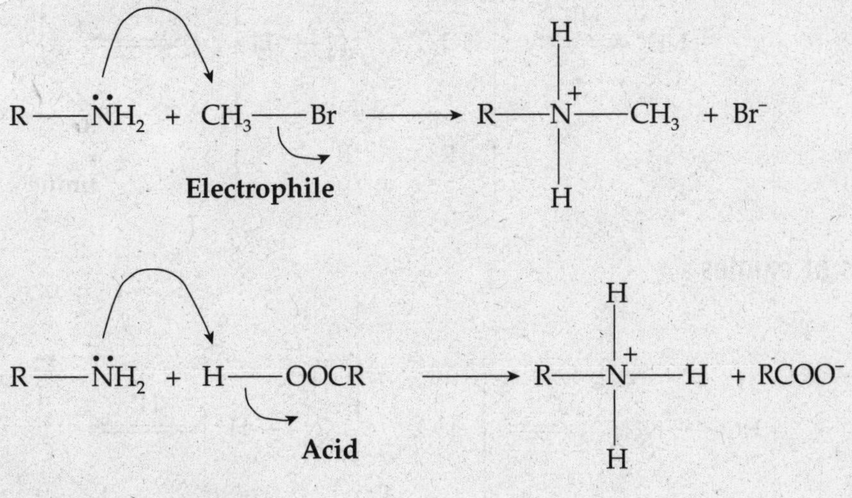

$$R{-}\ddot{N}H_2 + CH_3{-}Br \longrightarrow R{-}\overset{+}{N}(H)(H){-}CH_3 + Br^-$$

Electrophile

$$R{-}\ddot{N}H_2 + H{-}OOCR \longrightarrow R{-}\overset{+}{N}(H)(H){-}H + RCOO^-$$

Acid

SYNTHESIS OF AMINES

1.   Alkylation

$RCH_2X + NH_3 \rightarrow RCH_2NH_2$ (primary amine)

$RNH_2 + R'X \rightarrow RR'NH$ (secondary amine)

$3RX + NH_3 \rightarrow R_3N$ (tertiary amine)

2. Reduction

$RC\equiv N + :H^- \rightarrow RCH_2NH_2$ (primary amine)

$RCONH_2 + :H^- \rightarrow RCH_2NH_2$ (primary amine)

$RCH_2N_3 + :H^- \rightarrow RCH_2NH_2$ (primary amine)

$RCH_2NO_2 + :H^- \rightarrow RCH_2NH_2$ (primary amine)

$R-N\equiv C + H_2 \rightarrow RNHCH_3$ (secondary amine derivative)

$R-CH=NR' + H_2^- \rightarrow RCH_2NHR'$ (secondary amine derivative)

$ArNO + H_2 \rightarrow ArNH_2$ (primary aromatic amine)

$ArNHOH + H_2 \rightarrow ArNH_2$ (primary aromatic amine)

$ArNHNHAr + H_2 \rightarrow ArNH_2$ (primary aromatic amine)

$ArNH_2 + RX \rightarrow ArNHR$ (secondary aromatic amine)

REACTIONS OF AMINES

1. Conversion to salts

$R-CH_2NH_2 + H-X \rightarrow RCH_2NH_3^+ + X^-$ (ammonium salt)

2. Synthesis of imines

Ketone   Imine = Schiff base

3. Synthesis of oximes

Ketone   Oxime

4. Alkylation

$R-NH_2 + R'CH_2-X \rightarrow R-N^+H_2-CH_2-R'\ ^-X$ (salt of a 2° amine)

5. Acylation

$$RCOCl + R'-NH_2 \rightarrow R-CO-NH-R' + HCl \qquad \text{(amide)}$$

Example:

Aniline + Acetyl chloride → Acetanilide + HCl (Hydrogen chloride)

6. Oxidation of 2° amines

$$RR'NH + H_2O_2 \rightarrow RRNOH + H_2O \qquad \text{(secondary hydroxylamine)}$$

7. Oxidation of 3° amines

$$R_3N + H_2O_2 \rightarrow R_3N^+-O^- + H_2O \qquad \text{(tertiary amine oxide)}$$

8. Diazotization

$$R-NH_2 + NaNO_2/HCl \rightarrow R-N^+\equiv N \ ^-Cl \qquad \text{(alkane diazonium salt)}$$

REACTIVE INTERMEDIATES

Reactive intermediates are species that are involved at one point or another in many organic reactions. Six topics are covered under this heading: The chemistry and nature of carbocations, carbanions, free radicals, carbenes, benzynes, and enols.

CARBOCATIONS

A **carbocation** is a positive ion in which a positive charge resides on a carbon atom; one example of a carbocation is the *tert*-butyl cation, $(CH_3)C^+$. Carbocations are unstable species and cannot be isolated. They occur as intermediates in reactions of the S_N1 and E1 type. Carbocations can be primary, secondary, or tertiary, and in numbering their chains, the positive carbon is assigned as 1:

Propyl cation, primary   1-Methylpropyl cation, secondary   1-Ethylcyclohexyl cation, tertiary

The properties of carbocations are a function of their structure. In the methyl cation, CH_3^+, the carbon atom contributes three electrons, and each hydrogen contributes one, for a total of six electrons. A carbon bonded to three atoms is sp^2 hybridized and has a trigonal planar geometry. In CH_3^+, the three σ C–H bonds are coplanar, and the fourth orbital of carbon is a vacant, unhybridized 2π orbital, perpendicular to the plane of the ion:

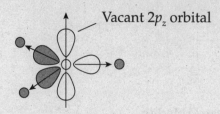

Vacant $2p_z$ orbital

Any factor that disperses the positive charge stabilizes the carbocation. In alkyl cations, the inductive effect stabilizes them because the electron density of the σ bonds is shifted toward the positive carbon:

This shift of electron density creates a partial positive charge on the adjacent carbon atoms, and the positive charge on the central carbon is said to be dispersed. The more alkyl groups attached to the cation, the greater its stability:

$$\overset{+}{C}H_3 \ < \ CH_3\overset{+}{C}H_2 \ < \ (CH_3)_2\overset{+}{C}H \ < \ (CH_3)_3\overset{+}{C}$$

Example:

What is the most stable carbocation that has the formula $C_5H_{11}^+$?

Answer:

Write down all possible isomeric $C_5H_{11}^+$ carbocations. There are two possible primary and three secondary isomers, as well as one tertiary isomer, $(CH_3)_2C^+CH_2CH_3$. The $3°$ carbocation is the most stable because it has the greater number of alkyl groups.

Another stabilizing factor is the delocalization of electrons into the vacant p orbital of the positive carbon atom because this also enhances the dispersal of the positive charge.

A good substituent group must have a filled σ orbital available to overlap with the vacant p orbital of the carbocation. The more alkyl substituents attached to the positive carbon, the more delocalization and the greater the dispersal of the positive charge and subsequent carbocation stability. This phenomenon is called **hyperconjugation**.

The positive charge of the carbon and the vacant p orbital combine to make carbocations very **electrophilic** (electron-loving). Electrophiles combine with nucleophiles (nucleus or positive charge-loving); an unshared pair of electrons on a nucleophile can interact with the vacant $2p$ orbital of a carbocation.

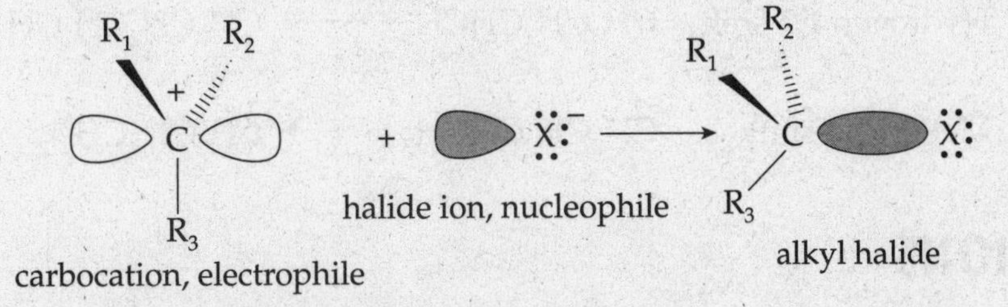

carbocation, electrophile   halide ion, nucleophile   alkyl halide

Carbocations are **Lewis acids** because they are **electron-pair acceptors**. Halide ions are **Lewis bases** because they are **electron-pair donors**.

During the course of S_N1 and E1 reactions, carbocation rearrangement often occurs:

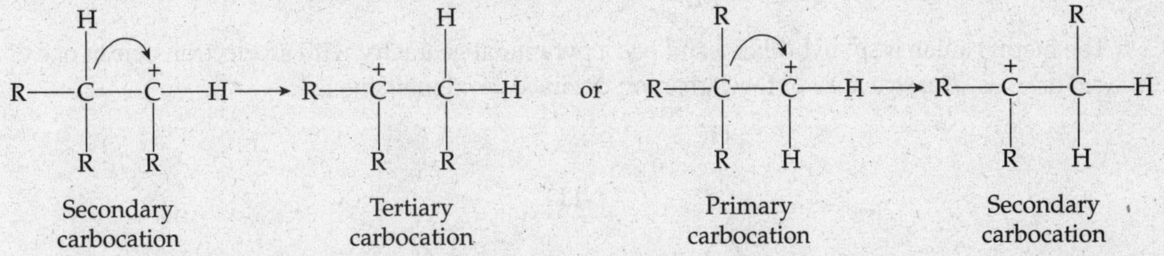

Secondary carbocation   Tertiary carbocation   or   Primary carbocation   Secondary carbocation

The energy of a secondary carbocation is higher than that of a tertiary carbocation, so this energy is lowered by the shift of an –H atom or a –CH_3 group with its bonding electrons from an adjacent carbon atom. This means that a secondary carbocation can rearrange into a more stable tertiary carbocation in a process called a **1,2-shift**, or a **Wagner-Meerwein transposition**.

Example:

What S_N1 products can be obtained by the reaction of 2-bromo-3,3-dimethylbutane with methanol? Show the structure of the carbocation intermediate involved.

Answer: The first step of this reaction involves the formation of a secondary carbocation, which can rearrange by a 1,2-shift into a more stable carbocation, followed by reaction of the intermediates with methanol to give two distinct methoxy compounds:

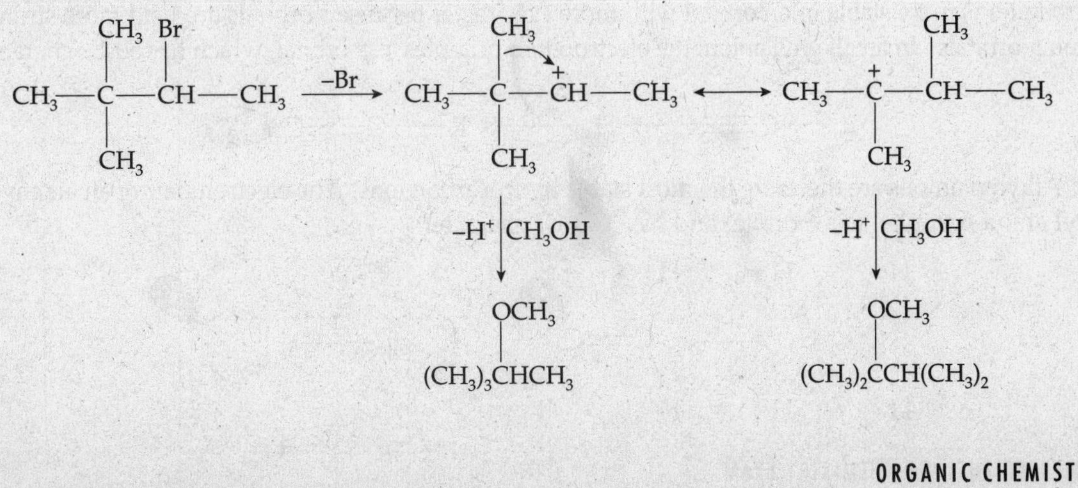

The secondary carbocation leads to the "normal" product and the tertiary carbocation leads to the rearrangement product. If a more stable carbocation or another carbocation with equal stability can be easily formed, rearrangement can occur.

Example:

Can $CH_3CH_2CH^+CH_3$ undergo rearrangement?

Answer: This is a secondary carbocation. Hydrogen and methyl 1,2-shifts would lead to a less stable primary carbocation, so rearrangement is not likely to occur:

Hydrogen 1,2-shift: $CH_3CH_2\overset{+}{C}HCH_3 \longrightarrow CH_3CH_2CH_2\overset{+}{C}H_2$

Methyl 1,2-shift: $CH_3CH_2\overset{+}{C}HCH_3 \longrightarrow \overset{+}{C}H_2CH(CH_3)_2$

CARBANIONS

A **carbanion** is an ion in which the negative charge is carried by a carbon atom. It is formed by **heterolytic cleavage** of the bond between a carbon atom and a less electronegative atom, such as a metal:

$$RCH_2\!\!-\!\!MgX \longrightarrow RCH_2^- + {}^+MgX$$

The methyl anion is sp^3-hybridized and has a pyramidal geometry with an electron pair in one of the sp^3 orbitals. The structure of the carbanion obtained from methane is

Carbanions are **conjugate bases** of hydrocarbons. The pK_a of methane is 60, so it is a very weak acid, and CH_3^- is a very strong base. Hydrocarbons display a great range of acidity; alkynes are far stronger acids than alkenes, and alkenes are stronger than alkanes:

$$HC\!\equiv\!CH > H_2C\!=\!CH_2 > CH_3CH_3$$

$$(pK_a = 25) \qquad (pK_a = 45) \qquad (pK_a = 65)$$

The acidity of a proton depends on the hybridization of the carbon atom. The electron doublet of a carbanion is more stable in an orbital with more s character because s orbitals are held more strongly than p-orbitals. In an alkynyl anion, the electron pair occupies a sp orbital, which has 50% s character.

Alkynyl anions are therefore the most stable hydrocarbon ions. The electron pair of an alkenyl or aryl anion occupies an sp^2 orbital and has 33.3% s character:

The electron pair of an alkyl anion occupies an sp^3 orbital and has 25% s character. They are the least stable of all hydrocarbon carbanions.

Electronegative substituents have a strong influence on the stability of carbanions. For example, nitromethane ($pK_a = -1.4$) is acidic enough to react with alkali because the anion formed is stable:

$$NO_2CH_3 \xrightarrow{+OH^+} \left[\quad \longleftrightarrow \quad \longleftrightarrow \quad \right]$$

The stability of the ion is due to the electronegativity of the oxygen atoms. The inductive and resonance effects draw the negative charge from the carbon atom into the nitro group. In order of decreasing electron-withdrawing ability, the most common substituent groups are ordered in this way: $-NO_2 > -SO_2R > -CN > -C=O > -CO_2R > -Ph > C=C > -X > -H$.

A group located between $-SO_2R$ and $-CO_2R$ in that listing is not electronegative enough to yield a compound with a measurable acidity relative to water. However, two such groups attached to a carbon atom greatly enhance the acidity of a C–H bond. For example, ethyl acetate does not react with ethyl alcohol to a significant extent:

However, maleic ester does:

FREE RADICALS

A **free radical** is a neutral species that contains unpaired electrons. These electrons result from **homolytic bond cleaveage**; each fragment carries one electron from the broken bond.

$$RCH_2 : H \longrightarrow RCH_2\cdot + H\cdot$$

Free radicals are very reactive and can even react between themselves:

$$RCH_2\cdot + \cdot CH_2R \longrightarrow RCH_2CH_2R$$

Alkyl radicals are classified as primary, secondary, and tertiary. The methyl radical can be compared with the methyl cation, in that it has six electrons in three σ bonds between aN sp^2 carbon and three hydrogen atoms, as well as an unpaired electron in a $2p$ orbital, so the $2p$ orbital is half-full, and the geometry of the methyl radical is nearly planar:

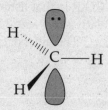

Free radicals have an unfilled $2p$ orbital and are stabilized by electron-donating substitutents, such as alkyl groups. Their order of increasing stability is

$$\cdot CH_3 < R\dot{C}H_2 < R_2\dot{C}H < R_3C\cdot$$
$$\qquad\quad 1° \qquad\; 2° \qquad 3°$$

Example:

What is the most stable radical that has the formula C_5H_{11}?
Answer: Write down all possible isomers of C_5H_{11}. Of these, the radical with an unpaired electron on a tertiary carbon is the most stable:

$$CH_3CH_2\dot{C}(CH_3)_2$$

The stability of free radicals is related to their bond dissociation energies (BDE); the lower the BDE, the more stable the radical.

The chlorination of methane provides the classic example of free-radical involvement in a reaction. The net result is the substitution of one or more chlorine atoms for hydrogen atoms:

$$CH_4 + Cl_2 \xrightarrow{hv} CH_3Cl + CH_2Cl_2 + CHCl_3 + CCl_4 + HCl$$

This prototypical free-radical reaction proceeds in three steps:

(1) Initiation: dissociation of the radical precursor molecule and the formation of two free radicals under light or high temperature;

$$Cl \overset{\curvearrowleft}{\underset{\curvearrowright}{\vdots}} Cl \xrightarrow{h\nu} 2\, Cl\cdot$$

(2) Chain propagation: the free radical abstracts a hydrogen atom from the alkane:

$$Cl\cdot \quad H \overset{\curvearrowleft}{\underset{\curvearrowright}{\vdots}} CH_3 \longrightarrow Cl \overset{\cdot}{\underset{\cdot}{}} H + \cdot CH_3$$

Then the alkyl radical reacts with another precursor molecule:

$$CH_3\cdot \quad Cl \overset{\curvearrowleft}{\underset{\curvearrowright}{\vdots}} Cl \longrightarrow CH_3Cl + Cl\cdot$$

This step yields one of the products of the reaction and generates a new free radical that can abstract a hydrogen atom from another alkane molecule. The reaction is self-perpetuating. The number of possible passes through the propagation step is called the **chain length** and depends partly on the energy of the free radicals generated. For the chlorination of hydrocarbons, the chain length is about 10,000.

(3) **Termination of the propagation cycle**: occurs when free radicals combine with other free radicals:

$$CH_3\cdot \ + \ \cdot Cl \longrightarrow CH_3Cl \quad \text{or} \quad Cl\cdot + Cl\cdot \longrightarrow Cl_2 \quad \text{or}$$

$$CH_3\cdot \ + \ \cdot CH_3 \longrightarrow CH_3CH_3$$

There can be many products in a free-radical reaction because the high-energy free radical is not particularly selective about which hydrogen it abstracts during propagation.

Example:
Write the propagation steps that lead to the formation of dichloromethane from chloromethane.
Answer:
Remember the two parts of the propagation step: formation of the chloromethane radical followed by its reaction with molecular chlorine:

$$Cl\cdot \ + \ CH_3Cl \longrightarrow \cdot CH_2Cl + HCl$$

$$\cdot CH_2Cl \ + \ Cl_2 \longrightarrow CH_2Cl_2 + Cl\cdot$$

If a hydrogen is abstracted from the chiral carbon of a pure enantiomer, **racemization** is observed:

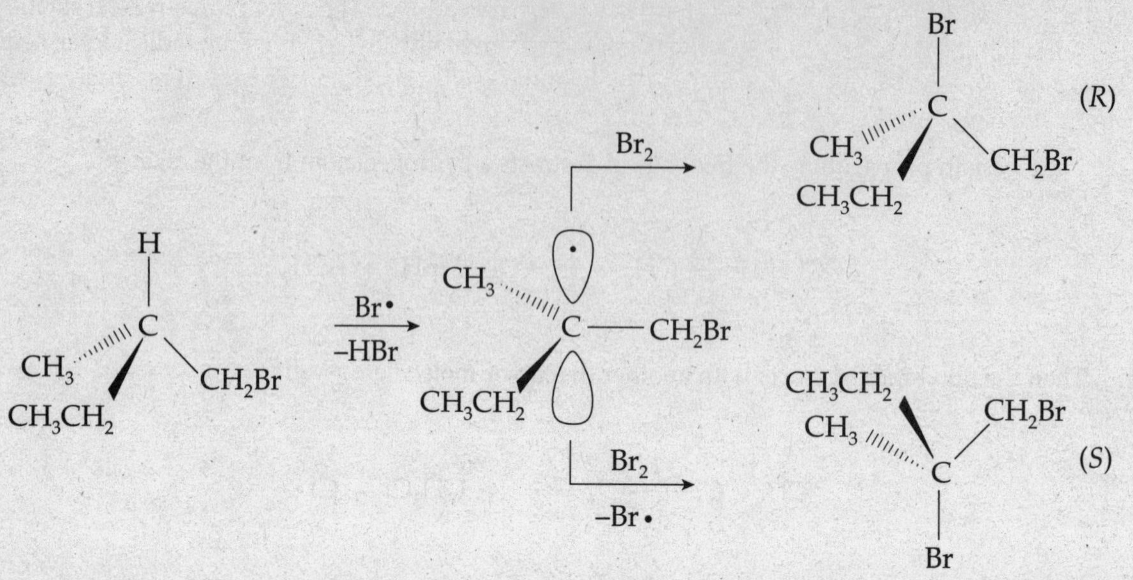

This reaction can have several products, including trichloro- and tetrachloroalkanes. Examining only the products that result from chlorination at the chiral carbon, we obtain a racemic mixture, and the bromide radical can attack on both lobes of the p orbital.

The relative rates of free radical chlorination are as follows:

tertiary (5.0) > secondary (4.0) > primary (1.0)

The relative rates of bromination are

tertiary (1600) > secondary (80) > primary (1)

Therefore, bromine is more **regioselective** than chlorine in the substitution of tertiary hydrogens.

Example:

What is the structure of the main product formed by free-radical bromination of 2,2,4-trimethylpentane?

Answer: Write the structure of the hydrocarbon and identify any tertiary hydrogen. The only tertiary hydrogen of 2,2,4-trimethylpentane is attached to C_4, and it is replaced by bromine:

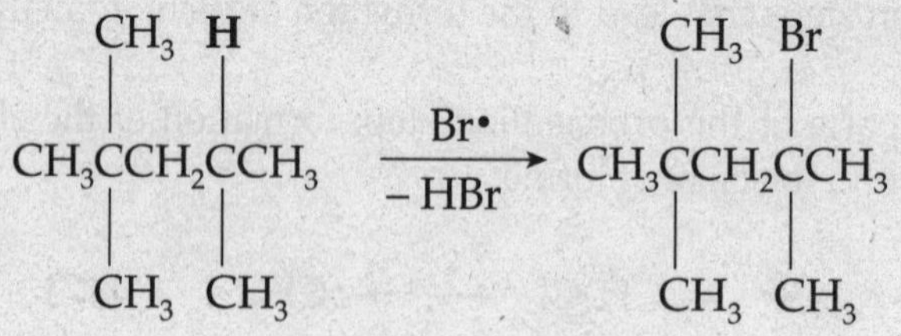

The tertiary hydrogens are abstracted more easily because of the lower bond dissociation energy of the C–H bond. BDE decreases from primary to tertiary carbons. The order of free-radical stability is similar to that of carbocation stability: it increases from methyl to tertiary. Free-radical intermediates can also be stabilized by hyperconjugation, and there is enhanced free-radical reactivity at the **allylic** (carbon next to a C=C double bond) and **benzylic** (carbon next to a benzene ring) positions, due to the resonance stabilization of the intermediate.

Example:

Write resonance structures for the $CH_2=CHCH_2 \cdot$ and the $Ph\text{-}CH_2 \cdot$ free radicals.

Answer: Use half-arrows to show the movement of individual electrons between the carbon bearing the unpaired electron and the adjacent double bond:

$$CH_2=CH-\overset{\bullet}{C}H_2 \longleftrightarrow \overset{\bullet}{C}H_2-CH=CH_2$$

Free radicals and carbocations are both planar and sp^2-hybridized. They also both undergo racemization at a chiral carbon, but unlike carbocations, free radicals do not tend to undergo rearrangement toward more stable species.

CARBENES

Carbenes are neutral molecules of general formula $R_2C:$ in which a carbon atom has two bonds and two electrons. There are two types of carbenes: **singlet carbenes**, which have two paired electrons in the same sp^2 orbital, and **triplet carbenes**, which have two unpaired electrons of the same spin in separate p-orbitals:

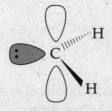

singlet methylene
(C is sp^2)

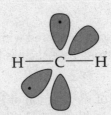

triplet methylene
(C is sp)

Singlet carbenes are useful in organic synthesis. For instance, methylene is prepared by photolysis of the very reactive diazomethane:

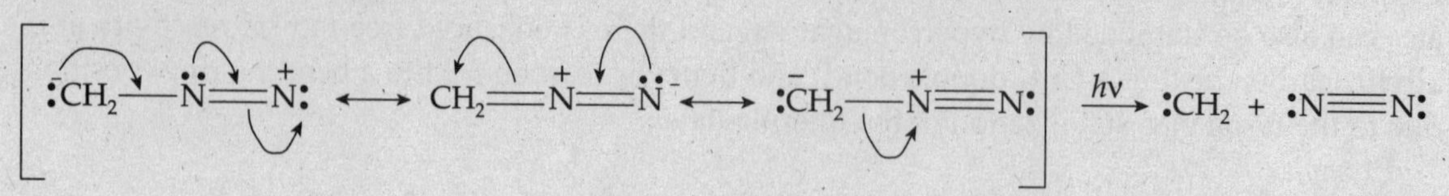

The carbon in methylene has only six electrons and is electrophilic. Carbenes form during the conversion of alkenes to cyclopropenes The reaction is stereospecific: *cis* alkenes yield *cis* cyclopropenes and *trans* alkenes yield *trans* cyclopropenes.

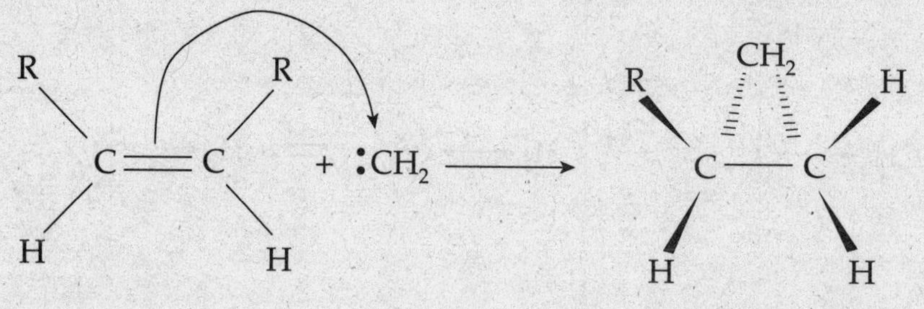

cis

cis-Dialkylcyclopropane
(*meso*)

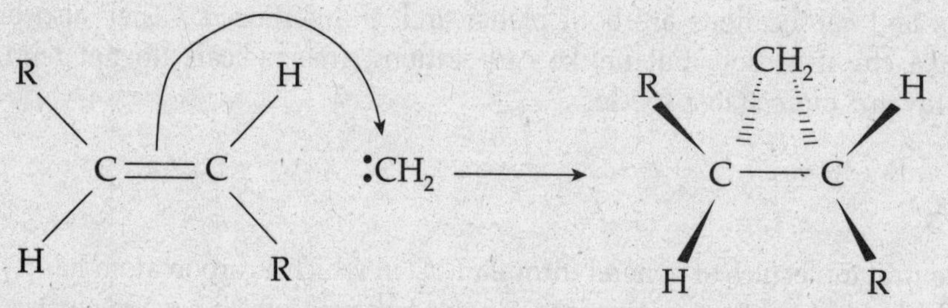

trans

trans-Dialkylcyclopropane
(racemic)

Dihalopropanes can also be prepared with dihalocarbenes, which are obtained by the reaction of a trihalomethane with a strong base such as $KOC(CH_3)_3$.

Example:

What are the products of the reaction of 1,2-dimethyl-1,4-cyclobutadiene with tribromomethane in the presence of sodium tert-butoxide? Which product predominates?

Answer: First write the equation for the generation of the carbene; then the formula of the other reactant. Remember that the alkyl-substituted double bond is a better nucleophile than the nonsubstituted bond, and so it should yield the predominant product:

$$CHBr_3 \; + \; (CH_3)_3CO^- \longrightarrow \; :CBr_2 \; + \; (CH_3)_3COH \; + \; Br^-$$

(by-product)

BENZYNES

Benzynes are compounds that are formed as reactive intermediates in the reaction of alkyl halides with strong bases (nucleophilic aromatic substitution). Their general structure is

The first two components of the triple bond are part of the delocalized π-electron system. The other component results from two overlapping sp^2 orbitals and lies in the plane of the ring. This bond is very weak because the sp^2 orbitals in the plane of the ring are not properly aligned for effective overlap. Also, the C–C≡C–C unit is not linear, so the structure is strained, and benzyne is highly reactive.

The elimination-addition mechanism illustrates the role of benzyne in nucleophilic aromatic substitution. This reaction proceeds in three steps:

Step 1: Elimination stage: dihydrohalogenation of chlorobenzyne by the amide ion:

Step 2: Beginning of the addition phase: the amide ion reacts with benzyne to form a carbanion:

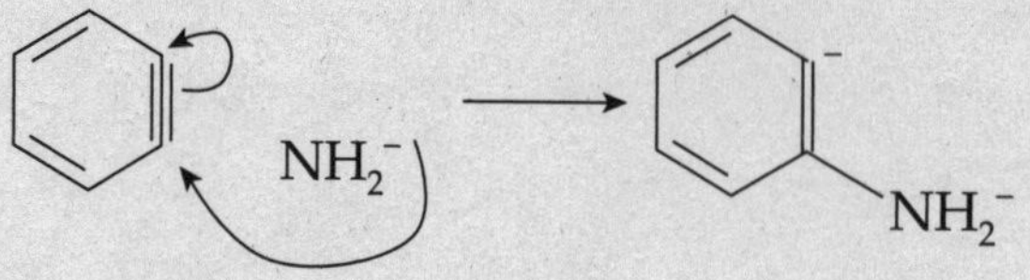

Step 3: End of the addition phase: the aryl anion reacts with solvent ammonia:

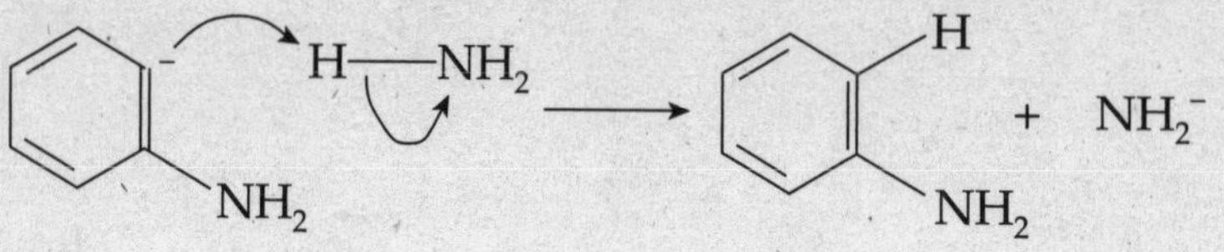

ENOLS

Enols are compounds that exist as an equilibrium mixture of ketone and aldehyde **tautomers**. The two tautomers, called the **keto form** and the **enol form**, interconvert by migration of an H atom and a C=C bond. For an enol form to exist, there must be a hydrogen atom on a carbon atom adjacent to the carbonyl group:

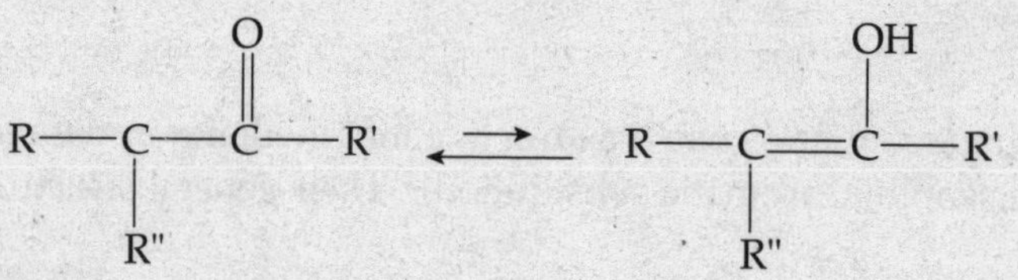

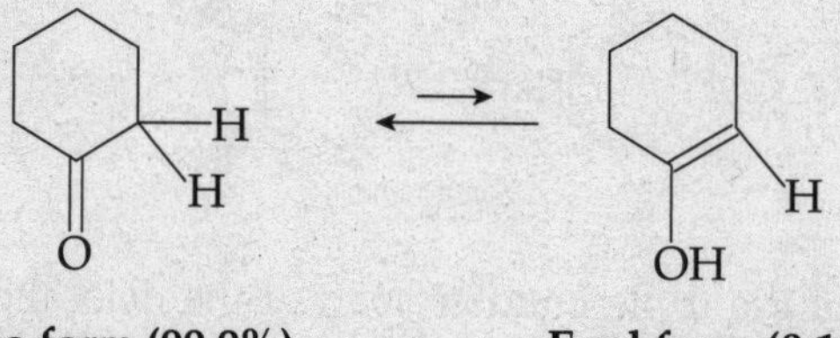

Keto form (99.9%)   Enol form (0.10%)

The keto form is more stable and predominates in simple ketones and aldehydes because the C–H and C=O bonds have greater bond energies than the C=C and O–H bonds. This is because the resonance energy of the carbonyl group is greater than that of the enol.

In a few cases, the enol form predominates. For example, in 2,4-pentanedione, the enol is stabilized by an intramolecular hydrogen bond and a conjugated system:

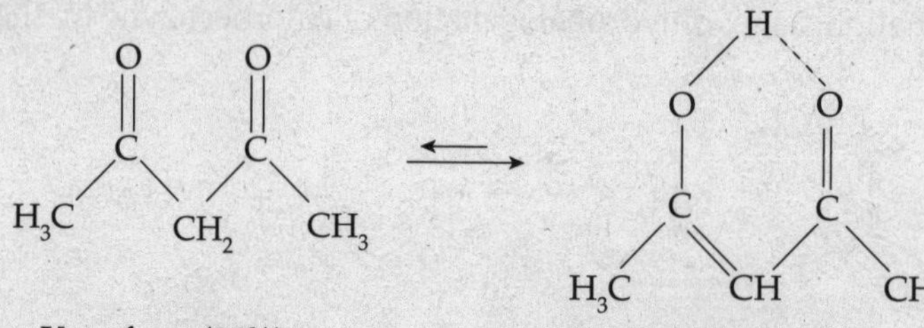

Keto form (25%)   Enol form (25%)

2,4-Pentanedione

Keto and enol tautomers are real species, and it is possible to isolate them under the appropriate experimental conditions.

Example:

What are the keto and enol forms of C_6H_5OH, and which tautomer predominates?

Answer:

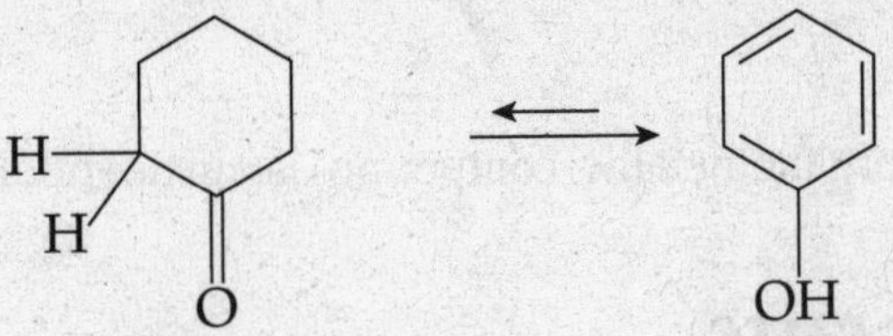

Keto form
Cyclohexa-2,4-diene-1-one

Enol form
Phenol

The enol form, phenol, predominates because it has a very stable aromatic ring.

Example:

2-Butanone exists in equilibrium in two enol forms. What are they, and which will predominate?

Answer:

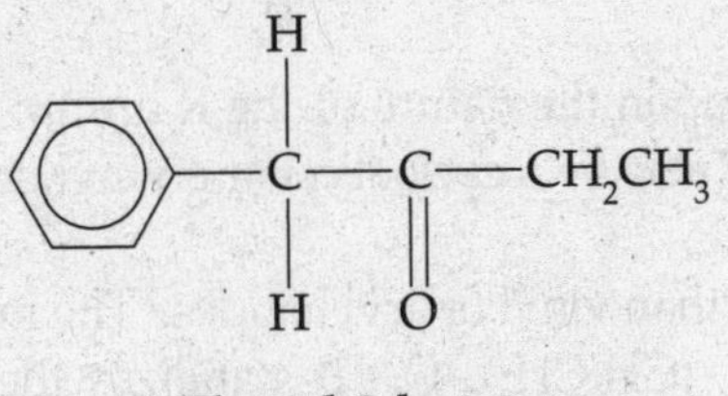

1-Phenyl-2-butanone

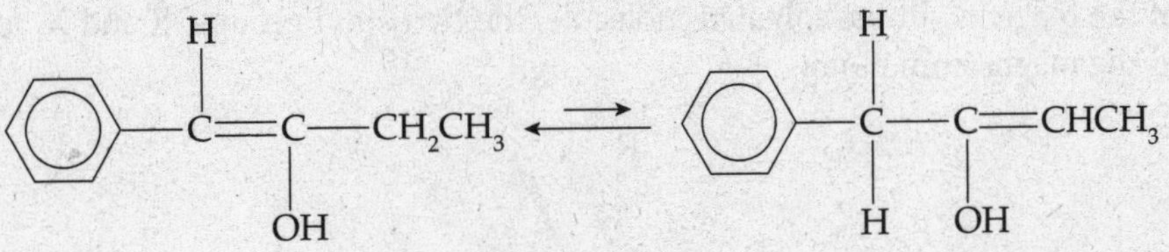

Enol forms

The enol structure on the left will predominate because the C=C is conjugated with the aromatic ring.

ORGANOMETALLICS

Organometallic compounds are compounds in which a nucleophilic carbon is bonded to a metal atom. This makes them very useful reagents. The topics covered under this heading include the preparation and reactions of Grignard and organolithium reagents, lithium organocuprates, and other main group and transition-metal reagents and catalysts.

ORGANOMETALLIC COMPOUNDS

An **organometallic** compound consists of a carbon atom covalently bonded to a metal. The electronegativity of carbon is 2.5; hence, it is electropositive and acquires a partial positive charge when it bonds to a more electronegative element (O, N, Cl, Br, I,...). But when carbon is bonded to a more electropositive element—such as Li, Mg, Al, or K which have the respective electronegativities 1.0, 1.3, 1.6, and 0.8 —then the partial positive charge resides on the metal, and carbon acquires a partial negative charge:

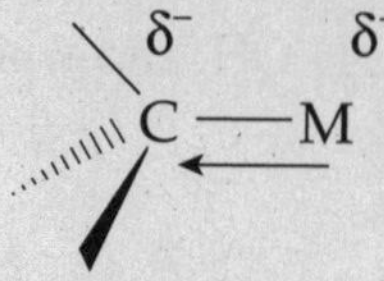

$$\delta^- \quad \delta^+$$

$$C \text{---} M$$

So the carbon of an organometallic compound is nucleophilic, and organometallics have a carbanionic character.

GRIGNARD REAGENTS

Organomagnesium halides with the general formula **(RMgX)** are called **Grignard reagents**. A Grignard reagent is prepared by a free radical reaction between magnesium and an alkyl halide (RX) in an ether solvent, which stabilizes the Grignard reagent as it forms.

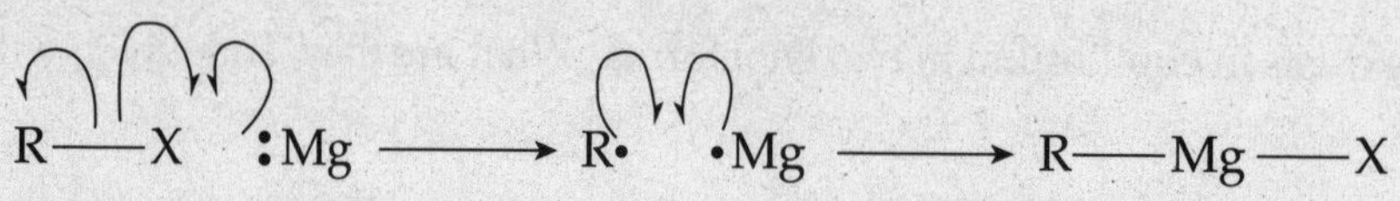

$$R \text{---} X \quad :Mg \longrightarrow R\cdot \quad \cdot Mg \longrightarrow R \text{---} Mg \text{---} X$$

The reaction does not depend upon the nature of the R group; R can be a methyl or a primary, secondary, or tertiary alkyl; it may also be a cycloalkyl or a vinyl or aryl group. The order of halide reactivity is I > Br > Cl > F.

Alkyl halides are more reactive than vinyl or aryl halides. The most common solvent for use with Grignard reagents is diethylether, $(CH_3CH_2)_2\text{-}O$. It stabilizes the reagent by donating unshared electrons to the empty orbitals of the magnesium atom, and its two ethyl groups solvate the alkyl fragments of the reagents. In the solvated molecule, the two ethyl groups, R and X, form a tetrahedron around the magnesium atom:

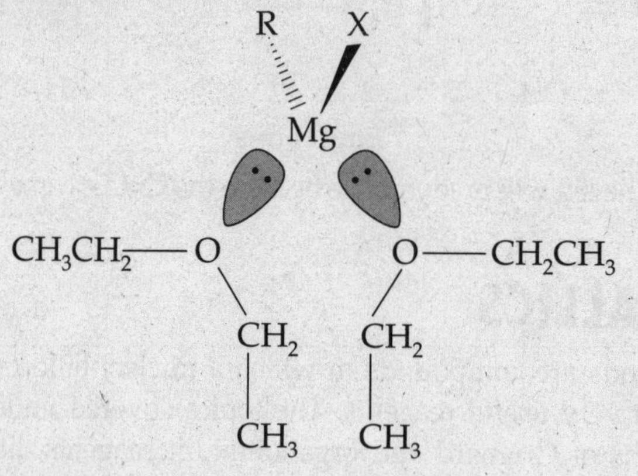

Example:

What is the product formed by reaction of p-chloroiodobenzene with magnesium in diethylether?
Answer:

Iodine reacts faster than chlorine. Chlorine is left on the ring as a carbon–magnesium bond replaces the carbon–iodine bond:

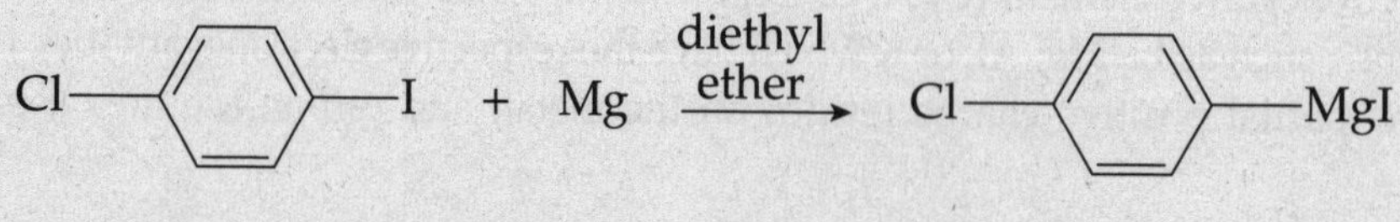

Grignard reagents have a carbanionic character, so they are very strong bases that react quickly with proton donors to form alkanes:

$$CH_3CH_2CH_2 \!\!-\!\! MgBr \ + \ H\!\!-\!\!OCH_3 \longrightarrow CH_3CH_2CH_3 \ + \ CH_3OMgBr$$

Because they are such strong bases, Grignard reagents cannot be used with solvents or reactants that can act as proton donors (e.g., H_2O, alcohols, –NH, and –SH groups). Their alkyl or aryl groups act as nucleophiles in chemical reactions.

The most important reactions of Grignard reagents are reactions with carbonyl compounds. The carbon of the carbonyl group bears a partial positive charge, and it is readily attacked by the nucleophilic carbon of the Grignard:

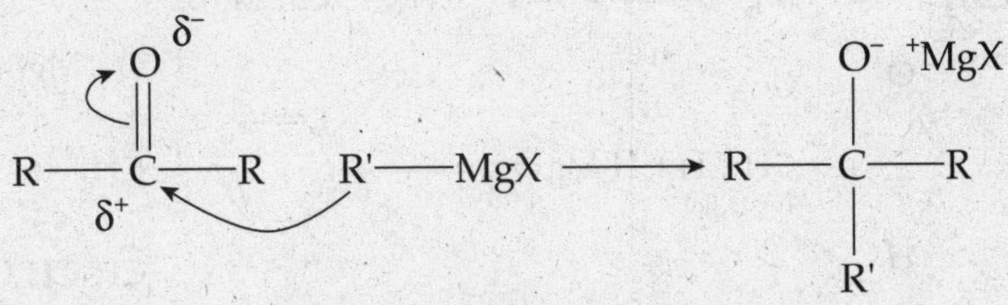

The product is the magnesium salt of an alcohol. Treatment of the salt with water or aqueous acid yields the alcohol and a mixed inorganic magnesium salt:

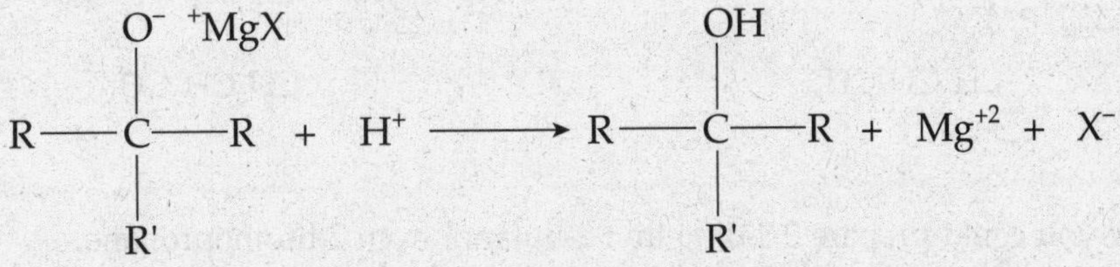

The two steps of a Grignard reaction are usually combined into a single equation:

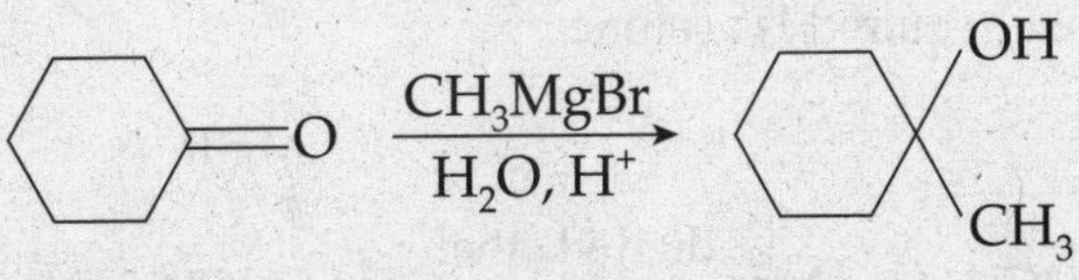

The reaction with carbon dioxide is slightly different; it yields a magnesium carboxylate salt that is insoluble in ether. This means that only one of the carbonyl groups reacts. Treatment of the salt with acid produces a carboxylic acid.

Some important products obtained with Grignard reagents are

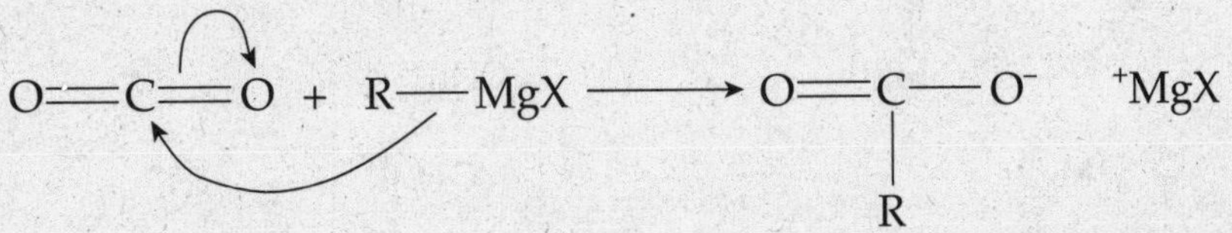

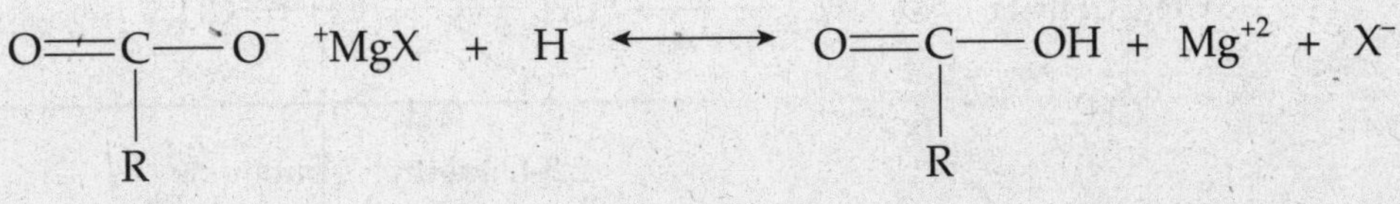

- Formaldehyde + RMgX → primary alcohol (RCH_2OH)

- Aldehyde (RCOH) + RMgX → secondary alcohol (RCHOHR′)

- Ketones (RCOR′) + RMgX → tertiary alcohol (RCOHR′R″)

- CO_2 + RMgX → carboxylic acid (RCOOH)

Example:

What is the final product of the reaction of bromopropane with magnesium in diethyl ether, followed by reaction with benzaldehyde and the addition of dilute hydrochloric acid?

Answer: The equation for the formation of the Grignard reagent should be written first, followed by that of Grignard reaction with the aldehyde and H^+, which yields a secondary alcohol:

$$CH_3CH_2CH_2Br \ + \ Mg \ \xrightarrow{(CH_3CH_2)_2O} \ CH_3CH_2CH_2MgBr$$

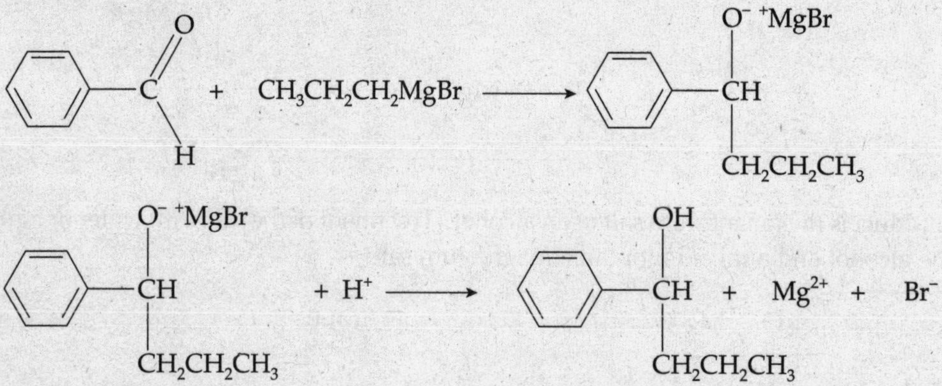

Example:

Show how you could prepare 2,3-dimethyl-2-butanol from 2-bromopropane.

Answer: You must recognize that the product is a tertiary alcohol and thus be obtained by reaction of a ketone with a Grignard. The Grignard formula is RMgX so 2-bromopropane is used to prepare RMgBr. The ketone required is acetone.

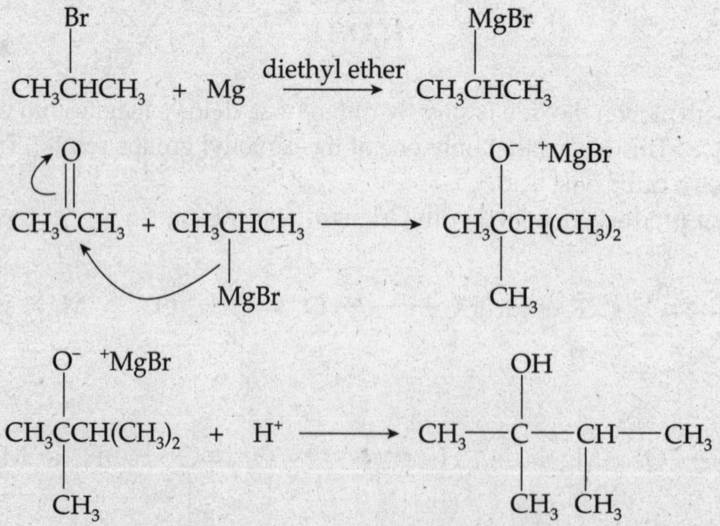

2,3-Dimethyl-2-butanone

ORGANOLITHIUM REAGENTS

Organolithium reagents and other Group I organometallics are prepared by the reaction of an alkyl halide (RX) with the desired metal in a wide variety of solvents. Unlike the preparation of RMgX, ether is not required:

$$RX + 2M \text{ (Group I)} \longrightarrow RM + M^+X^-$$

$$CH_3CH_2CH_2Br + 2Li \longrightarrow CH_3CH_2CH_2Li + LiBr$$

The reaction takes place at the metal surface. First, an electron is transferred from the metal to the alkyl halide; this produces an anion radical.

The extra electron is in an antibonding orbital. After dissociation, the alkyl radical combines with a lithium atom to form the organolithium reagent:

$$R{-\!\!-}X^{\cdot} \longrightarrow R + X^-$$

$$R\cdot + Li\cdot \longrightarrow R{-\!\!-}Li$$

Lithium is more electropositive than magnesium, so organolithium reagents are more reactive nucleophiles than Grignard reagents because the carbon atom carrying the lithium is more negative. Like Grignard reagents, they react with carbonyl compounds to form alcohols:

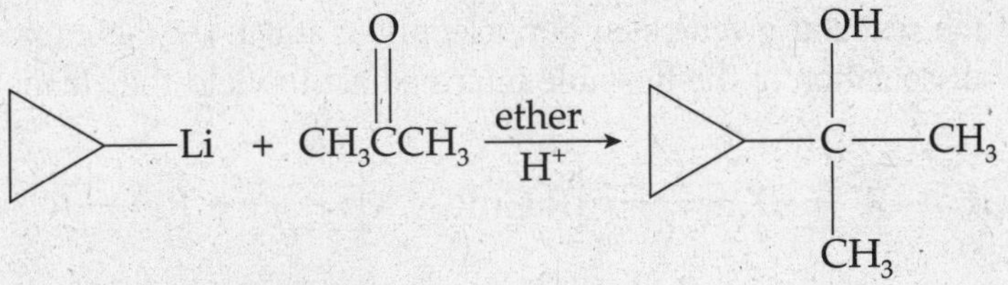

LITHIUM ORGANOCUPRATES

Lithium organocuprates are particularly useful in coupling two alkyl fragments to produce a larger alkane in a synthesis called the **Corey-House reaction**.

Lithium dialkylcuprates (R_2–Cu–Li) are the preferred organometallic reagents for this reaction, and the most commonly used are

- $(CH_3)_2$–Cu–Li, lithium dimethylcuprate;
- $(H_2C=CH)_2$–Cu–Li, lithium divinylcuprate.

A dialkylcuprate is obtained from the reaction of a copper (I) halide with two equivalents of an alkyl lithium:

$$2RLi + CuX \longrightarrow R_2CuLi + LiX$$

The reaction proceeds in two steps:

1. One molar equivalent of alkyllithium reacts with CuX to yield an alkylcopper (I);
2. The second molar equivalent of alkyllithium reacts with the alkylcopper to give a dialklylcuprate, formed as a lithium salt:

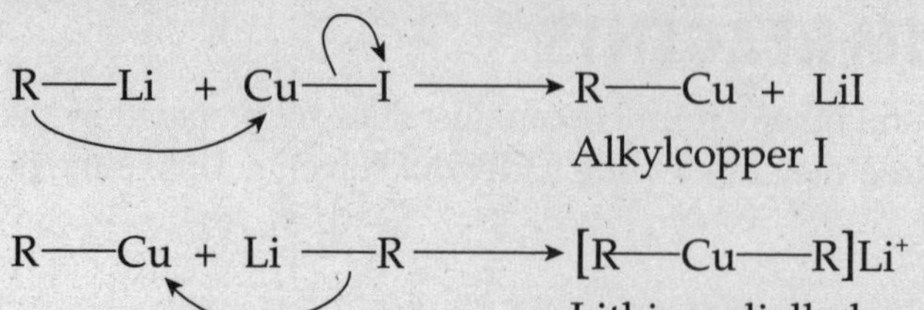

$$R\!-\!Li \ + \ Cu\!-\!I \longrightarrow R\!-\!Cu \ + \ LiI$$

Alkylcopper I

$$R\!-\!Cu \ + \ Li\!-\!R \longrightarrow \big[R\!-\!Cu\!-\!R\big]Li^{+}$$

Lithium dialkylcuprate

Lithium diarylcuprates are prepared in the same way. These reagents are useful for the synthesis of unsymmetrical alkanes of the type R–R′, where R′ (primary or secondary alkyl group, vinyl, or aryl group) comes from the alkyl halide:

$$R_2CuLi \ + \ R'X \longrightarrow RR'$$

$$(CH_3)_2CuLi \ + \ CH_3(CH_2)_8CH_2I \longrightarrow CH_3(CH_2)_8CH_2CH_3$$

| Lithium dimethylcuprate | 1-Iodododecane | Undecane |

The reaction of cuprates with alkyl halides follows the S_N2 order of reactivity:

$$CH_3 > primary > secondary > tertiary, \ and \ I > Br > Cl > F.$$

For secondary and tertiary halides, elimination becomes important. Organocuprates bearing primary halide groups are preferred because those bearing secondary or tertiary alkyl groups are less reactive toward alkyl halides.

The key step of the reaction mechanism is nucleophilic attack by the cuprate ion on the alkyl halide, followed by dissociation of the unstable intermediate to yield the alkane:

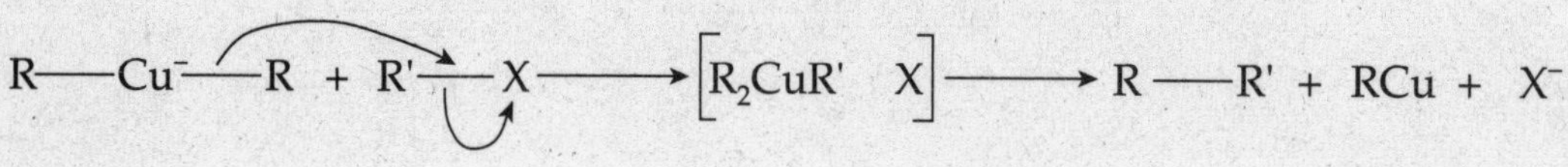

$$R\!-\!Cu^{-}\!-\!R \ + \ R'\!-\!X \longrightarrow \big[R_2CuR' \ \ X\big] \longrightarrow R\!-\!R' \ + \ RCu \ + \ X^{-}$$

Example:

What combination of alkyl halide and cuprate reagent would you use for the preparation of 2-methylpentane? (There may be several correct answers.)

Answer: Examine the structure of 2-methyl pentane and determine which C–C bonds can be formed. Remember that neither the alkyl halide nor the cuprate reagent should have secondary or tertiary alkyl groups. The C_3–C_4 or C_4–C_5 bonds could be formed in four different ways:

$$(CH_3)_2CuLi \ + \ BrCH_2CH_2CH(CH_3)_3 \longrightarrow CH_3\!-\!CH_2CH_2CH(CH_3)_2$$

$$(CH_3CH_2)_2CuLi \ + \ BrCH_2CH(CH_3)_3 \longrightarrow CH_3CH_2\!-\!CH_2CH(CH_3)_2$$

$$\Big[(CH_3)_2CHCH_2CH_2\Big]CuLi \ + \ CH_3Br \longrightarrow (CH_3)_2CHCH_2CH_2\!-\!CH_3$$

$$\Big[(CH_3)_2CHCH_2\Big]CuLi \ + \ CH_3CH_2Br \longrightarrow (CH_3)_2CHCH_2\!-\!CH_2CH_3$$

Grignard and organolithium reagents are very strong bases, they react rapidly with acidic hydrogens to yield hydrocarbons and metal salts:

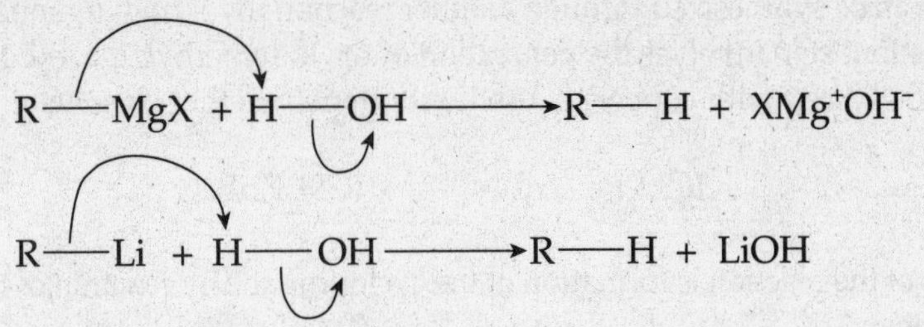

$$R\overset{\frown}{\longrightarrow}MgX + H\overset{\frown}{\longrightarrow}OH \longrightarrow R\longrightarrow H + XMg^+OH^-$$

$$R\overset{\frown}{\longrightarrow}Li + H\overset{\frown}{\longrightarrow}OH \longrightarrow R\longrightarrow H + LiOH$$

Grignard and lithium are stronger bases than OH^-, RO^- and NH_2^-. The hydrogens bonded to oxygen, nitrogen, and sp-hybridized carbons can easily be abstracted from these reagents.

Example:

Could a Grignard reagent be prepared with 3-amino-1-bromobutane?

Answer: Yes, because the carbon of the Grignard reagent is partially negative and so can react with a positive group, such as the acidic hydrogen on the amino group.

OTHER ORGANOMETALLIC REAGENTS

Organozinc reagents are prepared in the same way as other organometallic reagents:

$$RX + Zn \xrightarrow{\text{ether}} RZnX$$

They are not as reactive toward carbonyl compounds as organolithium or organomagnesium reagents.

They are often involved as reaction intermediates in reactions between alkyl halides and zinc in acid media:

$$RX + Zn \longrightarrow \overset{\delta^-}{R}\longrightarrow \overset{\delta^+}{ZnX} + HX \longrightarrow RH + ZnX_2$$

1,2-Dihalides undergo dehalogenation by reaction with zinc. Here the C–Zn bond of the intermediate provides electrons for a β-elimination:

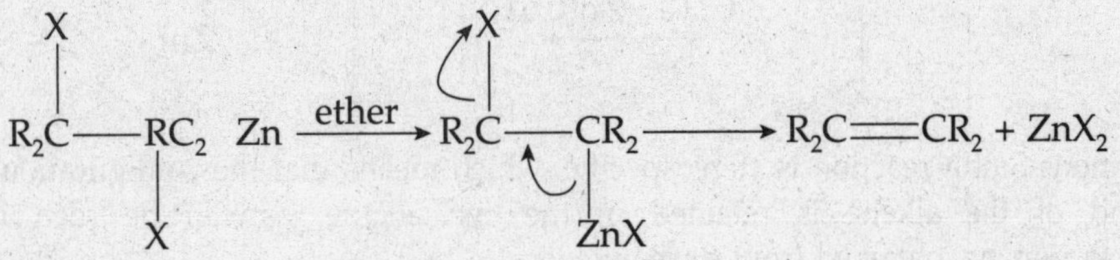

1,3-Dihalides are converted to cyclopropanes by treatment with zinc. The negative C–Zn bond acts as an internal nucleophile during cycloformation:

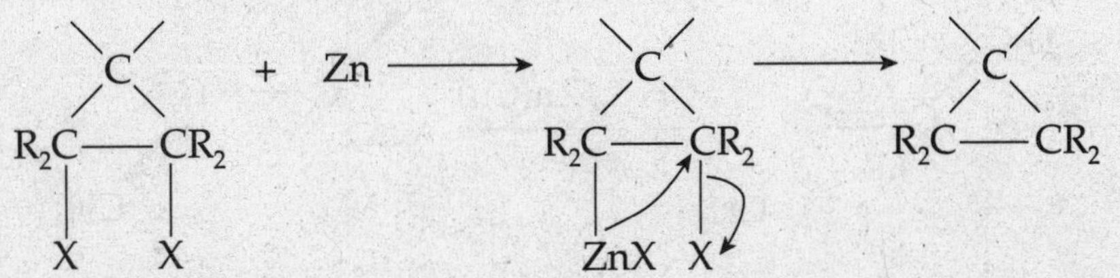

Cyclopropanes can be synthesized through another reaction involving organozinc: the **Simmons-Smith reaction**. The first step involves the generation of the iodomethylzinc iodide reactant. A zinc-copper couple (zinc covered with copper) is used with dimethylether as solvent:

$$ICH_2I + Zn \xrightarrow[Cu]{ether} ICH_2ZnI$$

The second step of the reaction is formation of the cyclopropane by reaction of the iodomethylzinc iodide with an alkene:

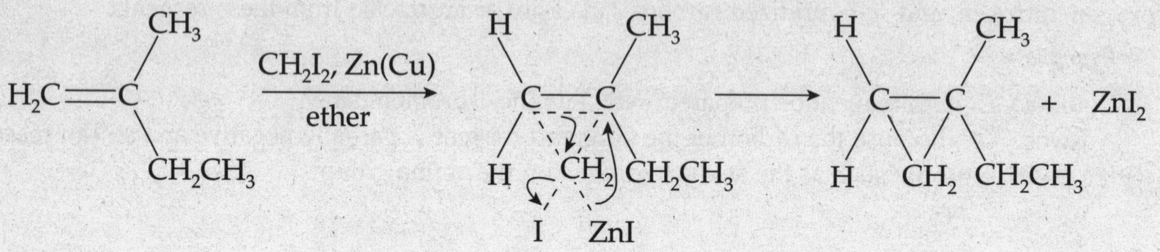

Example:

How could you use the Simmons-Smith reaction to synthesize:

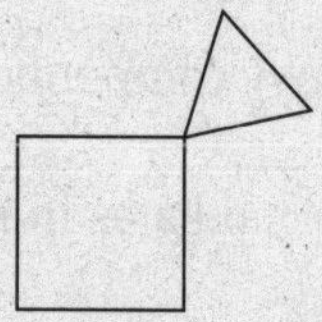

Answer: In the Simmons-Smith reaction, a CH_2 group is transferred from the organometallic compound to the alkene. Therefore, disconnect a CH_2 unit from the cyclopropene ring to identify the substrate:

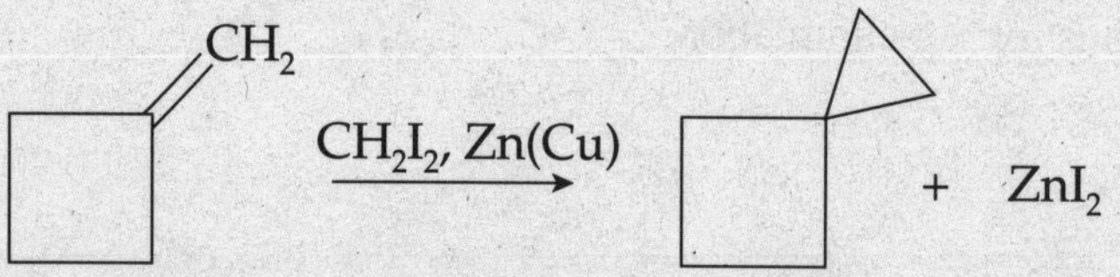

The Simmons-Smith reaction is stereospecific, which means that the configuration around the double bond of the alkene is retained in the cycloalkane, as can be seen in *trans*-1,2-dimethylcyclopropane, obtained from *trans*-butene:

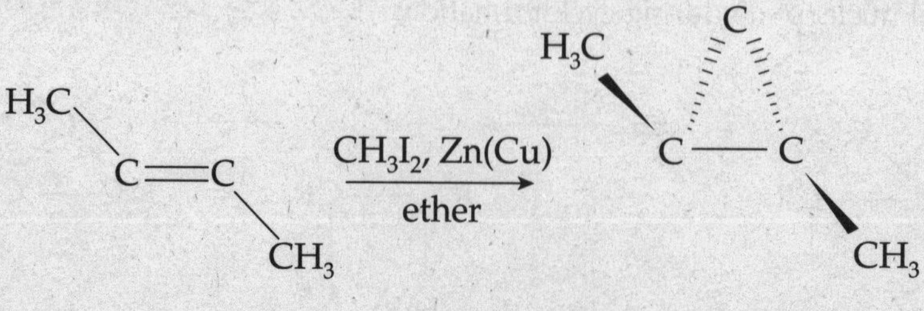

The most useful **organomercury** compounds are formed when mercury (II) acetate, $Hg(O_2CCH_3)_2$, reacts with alkenes in a mixture of water and tetrahydrofuran (THF). This reaction is called **oxymercuration**, and the product formed is a β-hydroxyalkylmercury(II) acetate:

$$\text{C==C} + Hg(O_2CCH_3)_2 + H_2O \longrightarrow HO-C-C-HgO_2CCH_3 + CH_3CO_2H$$

β-Hydroxyalkyl-
mercury(II) acetate

The product of an oxymercuration is not isolated; it's treated with a basic solution of sodium borohydride ($NaBH_4$) in a subsequent reaction called **demercuration**, which yields an alcohol.

Oxymercuration-demercuration gives better yields than the simple addition of water with H_2SO_4. The reaction sequence occurs according to Markovnikov's rule: the hydrogen atom introduced in step two attaches to the carbon that has the greater number of hydrogen substituents, and the hydroxyl group introduced in step one goes to the carbon atom that has the fewer hydrogen substituents:

$$HO-C-C-HgO_2CCH_3 \xrightarrow[OH^-]{NaBH_4} HO-C-C-H + Hg + CH_3CO_2^-$$

Example:

What is the oxymercuration-demercuration product of 1-pentene?

Answer: Considering Markovnikov's rule, determine on which carbon the hydrogen and hydroxyl groups will attach: C_2 has fewer hydrogens and so will gain the –OH group:

$$CH_3CH_2CH_2CH=CH_2 \xrightarrow[NaBH_4,\ OH^-]{Hg(OAc)_2, H_2O-THF} CH_3CH_2CH_2\overset{\overset{\displaystyle OH}{|}}{C}H-CH_3$$

1-Pentene   2-Pentanol

Example:

What is the structure of the two alkenes that could produce 1-methylcyclopentanol by oxymercuration-demercuration?

Answer: Examine the structure of the alcohol: the hydroxyl group is on a tertiary carbon. Therefore, an alkene with a double bond located either in the ring, between C_1 and C_2, or out of the ring at position C_1 could undergo reaction according to Markovnikov's rule:

The oxymercuration-demercuration reaction has three steps. The first is the dissociation of mercury(II) acetate:

$$Hg(O_2CCH_3)_2 \rightleftharpoons {}^+HgO_2CCH_3 + {}^-O_2CCH_3$$

mercury(II) cation

The second step is the electrophilic attack of the π electrons of the C=C bond by the mercury cation, with formation of a bridged intermediate:

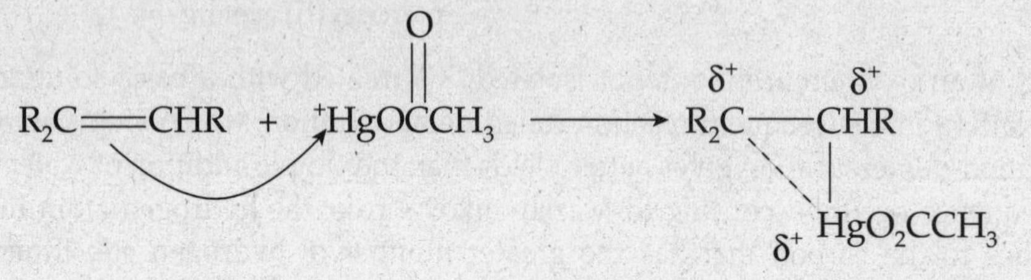

Bridged carbocation intermediate

The final step is attack by H_2O and proton loss:

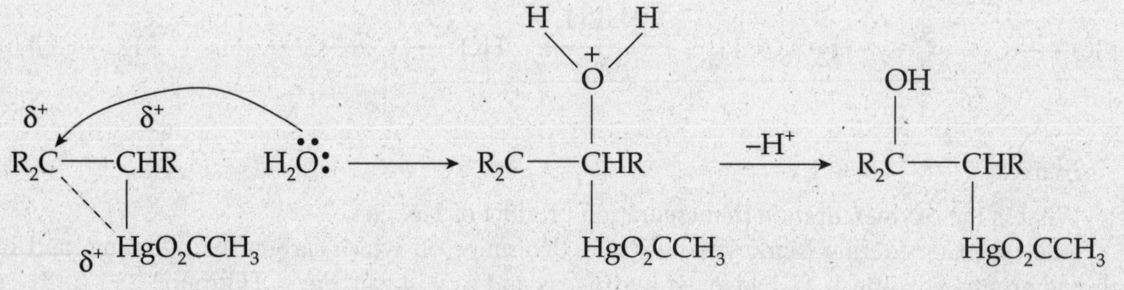

H_2O attacks the more positive carbon of the bridge intermediate, which you can identify if you remember the order of carbocation stability (tertiary > secondary > primary).

Oxymercuration-demercuration can be applied to the synthesis of ethers by substituting an alcohol for THF—the reaction is called **solvomercuration-demercuration**:

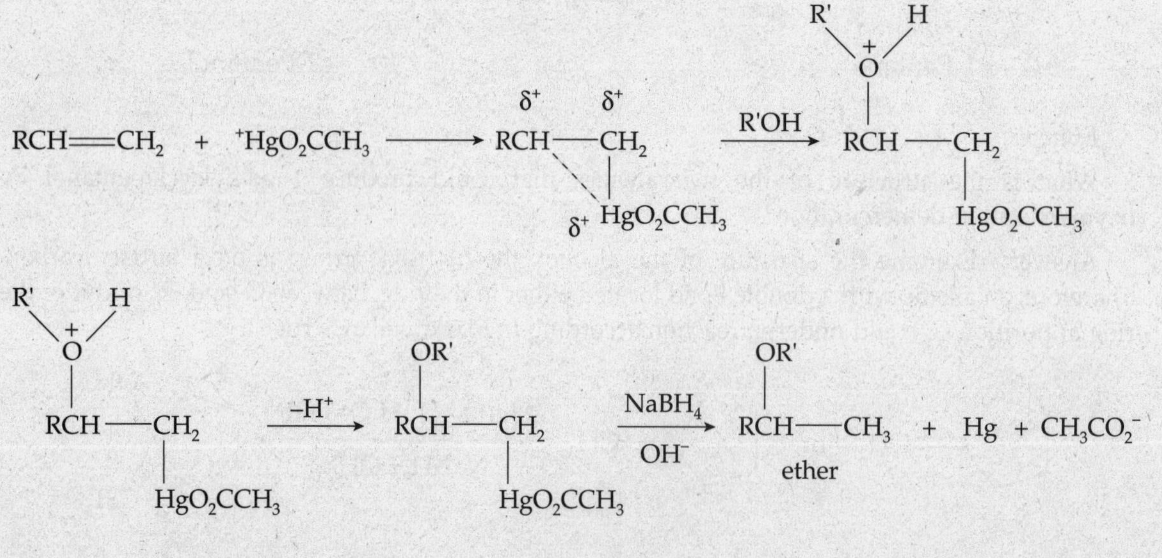

Example:

How would you prepare 2-methoxy-2-phenylpropane by solvomercuration?

Answer: Examine the structure of this product. The methoxy group is on a tertiary carbon. According to Markovnikov's rule, ethers such as this are obtained only if the alkene substrate has its double bond between this carbon and an adjacent one. The solvent is methanol:

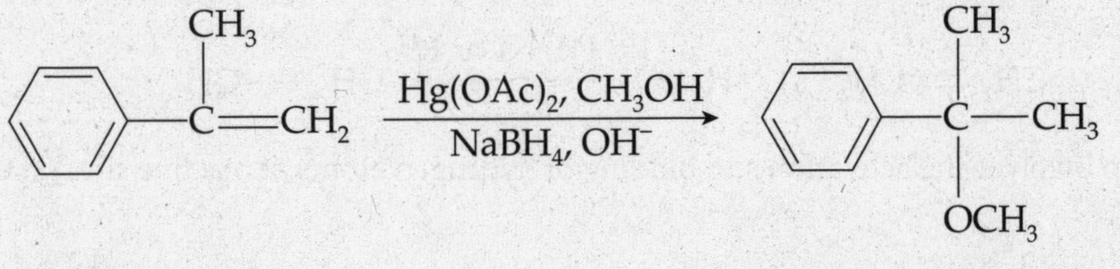

2-Phenylpropene   2-Methoxy-2-phenylpropane

Many organometallic compounds are derived from transition metals such as iron, chromium, nickel, platinum, or rhodium. In these compounds, the organic group is bonded to the metal through its π electron system. For example, **benzenetricarbonyl chromium** has three σ bonds between the CO groups and Cr and a benzene ring (not a phenyl group) attached to the metal:

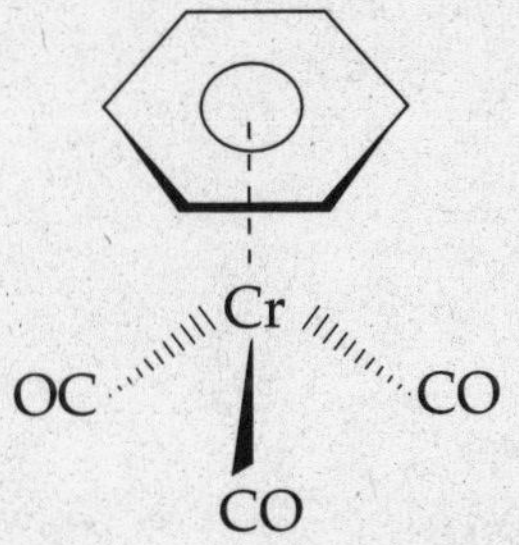

The bond between benzene and the chromium atom is very strong. Systems like these are referred to as π complexes. Bonding with a metal stabilizes species that are highly reactive in their free state. For example, **cyclobutadiene tricarbonyliron**:

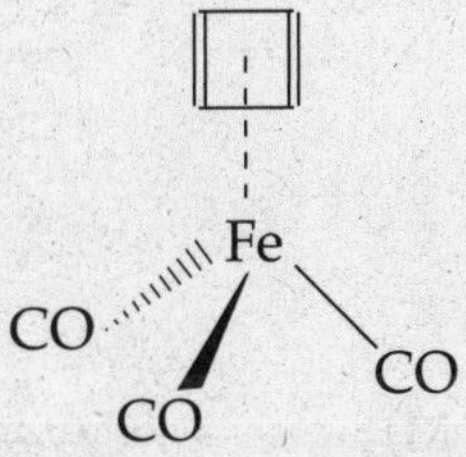

Ferrocene is a well-known π bonded organometallic compound, in which two cyclopentadienyl radicals are held together by an iron atom.

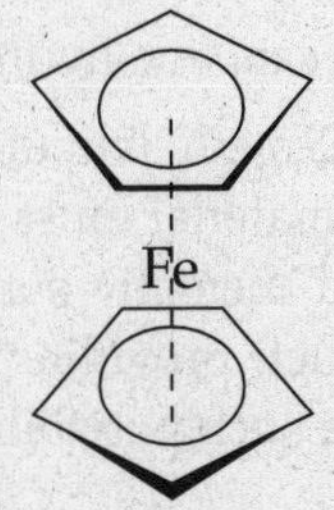

The iron atom donates two of its electrons to form a stable iron(II) ion, and the cyclopentadienyls become anions.

The compound holds together as a neutral, stable π bonded sandwich structure.

Metals and their complexes catalyze many important industrial organic processes. For example, the hydrogenation of alkenes is carried out in the presence of metals such as palladium, platinum, nickel, and rhodium:

$$CH_2{=\!=}CH_2 \; + \; H_2 \; \xrightarrow{\text{Pt, Pd, Ni or Rh}} \; CH_3{-\!-}CH_3$$

The first step involves the activation and binding of hydrogen atoms at reactive sites on the metal surface:

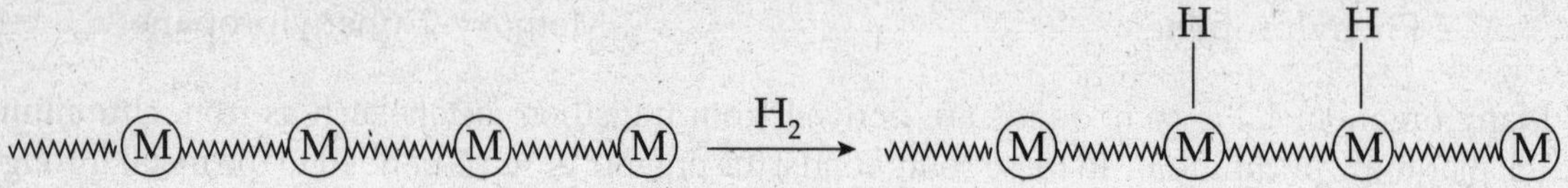

A second step transfers a hydrogen atom from the surface of the catalyst to one of the carbons of the alkene. The other carbon then binds to the metal:

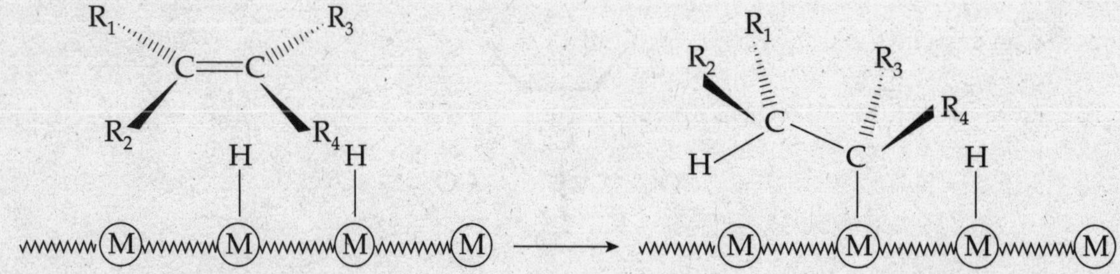

During the final reaction step, the second hydrogen is transferred. An alkane is obtained, and the catalyst is regenerated:

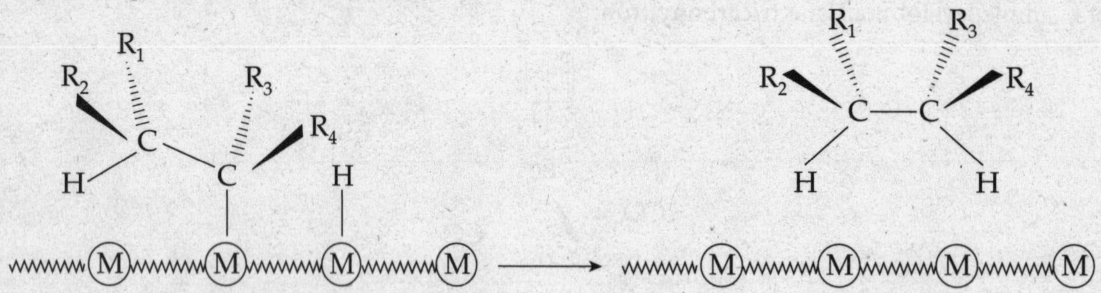

Example:

How can 2-methylbutane be formed by catalytic hydrogenation?

Answer: First you must recognize that 2-methylbutane is a substituted alkane and that to obtain it by cayalytic hydrogenation, the starting material must be an alkene. To identify this alkene, you must simply examine the final alkane and mentally subtract two hydrogen atoms. Any pair of hydrogen atoms will yield the final product, providing that they are placed on adjacent carbon atoms. For 2-methylbutane, there are three such possibilities:

(a) Subtract one H from C_1 and one H from C_2. The resulting alkene is 2-methyl-1-butene: $CH_2=C(CH_3)-CH_2-CH_3$;

(b) Subtract one H from C_2 and one H from C_3. The resulting alkene is 2-methyl-2-butene: $CH_3-C(CH_3)=CH-CH_3$;

(c) Subtract one H from C_2 and one H from C_3 with the methyl substituent on C_3. The resulting alkene in this case is 3-methyl-1-butene: $CH_2=CH-CH(CH_3)-CH_3$.

SPECIAL TOPICS

Organic compounds, by virtue of their covalent bonding, easily form macromolecular assemblies, of which the most important are proteins and nucleic acids, the building blocks of life. The topics covered under this heading include: carbohydrates, nucleic acids, amino acids, peptides, proteins, and lipids.

CARBOHYDRATES

Carbohydrates or **saccharides** have the general formula $C_n(H_2O)_m$. They include aliphatic polyhydroxaldehydes (**aldoses**), polyhydroxyketones (**ketoses**), and all compounds that yield them upon hydrolysis. The simpler carbohydrates are also called **sugars**. They are synthesized by almost all living organisms—plant and animals—as a source of metabolic energy. The oxidation of **glucose** to CO_2 and H_2O provides energy for all cells, and the conversion of glucose to **starch** is the main energy storage mechanism of plants.

   Monosaccharides are saccharides that cannot be hydrolyzed to simpler structures.

Glucose, an aldose   Fructose, a ketose

A **disaccharide** can be hydrolyzed to yield two monosaccharides.

For example, sucrose, a disaccharide, can be hydrolyzed to one molecule of glucose and one molecule of fructose.

Carbohydrates are named as follows:

- **Aldoses** contain the aldehyde functional group, and **hexoses** contain the ketone group.

- The number of carbons in the chain determines the root name, and the names are followed by the suffix –*ose*.

  Triose = 3 carbons

  Tetrose = 4 carbons

  Pentose = 5 carbons

  Hexose = 6 carbons

  Heptose = 7 carbons

- The configuration of the chiral carbon farthest from the CO group confers to the carbohydrate a stereochemical prefix, either *D* or *L*.

The D prefix refers to carbohydrates that degrade to (+) glyceraldehyde and the L prefix designates those that degrade to (–) glyceraldehyde.

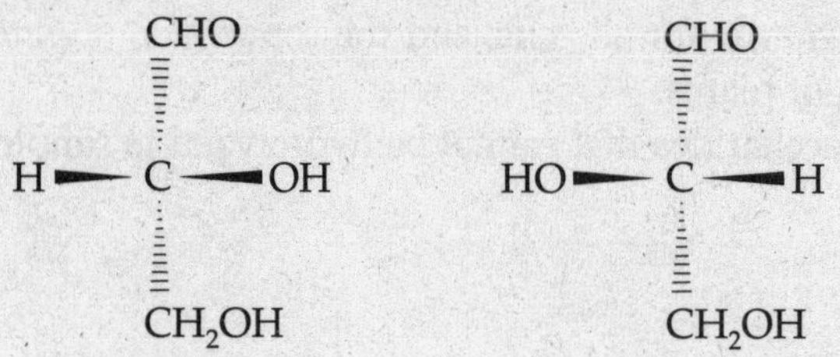

D-carbohydrates
degrade to
(+)-glyceraldehyde

L-carbohydrates
degrade to
(–)-glyceraldehyde

The *D*-carbohydrates have the –OH group in the bottom chiral carbon to the right in a Fisher projection.

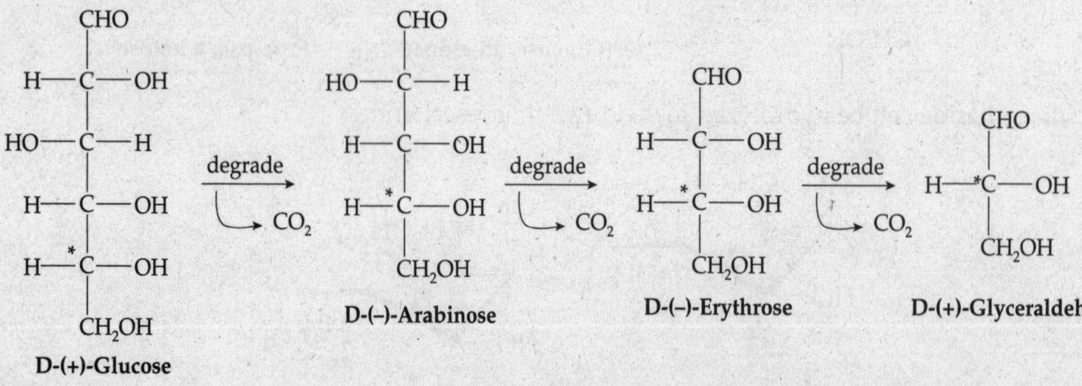

D-(+)-Glucose

D-(–)-Arabinose

D-(–)-Erythrose

D-(+)-Glyceraldehyde

The *D* and *L* convention is not indicative of optical activity. The (+) and (–) convention is required to show which way a compound will rotate the plane of polarized light. So this means that a *D*-carbohydrate can rotate the plane of polarized light either clockwise or counterclockwise.

Carbohydrates form **epimers**, compounds whose stereochemistry differs at only one carbon:

C₂ epimers of aldohexose

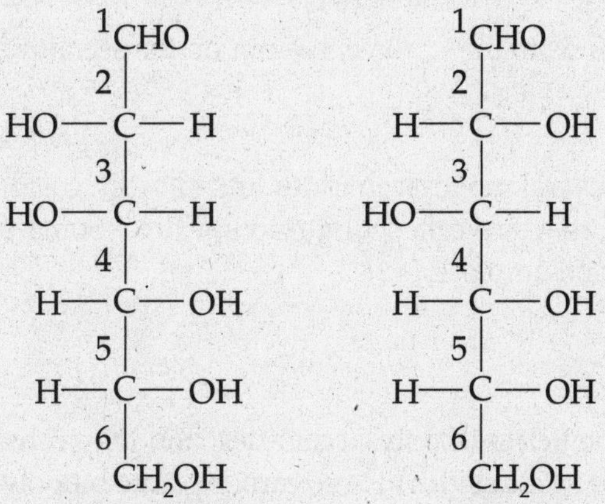

D-mannose   *D*-glucose

Cyclic Carbohydrates

In the solid state, aldoses exist as cyclic hemiacetals. In the liquid state, although they exist in both cyclic and open-chain forms, equilibrium generally favors the hemiacetal form.

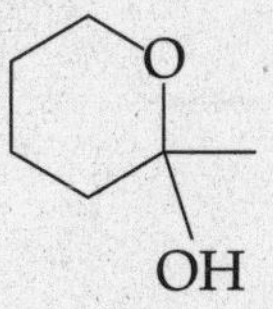

Hemiacetal

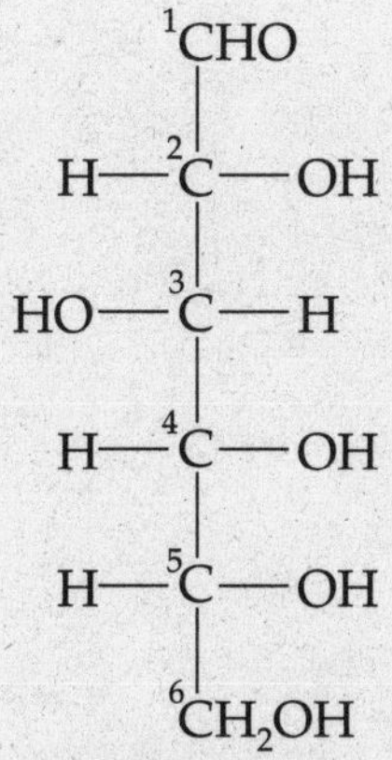

D-glucose

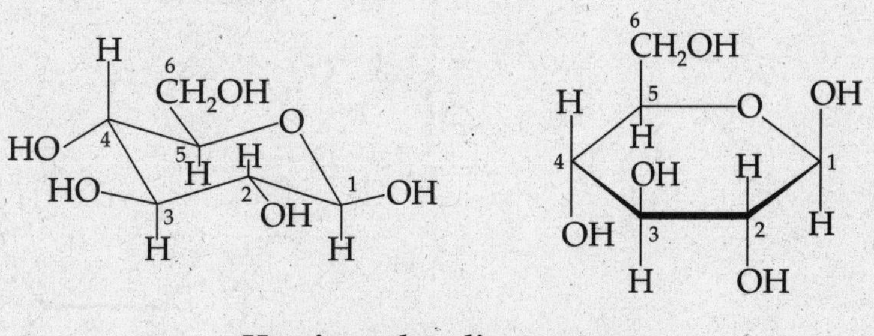

Hemiacetal cyclic structures

When the hemiacetal ring closes, carbon 1 becomes a chiral carbon, and the –OH group of this hemiacetal carbon can be oriented either up or down. These two possible orientations give rise to diastereomers called **anomers**, and the hemiacetal carbon (C_1) is called an **anomeric carbon**. When this carbon reacts with the –OH group of an alcohol, the acetal product is called a **glycoside**. If the –OH group belongs to another carbohydrate molecule, the glycoside is a **disaccharide**. In disaccharide formation, anomeric carbons can adopt the following glycosidic bonding schemes:

1. The 1,1' link: C_1 binds to the C_1 oxygen atom on the second carbohydrate.

2. The 1,4' link: C_1 binds to the C_4 oxygen atom on the second carbohydrate.

3. The 1,6' link: C_1 binds to the C_6 oxygen atom on the second carbohydrate.

Polysaccharides

Polysaccharides consist of several monosaccharides linked by glycosidic bonds. When they contain up to ten monosaccharides, they are called **oligosaccharides**. Some common polysaccharides are starch, glycogen, cellulose, and amylose.

NUCLEIC ACIDS

Nucleic acids are an important class of polysaccharides, and they consist of both **RNA** (ribonucleic acids) and **DNA** (deoxyribonucleic acids). These carbohydrate biopolymers consist of ribofuranose chains linked by phosphate ester groups. Illustrated below is DNA:

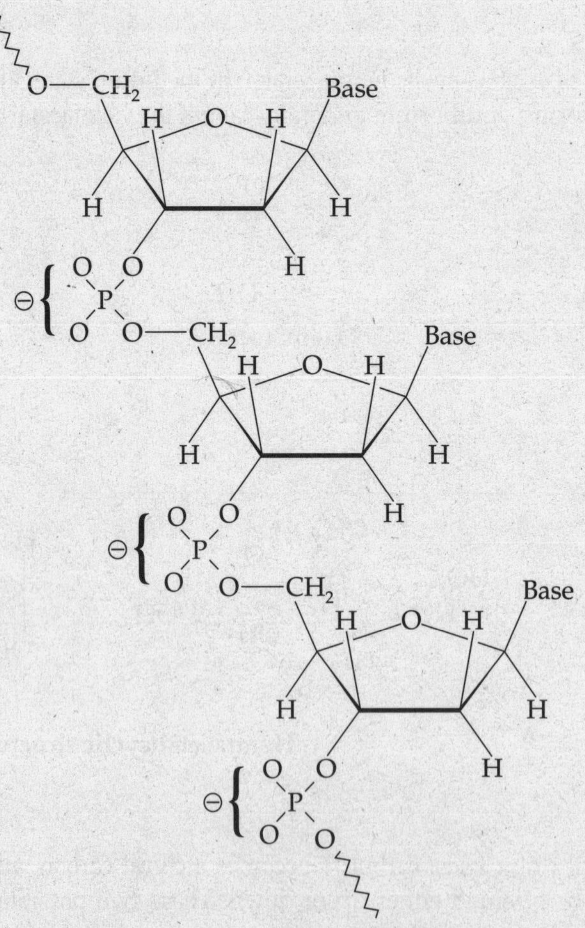

The building blocks of nucleic acids are **ribonucleosides**, which are glycosides of ribofuranose—or ribofuranosides β, derived from cyclic *D*-ribose:

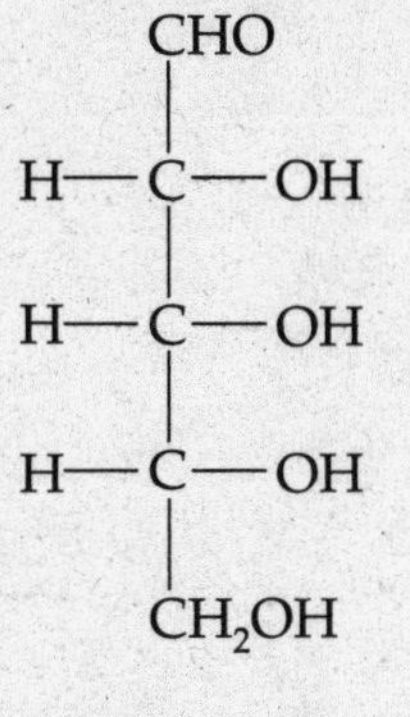

D-Ribose 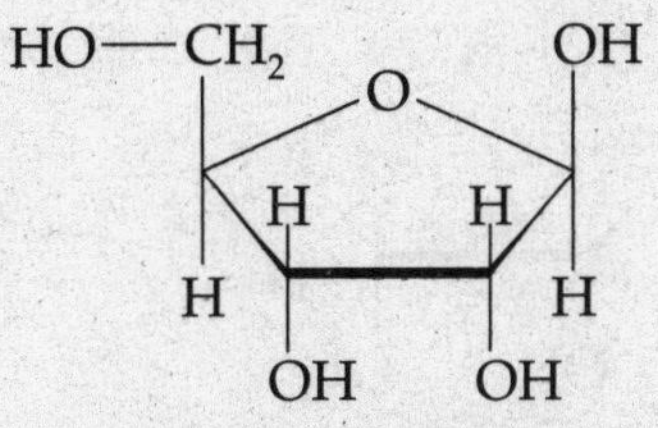   **β-D-Ribofuranose** 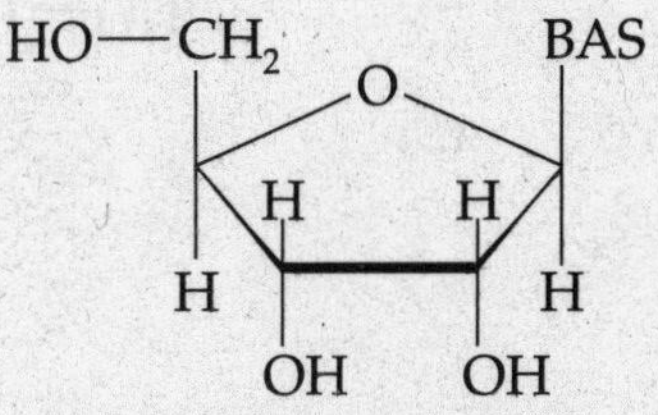   **Ribonucleoside**

The most well-known ribonucleoside bases are the single ring **pyrimidine** bases and the two ring **purine**, which carry the genetic information:

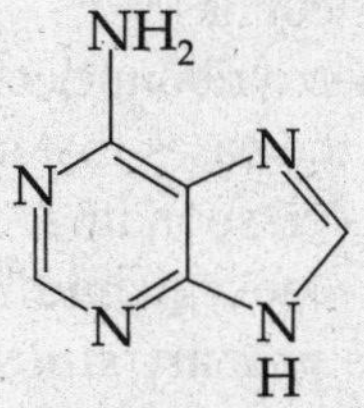

Adenine (A) 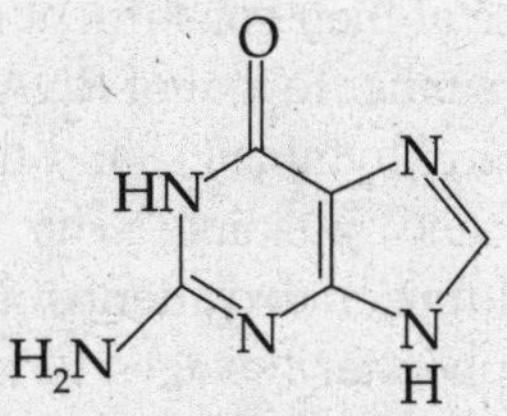   **Guanine (G)**

Purine bases

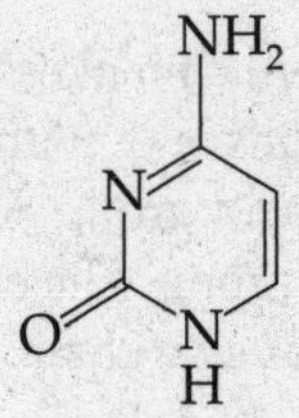

Cytosine (C) 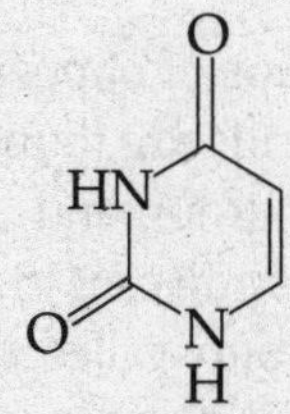   **Uracil (U)**

Pyrimidine bases

The four corresponding ribonucleosides are **cytidine** (C), **uridine** (U) **adenosine** (A), and **guanosine** (G). When ribonucleosides are phosphorylated at their C_5 carbon, they are called **ribonucleotides**. The four common ribonucleotides of RNA are **cytidine monophosphate (CMP)**, **uridine monophosphate (UMP)**, **adenosine monophosphate (AMP)**, and **guanosine monophosphate (GMP)**.

5'-Adenylic acid (AMP)

The phosphate group on the 5' carbon of a ribonucleotide can link with the –OH group of a 3' carbon in another ribonucleotide. This bond is called a phosphoester linkage. When many ribonucleotide units are linked by these bonds, a RNA polymer is created. RNA polymers differ from one another only in the sequence of their constituent ribonucleotides.

The structure of **DNA** is similar to that of RNA. The deoxyribonucleosides are derived from *D-2-deoxyribose* and the bases are thymine (T) and three of the bases that are also found in ribonucleotides: cytosine, adenine and guanine. The four corresponding deoxyribonucleosides are: **deoxycytidine, deoxythimidine, deoxyadenosine,** and **deoxyguanidine.** When phosphorylated, they too, can link via phosphoester linkages to form the **primary structure** of a DNA strand. The bases can hydrogen bond with other bases in a process called **base pairing**. So cytosine and guanine can form one **base pair**, and thymine (uracil in RNA) and adenine can form another. The DNA molecule consists of a double chain of polynucleotides held together by hydrogen-bonded base pairs.

AMINO ACIDS

Amino acids bear charged groups of opposite polarity, which makes them dipolar ions, or **zwitterions**. Twenty common amino acids are found in all proteins and, with the exception of proline, they all consist of a primary amino group and a carboxylic acid group substituted to the same carbon, called the α-carbon because it is adjacent to the carboxyl group. The other two carbon bonds are to a hydrogen and a substitutent group, called the R group, or side chain. The 20 naturally occurring α-**amino acids** have the same basic structure:

At physiological pH around pH 7, both –NH$_2$ and –COOH groups are completely ionized in solution, and the amino acid can act as an acid or a base, whereby the amino group is protonated (–NH$_3^+$) and the carboxyl group is dissociated (–COO$^-$). They are accordingly referred to as **amphoteric** substances. Some amino acids have a third ionizable group in their R group. The ionization state of an amino acid is pH-dependent. At acidic pH (pH ≈ 1), the carboxyl group is undissociated and protonated (–COOH), and the amino group is protonated (–NH$_3^+$). At alkaline pH (pH ≈ 10), the carboxyl group is ionized (–COO$^-$), and the amino group is not ionized (NH$_2$).

| Glycine at pH < 2.3 | Glycine at pH 7 | Glycine at pH > 9 |

The following table lists the pK_a values of the 20 naturally occurring amino acids. All have pK_a values for the amino and carboxyl groups. The amino acids that have ionizable side chains show a third pK_a.

Amino acid	R group	pI	pK_a, α-COOH α-NH$_3^+$, R group
Gly	–H	6.0	2.35, 9.78
Ala	–CH$_3$	6.0	2.35, 9.87
Val	–CH(CH$_3$)	6.0	2.29, 9.74
Leu	–CH$_2$CH(CH$_3$)$_2$	6.0	2.33, 9.74
Ile	–CHCH$_3$CH$_2$CH$_3$	6.0	2.32, 9.76
Phe	–CH$_2$Ar	5.5	2.16, 9.18
Tyr	–CH$_2$Ar–OH	5.7	2.20, 9.11, 10.13
Trp	–CH$_2$–indole	5.9	2.43, 9.44
Ser	–CH$_2$OH	5.7	2.19, 9.21
Thr	–CHCH$_3$OH	5.6	2.09, 9.11
Cys	–CH$_2$SH	5.0	1.92, 8.35, 10.46
Met	–CH$_2$CH$_2$SCH$_3$	5.7	2.13, 9.28
Asn	–CH$_2$C=ONH$_2$	5.4	2.11, 8.84
Gln	–(CH$_2$)$_2$C=ONH$_2$	5.7	1.99, 3.90, 9.90
Glu	–(CH$_2$)$_2$C=COOH	3.2	1.99, 3.90, 9.90
Asp	–CH$_2$COOH	2.8	2.10, 4.07, 9.46
Lys	–(CH$_2$)$_4$NH$_3^+$	9.7	2.16, 9.18, 10.79
Arg	–CH$_2$–imidazole	10.8	1.82, 8.99, 12.48
His	–pyrrilidine–COOH	7.6	1.80, 6.04, 9.33

The pH at which the amino acid exists as an equilibrium mixture of anionic and cationic forms is called the **isoelectric point** (pI). The amino acids with nonionizable R groups have pI values close to 5. This is due to the fact that their $-NH_3^+$ group is somewhat more acidic than their $-COO^-$ group is basic. Asp and Glu both have R groups that contain an acidic carboxyl group; this lowers their pI values to ~ 3. Similarly, His, Lys, and Arg, respectively, have an imidazole, an amino group, and a guanidine in their R groups, and this is reflected in their high pI values.

Glycine (Gly, G)   **Alanine (Ala, A)**   **Valine (Val, V)**   **Leucine (Leu, L)**

Isoleucine (Ile, I)   **Phenylalanine (Phe, F)**   **Tyrosine (Tyr, T)**

Tryptophan (Trp, W)   **Serine (Ser, S)**   **Threonine (Thr, T)**   **Cysteine (Cys, C)**

Methionine (Met, M)   **Asparagine (Asn, D)**   **Glutamine (Gln, Q)**

Aspartic acid (Asp, D)   **Glutamic acid (Glu, E)**   **Lysine (Lys, K)**

Arginine (Arg, R)   **Histidine (His, H)**   **Proline (Pro, P)**

PEPTIDES

Amino acids can link to form **peptides** via amide linkages called **peptide bonds**:

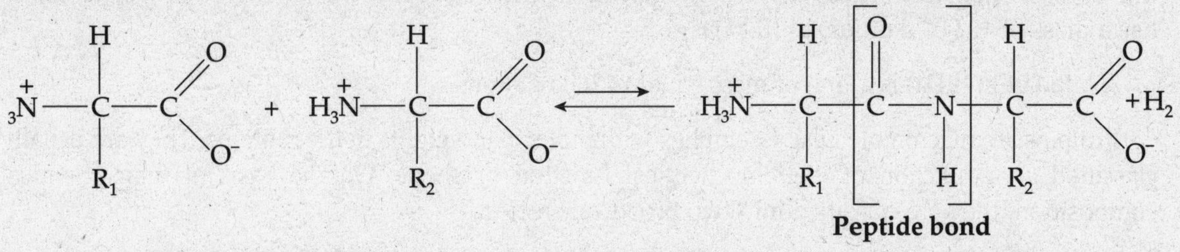

Peptide bond

When several amino acids are joined by peptide bonds, a structure called a **polypeptide** is formed:

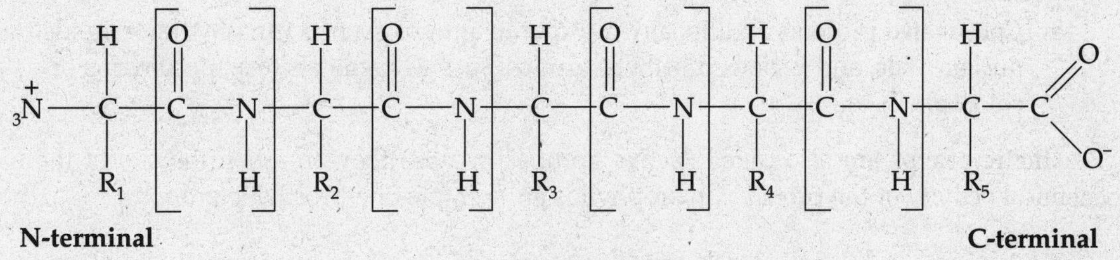

N-terminal **C-terminal**

A pentapeptide

Polypeptide chains are oriented. By convention, the amino end is considered the starting point of the chain and is referred to as the "amino" or "N-terminal," and the end of the chain is called the "carboxyl" or "C-terminal." So a polypeptide consists of repeating amino acid units called the **backbone**, to which are attached distinctive **side chains** (R groups). The **sequence** of a polypeptide is given by using the abbreviations of its constituent amino acids. By convention, the first amino acid in the sequence is the N-terminal: Arg-Ala-Cys-Pro-Tyr-Glu-Asn. This heptapeptide starts with an arginine residue and terminates with an asparagine residue.

Besides the peptide bond, two polypeptide chains can be linked together by a covalent bond formed between two cysteine residues, called a **disulfide bridge**.. This is a mild oxidation reaction, which converts two thiols to a disulfide. Two such cross-linked cysteines are called a **cystine:**

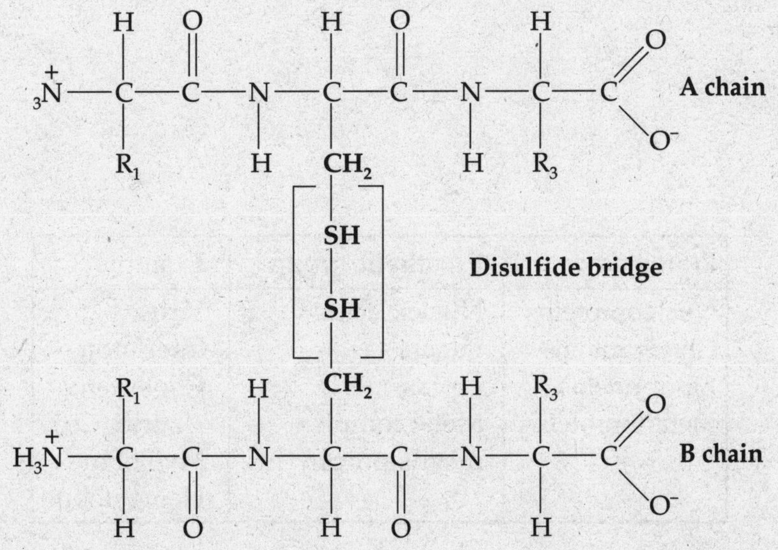

A chain

Disulfide bridge

B chain

PROTEINS

Polypeptides have molecular weights that range between 5,000 and 200,000 daltons. The **dalton** is a unit of mass equal to the mass of one hydrogen atom. Thus, a polypeptide of molecular weight 10,000 has a mass of 10,000 daltons, or 10 kDa.

A kilodalton (kDa) is a unit of mass equal to 1000 daltons.

Proteins are macromolecular assemblies with molecular weights in the millions. They are usually classified as a function of their biochemical function or shape. On the basis of their chemical composition, they are classified into two broad categories:

- **Simple proteins** are polypeptide assemblies that hydrolyze to their constituent amino acid residues.

- **Conjugated proteins** additionally incorporate groups such as carbohydrates, lipids, nucleic acids, and various prosthetic groups, such as pigments (e.g., porphyrins or chlorophyll).

Prosthetic groups are also called "active groups" because they are often the site of the main biochemical activity of the protein. Chlorophyll is an example of a prosthetic group:

Proteins	Prosthetic group	Example
Nucleoproteins	Nucleic acids	Viruses
Glycoproteins	Sugars	Interferon
Lipoproteins	Lipids, fats	Cholesterol
Metalloproteins	Metal complex, metalloporphyrins	Azurin (Cu) Myglobin Hemoglobin

The structure of proteins is organized at different levels:

- The **primary structure** refers to the covalent assembly, i.e., the amino acid sequence and the presence of disulfide bridges.

- The **secondary structure** refers to the arrangements adopted by the amino acid sequence. Three are possible: the α-helix, the β-**pleated sheet,** and the **random coil,** and they can coexist in the same protein.

> *An* α-helix *is a polypeptide arrangement in which the carbonyl groups on one turn of the helix hydrogen bond to the hydrogens of the peptide N–H bond of the next turn. A* β-pleated sheet *is a polypeptide arrangement in which the chains line up side by side with the carbonyl groups of one chain hydrogen bonded to the hydrogens of the N–H bond of the adjacent chain. A* random coil *is any nonhelical or nonpleated sheet polypeptide arrangement.*

- The **tertiary structure** represents the complete three-dimensional conformation of the protein and the folding pattern of its secondary structure.

- The **quaternary structure** is the "sum total" of the protein assembly, including complexation with ligands, inhibitors, etc.

For example, hemoglobin is made up of four monomeric units that consist of the same amino acid sequence incorporating a heme prosthetic group (iron porphyrin complex). These monomers define its tertiary structure, but the quaternary structure of hemoglobin includes all four monomers.

LIPIDS

Lipids are a major component of cells and animal tissues, and can be extracted by nonpolar organic solvents. **Simple lipids** are very difficult to hydrolyze with acidic or basic solvents. They include **terpenes**—compounds with general formula $(C_5H_8)_n$—**steroids**, and **prostaglandins**.

General steroid structure

Cholesterol

**Isoprene unit
contained in terpenes**

**Vitamin A
a terpene with two isoprene units**

Complex lipids are esters of carboxylic acids; they are easy to hydrolyze to acids and alcohols. They include **glycerides** and **waxes**.

Complex lipids are also called **fatty acids**; so glycerides are the fatty acid esters of glycerol. Triglycerides are called **fats** if they are solid at room temperature and **oils** if they are liquid.

Their carboxylic acids are straight chains that contain between 12 and 20 carbons, and they can be either saturated or unsaturated.

Saturated Fatty Acids

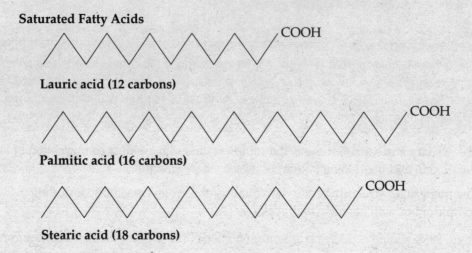

Lauric acid (12 carbons)

Palmitic acid (16 carbons)

Stearic acid (18 carbons)

Unsaturated Fatty Acids

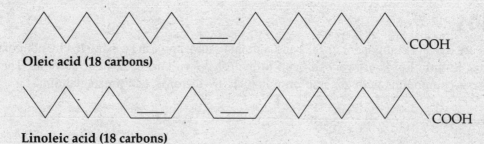

Oleic acid (18 carbons)

Linoleic acid (18 carbons)

ORGANIC CHEMISTRY: WORKED-OUT PROBLEM SET

1. 2,3-Pentandiol has four possible conformations. Which are enantiomers? Which are diastereomers?

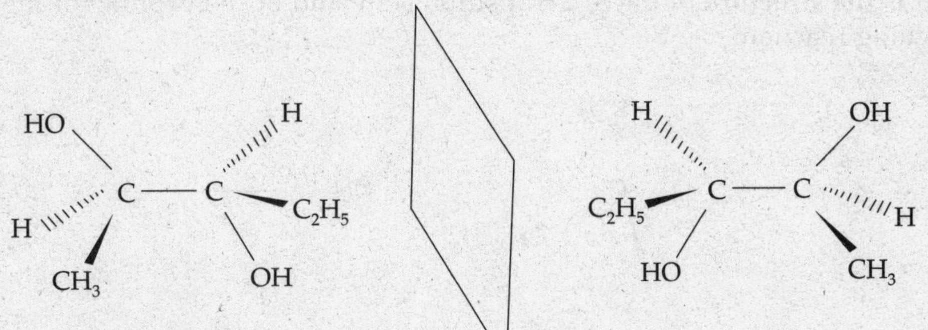

(a)

(b)

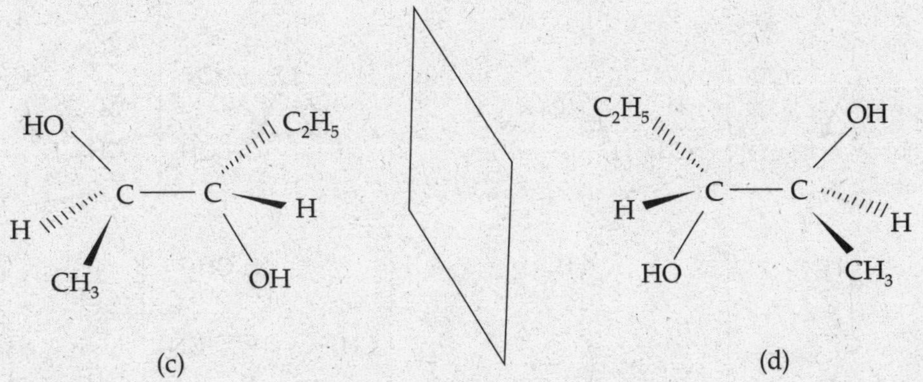

(c)

(d)

Answers:

- (a) and (b) are enantiomers (mirror images that are not superimposable)
- (c) and (d) are also enantiomers
- (a) and (c) are diastereomers (stereoisomers that are not mirror images)
- (b) and (d) are diastereomers
- (a) and (d) are diastereomers
- (b) and (c) are diasteroemers

2. Which of the following sets of characteristics best describes an S_N2 reaction?

   (A) Homolytic cleavage, no carbocation intermediate, bimolecular process.

   (B) Heterolytic cleavage, no carbocation intermediate, unimolecular process.

   (C) Heterolytic cleavage, no carbocation intermediate, bimolecular process.

   (D) Homolytic cleavage, carbocation intermediate, unimolecular process.

   (E) Heterolytic cleavage, carbocation intermediate, unimolecular process.

(C) is correct. The number 2 in S_N2 indicates that both the nucleophile and the substrate are involved in the transition state. The process is therefore bimolecular. In all substitution and elimination reactions, the bonds are broken heterolytically. Carbocations intermediates are involved only in S_N1 and E1 reactions.

3. What is the structure of the S_N2 transition state and of the product of the following reaction:

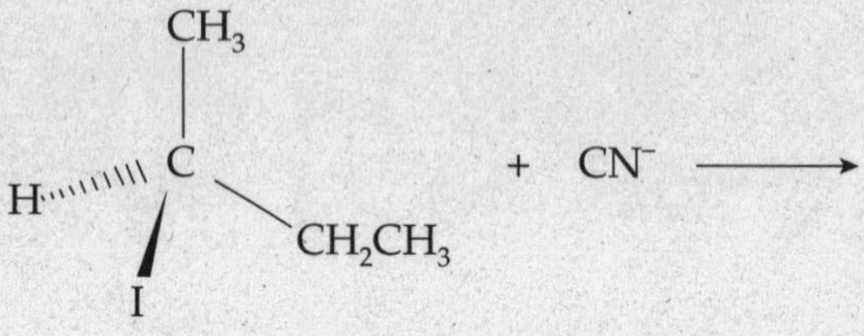

(A)

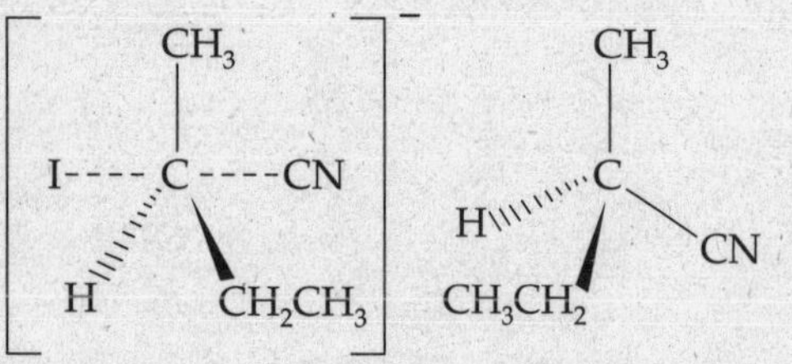

(B)

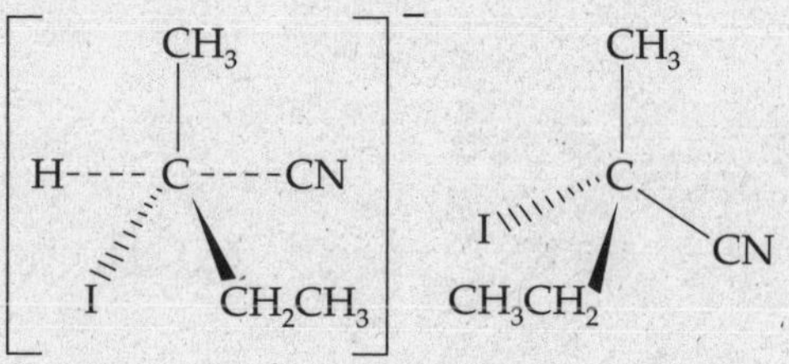

(C)

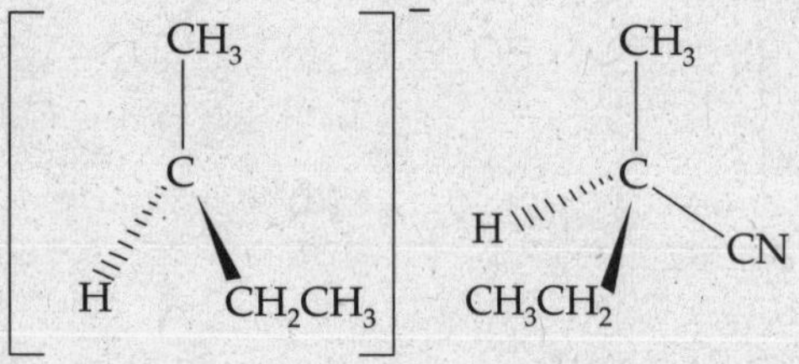

(D)

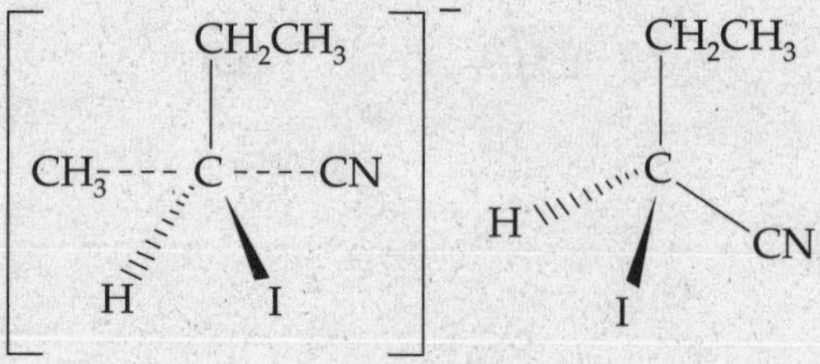

(E)

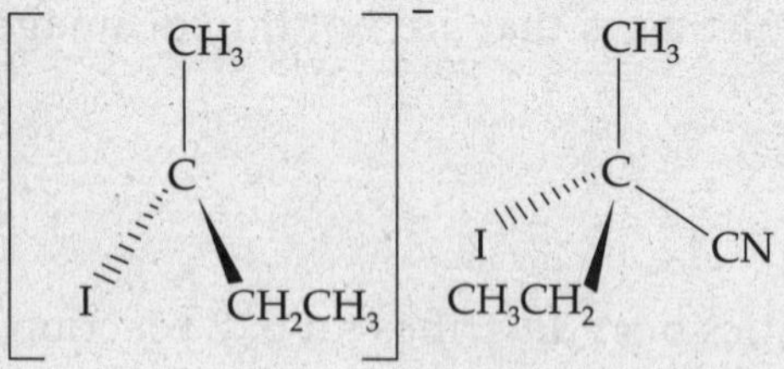

(B) is correct. I is the leaving group. The nucleophile attacks the carbon atom on the opposite side of the leaving group, and the reaction proceeds with inversion of configuration. The intermediate shows the nucleophile and the leaving group aligned with the hydrogen and methyl and ethyl substituents in the same plane as the carbon atom.

4. What is the order of increasing rate of S_N2 reaction for the following alkyl halides?

   (a) CH_3Br

   (b) $CH_3CHBrCH_3$

   (c) $CH_3CH_2CH_2Br$

   (d) CH_3CH_2Br

   (e) $(CH_3)_3CBr$

   (f) $CH_3CH_2CHBrCH_2CH_3$

   (A) $a < f < b < c < d < e$

   (B) $a < d < c < b < f < e$

   (C) $f < b < e < c < d < a$

   (D) $e < b < f < d < c < a$

   (E) $e < f < b < c < d < a$

(E) is correct. Here you should consider the steric hindrance around the head carbon. As the number of substituents increases, the transition state becomes increasingly crowded, and the rate of reaction decreases. Therefore, the order of the increasing rate of the S_N2 reaction is tertiary < secondary < primary < methyl. When comparing two secondary halides, the one with the fastest rate is the one with the less bulky substituents.

5. Which of the following best describes a S_N1 mechanism for the substitution of alkyl halides?

   (A) Ionization reaction, unimolecular reaction, first-order reaction, racemization, relative rate: $3°$ RX > $2°$ RX.

   (B) Ionization reaction, bimolecular reaction, second-order reaction, racemization, relative rate: $3°$ RX > $2°$ RX.

   (C) Concerted back-side attack, unimolecular reaction, first-order reaction, inversion of configuration, relative rate: CH_3X > $1°$ RX > $2°$ RX.

   (D) Concerted back-side attack, bimolecular reaction, second-order reaction, racemization, relative rate: $3°$ RX > $2°$ RX.

   (E) Ionization reaction, unimolecular reaction, first-order reaction, racemization, relative rate: CH_3X > $1°$ RX > $2°$ RX.

(A) is correct. The rate-determining step in an S_N1 reaction is ionization of the tertiary or secondary halide to form a carbocation. The reaction is therefore unimolecular. The 1 means that the rate-determining step is unimolecular.

6. What is the correct order of S_N1 reactivity for the following compounds? Assume that there is no Wagner-Meerwein transposition.

   (a) 3-iodopentane

   (b) 2-iodobutane

   (c) 1-iodobutane

   (d) 2-iodopropane

   (A) c < b < d < a

   (B) b < d < a < c

   (C) c < d < b < a

   (D) c < d < a < b

   (E) d < b < a < c

(C) is correct. S_N1 reactivity follows the order of carbocation stability. The order of increasing stability is primary < secondary < tertiary. Write each structure separately and determine the type of carbocation formed. You should recognize that (C) leads to a primary carbocation and that the other three compounds lead to secondary carbocations. To determine which of the secondary carbocations is the most stable, examine the size of the alkyl groups attached to the positive carbon. A large alkyl substituent has a larger stabilizing effect than a small one, because it allows for more dispersion of the positive charge.

7. Which of the following best describes an E2 mechanism for substitution in alkyl halides?

   (A) Concerted and bimolecular reaction, antielimination of H and X, rate of reaction: $1°$ RX > $2°$ RX > $3°$ RX.

   (B) Ionization reaction, antielimination of H and X, rate of reaction: $3°$ RX > $2°$ RX > $1°$ RX.

   (C) Concerted and bimolecular reaction, no stereospecificity, rate of reaction: $3°$ RX > $2°$ RX > $1°$ RX.

   (D) Ionization reaction, no stereospecificity, rate of reaction: $3°$ RX > $2°$ RX .

   (E) Concerted and bimolecular reaction, antielimination of H and X, rate of reaction: $3°$ RX > $2°$ RX > $1°$ RX.

(E) is correct. In the transition state of an E2 reaction, the attacking base and the leaving group want to be as far apart as possible. This *anti* positioning of H and X determines the stereochemistry of the alkene intermediate. Saytzeff's rule applies: the more highly substituted alkenes are more stable than less substituted ones.

8. What is the correct order of stability for the following alkenes:

(a) *trans*-$C_6H_5CH=CHCH_3$

(b) *trans*-$CH_3CH_2CH=CHCH_3$

(c) *cis*-$CH_3CH_2CH=CHCH_3$

(d) $CH_3CH_2CH=CH_2$

(A) d < b < c < a

(B) c < d < b < a

(C) d < c < b < a

(D) a < b < c < d

(E) d < c < a < b

(C) is correct. The stability of an alkene depends upon the number of substituents on the double bond, the most stable alkene is the most substituted. Alkene (c) is less stable than alkene (b) because of steric hindrance. Alkene (a) is the most stable because the double bond is conjugated with the benzene ring.

9. What is the Hofmann product of the following elimination?

$$
\begin{array}{c}
\text{Br} \\
|
\end{array}
$$

$$CH_3CH_2CH_2C(CH_3)_2 \quad + \quad {}^-OC(CH_3)_3 \longrightarrow$$

(A) $CH_3CH_2CH_2C(CH_3)=CH_2$

(B) $CH_3CH_2CH=C(CH_3)_2$

(C) $CH_2=CHCH_2CH(CH_3)_2$

(D) $CH_3CH_2CH_2C(CH_3)_2OC(CH_3)_3$

(E) none of the above

(A) is correct. Hoffman's rule states that the less substituted alkene will predominate, and A represents the least substituted alkene. Here, the bulky *t*-butoxide ion preferentially attacks the least sterically hindered hydrogen atom.

10. What would be the most abundant product of the following S_N1 reaction?

$$\underset{\text{Br}}{\overset{|}{(CH_3)_2CHCHCH_2CH_2CH_3}} + CH_3CH_2OH \longrightarrow$$

(A) $(CH_3)_2CH\underset{\text{OCH}_2CH_3}{\overset{|}{CH}}CH_2CH_2CH_3$

(B) $(CH_3)_2\underset{\text{OCH}_2CH_3}{\overset{|}{C}}CH_2CH_2CH_2CH_3$

(C) $(CH_3)_2CHCH_2\underset{\text{OCH}_2CH_3}{\overset{|}{CH}}CH_2CH_3$

(D) $(CH_3)_2CHCH_2CH_2\underset{\text{OCH}_2CH_3}{\overset{|}{CH}}CH_3$

(E) none of the above

(B) is correct. One could expect this alkyl halide to form a secondary carbocation, which would yield product (A). However, this carbocation will undergo a 1,2-shift to form a more stable tertiary carbocation. So product (A) is the normal product, product (B) is the rearrangement product, and the rearrangement product predominates.

11. Which of the following statements are true for the following Diels-Alder reaction:

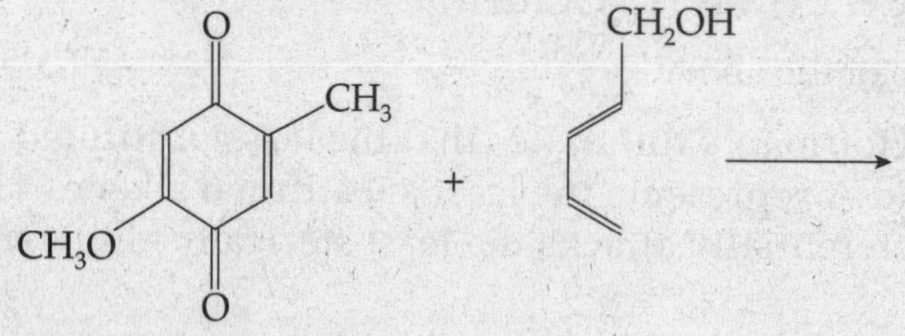

(a) The second reactant is the dienophile.

(b) The product of the reaction contains two rings.

(c) The product contains a cyclopentadiene ring.

(d) The reaction is stereospecific.

(A) a only

(B) b only

(C) d only

(D) b, c, and d

(E) b and d

(F) is correct. A Diels-Alder reaction occurs between a conjugated diene (the second reactant above) and a dienophile. The product always contains one more ring than was present in the reactants. The Diels-Alder reaction is stereospecific.

12. Which of the following statements are true concerning nucleophilic aromatic substitution?

    (a) Aryl halides undergo substitution in the presence of electron-withdrawing substituents on the ring.

    (b) When an electron-withdrawing substituent is attached to the ring, a carbanion intermediate is observed.

    (c) In the absence of electron-withdrawing substituents, a benzyne intermediate is observed.

  (A) all of the above

  (B) a and c

  (C) b and c

  (D) a and b

  (E) none of the above

(A) is correct. Aryl halides do not undergo substitution reactions as readily as alkyl halides do. Electron-withdrawing substituents such as nitro groups on the ring are required. When such groups are present, carbanions occur; when they are not present, benzyne intermediates result.

13. This reaction is an example of

$$\text{benzene} + (CH_3CH_2)_2CHCl \xrightarrow{AlCl_3} \text{benzene}-CH(CH_2CH_3)_2 + HCl$$

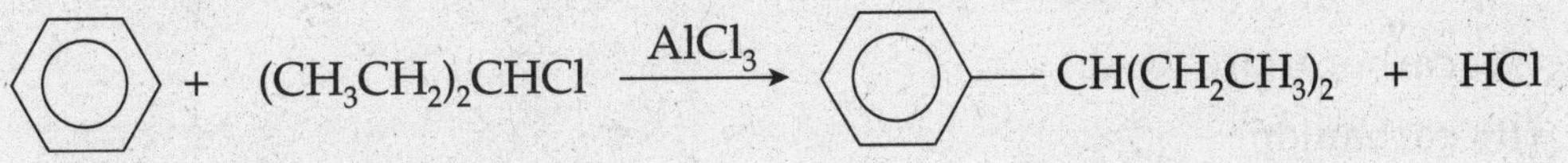

  (A) Saytzeff's elimination

  (B) Nucleophilic aromatic substitution

  (C) Diels-Alder reaction

  (D) Friedel-Crafts acylation

  (E) Hofmann's elimination

(D) is correct. The Friedel-Crafts reaction is an example of electrophilic aromatic substitution. In the first step of the reaction, a carbocation is generated by reaction of the alkyl halide with aluminum trichloride. The second step is electrophilic attack on benzene to form the alkylbenzene.

14. The following process describes the formation of

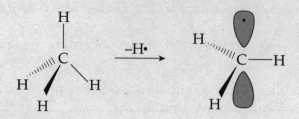

   (A) a carbocation
   (B) a carbanion
   (C) a free radical
   (D) a carbene intermediate
   (E) a heterolytic bond cleavage

(C) is correct. The process illustrates a homolytic C–H bond cleavage, which results in the formation of a free radical. The intermediate is neutral and almost planar, and the unpaired electron in a *p* orbital is perpendicular to the plane of the atoms.

15. To what species can the following set of characteristics be ascribed:

   (a) heterolytic, or asymmetric, bond cleavage between a carbon atom and a less electronegative atom, such as a metal.

   (b) pyramidal, or sp^3-hybridized, ion.

   (c) one sp^3 orbital contains a nonbonding pair of electrons.

   (A) carbocation
   (B) carbanion
   (C) free radical
   (D) carbene intermediate
   (E) a heterolytic bond rupture

(B) is correct. Carbanions are formed after heterolytic cleavage of a bond between a carbon and a less electronegative atom. The resulting species has one additional electron, and it is therefore negatively charged.

16. What is the order of increasing stability for the following free radicals:

(a)

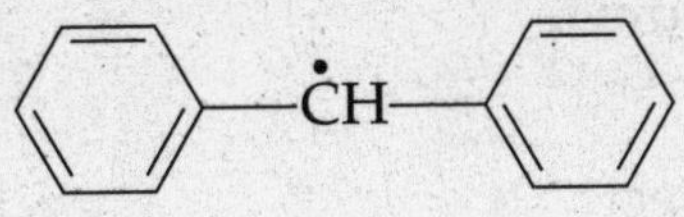

(c) 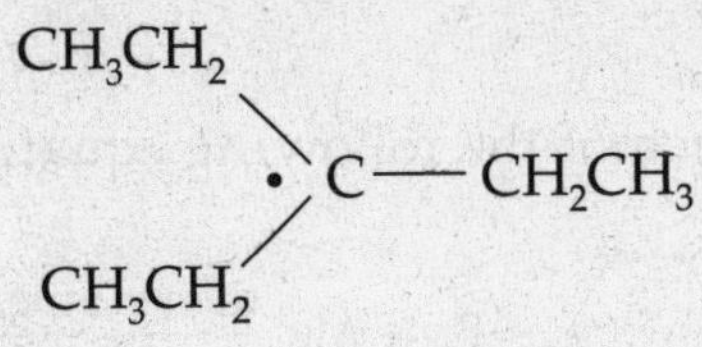 CH_3CH_2

$\cdot C \!\!-\!\! CH_2CH_3$

CH_3CH_2

(b)

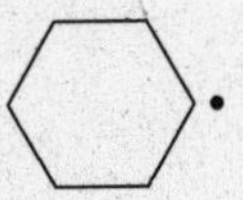

(d)

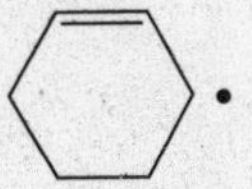

(A) c < b < d < a
(B) b < c < a < d
(C) b < a < d < c
(D) d < b < c < a
(E) b< c <d < a

(E) is correct. The order of stability of free radicals is methyl < primary < secondary < tertiary. Therefore, (b) is less stable than (c). Free radicals (a) and (d), though secondary, are stabilized by resonance and are more stable than (c).

17. Which of the following equations represents a propagation step?

(a) $Cl\cdot$ + $CH_2 \!\!=\!\! CH_2$ $\longrightarrow$ $\cdot CH_2CH_2Cl$

(b)

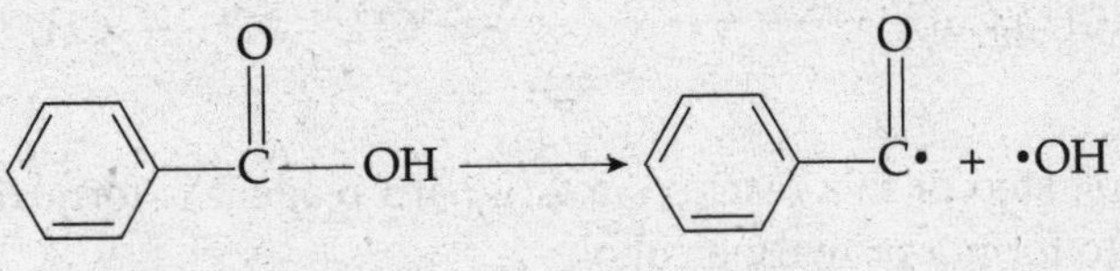

(c) $2CH_3\cdot$ $\longrightarrow$ CH_3CH_3

(d)

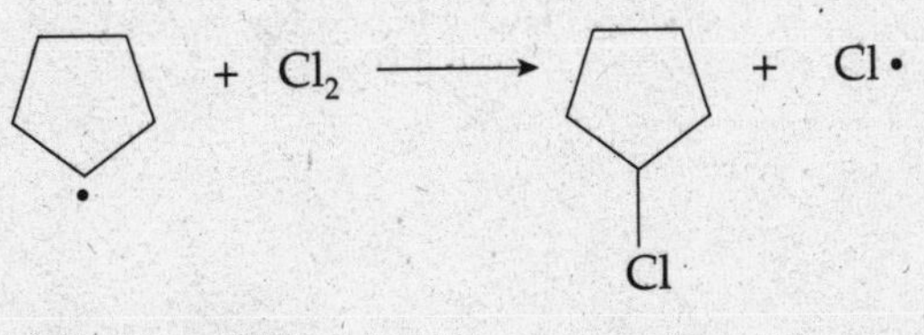

(A) a and d
(B) a only
(C) a and c
(D) b and c
(E) d only

(A) is correct. (a) describes the propagation step of a free-radical reaction, in which an alkyl free radical is generated and (d) is a termination step, in which free-radical reactants lead to nonradical products.

18. Which of the following equations is not correct?

(a) —Br + Mg $\xrightarrow{\text{diethyl ether}}$ —MgBr

(b) —Cl $\xrightarrow[\text{(2) HCHO} \\ \text{(3) H}_2\text{O, H}^+]{\text{(1) Mg, diethyl ether}}$

(c) =O $\xrightarrow[\text{(2) H}_2\text{O, H}^+]{\text{(1) CH}_3\text{MgBr}}$

(d) —CH=CHCH $\xrightarrow[\text{(2) H}_2\text{O, H}^+]{\text{(1) CH}_3\text{C}\equiv\text{CMgI}}$ —CH=CH—C—C≡C—CH$_3$

(e) —CH=CHBr + (CH$_3$)$_2$CuLi $\longrightarrow$ —CH=CH—CH$_3$

(B) is the correct answer. In the first step of this reaction, a Grignard reagent is formed, and it should then react with formaldehyde to form a primary alcohol:

—Cl + Mg $\longrightarrow$ —MgCl $\xrightarrow[\text{H}_2\text{O, H}^+]{\text{HCHO}}$ —CH$_2$

19. What is the formula of the carbonyl compound required for the following conversion?

$$CH_3CH_2CH_2MgBr \longrightarrow CH_3CH_2CH_2-\overset{\overset{\displaystyle O}{\|}}{C}-OH$$

(A) CH_3COCl
(B) $HCOCH_3$
(C) $HCHO$
(D) CO_2
(E) none of the above

(D) is correct. The reaction of a Grignard reagent with a ketone yields a tertiary alcohol, the reaction of a Grignard reagent with an aldehyde yields a secondary alcohol, and a Grignard reagent plus formaldehyde yields a primary alcohol, whereas a Grigard reagent plus CO_2 yields a carboxylic acid.

20. Which of the following compounds could yield a Grignard reagent?

(a)

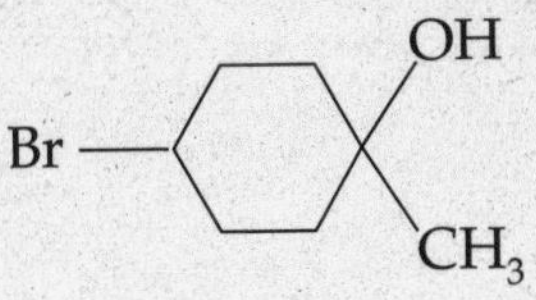

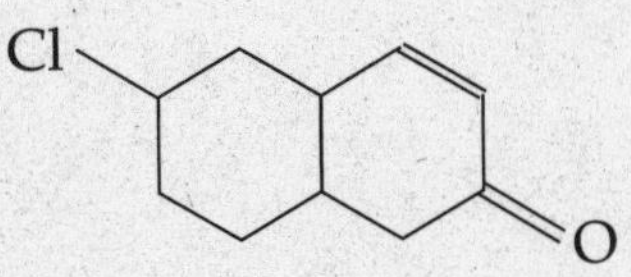

(d) $CH_3OCH_2CH_2I$

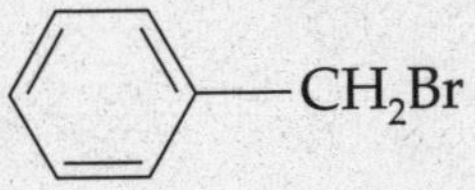

(b) —CH_2Br

(e) $(CH_3)_3CCHCH_2CH_3$ with Br

(c)

(f) 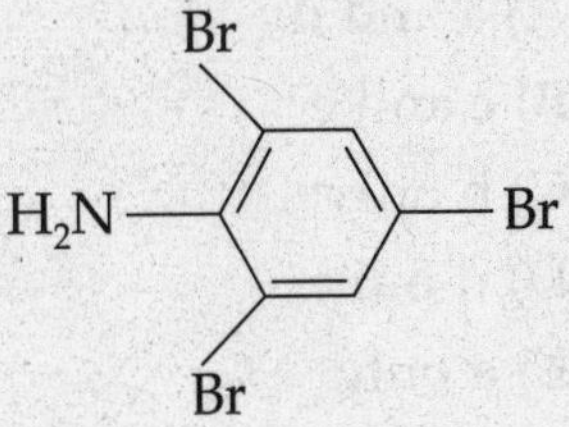 H_2N— with Br substituents

(A) b and e
(B) b, d, and e
(C) a, c, and f
(D) b, d, and f
(E) a, b, and f

(B) is correct. Compounds (a), (c), and (f) contain a functional group that would react with the Grignard reagent as soon as it is formed.

21. Which of the following reactions would produce a tertiary alcohol?

(a) 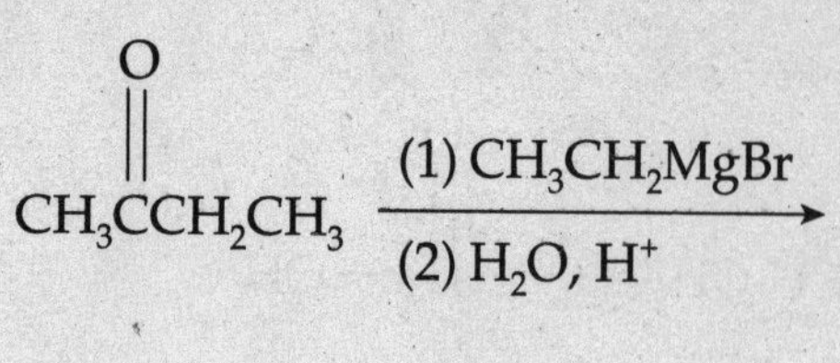 $CH_3CCH_2CH_3$ (with $=O$ above the C) $\xrightarrow[\text{(2) } H_2O, H^+]{\text{(1) } CH_3CH_2MgBr}$

(b) $(CH_3)_3CMgBr$ $\xrightarrow[\text{(2) } H_2O, H^+]{\text{(1) } CO_2}$

(c) 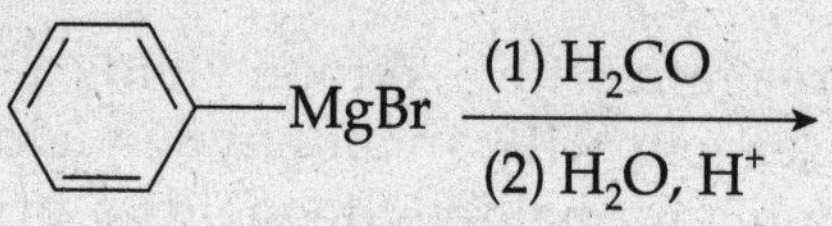 $\langle\text{phenyl}\rangle$—MgBr $\xrightarrow[\text{(2) } H_2O, H^+]{\text{(1) } H_2CO}$

(d) 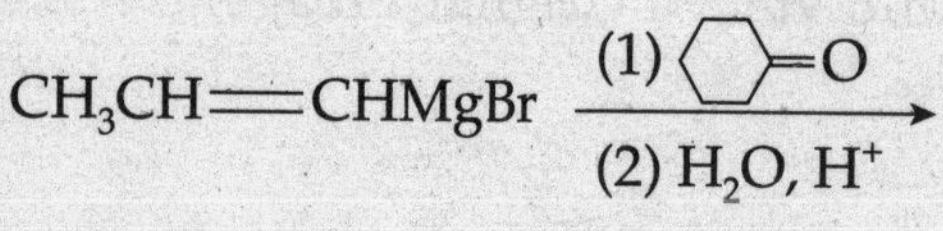 $CH_3CH=CHMgBr$ $\xrightarrow[\text{(2) } H_2O, H^+]{\text{(1) } \langle\text{cyclohexanone}\rangle=O}$

(e) CH_3CHO $\xrightarrow[\text{(2) } H_2O, H^+]{\text{(1) } CH_3CH_2CH_2CH_2MgBr}$

(A) a and d
(B) c and e
(C) b only
(D) d only
(E) a only

(E) is correct. A Grignard reagent reacts with a ketone to produce a tertiary alcohol.

IV. PHYSICAL CHEMISTRY

THERMODYNAMICS

Thermodynamics deals with systems and their surroundings. It is the study of the transformations of various kinds of energies and the exchange of energy between systems and their surroundings. Nine topics are covered under this heading: the First, second, and third laws of thermodynamics, thermochemistry, ideal and real gases and solutions, Gibbs and Helmholtz energy, chemical potential, chemical equilibria, phase equilibria, colligative properties, and statistical mechanics.

Some Definitions

Units and constants

Pressure (P):
$1 \, Pa = 1 \, kg \, m^{-1} \, s^{-2}$
$1 \, atm = 760 \, mmHg = 101325 \, Pa = 1.01325 \, bars$

Volume (V):
$1 \, l = 1000 \, mL = 10^3 \, mL$
$1 \, m^3 = 10^6 \, cc = 1000 \, L$

Energy (E, U)
$1 \, J = 1 \, kg \, m^2 \, s^{-2} = 1 \, N \, m$
$1 \, erg = 10^{-7} \, J$
$1 \, cal = 4.184 \, J$

Force (F)
$1 \, N = 1 \, kg \, m \, s^{-2}$

Gas constant
$R = 1.987 \, cal \, K^{-1} \, mol^{-1} = 0.08206 \, l \, atm \, K^{-1} \, mol^{-1}$

SYSTEM AND SURROUNDINGS

- **System**: A system is any part of the universe, any object, and any quantity of matter. The systems of interest are *finite* and *macroscopic*, rather than microscopic: only *state properties*, i.e., measurable variables, are considered thermodynamic parameters. The detailed structure of matter is not taken into account.

- **Surroundings**: everything around the system.

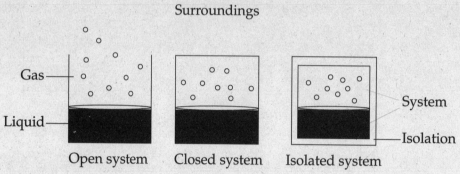

- **Boundary**: The boundary of a system is what encloses a system, setting it apart from its surroundings. This is an imaginary construct, which serves either to (a) completely isolate the system from its surroundings or (b) allow interactions between the system and its surroundings. Two types of transfer can occur between a system and its surroundings: (1) energy transfer and (2) matter transfer through the movement of particles (across the boundary between the system and its surroundings).

- **Types of systems**: Three types of systems can be defined on the basis of these two types of transfer: (1) *isolated systems*, in which no exchange of energy or matter occurs across boundaries. (2) *closed systems*, in which there is an exchange of energy, but not of matter, and (3) *open systems*, in which there is an exchange of both energy and matter.

STATE PROPERTIES

The state of a system in equilibrium is defined by a set of thermodynamic parameters called **state properties** or state variables. *A state property defines the state of the system.* These properties are interrelated; if one varies, at least one other property also varies. State properties are measurable; some include

- temperature (T)
- volume (V)
- pressure (P)
- internal energy (ΔU)
- enthalpy (ΔH)
- entropy (ΔE)

A state property does not depend on the path taken by a system as it changes states:

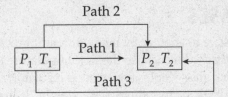

When thermodynamic quantities are path-dependent, as are heat (Q) and work (W), they are not considered state properties. This is because the differentials of all state properties must be *exact*, such as dV in the case of volume, which remains the same for all processes occurring between the different states reached by a system. So a quantity whose differential is not exact, is not a state property. Heat and work are then called *path functions* because the quantities Q and W are different for different processes, i.e., dQ or dW are *inexact* differentials.

INTENSIVE AND EXTENSIVE PROPERTIES

Properties of a system can be either extensive or intensive.

Extensive properties—or capacity factors—depend on the amount of matter present in terms of mass. Examples are the total volume or the total energy of a system. They are equal to the sum of the parts, i.e., they are additive.

Intensive properties—or intensity factors—do not depend on the quantity of material present. Examples include temperature, molar volume, density, pressure, viscosity, refractive index, etc. At equilibrium, they are the same for every part of the system, i.e., they are not additive.

The equation that relates the thermodynamic properties of a system in a state of equilibrium is called an **equation of state**. The simplest equation of state is that for an ideal gas: $PV = nRT$, where n is the number of moles and R is the gas constant ($R = 8.3143$ JK^{-1}mol^{-1}).

EQUILIBRIUM SYSTEMS AND THERMODYNAMIC PROCESSES

A system is in a **state of equilibrium** when its properties do not vary with time. This implies the following conditions:

(a) thermal equilibrium (T is the same everywhere in the system),

(b) mechanical equilibrium (P is the same everywhere in the system), and

(c) chemical equilibrium (the chemical composition of the system does not vary).

When a closed system is displaced from equilibrium, it undergoes a process during which its properties change until a new state of equilibrium is reached. This process can be **isobaric** (occurring at constant pressure), **isochoric** (occurring at constant volume), **isothermal** (occurring at constant temperature), **adiabatic** (occurring with no exchange of heat between the system and its surroundings), and **cyclic** (initial state = final state).

Constant P = isobaric, constant T = isothermal, and constant V = isochoric. If no heat flows in or out of the system, Q = 0, and the conditions are adiabatic.

In addition to this, a process is **reversible** if its direction can be reversed at any point by a change in external conditions or **irreversible**, if its direction cannot be reversed.

ADIABATIC PROCESSES

Systems can change from one state to another by many different processes. A process is **adiabatic** if the system is enclosed by an *adiabatic boundary* so that its temperature is independent from that of its surroundings. For example, thick glass wool is a very good insulator, and a vessel wrapped in it will reach thermal equilibrium with its surroundings very slowly. If glass wool totally prevents the exchange of heat (and thermal equilibrium between the vessel and its surroundings), it is an adiabatic boundary. A system enclosed in an adiabatic boundary remains at a temperature different from that of its surroundings; it never achieves thermal equilibrium with them. So an ideal adiabatic boundary is one across which the flow of heat is zero, even though there may be different temperatures on the two sides of the boundary.

THE IDEAL GAS

The simplest thermodynamic system is that of the **ideal gas**. Gases are composed of molecules in random motion. If the collisions between molecules are perfectly elastic and if the molecules don't attract each other, then the gas is said to be ideal. The collisions between the molecules and the walls of their container define the pressure P of the system (P = force per unit area). The temperature T of the system is directly related to the speed of the molecules and is also directly related to the average kinetic energy of any molecule in the system. The **internal energy (U)** of the system is the sum of the energies of the constituent molecules; it is a state property of the system. In an ideal gas, the internal energy depends only on the temperature and the number of particles; it does not depend on the volume occupied by the gas. The following equations describe the behavior of an ideal gas at all temperatures and pressures:

$$PV = nRT$$

$$U = U(T)$$

But no real gas *exactly* satisfies these equations.

THE VAN DER WAALS EQUATION

Real gases have a more complicated equation of state because intermolecular interactions must be taken into account; molecules in a real gas attract each other. The equation for real gases is the modified ideal gas law, or the **van der Waals equation**:

$$(P + an^2/V^2)(V - nb) = nRT$$

where a is a constant that accounts for the force of interactions between gas particles and b is another constant, which accounts for the excluded volume.

WORK AND HEAT

$$\Delta U = Q + W$$

expresses the relationship between heat and work, where ΔU is the internal energy, Q is heat, and W is work. We can come to an understanding of W from the following example:

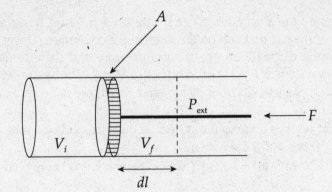

A = cross-sectional area of piston
d = distance travelled by piston
P_{ext} = external pressure
F = force applied

$$W = -P_{ext}(V_f - V_i)$$

Given the piston in the above illustration, we can write

$$W = F_{ext} \times l$$

or $$\Delta W = F_{ext} \times dl = (F_{ext}/A) \times dl$$

And: $$\Delta W = P_{ext} \times Adl = P_{ext} \times dV$$

Then the work done by this system as the piston moves from V_i to V_f is

$$W = -\int P_{ext}\, dV$$
$$W = -P_{ext} \int dV$$
$$W = -P_{ext} \mid dV$$
$$W = -P_{ext}(V_f) - (-P_{ext}V_i)$$
And $$W = -P_{ext}(V_f - V_i)$$

The exchange of energy can occur through heat or work. **Heat (Q)** is thermal energy that flows from a hot body to a cold one. When hot and cold bodies are in contact, a transfer of thermal energy takes place until a state of thermal equilibrium is achieved.

When energy is added as heat to a system, it is stored as kinetic and potential energy by the molecules of the system. The units of heat (a form of energy) are joules (J).

Work (W) involves the movement of matter from one place to another. Examples of work include pressure-volume (PV) work (which involves the expansion and compression of gases) and electrical or mechanical work. In thermodynamics, work always involves the exchange of energy between a system and its surroundings. **Mechanical work** occurs when a force, acting on a system, moves through a distance, as illustrated in the previous piston example.

If heat (Q) is added to a system, Q is positive. If heat (Q) is removed from a system, Q is negative.

If work (W) is done on a system, W is positive. If work (W) is done by a system, W is negative.

Example:

A gas is confined by a piston to a volume V_1 in a cylinder. When the piston is released, it moves outward because of the internal pressure of the gas that acts on the internal piston surface. The gas expands to a volume V_2 until equilibrium is reached between the gas pressure and the external pressure P. Calculate the work done by the system, if $P = 130$ kPa and if $V_2 - V_1 = 0.01$ m^3, assuming that the system is made up of the cylinder, the gas, and the piston, and that there is no friction between the cylinder and the piston.

Answer: First you should recognize that work is done *by* the system *on* the surroundings, which means that W is positive. Next, 1 kPa $= 1$ N $\cdot$ m^{-2} and 1 J $= 1$ N $\cdot$ m.

So $W = P\Delta V = (130$ kPa$)(0.01$ m$^3) = 1.30$ kN $\cdot$ m$^{-2} \cdot$ m$^3 = 1.30$ kJ. (Notice that work and energy have the same units).

THE FIRST LAW OF THERMODYNAMICS

The first law of thermodynamics states that even though energy can be exchanged between a system and its surroundings, it remains constant.

The total energy of a system and its surroundings is always constant.

Heat and work are both means by which the energy of a system can be changed. They are also measurable quantities. If a closed system is allowed to exchange only heat and work with its surroundings, the first law of thermodynamics can be written as follows:

$$\Delta U = Q - W$$

where ΔU is the **total internal energy** of the system, Q is the heat added to the system, and W is the work done by the system. ΔU is independent of the path taken by the system from its initial to its final state.

The **total energy of the system (E)** includes several contributions besides U:

$$\Delta E = \Delta E_K + \Delta E_P + \Delta U$$

Here ΔE_K is the kinetic energy of the system ($\Delta E_K = \frac{1}{2} mv^2$, where m is the mass and v is the velocity) and ΔE_P is the potential energy of the system ($\Delta E_P = mgh$, where g is the acceleration due to gravity, and h is the height).

The internal energy of the system is a specific thermodynamic quantity; it is the sum of the kinetic and potential energies of all the molecules, atoms, and subatomic particles of the system. Absolute values of U cannot be determined, but values for ΔU can be determined experimentally, since Q and W are measurable. The first law can be expanded to

$$\Delta E_K + \Delta E_P + \Delta U = Q - W$$

In most cases, the kinetic and potential energies of the system do not change, so this equation can be simplified to

$$\Delta U = Q - W$$

or, in differential form: $dU = dQ - dW$. This means that the energy exchange with the surroundings acts only on the *internal* energy.

If the process is **adiabatic**, that is, if there is no exchange of heat between the system and its surroundings ($dQ = 0$), we can write $\Delta U = -W$.

Note that U is a system property, and its value depends on the state of the system. So a process that changes the system also changes U. Therefore, the integration of dU gives the difference between two values of the internal energy: $\int dU$ (from U_1 to U_2) $= \Delta U$. On the other hand, Q and W are *quantities* (i.e., not state properties of the system) and depend only on the path of the process. So dQ and dW denote infinitesimal quantities, and their integration gives a finite quantity:

$$\int dQ = Q \text{ and } \int dW = W$$

Therefore, $\int dU = \int dQ - \int dW$ leads to $\Delta U = Q - W$.

ENTHALPY (*H*)

Enthalpy is expressed as follows:

$$H = U + PV$$

U, H, and PV have units of energy (joules). U, P and V are also system properties, so it follows that H is also a system property.

For any process, the change in H is

$$\Delta H = \Delta U + \Delta(PV) = \Delta U + P\Delta V + V\Delta P$$

For a constant pressure process, the last term is zero, and the equation becomes

$$\Delta H = \Delta U + P\Delta V.$$

HEAT CAPACITY: C_P AND C_V

The effect of temperature on the energy of chemical reactions is treated in terms of heat capacities.

Heat capacity is defined as the thermal energy that must be added to raise the temperature of a system by $1°C$, under specified conditions. We can calculate the heat capacity of reversible processes, for which the path is fully specified.

Heat capacity measured at constant volume (C_V) is

$$C_V = (\partial Q / \partial T)_V$$

In this equation, heat capacity is a measure of the amount of heat required to increase the temperature by ∂T, when the system is heated in a reversible process at constant volume. Under this restriction, no work can be done by the system. From the mathematical definition of the first law, $dU = dQ - dW = dQ - P\Delta V$ at constant volume, $\Delta V = 0$ and $dU = dQ$. So we can write

$$C_V = (\partial U / \partial T)_V$$

as an alternative definition of C_V. Since U, T, and V are system properties, so is C_V.

The heat capacity measured at constant pressure (C_P) is

$$C_P = (\partial Q / \partial T)_P$$

As for C_V, this is a measure of the amount of heat required to increase the temperature by ∂T when the system is heated in a reversible process at constant pressure. We know that at constant pressure,

$d\text{H} = d\text{U} + P\Delta V$. We also know that $d\text{U} = dQ - dW$ and that $dW = P\Delta V$ for a reversible process. Therefore, $d\text{H} = dQ$ and we can write another expression for C_P:

$$C_P = (\partial H / \partial T)_P$$

which shows that C_P is also a system property. The two equations above can also be written in the following form:

$$dU = C_V dT \text{ and } dH = C_P dT$$

These two equations are always valid for an ideal gas. Since real gases approach ideal gas behavior at low pressure, these equations provide good approximations of real gas behavior in the $P \rightarrow 0$ limit. It can also be shown that the following relationship exists between C_P and C_V for an ideal gas:

$$C_P - C_V = R$$

where R is the gas constant. The ratio of heat capacities is often given as $g = C_P / C_V$. Combining this equation with $C_P - C_V = R$, we obtain an alternate expression:

$$R / C_V = \gamma - 1.$$

At the zero-pressure limit, real gases approach ideal behavior. If a real gas is compressed to a finite pressure while retaining ideal gas behavior, the resulting state is then called an **ideal-gas state**. Ideal-gas heat capacities are used (^{ig}C) to describe a gas such as this. These ^{ig}C values are different for different gases and are a function only of temperature. For monoatomic gases such as helium and argon, the effect of temperature on molar heat capacity (heat capacity per mol of gas) in the ideal-gas state is negligible. The heat capacities are given by

$$^{ig}C_V = \left(\frac{3}{2}\right)R \qquad ^{ig}C_P = \left(\frac{5}{2}\right)R \qquad \gamma = 1.67$$

For diatomic gases such as H_2, O_2, and N_2, heat capacities change very slowly with temperature. Near 20°C, the values are

$$^{ig}C_V = \left(\frac{5}{2}\right)R \qquad ^{ig}C_P = \left(\frac{7}{2}\right)R \qquad \gamma = 1.40$$

For polyatomic gases, such as CO_2 and CH_4, heat capacity varies significantly with temperature; γ is usually less than 1.3

Example:

An ideal, monoatomic gas expands reversibly and adiabatically from an initial state with $T_1 = 400$ K and $V_1 = 5$ liters to a final volume of $V_2 = 7$ liters. Calculate the final temperature, the work done during the process, and the enthalpy change ΔH.

Answer:

First we must derive an equation that describes a system with constant heat capacity that's undergoing reversible adiabatic expansion or contraction. Since the process is adiabatic, $dQ = 0$ and $dU = -dW = -PdV = (RT/V)dV$. We also know that $dU = C_V dT$. Substituting $C_V dT$ for dU in the first equation, we obtain:

$C_V dT = -(RT/V)dV$

or

$dT/T = -(R/C_V)(dV/V).$

We can substitute $(\gamma - 1)$ for (R/C_V) and integrate from T_1 to T_2 and from V_1 to V_2:

$\ln(T_2/T_1) = (\gamma - 1)\ln(V_1/V_2)$ or, more simply,

$$(T_2/T_1) = (V_1/V_2)^{\gamma-1}$$

This is a general equation for an ideal gas undergoing reversible, adiabatic expansion or contraction. For an ideal, monoatomic gas, $\gamma = 1.67$. The final temperature is given by

$$T_2 = T_1(V_1/V_2)^{\gamma-1} = (400 \text{ K})(5L/7L)^{0.67} = 319 \text{ K}$$

The work done is $W = -\Delta U = \Delta C_V\_T = -(3/2)(8.314 \text{ J} \cdot \text{mol}^{-1} \cdot \text{K}^{-1})(319 \text{ K} - 400 \text{ K}) = 1010 \text{ J/mol}$. The positive sign tells us that expansion work is done by the system.

The enthalpy change is $\Delta H = C_P\Delta T = (5/2)(8.314)(319 - 400) = -1684 \text{ J/mol}$.

THE SECOND LAW OF THERMODYNAMICS

ENTROPY

A large part of chemistry is concerned with the state of equilibrium and the tendency of systems to move toward the equilibrium state. Internal energy and enthalpy changes are not reliable indicators of the equilibrium state and of the tendency of a reaction to proceed, so another thermodynamic function is required to measure the equilibrium state. The function that's used is called **entropy (S)**. Entropy is a measure of the disorder of a system and, like internal energy, it is an intrinsic property. It is also related to measurable quantities that characterize the system. For a reversible process, the change in entropy is given by the expression:

$$dS = dQ/T$$

The second law of thermodynamics states that the entropy change of any system and its surroundings, considered as a whole, is positive and approaches zero for any reversible process. Or

The entropy of the universe tends to increase.

Perfectly reversible processes do not exist in nature, so all natural processes result in an increase in entropy. This is expressed as follows:

$$\Delta S_{\text{total}} \geq 0$$

where S_{total} refers to $S_{\text{system}} + S_{\text{surroundings}}$

The idea of entropy can be summarized as follows:

- The total energy of the universe is constant, but the entropy of the universe is always increasing;

- All natural processes are spontaneous, which means that they must occur with an increase in entropy.

So how can we use entropy? Well, suppose that we're studying a physical or chemical transformation that proceeds from state a to b and that ΔS_{system} can be calculated.

If $\Delta S > 0$, the reaction is spontaneous from a to b. If $\Delta S = 0$, the system is at equilibrium, and no spontaneous process will occur. If $\Delta S < 0$, the reaction is spontaneous from b to a.

For example, the second law can be used to show that the flow of heat between two reservoirs at temperatures T_H and T_C (where the subscripts H and C mean hot and cold) must be from the hotter to the colder body. When heat is added to or extracted from a system, the system undergoes a finite entropy change at constant temperature, and $\Delta S = Q/T$. The quantity Q is the same for both the hot and cold bodies, but Q_H and Q_C have opposite signs. Heat added to one body is considered positive, and heat extracted from a body is considered negative, so $Q_H = -Q_C$.

It follows that $\Delta S_H = Q_H/T_H = -Q_C/T_C$, and $\Delta S_C = Q_C/T_C$, so

$$\Delta S_{total} = \Delta S_H + \Delta S_C = -Q_C/T_H + Q_C/T_C = [Q_C(T_H - T_C)/T_H T_C]$$

According to the second law, ΔS_{total} must be positive, therefore, $Q_C(T_H - T_C) > 0$. So Q_C must be positive and represent the heat added to the cold body. Conclusion: heat flows from a hot body to a cold body.

The process described above is spontaneous, and the **driving force** is the difference in temperature between the two bodies.

THE CARNOT CYCLE

Consider a heat engine made up of a cylinder that contains an ideal gas at T_H, placed between two reservoirs, one of which is at a temperature slightly higher than the temperature of the gas in the cylinder ($T_H + dT$), the other at a temperature slightly lower ($T_C - dT$). In the **Carnot cycle**, heat is added to the engine, and work is done. The following illustration represents a Carnot engine at the start of the cycle:

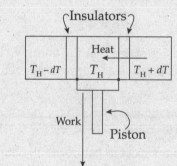

To mechanical reservoir

(The subscripts C and H mean cold and hot, respectively). The Carnot cycle consists of four steps, performed reversibly (heat flows by an infinitesimal temperature gradient and the pressure of the gas differs infinitesimally from that of the piston).

Step 1: Isothermal expansion

The insulators are removed. The temperature of the gas is constant at T_H. The gas goes from V_1 to V_2. For ideal gases, the internal energy depends only on temperature, and $DU_1 = 0$. So $W_1 = -Q_1$, where the subscript refers to the fact that this is step 1.

$$W_1 = -Q_1 = \int P dV = RT_H \int dV/V = RT_H \ln(V_2/V_1)$$

Step 2: Adiabatic expansion

The insulators are put in place. The gas goes from V_2 to V_3, and the temperature from T_H to T_C. $Q_2 = 0$ and $\Delta U_2 = W_2$; where the 2 subscript refers to step 2. We can write

$$\Delta U_2 = W_2 = C_V \Delta T = C_V(T_C - T_H)$$

Step 3: Isothermal contraction

The insulators are removed. Temperature is constant at T_C. The gas goes from V_3 to V_4. $\Delta U_3 = 0$, and $W_3 = -Q_3$.

$$W_3 = -Q_3 = \int P dV = RT_C \int dV/V = RT_C \ln(V_4/V_3)$$

Step 4: Adiabatic contraction

The insulators are replaced. The gas goes from V_4 to V_1, and the temperature, from T_C to T_H. $Q_4 = 0$, and $\Delta U_4 = W_4$

$$\Delta U_4 = W_4 = C_V\_T = C_V(T_H - T_C).$$

It can be easily shown that the cycle obeys the first law of thermodynamics. The net amount of work done is $W_{total} = W_1 + W_2 + W_3 + W_4$. W_2 and W_4 cancel each other out. So $W_{total} = W_1 + W_3 = RT_H \ln(V_2/V_1) + RT_C \ln(V_4/V_3)$.

Using the equation $(T_2/T_1) = (V_1/V_2)^{-1}$ (for reversible adiabatic expansion and compression; see the previous section), it can be shown that $(V_2/V_1) = (V_3/V_4)$, and

$$W_{total} = W_1 + W_3 = R(T_H - T_C)\ln(V_2/V_1).$$

Since $Q_2 = Q_4 = 0$, the total heat exchanged is $Q_{total} = Q_1 + Q_3$.

$Q_{total} = -RT_H \ln(V_2/V_1) - RT_C \ln(V_4/V_3) = -R(T_H - T_C)\ln(V_1/V_2)$.

The first law is obeyed because the energy given up by the thermal reservoirs is equal to that gained by the mechanical reservoir. It can also be shown that the sum of Q/T for each step of the Carnot cycle is zero:

$$\Delta S = \Delta S_1 + \Delta S_2 + \Delta S_3 + \Delta S_4 = \Delta S_1 + \Delta S_3$$

$$= -[RT_H \ln(V_2/V_1)]/T_H - [RT_C \ln(V_4/V_3)]/T_C = -R \ln(V_2/V_1) - R \ln(V_4/V_3)$$

$$= -R \ln(V_2/V_1) + R \ln(V_3/V_4) = -R \ln(V_2/V_1) + R \ln(V_2/V_1) = 0$$

The fact that $\Delta S = 0$ proves that the entropy of the system is a function of the state of the system. The entropy difference between the two states of a system is always the same, regardless of the path that connects the two states.

The efficiency of the Carnot engine is computed on the basis of the work produced for a given consumption of thermal energy:

Efficiency $= W/Q_H = [R(T_H - T_C)\ln(V_2/V_1)]/RT_H \ln(V_2/V_1) = 1 - (T_C/T_H)$.

To attain perfect efficiency, T_C should be 0 K, or T_H infinite (which is impossible).

This leads to the following equivalent statements of the second law:

1. It is impossible to build a cyclic engine that will extract heat from a reservoir and produce an equal amount of work with no other changes occurring.

2. It is impossible to build a cyclic engine that will transfer heat from a cold reservoir to a hot one with no other effects.

3. All reversible Carnot cycles operating between the same initial and final T must have the same efficiency.

Examples of hot reservoirs at T_H are furnaces and nuclear reactors. The best example of a heat reservoir at T_C, called a **heat sink**, is the environment. The discharge of waste heat into the environment, called thermal pollution, is a direct consequence of the second law of thermodynamics.

THE THIRD LAW OF THERMODYNAMICS

The first law of thermodynamics deals with the conservation of energy and the relationship between heat and work, and the second law deals with the spontaneous occurrence of chemical or physical processes. It defines only *changes* in entropy (DS), not entropy itself.

Absolute entropy values are the subject of the third law of thermodynamics, which deals primarily with the behavior of matter at very low (i.e., cryogenic) temperatures. Absolute zero (0 K) cannot be attained, and this is taken as evidence for the statement that the entropies of all crystalline materials are the same at absolute zero. This was first stated as the **Nernst heat theorem** but is widely known as the third law.

> *The entropy S of all perfect crystalline substances is the same at absolute zero.*

At 0 K, the atoms in a pure, perfect crystal are perfectly aligned and do not move. There is no entropy of mixing because the crystal is pure (contains only one element). This means that if the entropy of each element in a crystalline state is taken as zero at the absolute zero of temperature, then every substance has a positive, finite entropy.

The third law allows us to obtain absolute values for the entropy of chemical compounds by calorimetric measurements. We can obtain the difference in entropy between 0 K and T using reversible additions of heat to a heat reservoir:

$$S_T - S_0 = \int dQ/T.$$

The integration is performed from 0 to T. If a substance in a given phase is heated from T_1 to T_2, it gains entropy according to

$$S_2 - S_1 = \int dH/T = \int C_P(dT/T) = \int C_P d(\ln T).$$

Again, integration is between T_1 and T_2 and graphed with a plot of C_P/T versus T or C_P versus $\ln T$, if the required C_P values have been measured. However, C_P measurements are difficult below 15 K, so extrapolation to absolute zero is necessary. From 0 K to 25°C, the system undergoes a number of phase transitions. At each transition, C_P changes abruptly. The entropy change at the transition can be calculated using $\Delta S_{trans} = \Delta H_{trans}/T_{trans}$. By adding all of the contributions to entropy from 0 K to 25°C, we can get the standard entropy at 25°C, called $S°$.

Example:

The following C_P data were obtained for $Na_2SO_{4\,(s)}$:

T (K)	C_P (cal deg^{-1} mol^{-1})	C_P/T (cal deg^{-2} mol^{-1})
13.74	0.171	0.01244
16.25	0.286	0.01760
20.43	0.626	0.03064
27.73	1.615	0.05824
41.11	4.346	0.10571
52.72	7.032	0.13338
68.15	10.480	0.15377
82.96	13.280	0.160017

Calculate the absolute entropy of $Na_2SO_{4\,(s)}$ at 95.0 K.

Answer:

$dS = nC_p/T \, dt$ at constant P

Assume you have 1 mole of substance and integrate from 0 to 95 K:

$\int dS = \int C_p/T \, dt$ integration from 0 to 95 K.

But we have no data from 0 to 13.74 K, so we must break up the integral into two parts:

$$\int C_p/T \, dt \text{ (from 0 to 13.74 K)} + \int C_p/T \, dt \text{ (from 13.74 to 95 K)}$$

A plot of C_p/T vs. T looks like this:

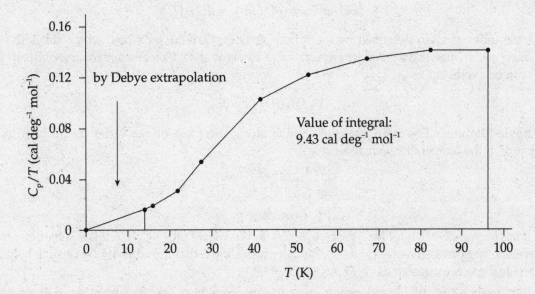

The value of the definite integral from 13.74 to 95 K corresponds to an entropy value of 9.43 cal K^{-1}.

The first integral for which we have no data can be evaluated by *Debye extrapolation*:

For a solid at low T, $C_v = C_p = aT^3$.

And $\int C_p/T \, dt = \int aT^3/T \, dt = \int aT^2 \, dt = aT^3/3$ from 0 to 13.74.

The lower limit is not used, so $a(13.74)^3/3 = C_p$ at 13.74 K.

Using the graph, $a(13.74)^3/3 = 0.171/3$, since $C_p = aT^3$.

And $aT^3/3$ from 0 to 13.74 corresponds to an entropy value of 0.06 cal K^{-1}.

And $\int C_p/T \, dt$ (from 0 to 13.74 K) + $\int C_p/T \, dt$ (from 13.74 to 95 K) equals

$$0.06 \text{ cal } K^{-1} + 9.43 \text{ cal } K^{-1} = 9.49 \text{ cal } K^{-1}.$$

A perfect crystalline solid at 0 K has $S = 0$, so $S_0 = 0$ and $S_{95} = 9.49$ cal K^{-1} or 39.71 JK^{-1}.

Standard entropies, along with standard enthalpies, constitute the thermodynamic basis for the study of chemical equilibria, and also define another important thermodynamic function, the standard Gibbs's free energy ($G°$).

IDEAL GASES AND SOLUTIONS

We saw that ideal gases were characterized by the absence of intermolecular forces and that the internal energy of an ideal gas does not depend on its volume:

$$\Delta U_T = 0$$

or

$$(\partial U/\partial V)_T = 0$$

At constant temperature, a change in V also leads to a change in P; therefore $(\partial U/\partial P)_T = 0$. This is known as **Joule's law**, which is basically a statement that the internal energy of a perfect gas depends only on the temperature:

$$(\partial U/\partial V)_T = (\partial U/\partial P)_T = dU/dT$$

Ideal gases are also described by the following laws: **Gay-Lussac's law,** which states that *the volume of a given mass of gas is directly proportional to its temperature, if the pressure remains constant*. This law can be expressed as

$$(V_2/V_1)P = (T_2/T_1)_P$$

Boyle-Mariotte's law states that the volume of a given mass of gas varies inversely with the pressure, if the temperature remains constant:

$$(V_2/V_1)_T = (P_1/P_2)_T$$

or

$$PV = \text{constant}$$

It has been shown that for ideal gases, $C_p - C_V = R$. We know that $\gamma = C_p/C_V$; this is sometimes more conveniently expressed as $\gamma - 1 = R/C_V$. We have also shown that the adiabatic, reversible behavior of an ideal gas is expressed as $(T_2/T_1) = (V_1/V_2)^{\gamma-1}$.

Real gases show PVT relationships that deviate from ideal gas behavior. At high pressure, calculations performed with Clapeyron's equation ($PV = nRT$) deviate by 2–3%. Van der Waals attributed the failure of the $PV = nRT$ relationship to the fact that it neglects (a) the volume occupied by the gas molecules and (b) the attractive forces among the molecules. The presence of molecules on nonnegligible size means that a certain volume (the **excluded volume**) is not available for molecules to move in. If b represents the excluded volume of a mole of a gas, then we can correct Clapeyron's equation to read $P(V - nb) = nRT$. Not surprisingly, the intermolecular attractions lower the mobility of each molecule. The pressure exerted by the gas is thus reduced, as if the number of molecules are effectively reduced. The second correction factor applies to pressure. Van der Waals' complete equation becomes $(P - an^2/V^2)(V - nb) = nRT$, where a is a proportionality factor. The factors a and b are characteristic for each gas and temperature.

A solution is a homogeneous system that contains at least two constituents. It can be gaseous, liquid, or solid. The characteristics of an ideal solution are

- $\Delta V_{mix} = 0$. An ideal solution is one in which the volume of the solution is equal to the volume of the unmixed components.

- $\Delta H_{mix} = 0$. There is no change of enthalpy in the system when the components are mixed to form a solution.

- The entropies of each component in an ideal solution are greater than the entropy of the pure, isolated materials.

If A and B represent the two components of a binary system, then $S_A(\text{lns}) = S°_A - R\ln(x_A)$, where $S°$ is the standard entropy of the pure component and x_A is the molar fraction of A in the mixture ($x_A = n_A/[n_A + n_B]$). Also, $S_B(\text{lns}) = S°_B - R\ln(x_B)$, where x_B is the molar fraction of B. Because x_A and x_B are both less than 1, $S_A > S°_A$, and $S_B > S°_B$.

A **real** solution is a solution in which the interactions between the molecules of the different components differ from the interactions between the molecules of the same components. Consider, for example, a solution of chloroform and acetone, in which intermolecular hydrogen bonding takes place: $Cl_3C-H\cdots\cdots O=C(CH_3)_2$. In this case, heat will be given off when the solution is formed, so $\Delta H_{mix} < 0$. The association between the molecules restricts their motion. This should give the system a less positive entropy than in an ideal solution.

THERMOCHEMISTRY

Thermochemistry is the application of the first law of thermodynamics to the study of chemical reactions. This subject deals with the measurement, or calculation, of the heat absorbed or released during a chemical reaction. Enthalpy is a state property. The enthalpy change of a reaction depends only on the enthalpies of the initial and final states, not on the path of the reaction. If a chemical reaction is represented by

$$\text{Reactants} \rightarrow \text{products}$$

the changes in internal energy and enthalpy for the reaction are

$\Delta U = U_{products} - U_{reactants}$

and

$\Delta H = H_{products} - H_{reactants}$

> *If heat is absorbed during a reaction, ΔH and ΔU are positive, and the reaction is said to be endothermic. If heat is given off, ΔH and ΔU are negative, and the reaction is exothermic.*

We have seen that $\Delta H = \Delta U + \Delta PV$. The difference between ΔH and ΔU is quite small if, at constant pressure, the change of volume during the reaction is slight, as is the case when solids and liquids are involved. If gases are involved, $P\Delta V$ can cause a significant difference between ΔU and ΔH. If the reaction produces a net change (Δn), the expression can be written as follows:

$$\Delta H = \Delta U + \Delta PV = \Delta U + \Delta(nRT) = \Delta U + RT\Delta n.$$

HESS'S LAW

Hess's law states that if a reaction can be broken down into a number of steps, ΔH of the overall process is equal the sum of the enthalpy changes of each step. This is true because H is a state property and is independent of the path.

Example:

The ΔH of the following reaction:

$$(1) \quad C\,(s) + \frac{1}{2}O_2\,(g) \rightarrow CO\,(g)$$

cannot be measured directly. Use the following information to calculate ΔH of the reaction:

(2) $C\ (s) + O_2\ (g) \rightarrow CO_2\ (g) + 393.5$ kJ

(3) $CO_2\ (g) + 283$ kJ $\rightarrow CO\ (g) + \dfrac{1}{2}O_2\ (g)$

Answer: Summing up equations 2 and 3 and canceling the identical terms gives

$$C\ (s) + O_2\ (g) + CO_2\ (g) + 283\text{ kJ} \rightarrow CO_2\ (g) + CO\ (g) + \dfrac{1}{2}O_2\ {}_{(g)} + 393.5\text{ kJ}$$

and

$$C\ (s) + \dfrac{1}{2}O_2\ (g) \rightarrow CO\ (g) + 103.5\text{ kJ}.$$

The result shows that heat has been released.

For this reaction, we could write that $\Delta H = -103.5$ kJ.

STANDARD ENTHALPY OF FORMATION (ΔH°_f)

The enthalpy change of a reaction can be evaluated from the standard enthalpies of formation (ΔH°_f) of the reactants and products. The standard state is defined by 1 atm pressure and 25°C, and one in which the substance is in a stable physical state under these conditions. The enthalpy of formation of the elements in the standard state is zero. For example, $\Delta H^\circ_f\ (H_2) = 0$ at 25°C. At higher temperatures, it becomes positive, and at lower temperatures it becomes negative. The standard enthalpy of formation of a compound is the enthalpy change that would occur if 1 mol of the compound were obtained directly from its elements at 1 atm and 25°C. For example, C (graphite) + $O_2\ (g) \rightarrow CO_2\ (g)$, ΔH° (298 K) = –393.5 kJ. Since the standard enthalpies of formation of C and O_2 are zero, $\Delta H^\circ_f\ (CO_2)$ = –393.5 kJ. The standard enthalpy of formation of compounds is often referred to as the **standard heat of formation**. The ΔH°_f of most compounds have been recorded.

STANDARD ENTHALPY OF REACTION (ΔH°_R)

The standard enthalpy of a reaction, ΔH°_R, is the difference in enthalpy between the products and the reactants, when both products and reactants are in their standard state at 298 K:

$$\Delta H^\circ_R = \Sigma(\Delta H^\circ_f \text{ of products}) - \Sigma(\Delta H^\circ_f \text{ of reactants})$$

This equation is more useful than $\Delta H_R = H_{products} - H_{reactants}$, because H cannot be measured. However, in accordance with Hess's law, we can evaluate ΔH°_R through a succession of steps: first the determination of ΔH°_f of the reactants, then the determination of the ΔH°_f of the products, and finally, the determination of ΔH°_R.

Example:

Calculate ΔH°_R for the reaction: $Fe_2O_3\ (s) + 3\ CO\ (g) \rightarrow 2\ Fe\ (s) + 3\ CO_2\ (g)$ using the following data: $\Delta H^\circ_f\ (Fe_2O_3)$ = –822.2 kJ/mol, $\Delta H^\circ_f\ (CO)$ = –110 kJ/mol, $\Delta H^\circ_f\ (CO_2)$ = –394 kJ/mol.

Answer:

Remember that the ΔH°_f of a pure element is zero, so $\Delta H^\circ_f\ (Fe) = 0$. And using

$$\Delta H^\circ_R = \Sigma(\Delta H^\circ_f \text{ of products}) - \Sigma(\Delta H^\circ_f \text{ of reactants})$$

gives us

$\Delta H^\circ_R = 3\Delta H^\circ_f\ (CO_2) - [\Delta H^\circ_f\ (Fe_2O_3) + 3\Delta H^\circ_f\ (Fe_2O_3)] = 3(-394) - (-822.2 - 110) = -249.8$ kJ/mol.

BOND DISSOCIATION ENERGY

Consider the reaction H–H + Cl–Cl → 2 H–Cl. The rupture of the H–H and Cl–Cl bonds is an endothermic process that requires 436 and 242 kJ/mol, respectively. The formation of the H–Cl bond, however, is an exothermic process that releases 431 kJ/mol of energy. In this reaction, the reactants absorb 436 + 242 = 678 kJ/mol and are dissociated. When the atoms combine to form 2 HCl molecules, $2 \times 431 = 862$ kJ of energy is liberated. ΔH_R for this reaction is the difference between the energy absorbed (called the endo phase) by the reactants and the energy liberated by the formation of the products (the exo phase).

$\Delta H_R = \Sigma \Delta H$(bond enthalpies of reactants) – ΔH(bond enthalpies of products) Here, $\Delta H_R = 678 - 862 = -184$ kJ for 2 mols of HCl, or $\Delta H_R = -92$ kJ/mol. The bond enthalpy is the average energy required to break a particular bond in one mole of gaseous molecules. For example, Cl_2 (g) → 2 Cl (g), $\Delta H = 242$ kJ/mol.

GIBBS AND HELMHOLTZ ENERGIES

Change in enthalpy and entropy are two factors that affect the spontaneity of a chemical reaction. The Gibbs free energy or molar free enthalpy (G) combines these two thermodynamic factors:

$$G = H - TS$$

For a process that occurs at constant temperature, the variation in free energy is given by

$$\Delta G = \Delta H - T \Delta S$$

Since H and S are state properties, G is also a state property. This fact allows us to study the influence of temperature on the spontaneity of a given process. We have seen that, if a reaction is spontaneous, $\Delta S = 0$, but it can be shown that $\Delta S = -\Delta G/T$ at constant P and T. Therefore, for ΔS to be positive, ΔG must be negative. Or

- if $\Delta G < 0$, the reactions is spontaneous;
- if $\Delta G > 0$, the reaction is not spontaneous;
- if $\Delta G = 0$, the system is in a state of equilibrium.

Let's examine a reaction in which the entropy of the system decreases. This means that the final term, $-T\Delta S$, will be positive. The reaction is spontaneous only if ΔH is negative and large enough to overcome $-T\Delta S$. If we want to convert the energy of the reaction to work, enough energy must be left as ΔH to be delivered to the surroundings after $-T\Delta S$ has been accounted for. Only energy in excess of $-T\Delta S$ is available for work. The free energy is a measure of the work that can be done by the system after the entropy demand has been supplied by ΔH. This is the meaning of the word free in free energy. The effect of temperature on spontaneity can be summarized as follows:

- $\Delta S > 0$ and $\Delta H < 0$ spontaneous at all temperatures
- $\Delta S > 0$ and $\Delta H > 0$ spontaneous at high temperatures
- $\Delta S < 0$ and $\Delta H < 0$ spontaneous at low temperatures
- $\Delta S < 0$ and $\Delta H > 0$ nonspontaneous at any temperature

The Gibbs free energy applies to constant pressure processes. For constant volume processes, the **Helmholtz free energy (A)** is used:

$$A = U - TS$$

We can define the **standard free energy** ($\Delta G°$) as the ΔG of a process occurring under standard conditions (1 atm, 25°C, and 1 M concentration). If we define $\Delta G°_f$ as the $\Delta G°$ that occurs when 1 mol of a compound in its standard state is formed from its elements (also in their standard states), then we can write

$$\Delta G°_R = \Sigma \Delta G°_f(\text{products}) - \Sigma \Delta G°_f(\text{reactants})$$

ENTHALPY

Symbol	Quantity	Type of property
H	Molar enthalpy Not measurable	Intensive
ΔH	Change in molar enthalpy e.g., ΔH_R change in enthalpy of reaction	Intensive Unit: J mol^{-1}
ΔH^0	Change in standard molar enthalpy, e.g., $\Delta H°_R$ change in standard enthalpy of reaction	Intensive Unit: J mol^{-1} Standard conditions
G	Molar free enthalpy or Gibb's free energy	Intensive Also called chemical potential, μ Not measurable
ΔG	Change in free energy	Intensive Units: J mol^{-1}
ΔG^0	Change in standard free energy e.g., $\Delta G°_R$ change in standard free energy of reaction	Intensive Units: J mol^{-1} Standard conditions

CHEMICAL POTENTIAL

Consider a system that consists of one phase but has more than one component. The chemical potential of the ith component of this system is defined as

$$\mu_i = \partial G / \partial n_i$$

where n_i is the number of moles of component i. Then the chemical potential is the variation in free energy of the component during an increase in its quantity, and the **chemical energy** is mdn.

Each type of energy is the product of two factors, an intensity factor (an intensive property) and a capacity factor (an extensive property):

Type of energy	Intensity factor	Capacity faqctor
Mechanical ($F dl$)	Force (F)	Displacement (dl)
"Volumetric" ($P dV$)	Pressure (P)	Change of volume (dV)
Kinetic ($1/2 v^2 dm$)	$v^2/2$	Change of mass (dm)
Chemical (μdn)	Chemical potential (μ)	Change of quality (dn)

The intensity factors are potentials, the "tension", or "driving force" of the type of energy considered. For instance, temperature is the driving force of a heat transition. When two systems with different potentials interact, equalization of the potentials takes place at the expense of the corresponding capacity factors. The chemical potential is a driving force during mass transfer.

Consider, for example, a system that consists of two phases, a and b. The chemical potentials of component i in each phase are $(\mu_i)_a$ and $(\mu_i)_b$. At constant T and P, a certain amount of i is transferred from one phase into the other. If dn_i mols of i goes from a to b, then $\Delta G_b = (\mu_i)_b dn_i$ and $\Delta G_a = (-\mu_i)_a dn_i$, and the total change in free energy is $\Delta G_{tot} = [(\mu_i)_b - (-\mu_i)_a]dn_i$.

Equilibrium between the two phases is achieved when $\Delta G_{tot} = 0$ or when $(\mu_i)_b = (-\mu_i)_a$.

> *When phase equilibrium is achieved, the chemical potential of a component is the same in both phases.*

CHEMICAL EQUILIBRIA

Consider the reaction

$$aA + bB \leftrightarrow cC + dD$$

The double arrow represents both the forward and reverse reactions. This type of reaction does not go to completion; the reactants and products still react in both directions. We can define a reaction quotient K as follows:

$$K = \frac{[C]^c [D]^d}{[A]^a [B]^b}$$

where the brackets refer to molar concentrations. The free energy change at nonstandard conditions for this reaction is

$$\Delta G = \Delta G° + RT \ln K$$

The values of ΔG and K change as the reaction proceeds to equilibrium. When the system reaches equilibrium, $\Delta G = 0$. Therefore, $\Delta G° = -Rt \ln K_{eq}$, where K_{eq}, the reaction quotient at equilibrium, is called the **equilibrium constant**. A large negative value of $\Delta G°$ means a large positive value of K_{eq}, and a large value of K_{eq} means that equilibrium favors the products.

Le Châtelier's principle is a general law that explains the consequence of applying a change, called a **stress**, to a system in a state of equilibrium and the subsequent shift in equilibrium. The following factors can shift equilibria:

- concentration: if a constituent (reactant or product) is added to or removed from a system in equilibrium, the concentrations of all of the species in the system will change until a new equilibrium is reached. If a reactant is added or a product is removed, the forward reaction will be favored. If a reactant is removed or a product added, the reverse reaction will be favored.

- temperature: if heat is added to a system in equilibrium, the system shifts in the direction that absorbs heat; this means that the endothermic reaction is favored. If heat is removed, the system shifts in the direction that gives out heat, or the exothermic direction.

For example, if heat is added to the reaction N_2 (g) + O_2 (g) + 181 kJ $\leftrightarrow$ 2 NO (g), the forward reaction is favored, and if heat is removed, the reverse reaction is favored.

- pressure: the pressure in a closed system can be modified by changing the volume of the container. If the volume of the container is decreased, the pressure of the system increases and the system reacts so as to decrease the number of molecules present in the system. If the volume is increased, the pressure inside the container is lowered and the system is displaced in the direction that produces the greatest number of molecules.

Take, for example, the following Haber process reaction: N_2 (g) + 3 H_2 (g) $\leftrightarrow$ 2 NH_3 (g). If the volume of the container is decreased, the pressure inside the container is increased and the forward reaction is favored, because it creates a reduced number of molecules in the system.

PHASE EQUILIBRIA

A phase is defined as any part of a system that's homogeneous. **Gibbs' phase rule** provides a good tool for studying heterogeneous equilibria:

$$f = c - p + 2$$

where c is the number of components in the system, p is the number of phases present, and f is the number of degrees of freedom of a system.

The number of degrees of freedom of a system is defined by the number of independent variables, such as temperature, pressure, and concentration, that may be varied without altering the number of phases in the system.

To illustrate this concept, let us consider a one-component system. From the phase rule, we know that $c = 1$ and that $f = 3 - p$.

- If $p = 1$ (the system contains one phase), $f = 2$, and the system is bivariant.
- If $p = 2$ (the system has two phases), $f = 1$, and the system is univariant.
- If $p = 3$ (three phases), $f = 0$, and the system is invariant.

Pure water is a one-component system. Water can exist in three phases: ice, liquid, and steam. Because water is a one component system, its maximum number of degrees of freedom is 2. The water system, as with any one-component system, can be represented by a two-dimensional diagram. The most convenient variables to plot are P and T:

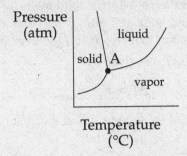

Pressure
(atm)

Temperature
(°C)

There are three areas, each of which represents a single phase. In these single-phase areas, the system is bivariant: P and T can be modified independently without altering the number of phases. The dividing lines between areas describe the conditions at which equilibrium exists. Along the lines, the system is univariant, and has only one degree of freedom: for a given temperature, there is only one pressure at which two phases may coexist. The curves intersect at point A, a point at which all three phases are simultaneously at equilibrium. At A, the system is invariant; there are no degrees of freedom, and neither P nor T can be altered without causing the disappearance of one of the phases.

COLLIGATIVE PROPERTIES

The presence of nonvolatile particles dissolved in a solvent can cause the physical properties of the solution, such as boiling point and freezing point, to differ from those of the solvent because the presence of a nonvolatile solute reduces the number of solvent particles per unit volume. The physical properties of dilute solutions that depend only on the number of molecules in solution, not on their chemical nature, are called **colligative properties**. The three most important colligative properties are freezing point depression, boiling point elevation, and osmotic pressure.

Raoult's law says that when a solute is added to a pure solvent, the vapor pressure above the solvent decreases. This is expressed as

$$P_{solution} = x_{solution} P^\circ_{solvent}$$

where $x_{solvent}$ is the molar fraction of the solvent. This is a linear equation, so a graph of $P_{solution}$ vs. $x_{solution}$ gives a straight line with an elevation equivalent to $P^\circ_{solvent}$.

Raoult's law also allows for the determination of the molecular mass of the solute. Because changes of state depend on vapor pressure, the presence of a solute also modifies the freezing and boiling points of a solvent. The phase diagram of a solution when a nonvolatile solute is added looks like this:

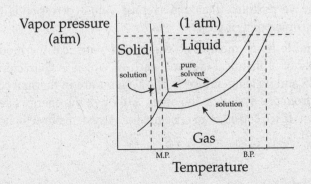

The phase diagram of the solution is generally lower than that of the pure solvent. Remembering that the melting point is the temperature at which a solid melts (at 1 atm) and that the boiling point is the temperature at which a liquid boils at 1 atm, it becomes obvious that a decrease in vapor pressure should cause the boiling point to increase and the freezing point to decrease.

The **freezing point depression (ΔT_f)** is given by:

$$\Delta T_f = K_f \cdot m_{solute}$$

where K_f is a constant characteristic of the solvent, called the molal cryoscopic constant, and m_{solute} is the molality of the solute (mol solute/kg of solvent).

The **boiling point elevation (ΔT_b)** is given by:

$$\Delta T_b = K_b \cdot m_{solute}$$

where K_b is a constant characteristic of the solvent, called the molal ebullioscopic constant, and m_{solute} is the molality of the solute.

The **osmotic pressure (π)**, defined as the pressure required to stop the migration of a solute across a semipermeable membrane, is the third colligative property:

$$\pi = CRT$$

where C is the concentration of the solution and T is the temperature in K. This equation shows that as C increases, so does osmotic pressure.

STATISTICAL THERMODYNAMICS

Statistical mechanics attempts to predict the probable behavior of a large collection (called an "ensemble") of molecules. Ensembles are characterized by specific macroscopic properties, such as volume, potential energy, pressure, and temperature. The individual molecules in an ensemble are distributed over a range of microscopic states; so they differ from each other. Instead of trying to precisely define the states of the constituent molecules of an ensemble, statistical mechanics describes their most probable states in an attempt to arrive at a good description of their macroscopic properties.

Statistical thermodynamics uses the distribution laws of statistical mechanics to calculate and predict the energies and molecular velocities of ensembles of molecules, as well as their most probable energies and velocities. A macroscopic system can be defined by a few properties, such as volume, pressure, density, or temperature. But from a microscopic point of view, there are a great number of quantum states consistent with the fixed macroscopic properties. In statistical thermodynamics, to calculate any property, such as energy, one calculates the value of that property in each quantum state. Supposing that each quantum state has the same weight, the average value of the property is taken. Then we postulate that this average value corresponds to the thermodynamic property from a macroscopic point of view.

The **canonical ensemble** is the most basic concept of statistical thermodynamics. A canonical ensemble is an assembly of A identical systems, each of which is characterized by its number of systems N, its volume V, and its temperature T. The systems are in thermal contact with each other, so energy can circulate from one system to the other. Although the energy of each system varies, the average energy is known. If we consider an ensemble of A systems in which A_i systems are distributed between macroscopic states (the states of the system defined by macroscopic quantities such as T, V, etc.) of energy E_i, then the probability of finding a system in a state of energy E_i is given by

$$P_i = A_i/A = G_i \cdot \exp(-E_i/KT) \, / \, \Sigma G_i \cdot \exp(-E_i/KT)$$

where G_i is the degeneracy of the state E_i. The denominator of this equation is called the **canonical partition function (Z_c)** of the system:

$$Z_c(N, T, V) = \Sigma G_I \cdot \exp(-E_i/KT).$$

This distribution law can be compared with the **Boltzman distribution**: for an isolated system with N particles that can occupy various energy levels e_i with degeneracy g_i, the distribution is

$$P_i = A_i/A = g_i \cdot \exp(-e_i/KT) \, / \, \Sigma g_i \cdot \exp(-e_i/KT)$$

The denominator of this equation is the **partition function (Z)** of the particle:

$$Z(T, V) = \Sigma g_i \cdot \exp(-e_i/KT).$$

The partition function is the bridge between the quantum mechanical energy states of a macroscopic state and the thermodynamic properties of the system. These properties can be expressed as a function of the partition function. For the canonical ensemble, examples include

$$U = KT^2(\partial \ln Z/\partial T)_{N,V}$$

$$P = KT(\partial \ln Z/\partial V)_{N,T}$$

$$S = KT(\partial \ln Z/\partial T)_{N,V} + K\ln Z$$

Since the Helmholtz energy is $A = E - TS$, we can also write

$$A = -KT\ln Z(N, V, T)$$

Statistical thermodynamics also uses other ensembles. For example, the **microcanonical ensemble**, in which N, V, and E are fixed, and **the isothermal-isobaric ensemble**, in which N, T, and P are fixed. Each ensemble leads to a particular partition function, and each partition function leads to characteristic thermodynamic functions. In the isothermal-isobaric ensemble, the partition function is $\Delta(N, T, P)$, and a characteristic thermodynamic function is the Gibbs's free energy:

$$G = -KT\ln\Delta(N, T, P)$$

For the microcanonical ensemble (used to describe isolated systems) the partition function, called $\Omega(N, V, E)$, can be related to the entropy of the system:

$$S = K\ln\Omega(N, V, E).$$

The partition function is a summation over all possible quantum states. Therefore, this last equation shows that, for an isolated system, the entropy is proportional to the logarithm of the number of states available to the system.

QUANTUM CHEMISTRY AND ITS APPLICATION TO SPECTROSCOPY

Quantum chemistry provides the key to understanding atomic and molecular structure, chemical bonding, and the spectra of molecules. Four topics are covered under this heading: classical experiments, principles of quantum mechanics, quantum numbers and atomic term symbols, and molecular spectroscopy.

CLASSICAL EXPERIMENTS

BLACKBODY RADIATION

If a tungsten filament is gradually heated up, it starts to glow dull red at 900 K. As the temperature is further increased, the filament glows bright red, then orange, then yellow and finally white, and at this point, T is 2300 K. This glowing radiation is called the **radiant excitance**. If you were to think of a perfect absorber, it would be a substance that absorbs all frequencies of light and emits none. This substance would be black and would be called a **blackbody**. The closest thing to a true blackbody is a hollow cavity with a very small hole that leads to it: of the light absorbed, very little can escape. At the turn of the century, the experimentally observed variation of the radiant excitance of a blackbody with wavelength could not be explained by any model because theory assumed that energy was divided equally between all the vibrations emitting radiation, with the result that the energy had to increase as the wavelength became shorter, since the short wavelengths had more vibrational modes. This is due to the reciprocal relationship between wavelength and frequency. In other words, theory could not explain experiment. This problem was solved in 1901 by Max Planck, who proposed that energy consisted of discrete units, called **quanta**, and that the energy of a quantum was directly proportional to the frequency of an oscillator:

$$E = h\nu$$

In the expression above, E is energy, n is frequency, and h is Planck's constant (6.626×10^{-34} J). This led to a new treatment of the variation of radiant excitance with wavelength in excellent agreement with experimental results, as illustrated below:

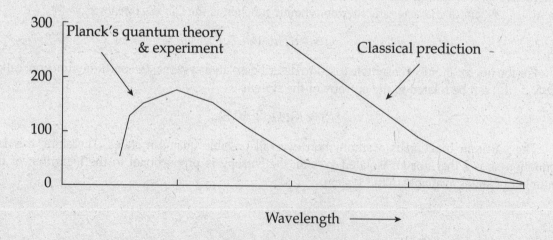

THE PHOTOELECTRIC EFFECT

In 1887, Hertz observed that electrons are emitted from a metal when the metal is irradiated with visible or ultraviolet radiation. He named this the **photoelectric effect**. It was quickly shown that (i) below a given cutoff frequency of incident radiation, no electrons were ejected from the metal surface, no matter how intense the radiation; (ii) above the cutoff frequency, the number of electrons emitted was directly proportional to the intensity of the radiation; and (iii) as the frequency of the incident radiation was increased, the maximum velocity of the ejected electrons increased. Classical theory could not explain these results, since it predicted that the emission of electrons should depend on the intensity of the radiation. This problem was solved by Einstein in 1905 with the help of Planck's quantum theory. He proposed that not only was the energy of an oscillator quantized, but that light itself consisted of particles—or **photons** with energy equal to hn. He explained the photoelectric effect by proposing that "work energy" (w) was required to remove an electron of given energy hn from the surface of the metal according to

$$hn = \frac{1}{2}mu^2 + w$$

where $\frac{1}{2}mu^2$ is the kinetic energy of the emitted electron. If the energy of the electron hn is less than w, the electron can not be emitted, and if it is greater, the electron is emitted. There is also a frequency equal to w/h that's just sufficient for the electron to be emitted. This clearly explained the frequency dependence of the photoelectric effect and the validity of the new quantum theory.

THE DUAL NATURE OF LIGHT

Explaining blackbody radiation and the photoelectric effect required understanding that light had particle properties, that it consists of particles called photons. However, it was quickly realized that other properties of light, such as refraction, could be explained only by considering light as a wave. This led to the quantum mechanical theory on the **dual nature of radiation**, elaborated by de Broglie in 1924. He proposed that electrons could also behave as waves with wavelength λ given by:

$$\lambda = h/p = h/mv$$

where p is the momentum of the electron, v its velocity, m its mass, and h is Planck's constant.

THE UNCERTAINTY PRINCIPLE

In 1926, Heisenberg realized that it was impossible to simultaneously measure the momentum and the position of a particle such as an electron, because performing one measurement would disturb the particle and prevent the accurate measurement of the second quantity. This is expressed in the **Heisenberg uncertainty principle**:

$$\Delta q \Delta p \approx h/4\pi$$

or you could say that the product of the uncertainty of the position of the particle (Δq) and the uncertainty in its momentum (Δp) is approximately equal to $h/4\pi$.

PRINCIPLES OF QUANTUM MECHANICS

The postulates of quantum mechanics:

1. The physical state of a particle can be fully described by a wave function of the type $(\Psi_{x,y,z,t})$

2. The $(\Psi_{x,y,z,t})$ wave functions are obtained by solving the appropriate Schrödinger equation. For time-independent systems, this equation is $(h^2/8\pi^2m) \nabla\Psi + [E - V(r)]\Psi = 0$

3. Every dynamic variable that correlates with a physically observable property is expressed as a linear operator

4. Operators that represent physical properties are derived from the classical expressions for these properties

5. The eigenvalues obtained by solving the appropriate Schrödinger equation represent all possible values of an individual measurement of the quantity in question

In quantum mechanical calculations, **operators** are represented with a circumflex accent over the symbol that represents the variable of interest. They are placed to the left of the function on which they are operating. For example, the classical variable for kinetic energy is E_k. The corresponding quantum mechanical operator is $\hat{E}_k$, and the operation that it performs on the function to which it is attached is $-(h^2/8p^2m) \nabla^2$. So $\hat{E}_k\phi$ means that the operator $\hat{E}_k$ is operating on the function ϕ.

SCHRÖDINGER'S EQUATION

Schrödinger's equation $(\Psi_{x,y,z,t})$ is a complex **wave function** used to describe the quantum mechanical state of a particle. It is a mathematical construct that cannot be experimentally verified. The wave function is used to describe the **probability density** of a particle, i.e., the probability of finding a particle (for instance, an electron) at time t at a given position $\mathbf{r} = x, y, z$ in a volume dV. This probability (w) is proportional to the square of the wave function:

$$W_{x,y,z,t} = |\Psi|^2 \, dV$$

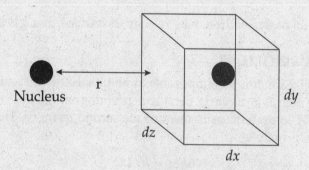

Electron "somewhere"
in a volume element dx, dy

The **time-dependent** wave function is used to describe the harmonic wave motion of a free particle:

$$\Psi(\mathbf{r}, t) = (a)e^{j[wt - (\mathbf{k.r})]}$$

where

a = amplitude in units of m$^{-3/2}$

j = imaginary unit (= 1)

w = frequency

$\mathbf{k}$ = wave number vector

$\mathbf{r}$ = radius vector describing the position of the particle in space.

The wave function is also used to describe the motion of an electromagnetic wave traveling in a vacuum. The **time-independent Schrödinger equation** is

$$(h^2/8\pi^2 m)\, \nabla\Psi + [E - V(\mathbf{r})]\Psi = 0$$

where

ψ = wave function in units of m$^{-3/2}$

m = mass in kg

∇ = Laplace operator in units of m^{-2}

$V(r)$ = potential in units of J

E = energy in units of J

h = Planck's constant

Eigenfunctions are the solutions to this equation, and they exist only for specific **eigenvalues** of energy E. The totality of the eigenvalues for E yield the entire energy spectrum of the particle.

If $\lim (r \to \infty)\, V(r) = 0$, then the energy eigenvalues yield a **discrete** spectrum in the $E < 0$ range, and a **continuum** in the $E \geq 0$ range.

THE HARMONIC OSCILLATOR

The harmonic oscillator is a particle that has mass m which, under the influence of a linearly applied force, will move in one or several directions with a frequency w_0. The Schrödinger equation for a **one-dimensional harmonic oscillator** is

$$d^2\Psi/dx^2 + 8\pi^2 m/h^2\, [E - (m\omega_0^2/2)x^2]\Psi = 0$$

The eigenvalues of the harmonic oscillator are **quantized** and **equidistant**:

$$E_n = hw_0\,(n + 1/2) = hv_0\left(n + \frac{1}{2}\right) \text{ with } n = 0, 1, 2, 3\ldots$$

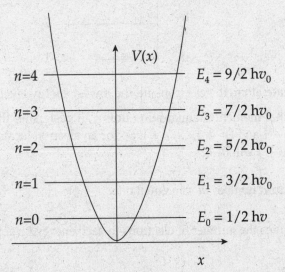

The **zero-point energy**, $E_0 = \frac{1}{2}h\nu_0$, is the lowest energy possible for the harmonic oscillator.

An **energy quantum** with $E = h\nu = \hbar\omega$ is also called a **photon**.

The harmonic oscillator is used to model:

- the vibrations of atoms and molecules; and
- the lattice vibrations of crystalline materials.

QUANTUM NUMBERS AND ATOMIC TERM SYMBOLS

QUANTUM NUMBERS

- Electrons are defined by three orbital quantum numbers: n, l, m_l and one spin quantum number, m_i.

You should be familiar with the Pauli exclusion principle, which states that in an atom, no two electrons can have the same set of quantum numbers n, l, m_l, and m_i.

- n is the principal quantum number; it defines the energy of electron shells. It can be a positive integer, 1, 2, 3, etc. In the diagram below, an electron located in the lowest shell, K, will have n equal to 1.

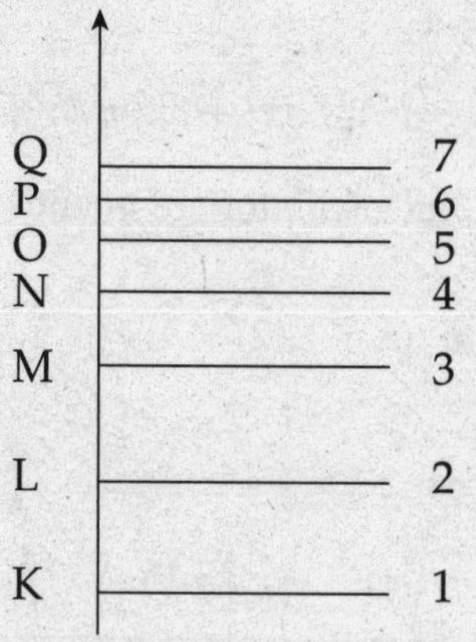

$$
\begin{array}{lll}
\text{Q} & \underline{\hspace{3cm}} & 7 \\
\text{P} & \underline{\hspace{3cm}} & 6 \\
\text{O} & \underline{\hspace{3cm}} & 5 \\
\text{N} & \underline{\hspace{3cm}} & 4 \\
\text{M} & \underline{\hspace{3cm}} & 3 \\
\text{L} & \underline{\hspace{3cm}} & 2 \\
\text{K} & \underline{\hspace{3cm}} & 1 \\
\end{array}
$$

- In a **ground state** atom, the electrons fill the lowest energy levels first.

- l is the azimuthal momentum quantum number; it designates the electron subshells. It is equal to $n - 1$ and $l = 0, 1, ..., n - 1$. So for an electron located in the K level with n equal to 1, l will be 0.

- The spin quantum number m_s can equal only $+\frac{1}{2}$ or $-\frac{1}{2}$.

The following table gives the number of electrons in each energy level for boron, aluminum, and neon:

n	1	2	2	3	3	..3
l	0	0	1	0	1	2
B	2e	2e	6e	2e	1e	
Ne	2e	2e	6e			

ATOMIC TERM SYMBOLS

- The **electron configuration** of an atom is the assignment of a number of electrons to specific orbitals (e.g., Na: $1s^2\,2s^2\,2p^6\,3s^1$). In this description, the number before the letter is n, the principal quantum number.

- A **term** is an **energy level.**

- A given electronic configuration gives rise to a number of energy levels and thus to a number of terms.

- A term—or energy level—is defined by its **total angular momentum L,** which is zero or a positive integer for a single electron, and by its **total spin angular momentum S,** which is zero, a positive integer, or $\dfrac{1}{2}$.

- A term is labeled using its L and S values using

$$(2S + 1)_X$$

where X adopts a value corresponding to a specific quantum number L:

if $L =$	0	1	2	3	4	5	6	...
then X =	s	p	d	f	g	h	i	...

- $(2s + 1)$ is the **multiplicity** of the term and is equal to the number of unpaired electrons plus one.

- Depending on the value of s, terms are called:

	singlet	doublet	triplet	quartet	quintet
when $s =$	0	1	2	3	4

Example: hydrogen term symbols:
The electronic configuration of H is $1s^1$ in the ground state, it has one electron, and L =1.

$n = 1$, $l = 0$ and its ground state term symbol is s.
In the first excited state, the electronic configuration of H is $2s^1$. So,

$n = 2$, $l = 0$ or 1, and the term symbols are s and p.

If more energy is supplied and the electron can be excited to the second excited state,

$n = 3$, $l = 0$, 1 or 2, and the term symbols are s, p, and d.

Spectroscopy provides direct evidence about electron "energy jumps" between states. The spectrum of hydrogen consists of a series of sharp lines, each of which results from an electron jumping from one energy level to another, while emitting a photon of energy equal to the energy difference between the two levels. For example, electron jumps from levels where $n > 3$, down to the $n = 3$ level yield the Paschen series of lines observed in the near IR.

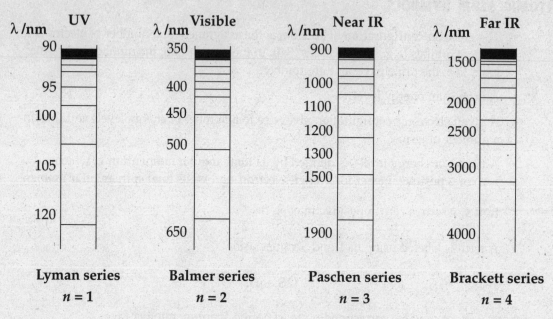

Line spectrum of the hydrogen atom

The energy of the electron in hydrogen depends on its principal quantum number n. So it will have the same energy whether it is found in the $2s$ or the $2p$ state, and this also applies to electrons in the $3s$, $3p$, and $3d$ states. However, this is only true for hydrogen-like atoms, i.e., atoms with only one electron in their valence shell. When atoms have more than one electron, coulombic interactions occur between them, and there is a significant energy difference between electrons that have different second quantum numbers.

The atomic term symbols—indicative of the total angular momentum L—are used to account for these coulombic interactions. For a hydrogen-like atom, the orbital angular momentum is:

$$L = \sqrt{[l(l+1)h/2\pi]}$$

And, for an atom with more than one electron:

$$L = \sum_i = \sqrt{[L(L+1)h/2p]}$$

where l = angular momentum vector of each electron in the atom

L = total angular momentum quantum number of the atom.

Atomic term symbols can be derived for all elements from their electronic configuration. Listed below are the electronic configurations and atomic term symbols of the elements of the *s* and *p* blocks:

Group	Electronic configuration	Atomic term symbol
I (alkali metals)	$[X]ns^1$	^2S
II (alkaline-earth metals)	$[X]ns^2$	$^1S_0$
III	$[X]ns^2np^1$	^2P
IV	$[X]ns^2np^2$	$^3P_0$
V	$[X]ns^2np^3$	$^4S_{3/2}$
VI	$[X]ns^2np^4$	$^3P_2$
VII (halogens)	$[X]ns^2np^5$	$^2P_{3/2}$
VIII (rare gases)	$[X]ns^2np^6$	$^1S_0$

MOLECULAR SPECTROSCOPY

THE ELECTROMAGNETIC SPECTRUM

All types of electromagnetic radiation (gamma rays, x-rays, UV, visible, infrared, radio frequency) travel at the same velocity: 3.0×10^8 m/s. Electromagnetic radiation is characterized by two properties, **amplitude** and **periodicity**, and these properties are described using any of the following quantities: wavelength (λ), wave number ($\bar{v}$) or frequency (v):

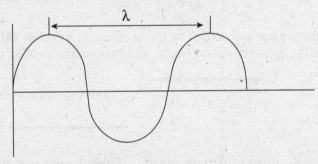

The wavelength (λ) is the distance from crest to crest on adjacent waves.

Radiation	Wavelength (μ)	Wavelength (nm)	Wave number (cm^{-1})	Frequency ($Hz \times 10^{-12}$)
Far UV	0.01 to 0.02	10 to 200	10^6 to 50,000	30,000 to 15,000
Near UV	0.20 to 0.38	200 to 390	50,000 to 26,300	1,500 to 787
Visible	0.38 to 0.78	390 to 790	26,300 to 12,800	787 to 385
Near infrared	0.78 to 3.00	790 to 3000	12,800 to 3,333	385 to 100
Infrared	3 to 30	3000 to 30,000	3,333 to 333	100 to 10
Far infrared	30 to 300	30,000 to 300,000	333 to 33.3	10 to 1
Microwave	300 to 10^6	300,000 to 10^9	33.3 to 0.01	1 to 0.0003

UNITS

1μ (micron) = 1000 nm = 10,000 Å (angstroms) = 0.0001 cm = 10^{-10} m

Frequency (n) is the number of waves that pass a given point in unit time. It is related to wavelength (λ) as follows:

$$\nu = c/\lambda$$

where c is the speed of light, 3.0×10^8 m/s

For example, UV electromagnetic radiation at 3,000 Å corresponds to a frequency of

$$\nu = c/\lambda = 3.00 \times 10^8 \text{ m s}^{-1} / 3.0 \times 10^{-7} \text{ m} = 10^{15} \text{ s}^{-1} \text{ or } 10^{15} \text{ Hz.}$$

A wavenumber ($\bar{\nu}$) is the number of waves per unit distance, so it has the units of reciprocal distance (cm^{-1}). A wavelength of 3000 Å corresponds to

$$\bar{\nu} \text{ (cm}^{-1}) = \text{number of Å in one cm}/\lambda = 10^8/3 \times 10^3 = 33,333 \text{ cm}^{-1}.$$

OPTICAL SPECTRA

The energy of a photon (E_p) is given by

$$E_p = h\nu$$

A molecule can absorb or emit this energy, thereby altering its rotational, vibrational, or electronic energy by an amount ΔE_m:

$$\Delta E_m = E_p = h\nu$$

If ΔE_m is positive, the photon is absorbed by the molecule in a process called **absorption**. If ΔE_m is negative, the photon is emitted by the molecule, and the process is called **emission**.

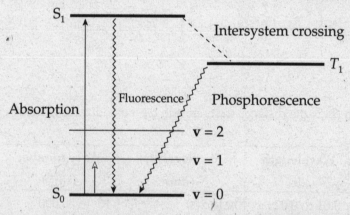

Electronic absorption takes place when the energy of the absorbed photon is in the UV or visible range. This is shown above by the S_0 to S_1 arrow. If the photon absorbed is in the infrared region, the absorption is vibrational (IR arrow above) and takes place between vibrational levels (labelled **v** above). Electronic absorption is allowed only between states of the same spin multiplicity (e.g., singlet to singlet) and is forbidden between states of different multiplicity (e.g., singlet to triplet). However, if two states of different multiplicity lie close to each other, the absorbed energy can be transferred between these states by a process called intersystem crossing. This is illustrated above by the dashed line.

Emission from the triplet state is called phosphorescence, and emission from the singlet state is called fluorescence.

A **spectrum** records the dependence of the absorption or emission intensity on wavelength or frequency.

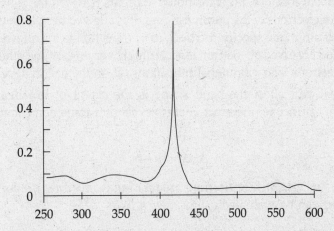

Above is the UV-Vis electronic absorption spectrum of a metalloporphyrin. Several factors affect the shape of its spectral bands, for instance, the **selection rules**, which determine whether or not a transition is allowed. This can be understood by taking a look at its (simplified) energy level diagram:

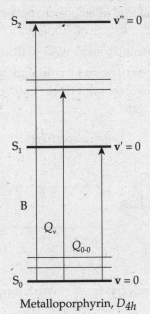

Metalloporphyrin, D_{4h}

A metalloporphyrin has the following structure:

Depending on the substituents on the ring, it can be assigned to a specific point group. The one shown in our spectrum belongs to the D_{4h} point group. **Group theory** is used to assign symmetries to the orbitals in which electrons reside, as well as to the energy levels involved in the transition. These symmetry assignments will determine whether or not a transition can occur, i.e., whether it is **allowed** or **forbidden**. For instance, the transition that occurs between the S_0 and S_2 levels is a $\pi \rightarrow \pi^*$ transition that involves electrons of the porphyrin ring. It is allowed by symmetry and is observed as a strong band at ~ 408 nm in the spectrum. The S_0 to S_1 transition is not allowed by symmetry, and the corresponding band observed at ~560 nm is accordingly very weak. The other weak band at ~ 540 nm is a mixture of electronic and vibrational transitions (Q_v in the energy level diagram).

Another factor that will affect the band shape is the extent of **broadening**. Because of the Heisenberg uncertainty principle, the exact energy levels of a transition cannot be known. This is expressed as follows:

$$\Delta E \Delta t \approx h/4\pi$$

The extent of this "uncertainty" or **lifetime broadening** is inversely proportional to the lifetime Δt, and the broadening can be evaluated using:

$$\Delta v/cm^{-1} \approx 2.7 \times 10^{-12}/\Delta t$$

Another broadening mechanism results from the **Doppler effect** due to the fact that molecules travel at high speeds in every possible direction. This causes Doppler shifts in the spectral lines, which broaden them. The effect is due to the fact that an object approaching an observer with speed v, while emitting radiation of wavelength λ, seems to be emitting from $[1 - (v/c)] \lambda$ rather than from λ.

The environment in which the transition takes place will also affect the spectrum.

For instance, the presence of a magnetic field will shift the energy levels between which the transition occurs, in what is called the **Zeeman effect**. Similarly, an electric field can shift spectral bands, and this is called the **Stark effect**:

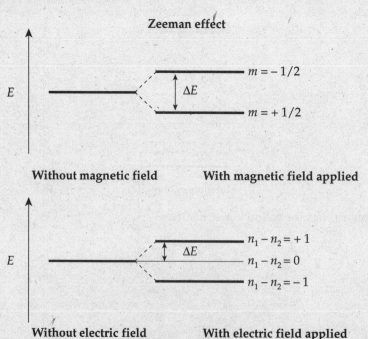

The Zeeman splitting is given by

$$\Delta E_Z = g \times m_j \times \mu_B \times B$$

where g = Landé factor

m_j = magnetic quantum number

μ_B = Bohr magneton

B = magnetic field

The Stark splitting is given by

$$\Delta E_{Stark} = (3/8\pi^2)(hm_eeZ)(n_1 - n_2)\, n\, |\mathbf{E}|$$

where h = Planck's constant

m_e = mass of the electron

Z = number of protons in nucleus

n_i = principal quantum number

$\mathbf{E}$ = electric field

CHEMICAL DYNAMICS

We saw that thermodynamics allows us to predict which processes will occur spontaneously, but it cannot help us predict the rate at which these processes occur. This is the subject of kinetics, which comes under the heading of chemical dynamics. Chemical dynamics is the study of the way chemical changes occur. Three topics are covered under this heading: experimental and theoretical chemical kinetics, solution and liquid dynamics, and photochemistry.

EXPERIMENTAL AND THEORETICAL CHEMICAL KINETICS

Chemical kinetics is the study of the rates and mechanisms of chemical reactions. The hydrolysis of ATP to yield ADP and phosphate is a thermodynamically favorable reaction with $\Delta G^o = -30.5$ kJ mol^{-1} at 298 K and pH 7. But a solution of ATP at pH 7 and 298 K remains stable. How can this be explained?

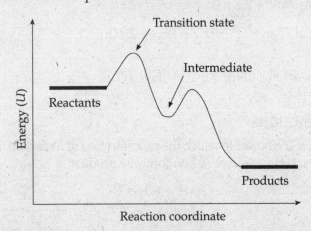

The energy profile shown above provides a clue. If we define the reaction coordinate (x axis) as the length of the P–O bond that needs to be broken in ATP for the reaction to proceed, we know that the cleavage of this bond requires a lot of energy, and therefore that the reaction proceeds uphill to the transition state or, in other words, there is a high energy barrier, which accounts for the stability of ATP.

The maximum of the energy profile curve is called the **transition state** and if a minimum occurs in the curve as the reaction proceeds to the reactants, it is called an **intermediate**. The **activation energy** is the difference between the energy of the reactants and that of the transition state (or activated complex).

THE REACTION RATE

A **homogeneous** reaction occurs entirely in one phase, and a **heterogenous** reaction occurs in more than one phase. Consider the following homogeneous reaction, which takes place in a closed system:

$$aA + bB \rightarrow cC + dD$$

A, B, C, and D represent different chemical substances, and a, b, c, and d are the stoichiometric coefficients of the balanced equation. The rate at which the reactants are consumed and the products are formed is proportional to these stoichiometric coefficients:

$$(dn_A/dt)/(dn_B/dt) = a/b$$

or

$$(1/a)\,(dn_A/dt) = (1/b)/(dn_B/dt),$$

where t represents the time and n the number of moles present.

The **rate of conversion** (J) is defined as:

$$J = -(1/a)\,(dn_A/dt) = -(1/b)/(dn_B/dt) = (1/c)/(dn_C/dt) = (1/d)/(dn_D/dt)$$

and since A and B are disappearing and C and D are being formed, J is positive.

The rate of conversion per unit volume is called the **reaction rate (r)**:

$$r = J/V = -(1/aV)\,(dn_A/dt)$$

If V remains constant throughout the reaction,

$$r = -(1/aV)\,(dn_A/dt) = -(1/a)[d(n_A/V)/dt] = -(1/a)(dC_A/dt) = -(1/a)(d[A]/dt)$$

where $[A]$ is the molar concentration of A.

Example:

What is the rate constant for the following reaction?

$$H_2 + Br_2 \rightarrow 2\,HBr$$

Answer: $r = -(d[H_2]/dt) = -(d[N_2]/dt) = \dfrac{1}{2}(d[HBr]/dt)$.

THE ORDER OF REACTIONS

The order of a reaction is the power to which the concentration of a reactant is raised. In the reaction below, x moles of A react with y moles of B to form the product P:

$$xA + yB \rightarrow P$$

If the rate of formation of P is $d[P]/dt$, then an expression for r can be written as follows:

$$r = d[P]/dt = k[A]^a[B]^b$$

Such an expression is a **rate law** and is expressed as a function of the reactant concentrations, set in square brackets, at constant temperature. The exponents are usually integers or half integers, and k is the **rate constant**. The above reaction is then of ath order in A, of bth order in B, and the overall order is $(a + b)$. The exponents a and b are the **partial orders**. The sum of the partial orders is the **total order** n. The exponents in the rate law can differ from the stoichiometric coefficients of the balanced equation. Therefore, rate laws cannot be derived from the reaction stoichiometry, they must be determined experimentally.

FIRST-ORDER REACTIONS

For a first-order reaction of the type

$$aA \rightarrow products$$

the rate law expression is

$$r = -(1/a)(d[A]/dt) = k[A]$$

If we define a rate constant for the rate of change of A, such that $k_A = a \cdot k$, then,

$$d[A]/dt = -k_A[A]$$

or $\quad d[A]/[A] = -k_A dt$

To solve this differential equation, we integrate from state 1 to state 2 and get

$$\int d[A]/[A] = -\int k_A dt$$

$$\ln([A]_2/[A]_1) = -k_A(t_2 - t_1)$$

If state 1 is the initial state of the reaction (at $t = 0$) and if $[A] = [A]_0$, the equation becomes

$$\ln([A]/[A]_0) = -k_A t$$

or: $\quad \ln[A] = -k_A t + \ln[A]_0$

$$[A] = [A]_0 \exp(-k_A t)$$

$[A]$ decreases exponentially for a first-order reaction, and a plot of $\ln([A]/[A]^0)$ vs. t gives a straight line with slope $-k_A$.

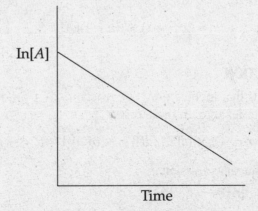

The **half-life** of the reaction is the time required for the initial concentration of the reactants to be reduced by half. So, for $[A] = [A]_0/2$ and $t = t_{\frac{1}{2}}$, we get $t_{\frac{1}{2}} = \ln 2/k_A$.

SECOND-ORDER REACTIONS

There are two common forms of second-order rate laws:

1. For a reaction of the type aA → products, $r = k[A]^2$

   The rate law is $d[A]/dt = -k_A[A]^2$, and again $k_A = a \cdot K$

It can be shown that $(1/[A]) - (1/[A]_0) = k_A t$, and that $t_{\frac{1}{2}} = 1/[A]_0 kA$.

A plot of $1/[A]$ vs. t gives a straight line with slope k_A.

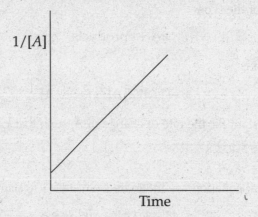

2. For a reaction of the type aA + bB → products, $r = k[A][B]$:

   The rate law takes a more complicated form:

   $$\{1/(a[B]_0 - b[A]_0)\}\ln\{([B]/[B]_0) / ([A]/[A]_0)\} = kt$$

NTH-ORDER REACTIONS

There are many nth-order rate laws. For those having the form $d[A]/dt = -kA[A]^n$, the rate law is as follows:

$$([A]/[A]_0)^{1-n} = 1 + [A]_0^{n-1}(n - 1)k_A t \quad n \neq 1$$

$$t_{\frac{1}{2}} = (2^{n-1} - 1) / \{(n - 1)[A]_0^{n-1}k_A\}$$

ZEROTH-ORDER REACTION

The order of most reactions that involve only one reactant, aA ‡ products, is either 1 or 2. A few reactions, however, are of order zero. In these cases,

$$r = -(1/a)(d[A]/dt]) = k, \text{ or } d[A]/dt = -k_A$$

Integration gives the general expression

$$[A] = -k_A t = [A]_0,$$

and
$$t_{\frac{1}{2}} = [A]_0/2k_A$$

For a zeroth-order reaction, a graph of $[A]$ vs. t gives a straight line with slope $-k_A$.

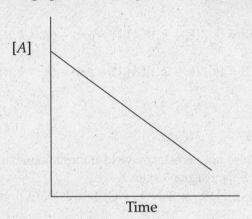

REVERSIBLE FIRST-ORDER REACTIONS

The reaction $A \leftrightarrow B$ is first order in both the forward and reverse directions, so that $r_f = k_f[A]$ and $r_r = k_r[B]$, where the subscripts f and r mean forward and reverse respectively. At equilibrium, the concentration of each species is constant. It can be show that

$$k_r[B]_0 = k_r[A]_0 = (k_f + k_r)[A]_{eq}$$

This equation relates the equilibrium concentration of A to the initial concentrations of A and B. It can also be shown that the rate law equation for a reversible first-order reaction is given by

$$[A] - [A]_{eq} = ([A]_0 - [A]_{eq})\exp{-(k_f + k_r)t}$$

CONSECUTIVE FIRST-ORDER REACTIONS

Consider two consecutive irreversible reactions:

$$A \rightarrow B \rightarrow C$$

The rate constant of the first reaction ($A \rightarrow B$) is k_1, and that of the second reaction ($B \rightarrow C$) is k_2. So

$$[A] = [A]_0\exp{-k_1t},$$

$$[B] = \{k_1/(k_2 - k_1)\}[A]_0[\exp(-k_1t) - \exp(-k_2t)]$$

$$[C] = [A]_0\{1 - [k_2/(k_2 - k_1)]\exp(-k_1t) + [k_1/(k_2 - k_1)]\exp(-k_2t)\}$$

COMPETING FIRST-ORDER REACTIONS

Let's consider the simplest case:

$$A \rightarrow B \text{ and } A \rightarrow C$$

with k_1 and k_2, respectively. The rate law is

$$d[A]/dt = -k_1[A] - k_2[A] = -(k_1 + k_2)[A]$$

which leads to

$$[B] = [k_1/(k_1 + k_2)][A]_0[1 - \exp - (k_1 + k_2)t]$$

$$[C] = [k_2/(k_1 + k_2)][A]_0[1 - \exp - (k_1 + k_2)t]$$

It is clear that $[B]/[C] = k_1/k_2$.

REACTION MECHANISMS

The reaction stoichiometry does not necessarily yield information about the **reaction mechanism**, which is the process by which the reaction occurs.

For example, the reaction $2 N_2O_5 \rightarrow 4 NO_2 + O_2$ ($r = k [N_2O_5]$), occurs through a three-step mechanism:

step 1:	$N_2O_5 \rightarrow NO_3 + NO_2$	$r_{step1} = k_{step1}[N_2O_5]$
step 2:	$NO_3 + NO_2 \rightarrow NO + O_2 + NO_2$	$r_{step2} = k_{step2}[NO_3][NO_2]$
step 3:	$NO + NO_3 \rightarrow 2 NO_2$	$r_{step3} = k_{step3}[NO][NO_3]$

To be accepted as valid, a mechanism must satisfy two conditions:

(a) the sum of its elementary steps must be equal to the balanced equation of the overall reaction; and

(b) the mechanism must be consistent with the experimentally determined rate equation.

Here, NO_3 and NO are **reaction intermediate**s: they are species that are formed in one step of the mechanism and consumed in a subsequent one. The NO produced in step 1 is consumed in step 3. For each occurrence of step 3, there must be one occurrence of step 2. However, steps 2 and 3 consume one NO_3 intermediate each. Therefore, there must be two occurences of step1 for each occurrence of step 2 and 3. The overall reaction is the sum of 2 steps 1 + 1 step 2 + 1 step 3. The number of occurrences of a step is called the **stoichiometric number (s)** of the step; each step is called an **elementary reaction**. A **simple reaction** consists of only one elementary reaction. A **complex reaction** consists of more than one elementary reaction.

In the example above, the rate of each step can be expressed in terms of its **molecularity**, which is defined as the number of molecules that must collide for the reaction to proceed. So step 1 is unimolecular, and steps 2 and 3 are bimolecular. The individual rates of the different steps of the reaction may differ. Since the overall rate of the reaction cannot exceed the rate of the slowest step, we call the slowest step **the rate-limiting step**.

In the decomposition reaction of N_2O_5, we can determine that the limiting step is the first, because its rate equation, obtained directly from its molecularity, corresponds to the rate equation of the overall reaction , which is obtained experimentally.

Let's look at another set of reactions, this time the decomposition of ozone. The reaction is

$$2 O_{3 (g)} \rightarrow 3 O_{2 (g)}, \text{ and } r = k [O_3]^2/[O_2]$$

and the suggested mechanism is

Step 1: $O_3 \leftrightarrow O_2 + O$ (fast), where $r_{forward} = k_1[O_3]$ and $r_{reverse} = k_{-1}[O_2][O]$

Step 2: $O + O_3 \rightarrow 2\,O_2$ (slow), where $r_2 = k_2[O][O_3]$

Step 2 is the rate-determining step, but its rate equation does not agree with the experimental rate equation for the overall reaction. Also, it contains [O], which is a reaction intermediate. But we can assume that $r_{forward} = r_{reverse}$, so

$$k_1[O_3] = k_{-1}[O_2][O]$$

and

$$[O] = (k_1/k_{-1})([O_3]/[O_2])$$

Substituting the [O] thus obtained in the rate equation of step 2 gives us

$$r = (k_2 k_1/k_{-1})[O_3]^2/[O_2] = k[O_3]^2/[O_2],$$

where $k = k_2 k_1/k_{-1}$.

MEASUREMENT OF REACTION RATES

The most common method for determining rate laws is called the initial-rate method. In this method, the initial rate (r_0) is measured for several runs of the reaction, and the initial concentration of one reactant at a time is varied. Consider for example the reaction

$$A + B \rightarrow C + D$$

its rate law is in the form $r = k[A]^a[B]^b$, where a and b are the partial orders in A and B, respectively. We wish to determine a and b from the following data:

Experiment	$[A]_{initial}$ (mol/L)	$[B]_{initial}$ (mol/L)	Initial rate (mol/L $\cdot$ s)
1	0.100	0.005	1.40×10^{-6}
2	0.100	0.010	2.80×10^{-6}
3	0.100	0.010	5.60×10^{-6}

From run 1 to run 2, [A] is kept constant, but [B] is doubled, and the initial rate is also doubled. This shows that the reaction is first order in B.

Mathematically, we obtain

$$([B]_1/[B]_2)^b = r_1/r_2,$$

where $(0.005/0.010)^b = (1.40/2.80)$, or $(\frac{1}{2})^b = (\frac{1}{2})^1$, and $b = 1$.

From run 2 to 3, $[B]$ is kept constant, but $[A]$ is doubled. In this case, the initial rate of the reaction also doubles, which shows that the reaction is also first order in A:

$$([A]_2/[A]_3)^a = r_2/r_{3,}$$

where $(0.100/0.200)^a = (2.80/5.60)$, or $(\frac{1}{2})^a = (\frac{1}{2})^1$, and $a = 1$.

Therefore the rate of the overall reaction is 2, and the experimental rate law is $r = k[A][B]$. The value of k can be obtained from the results of any experiment. From experiment 2,

$2.80 \cdot 10\text{--}6 \text{ mol} \cdot L^{-1}s^{-1} = k(0.100 \text{ mol} \cdot L^{-1})(0.010 \text{ mol} \cdot L^{-1})$, where $k = 2.80 \cdot 10^{-3} 1 \cdot \text{mol}^{-1} s^{-1}$.

Example:

For the reaction $2 \text{ NO } (g) + Cl_2 (g) \rightarrow 2 \text{ NOCl } (g)$, the following results were obtained:

$[NO]_0$ (mol/L)	$[Cl_2]_0$ (mol/L)	Initial rate (mol/L · min)
0.20	0.20	0.35
0.20	0.40	0.70
0.40	0.40	2.80

Determine the rate equation and the value of k.

Answer:

When $[Cl_2]$ doubles and $[NO]$ remains constant, the initial rate of the reaction doubles. So the partial rate is 1 with respect to Cl_2. When $[NO]$ doubles and $[Cl_2]$ remains constant, the initial rate of reaction increases by a factor of 4. Then this partial rate is 2 in NO.

Then the overall rate expression is $r = k[NO]^2[Cl_2]$. The value of k can be obtained from any of the four experiments; it is $k = 44 \text{ L}^2 \cdot \text{mol}^{-2} \cdot s^{-1}$.

COLLISION THEORY AND CHEMICAL KINETICS

The concentration dependence of a reaction rate is expressed by a rate law equation. Experiment also shows that most rate constants increase exponentially with temperature. Usually, k doubles for every 10°C temperature increase.

Collision theory states that reactants must collide to react. If temperature increases, so does the speed of the molecules and the frequency of collisions. However, the rate of a reaction is much slower than the calculated rate of collisions. This means that only a small collision percentage leads to an effective reaction. For every reaction, a threshold exists called **the activation energy**, which must be overcome for the reaction to occur. For example, in the reaction $2BrNO(g) \rightarrow 2NO(g) + Br_2(g)$, two Br–N bonds must be broken, and this requires energy. According to collision theory, this energy comes from the kinetic energy that the molecules have before colliding. This kinetic energy is transformed into potential energy, which is stored in a transition state called an **activated complex**. The Br–N bonds are broken in this activated complex and Br–Br bonds are formed. In our example, the reaction is exothermic. The rate of the reaction depends on the activation energy, not on the amount of energy liberated:

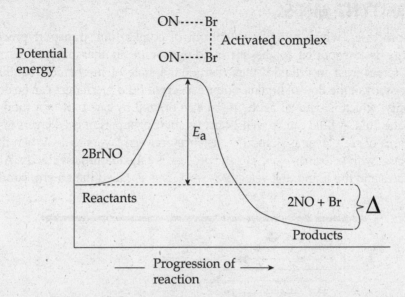

The above reaction energy profile shows that the colliding molecules must have an amount of kinetic energy at least equal to E_a. At a given temperature, only a fraction of the molecules have this required energy. The following graph shows the distribution of molecules as a function of the temperature:

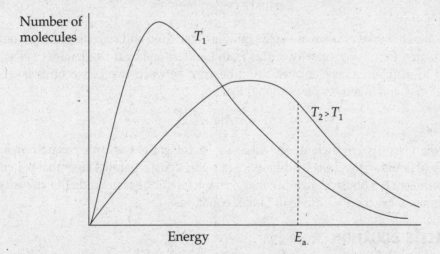

The number of molecules with energy greater than or equal to E_a at a temperature T_1 is given by the area under the curve. For $T_2 > T_1$, the area under the curve is clearly greater than for the T_1 area. Then the number of molecules that have energy greater than or equal to E_a is larger at $T_2 > T_1$ than at T_1. The number of effective collisions is also greater, and so is the reaction rate. Experiment also shows that not all collisions between molecules that have the required kinetic energy create new bonds. Only molecules that have a favorable orientation and with $E \geq E_a$ will actually lead to product formation. A favorable orientation is one that allows the new bonds to be formed.

Arrhenius's equation describes the relationship between k and E_a:

$$k = A \exp(-E_a/RT)$$

where k is the rate constant, R is the gas constant, T is the temperature in Kelvin, and A is a constant called the preexponential factor.

SOLUTION DYNAMICS

We call those processes, which bring a system out of equilibrium, **transport processes**, because matter or energy is transported to the surroundings or to another part of the system. When unequilibrated forces exist in a liquid, they disrupt the state of mechanical equilibrium. **Liquid dynamics** is the study of the flow of liquids. Some aspects of fluid mechanics can be described by the study of **viscosity,** which is defined as the resistance offered by one part of a fluid to the flow of another part of the fluid. A fluid can be seen as an ensemble of superimposed layers of molecules. We can define the area of each layer as A and the distance between layers as dx. When the layers move between two plates with velocities v_1, v_2, etc. the process is called **laminar velocity**. At the boundary between the plates and the liquid, the velocity is zero. This is called the **no-slip condition.**

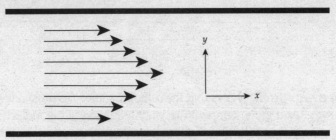

Motion of fluid between two plates

The velocities of the layers increase in the middle of the fluid and start decreasing from the middle toward the plates. Each layer velocity differs from the next one by dv. In laminar velocity, the force (F) required to maintain a constant velocity difference between two consecutive layers is directly proportional to A and inversely proportional to dx:

$$F = \eta A (dv/dx),$$

where η is the **viscosity coefficient**. The viscosity coefficient is the force per unit area required to move a layer of liquid with a velocity difference of 1 cm/s past a parallel layer that is 1 cm away. The viscosity coefficient is a physical quantity that is characteristic of each fluid. The viscosity of fluids is measured using either the Poisseuille or Stokes equations.

POISSEUILLE'S EQUATION

$$\eta = \frac{\pi P t r^4}{8LV}$$

where V is the volume of the liquid; t is the time required for this volume to flow through a capillary tube of radius r, length L; and P is the pressure at the start of the process. The viscosity of a liquid is determined by comparison with a reference liquid, usually water. The ratio of the viscosity coefficients of the two liquids is

$$\frac{\eta_1}{\eta_2} = \left(\frac{\pi P_1 r^4 t}{8LV} \right) \left(\frac{8LV}{\pi P_2 r^4 t} \right) = \frac{P_1 t_1}{P_2 t_2} = \frac{\rho_1 t_1}{\rho_2 t_2}$$

where P_1 and P_2 are proportional to ρ_1 and ρ_2, the densities of the liquids. When ρ_1, ρ_2 and η_2 are known, the viscosity coefficient η_1 of the liquid can be determined.

STOKES EQUATION

Stokes's law describes the fall of a spherical body of radius r and density ρ, falling by gravity through a fluid of density ρ_1. Stokes's equation is

$$F_1 = (4/3)\pi r^3(\rho - \rho_1)g,$$

where F_1 is the force acting on the spherical body and g is the acceleration due to gravity. This force F_1 is opposed by a frictional force due to the medium, which increases as the velocity of the falling sphere increases. When a uniform rate of fall is reached, the frictional force becomes equal to the gravitational force F_1. Stokes showed that F_2 the force due to friction is

$$F_2 = 6\pi r \eta v$$

where v is the velocity of the falling sphere, once it has become constant. When the gravitational and frictional forces are equal, $6prhv = (4/3)\pi r^3(\rho - \rho_1)g$, and

$$\eta = [2r^3(\rho - \rho_1)g] / 9v.$$

Stokes's equation is valid as long as the radius of the falling sphere is larger than the distance that separates the molecules of the fluid. **Fluidity** is a term often used in connection with viscosity. The fluidity of a substance ϕ is the reciprocal of the viscosity: $\phi = 1/\eta$.

PHOTOCHEMISTRY

Photochemistry is the study of chemical reactions induced by light. In chemical or thermal reactions, the activation energy is supplied by intermolecular collisions. In photochemical reactions, energy is supplied by absorption of light. Usually, there are as many photons absorbed as there are molecules undergoing a transition to an excited state. This is known as the **Stark-Einstein law**. During a photochemical reaction, a photon may promote a molecule to an excited electronic state where it is more likely to undergo a chemical reaction than in the ground state.

The absorption of energy by a molecule can be described as follows:

$$A + h\nu \rightarrow A^*$$

where A is the molecule in its ground state and A* is the molecule in an excited state. In most cases, all of the electrons of the ground state are paired. The total electronic spin (S) is zero and the multiplicity is $2S + 1 = 1$: the ground state is a singlet (S_0). In the excited states, if the unpaired electrons have opposite spins, S is also zero, and the excited states are also singlets (S_1, S_2, etc.). If the unpaired electrons have identical spins, $S = 1$ and the multiplicity is 3. This is called a triplet state.

During the course of a photochemical reaction, several processes can occur. The following diagram illustrates some of these processes.

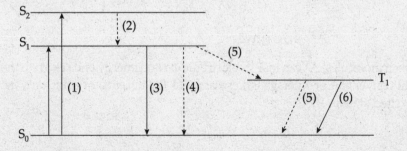

(1) Absorption
(2) Internal conversion
(3) Fluorescence
(4) Radiationless deactivation
(5) Intersystem crossing
(6) Phosphorescence

- **Vibrational relaxation**: A* is usually produced in an excited vibrational state. Intermolecular collisions transfer part of this vibrational energy to other molecules, and A* relaxes to the lowest excited vibrational level.

- **Internal conversion**: A molecule A* in its lowest vibrational state can make a radiationless transition to a different excited electronic state: A* → A*′. For this process to occur, A* and A*′ must have the same energy. The molecule A*′ is generally in a lower electronic state, but in a higher vibrational state than A*:

$$A^*(v = 0) \longrightarrow A^{*\prime}(v = 5)$$

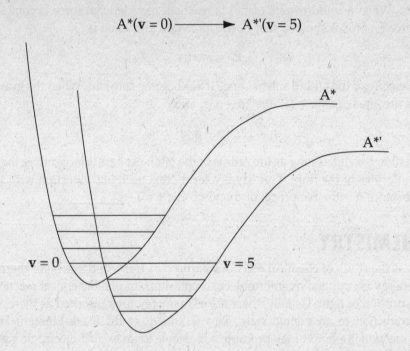

If A* and A*″ are both singlet or triplet states, the radiationless process is called **internal conversion**. If A* is a singlet electronic state and A*′ is a triplet electronic state, the radiationless process is called **intersystem crossing**.

- **Radiationless deactivation**: This occurs when A* transfers its electronic excited energy to another molecule and returns to its ground electronic state: A* + B → A + B*. The products A and B* can have additional translational, rotational, and vibrational energy.

- **Fluorescence:** Fluorescence occurs when light is emitted from an excited electronic state to a lower electronic state without spin change: $\Delta S = 0$. A* can lose its electronic energy by spontaneously emitting a photon, which brings it to the ground state:

$$A^* \rightarrow A + h\nu$$

If there are collisions between molecules, A* can lose its electronic excited energy and return to the ground state through internal conversion or intersystem crossing. In the absence of collisions, the typical lifetime of a singlet excited state is 10^{-8} s.

- **Phosphorescence:** This process is the emission of radiation from a triplet excited electronic state to a lower singlet state. This transition occurs with $\Delta S \neq 0$. Since the selection rule for electronic transitions is $\Delta S = 0$, phosphorescence has a very low probability. If there are intermolecular collisions, the excited electronic energy is lost to internal conversion and intersystem crossing. In the absence of collisions, however, the typical lifetime of an excited triplet state is 10^{-3} to 1 s.

A* is often formed in an excited vibrational level. If A* has enough vibrational energy, dissociation may occur:

$$A^* \rightarrow B + C$$

where the decomposition products may react further, especially if they are free radicals.

An example is that of an electronic transition in a diatomic molecule where A* has vibrational energy that exceeds the dissociation energy D_e:

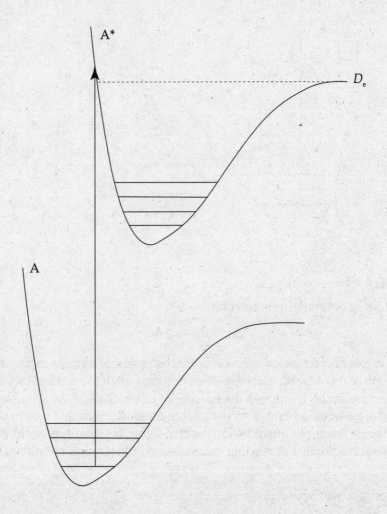

Excitation of a diatomic molecule to a repulsive electronic state (one in which there is no minimum in the potential energy curve) also leads to dissociation:

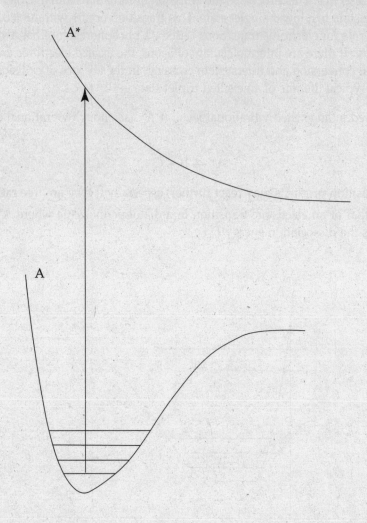

QUANTUM YIELD

Consider the following decomposition reaction:

$$A_2 + h\nu \rightarrow 2A$$

The first step in this photochemical reaction is the absorption of a single quantum of energy by a molecule. As a result of this activation, the molecule decomposes. If the products react no further, the number of reacting molecules is equal to the number of photons absorbed. If, however, the photochemically activated molecule initiates a sequence of thermal reactions that deactivate the molecule, less than one molecule reacts per quantum of absorbed light. The **quantum yield (Φ)** describes the relationship between the number of reacting molecules and the number of light quanta absorbed:

Φ = (number of moles reacting per unit time) / (number of moles of light absorbed per unit time)

PHOTOCHEMICAL KINETICS

Let's take a look at the kinetics of the above decomposition reaction. We assume that the reaction is following the a three-step mechanism:

Step 1 $A_2 + h\nu \rightarrow A_2^*$ (k_1)

Absorption of a quantum of light by A_2 and formation of an activated molecule.

Step 2 $A_2^* \rightarrow 2A$ (k_2)

Dissociation of the activated molecule.

Step 3 $A_2^* + A_2 \rightarrow 2A_2$ (k_3)

Deactivation of A_2^* by collision with an A_2 molecule.

The product is formed during step 2. The rate of formation of A is

$$d[A]/dt = k_2[A_2^*]$$

Since we do not know $[A_2^*]$, we need to express the concentration of A_2^* in terms of A_2.

To do this, we can use the **steady-state principle**, which says that the rate of formation of an intermediate is equal to the rate of its disappearance. A_2^* is formed in step 1. The rate of its formation is determined by the rate at which it absorbs light. Therefore:

$$d[A_2^*]/dt = k_1 I_a,$$

where I_a is the intensity of the absorbed light. The rate of disappearance of A_2^* is the sum of the rates of steps 2 and 3:

$$-d[A_2^*]/dt = k_2[A_2^*] + k_3[A_2^*][A_2]$$

So then we write

$$k_1 I_a = k_2[A_2^*] + k_3[A_2^*][A_2]$$

or:

$$[A_2^*] = (k_1 I_a) / (k_2 + k_3[A_2])$$

Then the rate of formation of A is given by

$$d[A]/dt = k_2[A_2^*] = (k_1 k_2 I_a) / (k_2 + k_3[A_2])$$

For every two molecules of A formed, one molecule of A_2, one quantum of light is absorbed, and the quantum yield of the process is given by

$$\Phi = [1/2(I_a)](d[A]/dt) = \frac{1}{2}\{(k_2 k_1) / (k_2 + k_3[A_2])\}$$

PHYSICAL CHEMISTRY: WORKED-OUT PROBLEM SET

Use the following data to answer questions 1 and 2.

At 25°C and 1 atm.

$$H_{2\,(g)} + \frac{1}{2}O_{2\,(g)} \rightarrow H_2O_{\,(l)} \qquad\qquad \Delta H = -285.839 \text{ kJ/mol}$$

$R = 8.3143 \text{ JK}^{-1}\text{mol}^{-1}$
$1 \text{ atm·l} = 101.3 \text{ J}$
Molar volume of water : 18 mL/mol

1. Calculate the value of PV for H_2, O_2 and H_2O.

   (A) $PV(H_2) = 2.478$ kJ/mol $PV(O_2) = 2.478$ kJ/mol $PV(H_2O) = 0.0018$ kJ/mol
   (B) $PV(H_2) = 1.239$ kJ/mol $PV(O_2) = 1.239$ kJ/mol $PV(H_2O) = 2.478$ kJ/mol
   (C) $PV(H_2) = 2.478$ kJ/mol · $PV(O_2) = 1.239$ kJ/mol $PV(H_2O) = 0.0018$ kJ/mol
   (D) $PV(H_2) = 1.239$ kJ/mol $PV(O_2) = 2.478$ kJ/mol $PV(H_2O) = 2.478$ kJ/mol
   (E) $PV(H_2) = 2.478$ kJ/mol $PV(O_2) = 1.239$ kJ/mol $PV(H_2O) = 0.0018$ kJ/mol

The correct answer is (C). First examine the physical state of the reactants and the products, as well as the stoichiometric coefficients. The reactants are both in the gas phase. Since P and T are known, $PV\,(H_2) = RT = (8.3143 \text{ JK}^{-1}\text{mol}^{-1})(298$ K) $= 2.478$ kJ/mol. Because of the stoichiometric coeficient, $PV\,(O_2) = \frac{1}{2}(2.478$ kJ/mol) $= 1.239$ kJ/mol. H_2O is a liquid. And so, $PV\,(H_2O) = (1\text{atm})(18 \times 10^{-3}$ L/mol) $= 18 \times 10^{-3}$ atm–L/mol $= 18 \times 10^{-3}\,(101.3 \text{ J})$/mol $= 1.8$ J/mol $= 0.0018$ kJ/mol.

2. Calculate the change in internal energy, ΔU, for this reaction.

   (A) $\Delta U = +282.124$ kJ/mol
   (B) $\Delta U = -3.715$ kJ/mol
   (C) $\Delta U = +3.715$ kJ/mol
   (D) $\Delta U = -282.124$ kJ/mol
   (E) $\Delta U = -285.839$ kJ/mol

The correct answer is (D). From the relationship $\Delta H = \Delta U + \Delta(PV)$, we obtain

$\Delta U = \Delta H - \Delta(PV)$. $\Delta(PV)$ can be calculated from the values calculated in question 1.

$\Delta(PV) = PV_{\text{products}} - PV_{\text{reactants}} = PV_{\text{H2O}} - (PV_{\text{H2}} + PV_{\text{O2}}) = 0.0018 - (2.478 + 1.239) = -3.715$ kJ/mol. Then, $\Delta U = \Delta H - \Delta(PV) = -285.839 - (-3.715) = -282.124$ kJ/mol.

Use the following diagram and data to answer questions 3 and 4:

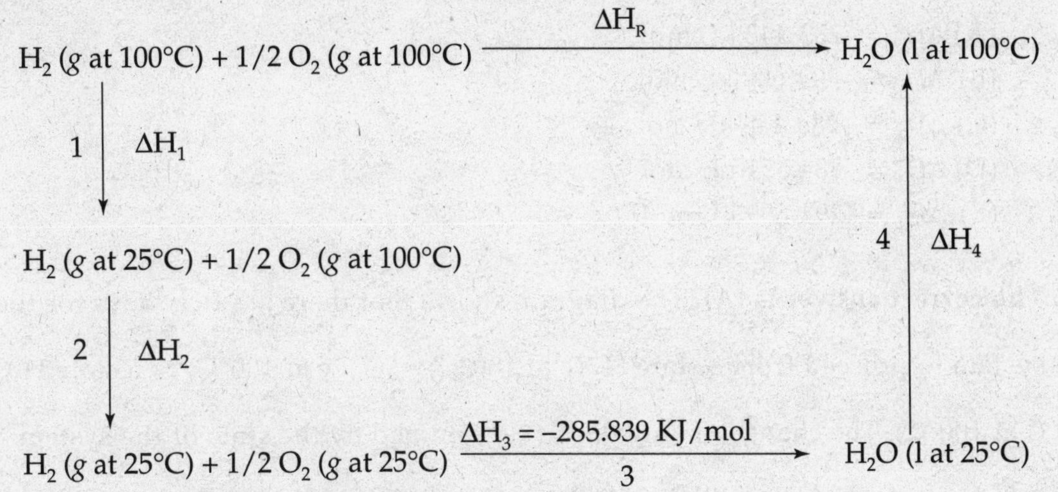

$$H_2 \text{ (}g\text{ at 100°C)} + 1/2\ O_2 \text{ (}g\text{ at 100°C)} \xrightarrow{\Delta H_R} H_2O \text{ (l at 100°C)}$$

1 │ ΔH_1

$$H_2 \text{ (}g\text{ at 25°C)} + 1/2\ O_2 \text{ (}g\text{ at 100°C)}$$

4 │ ΔH_4

2 │ ΔH_2

$$H_2 \text{ (}g\text{ at 25°C)} + 1/2\ O_2 \text{ (}g\text{ at 25°C)} \xrightarrow[3]{\Delta H_3 = -285.839\ KJ/mol} H_2O \text{ (l at 25°C)}$$

$C_P\ (H_2)$ from 25°C to 100°C = 28.9 J deg^{-1}mol^{-1}.
$C_P\ (O_2)$ from 25°C to 100°C = 29.4 J deg^{-1}mol^{-1}.
$C_P\ (H_2O)$ from 25°C to 100°C = 75.5 J deg^{-1}mol^{-1}.

3. Calculate ΔH_1, ΔH_2, and ΔH_4.

   (A) $\Delta H_1 = -2.168$ kJ/mol $\Delta H_2 = -2.206$ kJ/mol $\Delta H_3 = 5.662$ kJ/mol
   (B) $\Delta H_1 = -2.168$ kJ/mol $\Delta H_2 = -1.103$ kJ/mol $\Delta H_3 = -5.662$ kJ/mol
   (C) $\Delta H_1 = -2.168$ kJ/mol $\Delta H_2 = -2.206$ kJ/mol $\Delta H_3 = -5.662$ kJ/mol
   (D) $\Delta H_1 = +2.168$ kJ/mol $\Delta H_2 = +1.103$ kJ/mol $\Delta H_3 = -5.662$ kJ/mol
   (E) $\Delta H_1 = -2.168$ kJ/mol $\Delta H_2 = -1.103$ kJ/mol $\Delta H_3 = +5.662$ kJ/mol

The correct answer is (E). The heat contents of each step of the above process can be obtained from the relationship:

$$\Delta H = C_P dT.$$

Integrating, we obtain $\Delta H = \int C_P dT$, from the initial to the final temperature.

In the first step of the path, T goes from 100°C to 25°C.

So $\Delta H_1 = \int C_P dT = C_P(T_{final} - T_{initial}) = 28.9\ J \cdot deg^{-1} \cdot mol^{-1}\ (25°C - 100°C) = -2.168$

kJ/mol. Similarly, we can also obtain ΔH_2 and ΔH_4: $\Delta H_2 = (\frac{1}{2})\ (29.4)(25 - 100) =$

-1.103 kJ/mol, and $\Delta H_4 = 75.5\ (100 - 25) = +5.662$ kJ/mol.

4. Calculate ΔH for the reaction: $H_2\ (g) + \frac{1}{2}O_2\ (g) \to H_2O\ (l)$ at 1 atm and 100°C,

(A) $\Delta H_R = -283.448$ kJ/mol

(B) $\Delta H_R = +294.699$ kJ/mol

(C) $\Delta H_R = +283.448$ kJ/mol

(D) $\Delta H_R = -284.551$ kJ/mol

(E) $\Delta H_R = -294.699$ kJ/mol

The correct answer is (A). The diagram shows that there are two ways for the system to proceed from a state H_2 (g at 100°C), $\frac{1}{2}O_2$ (g at 100°C) to a state H_2O (l at 100°C). The change of enthalpy is determined by the state of the system and is independent of the path. In this case, $\Delta H_R = \Delta H_1 + \Delta H_2 + \Delta H_3 + \Delta H_4 = -2.168 - 1.103 - 285.839 + 5.662 = -283.448$ kJ/mol.

5. Which of the following reactions shows the greatest decrease in entropy?

(A) $C_3H_8\ (l) + 5\ O_2\ (g) \to 3\ CO_2\ (g) + 4\ H_2O\ (g)$

(B) $C_3H_8\ (g) + 5\ O_2(g) \to 3\ CO_2\ (g) + 4\ H_2O\ (g)$

(C) $C_3H_8\ (g) + 5\ O_2\ (g) \to 3\ CO_2\ (g) + 4\ H_2O\ (g)$

(D) $C_3H_8\ (g) + 5\ O_2\ (g) \to 3\ CO_2(g) + 4\ H_2O\ (l)$

(E) $C_3H_8\ (l) + 5\ O_2\ (g) \to 3\ CO_2\ (g) + 4\ H_2O\ (l)$

The correct answer is (D). To answer this question, look for the greatest decrease in the number of moles of gas. Remember that the gas phase is more disordered than the liquid or solid phases. The answer is D because $\Delta n_g = 3 - (1 + 5) = -3$. For A, B, C, and E, the values of Δn_g are +2, +1, –2 and –2, respectively.

6. A process can be spontaneous when

(A) $\Delta H°$ is positive and $\Delta S°$ is positive.

(B) $\Delta H°$ is negative and $\Delta S°$ is positive.

(C) $\Delta H°$ is negative and $\Delta S°$ is negative.

(D) $\Delta H°$ is positive and $\Delta S°$ is negative.

(E) none of the above.

The correct answer is (D). A process is nonspontaneous when its $\Delta G°$ is positive. According to the Gibbs's free-energy equation $\Delta G° = \Delta H° - T\Delta S°$, $\Delta G°$ is always positive when $\Delta H°$ is positive and $\Delta S°$ is negative.

7. The condensation of any gas to a liquid is expected to have

    (A) a negative ΔH and a negative ΔS.

    (B) a negative ΔH and a positive ΔS.

    (C) a positive ΔH and a negative ΔS.

    (D) a positive ΔH and a positive ΔS.

    (E) none of the above.

The correct answer is (A). The condensation of a gas releases energy. Therefore the enthalpy change ΔH is negative. During condensation, the system goes from a state of great disorder (a gas) to a state of greater order (a liquid). The entropy decreases, and ΔS is negative.

8. Which of the following equations is exothermic?

    I. $\frac{1}{2}N_2 + O_2 \rightarrow NO_2$ $\Delta H = +33.8$ kJ

    II. $C + O_2 \rightarrow CO_2 + 395$ kJ

    III. $H_2 + \frac{1}{2}O_2 \rightarrow H_2O$ $\Delta H = -241$ kJ

    IV. $2\,NaNO_3 + heat \rightarrow 2\,NaNO_2 + O_2$

    V. $N_2 + 3\,H_2 \rightarrow 2\,NH_3 + energy$

    (A) I and IV

    (B) I, II, and V

    (C) II, III, and V

    (D) II, III, and IV

    (E) I, II, and V

The correct answer is (C). A reaction is exothermic when heat is released with product formation. This can be expressed in the equation itself or as a ΔH with a negative value.

9. Which of the following statements is false about the reaction

$$N_2\,(g) + 3\,H_2\,(g) \rightarrow 2\,NH_3\,(g) + 92 \text{ kJ?}$$

    (A) The reaction is exothermic.

    (B) The energy content of the reactants is greater than that of he products.

    (C) If the system is cooled down, the equilibrium is displaced to the right.

    (D) If the pressure of the system is increased, the equilibrium is displaced to the left.

    (E) If some N_2 is taken from the system, the equilibrium is displaced to the left.

The correct answer is (D). The equation shows that 92 kJ of energy is released per mole of N_2. This means that the sum of the energies of the N_2 and H_2 molecules is greater than that of the NH_3 molecules formed and that the reaction is exothermic. If the system is cooled down, it will try to restore its thermal equilibrium by favoring the exothermic reaction. Therefore the equilibrium is to the right. If pressure is increased, the system will try to decrease it by reducing the number of particles: the equilibrium is displaced to the right. If N_2 is taken from the system, the equilibrium is displaced in the direction that allows the formation of N_2.

10. What reaction can be obtained from the following thermochemical data?

$$H_2SO_4 \,(l) + 811 \text{ kJ} \rightarrow H_2 \,_{(g)} \rightarrow 1/8 \, S_8 \,_{(s)} + 2 \, O_2 \,_{(g)}$$

$$H_2 \,(g) + \frac{1}{2}O_2 \,(g) \rightarrow H_2O \,(g) + 242 \text{ kJ}$$

$$1/8 \, S_8 \,(g) + O_2 \,(g) \rightarrow SO_2 \,(g) + 297 \text{ kJ}$$

(A) $H_2SO_4 \,(l) \rightarrow H_2O \,(g) + SO_2 \,(g) + \frac{1}{2}O_2 \,(g)$ $\Delta H = -272 \text{ kJ}$

(B) $H_2SO_4 \,(l) \rightarrow H_2O \,(g) + SO_2 \,(g) + \frac{1}{2}O_2 \,(g)$ $\Delta H = +272 \text{ kJ}$

(C) $H_2SO_4 \,(l) + H_2 \,(g) \rightarrow 2H_2O \,(g) + SO_2 \,(g)$ $\Delta H = +272 \text{ kJ}$

(D) $H_2SO_4 \,(l) \rightarrow H_2O \,(g) + SO_2 \,(g) + \frac{1}{2}O_2(g) + 272 \text{ kJ}$

(E) $H_2SO_4 \,(l) + H_2 \,(g) \rightarrow H_2O \,(g) + SO_2 \,(g) + 272 \text{ kJ}$

The correct answer is (B). This is an application of Hess's law. Summing up the enthalpies and all of the reactants and the products and canceling the identical terms yields equation B. Hess's law results from the fact that the enthalpy change of a reaction depends on the final and initial states of the system, not on the path taken to reach the final state.

11. Evaluate the heat of reaction for the reaction

$$\frac{1}{2}Cl_2 \,(g) + NaBr \,(g) \rightarrow NaCl \,(s) + \frac{1}{2}Br_2 \,(g)$$

from the following data:

(1) $CaOCl_2 \,(g) \rightarrow CaO \,(g) + Cl_2 \,(g)$ $\Delta H° = +111 \text{ kJ}$

(2) $H_2O \,(l) + CaOCl_2 \,(g) + 2 \, NaBr \,(s) \rightarrow 2 \, NaCl \,(s) + Ca(OH)_2 \,(s) + Br_2 \,(g)$

                                                         $\Delta H° = -60 \text{ kJ}$

(3) $Ca(OH)_2 \,(s) \rightarrow CaO \,(s) + H_2O \,(l)$ $\Delta H° = + 65 \text{ kJ}$

(A) $\Delta H^{\circ}_{R} = +116$ kJ

(B) $\Delta H^{\circ}_{R} = -106$ kJ

(C) $\Delta H^{\circ}_{R} = +53$ kJ

(D) $\Delta H^{\circ}_{R} = +106$ kJ

(E) $\Delta H^{\circ}_{R} = -53$ kJ

The correct answer is (E). This is another application of Hess's law. Before solving this kind of problem, examine each term in the main equation and look where it appears in the data. For example, Cl_2 (g) appears in the first equation. Before applying Hess's law, one must reverse the reaction, as well as the sign of the enthalpy. In this case, the solution is $(-1) + (2) + (3)$.

12. Which of the following statements applies to a first-order reaction:

$$2\,N_2O_5\,(sln) \rightarrow 4\,NO_2\,(sln) + O_2\,(g)$$

I. $v = k[N_2O_5]$

II. $t_{\frac{1}{2}} = \ln 2 / k$

III. $[N_2O_5] = -kt + [N_2O_5]_0$

IV. $v = k[N_2O_5]^2$

V. $\ln[N_2O_5] = -kt + \ln[N_2O_5]_0$

VI. $t_{\frac{1}{2}} = [N_2O_5]_0 / 2k$

(A) I, II, and V

(B) I, II, and VI

(C) II, V, and VI

(D) I, II, and III

(E) I, III, and VI

The correct answer is (A). III and VI are characteristic of a zeroth-order reaction, and IV would be the rate equation if the reaction were second-order.

The reaction I^- (aq) + OCl^- (aq) $\rightarrow$ IO^- (aq) + Cl^- (aq) is believed to proceed through the following three-step mechanism:

step 1 $OCl^- + H_2O \underset{k_{-1}}{\overset{k_1}{\rightleftharpoons}} HOCl + OH$ fast equilibrium

step 2 $I^- + HOCl \overset{k_2}{\rightleftharpoons} HOI + Cl^-$ slow equilibrium

step 3 $HOI + OH^- \overset{k_3}{\rightleftharpoons} H_2O + IO^-$ fast equilibrium

Using this data, answer questions 13 and 14.

13. Identify the false statement:

    (A) The molecularity of each step is 2.
    (B) The limiting step is the second one.
    (C) HOCl is the only reaction intermediate.
    (D) The reaction is a complex reaction.
    (E) All the above statements are true.

The correct answer is (C). The molecularity is the number of reactant molecules involved in a particular step. The reaction is complex because it involves more than one elementary step. The limiting step of a complex reaction is always the slowest. The reaction intermediates appear in one step and disappear in the next. HOCl is an intermediate because it appears in step1 and disappears in step 2. HOI is also an intermediate because it appears in step 2 and disappears in step 3.

14. What is the rate equation of the reaction?

    (A) $r = (k_2 k_1 / k_{-1})\{[I^-][OCl^-] \, / \, [OH^-]\}$
    (B) $r = k_2[I^-][HOCl]$
    (C) $r = (k_2 k_{-1} / k_1)\{[I^-][OCl^-] \, / \, [OH^-]\}$
    (D) $r = (k_2 k_1 / k_{-1})\{[I^-][OH^-] \, / \, [Cl^-]\}$
    (E) $r = k_1 k_2 [OCl^-][I^-]$

The correct answer is (A). The rate of this reaction should be the rate of its slowest step: $r = k_2[I^-][HOCl]$. HOCl is a reaction intermediate, and its concentration cannot be evaluated directly. However, we can replace it with an expression obtained from the equilibrium of step 1. For step 1, when a state of equilibrium is achieved, the rates of the forward and the reverse reactions are equal:

$$k_1[OCl^-] = k_{-1}[HOCl][OH^-].$$

We omit $[H_2O]$ because it remains constant throughout the reaction. Isolating [HOCl], we obtain

$$[HOCl] = (k_1 / k_{-1})([OCl^-] \, / \, [OH^-].$$

Finally,

$$r = k_2[I^-][HOCl] = k_2[I^-](k_1 / k_{-1})([OCl^-] \, / \, [OH^-] = (k_2 k_1 / k_{-1})(\, [I^-][OCl^-] \, / \, [OH^-].$$

15. A solution contains 5.36×10^{-2} mol of a nonvolatile solute in 154 g of CCl_4 at 64°C. The vapor pressure of pure CCl_4 is 531 mmHg at 64°C. What is the vapor pressure of the solution?

   (A) 503 mmHg

   (B) 504 mmHg

   (C) 505 mmHg

   (D) 506 mmHg

   (E) 507 mmHg

The correct answer is (B). According to Raoult's law, $P_{solution} = x_{solvent}P°_{solvent}$, where $x_{solvent}$ is the molar fraction of the solvent.

$$x_{solvent} = \text{(mole of solvent) / (mole of solvent + mole of solute)} =$$
$$(154g / 154 \text{ g} \cdot \text{mol}^{-1}) / (154g / 154 \text{ g} \cdot \text{mol}^{-1} + 5.36 \cdot 10^{-2} \text{ mol}) = 0.949.$$

Then, $P_{solution} = x_{solvent}P°_{solvent} = (0.949)(531 \text{ mmHg}) = 504 \text{ mmHg}$.

16. The vapor pressure of water is 23.7 torr at 25 °C. A solution of 5.00 g of a nonvolatile solute in 100 g of water has a vapor pressure of 23.3 torr at 25°C. What is the molar mass of the solute?

   (A) 54.6 g/mol

   (B) 46.8 g/mol

   (C) 58.4 g/mol

   (D) 52.5 g/mol

   (E) 56.0 g/mol

The correct answer is (A). One of the most interesting aspects of Raoult's law is that it allows the determination of the molar masses of solutes. One can write

$$x_{solvent} = (P_{solution})/(P_{solvent}) = 23.3 / 23.7 = 0.983.$$

Therefore, if x is the molar mass,

$$x_{solvent} = (100 \text{ g} / 18.0 \text{ g} \cdot \text{mol}^{-1}) / (100 \text{ g} / 18.0 \text{ g} \cdot \text{mol}^{-1} + 5.00 \text{ g} / x) = 0.983.$$

Solving this equation for x, one obtains x = molar mass = 54.6 g/mol.

17. A solution of 0.40 g of a polypeptide in 1.0 L of aqueous solution has an osmotic pressure of 4.92×10^{-3} atm at 300 K. What is the molar mass of the polypeptide? ($R = 0.08206$ L $\cdot$ atm $\cdot$ K^{-1} $\cdot$ mol^{-1})

   (A) 2.0×10^6

   (B) 2.5×10^6

   (C) 2.0×10^2

   (D) 2.0×10^3

   (E) 2.0×10^4

The correct answer is (D). The osmotic pressure is one of the colligative properties: $\pi = CRT$. The molar mass can be evaluated in the following way: (π/RT) = C = (mass of solute / molar mass of solute) / V. The molar mass is: molar mass = (m/π)RT = [(0.40)(0.08206)(300)] / [(0.00492)(1.00)] = 2.0×10^3 g/mol.

18. The freezing point of a solution of 2.40 g of biphenyl (molar mass = 154 g/mol) in 75.0 g of benzene is 1.10°C lower than that of pure benzene. What is the value of the molal cryoscopic constant of benzene in °C/m?

   (A) −4.4

   (B) −5.4

   (C) −4.6

   (D) −5.0

   (E) −5.3

The correct answer is (E). The freezing point depression is another colligative property. It is given by

$$\Delta T_f = -K_f m_{solute}$$

where m is the molality of the solute. The molal cryoscopic constant is

$$K_f = -(\Delta T_f / m) = -(1.10°C) / [(2.40 \text{ g} / 140 \text{ g/mol}) / 0.0750 \text{ kg}] = -5.3°C/m.$$

Remember that the molality is defined as the number of moles of solute dissolved in 1 kg of solvent. The units mol/kg are abbreviated as the lower case letter m.

19. Use the average bond energies at 25°C to calculate the $\Delta H°_f$ of the hydrazine (H_2N-NH_2). $\Delta H°(N-N) = 944$ kJ/mol, $\Delta H°(N-N) = 163$ kJ/mol, $\Delta H°(H-H) = 436$ kJ/mol, $\Delta H°(N-H) = 388$ kJ/mol.

Answer: The reaction of formation of hydrazine is given by $N_2 + 2 H_2 \rightarrow H_2N-NH_2$. The energy required to break the bonds of the reactants is $944 + 2(436) = 1816$ kJ/mol. The energy liberated by the formation of the products is $163 + 4(388) = 1715$ kJ/mol. So, $\Delta H°_f$ = sum of the bond energies of the reactants – sum of the bond energies of the products = $1816 - 1715 = 101$ kJ/mol.

A catalyst increases the rate of a reaction by lowering its activation energy. Use this statement and the following diagram for the reversible catalyzed and non-catalyzed reversible reaction to answer questions 20 and 21.

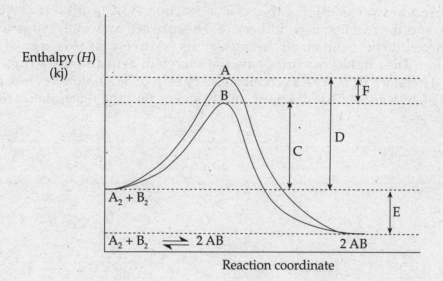

20. The energy of activation of the reverse catalyzed reaction is

    (A) E

    (B) E + C

    (C) E + D

    (D) F

    (E) C + F

The correct answer is (B). The energy of activation of the reverse catalyzed reaction is the difference between the energy of the activated complex (point B) and the energy of the reactants of the reverse reaction (AB). On the diagram, it is the sum E + C.

21. Which of the following statements are true?

    I. The reverse catalyzed reaction is exothermic.

   II. The forward noncatalyzed reaction is spontaneous.

  III. ΔH of the forward reaction = ΔH of the reverse reaction.

   V. The mechanism of this reaction consists of only one step.

    (A) I and II

    (B) II and IV

    (C) II and III

    (D) II and IV

    (E) I and IV

The correct answer is (B). For the reverse reaction H (A_2 + B_2) > H (2 AB).
$\Delta H > 0$, and the reaction is endothermic. The forward noncatalyzed reaction is
not expected to be spontaneous because of its relatively large energy of
activation. The catalyst modifies only the energy of activation of a reaction, not
its ΔH. Therefore III is true. Each elementary step of a reaction has its own
energy of activation. This diagram clearly shows that the reaction has only one
step.

V. The Princeton Review GRE Chemistry Diagnostic Exam

Directions: Each of the questions or incomplete statements below is followed by five suggested answers or completions. Select the one that is best in each case.

1. Choose the answer below that accurately describes the hybridization of the central atom and the molecular geometry of BF_3.

   A) sd^2, trigonal planar
   B) sp^2, pyramidal
   C) sp^2, trigonal planar
   D) sd^2, pyramidal
   E) spd, trigonal planar

2.   I   II   III

   SO_3^{2-} O^{2-} H_2S

   Using Hard/Soft Acid/Base theory, rank the bases above in increasing order of hardness.

   A) II < I < III
   B) II < III < I
   C) III < I < II
   D) III < II < I
   E) I < II < III

3. How many unpaired electrons are there in a ground-state tungsten atom?

   A) Zero
   B) One
   C) Two
   D) Three
   E) Four

4. Which of the following substances is a good reducing agent?

   A) NaCl
   B) BH_3
   C) N_2

   D) K^+

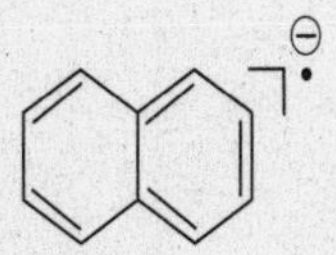

   E) $KMnO_4$

5. Which of the following molecules has the greatest first ionization potential?

   A) Li
   B) Na
   C) H
   D) Ca
   E) Be

6.  $+ (BH_3)_2 \longrightarrow$

   After treatment of the reaction mixture above with hydrogen peroxide, sodium hydroxide, and water, what is the product of the reaction?

   A)

   B)

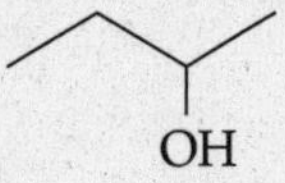

   C)

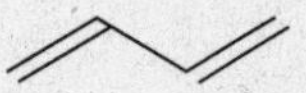

   D)

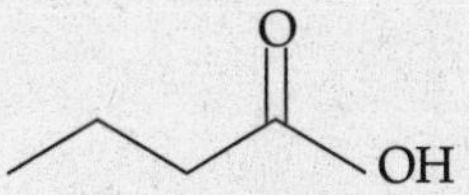

   E)

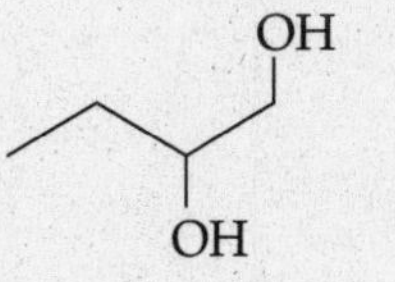

GO ON TO THE NEXT PAGE

7.

$$\begin{array}{c}
OOH \\
HO-H \\
H-HO \\
H-HO \\
HO-H \\
CH_2OH
\end{array}$$

Which of the following compounds is an epimer of the molecule above?

A)

$$\begin{array}{c}
OOH \\
H-OH \\
H-OH \\
H-OH \\
H-OH \\
CH_2OH
\end{array}$$

B)

$$\begin{array}{c}
OOH \\
HO-H \\
HO-H \\
HO-H \\
HO-H \\
CH_2OH
\end{array}$$

C)

$$\begin{array}{c}
HOO \\
HO-H \\
H-OH \\
H-OH \\
HO-H \\
CH_2OH
\end{array}$$

D)

$$\begin{array}{c}
OOH \\
HO-H \\
H-OH \\
H-OH \\
H-OH \\
CH_2OH
\end{array}$$

E)

$$\begin{array}{c}
OOH \\
H-OH \\
HO-H \\
HO-H \\
H-OH \\
CH_2OH
\end{array}$$

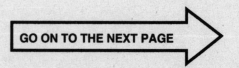

8. Which of the following molecules contains the aldehyde functionality of exo stereochemistry?

A)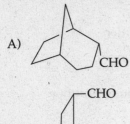

B)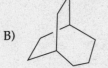

C)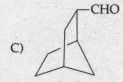

D)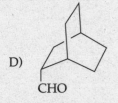

E)

9. Which of the following resonance structures best depicts why the major regiochemical product of the reaction between nitrobenzene, Br_2, and $FeBr_3$ is p-bromonitrobenzene?

A)

B)

C)

D)

E)

GO ON TO THE NEXT PAGE

10.

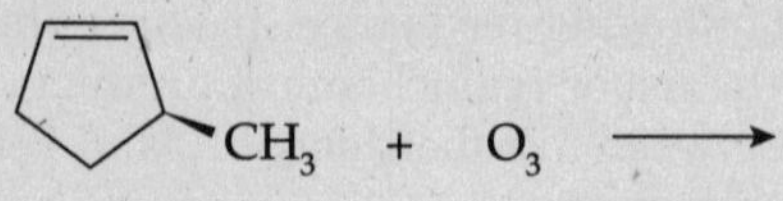

+ O₃ ⟶

After treatment with Zn/H_2O, what is the product of the reaction above?

A)

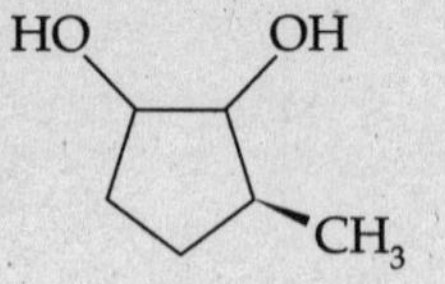

B)

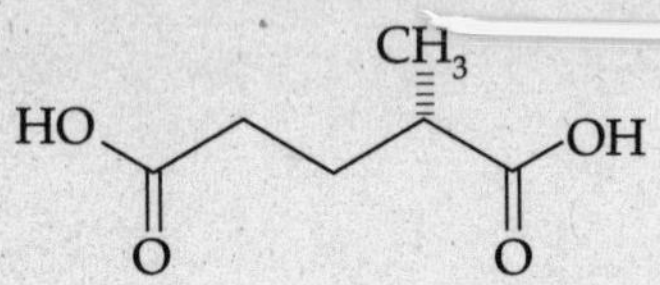

C)

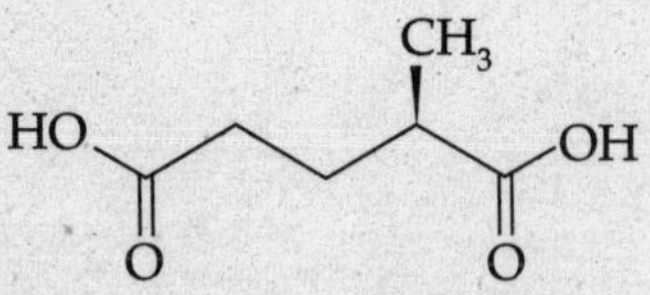

D)

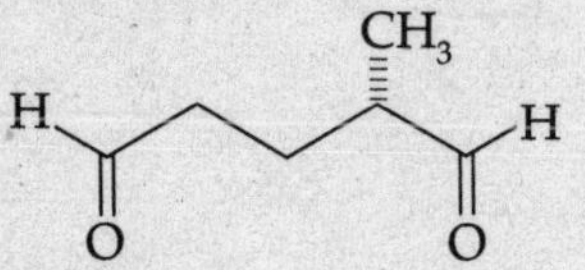

E)

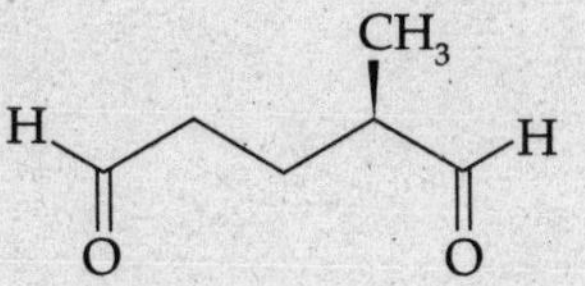

11. $Ph(Et)_2N$ + CH_3CH_2I → $PhN(Et)_3^+$ I^-

The reaction above is an example of which of the following?

A) nucleophilic substitution
B) electrophilic addition
C) radical chain reaction
D) elimination
E) electrophilic aromatic substitution

GO ON TO THE NEXT PAGE

12. Which of the following reactions would be most likely to produce acylium ions (OC^+CH_3) as intermediates in the reaction mechanism?

A)

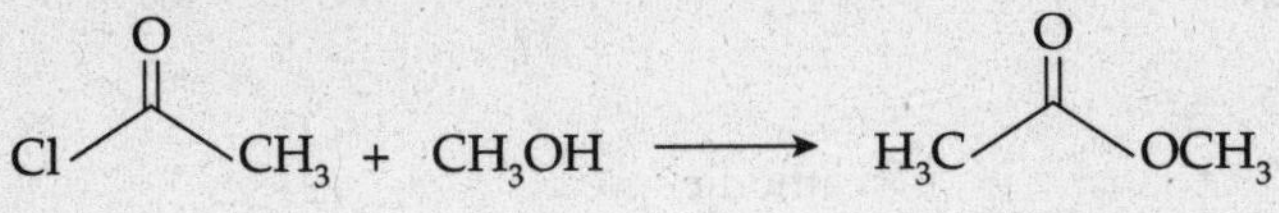

B)

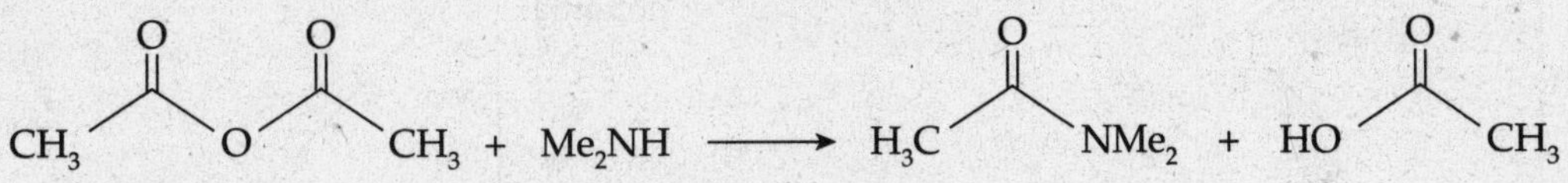

C)

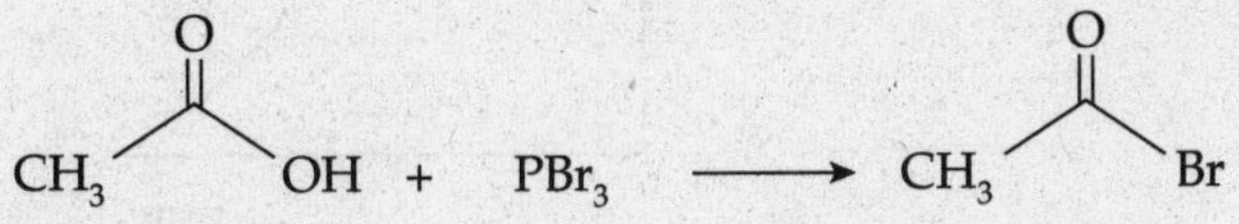

D)

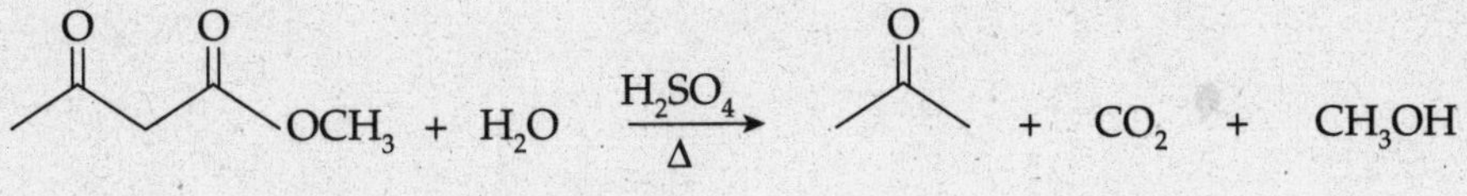

E)

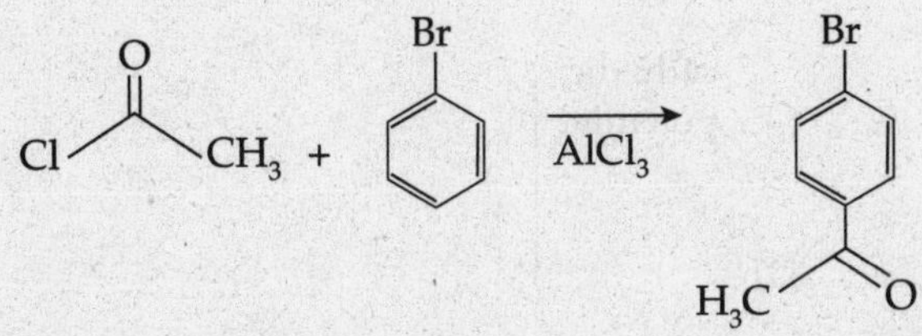

13. Which of the following is not commonly used as a primary standard for acid/base titrations?

A) sodium carbonate
B) potassium hydrogen phthalate
C) potassium hydroxide
D) borax ($Na_2B_4O_2$)
E) HgO

GO ON TO THE NEXT PAGE

14. Which of the following graphs accurately represents the potential applied to the working electrode in a typical cyclic voltammetry experiment?

A)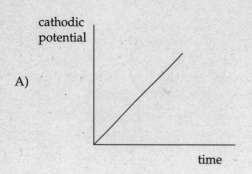

B)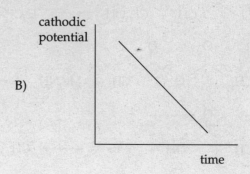

C)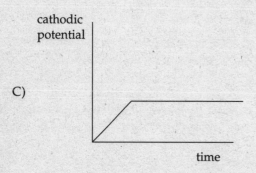

D)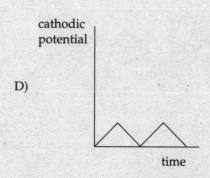

E)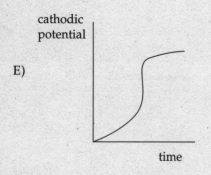

GO ON TO THE NEXT PAGE

15. Which of the following conjugate acid/base pairs should be used to prepare a buffer with pH near 7.15?

A) succinic acid/sodium succinate (pK_a = 5.64)
B) phosphoric acid/sodium dihydrogen phosphate (pK_{a1} = 2.15)
C) sodium dihydrogen phosphate/sodium hydrogen phosphate (pK_{a2} = 7.20)
D) glycylglycine/sodium glycylglycate (pK_a = 8.35)
E) formic acid/sodium formate (pK_a = 3.74)

16. Which of the following compounds is a Lewis acid, but not a Brönsted acid?

A) HCl
B) B_2H_6
C) HCO_2H
D) HNO_3
E) Phenol

17. $A \leftrightarrow B$

The instantaneous free energy (ΔG) of the reaction shown above is defined as $\Delta G = RT \ln \frac{Q}{K}$, where R = the gas constant, T = temperature (K), Q = the reaction quotient, and K = the equilibrium constant. Under what conditions does $\Delta G = \Delta G°$, the standard reaction free energy?

A) when [B] >> [A]
B) when $Q = K$
C) when Q is negative
D) when [B] = [A]
E) when [A] = 0

18. The fastest rate at which a bimolecular reaction can reasonably occur is

A) infinite
B) 10^{-13} s^{-1}
C) 10^{-13} $m^{-1}s^{-1}$
D) 10^{-9} ms^{-1}
E) 10^9 $m^{-1}s^{-1}$

19. The kinetic energy (K) of a revolving particle is described by

A) $K = \frac{1}{2}mI^2$

B) $K = \frac{1}{2}I\omega$

C) $K = \sqrt{\frac{1}{2}mv^2}$

D) $K = \frac{1}{2}I\omega^2$

E) $K = \sqrt{\frac{1}{2}I\omega^2}$

20. Which of the following properties is/are intensive?

A) volume
B) mass
C) temperature
D) energy
E) all of the above

21. $\Delta E_{univ.} = \Delta E_{sys.} + \Delta E_{surr.} = 0$ can also be stated as:

A) $H = E + PV$
B) $\Delta H = NC_p\Delta T$
C) $\Delta S_{total} < 0$
D) $\Delta G = \Delta H - T\Delta S$
E) $\Delta E = q + w$

22. For a given reaction with a rate constant k and an activation energy E_a, the Arrhenius equation is given by

A) $\ln k = \ln A - \frac{E_a}{RT}$

B) $k = Ae^{-RT/E_a}$

C) $k = Ae^{E_a/RT}$

D) $\ln k = \ln A + \frac{E_a}{RT}$

E) $k = E_a e^{-A/RT}$

GO ON TO THE NEXT PAGE

23. Which of the following expressions accurately describes the radii of electron orbits allowed within the Bohr model of the hydrogen atom?

A) $r = \dfrac{\varepsilon_0 \hbar^2 n^2}{4\pi m e^2}$, $n = 1, 2....$

B) $r = \dfrac{4\pi \varepsilon \hbar^2 n^2}{m e^2}$, $n = 1, 2....$

C) $r = \dfrac{4\pi m e^2}{\varepsilon \hbar^2 n^2}$, $n = 1, 2....$

D) $r = a_o$

E) $a_o = \dfrac{4\pi \varepsilon_o \hbar^2 n^2}{m e}$, $n = 1, 2, 3....$

24. The Frank-Condon principle provides an estimate of which of the following values?

A) force constant of a bond
B) bond strength
C) intensity of vibronic transitions
D) extent of internal conversion
E) dipole moment

25. The exact solution of the Schrodinger equation for He cannot be obtained due to

A) the size of the atom
B) intersystem crossing
C) internal vibrations
D) interelectronic repulsion
E) j – j coupling

26. Which process is spontaneous at constant temperature and pressure?

A) $\Delta G_{sys} < 0$
B) $\Delta G_{sys} = 0$
C) $\Delta G_{sys} > 0$
D) Both A and B
E) Both B and C

27. Which labels are correct for the following phase diagram of H_2O?

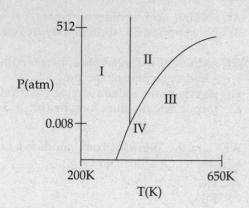

A) I solid; II liquid; III gas; IV triple point; V critical point
B) I liquid; II solid; III gas; IV triple point; V critical point
C) I gas; II liquid; III solid; IV critical point; V triple point
D) I gas; II liquid; III solid; IV triple point; V critical point
E) I critical point; II liquid; III solid; IV gas; V triple point

28. Isothermal bulk compressibility is defined by $\kappa = \dfrac{-1}{V}\left(\dfrac{\partial V}{\partial P}\right)_T$. For an ideal gas obeying the equation of state $PV = nRT$, which expression defines κ^2?

A) $\dfrac{1}{T}$

B) $\dfrac{nR}{T}$

C) $\dfrac{PV}{T}$

D) $\dfrac{PV}{nR}$

E) $\dfrac{1}{P}$

GO ON TO THE NEXT PAGE

29. Calculate the work done by a system of 1.00 mol of ideal gas as it expands irreversibly at constant $T = 100K$ from a P of 100 atm to 10 atm. The external pressure is held constant at 1 atm. [$R = 0.08206$ L $\cdot$ atm/mol $\cdot$ κ].

   A) 0.739 L $\cdot$ atm
   B) 0.0739 L $\cdot$ atm
   C) 7.39 L $\cdot$ atm
   D) –0.739 L $\cdot$ atm
   E) –0.0739 L $\cdot$ atm

30. Coulometric titration relies on detecting of the number of electrons generated in a chemical reaction. For example, hexene can be titrated with Br_2 generated by the electrolytic oxidation of Br^-:

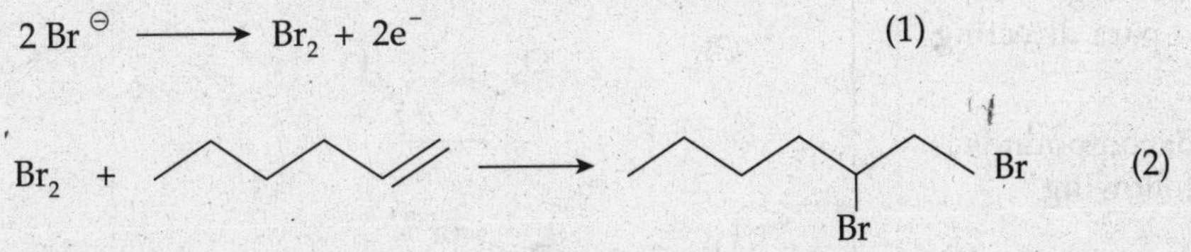

   Where does reaction (1) occur?
   I. Cathode
   II. Anode
   III. In the vapor phase above the solution
   A) I
   B) II
   C) III
   D) I + III
   E) II + III

31. If the signal-to-noise ratio for a one-scan NMR spectrum is 3, what is the signal-to-noise ratio for an average of 36 scans for the same sample?

   A) 3
   B) 6
   C) 9
   D) 12
   E) 18

32. Which of the following numbers balances the stoichiometry of this reaction?

   $2Ca_3(PO_4)_2$ (s) + $6SiO_2$ (s) + $10C$ (s) →
   P_4 (g) + ...$CaSiO_3$ (s) + $10CO$ (g)
   A) 2
   B) 6
   C) 8
   D) 4
   E) 5

GO ON TO THE NEXT PAGE

33. In which of the following titrations does pH = 7.0 at the equivalence point?

    I.   Strong acid/strong base
   II. Weak acid/strong base
  III. Strong acid/weak base
  A) I only
  B) II only
  C) III only
  D) II and III only
  E) I, II, and III

34. Which of the following describes the amino group as a substituent in electrophilic aromatic substitution?

  A) Weakly activating, ortho-para directing
  B) Strongly activating, ortho-para directing
  C) Weakly deactivating, meta directing
  D) Strongly activating, meta directing
  E) Strongly deactivating, ortho-para directing

35. Which of the following classes of compounds is most prone to decarboxylation following hydrolysis?

  A) β–keto esters
  B) δ–keto esters
  C) α–halo amides
  D) α–halo esters
  E) β–hydroxy acids

36.

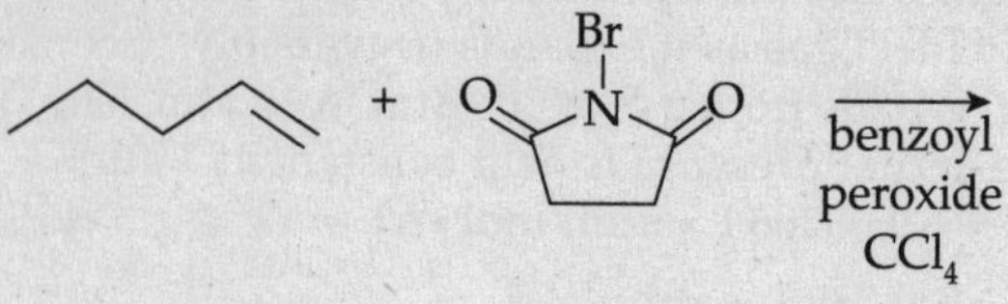

Predict the product of the reaction shown above.

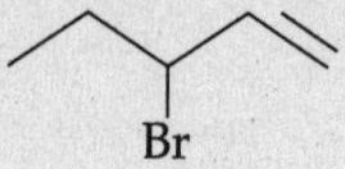

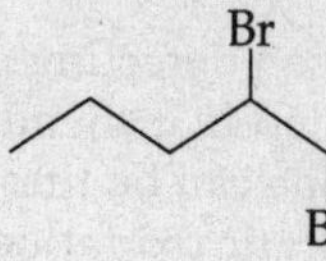

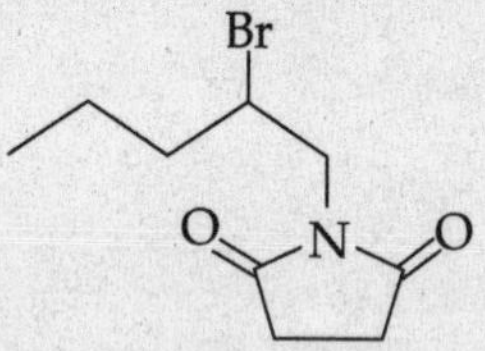

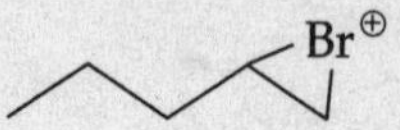

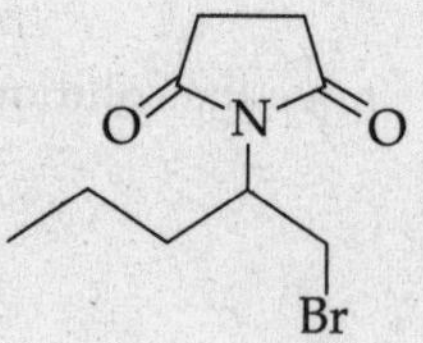

GO ON TO THE NEXT PAGE

37.

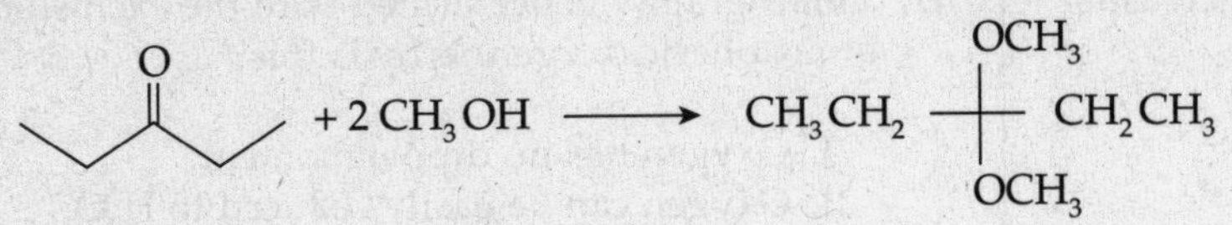

$$\text{(ketone)} + 2\,CH_3OH \longrightarrow CH_3CH_2 \overset{OCH_3}{\underset{OCH_3}{\text{—C—}}} CH_2CH_3$$

Which of the following is an intermediate in the ketal-forming reaction shown above?

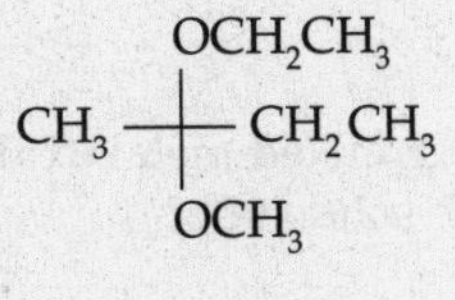

A) 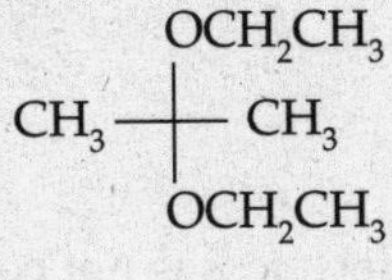 $CH_3 \overset{OCH_2CH_3}{\underset{OCH_2CH_3}{\text{—C—}}} CH_3$

B) $CH_3 \overset{OCH_2CH_3}{\underset{OCH_3}{\text{—C—}}} CH_2CH_3$

C) $CH_3\text{—C(}^+OH\text{)—}CH_2CH_3$

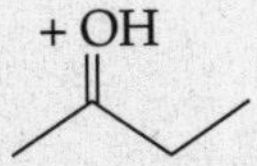

D) 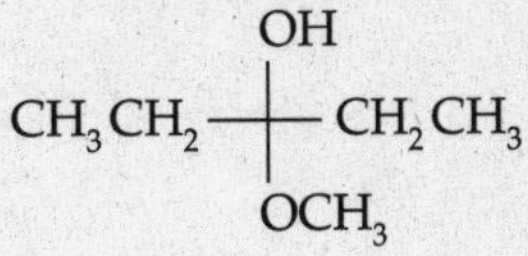 $CH_3CH_2 \overset{OH}{\underset{OCH_3}{\text{—C—}}} CH_2CH_3$

E) 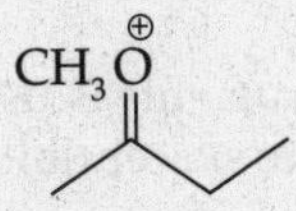 $CH_3\overset{\oplus}{O}\text{—C—}CH_2CH_3$

38.

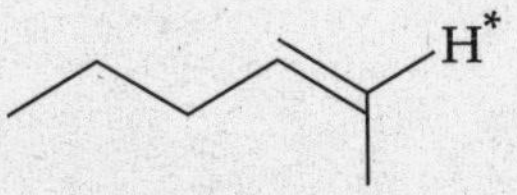

In the structure above, the position of the indicated (*) hydrogen is best described as which of the following?

A) geminalic
B) vicinylic
C) vinylic
D) allylic
E) acetylinic

39. Rank the following radicals in order of increasing stability.

I. $\cdot CH_3$
II. $\cdot C(CH_3)_3$
III. $\cdot C(CH_3)_2H$

A) I < II < III
B) I < III < II
C) II < I < III
D) II < III < I
E) III < II < I

40. In the mass spectrum of 2-hexanone, which of the following is LEAST likely to be an observed species?

A) 85 m/z
B) 37 m/z
C) 100 m/z
D) 58 m/z
E) 43 m/z

41. In which of the following molecules is the bonding most ionic?

A) $NiCl_2$
B) CsF
C) BCl_3
D) Br_2
E) PH_3

GO ON TO THE NEXT PAGE

42. Rank the following ligands in order of increasing field strength.

$$H_2O \qquad CO \qquad I^- \qquad ^-OH$$
$$I \qquad\quad II \qquad III \qquad IV$$

A) II < I < IV < III
B) II < I < III < IV
C) III < IV < I < II
D) III < IV < II < I
E) IV < III < I < II

43. Which of the following mixed metal oxides has a spinel structure in the solid state?

A) $MgTiO_3$
B) RuO_2
C) $FeCr_2O_4$
D) Cr_2O_3
E) $KNbO_3$

44. According to the 18-electron rule, which of the following compounds would be expected to be most reactive? (Atomic numbers: Fe = 26, Os = 76, Co = 27, Ir = 77, W = 74, Cp = cyclopentadienide.)

A) $H_2Fe(CO)_4$
B) Cp_2Os
C) $(PMe_3)_3Co(Me)_2Br$
D) $(PPh_3)_2Ir(CO)Cl$
E) $W(CO)_3(PEt_3)_2Cl_2$

45. A 100-mL solution containing ClO_4^- was treated with excess KCl to precipitate 0.72 g $KClO_4$ (MW = 138.4). What was the molarity of perchlorate in the solution?

A) $1.4 \times 10^{-2}\,M$
B) $1.9 \times 10^{-3}\,M$
C) $7.1 \times 10^{-2}\,M$
D) $1.4 \times 10^{-3}\,M$
E) $5.2 \times 10^{-2}\,M$

46. The ionic strength of an aqueous solution containing 0.05M NaCl and 0.02 M Na_2SO_4 is

A) 0.11 M
B) 0 M
C) 0.09 M
D) 0.19 M
E) 0.15 M

47. Polarography is performed with the exclusion of atmospheric oxygen. Why is this?

I. Oxygen has no dipole moment.
II. Oxygen can be easily reduced to H_2O.
III. Oxygen is in equilibrium with O_3^-, a highly polar molecule.

A) I, II, and III
B) I and II only
C) I only
D) II only
E) III only

48. Which of the following detectors is not commonly paired with a gas chromatograph?

A) flame ionization detector
B) electron capture detector
C) interferometer
D) thermal conductivity detector
E) mass spectrometer

49. Which of the following instruments is used for the measurement of magnetic susceptibilities?

A) NMR spectrometer
B) Microwave spectrometer
C) IR spectrometer
D) Raman spectrometer
E) Gouy balance

50. Which of the following homoleptic carbonyl complexes would be expected to be the most reactive?

A) $Cr(CO)_6$
B) $Fe(CO)_5$
C) $Mn_2(CO)_{10}$
D) $Co_2(CO)_8$
E) $V(CO)_6$

51. Which of the following point groups contains an inversion center (i) as one of its symmetry elements?

A) C_{4v}
B) C_s
C) T_d
D) D_{2d}
E) C_{Gh}

GO ON TO THE NEXT PAGE

52. How many resonances in the ^{31}P NMR spectrum (^{31}P is 100% abundant with a nuclear spin of $\frac{1}{2}$) would you expect for trans-$(P(Ph_3))_4RuH_2$?

A) 0
B) 1
C) 2
D) 3
E) 4

53. Which of the following equations accurately describes electron affinity (EA)?

$ion^-_{(g)} \rightarrow atom_{(g)} + e^- \qquad \Delta E = EA$

$atom_{(g)} \rightarrow ion^{\oplus}_{(g)} + e^- \qquad \Delta E = EA$

$atom_{(g)} + e^- \rightarrow ion^-_{(g)} \qquad \Delta E = EA$

$ion^{\oplus}_{(g)} + e^- \rightarrow atom_{(g)} \qquad \Delta E = EA$

$ion^{2-}_{(g)} \rightarrow ion^-_{(g)} + e^- \qquad \Delta E = EA$

54. Which of the following molecules is NOT subject to Jahn-Teller distortion?

A) VCl_4
B) ReF_6
C) $Ti(H_2O)_6^{3+}$
D) $Cu(NH_3)_6^{2+}$
E) $Ni(CO)_4$

55.

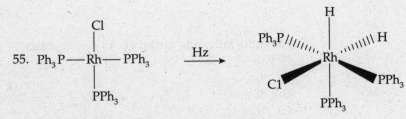

The transformation reaction shown above is known as what kind of reaction?

A) reductive elimination
B) oxidative addition
C) ligand substitution
D) migratory insertion
E) migratory deinsertion

56. Which of the following accurately describes the Lux-Flood definition of acidity?

$HCl + NaOH \rightarrow NaCl + H_2O$

$CaO + SiO_2 \rightarrow CaSiO_3$

$BH_3 + NH_3 \rightarrow H_3N-BH_3$

$2H_2O \Leftrightarrow H_3O^+ + OH^-$

$Ni + 4CO \rightarrow Ni(CO)_4$

57. Which of the following does not describe structure-types of polyhedral polyboron-hydride cage compounds?

A) quadro-
B) nido-
C) arachno-
D) closo-
E) klado-

GO ON TO THE NEXT PAGE

58.

In the nucleophilic aromatic substitution reaction undergone by the reagents shown above, the piperidine attacks which position of the aromatic ring?

A) ortho to the fluorine substituent
B) meta to the fluorine substituent
C) para to the fluorine substituent
D) ipso to the fluorine substituent
E) meso to the fluorine substituent

59. Which of the following compounds is NOT aromatic?

A)

B)

C)

D)

E)

60. Which of the following molecules would be the LEAST likely to undergo 1,3-dipolar cycloaddition reactions in the presence of a dipolarophile?

A) $Ph-N_3$
B) O_3
C) $Ph-N_2^+ Cl^-$
D) CH_2N_2
E)

61. Which of the following compounds is achiral?

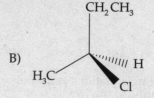

A)

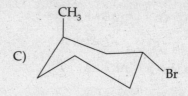

B)

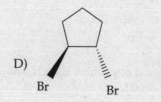

C)

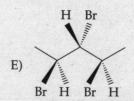

D)

E)

62. All of the following are powerful electrophiles except:

A) BF_3
B) Br^+
C) NO^+
D) PH_3
E) $AlCl_3$

GO ON TO THE NEXT PAGE

63. For the synthesis of dioxin shown below, the first step of the reaction mechanism is best described as

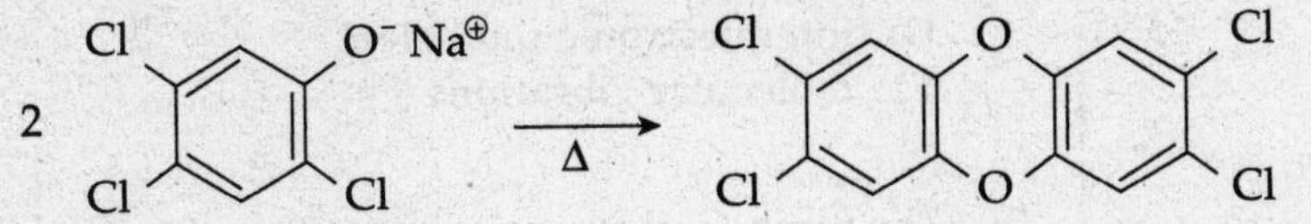

dioxin

A) radical cyclization
B) electrophilic substitution
C) free radical addition
D) nucleophilic addition
E) chloride elimination

64.

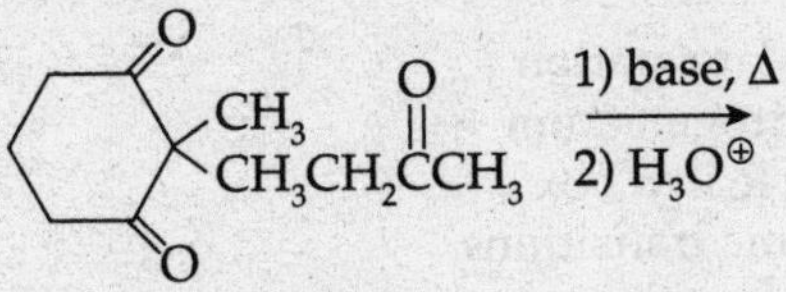

Predict the major product of the reaction mechanism above.

A)

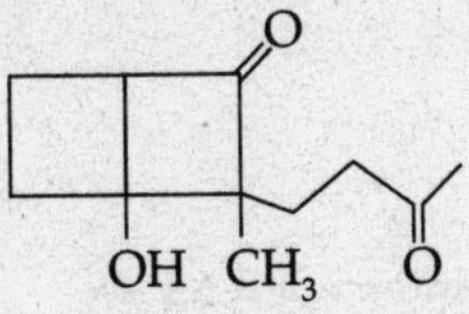

B)

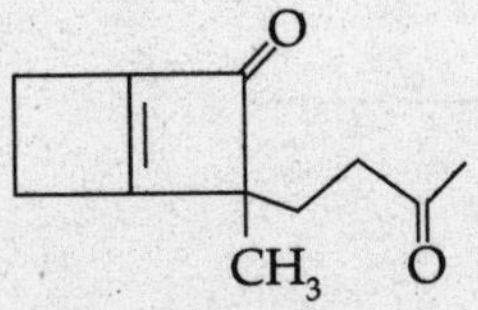

C)

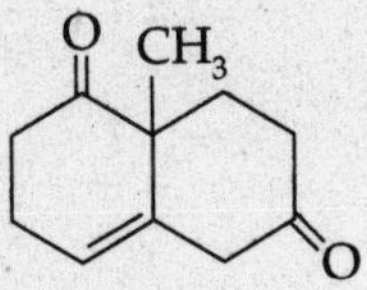

D)

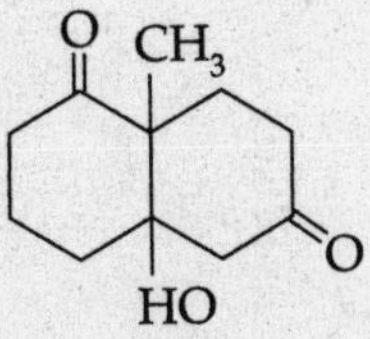

E)

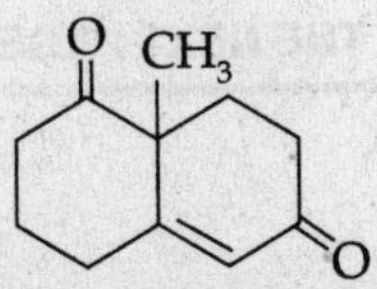

65. What is the bond order of He_2^+?

A) 0

B) $\frac{1}{2}$

C) 1

D) $1\frac{1}{2}$

E) 2

66. Which of the following statements is a valid derivative of the steady-state approximation?

A) A viable kinetic model can be generated if the concentrations of all reactants are assumed to be constant.
B) A system at equilibrium tends to stay at equilibrium.
C) In a two-step reaction where only the first step is reversible, the concentration of the intermediate is negligibly small.
D) In a two-step reaction where the first step is irreversible and the second step is reversible, the concentration of the intermediate is negligibly small.
E) None of the above.

GO ON TO THE NEXT PAGE

67. A Hermitian operator ($\hat{A}$) can be generally defined by which of the following? (Assume f and g are well-behaved functions.)

A) $\int_{-\infty}^{\infty} g^* \hat{A} f \, dx = \int_{-\infty}^{\infty} f \hat{A}^* g^* \, dx$

B) $\int_{-\infty}^{\infty} f^* f \, dx = \int_{-\infty}^{\infty} g^* g \, dx$

C) $\int_{-\infty}^{\infty} g^* \hat{A} \, dx = \int_{-\infty}^{\infty} f^* \hat{A} \, dx$

D) $\int_{-\infty}^{\infty} \hat{A} f g^* \, dx = \int_{-\infty}^{\infty} \hat{A} g^* f \, dx$

E) $\int_{-\infty}^{\infty} f^* \hat{A} g^* \, dx = \int_{-\infty}^{\infty} f^* \hat{A} g^* \, dx$

68. Orbital energies obtained from Hartree-Fock calculations can be used to approximate which of the following values?

A) rotational energy levels
B) ionization energy of an atom
C) vibrational energy levels
D) bond dissociation energies
E) potential energies

69. Which expression describes the force between the proton and electron (ε_0 = permittivity of free space)?

A) $\dfrac{\varepsilon_0 e^2}{\pi r^2}$

B) $\dfrac{4\pi e^2}{\varepsilon_0 r^2}$

C) $\dfrac{4\pi \varepsilon_0}{r^2 e^2}$

D) $\dfrac{r^2}{4\pi \varepsilon_0 e^2}$

E) $\dfrac{e^2}{4\pi \varepsilon_0 r^2}$

70. The Born-Oppenheimer approximation neglects

A) spin
B) coupling
C) nuclear motion
D) interelectronic repulsion
E) molecular vibrations

71. The Stern-Gerlach experiment demonstrated the existence of

A) mass
B) charge
C) spin
D) waves
E) particles

72. A harmonic oscillator is used as a model for

A) molecular rotation
B) the hydrogen atom
C) a particle in a box
D) electronic transitions
E) molecular vibration

73. What is the slope of the following line?

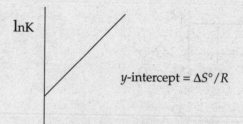

$y\text{-intercept} = \Delta S^\circ / R$

A) $\dfrac{1}{T \ln K}$

B) $\dfrac{-\Delta H^\circ}{R}$

C) $\dfrac{\Delta S^\circ T}{R}$

D) $\dfrac{\ln K}{T}$

E) $\dfrac{-\Delta H^\circ R}{T}$

GO ON TO THE NEXT PAGE

74. When will a spontaneous process in an isolated system have $\Delta S_{sys} < 0$?

    A) always
    B) for reversible processes
    C) at high P
    D) at high T
    E) never

75. What is the eigenvalue of the momentum operator, $\hat{P}_x = -i\hbar \dfrac{\partial}{\partial x}$ with eigenfunction e^{ikx}?

    A) ik
    B) $-i\hbar k$
    C) $\hbar k$
    D) ikx
    E) e^{ikx}

76. Which diagram illustrates the probability density for a particle in a one-dimensional box?

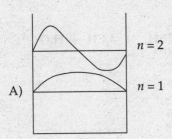

    A)

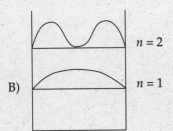

    B)

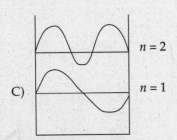

    C)

    D) both B and C
    E) both A and B

77. Which of the following procedures will increase the retention time of an analyte on a GC column?

    I. Increasing the column length
    II. Raising the % of the stationary phase
    III. Increasing the column temperature

    A) I only
    B) III only
    C) I, II, and III
    D) I and II only
    E) II and III only

78. The "common ion effect" addresses the solubility of salts in polar solvents. Which of the following statements encapsulates the "common ion effect?"

    A) Polar solvents dissolve polar solutes. Likewise, nonpolar solvents dissolve nonpolar solvents.
    B) A salt will be more soluble if one of its constituent ions is already present in solution.
    C) In a polar solvent, salts with the same anion will have similar solubilities.
    D) A salt will be less soluble if one of its constituent ions is already present in solution.
    E) Increasing the ionic strength of a solution increases the solubility of salts in it.

79. The intermolecular forces in benzene at room temperature can be described as

    A) only covalent
    B) only electrostatic
    C) both covalent and electrostatic
    D) gravitational
    E) repulsive

GO ON TO THE NEXT PAGE

80. For citric acid $(C_6O_7H_8)$, $pK_{a1} = 3.13$, $pK_{a2} = 4.76$, $pK_{a3} = 6.40$. Which of the following statements about the relative concentrations of the listed species at pH = 2.0 is true?

I. $C_6O_7H_5^{3-}$
II. $C_6O_7H_6^{2-}$
III. $C_6O_7H_7^{1-}$
IV. $C_6O_7H_8$

A) I > II > III > IV
B) II > III > IV > I
C) IV > III > I > II
D) III > IV > II > I
E) IV > III > II > I

81. The reaction of benzoic acid with phosphorus tribromide yields which of the following?

A)

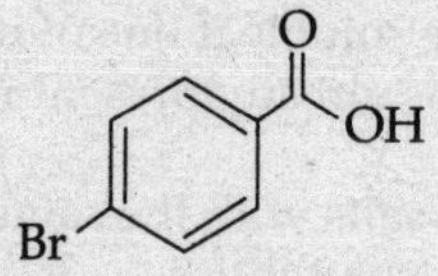

Br—⬡—C(=O)OH

B)

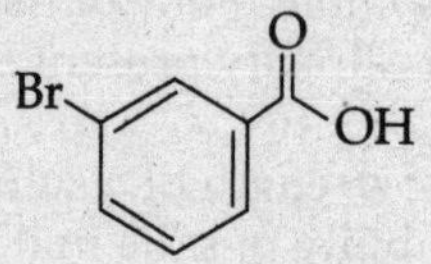

Br—⬡—C(=O)OH

C)

Br—⬡—C(=O)—Br

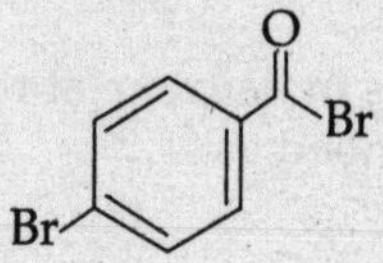

D)

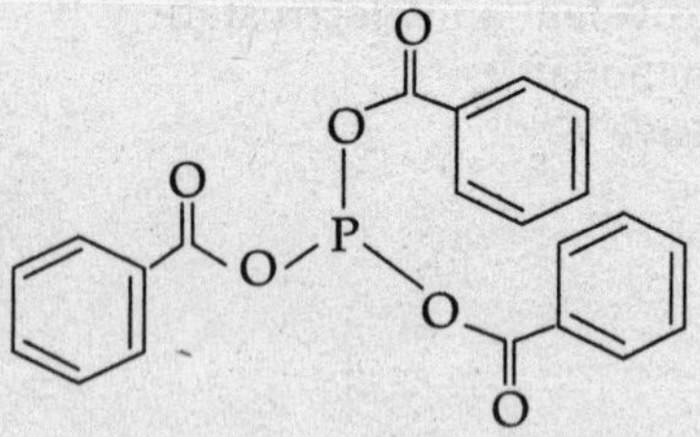

⬡—C(=O)—O—P(—O—C(=O)—⬡)—O—C(=O)—⬡

E)

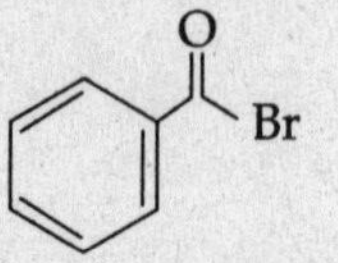

⬡—C(=O)—Br

82.

CH_3—C(=O)—H + I_2 $\xrightarrow[\text{H}_2\text{O}]{\text{NaOH}}$

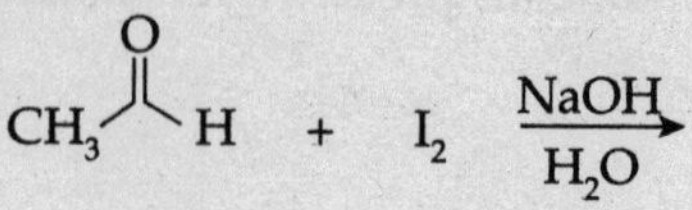

The iodoform reaction shown above gives which of the following as products/byproducts?

A)

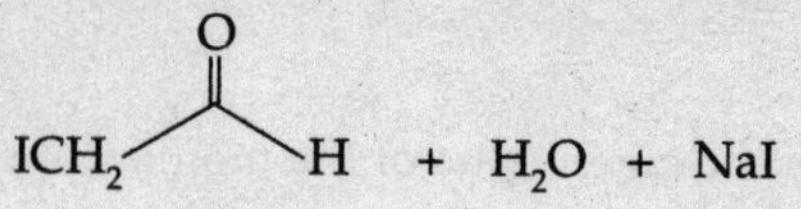

ICH_2—C(=O)—H + H_2O + NaI

B)

CH_3—C(=O)—I + H_2O + NaI

C)

ICH_2—C(=O)—I + H_2O

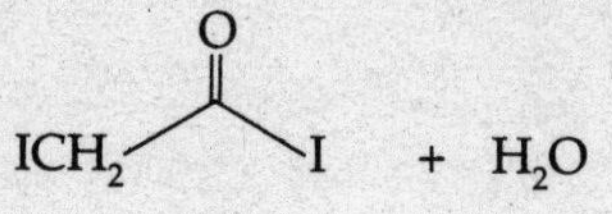

D)

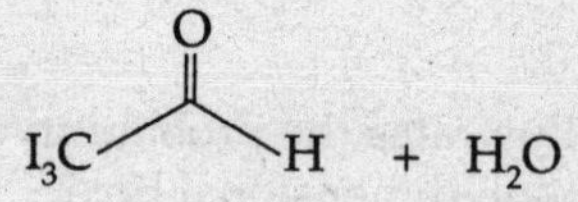

I_3C—C(=O)—H + H_2O

E)

$Na^{\oplus}O^{\ominus}$—C(=O)—H + I_3CH + H_2O

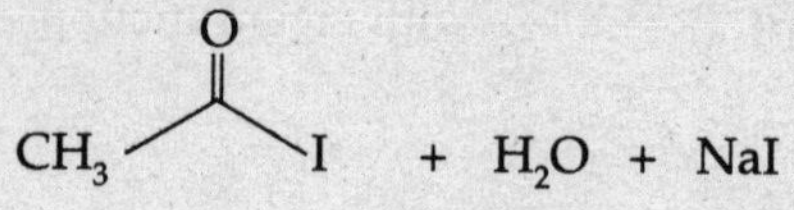

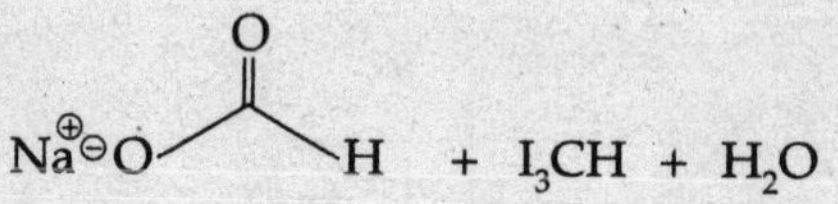

GO ON TO THE NEXT PAGE

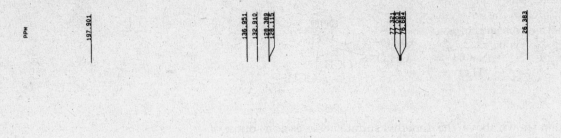

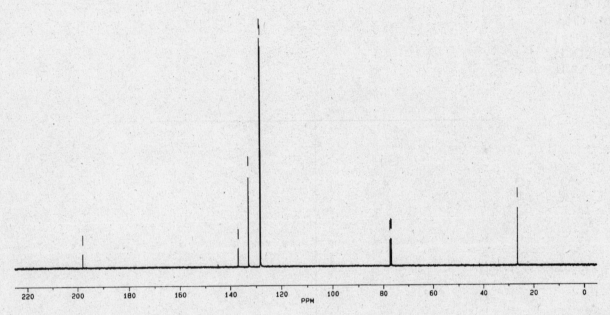

83. The 100-megahertz carbon nuclear magnetic resonance (proton decoupled) shown above is consistent with which of the following structures? (Ignore the 3 resonances at ~ 77ppm as they belong to the solvent, not the analyte.)

A) Ph—CH(OH)—CH₃

B) Ph—CHO

C) Ph—O—CH₂CH₃

D) Ph—C(O)—CH₃

E) 4-Br-C₆H₄—COOH

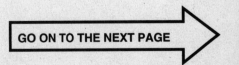

GO ON TO THE NEXT PAGE

84.

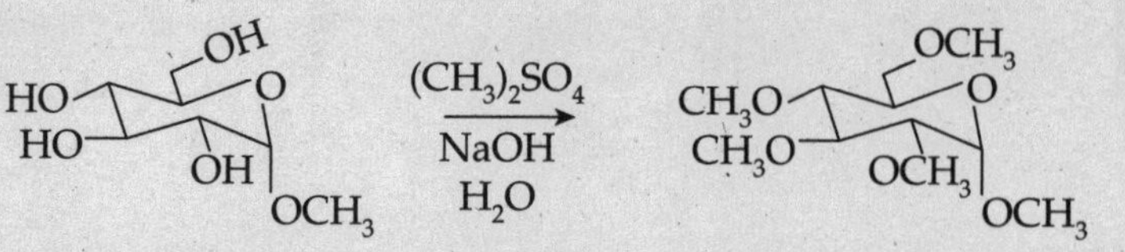

In the reaction shown above, the dimethyl sulfate behaves as a source of

A) CH_3^-
B) $CH_3 \cdot$
C) CH_3^+
D) $^+OCH_3$
E) $^-OCH_3$

85. I.

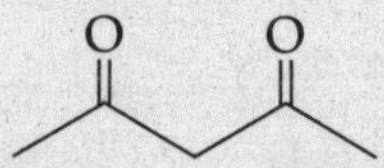

II.

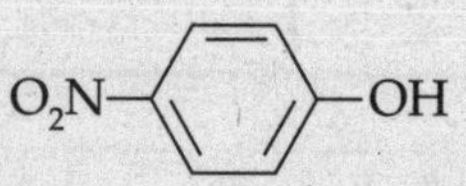

III.

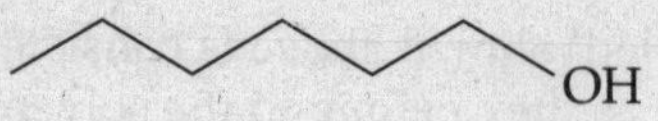

IV.

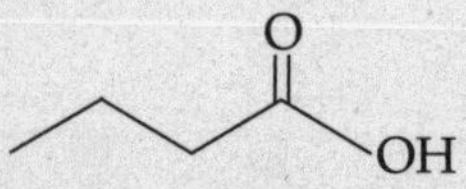

Which of the following indicates the order of decreasing acidity of the four molecules shown above?

A) III > I > II > IV
B) III > I > IV > II
C) III > II > I > IV
D) IV > I > II > III
E) IV > II > I > III

GO ON TO THE NEXT PAGE

86. 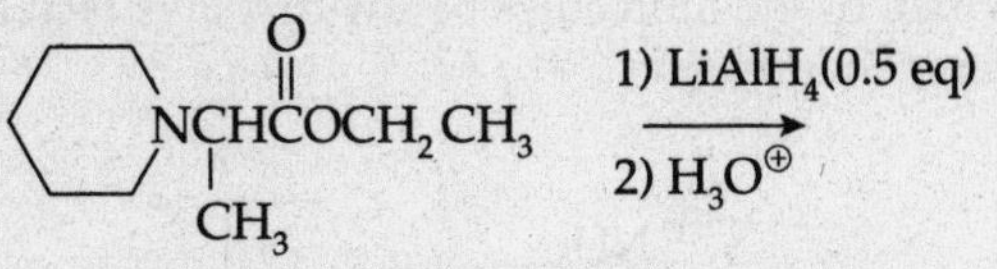
O
NCHCOCH2CH3
CH3
1) LiAlH4(0.5 eq)
2) H3O⊕

Which of the compounds below is obtained by the reaction shown above?

A) 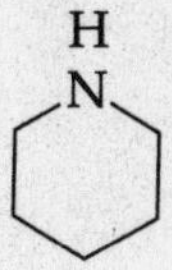
H
N

B) 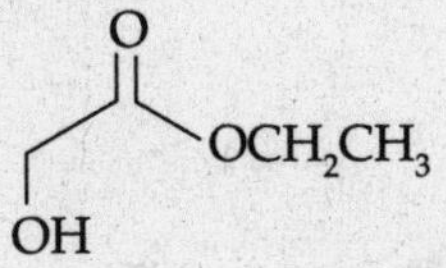
O
OCH2CH3
OH

C) 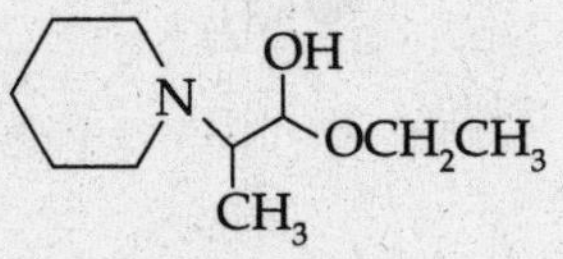
OH
N
OCH2CH3
CH3

D) 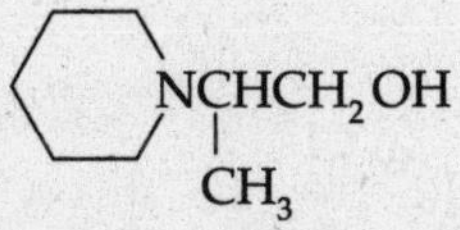
NCHCH2OH
CH3

E) 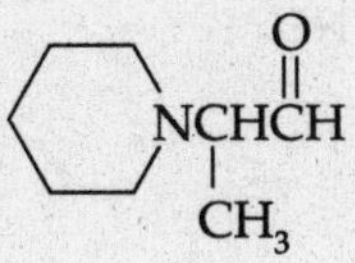
O
NCHCH
CH3

88. 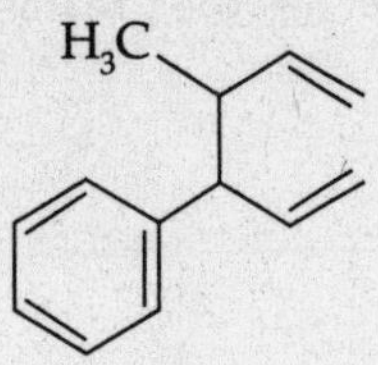
H3C

If the molecule above were to undergo a [3,3] sigmatropic rearrangement, which of the following would be the product?

A) 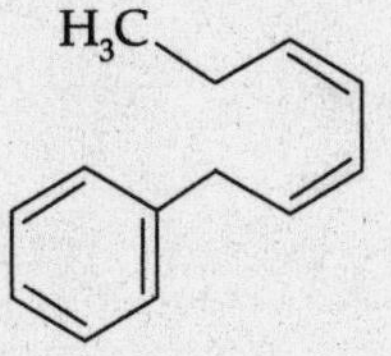
H3C

B) 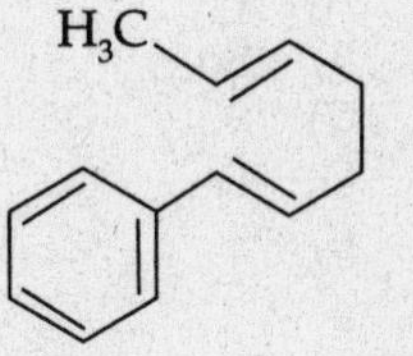
H3C

C) 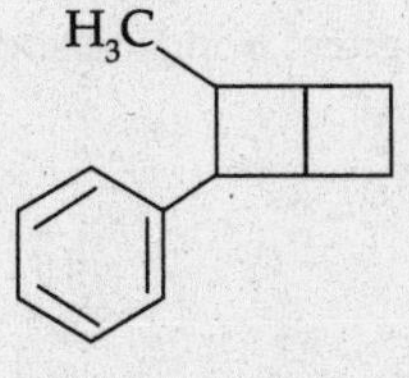
H3C

D) 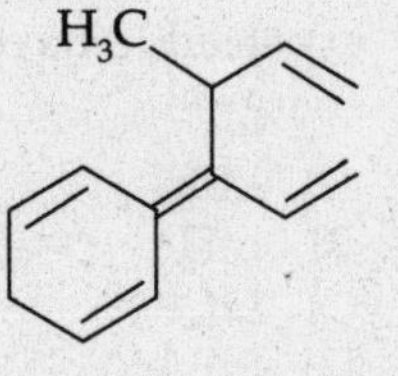
H3C

E) 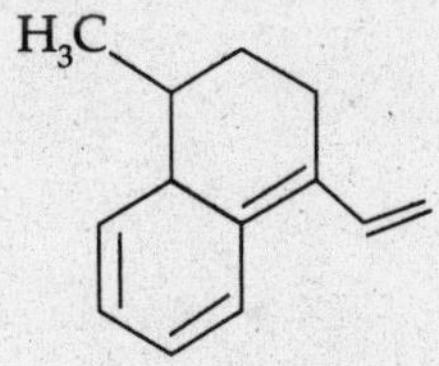
H3C

87. 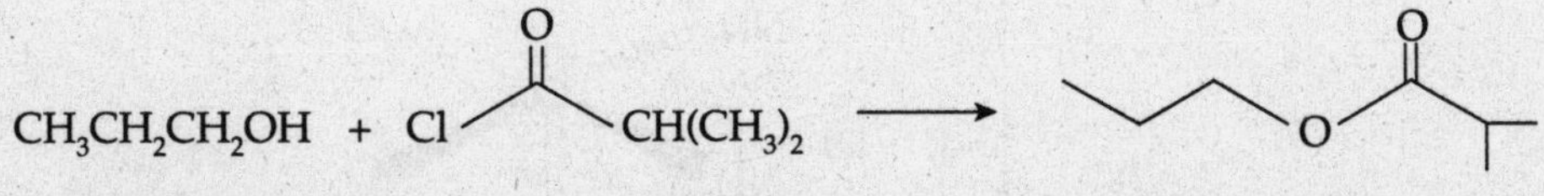
CH3CH2CH2OH + Cl
O
CH(CH3)2
O
O

Which of the following reaction categories best describes the reaction shown above?

A) amination
B) alkylation
C) acylation
D) oxidation
E) reduction

GO ON TO THE NEXT PAGE

89. Which of the following atoms has the greatest atomic radius?

    A) Al
    B) Li
    C) O
    D) K
    E) Br

90. Which of the following is the ground-state term symbol for a neon atom?

    A) ^1P_o
    B) ^1S_o
    C) $^2S_{1/2}$
    D) $^2D_{1/2}$
    E) $^1S_{3/2}$

91. Which of the following molecules would be expected to have the highest bond dissociation energy?

    A) LiBr
    B) LiH
    C) LiCl
    D) LiF
    E) LiI

92. Which of the molecules below displays facial stereochemistry?

A)
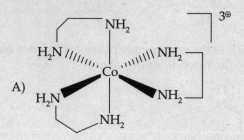

B)
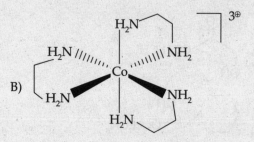

C)
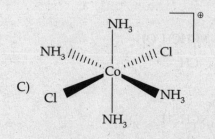

D)
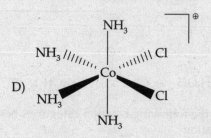

E)
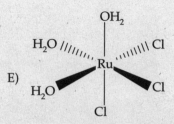

GO ON TO THE NEXT PAGE

93. According to the solvent system definition, which of the following is the strongest base?

A) CH_3CO_2H
B) NH_3
C) H_2SO_4
D) C_2H_5OH
E) H_2O

94. Which of the following is NOT a normal vibrational mode of BCl_3?

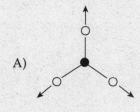

A)

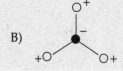

B)

C)

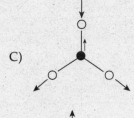

D)

E)

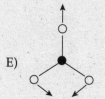

95. Approximately what percentage of NO molecules are in the ground vibrational state at 300 K?

A) 0
B) 25
C) 50
D) 75
E) 100

96. The lines in a rotational spectrum are not equally spaced due to

A) anharmonicity
B) antifugal repulsion
C) interelectronic repulsion
D) reduced mass
E) isotope effects

97. List the following molecules in order of increasing dipole moment.

I. H_2
II. CO
III. HCl
IV. NaCl

A) I < II < III < IV
B) II < I < III < IV
C) I < III < II < IV
D) IV < III < II < I
E) III < IV < II < I

98.

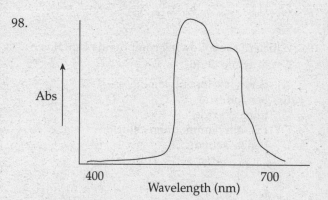

What is the most likely color of the substance whose UV-Vis spectrum is shown above?
A) red
B) black
C) blue
D) orange
E) colorless

GO ON TO THE NEXT PAGE

99. Assuming equal volumes, pressures, and temperatures, which gas contains the most particles?

A) H_2O
B) NH_3
C) NO
D) C = B
E) A = B = C

100. Which of the following reaction sequences offers the best combination of reagents to give the highest yield of methylamine, CH_3NH_2?

A) NH_3 + $ClMgCH_3$

B) NH_2–NH_2 +

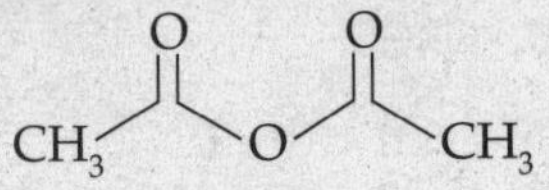

C) 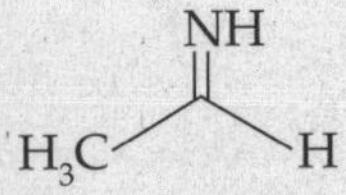 + $NaBH_4$

D) NH_3 + CH_3I
E) H_3CN_3 + $LiAlH_4$

101. Which of the following compounds contains a C≡N triple bond?

A) benzylcyclopentylamine
B) benzonitrile
C) phenyl azide
D) trimethylammonium chloride
E) benzaldehyde

102. The Dieckmann condensation of diethyl hexane-dioate, $CH_3CH_2OC(O)CH_2CH_2CH_2CH_2C(O)OCH_2CH_3$, in the presence of sodium metal leads to formation of which of the following products?

A)

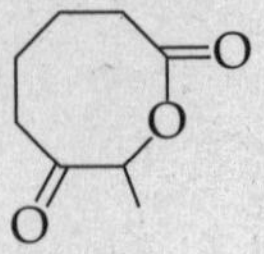

B)

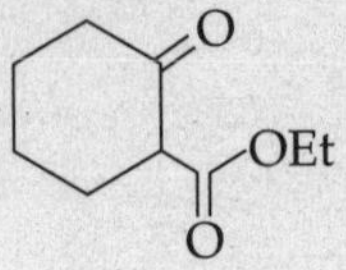

C)

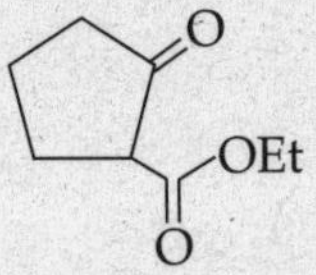

D)

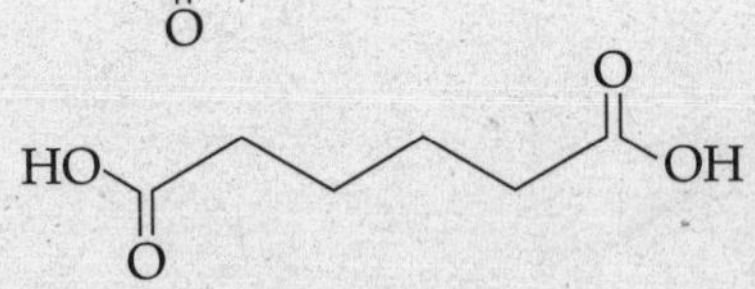

E)

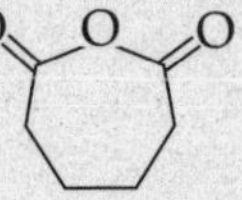

GO ON TO THE NEXT PAGE

103. Which of the following represents the correct structure of the dipeptide valylvaline (val-val)?

A)

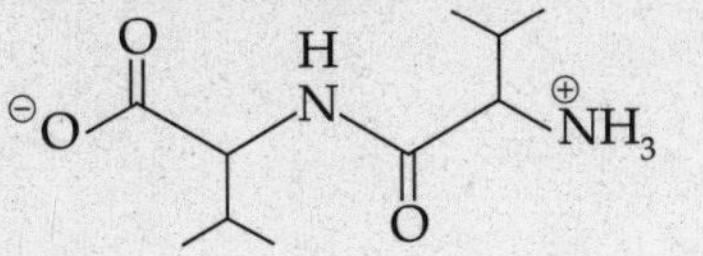

B)

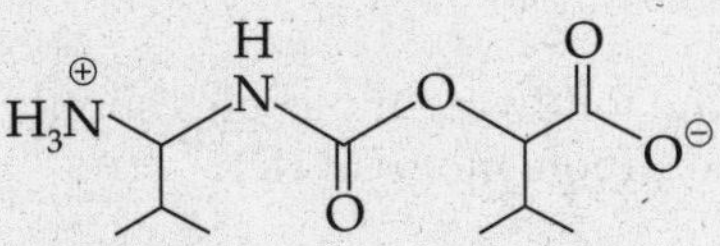

C)

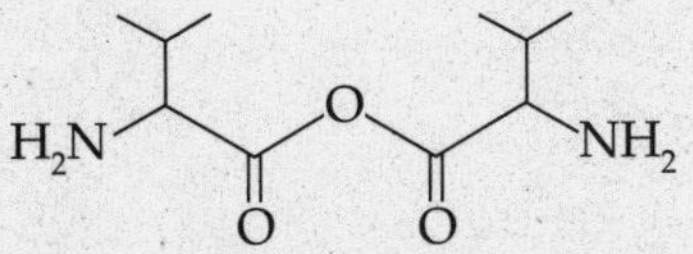

D)

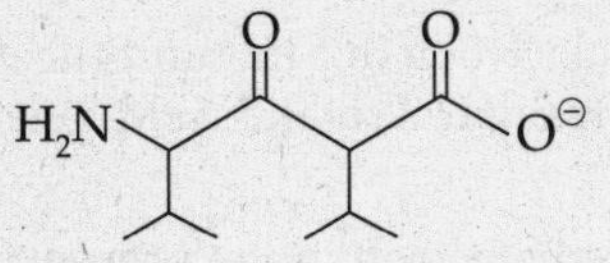

E)

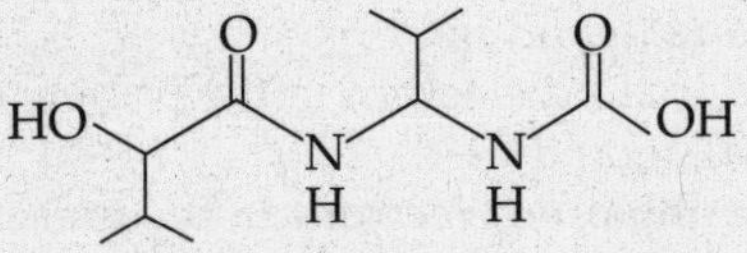

104.

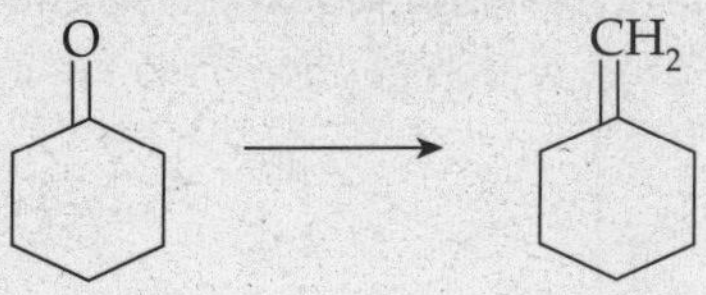

The reaction shown above could successfully be performed using which of the following reagents?

A) Ph_3PCH_2

B)

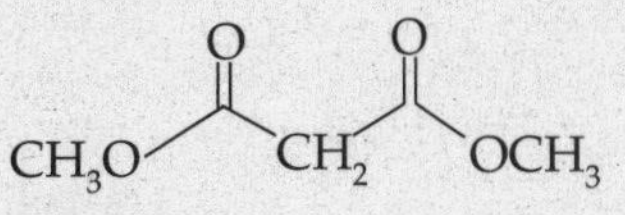

C) CH_2Br_2
D) $CH_2=O$
E) PCC

105. A 5g sample of menthol in 100 mL of ethanol has an optical rotation of +2.46° at 20°C using a 10-cm sample tube and a sodium lamp (D line, $\lambda = 589.3$ nm). What is the specific rotation of menthol?

A) −49.2°
B) +49.2°
C) +2.46°
D) −2.46°
E) +4.92°

GO ON TO THE NEXT PAGE

106. Which of the reaction sequences below produces

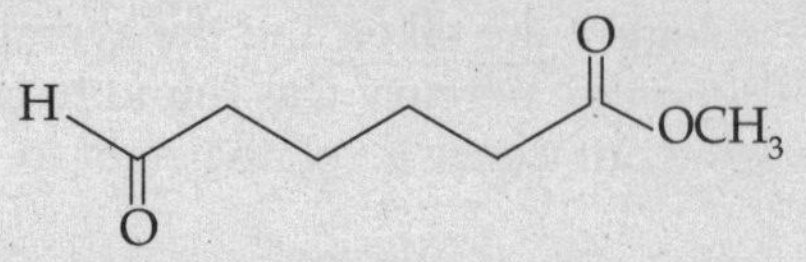

H
O
O
OCH3

as the major product?

A) 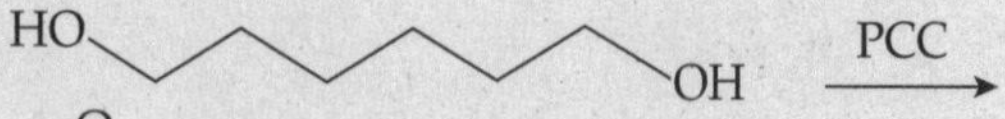

HO
OH
PCC

B) 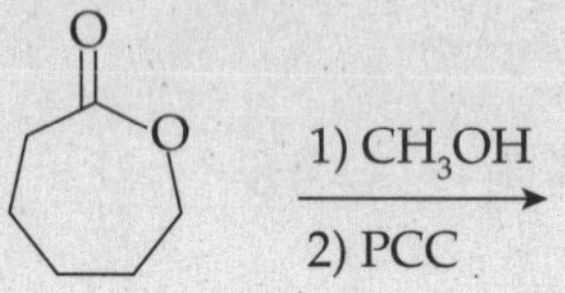

O
O
1) CH3OH
2) PCC

C) 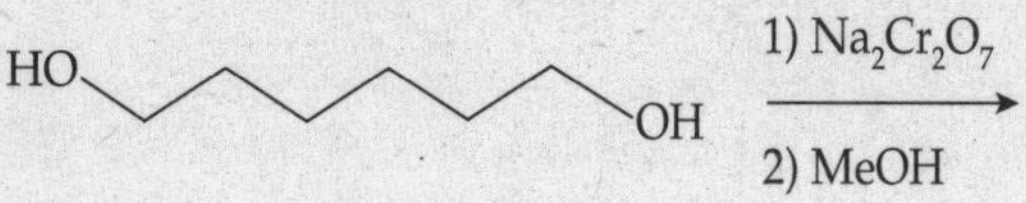

HO
OH
1) Na2Cr2O7
2) MeOH

D) 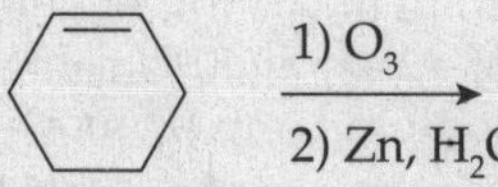

1) O3
2) Zn, H2O

E) 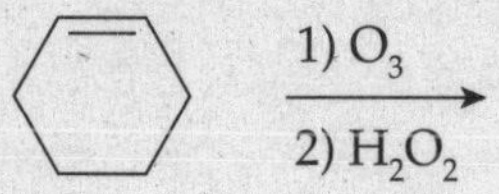

1) O3
2) H2O2

107. $SnCl_4 + 2Li$ Æ $SnCl_4L_2$

The acid-base reaction illustrated above is best described by which of the following definitions?

A) Brönsted-Lowry definition
B) Lux-Flood definition
C) Lewis definition
D) Solvent system definition
E) Usanovich definition

108. Which of the following forms an acidic solution upon dissolving in water?

A) N_2
B) Ar
C) O_2
D) CO
E) CO_2

109. Which of the following molecules should have the greatest dipole moment (D)?

A) LiH
B) CO
C) BrF
D) NO
E) O_2

110. If there are 5 *d* electrons in Mn^{2+} and the *d* orbitals are split by a tetrahedral ligand field, one could expect to find

A) one unpaired electron in the presence of a strong ligand field
B) one unpaired electron in the presence of a weak ligand field
C) three unpaired electrons in the presence of a strong ligand field
D) three unpaired electrons in the presence of a weak ligand field
E) five unpaired electrons in the presence of a strong ligand field

111. 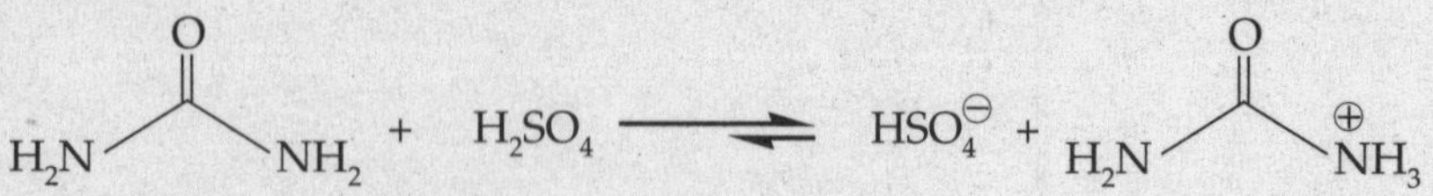

O
H2N
NH2
+
H2SO4
HSO4
+
O
H2N
NH3

In the equilibrium shown above, hydrogen sulfate ion acts as

A) a catalyst
B) an acid
C) a base
D) a spectator ion
E) an oxidizing agent

GO ON TO THE NEXT PAGE

112. Which of the following is the most common oxidation state of the lanthanide elements?

A) +1
B) −1
C) +2
D) −2
E) +3

113. In the electrochemical cell described by the following schematic, what reaction occurs at the anode? $Zn(s)|ZnCl_2(s)|Cl^-(aq)|Cl_2(l)|C(s)$

A) $Zn^\circ \rightarrow Zn^{2+} + 2e^-$
B) $Zn^{2+} + 2e^- \rightarrow Zn^\circ$
C) $Cl_2 + 2e^- \rightarrow 2Cl^-$
D) $2Cl^- \rightarrow Cl_2 + 2e^-$
E) $Zn + Cl_2 \rightarrow ZnCl_2$

114. Vessel A (volume = 300 mL) is charged with 150 torr of ethylene at room temperature. Using ligand N_2 as a refrigerant, the gas is quantitatively condensed into vessel B (volume = 5 mL). What is the pressure inside vessel B if it is sealed and warmed to room temperature?

A) 1,500 torr
B) 3,000 torr
C) 6,000 torr
D) 9,000 torr
E) 45,000 torr

115. A 10.0 ± 0.1 mL sample of trimethyl aluminum was found to have a mass of 7.52 ± 0.08g. What is the percent uncertainty in the density calculated from these values?

A) 14%
B) 7.2%
C) 1.4%
D) 0.14%
E) 0.72%

116. The concentration of mercury in a coastal stream was tested over five years. During this time, 260 measurements were taken and the average concentration of mercury was found to be 20 ppb. At the 95% confidence level, the error in this measurement is 4 ppb. What is the relationship between the confidence level and experimental uncertainty?

A) 95% of the measurements were between 16 and 24 ppb.
B) There is a 95% chance that the true concentration is between 16 and 24 ppb.
C) The true mean must be between 22.8 and 15.2 ppb.
D) The experimenters are 95% sure that the error is 4 ppb.
E) None of the above.

117. Solute A has a partition coefficient of 4 between diethyl ether and H_2O. If 100 mL of a 0.1 M aqueous solution of solute A is extracted twice with 100 mL of diethyl ether, what is the molarity of A in the aqueous layer?

A) $1.7 \times 10^{-3} M$
B) $1.6 \times 10^{-2} M$
C) $5.6 \times 10^{-2} M$
D) $6.3 \times 10^{-2} M$
E) $5.6 \times 10^{-3} M$

GO ON TO THE NEXT PAGE

118. Which of the following rate laws is consistent with the mechanism proposed for the conversion $NO_3 + NO \longrightarrow 2NO_2$?

Proposed mechanism:

$$NO_2 + NO_3 \xrightarrow{\ k_1\ } N_2O_5$$

$$NO + N_2O_5 \xrightarrow{\ k_2\ } 3NO_2$$

A) $\dfrac{d[NO_3]}{dt} = k_1 k_2 [NO_2][NO_3]$

B) $\dfrac{d[NO_3]}{dt} = -k_1 k_2 [NO_2][NO_3]$

C) $\dfrac{d[NO_3]}{dt} = -k_1 k_2 [NO_3][NO]$

D) $\dfrac{d[NO_3]}{dt} = -k_1 [NO_2][NO_3]$

E) $\dfrac{d[NO_3]}{dt} = k_1 [NO_2][NO_3]$

119. The classical wave equation is defined by which of the following [$u(x,t)$ is the amplitude, v is the speed]?

A) $\dfrac{\partial^2 u}{\partial x^2} = \dfrac{1}{v}\dfrac{\partial^2 u}{\partial t^2}$

B) $\dfrac{\partial^2 u}{\partial t^2} = \dfrac{1}{v}\dfrac{\partial^2 u}{\partial t^2}$

C) $\dfrac{\partial^2 u}{\partial x^2} = v\dfrac{\partial^2 u}{\partial t^2}$

D) $\dfrac{\partial^2 u}{\partial t^2} = v\dfrac{\partial^2 u}{\partial t^2}$

E) $\dfrac{\partial^2 u}{\partial t^2} = t\dfrac{\partial^2 v}{\partial t^2}$

120. For the following reaction, $2P_2(g) \Leftrightarrow P_4(g)$ a decrease in volume (at constant temperature) will have what effect on the system?

A) no change
B) increase in the partial pressure of P_4
C) increase in the partial pressure of P_2
D) increase in the partial pressure of BOTH P_2 and P_4
E) decrease in the partial pressure of BOTH P_2 and P_4

121. Which reaction best illustrates a redox reaction?

A) $H_2S(aq) \rightarrow H^+(aq) + SH^-(aq)$
B) $H_2(g) + Cl_2 \rightarrow 2HCl(g)$
C) $CaCO_3(s) \rightarrow CaO(s) + CO_2(g)$
D) $K_2O(s) + CO_2(g) \rightarrow K_2CO_3(s)$
E) $MgO(s) + SO_3(g) \rightarrow MgSO_4(s)$

122. Calculate the change in entropy when 1.00 mol of H_2O is vaporized under ambient conditions.

$$[\Delta H_{vap} = 40.66 \text{ kJ/mol}]$$

A) 109 J/K·mol
B) 52 J/K·mol
C) 520 J/K·mol
D) 1090 J/K·mol
E) 5.20 J/K·mol

123. The number of mictrostates (Ω) available to a system of N particles confined to a volume (V) can be expressed by the equation, $\Omega = (cV)^N$ where c is a constant. This is best explained by the fact that

A) Entropy is an extensive property.
B) Entropy is an intrusive property.
C) The number of states scales linearly with particle number.
D) The number of states is independent of particle number.
E) Enthalpy is an intensive property.

GO ON TO THE NEXT PAGE

124. Atomic absorption spectroscopy (AA) was used to analyze the calcium content of milk. Solution 1 was prepared by mixing 10.00 mL of milk with 5.00 mL of a 0.1 mmolar solution of Ca^{2+}, then diluting to a total volume of 100.0 mL. Solution 1 gave an absorbance of 3.0 units. Solution 2 was prepared by diluting 10.00 mL of milk to 100.0 mL and gave an absorbance of 2.0 units. What was the concentration of Ca^{2+} in the original milk sample?

A) 1.0×10^{-4} M
B) 5.0×10^{-5} M
C) 2.0×10^{-4} M
D) 1.0×10^{-3} M
E) 1.5×10^{-4} M

125. Which of the following indications would be most useful in titrating a strong acid with a strong base?

A) Cresol purple, transition range = 1.2–2.8
B) Bromothymol blue, transition range = 6.0–7.6
C) Phenolphthalein, transition range = 8.0–9.6
D) Alizarin yellow, transition range = 10.1–12.0
E) Litmus, transition range = 5.0–8.0

126. The units on the x axis of a mass spectrum are

A) mz
B) m
C) cm^{-1}
D) m/z
E) ppm

127. Which of the following solids is most ionic?

A) C_{60}
B) Mn
C) SiO_2
D) BN
E) $NaBH_4$

128. The concentration of ions in solution can be described by the solubility product (K_{sp}) for the salt and the activities (δ) of the ions. Which of the following expressions describes the concentration of Cr^{3+} in a solution of $Cr(IO_3)_3$?

A) $\left[Cr^{3+}\right] = \dfrac{K_{sp}\left[IO_3^-\right]^3}{\delta Cr^{3+}\delta IO_3^-}$

B) $\left[Cr^{3+}\right] = \dfrac{K_{sp}}{\delta Cr^{3+}\left[IO_3^-\right]^3\delta IO_3^-}$

C) $\left[Cr^{3+}\right] = \dfrac{K_{sp}\delta Cr^{3+}\left(\delta IO_3^-\right)^3}{\left[IO_3^-\right]^3}$

D) $\left[Cr^{3+}\right] = \dfrac{K_{sp}}{\delta Cr^{3+}\left[IO_3^-\right]^3\left(\delta IO_3^-\right)^3}$

E) $\left[Cr^{3+}\right] = \dfrac{K_{sp}\delta Cr^{3+}\delta IO_3^-}{\left[IO_3^-\right]^3}$

GO ON TO THE NEXT PAGE

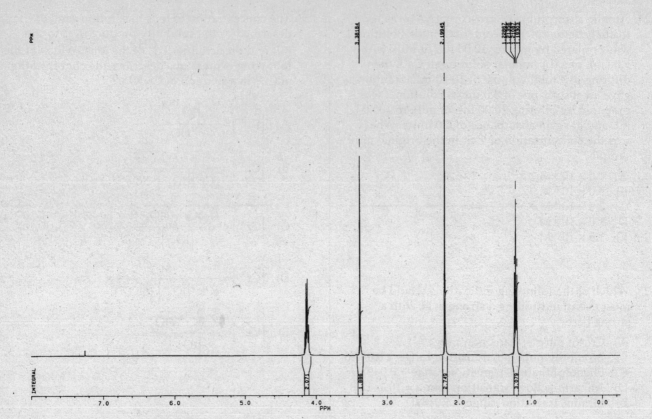

129.

The 400-megahertz proton nuclear magnetic resonance spectrum above is consistent with which of the following structures?

A)

B)

C)

D)

E)

GO ON TO THE NEXT PAGE

130. Which of the following is a Haworth projection?

A)

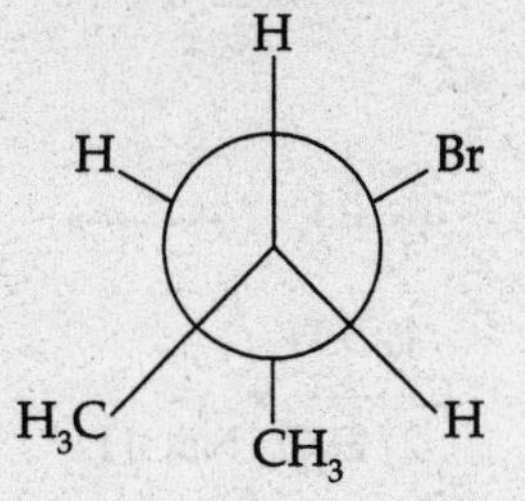

B)

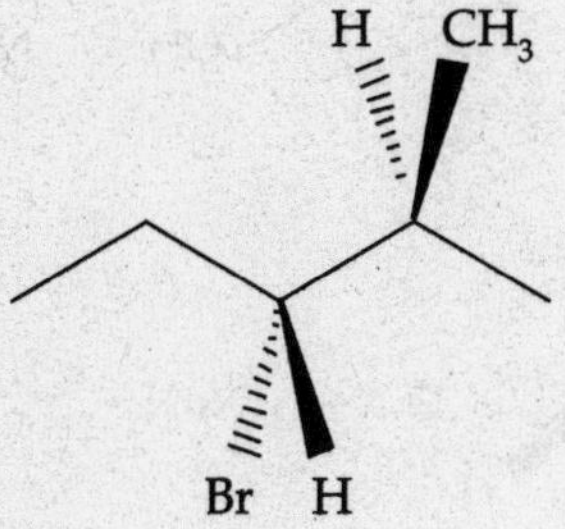

C)

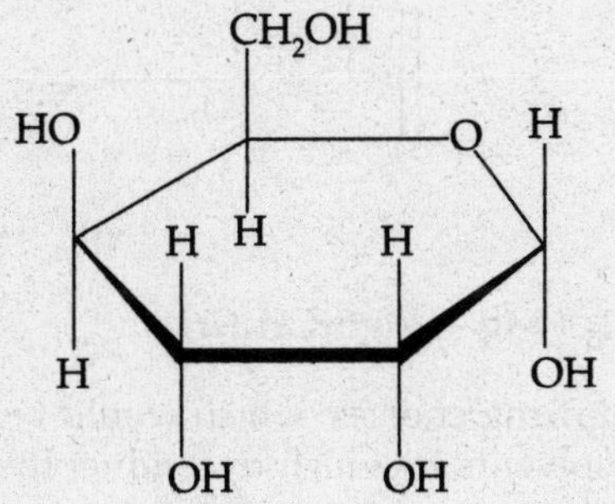

D) 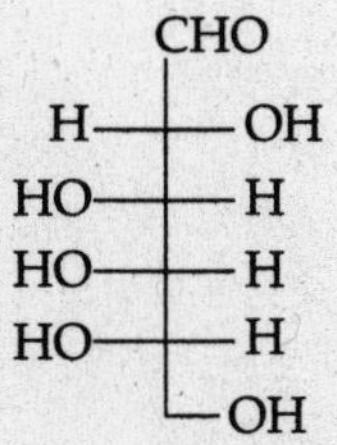
$$\begin{array}{c} CHO \\ H{-}OH \\ HO{-}H \\ HO{-}H \\ HO{-}H \\ {-}OH \end{array}$$

E)

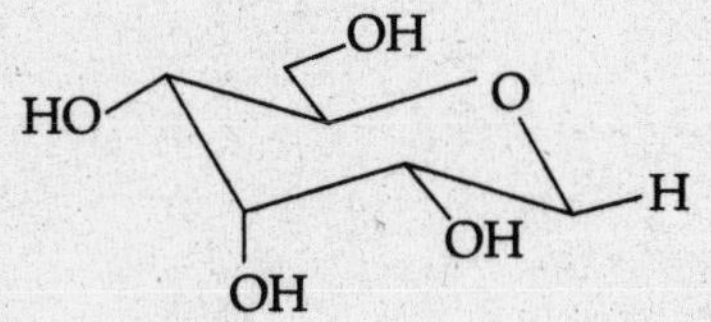

131. I. $CH_3CH_2CH{=}CH_2$

II.

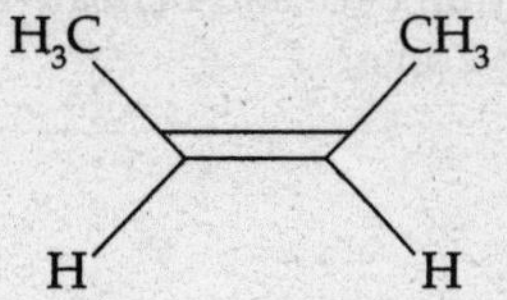

III.

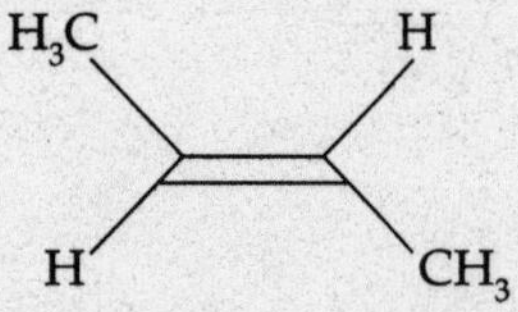

Rank the three alkenes shown above in order of increasing heats of hydrogenation.

A) I < II < III
B) I < III < II
C) II < I < III
D) II < III < I
E) III < II < I

GO ON TO THE NEXT PAGE

132. Which of the following represents the product of an aldol condensation between benzaldehyde and 3,3-dimethylbutan-2-one?

A)

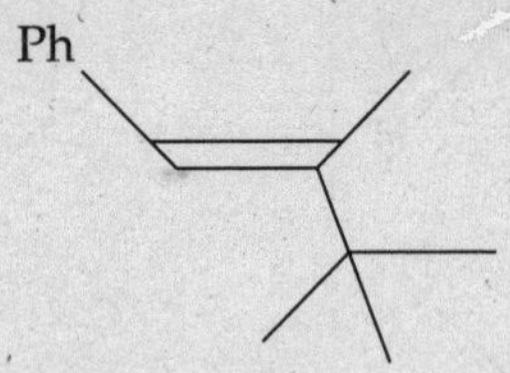

B)

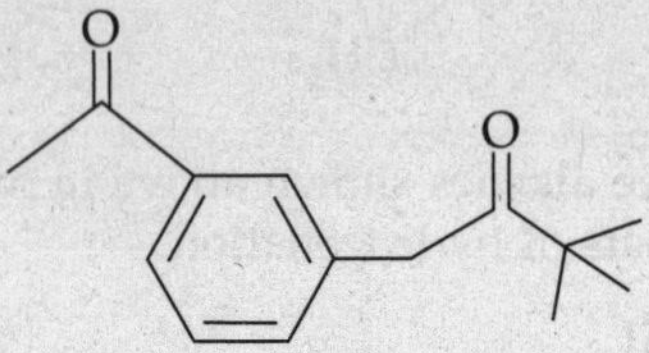

C) 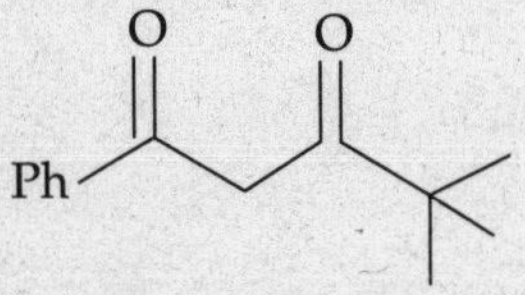 Ph

D) 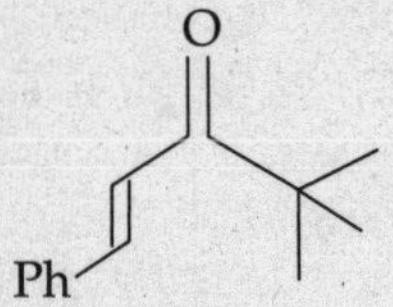 Ph

E) 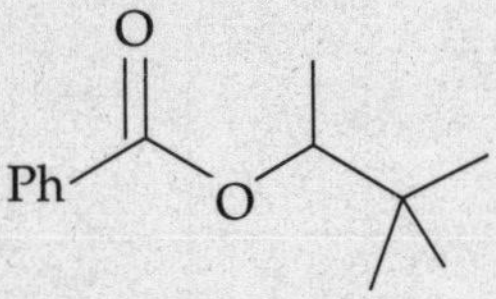 Ph

133. Which of the following reactions is known for being regioselective?

A)

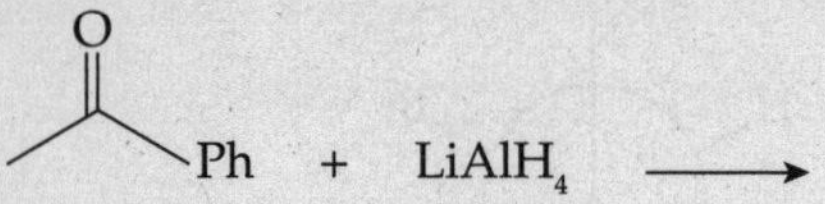

$$\text{Ph} \quad + \quad \text{LiAlH}_4 \quad \longrightarrow$$

B)

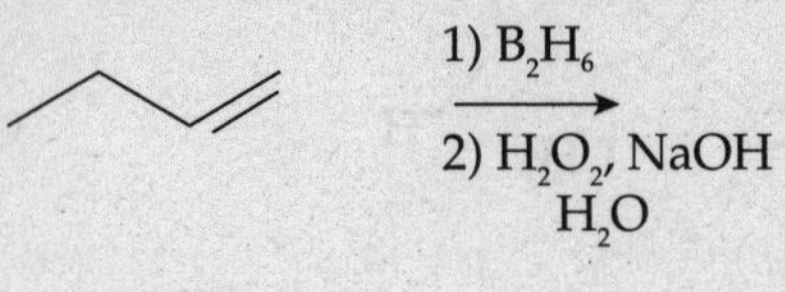

$$\xrightarrow[\begin{array}{c}2)\ H_2O_2,\ NaOH \\ H_2O\end{array}]{1)\ B_2H_6}$$

C) HO——————OH + NaH——→

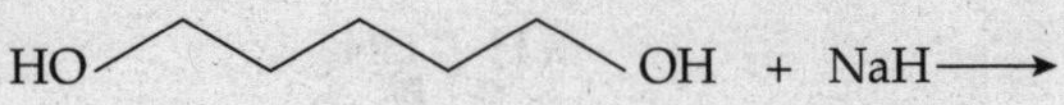

D)

$$H_3C \quad \overset{Br}{\underset{H}{\bigwedge}} \quad D \quad + \quad NaN_3 \quad \longrightarrow$$

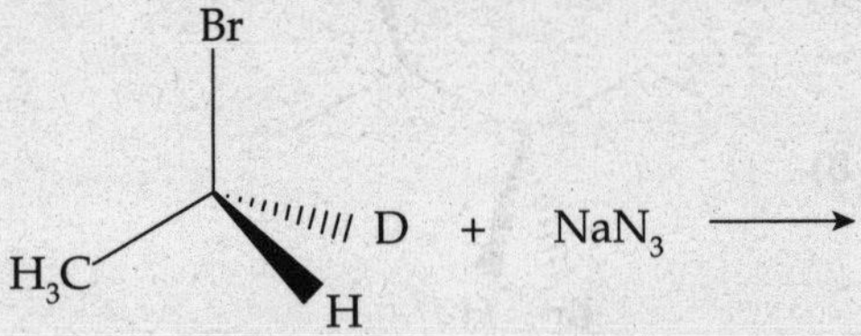

E)

$$+ \quad \longrightarrow$$

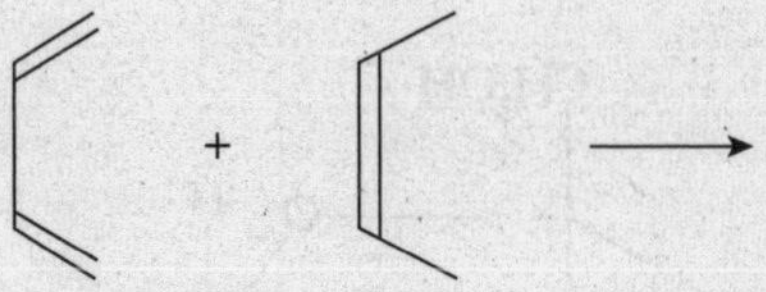

134. $BrCH_2CH_3 + Mg \rightarrow MgBrCH_2CH_3$

Of the following choices, which would be the best choice of solvents in which to conduct the reaction shown above?

A) acetone
B) acetonitrile
C) ether
D) methanol
E) ethyl acetate

GO ON TO THE NEXT PAGE

135. Which of the following compounds would NOT become partially deuterated upon treatment with NaOD and D_2O?

A)

B) $EtNH_2$
C) Ph–O–Me

D) $\sim\sim SH$

E) (structure with CO_2H group)

136. Which of the following sets of reaction conditions will turn a hydroxyl group into a better leaving group?

A) KOH, H_2O_2
B) Cl–SiMe$_3$

C) Cl–C(=O)–CH$_3$

D) (tosyl chloride structure) , (pyridine structure)

E) HS$\sim\sim$SH,   NaOH

137. Predict the geometry of the molecule ClF$_3$ based on VSEPR theory.

A) trigonal planar
B) pyramidal
C) seesaw
D) T-shaped
E) Linear

138. Which of the following does NOT describe an atomic orbital with principal quantum number (n) equal to 3.

A) dz^2
B) $dz^2 + y^2$
C) dzy
D) dzz
E) dyz

139. What is the bond order for the species $Cl_2{}^+$?

A) 0
B) $\dfrac{1}{2}$
C) 1
D) $1\dfrac{1}{2}$
E) 2

140. Lithium nitrate has the calcite structure (rhombohedral $R\bar{3}c$). What is the coordination number of the metal atom?

A) 2
B) 4
C) 5
D) 6
E) 8

141. $^2_1H + ^1_1H \rightarrow ^3_2He + ?$

In the reaction shown above, which of the following is a byproduct of the reaction?

A) gamma ray
B) proton
C) electron
D) neutron
E) positron

STOP
IF YOU FINISH BEFORE TIME IS CALLED,
YOU MAY CHECK YOUR WORK
ON THIS SECTION.

DO NOT GO ON
UNTIL YOU ARE TOLD TO DO SO.

V. Answers and Explanations to The Princeton Review GRE Chemistry Diagnostic Exam

1. C Boron is sp^2 hybridized since it has three substituents and an empty p-orbital. This requires a trigonal planar geometry.

2. C H_2S is very soft since it is charge neutral and sulfur is large and polarizable. This eliminates choices A, B, and E. SO_3^{2-} is softer than O^{2-} since it is resonance stabilized.

3. E The electron configuration for W is [Xe] $4f^{14}5d^46s^2$. The four unpaired electrons are in the $5d$ orbitals.

4.

   is an excellent reducing agent since it easily loses an electron to form napthalene.

5. C Ionization potential, the energy required to remove an electron from an atom in the gas phase, roughly tracks with electronegativity. Therefore H (choice C) is the best answer.

6. A Hydroboration/oxidation of an alkene results in the formation of the anti-Markovnikov (less substituted) alcohol.

7. D Epimers are stereoisomers that differ at one and only one stereocenter.

8. C The term "exo" is used for bicyclic systems to denote whether a substituent on a bridge is on the side of the smaller bridge. "Endo" refers to a substituent on a bridge that is on the side of the larger bridge.

9. B Choices B, C, D, and E all depict carbocation character at the para position. However, choice D is a bad resonance form since N does not have an octet. C and E are poor choices since there is a negative charge on carbon in each of the choices.

10. E Ozonolysis followed by a reductive workup cleaves alkenes to form aldehydes. It does not disturb stereochemistry in the carbon chain.

11. A This is an ordinary S_N2 reaction.

12. E The acylium is most likely formed when the strong Lewis acid ($AlCl_3$) removes the Cl^- from acetyl chloride.

13. C Potassium hydroxide is very hygroscopic, and its weight is difficult to determine accurately. This is why KOH solutions for weak acid/strong base titrations are always "standardized."

14. D The key to this answer is the cyclic nature of the experiment. A linear voltage ramp is applied between t_0 and t_1. Between t_1 and t_2 the potential is brought back to the starting value. None of the other graphs show a cyclic potential.

15. C According to the Henderson-Hasselbach equation, when pH = pK_a, [HA] = [A$^-$]. Hence, a buffer is best able to resist changes in pH ranges near its pK_a.

16. B A Brönsted acid is a proton donor. All of the compounds but B_2H_6 have acidic protons. Although B_2H_6 is electron-deficient (Lewis acidic), it cannot sacrifice any protons and therefore is not a Brönsted acid.

17. D When [B] = [A], $Q = 1$. This means that $\Delta G = RT \ln 1/K$, which is easily rearranged to $\Delta G = -RT \ln K$. This is familiar as the expression for $\Delta G°$.

18. E This is the diffusion limit, which is how fast the species can come together in solution. Notice that the units are $m^{-1}s^{-1}$, which is indicative of a bimolecular reaction.

19. D Starting with the familiar form for kinetic energy, $K = \frac{1}{2}mv^2$ (where m = mass and v = linear velocity), we can make a few simple substitutions to arrive at the expression for a rigid rotator. The velocity of a rotating particle has units of radians/second and is called angular velocity (ω). This is related to linear velocity by the following expression $v = r\omega_{rot}$ (where r is the radius of rotation). The moment of inertia (I) is given by $I = mr^2$. Using simple algebraic substitution, we arrive at $K = \frac{1}{2} I\omega^2$.

20. C An intensive property is one which is independent of the sample size. Of the properties listed, mass (b) and volume (a) are clearly not intensive because they are measures of size. Energy (d) is proportional to size, so it is also not intensive. Hence, of the properties listed, only temperature is intensive.

21. E Both are statements of the first law of thermodynamics.

22. A The expression $\ln k = \ln A - \dfrac{E_a}{RT}$ can easily be rearranged to the more familiar $k = Ae^{\frac{-Ea}{RT}}$. Both expressions give a linear plot of $\ln k$ vs. $\dfrac{1}{T}$, which is the empirical observation that underlies the Arrhenius equation.

23. B The Bohr model relies on two assumptions: First, the force holding the electron in a circular orbit around the nucleus is supplied by the electrostatic attraction between the proton and the electron: $\dfrac{e^2}{4\pi\varepsilon_0 r^2} = \dfrac{mv^2}{r}$.

Second, angular momentum is quantized: $mvr = n\hbar$, $n = 1, 2, \ldots$. Combining these assumptions gives B.

24. C Like the Born-Oppenheimer approximation, the Frank-Condon principle states that because nuclei are so much more massive than electrons, electronic motion is almost instantaneous relative to nuclear motion. This allows us to calculate the probabilities (and hence, intensities) of vibronic transitions from the individual electronic and vibrational transitions.

25. D The complete Schrodinger equation for the He atom includes three terms, two of which are hydrogenic Hamiltonians and one of which accounts for the interaction of the two electrons with each other. It is this third term that makes an exact solution possible.

26. A $\Delta G_{sys} < \varnothing$

$$G = H - TS$$

$$\Delta S_{surr} = \frac{\Delta H_{sys}}{T} \qquad\qquad \Delta H_{sys} = -T\Delta S_{surr}$$

$$\Delta G = -T\Delta S_{surr} - T\Delta S_{sys} = -T\Delta S_{tot} \leq \varnothing$$

$\Delta G_{sys} = 0$ is reversible.

27. A

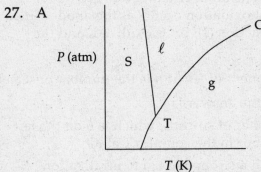

This is easiest by reasoning that the solid is favored at high pressure and low temperature, the liquid is intermediate, and the gas is favored at low pressure and high temperature.

28. E   Using $K = \frac{-1}{V}\left(\frac{\partial V}{\partial P}\right)_T$

$$PV = nRT$$

$$V = \frac{nRT}{P}$$

$$\left(\frac{\partial V}{\partial P}\right)_T = \frac{-nRT}{P^2}$$

$$K = \frac{-nRT}{VP^2}$$

This expression simplifies to

$$K = \frac{nRT}{nRTp^{-1}p^{-2}} = \frac{1}{P}.$$

29. A $V_1 = \dfrac{nRT}{P_1} = \dfrac{(1\text{ mol})\left(0.08206\,\dfrac{L\cdot atm}{mol\cdot K}\right)(100\,K)}{100\text{ atm}} = 0.0821L$

$V_2 = 10V_1 = (0.0821L)(10) = 0.821L$

Work $= W = -P_{ext}\Delta V = -(1.0\text{ atm})(0.821 - 0.0821)$

$= 0.739\ L\cdot atm$

30. B Answer III can be eliminated immediately because vaporizing an ion (like Br^-) is a very high energy process. The other two answers are distinguished by remembering that oxidation occurs at the anode. Since electrons appear as a product in reaction (I), Br^- is oxidized, and the reaction must occur at the anode.

31. E Averaging scans gives an improvement of $\sqrt{n}$ (if n is the number of scans). In this case, $n = 36$, so $\sqrt{n} = 6$, and the answer is E.

32. B This is most obvious from the number of silicons, which is 6 on the left and appears nowhere on the right but in the complex $CaSiO_3$.

33. A In the titration of a strong acid with a strong base, a neutralization reaction occurs. For example, $HCl + NaOH \rightarrow H_2O + NaCl$, clearly, at equivalence, pH = 7.0 (neglecting small variations from dissolved atmospheric CO_2). In titrating a weak acid with a strong base, the following reaction occurs: $HA + NaOH \rightarrow H_2O + A^-Na^+$. Here the conjugate base of the weak acid is present in solution at the equivalence point, raising the pH above 7.0. A similar case can be made for the strong acid/weak base titration.

34. B The amino group directs to the ortho and para positions due to resonance and makes the aromatic ring much more electron-rich, which is strongly activating.

35. A β-Keto esters decarboxylate upon hydrolysis by loss of CO_2 from the carboxylic acid intermediate.

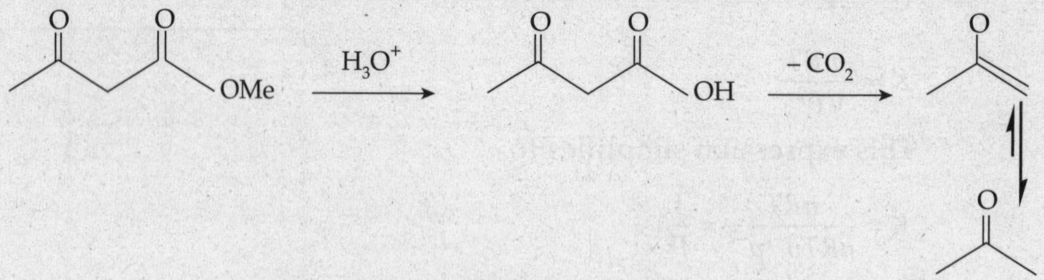

36. A N-Bromosuccinimide is a good source of $Br\cdot$ and monobrominates the allylic position of alkenes. It does not add across alkenes.

37. D Only hemiketal (D) is an intermediate in the formation of the ketal.

38. C Two substituents are said to be geminal if they are on the same carbon atom, this eliminates choice A. Two substituents are said to be vicinal if they are on adjacent carbon atoms, this eliminates choice B. The allylic position is one carbon removed from an alkene, and the acetylenic position is that of the carbon atom of a $C \equiv C$ triple bond. The indicated H atom, which is attached to the carbon atom of a $C = C$ double bond is in the vinylic position.

39. B Since radicals are deficient 1 electron, like carbocations, they are more stable when they are more substituted.

40. B The radical cation of 2-hexanone is likely to fragment in a mass spectrometer as illustrated below:

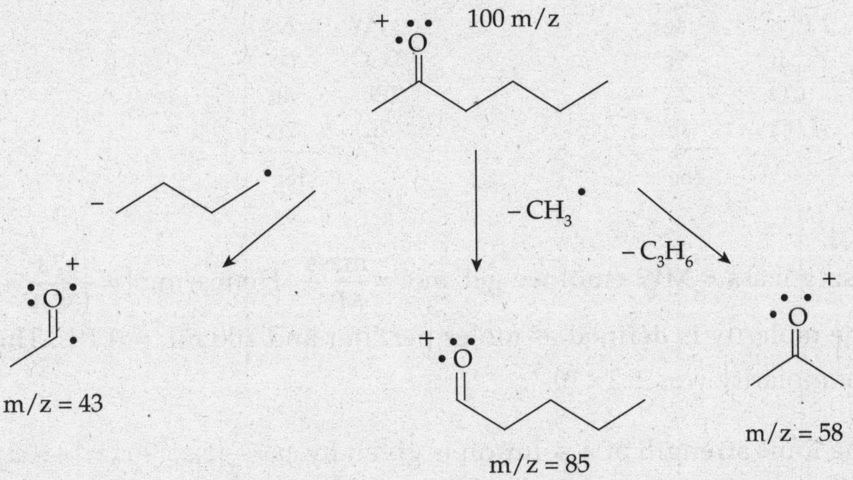

41. B The bonding is most ionic in CsF since the difference in electronegativity between Cs and F is greatest.

42. C Ligands are ranked in the spectrochemical series according to how much they tend to increase the splitting of orbitals, D. Since CO is a very strong field (low spin) ligand relative to the others, we can eliminate choices A and B. Since iodide is a very weak field (high spin) ligand, the correct choice is C.

43. C Spinel structures are usually adopted by compounds with the formula $M^{II}M_2^{III}O_4$.

44. **D** The electron count for each complex is given below, using the covalent method.

$H_2 Fe(CO)_4$	
2H	$2e^-$
Fe	$8e^-$
4CO	$8e^-$
	$18e^-$

Cp_2O_5	
2Cp	$10e^-$
Os	$8e^-$
	$18e^-$

$(PMe_3)_3 Co(Me)_2Br$	
$3PMe_3$	$6e^-$
CO	$9e^-$
2Me	$2e^-$
Br	$1e^-$
	$18e^-$

$(PPh_3)_2 Ir(CO)Cl$	
$2 PPh_3$	$4e^-$
Ir	$9e^-$
CO	$2e^-$
Cl	$1e^-$
	$16e^-$

$W (CO)_3(PEt_3)_2Cl_2$	
W	$6e^-$
3 CO	$6e^-$
$2PEt_3$	$4e^-$
2Cl	$2e^-$
	$18e^-$

45. **E** Using mass = MW · mol we get $mol = \dfrac{mass}{MW}$. Hence, $mol = \dfrac{0.72}{138.4} = 5.2 \times 10^{-3}$. The molarity is defined as moles per liter and 100 mL = 0.1 L. Therefore, the molarity was 5.2×10^{-3}.

46. **A** The ionic strength of a solution is given by $\mu = \dfrac{1}{2}\left(c_1 z_1^2 + c_2 z_2^2 + \dots c_n z_n^2\right)$

where c_i is the concentration of the ith species and z_i is the charge on that species. For this solution,

$c_{Na} = 0.05 + 0.04 = 0.09 M$

$\left(z_{Na^+}\right)^2 = (1)^2 = 1$

$c_{Cl} = 0.05 M$ $\qquad$ $c_{SO_4^{2-}} = 0.02 M$

$\left(z_{Cl^-}\right)^2 = (-1)^2 = 1$ $\qquad$ $\left(z_{SO_4^{2-}}\right)^2 = (-2)^2 = 4$

Plugging in, we get

$\mu = \dfrac{1}{2}(0.09 + 0.05 + 0.08)M$

$\mu = 0.11 M$

47. **D** In polarography, the current is measured as a function of the potential of the working electrode. For example, cyclic voltammetry is a polarographic technique. Redox chemistry is relevant here, whereas polarity of the molecule (answers I and III) is not.

48. **C** Interferometers are used for Fourier transform techniques. Gas chromatography never gives data that can be interpreted by an interferometer. The other detectors are commonly used with GCs.

49. **E** Of the choices listed, only a Gouy balance may be used to measure magnetic susceptibilities. The other common means is the Faraday method.

50. **E** The electron counts for all of the choices are given below. $V(CO)_6$ is predicted to be the most reactive of these compounds since it has only 17 electrons.

$Cr(CO)_6$	
Cr	$6e^-$
6 CO	$12e^-$
	$18e^-$

$Fe(CO)_5$	
Fe	$8e^-$
5 CO	$10e^-$
	$18e^-$

$Mn_2(CO)_{10}$	
2 Mn	$14e^-$
10 CO	$20e^-$
Mn–Mn	$2e^-$
	$36e^-$

(or $18e^-$/min)

$Co_2(CO)_8$	
2 Co	$18e^-$
8 CO	$16e^-$
Co–Co	$2e^-$
	$36e^-$

(or $18e^-$/Co)

$V(CO)_6$	
V	$5e^-$
6 CO	$12e^-$
	$17e^-$

51. **E** Only C_{6h} contains an inversion center (I). Listed below are all the symmetry elements present in each of the point groups listed.

C_{4v}: E, $2C_4$,C_z, $2\sigma_v$, $2\sigma_d$

C_s: $E\sigma_h$

T_d: E, $8C_3$, $3C_2$, $6C_4$, $6\sigma_d$

D_{2d}: E, $2S_4$, C_z, $2C_z^1$, $2\sigma_d$

C_{6h}: E, C_6, C_3, C_2, C_3^2, C_6^5, i, S_3^5, S_6^5, σ_n, S_6, S_3

52. B *trans*-$(PPh_3)_4RhH_2$ will have only one ^{31}P NMR resonance since all four PPh_3 groups are equivalent.

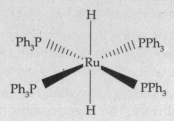

53. A Electron affinity is defined as the energy required to remove an electron from an ion in the gas phase to give a neutral gas phase atom.

54. E Molecules are subject to Jahn-Teller distortions if they are nonlinear molecules in an electronically degenerate state. Distortion occurs to lower symmetry and remove the degeneracy and hence lower the energy. Since Ni^0 is d^{10}, it can not undergo a Jahn-Teller distortion.

55. B This is an oxidative addition reaction since the metal gains two ligands and increases its oxidation state by 2 (from Rh^{+1} to Rh^{+3}).

56. B Choices A and D are best thought of in Brönsted-Lowry acidity terms. Choices C and E are best thought of in Lewis acidity terms. Choice B, in which oxide transfer occurs, is best thought of according to the Lux-Flood definition.

57. A Choices B, C, D, and E describe polyhedral polyboronhydride cage compounds. The prefix quadro- describes four atoms bound in a quadrangle (e.g., a square).

58. D In nucleophilic aromatic substitution, the incoming nucleophile always attacks an aromatic carbon atom that is substituted with a good leaving group. This is in sharp contrast to electrophilic aromatic substitution, where the incoming electrophile attacks an unsubstituted carbon atom of the aromatic framework.

59. B Hückels' rule tells us that an aromatic compounds must have a cyclic array of p orbitals and $4n + 2$ π electrons. All of the choices except B fit these qualifications.

60. C Only choice C cannot be drawn as a 1,3-dipole. The other choices are drawn below as 1,3-dipolar molecules.

61. **E** Choice E is achiral since it has an internal plane of symmetry (meso).

62. **D** PH_3 is not an electrophile since, like ammonia, it has a lone pair (on P). The other choices are all electron-deficient.

63. **D** The first step is nucleophilic addition. This reaction is an example of a double-nucleophilic aromatic substitution.

64. **E** Choices A and B are extremely unlikely due to ring strain.

Choice C is incorrect, even though it is an elimination product of the second intermediate. Choice E is more likely since it forms an α, β-unsaturated product. Choice D is incorrect since it reacts with acid to form E.

65. **B** The ground-state electronic configuration of He_2^+ is given by $(\sigma_{1s})^2(\sigma_{1s})^1$. There are two bonding electrons and one antibonding electron. Bond order is defined as BO = $\frac{1}{2}$ (# of bonding electrons – # of antibonding electrons). For He_2^+, this is BO = $\frac{1}{2}(2-1) = \frac{1}{2}$.

66. **C** Answer A can be eliminated because no reaction would occur if concentrations of reactants were constant. Answer B can be eliminated because the steady-state approximation applies to kinetics, not thermodynamics. Answer D can be eliminated because the intermediate can build up in the situation described. Answer C is correct because if the concentration of the intermediate is close to zero, it can be assumed to be constant—simplifying the algebra of the corresponding rate equation.

67. **A** This is the definition of a Hermitian operator.

68. B Koopman's theorem allows us to use the same orbitals to calculate the energies of both the neutral atom and the ion. The ionization energy is calculated by subtracting the HF energy of the atom from the exact energy of the ion.

69. E The coulombic force between two charged particles is defined as

$$\text{Force} = \frac{e^2}{4\pi\varepsilon r^2}.$$

70. C The Born-Oppenheimer approximation was first used to solve the Schroedinger equation for H_2. For this two-nucleus, two-electron system, the equation can be simplified by noting that electrons move much more quickly than the nuclei can respond. Hence, it was assumed that nuclear motion can be neglected.

71. C A beam of silver atoms passed through a nonhomogeneous magnetic field was split into two components corresponding to $2l + 1 = 2$, $l = \frac{1}{2}$. This proved the existence of spin.

72. E Analysis of molecular vibration assumes that a chemical bond is analogous to two weights connected by a spring. The classical approximation is termed "the harmonic oscillator," and its differential equations can be applied to the molecular situation.

73. B This is a van't Hoff plot, which is used to determine ΔH^o and ΔS^o from thermodynamic data. Starting with $\Delta G^o = RT \ln k = \Delta H - T\Delta S$, we can easily rearrange to $\ln k = \frac{-\Delta H^o}{RT} + \frac{\Delta S^o}{R}$.

If $\ln k$ is plotted vs. $\frac{1}{T}$, the slope will be $\frac{-\Delta H}{RT}$.

74. E A spontaneous process is defined as one in which the entropy of the system increases. Hence, by definition, ΔS_{sys} can never be less than 0 if the process is spontaneous.

75. C To operate on the eigenfunction e^{ikx} with the operator $P_x = -i\hbar\frac{\partial}{\partial x}$, first take the partial derivative of the eigenfunction with respect to x. This gives $\frac{\partial}{\partial x}\left(e^{ikx}\right) = ike^{ikx}$. Multiplying by $-i\hbar$ (as dictated by the operator) gives

$(-i\hbar)(ik)e^{ikx} = -i^2\hbar k e^{ikx}$

$= (-1)(-1)\hbar k e^{ikx}$

$= \hbar k e^{ikx}.$

Hence the eigenvalue is $\hbar k$.

76. B The general wave function for a particle in a one-dimensional box is given by: $\lambda(x) = B\sin\left(\dfrac{n\pi x}{a}\right)$ where B is a constant, a is the length of the box, and n is the energy level. The probability density is given by $\lambda^2(x)$, which looks like the graphs in B.

77. D Retention time in GC is governed by the equilibrium of the analyte between the solid and gas phases of the column. Increasing the column length (I) and percent stationary phase (II) both increase the amount of solid phase and concommitantly the amount of time the analyte can spend interacting with the solid (i.e., not moving down the column). Increasing the column temperature makes the analyte more volatile, and hence it spends more time in the vapor phase. This means that the analyte will have a smaller retention time.

78. D Although A and E are both true, neither is the "common ion effect." The common ion effect is a direct extention of LeChatelier's principle. Hence, the answer is D.

79. B Intermolecular forces are forces between molecules, not within molecules. (If the question had been asked about intramolecular forces, C would have been correct.) To answer this question, you have to know that benzene is a liquid at room temperature. Clearly, the forces cannot be repulsive (eliminating E), or the liquid would not have any cohesive properties. The primary intermolecular forces are dipole and quadrupolar interactions and van der Waals (or London dispersion) interactions. These are all electrostatic interactions.

80. E At pH = 3.13, pH = pK_a, and H_3A should be roughly the same concentration as H_2A^-. Since pH 2.0 is roughly 1 unit lower than 3.13, $H_3A:H_2A^-$ should be about 10:1. Hence, H_3A is the dominant species in solution.

81. D The NMR resonances are summarized below:

198 ppm

137 ppm

132 ppm

128.3 ppm

128.1 ppm

26 ppm

Although the four resonances between 128 and 137 ppm indicate the presence of a phenyl group, this does not allow us to eliminate any of the answer choices. We can eliminate B, however, since the spectrum contains two additional resonances and choice B contains only one additional carbon atom. Of the remaining choices, (A, C, D, and E), only choice D with its carbonyl functional group would have a resonance of around 200 ppm.

82. E PBr_3 reacts with alcohols and carboxylic acids to make bromoalkanes and acid bromides, respectively. It does not undergo electrophilic aromatic substitution reactions.

83. E This reaction is called the iodoform reaction because iodoform (I_3CH) is the product. Under acidic conditions, I_2 reacts with methyl ketones to form the α-I ketone in choice A.

84. C The reactions of R–OH groups with dimethyl sulfate is a simple substitution reaction where oxygen acts as the nucleophile, and Me_2SO_4 is a source of $^+CH_3$.

85. A Since carboxylic acids are much more acidic than carbonyl compounds, phenols, or alcohols, we can eliminate choices B, D, and E. *p*-Nitrophenol (which is even more acidic than phenol due to the nitro group) is more acidic than 2,4-pentadione.

86. D $LiAlH_4$ is a strong source of 4 equivalents of H$^-$ (hydride). Therefore, 0.5 equivalents will provide two equivalents of hydride, which will reduce the ester to an alcohol via an aldehyde.

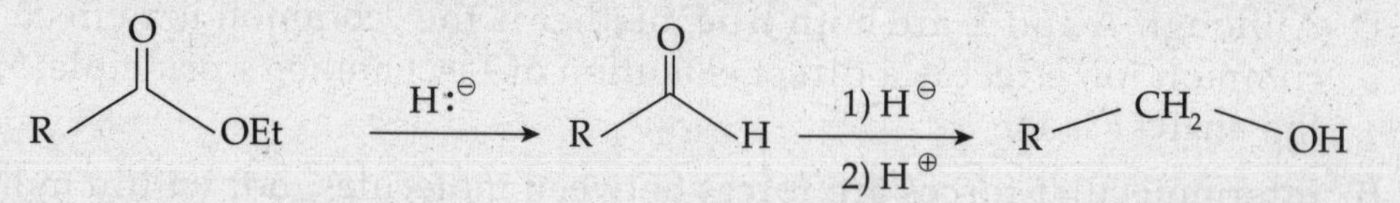

87. C This is an acylation reaction since an acyl group is transferred to the alcohol.

88. B This reaction, called a Cope rearrangement, involves redistribution of six electrons ($4\,\pi$, $6\,\sigma$) as shown below.

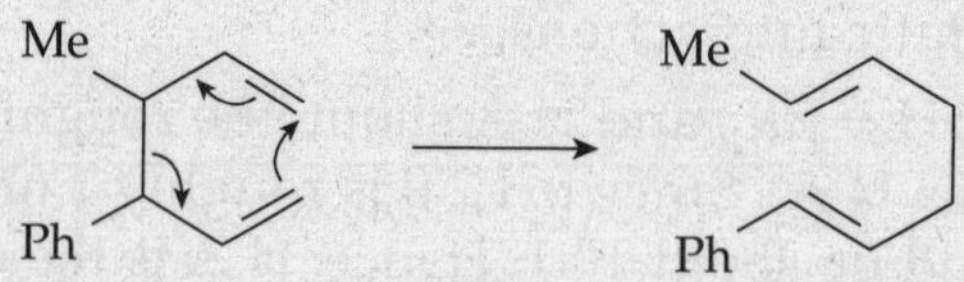

89. D In a row (period), atomic radius decreases going left to right. In a column, (group) atomic radius increases going down. Therefore choice D is the largest.

90. B For neon, L = 0, S = 0, and J = 0. Therefore, the ground-state term symbol is $^1S_0$.

91. D Since all of the cations are Li, we can focus on the anion. Bond energies for salts can be thought of in terms of size matching the ions and differences in electronegativity. Ions that are similar in size will have higher bond energies than ions of very different sizes. Also, a large electronegativity difference will lead to a higher bond energy.

92. E Facial (fac) stereochemistry is used to denote three ligands that share a face of an octahedron.

93. B NH_3 is the strongest base among the choices by any of the common definitions. According to the solvent system definition, a base is a species that increases the concentration of the characteristic anion.

94. **D** Only choice D is not a normal vibrational mode since it does not preserve the center of mass of the molecule.

95. **E** The actual value is 0.99989 = 100% according to the Boltzmann distribution.

96. **B** As rotation increases, the centrifugal force causes the bond to stretch. This results in the uneven spacing between lines of a rotational spectrum.

97. **A** Actual values (D) $H_2 = 0$

   $CO = 0.112$

   $HCl = 1.109$

   $NaCl = 9.001$

   It is easiest to see that H_2 has the lowest dipole moment by looking at the electronegativity differences between the two atoms. For a homonuclear diatomic, the difference is 0, and the dipole moment is also 0.

98. **C** The sample absorbs in the orange-red region, so the sample transmits blue.

99. **E** This is a statement of Avogadro's principle. For example, at 25°C, 22.4 L of any gas contains 6.02×10^{24} molecules.

100. **E** A can be ruled out since both reagents are strong nucleophiles and bases. In B, the electrophile is an acylation agent, not a methylation agent. C would produce ethylamine, not methylamine. D would produce a mixture of $MeNH_2$, Me_2NH, Me_3N, and Me_4N^+I. Only E, reduction of methyl azide, will give a good yield of $MeNH_2$.

101. **B** The $C \equiv N$ functional group is called a nitrile. Therefore, B is the correct choice.

102. **C** The Dieckmann condensation is an intramolecular version of the Claisen condensation. Choice C correctly depicts the product.

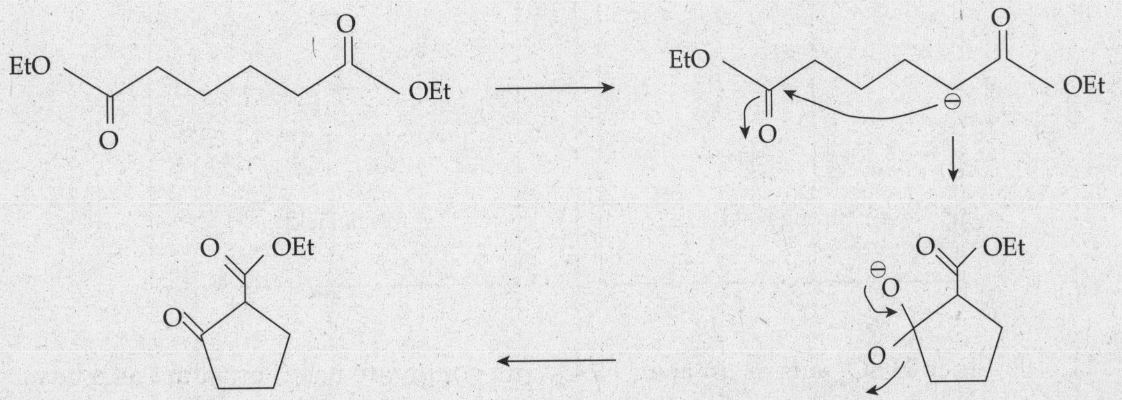

103. A Valine 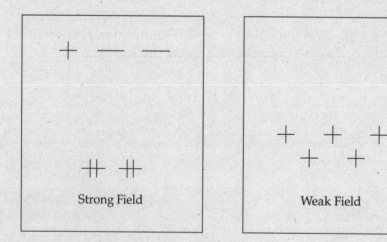 can form a peptide (amide) bond with

another valine to form val-val, choice A.

104. A This reaction, known as a Wittig reaction, can be performed only with A.

105. B Specific rotation is determined by the following equation: $[\alpha]_D^{20} = \dfrac{\alpha}{l \cdot c}$

where $[\alpha]_D^{20}$ is the specific rotation, α is the observed optical rotation (o), l is the sample path length (dm), and c is the concentration (g/mL).

106. B Choices A and D would give the dialdehyde. Choices C and E would give the dicarboxylic acid. Only B would give the desired product.

107. C Since $SnCl_4$ is accepting two equivalents of :L, it is best thought of as an electron pair acceptor.

108. E CO_2 dissolves in water to form carbonic acid, H_2CO_3.

109. A LiH (choice A) will have the highest dipole moment due (in part) to the large difference in electronegativity and no possibility for resonance.

110. A The strong field (Td) and weak field (td) splittings are shown below with five electrons.

Strong Field

Weak Field

111. C Since H_2SO_4 acts as an acid, HSO_4^- (its conjugate base) must act as a base.

112. E The lanthanides generally prefer +3 as an oxidation state.

113. A The vital piece of information here is that oxidation occurs at the anode, eliminating B and C. E is eliminated because the schematic makes it clear that Zn and Cl_2 are not in the same solution. D is eliminated because Cl^- is not one of the starting reagents.

114. D This is a simple application of the ideal gas law: $PV = nRT$. If P_1 is 150 torr and $V_1 = 300$ mL, $T_1 = T_2$, $n_1 = n_2$, and R is constant, $\dfrac{P_2}{P_1} = \dfrac{V_2}{V_1}$. $\therefore P_2 = \left(\dfrac{V_2}{V_1}\right)(P_1)$.

115. C For division, all absolute uncertainties are first converted into relative uncertainties (percents). Then, these are analyzed using

$$\left(\frac{\Delta d}{d}\right)^2 = \left(\frac{\Delta m}{m}\right)^2 + \left(\frac{\Delta V}{V}\right)^2$$

$$\frac{\Delta d}{d} = \sqrt{\left(\frac{\Delta m}{m}\right)^2 + \left(\frac{\Delta V}{V}\right)^2} \quad \frac{\Delta d}{d} = \sqrt{\left(\frac{0.1}{10}\right)^2 + \left(\frac{0.08}{8}\right)^2}$$

$$\frac{\Delta d}{d} = \sqrt{(0.01)^2 + (0.01)^2} \quad \frac{\Delta d}{d} = \sqrt{2 \times 10^{-4}}$$

$$\frac{\Delta d}{d} = 1.4 \times 10^{-2}$$

and the percent uncertainty is 1.4%

116. B This answer encapsulates the definition of a confidence interval.

117. D The partition coefficient is 4, which means $\dfrac{[A]_{Et_2O}}{[A]_{H_2O}}$. Since the volumes of the two layers are equal, this means that 75% of A will be in the organic layer on the first extraction. The second extraction will remove 75% of the remaining A.

Start: 0.1 M = concentration of A in H_2O.

Extract once: 0.025 M = concentration of A in H_2O.

Extract twice: 0.00625 M = concentration of A in H_2O.

118. D The rate in all of the choices is expressed in terms of the disappearance of NO_3. Since NO_3 appears only in the first elementary step, the rate is given by the rate of disappearance of NO_3 in this step. Most notably, answer C is incorrect because this is an expression of the overall reaction, not the first elementary step.

119. A $\dfrac{\partial^2 u}{\partial x^2} = \dfrac{1}{v}\dfrac{\partial^2 u}{\partial t^2}$ is the definition of the classical wave equation.

120. C This is an example of LeChatelier's principle and the ideal gas law. An increase in volume will result in a decrease in pressure in the system. The system will respond by shifting to the left, where there are two equivalents of gaseous molecules.

121. B A is an acid-base reaction. C, D, and E show no change in oxidation number. For the reaction shown in answer B, the hydrogens in H_2 have an oxidation state of 0, and the chlorine atoms in Cl_2 also have an oxidation state of 0. However, in the product HCl, the hydrogen is +1 and chlorine is –1.

122. A The following equation applies: $\Delta S_{vap} = \dfrac{\Delta H_{vap}}{T_b}$ where T_b is the temperature of vaporization in Kelvin. Since the boiling point of H_2O is 373 K, the calculation is $\dfrac{40.66 \text{ kJ}/\text{mol}}{373 \text{ K}} = 109 \text{ J}/\text{K}\cdot\text{mol}$

123. A The number of particles N must be an exponent in the equation since entropy is an extensive property and it scales with the number of particles according to the Boltzmann equation, $S = k \ln \Omega$.

124. A This is an example of standard addition. The relevant equation is

$$\frac{[\text{analyte}] \text{ in solution 1}}{[\text{analyte}] \text{ in solution 2}} = \frac{\text{Absorbance of solution 1}}{\text{Absorbance of solution 2}}$$

For solution 1, $\left[Ca^{2+}\right] = \dfrac{(10.00)([Ca^{2+}\text{in milk}]) + (5.00)(1.0\times10^{-4}M)}{100}$

$\left[Ca^{2+}\right] = \dfrac{10x + 5\times10^{-4}}{100}M$

For solution 2, $\left[Ca^{2+}\right] = \dfrac{(10.00)([Ca^{2+}\text{in milk})}{100}M$

$\therefore \dfrac{10x + 5\times10^{-4}}{10x} = \dfrac{3}{2}$

$30x = 20\,x + 1\times10^{-3}\,M$

$10\,x = 1\times10^{-3}\,M$

$x = 1\times10^{-4}\,M$

125. B The endpoint of a strong acid/strong base titration is pH = 7.0. The indicator should have a color transition at the endpoint. The only indicators listed that fit this requirement are bromothymol blue (B) and litmus (E). Since litmus has a broader transition range, it is the inferior indicator.

126. D Mass spectrometry gives results as a mass to charge ratio.

127. E A and B cannot be ionic because they are composed of only one element each. BN (D) has a graphite-like structure with covalent bonding between B and N atoms. Although the Si–O bonds in SiO_2 are polar, the $Na^+BH_4^-$ interaction is a purely ionic interaction because BH_4^- has eight valence electrons and cannot accept another covalent bond.

128. D Including activities, K_{sp} is defined as $K_{sp} = Cr^{3+}\left[Cr^{3+}\right](gIO_3^-)^3[IO_3^-]^3$. This is easily arranged to give D.

129. **B** The NMR resonances are summarized below:

4.1 ppm	quartet	2H
3.4 ppm	singlet	2H
2.2 ppm	singlet	2H
1.2 ppm	triplet	3H

The presence of both a triplet and a quartet indicates the presence of an ethyl group. This eliminates choices C and E. The fact that the quartet is at 4.1 ppm indicates that it is bonded to a very electronegative atom. This eliminates choice E. Of the remaining choices (A and B), only choice B would give two singlets.

130. **C** Choice A is a Newman projection.

Choice B is a dashed-wedged-line notation.

Choice C is a Haworth projection.

Choice D is a Fischer projection.

Choice E is a chair notation.

131. **E** Since these are all isomers of one another, the heats of hydrogenation will track with the degree of substitution. The monosubstituted alkene (I) will be the greatest. The cis-disubstituted will be greater than the trans compound.

132. **D**

Since there is only one site (the alpha methyl group) for tautomerization, the enol/enolate can only form in one place. This makes D the only possible choice.

133. **B** A reaction is regioselective when there are two (or more) possible sites (regions) for reactivity, but one is preferred over the other. Hydroboration is regioselective since is prefers to give the less substituted (not the more substituted) alcohol.

134. **C** This must be conducted in an aprotic nonelectrophilic solvent.

135. **C** Of the choices, only Ph–O–Me is a weak enough acid to not be deprotonated by NaOD.

136. **D** The usual method for making an –OH group into a better leaving group is to form a tosylate (Ots) group by reacting the alcohol with tosyl chloride (TsCl) and pyridine.

137. D ClF_3 will be T-shaped since it has three substituents and two lone pairs.

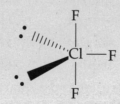

138. B The *d*-orbitals ($n = 3$) are d_{z^2}, d_{xy}, d_{xz}, d_{yz}, and $d_{x^2-y^2}$.

139. D Below are the molecular orbital diagrams for Cl_2 and Cl_2^+.

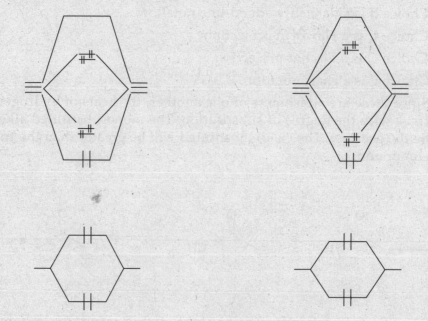

140. D The calcite structure of CO_3^{2-} (carbonate ion) is adopted by many other species including $MgCO_3$, $FeCO_3$, $LiNO_3$, $NaNO_3$, and YBO_3. The coordination number of the metal ion is 6.

141. A Since the product contains the sum of both the materials and the charge of the starting materials, it must have given off a massless, chargeless particle, a gamma ray.

ABOUT THE AUTHOR

Dr. Laberge has been a Reseach Associate in the Department of Biochemistry and Biophysics at the University of Pennsylvania since 1996, investigating protein structure-function problems, using a combined laser spectroscopy/computational approach. She is presently on leave of absence to the SOTE Institute of Biophysics in Budapest.

NOTES

NOTES

NOTES

NOTES

www.review.com

Expert Advice

Talk About It

www.review.com

Pop Surveys

Paying for it

www.review.com

www.review.com

THE PRINCETON REVIEW

Getting in

Word du Jour

www.review.com

Find-O-Rama School & Career Search

www.review.com

Best Schools

Finding it

FIND US...

International

Hong Kong
4/F Sun Hung Kai Centre
30 Harbour Road, Wan Chai,
Hong Kong
Tel: (011)85-2-517-3016

Japan
Fuji Building 40, 15-14
Sakuragaokacho, Shibuya Ku,
Tokyo 150, Japan
Tel: (011)81-3-3463-1343

Korea
Tae Young Bldg, 944-24,
Daechi- Dong, Kangnam-Ku
The Princeton Review—ANC
Seoul, Korea 135-280,
South Korea
Tel: (011)82-2-554-7763

Mexico City
PR Mex S De RL De Cv
Guanajuato 228 Col. Roma
06700 Mexico D.F., Mexico
Tel: 525-564-9468

Montreal
666 Sherbrooke St.
West, Suite 202
Montreal, QC H3A 1E7 Canada
Tel: 514-499-0870

Pakistan
1 Bawa Park - 90 Upper Mall
Lahore, Pakistan
Tel: (011)92-42-571-2315

Spain
Pza. Castilla, 3 - 5º A, 28046
Madrid, Spain
Tel: (011)341-323-4212

Taiwan
155 Chung Hsiao East Road
Section 4 - 4th Floor,
Taipei R.O.C., Taiwan
Tel: (011)886-2-751-1243

Thailand
Building One, 99 Wireless Road
Bangkok, Thailand 10330
Tel: 662-256-7080

Toronto
1240 Bay Street, Suite 300
Toronto M5R 2A7 Canada
Tel: 800-495-7737
Tel: 716-839-4391

locations

Vancouver
4212 University Way NE,
Suite 204
Seattle, WA 98105
Tel: 206-548-1100

National (U.S.)
We have more than 60 offices around the U.S. and
run courses at over 400 sites. For courses and locations
within the U.S. call 1-800-2-Review and you will be
routed to the nearest office.

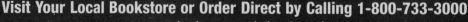